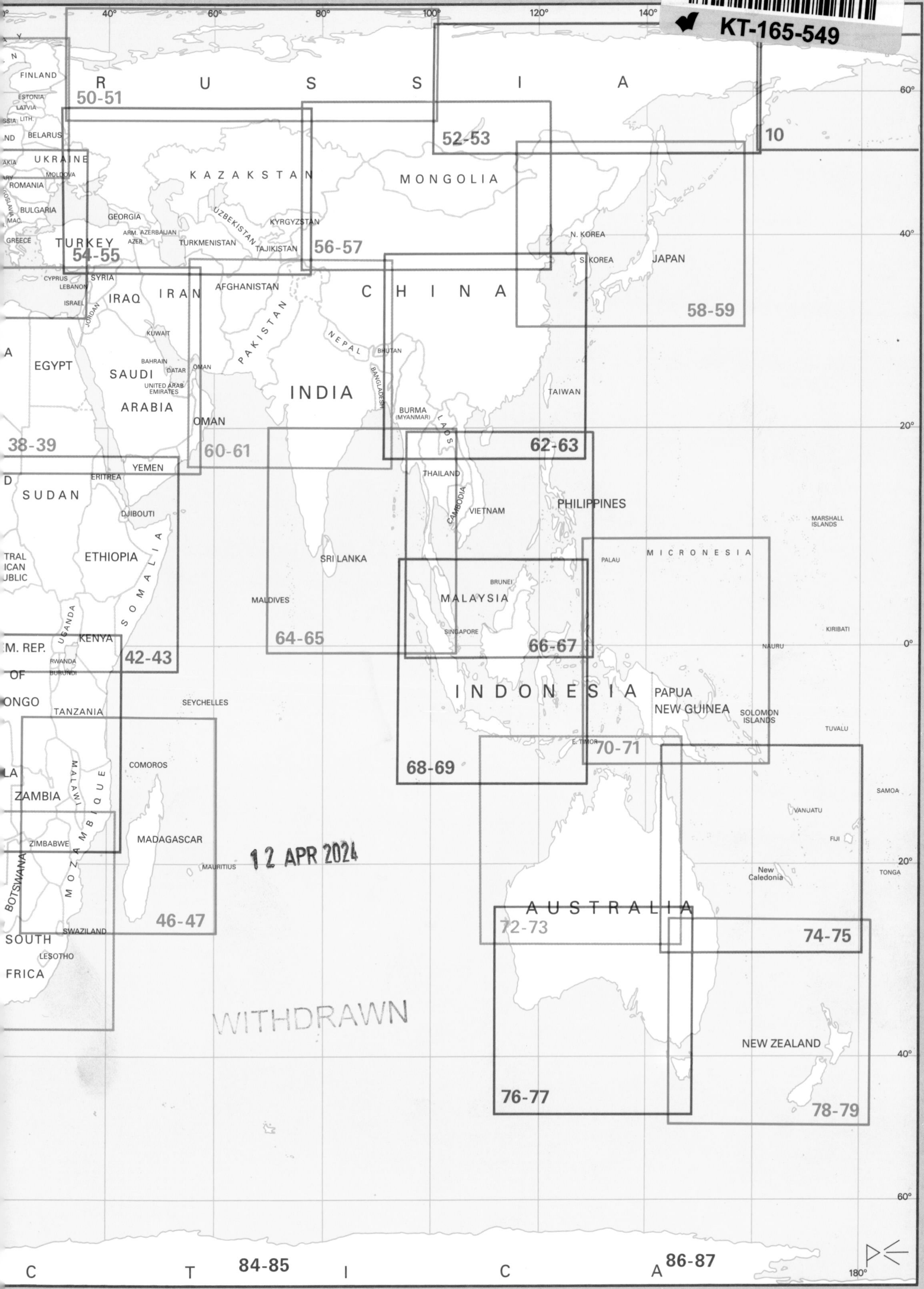

OPOGRAPHIC MAPS

The Peters World Atlas

Based on the Peters World Map

The Earth in its true proportion

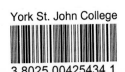

Contributors and Consultants:

Dr. E.C. Barrett
Professor Ulrich Bleil
Michael Benckert
Wolfgang Behr
Professor Heinz Bosse
Professor Walter Buchholz
Dr. Nicola Bradbear
Carol Claxton
Professor Heinrich Dathe
Mick Dyer
Hellmuth Färber
Jean Fernand-Laurent
Kurt Ficker
Professor Fritz Fischer
Karlheinz Gieseler
Professor Manfred Görlach
Professor Ulrich Grosse
Arnulf Hader
Hazel Hand
Max Hann
Dirk Hansohm
Dr. Günther Heidmann
Professor Wolf Herre
Karl-Heinz Ingenhaag
Jeff Jones
Dr. Andreas Kaiser
Professor Günther Krause
Dr. Manfred Kummer
Daniel Lloyd
Konrad G. Lohse
Wolfgang Mache
Dr. Udo Moll
Georg Möller
Olive Pearson
Dr. Aribert Peters
Birgit Peters
Werner Peters
Thomas Plümer
Detlev Quintern
D.H. Reichstein
Hellmut Schlien
Professor Hermann Schulz
Professor Axel Sell
Eduard Spescha
Piet Summerfield
Jürgen Wendler
Thorsten Wieland
Professor Adolf Witte
Professor Karl Wohlmuth
Judith Wood
Siegfried Zademack
Madeleine Zeller

Cartography:

Kümmerly+Frey, Bern (graticules, coastlines, borders, seas, rivers and lakes).
Oxford Cartographers (topographic and thematic maps). www.oxfordcarto.com
Cartographic editor: Terry Hardaker, Oxford Cartographers.

This edition published by:

New Internationalist Publications Ltd
55 Rectory Road, Oxford OX4 1BW, United Kingdom
www.newint.org

Oxford Cartographers
Oasis Park, Eynsham, Oxford OX29 4TP, United Kingdom
www.oxfordcarto.com

ISBN 0-9540499-5-0 The Peters World Atlas

Printed and bound in Germany by Neue Stalling GmbH & Co KG, Ammergaustraße 72-74, D-26123 Oldenburg, Germany

FOREWORD

In 1493 – one year after Columbus's first voyage to America – the Pope apportioned the non-European world among the most powerful nations of his own continent. By the time Mercator completed his Atlas 100 years later, European domination had spread across the world, and Mercator's Atlas was the embodiment of Europe's geographical conception of the world in an age of colonialism.

Since then thousands of atlases have been published. They differ in many respects from Mercator's, but all have a common feature: they focus on the industrialised countries. The country and continent of origin are represented at a larger scale than other countries and continents. If, together with the age of colonialism, the view of the world that underpinned it is to come to an end, we need a new geography – one that is based on the equal status of all peoples.

This Atlas represents all countries and continents at the same scale. Their actual size and their position in the world can thus be taken directly from the map. This equal presentation is an expression of the consciousness that is gradually replacing our traditional world view.

The use of a single scale for all topographic maps; the principle of fidelity of area; and a new, universally applicable presentation of relief; together, these now make it possible to alter our conception of the world. All 246 thematic maps are also equal-area world maps. The comprehensive presentation in these thematic maps of man, nature, and society is based on the same principle of equality as that underlying the topographic maps.

This Atlas, therefore, offers a way of understanding the history underlying the North-South divide, as well as the tensions between East and West – so often the outcome of the gulf which separates rich and poor.

Arno Peters

CONTENTS

Map Finder for the Topographic Maps . . . . . Front Endpaper
Foreword 3
Introduction 6–7
Page Finder for Countries 8
Key to the Topographic Section 9
Sources for Thematic Section 96
Introduction to the Thematic Section 97
Political World Map 112–113
Relief and Vegetation of the World 230–231

THE WORLD IN 43 MAPS AT THE SAME SCALE

THE AMERICAS

Alaska. Canada (North-West) 11
Canada (North) 12–13
Canada (South-West). USA (West) 14–15
Canada (South-East). USA (East) 16–17
USA (South). Mexico. Hawaii 18–19
USA (South-East). Cuba. Caribbean 20–21
Central America. South America (North) . . 22–23
South America (West) 24–25
South America (East) 26–27
South America (Central) 28–29
South America (South) 30–31

EUROPE

Northern Europe 32–33
Southern Europe 34–35
Eastern Europe 50

AFRICA

Africa (North-West) 36–37
Africa (North-East) 38
Africa (West) 40–41
Africa (East) 42–43
Africa (South-West) 44–45
Africa (South-East). Madagascar 46–47
Africa (Southern) 48–49

ASIA

Russia (North-Western Siberia) 51
Russia (Northern Siberia) 52–53
Russia (North-Eastern Siberia) 10
Asia (North-West) 54–55
Russia (South-East). Kazakstan. Mongolia. China (North) 56–57
China (North-East). Korea. Japan 58–59
China (South-East). South-East Asia (North) 62–63
Asia Minor 35, 54
Arabian Peninsula 38–39
Asia (South) with India (North) 60–61
India (South). South-East Asia 64–65
South-East Asia. Philippines. Borneo 66–67
Indonesia. Malaysia 68–69
New Guinea. South Pacific 70–71

AUSTRALASIA

Australia (West) 72–73
Australia (North-East). South Pacific 74–75
Australia (South) 76–77
Australia (South-East). New Zealand 78–79

ANTARCTICA

Antarctica (Byrd Land) 80–81
Antarctica (Graham Land) 82–83
Antarctica (Maud Land) 84–85
Antarctica (Wilkes Land) 86–87

THE ARCTIC

Arctic (Canada) 88–89
Arctic (Greenland) 90–91
Arctic (Novaya Zemlya) 92–93
Arctic (Siberia) 94–95

NATURE, HUMANKIND AND SOCIETY IN 246 THEMATIC WORLD MAPS

The Continents 98–99
560 Million Years Ago · 280 Million Years Ago · 180 Million Years Ago · 120 Million Years Ago · 60 Million Years Ago · Today

Mountains 100–101

Rivers and Seas 102–103

Sun and Climate 104–105
Hours of Sunshine · Incidence of Rays · Evaporation · Temperature · Temperature Variation · Precipitation

Natural Dangers 106–107
Volcanoes · Earthquakes · Maritime Earthquakes · Hurricanes

Vegetation 108–109
Woodland · Pastureland · Arable Land · Barren Land

People and Cities 110–111

States 112–113

Languages 114–115
French · Spanish · Portuguese · English · German · Russian · Italian · Bengali · Malay · Arabic · Chinese · Japanese · Hindi · Swahili

Scripts 116–117
Scripts of Chinese Origin · Scripts of Indian Origin · Scripts of Greek Origin · Scripts of Latin Origin · Scripts of Arabic Origin · The Direction of Writing

Religions 118–119
Natural Religions · Hinduism · Christianity · Islam · Buddhism · Confucianism · Shinto · No Religion

Education 120–121
Illiteracy · Primary Education · Secondary Education · University · Pupil/Teacher Ratio · Expenditure on Education

The Sciences 122–123
University Teachers · Publication of Scientific Books · Researchers and Engineers · Expenditure on the Sciences

Information 124–125
Newspapers · Radio · Television · Books

Communications 126–127
Letters · Telephones · Fax · Internet

Traffic Density 128–129
Railways · Cars · Air Traffic · Shipping

Population Structure 130–131
Population Density · Population Growth · Adults/Children Ratio · Men/Women Ratio

Life Expectancy 132–133

Health 134–135
Medical Attention · Available Hospital Beds · Drinking Water Supplies · Infant Mortality

Sport 136–137
Running Events · Jumping Events · Throwing Events · Gymnastics · Skiing · Ski Jumping · Tobogganing and Bob-Sled Events · Speed Skating · Swimming Events · Rowing Events · Sailing Events · Figure Skating · Cycling Events · Equestrian Events · Single Combat · Ball Games

Nutrition 138–139
Calorie Consumption · Carbohydrates · Vegetables and Fruit · Meat · Protein · Fat

Soil Cultivation 140–141

Crop Yield 142–143

Staple Foodstuffs 144–145
Wheat · Barley · Rye · Oats · Millet · Soya · Maize · Sorghum · Rice

Animal Husbandry 146–147
Cattle · Horses · Mules · Donkeys · Camels · Buffalo · Elephant · Reindeer · Sheep · Pigs · Goats · Bees · Chickens · Ducks · Turkeys · Silkworm

Fishing 148–149
Size of Catches · Herring · Cod · Tuna · Flatfish · Squid

Hunting 150–151
Hare, Rabbit · Roe Deer · Red Deer · Elk · Fox · Wolf · Bear · Jackal · Antelope · Gazelle · Kangaroo · Lynx · Opossum · Beaver · Pheasant · Partridge

Natural Products 152–153
Wood · Rubber · Silk · Cotton · Wool · Skins · Hemp · Flax · Honey · Eggs · Grain · Meat · Vegetables · Fruit · Sugar · Milk

Mineral Resources 154–155
Iron · Copper · Tin · Lead · Gold · Silver · Platinum · Diamonds · Aluminium · Zinc · Manganese · Nickel · Chrome · Sulphur · Potassium · Phosphate

Energy 156–157
Oil · Natural Gas · Water Power · Uranium · Coal · Total Consumption

Industrial Products 158–159
Metals and Metal Goods · Machines · Electrical Appliances · Means of Transport · Chemical Products · Glass, Porcelain, Ceramics · Oil and Coal Products · Paper, Paper Products · Textile Products · Wood Products · Food Products · Plastic Products · Rubber · Scientific Instruments · Leather and Fur · Shoes

Urbanisation 160–161

World Trade 162–163
Natural Products (Import) · Natural Products (Export) · Industrial Products (Import) · Industrial Products (Export)

Poor Nations – Rich Nations 164–165

Economic Growth 166–167

Employment Structure 168–169
Agriculture · Transport · Industry · Mining · Building · Trade · Energy · Social Professions · Banking

Economic Order 170–171

Unemployment 172–173

Inflation 174–175

Child Labour 176–177

Inequality 178–179

Prostitution 180–181

The Status of Women 182–183
Paid Employment · Housework · Number of Children · Monogamy/Polygamy · Participation in Legislation · Higher Education

Relative Military Strength 184–185
Armed Forces · Tanks · Fighter Planes · Naval Vessels · Nuclear Weapons · Reserve Forces

The Conquest of Space 186–187
Launching Sites for Space Flights · Earth Satellites · Manned Space Flights · Interplanetary Space Flights

Instructions for Use of the Index 188
Index 189–228

CARTOGRAPHIC INTRODUCTION

It may come as a shock to realise that all of the atlases we have known until now present a distorted picture of the world. The nature of this distortion, and the reason for it, are now so obvious that it seems hardly possible to have overlooked it for 400 years. The distortion caused by attempting to represent the spherical earth on flat paper is more or less unavoidable, but the distortion caused by the use of inconsistent scales, which has acquired the unquestioned sanction of habit, is not.

We have come to accept as "natural" a representation of the world that devotes disproportionate space to large-scale maps of areas perceived as important, while consigning other areas to small-scale general maps. And it is because our image of the world has become thus conditioned, that we have for so long failed to recognise the distortion for what it is – the equivalent of peering at Europe and North America through a magnifying glass and then surveying the rest of the world through the wrong end of a telescope.

There is nothing "natural" about such a view of the world. It is the remnant of a way of thinking born even before the age of colonialism and fired by that age. Few thinking people today would subscribe to a world-view of this kind. Yet, until now, no atlas has existed that provided a picture of the world undistorted by varying scales.

A single scale

All topographic maps in this atlas are at the same scale: each double-page map shows one-sixtieth of the earth's surface. This means that all the topographic maps can be directly compared with one another. Among the many surprises this unique feature offers may be, for some users, the relative sizes of Great Britain (page 32) and the island of Madagascar (page 47); or, perhaps, the areas respectively covered by Europe (pages 32–33) and North Africa (pages 36–37). For most people it will soon become apparent that their hazy and long-held notions of the sizes of different countries and regions are, in a lot of cases, quite drastically wrong.

But what do we mean by scale? The scale indicator that appears on reference maps only shows distance scale. It enables the user to calculate the factor needed to multiply distances so as to compare them with those on other maps. This is a complex and somewhat tedious exercise that the great majority of users understandably neglects to carry out. Moreover, the number of different scales in conventional atlases is surprisingly high, in general beween twenty and fifty. Thus, the concept of relative scale must become increasingly vague in the user's mind. What is generally not mentioned is that, because it is impossible to transfer the curved surface of the globe correctly to a flat plane, the scale indicator on a map is only valid for a single part of the map, such as a line of latitude.

Distance is only one aspect of scale. Area has also to be considered. Whereas there can be no maps with absolute fidelity of distance, there can be maps with fidelity of area. Fidelity of area (or equal area) means that all countries are shown at the correct size in relation to others. The maps in this atlas preserve fidelity of area, a feature never previously achieved in an atlas. In the Peters Atlas all topographic maps have equal area scale: 1 square centimetre on the maps equals 6,000 square kilometres in reality.

While uniform scale for all parts of the world enables comparisons between all places on an equal footing, the local geography covered at larger scales in other world atlases is omitted from the Peters Atlas. To include enlargements of the more densly populated regions would be to defeat the purpose of this atlas.

A single symbology

This equality of scale offers further advantages besides direct comparability. The basis of any map compilation is the simplification of reality, which cartographers call "generalisation." This transfer of the real character of the earth's surface into a system of lines and symbols, which can be graphically represented, has to be adapted to the scale employed. Thus a river or road with all its turns and windings at a scale of 1:100,000 can be drawn nearer to reality (that is, with more detail) than at a scale of 1:1,000,000. Symbols also vary for different scales. Thus the same symbol can mean a town with 50–100,000 inhabitants at one scale, but a city with 1–5 million inhabitants at another. The same elevation may be differently coloured on maps of different scales. All such difficulties vanish in this atlas, which by way of its single scale has only one level of generalisation and a single set of symbols.

Topographic map colours

The green/brown colouring of most current atlases represents the topographic relief of the region; green stands for low-lying areas, brown for mountainous country, with different shades of the two colours for different elevations. Since, however, both colours (as also the blue of the sea and the white of snow-covered mountains) are borrowed from nature, the user of the atlas may be forgiven for assuming the green parts on the map to represent areas with vegetation and the brown parts to be the barren land. Although this is broadly true in Europe it may not be so elsewhere. For example, in North Africa the lower areas, even those below sea level, are usually deserts, and it is only above a certain height in the mountains that vegetation begins. The green/brown colouring is thus unsuitable for representing relief in an atlas dedicated to an accurate worldview. So in this atlas green represents vegetation, brown barren land, and a mixture of the two colours represents thin or scattered vegetation. Global vegetation data were obtained from 1985–86 satellite photography with the help of the Remote Sensing Unit at the Department of Geography of Bristol University. The resolution of this imagery down to individual units of 20 square kilometres, and its conversion to the Peters base maps by the Remote Sensing Unit, makes this the most up-to-date statement available of the distribution of world vegetation.

Topographic map relief

The tradition of showing relief by coloured layers running from green in lowlands, through brown to purple, mauve or white in high mountains, has one further serious disadvantage. The features of the land surface are only shown along the contours, or lines joining points of equal height. In between, we receive no information about the surface of the land. "Hillshading," or rendering the complete landscape with 3-D shadows to depict the relief, overcomes this. Cartographers have struggled with the best way to create hillshading for hundreds of years. In this atlas the 3-D relief comes from photographing specially made plaster relief models and blending these photos with hand-rendered colouring. In the blending, the relief shading has also been enhanced to eliminate awkward shadows, as for example when the angle of the light from the photo ran directly down a mountain chain thus reducing its impact. The addition of "spot heights" for selected peaks and other points on the map lends precision to the artwork.

The Peters Projection

Anyone who has ever tried to peel an orange and press the peel into a continuous flat piece without tearing will have grasped the fundamental impossibility that lies at the heart of all cartographic endeavour: that fidelity of shape, distance and angle are of necessity lost in flattening the surface of a sphere. On the other hand it is possible to retain three other qualities: fidelity of area, fidelity of axis and fidelity of position. Fidelity of area makes it possible to compare various parts of a map directly with one another, and fidelity of axis and position guarantee correct relationships of north-south and east-west axes by way of a rectangular grid.

In 1973 Arno Peters published his world map, which unites in a single flat map all three achievable qualities – fidelity of area, fidelity of axis and fidelity of position. In this way the real comparative sizes of all countries in the world are clearly visible. For this atlas Arno Peters has generalised the projection principle upon which his World Map was based, so that now each regional map represents the maximum possible freedom from distortion, of area as well as shape. Since map distortions through a projection decrease in proportion to the size of the area depicted – the smaller the area, the smaller the distortion – the forty-three topographical maps in this atlas are considerably closer to reality than is the Peters World Map. In particular these individual maps correct the distortions which are unavoidable on the Peters World Map in the equatorial and polar regions. An indication of how this has been applied can be seen from the shapes of the page areas on the Map Finder (front endpaper). In the north they are horizontal and thin while towards the Equator they are nearly square. The degree of departure from the normal page proportion is a guide to the amount of shape correction applied to the regional maps.

The eight polar maps on pages 80–95 have the same scale as all the other topographical maps. They also have fidelity of area, and represent one-sixtieth of the earth's surface on each double page. Thus the size of the countries and continents shown on them can be directly compared with all the other 35 topographical maps. The fidelity of position and axis which is necessarily lost on polar maps is also absent on these maps.

The thematic maps

The second part of this atlas directs attention to the whole earth. The author has collected data for 246 individual world thematic maps under 45 subject headings. Each of these subject headings is given a double page spread, but if more than one topic is covered under any subject, separate maps are given. Thus under the subject heading "Life Expectancy" only one topic is covered so the double spread comprises a single map, whereas the subject heading "Animal Husbandry" requires sixteen topics and therefore displays sixteen individual maps. The principle of one topic per map also enables all the maps to be represented by simple grades of colour, with, usually, a single hue chosen for each topic. Within this hue the range from light to dark colour represents low to high values of the topic. In this way all the thematic maps can be understood at a glance, without the necessity for complicated symbols or explanations.

The graticule

The traditional zero meridian running through Greenwich was adopted worldwide in 1884, when Britain was the strongest European colonial power and ruled over a quarter of the world. After the ending of colonialism and with the closure of Greenwich Observatory, there is no reason other than custom for retaining this zero meridian. The international dateline, which is dependent upon the zero meridian, also needs correction, since over its whole length it has been partially diverted where it cuts an inhabited area. The retention of the division into 360 degrees is also, it can be argued, an anomaly in the age of almost worldwide decimalisation.

Arno Peters has therefore proposed a new decimal grid in which the zero meridian and the international dateline would become a single line placed in the middle of the Bering Strait, and the earth is divided into 100 decimal degrees east-west and north-south. While for practical reasons the Greenwich system is retained throughout the bulk of the atlas, the new decimal grid is shown on pages 230–231.

The index

Someone consulting an index in search of a district, town or river has until now had to memorise, besides the page number, at least two grid figures, two letters, or a letter and a number. There can be few users of an atlas who have not experienced the irritation of forgetting at least one item in this unwieldy string of digits by the time the relevant map has been located, and the time-consuming exercise of turning back to the index to recall this information. In the Peters Atlas there is, apart from the page number, only a single letter, which can be easily remembered. This innovatory and simple indexing system is explained on page 188.

Digital cartography

The thematic maps in this edition have been revised using the latest available data and completely redrawn digitally, using Apple Mac technology.

The original edition of the atlas used computer techniques to adapt the world map to the 43 individual double spreads in the topographic section, minimising shape distortion on each spread. This process used Scitex technology with geographic data from the Erdgenössische Technische Hochschule in Berne. The same process is employed in the present edition, which also continues to feature the hand-crafted workmanship of the land surface colouring. The atlas thus reconciles the traditional and digital approaches.

Terry Hardaker

Chief Cartographer
Oxford Cartographers

PAGE FINDER FOR COUNTRIES

Afghanistan 60
Albania 35
Algeria 36–37
Andorra 34
Angola 44
Antigua & Barbuda 21
Argentina 28–29, 30–31
Armenia 54
Australia 72–73, 74, 76–77, 78
Austria 34–35
Azerbaijan 54
Bahamas 21
Bahrain 39
Bangladesh 61
Barbados 23
Belarus 33
Belgium 32–33
Belize 19
Benin 41
Bhutan 61
Bolivia 25, 28
Bosnia-Herzegovina 35
Botswana 48–49
Brazil 23, 24–25, 26–27, 28–29
Brunei 69
Bulgaria 35
Burkina Faso 40–41
Burma (Myanmar) 62, 65
Burundi 45
Cambodia 65, 66
Cameroon 41
Canada 11, 12–13, 14–15
Cape Verde 230
Central African Republic 41, 42
Chad 37, 38, 41, 42
Chile 28, 30
China 56–57, 58, 61, 62–63
Colombia 22–23, 24–25
Comoros 47
Congo 41, 42, 44
Congo, Dem. Rep. of . 42, 44–45, 46
Costa Rica 22
Côte d'Ivoire 40
Croatia 35
Cuba 20–21
Cyprus 35
Czech Republic 33, 34–35
Denmark 33
Djibouti 43
Dominica 23
Dominican Republic 21
Ecuador 24
East Timor 69, 72
Egypt 38
El Salvador 22
Equatorial Guinea 41
Eritrea 38–39, 43
Estonia 33
Ethiopia 43
Fiji 75
Finland 33
France 34
French Guiana 26
Gabon 41, 44
Gambia 40
Georgia 54
Germany 33
Ghana 40
Great Britain & Northern Ireland . . 32
Greece 35
Greenland 90–91
Grenada 23
Guatemala 19, 22
Guinea 40
Guinea-Bissau 40
Guyana 23
Haiti 21
Honduras 19, 22
Hungary 35
Iceland 32
India 60–61, 64
Indonesia 68–69, 70
Iran 39, 54–55, 60
Iraq 39
Ireland 32
Israel 38
Italy 34–35
Jamaica 21
Japan 58–59
Jordan 38
Kazakstan 54–55, 56
Kenya 43, 45
Kiribati 231
Korea, North 58
Korea, South 58
Kuwait 39
Kyrgyzstan 55, 56
Laos 62, 66, 66
Latvia 33
Lebanon 38
Lesotho 49
Liberia 40
Libya 37, 38
Liechtenstein 34
Lithuania 33
Luxembourg 33
Macedonia 35
Madagascar 47
Malawi 45
Malaysia 66–67
Maldives 64
Mali 36–37, 40–41
Malta 35
Marshall Islands 231
Mauritania 36, 40
Mauritius 47
Mexico 18–19
Micronesia 71
Moldova 33, 35
Monaco 34
Mongolia 56–57
Morocco 36
Mozambique 46
Myanmar 62, 65
Namibia 48
Nauru 231
Nepal 61
Netherlands 33
New Zealand 79
Nicaragua 22
Niger 37, 41
Nigeria 41
Norway 33
Oman 39, 60
Pakistan 60
Palau 71
Panama 22
Papua New Guinea 70–71
Paraguay 28–29
Peru 24–25
Philippines 67
Poland 33
Portugal 34
Qatar 39
Romania 35
Russia 10, 33, 50–51, 52–53, 54–55, 56–57, 58–59
Rwanda 45
St. Kitts Nevis 21
St. Lucia 23
St. Vincent & the Grenadines 23
Samoa 231
San Marino 34
Sao Tomé & Principe 41
Saudi Arabia 38–39
Senegal 40
Seychelles 231
Sierra Leone 40
Singapore 66
Slovakia 33, 35
Slovenia 35
Solomon Islands 71
Somalia 43
South Africa 48–49
Spain 34
Sri Lanka 64
Sudan 38, 42
Suriname 26
Swaziland 49
Sweden 33
Switzerland 34
Syria 38–39
Taiwan 61
Tajikistan 55
Tanzania 45, 46
Thailand 62, 66
Togo 41
Tonga 231
Trinidad and Tobago 23
Tunisia 34, 36–37
Turkey 35, 54
Turkmenistan 54–55, 60
Tuvalu 231
Uganda 42, 45
Ukraine 33, 35, 54
United Arab Emirates 39
Uruguay 28–29
USA . . 11, 14–15, 16–17, 18–19, 20
Uzbekistan 55
Vanuatu 75
Venezuela 23
Vietnam 62, 66
Western Sahara 36
Yemen 39, 43
Yugoslavia 35
Zambia 44–45
Zimbabwe 49

THE WORLD IN 43 MAPS AT THE SAME SCALE
EACH MAP SHOWS ONE-SIXTIETH OF THE EARTH'S SURFACE.

The colours used on the maps simulate those found in nature.

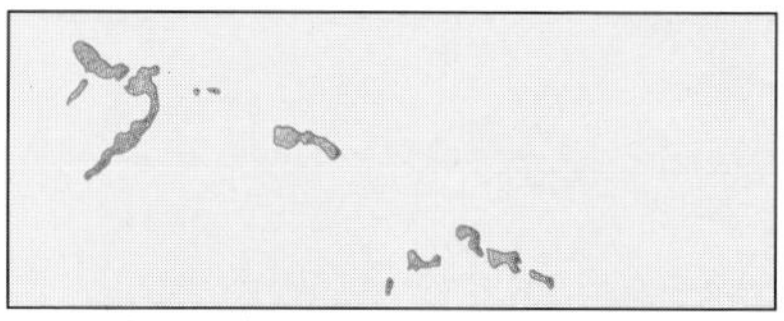
Water (Lakes, Seas, Oceans)

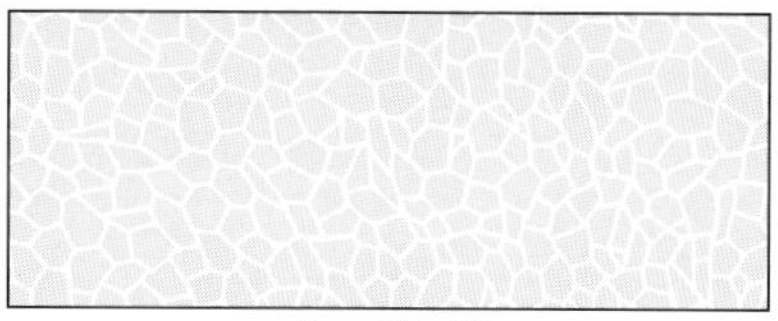
Ice Shelf

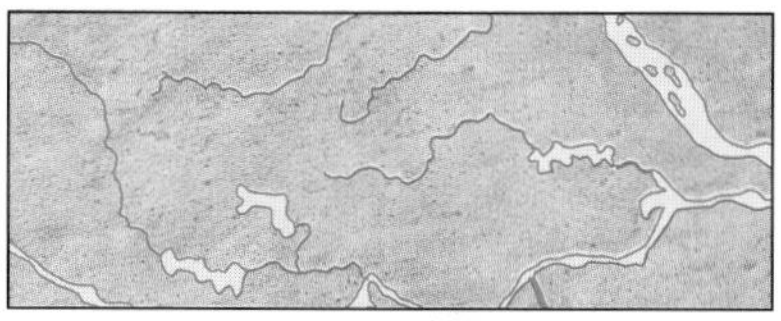
Vegetation (Plains)

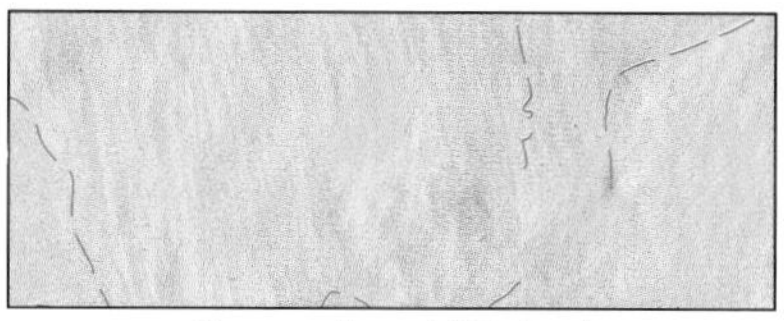
Barren Land (Plains)

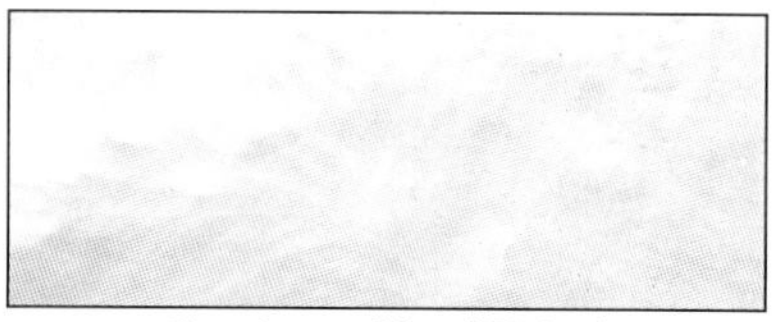
Continental Ice (Plains)

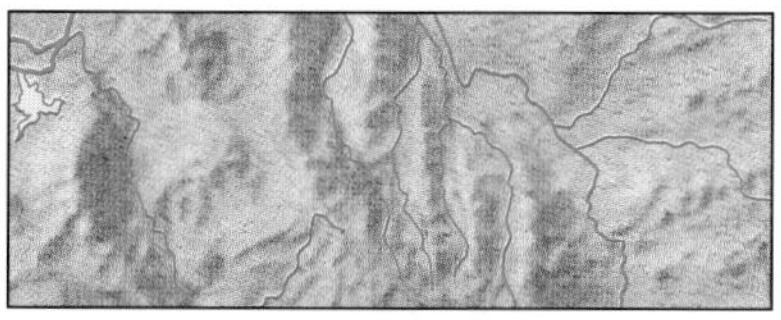
Vegetation (Hills)

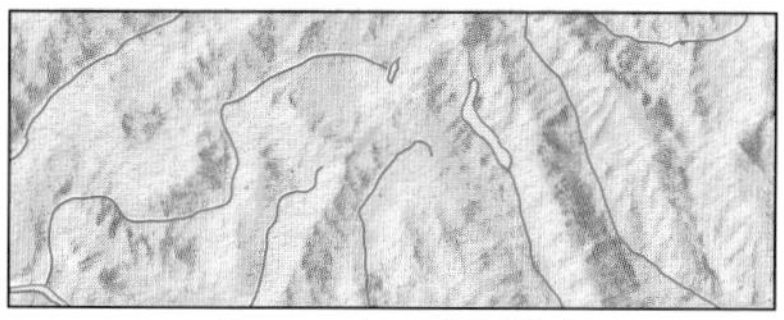
Barren Land (Hills)

Continental Ice (Hills)

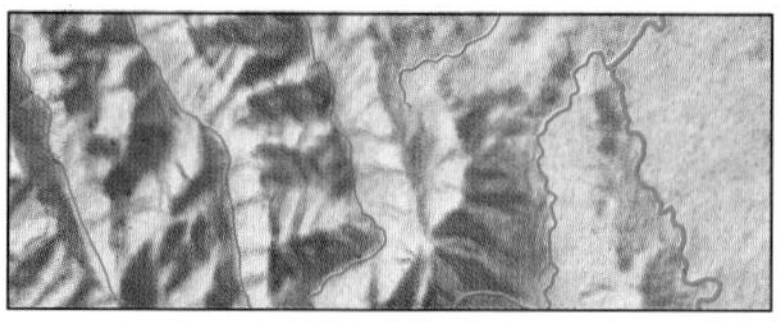
Vegetation (Mountains)

Barren Land (Mountains)

Continental Ice (Mountains)

Spot Heights:

- ·1236 — 1236 Metres above Sea Level
- ·-25 — 25 Metres below Sea Level

Communications:

- Railway
- Road
- Motorway
- Motorway in Tunnel
- River
- Canal

Boundaries:

- International Boundary
- International Boundary on River
- Disputed International Boundary
- State Boundary

On each double page the 1000 largest and most important cities and towns are shown; if the double page shows sea as well as land, there are proportionately fewer:

- fewer than 100,000 inhabitants
- 100,000 – 1,000,000 inhabitants
- 1,000,000 – 5,000,000 inhabitants
- over 5,000,000 inhabitants

Adjoining map indicator:

25 — Map of adjoining area is on page 25.

Other physical features:

- Waterfall
- Swamp, Marsh
- Salt Lake
- Coral Reef

Other man-made features:

- Archaeological Site
- Great Wall of China

Latitude and Longitude:

- 25°E — 25 degrees Longitude East
- 50°W — 50 degrees Longitude West
- 30°N — 30 degrees Latitude North
- 60°S — 60 degrees Latitude South
- Tropics

Type styles:

- *Mato Grosso* — Physical Features
- Kolhapur — Cities and towns (capital cities underlined)
- **BELGIUM** — Countries
- T E X A S — States
- *INDIAN OCEAN* — Oceans, Seas

Peters Projection (fidelity of area, axis and position)

165°E 170°E 175°E 180° 175°W 170°W

A R C T I C

1097
De Long Strait
Wrangel Island

70°N

C H U K C H I

S E A

Cape Lisburne

Ambarchik
Mal. Baranikha
Pevek
Krasnoarmeyskiy
Cherskiy

North Anyuskiy Mts.

Retkucha
Ostrovnoy ·1641
Little Anyuy
Ilirney

Plamennyy
Mys Shmidta
Iultin
·1707 2300

Point Hope

RUSSIA
South Anyuskiy Mts.

1508

Kotze Sou

Arctic Circle
Great Anyuy
·1313
·1504

Egvekinot

Chukot Peninsula
1250
Krasnaya Yaranga

Uelen
Shishmaref

Oloyskiy Mts.
·2200
Yeropol
Petushkova
Morokovo
Ust'-Belaya

Uel'kal

Akkani
Little Diomede
Wales
Tel

65°N
Markovo
Anadyr'
Anadyr'

Nunligran

Providseniya

Bering Strait

Gulf of Anadyr

Penzhino

Tumanskiy

Gambell
Saint Lawrence Island
(U.S.A.)

Kolymskiy Mts.
Berezovo
Velikaya

Alak

Koryak Mountains
Beringovskiy

Kovrizhka
Manily
Maynopil'gyn
Cape Navarin

Hooper Bay

Dana
·2562
Khatyrka

Penzhinskiy Mts.
Vatyna
·1285
Verkh.
Pakhacha
Apuka
Chukotskaya

Saint Matthew

Nunivak

Gulf of Penzhinskaya
Olyutorskiy

Il'pyrskiy
Korf
Cape Olyutorskiy

60°N

B E R I N G

53

·1700
Ossora
Ostrovnoy
Karaginskiy Island

S E A

Pribilof Islands

Kamchatsk

Kamchatka
·2412

Podutesnaya
55°N
·1327
Komandor Islands
(Russia)

Unalaska
De Ha

Umnak

Fox Isla

Attu
Near Islands
(U.S.A.)

Andreanof Islands
Atka

Kiska
Rai Islands
(U.S.A.)
Amchitka
Adak

A l e u t i a n   I s l a

165°E 170°E 175°E 180° 175°W 170°W

This map shows 1/60 of the earth's surface

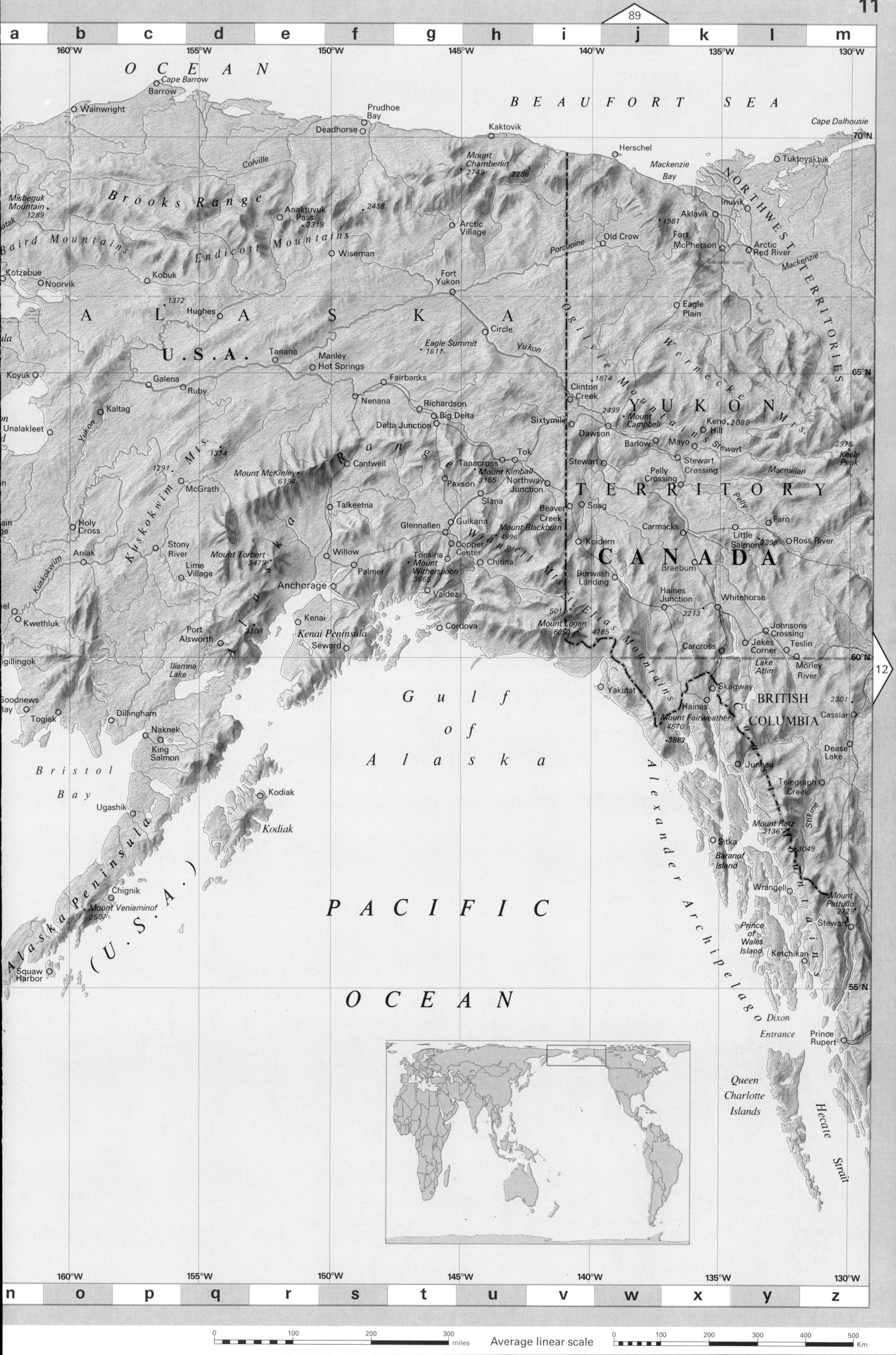
89
a b c d e f g h i j k l m
160°W 155°W 150°W 145°W 140°W 135°W 130°W
O C E A N
Cape Barrow
Barrow
Wainwright
Prudhoe Bay
Deadhorse
Kaktovik
B E A U F O R T S E A
Cape Dalhousie
70°N
Herschel
Mackenzie Bay
Tuktoyaktuk
Colville
Mount Chamberlin 2749
2286
Misheguk Mountain 1289
Brooks Range
Anaktuvuk Pass 2319
2438
Arctic Village
1981
Aklavik
Inuvik
NORTHWEST TERRITORIES
Baird Mountains
Endicott Mountains
Wiseman
Porcupine
Old Crow
Fort McPherson
Arctic Red River
Mackenzie
Kotzebue
Noorvik
Kobuk
Fort Yukon
1372
Hughes
A L A S K A
Circle
Eagle Plain
Ogilvie Mountains
Wernecke Mts.
U.S.A.
Tanana
Manley Hot Springs
Eagle Summit 1611
Yukon
Koyuk
Galena
Ruby
Fairbanks
1874
Clinton Creek
65°N
Nenana
Richardson
Big Delta
YUKON
2499
Mount Campbell
Keno Hill
2088
Kaltag
Unalakleet
Delta Junction
Sixtymile
Dawson
Barlow
Mayo
Stewart
Kuskokwim Mts.
1374
Alaska Range
Tok
Stewart Crossing
2975
Keele Peak
1291
Mount McKinley 6194
Cantwell
Tanacross
Mount Kimball 3155
Northway Junction
Stewart
Macmillan
McGrath
Paxson
Pelly Crossing
TERRITORY
Pelly
Slana
Talkeetna
Beaver Creek
Snag
Faro
Holy Cross
Glennallen
Gulkana
Wrangell Mts.
Mount Blackburn 4996
Carmacks
Little Salmon 2398
Ross River
Stony River
Koidern
Aniak
Mount Torbert 3479
Willow
Tonsina
Copper Center
Chitina
CANADA
Kuskokwim
Lime Village
Palmer
Mount Witherspoon 3665
Braeburn
Burwash Landing
Anchorage
Valdez
Haines Junction
Whitehorse
Kwethluk
Kenai
501
St. Elias Mountains
2213
Kenai Peninsula
Cordova
Mount Logan 6050
4785
Johnsons Crossing
Port Alsworth
3108
Seward
Jakes Corner
Teslin
Carcross
60°N
Togiak
Iliamna Lake
Lake Atlin
Morley River
12
Goodnews Bay
Yakutat
Skagway
BRITISH COLUMBIA
2301
Cassiar
Dillingham
Gulf of Alaska
Haines
Naknek
Mount Fairweather 4670
Coast Mountains
King Salmon
3882
Dease Lake
Bristol Bay
Juneau
Kodiak
Telegraph Creek
Ugashik
Alexander Archipelago
Stikine
Mount Ratz 3136
Sitka
3049
Baranof Island
Alaska Peninsula
(U.S.A.)
Chignik
Mount Veniaminof 2507
Wrangell
PACIFIC
Mount Pattullo 2725
Stewart
Prince of Wales Island
Ketchikan
Squaw Harbor
55°N
O C E A N
Dixon Entrance
Prince Rupert
Queen Charlotte Islands
Hecate Strait
n o p q r s t u v w x y z
0 100 200 300 miles
Average linear scale
0 100 200 300 400 500 Km

125°W   120°W   115°W   110°W   105°W   100°W

ARCTIC

80°N

OCEAN

Queen

E l i z a b e t h   I s l a n

Meighen Island

Borden Island

Prince Gustav Adolf

S v e r d r u

Ellef Ringnes Island

Hassel Sound

Amund R
Island

·457

Sea

Magnetic
North Pole (1992)

Mackenzie-King Island

Lougheed Island

B E A U F O R T

Prince Patrick Island

Mould Bay

·320

Parry Islands

Bathurst Island

S E A

·1067

Melville Island

·457

75°N

McClure Strait

Dundas Peninsula

Viscount Melville Sound

Cape
Prince Alfred

·248

Cape
Prince Alfred

Prince of Wales Strait

Stefansson
Island

Storkerson
Peninsula

McClintock Channel

Prince of Wales Island

B a n k s   I s l a n d

Prince Albert
Peninsula

Hadley Bay

Franklin
Strait

Sachs Harbour

·640

·762

Minto Inlet

V i c t o r i a

Cape
Bathurst

Holman Island

I s l a n d

Cape Parry

Amundsen Gulf

Prince   Albert   Sound

Victoria Strait

King Willia
Island

70°N

Cape Baring

Wollaston
Peninsula

·518

Read Island

Dease Strait

Cambridge Bay

Queen   Maud   Gulf

Adelai
She
Ba
Peninsula

Paulatuk

·366

Dolphin and Union Strait

·221

·609

Coronation   Gulf

Bluenose Lake

Perry Island

Colville Lake

Coppermine
(Kugluktuk)

·244

MacAlpine
Lake

460·

·518

Bathurst
Inlet

Arctic Circle

Fort Good
Hope

Great Bear Lake

Port Radium
(Echo Bay)

Takijuk Lake

·823

N U N

N

Garry Lake

·1003

Fort Franklin
(Déline)

Contwoyto
Lake

Aberdeen Lake

Norman
Wells

Hottah Lake

65°N

11

Fort Norman
(Tulit'a)

·704

N O R T H - W E S T

Aylmer Lake

Thelon

·2164

Rae Lakes

Warburton
Lake

Clinton
Colden
Lake

·413

Dubawnt
Lake

Mackenzie   Mountains

Lac
La Martre

Snare River

Artillery Lake

Yathkyed
Lake

Wrigley

·1577

Lac la Martre

Edzo   Rae

·221

Reliance

T E R R I T O R I E S

Yellowknife

Whitefish
Lake

Mount
Sir James
McBrien
2762

C

Snowdrift
(Lutselk'e)

·354

N

Mount
Hunt
2748

Fort Simpson

Great
Slave
Lake

A

Nonacho
Lake

Ennadai
Lake

·1548

Mackenzie

Fort
Providence

Fort Resolution

YUKON

Nahanni Butte

Hay River

Dawson Landing

Wholdaia
Lake

Kasba Lake

·349

TERRITORY

Enterprise

Watson
Lake

Fort Liard

Tathlina
Lake

Fort Smith

·594

Nueltin Lake

60°N

·1763

Nelson Forks

Caribou

Uranium
City   Eldorado

Caribo

Liard

·1036
Mountains

River

·236

Stony Rapids

Fort Chipewyan

Lake
Athabasca

B R I T I S H

Hay River

Fort Nelson

Steamboat

Churchill Peak
3049

Peace River

High Level

Rabbit Lake

Mount Pattullo
2729

3048

Wollaston
Lake

·674

Cree Lake

Reindeer
Lake

C O L U M B I A

Fort Burden
2324

Fort
St. John

A L B E R T A

·859

Athabasca

·672

S A S K A T C H E W A N

Kinoosao

Southern
Indian
Lake

·2047

Manning

Lynn Lake

M A N I

·3

·1094

Fort McMurray

Frobisher Lake

Southend

·390

Lake
Williston

Dawson Creek

Peace River

Peter
Pond
Lake

Churchill
Lake

Chetwynd
869

Rycroft   McLennan

Thompson

Mackenzie

Tupper

High Prairie

Lesser
Slave Lake

Buffalo
Narrows

Churchill

Island Falls

Hazelton

McLeod Lake

Grande Prairie

Valleyview
1259

Slave Lake   Smith

·553
Fort Black

Lac
La Ronge

Flin Flon

Wabowde

55°N

125°W   120°W   115°W   110°W   100°W

This map shows 1/60 of the earth's surface

90
a b c d e f g h i j k l m
90°W 85°W 80°W 75°W 70°W 65°W
Nansen Sound
Eureka
Agassiz Ice Cap
Axel Heiberg Island
Islands
Ellesmere Island
Norwegian Bay
Bjorne Peninsula
Sydney Ice Cap • 1328
Graham Island
Smith Bay
North Lincoln Land
Grise Fjord
Jones Sound
Devon Island
•1887
Dundas Harbour
Baffin Bay
Strait
Cape Clarence
Lancaster Sound
set Island
Prince Regent Inlet
Admiralty Inlet
Arctic Bay
•1189
Borden Peninsula
Bylot Island
•2134
Eclipse Sound
Pond Inlet
•549
Brodeur Peninsula
244•
Buchan Gulf
Bernier Bay
Gulf of Boothia
518
•1554
Clyde
Baffin Island
Barnes Ice Cap
•1250
Spence Bay (Taloyoak)
Fury and Hecla Strait
•558
Jens Munk Island
Rowley Island
Foley
Henry Kater Pen.
Home Bay
Davis Strait
Pelly Bay
Simpson Peninsula
Pelly Bay
Committee Bay
Wales Island
Melville Peninsula
Hall Beach
Prince Charles Island
•30
Kivitoo
Penny Ice Cap
•2591
Broughton Island
Peninsula
Rae Isthmus
Repulse Bay
381•
Foxe Basin
Koukdjuak
Nettiling Lake
Nunatak
Cumberland Peninsula
•2134
Cape Dyer
Exeter Sound
Pangnirtung
Lyon Inlet
V U T
Wager Bay
Vansittart Island
Nabukjuak
Cumberland Sound
Hoare Bay
Kigisa
Roes Welcome Sound
Southampton Island
•625
Foxe Channel
Foxe Peninsula
•411
Cape Dorset
Amadjuak Lake
Hall Peninsula
•1148
Coral Harbour
Bell Peninsula
Chesterfield Inlet
Chesterfield Inlet (Igluligaarjuk)
Salisbury Island
305
Iqaluit (Frobisher Bay)
Hudson Strait
Evans Strait
Fisher Strait
Nottingham Island
Meta Incognita Peninsula
Frobisher Bay
Labrador
Rankin Inlet
Coats Island
Big Island
Lake Harbour
Loks Land
Whale Cove
D A
Mansel Island
Ivujivik
•540
Salluit
Purtuniq
•661
Kangiqsujuaq
Resolution Island
mo Point (Arviat)
Sea
Cape Hopes Advance
Akulivik
Ungava
Akpatok Island
Port Burwell
Cape Chidley
ATLANTIC OCEAN
Hudson
Povungnituk
Ungava Bay
Ottawa Islands
Torngat Mountains
1621
Ramah
Peninsula
390•
NEWFOUNDLAND
rchill
Bay
Inukjuak
Kangiqsualujjuaq
Kuujjuaq
aux Feuilles
Koksoak
Labrador
Nutak
tock
•472
Lake Minto
QUEBEC
•1076
son
York Factory
•451
Fraser
Nain
Belcher Islands
196•
Fort Severn
Lac à l'Eau-Claire
241
Shamattawa
ONTARIO
Severn
Winisk
Cape Henrietta Maria
Kuujjuarapik
Caniapiscau
•876
Lake Bienville
Hopedale
90°W 85°W 80°W 75°W 70°W 65°W 55°W
80°N 75°N 70°N 65°N 60°N 55°N
n o p q r s t u v w x y z
16
17
90
0 100 200 300 miles
Average linear scale
0 100 200 300 400 500 Km

a   b   c   d   e   f   g   h   i   j   k   l   m

130°W   125°W   120°W   115°W

55°N

Dixon Entrance

Hazelton
McLeod
Lake
Endako
Prince Rupert
Skeena Terrace Walcott
Kitimat *1931*

Grande Prairie   Valleyview   *869*   Slave Lake   Smith   Atha

Whitecourt   Westlock
Barrhead   Edmonto

Hecate Strait

Ocean Falls

Queen Charlotte Islands

Prince George   Sinclair Mills   Grande Cache   Edson   Leduc   Wetaskiwin   Ve

B R I T I S H   C

Quesnel   *1000*   Mt Robson *3953* Red Pass   Jasper   Rocky Mountain House   Red Deer   A   L B E R T

Williams Lake   *2543*   Blue River   *3394*   Olds   Dru

Nechako Reservoir

Mount Waddington 4042

C O L U M B I A   Blackpool   Beavermouth   Golden   Banff   Calgary

Cache Creek   *2500*   Revelstoke   *2537*   High River

Kamloops   Armstrong   Fort Macleod   Mil

50°N

Port Hardy   *Queen Charlotte Strait*   *1749*   Powell River *1966*   Kelowna   Nelson   Cranbrook

Vancouver   Campbell River   Penticton   Trail   *2304*   Bonners Ferry   Browni

Strait of Georgia   Vancouver   Hope   Chilliwack   Oroville   Libby   Kalispell

Nanaimo   *Island*   Bellingham   Omak   Sandpoint   *Lake Flathead*   Cho

Victoria   Mount Vernon   Coeur d'Alene   Thompson Falls   Polson

Strait of Juan de Fuca   Port Angeles   Everett   Spokane   Wallace

Cape Flattery   Seattle   W A S H I N G T O N   Wenatchee   Moses Lake   M

Bremerton   Tacoma   Ellensburg   Pullman   Moscow   Missoula

P A C I F I C   Aberdeen   Olympia   *822*   Lewiston   Pierce   Hamilton

Centralia   Mt Rainier *4392*   Yakima   Richland   Snake   Walla Walla   Anaconda

Astoria   Longview   Grangeville   Wo

Tillamook   Vancouver   *Columbia*   Pendleton   Riggins   Salmon

Portland   The Dalles   Heppner   La Grande   New Meadows   Salmon

Salem   *1018*   John Day   Baker   Cascade   *2420*   I D A H O

O C E A N   Albany   Madras   *3857*   Borah Peak

O R E G O N   John Day   Weiser   *Salmon River*

Eugene   Bend   Ontario   Caldwell   *Mountains*   Hyndman Peak *3632*   Areo

2441   Hampton   Boise

Coos Bay   Chemult   *1982*   Burns   Poc

Roseburg   *Malheur Lake*   Burns Junction   *1000*   Glenns Ferry   Gooding

Wagontire   Twin Falls

Grants Pass   Medford   Klamath Falls   Lakeview   Riddle   Malad

McDermitt   Contact   Great Salt Lake

Crescent City   Yreka   Orovada   North Fork

Mount Shasta   Alturas   Wells   *3265*   Salt L

Mount Shasta *4317*   Winnemucca   Elko   Wendover

Burney   *2390*   Battle Mountain

Eureka   Susanville

Cape Mendocino   Redding   Pyramid Lake   Lovelock   *Great*

Garberville   Red Bluff   *2466*   *Basin*

40°N   *50*   Chico   Reno *1869*   Fallon   N E V A D A

Oroville   Carson City   Austin   Eureka   Ely

Yuba City   Wheeler Peak *3982*

Ukiah   Hawthorne   Currant   Milford

Santa Rosa   Sacramento   *2620*

Vallejo   Stockton   Tonopah

Oakland   Modesto   Boundary Peak *4007*   Goldfield   Caliente

San Francisco   C

San Jose   Merced   Bishop   Ce

Santa Cruz   *100*   Beatty   St. George

Salinas   Fresno   Death Valley   Las Vegas   A

Monterey   *1345*   Mount Whitney *4418*   *-86*   Lake Mead

King City   Visalia   Boulder City

Avenal   Delano   Ridgecrest   Searchlight

San Luis Obispo   *2449*   Colorado

Bakersfield   Baker   Kingman

Mojave   Barstow   Ludlow   Pre

Santa Barbara   Lancaster   *Lake Havasu City*

Ventura   A

35°N

n   o   p   q   r   s   t   u   v   w   x   y   z

130°W   125°W   120°W   115°W

This map shows 1/60 of the earth's surface

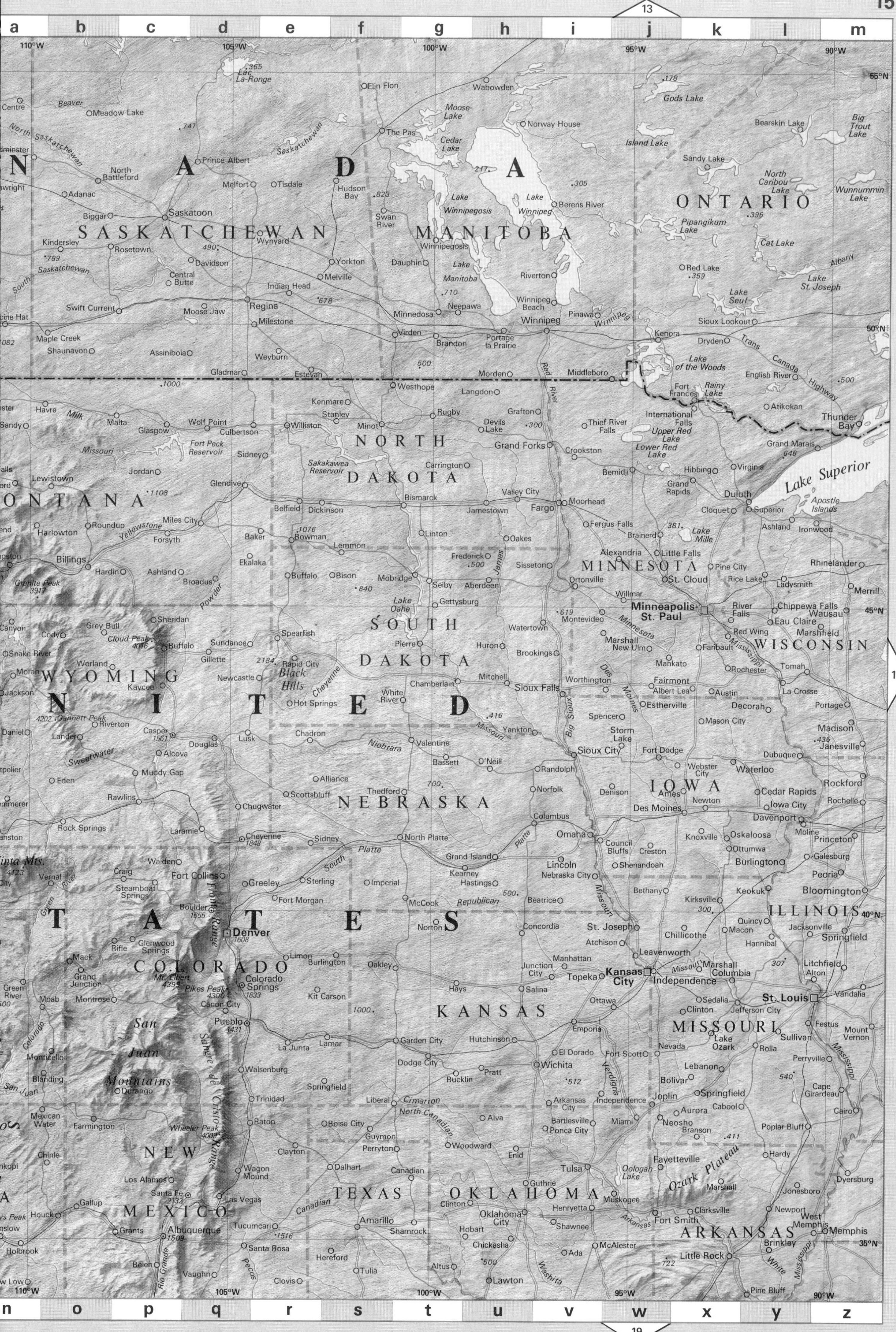

110°W   105°W   100°W   95°W   90°W

55°N

·365
Lac
La-Ronge

N
Centre
Beaver
Meadow Lake
Elin Flon
Wabowden
Moose-
Lake
Gods Lake
·178

·747
Norway House
Bearskin Lake
Big
Trout
Lake

Prince Albert
The Pas
Cedar
Lake
Island Lake
Wunnummin
Lake

North
Battleford
Adanac
Melfort
Tisdale
Hudson
Bay
·823
·217
A
·305
North
Caribou
Lake
Sandy Lake

Biggar
Saskatoon
Lake
Winnipegosis
Lake
Winnipeg
Berens River
ONTARIO
·396

SASKATCHEWAN
MANITOBA
Pipangikum
Lake
·305
Cat Lake

Kindersley
Rosetown
Wynyard
·490
Winnipegosis
Red Lake
·359
Lake
St. Joseph

·789
Davidson
Yorkton
Dauphin
Lake
Manitoba
Riverton
Lake
Seul

Central
Butte
Melville
Neepawa
·710
Winnipeg
Beach
Sioux Lookout

Swift Current
Indian Head
Minnedosa
Winnipeg
Pinawa
Winnipeg

cine Hat
Moose Jaw
Regina
Milestone
·678
Virden
Brandon
Portage
la Prairie
Kenora
Dryden
Trans
Canada
Highway
50°N

·1082
Maple Creek
Weyburn
Morden
Middleboro
Lake
of the Woods
English River
·500

Shaunavon
Assiniboia
Gladmar
Estevan
·1000
Westhope
Langdon
Morden
Red
River
Fort
Frances
Rainy
Lake
Atikokan
Thunder
Bay

Havre
Malta
Wolf Point
Kenmare
Stanley
Rugby
Grafton
Thief River
Falls
International
Falls
Upper Red
Lake
Grand Marais
·646

Sandy
Glasgow
Culbertson
Williston
Minot
Devils
Lake
·300
Crookston
Lower Red
Lake
Lake Superior

MONTANA
Fort Peck
Reservoir
Sidney
Sakakawea
Reservoir
NORTH
Carrington
Grand Forks
Bemidji
Grand
Rapids
Hibbing
Virginia
Duluth
Apostle
Islands

Lewistown
Jordan
Glendive
DAKOTA
Valley City
Moorhead
Fergus Falls
·381
Cloquet
Superior
Ashland
Ironwood

·1108
Miles City
Belfield
Dickinson
Bismarck
Jamestown
Fargo
Little Falls
Lake
Mille
Pine City
Rhinelander

Harlowton
Roundup
Baker
·1076
Bowman
Lemmon
Linton
Oakes
Alexandria
Brainerd
MINNESOTA
Rice Lake
Ladysmith
Merrill

Billings
Forsyth
Ekalaka
Buffalo
Bison
Frederick
·500
Sisseton
Ortonville
St. Cloud
Chippewa Falls
Wausau
45°N

Granite Peak
3917
Hardin
Ashland
Broadus
Powder
·840
Mobridge
Selby
Aberdeen
Willmar
Minneapolis
St. Paul
River Falls
Eau Claire
Marshfield

Cody
Sheridan
Sundance
Lake
Oahe
Gettysburg
·619
Montevideo
Red Wing
Faribault
Tomah
WISCONSIN

Grey Bull
Cloud Peak
4016
Buffalo
Gillette
2184
Rapid City
Pierre
SOUTH
Watertown
Marshall
New Ulm
Mankato
Rochester
La Crosse

Worland
Newcastle
Black
Hills
Chamberlain
DAKOTA
Huron
Brookings
Worthington
Albert Lea
Austin
Decorah
16

WYOMING
UNITED
Spearfish
Cheyenne
White
River
Mitchell
Sioux Falls
Spencer
Estherville
Mason City
Portage

Moran
Jackson
4202
Gannett Peak
Riverton
Lander
Hot Springs
·416
Yankton
Storm
Lake
Fort Dodge
Dubuque
Madison
·436
Janesville

Casper
1561
Douglas
Lusk
Chadron
Niobrara
Valentine
Missouri
Sioux City
Webster
City
Waterloo
Rockford

Daniel
Alcova
Muddy Gap
Bassett
O'Neill
Randolph
IOWA
Cedar Rapids
Iowa City
Rochelle

Sweetwater
Eden
Rawlins
Alliance
Thedford
·700
Norfolk
Denison
Ames
Newton
Davenport
Moline
Princeton

emmerer
Rock Springs
Scottsbluff
Chugwater
NEBRASKA
Columbus
Des Moines
Knoxville
Oskaloosa
Ottumwa
Galesburg

Laramie
Cheyenne
1848
Sidney
North Platte
Omaha
Council
Bluffs
Creston
Shenandoah
Burlington
Peoria

inta Mts.
4123
Vernal
Walden
Craig
Fort Collins
Greeley
Sterling
South
Platte
Imperial
Grand Island
Kearney
Hastings
Platte
Lincoln
Nebraska City
Bethany
Kirksville
·300
Keokuk
Bloomington

T
A
T
E
S
Steamboat
Springs
Boulder
1655
Fort Morgan
McCook
Republican
·500
Beatrice
Missouri
Concordia
St. Joseph
Chillicothe
Quincy
Macon
Jacksonville
ILLINOIS
40°N

Rifle
Glenwood
Springs
Denver
1608
Limon
Burlington
Oakley
Norton
St. Joseph
Atchison
Leavenworth
Hannibal
Springfield

Mack
Grand
Junction
COLORADO
Colorado
Springs
1833
Kit Carson
Junction
City
Manhattan
Topeka
Kansas
City
Independence
Marshall
Columbia
·307
Litchfield
Alton

Green
River
Moab
Montrose
Mt. Elbert
4399
Pikes Peak
4300
Canon City
Hays
Salina
Ottawa
Sedalia
Jefferson City
St. Louis
Vandalia

·500
Blanding
Pueblo
1431
KANSAS
Emporia
Clinton
MISSOURI
Sullivan
Festus
Mount
Vernon

Monticello
San
Juan
La Junta
Lamar
Garden City
Hutchinson
Nevada
Lake
Ozark
Rolla
Perryville

Mexican
Water
Farmington
Durango
Mountains
Walsenburg
Trinidad
Springfield
Dodge City
Pratt
Bucklin
Wichita
El Dorado
Fort Scott
Lebanon
Bolivar
Springfield
·540
Cape
Girardeau

San Juan
Blanding
Sangre de Cristo Range
Raton
Clayton
Liberal
Boise City
Cimarron
North Canadian
Alva
Arkansas
City
Bartlesville
Independence
Joplin
Aurora
Caboo!
Cairo

NEW
Wheeler
Peak
4000
Wagon
Mound
Dalhart
Perryton
Guymon
Woodward
Enid
Ponca City
Miami
Neosho
Branson
·411
Poplar Bluff

ys Peak
Houck
MEXICO
Santa Fe
2132
Las Vegas
Clayton
Canadian
Tulsa
Oologah
Lake
Fayetteville
Marshall
Hardy
Dyersburg

Chinle
Gallup
Albuquerque
1509
Tucumcari
·1516
Amarillo
Shamrock
TEXAS
OKLAHOMA
Guthrie
Clinton
Henryetta
Muskogee
Fort Smith
Clarksville
Newport
West
Memphis
Memphis

Grants
Santa Rosa
Hereford
Tulia
·500
Chickasha
Oklahoma
City
Shawnee
McAlester
ARKANSAS
Brinkley
35°N

Belen
Vaughn
Clovis
Altus
Lawton
Ada
·722
Little Rock
Pine Bluff

110°W   105°W   100°W   95°W   90°W

0   100   200   300   miles   Average linear scale   0   100   200   300   400   500   Km

12

a b c d e f g h i j k l m

95°W 90°W 85°W 80°W 75°W

MANITOBA

Shamattawa

Hudson Bay

Belcher Islands

Great Whale

55°N

Gods Lake

Winisk

Cape Henrietta Maria

Kuujjuarapik

.168

Kanaaupscow

Island Lake

Bearskin Lake

Big Trout Lake

Point Louis XIV

Chisasibi

La Radisson

Sakami

Sandy Lake 276

North Caribou Lake

Winisk Lake

.88

James Bay

Akimiki Island

.195

North Caribou Lake

Wunnummin Lake

Attawapiskat

.100

Pipangikum Lake

Attawapiskat Lake

Lake River

Eastmain

Eastmain

.396

Cat Lake

Fort Hope

268

Fort Albany

Q U

Red Lake

Lac Seul

268 Ogoki

Albany

Moosonee

Lake Evans .232

Chibougama

.359

Lake St. Joseph

Missinaibi

Abitibi

Fort Rupert

Rupert

Pinawa

.317

358 Armstrong

Nakina

Hearst

Kesagami Lake

U

50°N

Kenora Dryden

Sioux Lookout

Lake Nipigon

Longlac

Geraldton

Fraserdale

Matagami

.556 Chapais

Middleboro

Trans Canada Highway

English River

Nipigon

Manitouwadge

Kapuskasing

Cochrane

Monts Deloge .533

Senneterre

.GR

Fort Frances Atikokan

Schreiber

Marathon

White River

390.

Timmins

Lake Abitibi

Noranda Val-d'Or

International Falls

Rainy Lake

Thunder Bay

Isle Royale

New Liskeard

Kirkland Lake

.609

Thief River Falls

Upper Red Lake

Grand Marais

.693

Témiscaming

Cabonga Reservoir

358

Lower Red Lake

.646

Lake Superior

Copper Harbor

Chapleau

.640

Sudbury

Sturgeon Falls

Mont Laurier

Maniwaki

Hibbing

Virginia

Houghton

.665

Blind River

Espanola

North Bay

Pembroke

Buckingham

Bemidji

436.

Grand Rapids

Duluth

Apostle Islands

.603

Marquette

Sault Ste. Marie

.196

Ottawa

Hull

Mon

Fergus Falls

471

Cloquet

Superior

Ironwood

Ashland

.573

Iron Mountain

Seney

322

Little Current

Manitoulin Island

Georgian Bay

Parry Sound

Huntsville

Bancroft .419

Ste-Agathe-des-Mont

Ottawa

MINNESOTA

381

Mille Lacs

Rhinelander

Escanaba

Mackinaw City

Tobermory

Orillia L. Simcoe

Cornwall

Brainerd

Little Falls

Rice Lake

Ladysmith

Menominee

Petoskey

.573

Midland

Barrie

Perth

Smith's Falls

Alexandria

St. Cloud

Merrill

Wausau

Marinette

Alpena

Owen Sound

Port Elgin

Brockville

Willmar

Pine City

Chippewa Falls

Eau Claire

Marshfield

Sturgeon Bay

MICHIGAN

Goderich

Kitchener-Waterloo

Peterborough

Kingston

45°N

Minneapolis St. Paul

Red Wing

Stevens Point

Green Bay

Grayling

.200

Hamilton

Toronto

Oshawa

Belleville

Watertown

15

Marshall New Ulm

Faribault

WISCONSIN

Appleton

Manitowoc

Bay City

Saginaw

Sarnia

London

St. Catharines

Rochester Syracuse

.637

NEW

.510

Mankato

Rochester

Winona

Oshkosh

.223

Sheboygan

Cadillac

Ludington

Midland

Flint

St. Thomas

Niagara Falls

Utica

YORK

Fairmont

Albert Lea

Austin

La Crosse

Fond du Lac

Portage

.369

Muskegon

Lansing

.385

Détroit

Buffalo

Fredonia

Seneca Lake

Schenec

Worthington Estherville

Spencer

Mason City

.300

Madison

Milwaukee

Racine

Grand Rapids

Ann Arbor

Windsor

Erie

Dansville

Ithaca

Kin

Storm Lake

Webster City

Dubuque

Janesville

Beloit Kenosha

Battle Creek

Jackson

.358

Ashtabula

Meadville

Olean

Binghampton

Caskill Mountains

IOWA

Fort Dodge

Waterloo

Cedar Rapids

Freeport Rockford

Elgin

Rochelle

De Kalb

Chicago

South Bend

Toledo

Sandusky

.424

Cleveland

Youngstown

Williamsport

Clearfield

Kane Mansfield

Scran

Newbur

Denison

Ames

.1290

Newton

Iowa City

Princeton

Morris

Joliet

Gary

Napoleon

PENNSYLVANIA

Des Moines

Davenport

Moline

Kankakee

Fort Wayne

Findlay

Canton

Paters

Omaha

Council Bluffs

Knoxville

Oskaloosa

Ottumwa

Burlington

Galesburg

236

Peoria

Lafayette

Kokomo

Lima

Mansfield

Pittsburgh

Johnstown

Altoona

Harrisburg

.706

Newar

Elizabet

Shenandoah

Nebraska City

Bethany

Kirksville

Keokuk

Bloomington

Rantoul

Danville

Muncie

Columbus

Newark

.424 Wheeling

Greensburg

956

Reading

Allentow

Trenton

40°N

St. Joseph

Atchison

.300

Champaign

ILLINOIS

Beardstown

Decatur

Springfield

Anderson

Springfield

Dayton

Cambridge

Cumberland

Wilmington

Lancaster

Phila

Leavenworth

367

Chillicothe

Macon

Quincy

Jacksonville

INDIANA

Richmond

Washington Court House

Fairmont Marietta

Hagerstown

MARYLAND

NEW J

Kansas City

Independence

Hannibal

.307

Terre Haute

Indianapolis

Chillicothe

Athens

Parkersburg

Clarksburg

Bickle Knob

Baltimore

Washington DC

Annapolis

Vineland

Topeka

Sedalia

Columbia

Litchfield

Alton

Bloomington

Effingham

322

Cincinnatti

Hillsboro

412.

Portsmouth

1222

Elkins

Arlington

Alexandria

Cambridge

Cape May

St Louis

Jefferson City

Festus

Vandalia

Bedford

Ohio

Maysville

WEST

Charleston

1476

Culpeper

ederickbsurg

.23

MISSOURI

Sullivan

Rolla

Mt. Vernon

Jasper

Louisville

Lexington

Huntington

Morehead

VIRGINIA

Richwood

Spruce Knob

Lexington

Park Salisbury

Charlottesville

Emporia

Ottawa

Lake Ozark

Perryville

Evansville

Owensboro

Elizabethtown

Berea

Williamson

Pikeville

Bluefield

VIRGINIA

Richmond

Fort Scott

Nevada

Lebanon

.300

540

West Frankfort

314

Cape Girardeau

Central City

Hazard

Roanoke

Lynchburg

Williamsburg

Petersburg

Hampton

Independence

Bolivar

Springfield

.510

Caboel

Cairo

Paducah

KENTUCKY

Somerset

.532

Wytheville

Marion

25°

Martinsville

Danville

Portsmouth

Newport News

Miami

Bartlesville

Joplin

Aurora

Neosho

Branson

Hardy

Poplar Bluff

Blytheville

Bowling Green

Glasgow

Lake Cumberland

307

Kingsport

1743 Mount Rogers

784

Mount Airy

Winston Salem

Greensboro

Durham

Rocky Mount

Roanoke Rapids

Elizabeth City

Tulsa

Vinita

Fayetteville

Marshall

Clarksville

Dyersburg

Clarksville

Cumberland

High Knob 1916

Knoxville

Newport

2025

Hickory

Raleigh

Greenville

Goldsboro

Henrietta

ARKANSAS

Jonesboro

Jackson

Columbia

Nashville

Murfreesboro

Tennessee

.829

Rockwood

Clingmans Dome

2290

Ridge

Asheville

Hendersonville

Charlotte

NORTH CAROLINA

Fayetteville

New Bern

Fort Smith

Poteau

Conway

West Memphis

.100

TENNESSEE

Lawrenceburg

Fayetteville

Huntsville

Chattanooga

Cleveland

Greenville

Spartanburg

Rockingham

Morehead City

Cape Hatteras

Pamlico Sound

35°N

McAlester

95°W

Little Rock

Brinkley

Memphis

Savannah

Florence

90°W

85°W

80°W

75°W

n o p q r s t u v w x y z

19 20

This map shows 1/60 of the earth's surface

13
90
a b c d e f g h i j k l m
70°W
65°W
60°W
55°W
55°N
50°N
45°N
40°N
35°N
N E W F O U N D L A N D
Hopedale
Makkovik
Caniapiscau
Attikamagen Lake
Schefferville
Canairiktok
Petitsikapau Lake
Caniapiscau Reservoir
945
Smallwood Reservoir
Naskaupi
Hamilton Inlet
Rigolet
Cartwright
Lookout Mountain
Twin Falls
562
North-West River
Lake Melville
Happy Valley-Goose Bay
Churchill
914
Nitchequon
Labrador City
Wabush
L a b r a d o r
Atikonak Lake
989
120
1128
Otish Mountains
Lake Joseph
Fox Harbour
St.-Paul
St.-Augustin
Natashquan
Gagnon
Manicouagan Reservoir
948
Lake Plétipi
Ste-Marguerite
Romaine
Strait of Belle Isle
St. Anthony
Flower's Cove
St.-Augustin
805
E
B
E
C
Manicouagan
Sept-Iles
Port-Cartier
Havre-St-Pierre
125
Natashquan
Harrington Harbour
Cape Whittle
656
Long Range
806
Rocky Harbour
Nôtre Dame Bay
Péribonca
Pipmuacan Reservoir
D
Baie Comeau
St. Lawrence
Ste-Anne-des-Monts
A
Port Menier
Anticosti Island
312
Springdale
Corner Brook
Lewis Hill
814
Buchans
Windsor
Gander
Lake St-Jean
Alma
Saguenay
Escoumins
Matane
1268
Mount Jacques Cartier
Murdochville
Gaspé
Chandler
Gulf of
Stephenville
N E W F O U N D L A N D
381
Chicoutimi-Jonquière
Mont-Joli
Rimouski
New Richmond
Miscou Point
St. Lawrence
St.-Siméon
Campbelltown
Mount Carleton
820
493
Rivière-du-Loup
Edmundston
Bathurst
518
Channel-Port-aux-Basques
St. Alban's
St. John's
Tuque
Baie-St.-Paul
Cabot Strait
Magdalen Islands
Ile d'Orleans
Québec
Van Buren
Newcastle
Alberton
PRINCE EDWARD ISLAND
Cape North
Grand Bank
St. Pierre and Miquelon (France)
Ste-Foy
Montmagny
884
N E W
B R U N S W I C K
Presque Isle
Cap-de-la-Madeleine
Trois Rivières
St.-Eleanors
142
Charlottetown
531
Glace Bay
Sydney
Cape Race
Northumberland Strait
Woodstock
Moncton
St.-Georges
Drummondville
1605
East Millinocket
Fredericton
Amherst
367
Sherbrooke
New Glasgow
Mulgrave
Dover Foxcroft
St. Stephen
386
Saint John
Truro
M A I N E
331
Bangor
N O V A
S C O T I A
Bay of Fundy
Berlin
Rumford
Waterville
Middleton
Dartmouth
Halifax
Mount Washington
1917
Augusta
Hulls Cove
Bridgewater
85
Brunswick
NEW HAMPSHIRE
Lewiston
Yarmouth
Shelburne
Laconia
Portland
Cape Sable
Rochester
Portsmouth
Manchester
Haverhill
MASSACHUSETTS
Boston
Worcester
Cape Cod
Providence
New Bedford
RHODE ISLAND
CONNECTICUT
Southampton
Long Island
A T L A N T I C
O C E A N
n o p q r s t u v w x y z
21
0 100 200 300 miles
Average linear scale
0 100 200 300 400 500 Km

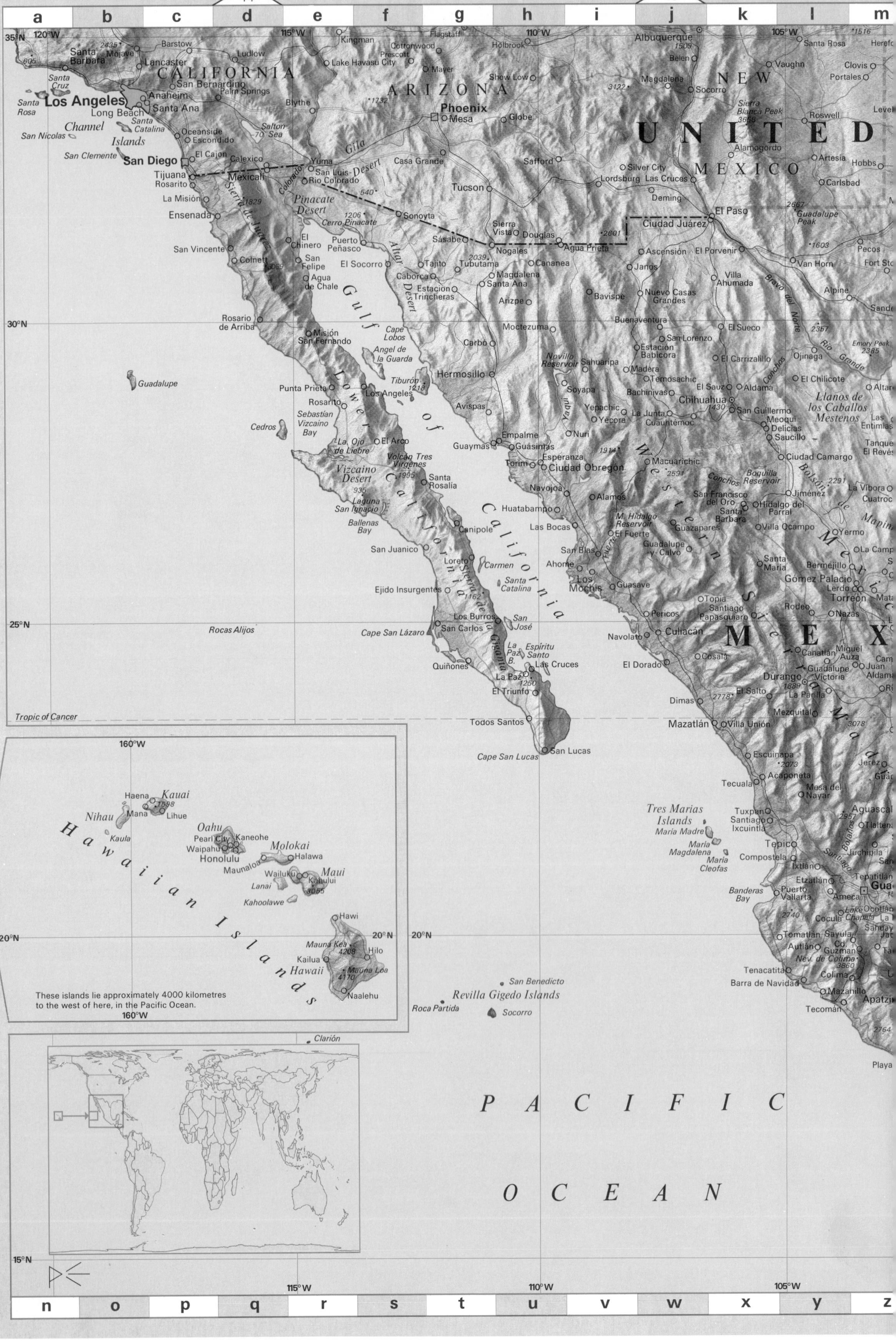

This map shows 1/60 of the earth's surface

a   b   c   d   14   e   f   g   h   i   15   j   k   l   m

35°N   120°W   115°W   110°W   Albuquerque   1509   105°W   Santa Rosa   Herefo   1516

Barstow   Kingman   Cottonwood   Flagstaff   Holbrook   Belen   Vaughn   Clovis   Portales   Leve

Santa   2435   Mojave   Lancaster   Ludlow   Lake Havasu City   Prescott   Mayer   Show Low   3122   Magdalena   Socorro

Barbara   605   CALIFORNIA   ARIZONA   Sierra Blanco Peak 3656   Roswell

Santa Cruz   Los Angeles   San Bernardino   Palm Springs   Blythe   Phoenix   Globe   Mesa   UNITED   Artesia   Hobbs

Santa   Long Beach   Anaheim   Santa Ana   Salton   70   Gila   NEW MEXICO   Carlsbad

Rosa   Channel   Santa Catalina   Oceanside   Escondido   Sea   Casa Grande   Safford   Silver City   Alamogordo

San Nicolas   Islands   El Cajon   Calexico   Yuma   Desert   Tucson   Lordsburg   Las Cruces   Deming   2667   Guadalupe Peak

San Clemente   San Diego   Tijuana   Mexicali   San Luis-   Rio Colorado   El Paso   Pecos

Rosarito   Colorado   540   Ciudad Juárez   1603   Van Horn   Fort Stoc

La Misión   1829   Pinacate Desert   Sonoyta   Sierra Vista   Douglas   2601   Ascensión   El Porvenir   Alpine

Ensenada   1206   Cerro Pinacate   Nogales   Agua Prieta   Janos   Sande

Sierra de Juárez   El Chinero   Puerto Peñasco   Altar Desert   2039   Tubutama   Cananea   Villa Ahumada

San Vincente   San Felipe   El Socorro   Tajito   Magdalena   Santa Ana   Nuevo Casas Grandes

Colnet   1969   Agua de Chale   Caborca   Estación Trincheras   Arizpe   Bavispe   El Sueco   2367

30°N   Rosario de Arriba   Gulf   Cape Lobos   Carbó   Moctezuma   Buenaventura   San Lorenzo   Ojinaga   Emory Peak 2385

Misión San Fernando   Angel de la Guarda   Hermosillo   Estación Babícora   El Carrizalillo   Rio Grande   El Chilcote

Lower   Tiburón   1218   Novillo Reservoir   Sahuaripa   Madera   Temósachic   Llanos de los Caballos Mestenos

Guadalupe   Punta Prieta   Los Angeles   Avispas   Soyapa   Bachiniyas   El Sauz   Aldama   Las Entimas

Rosarito   of   Yepachic   La Junta   Chihuahua   1430   San Guillermo

Sebastián Vizcaino Bay   Cedros   California   Guaymas   Empalme   Guásimas   Nuri   Yécora   Cuauhtémoc   Meoqui   Delicias

La Ojo de Liebre   El Arco   Volcán Tres Vírgenes   1995   Santa Rosalía   1914   Macuarichic   2591   Saucillo

Vizcaino Desert   935   Laguna San Ignacio   Torim   Ciudad Obregón   Conchos del Oro   Boquilla Reservoir   Ciudad Camargo   2291   La Vibora

Ballenas Bay   Navojoa   Alamos   San Francisco del Oro   Jiménez   Cuatro

San Juanico   Huatabampo   Las Bocas   M. Hidalgo Reservoir   Santa Barbara   Hidalgo del Parral   Yermo   La Camp

Canipole   Loreto   Carmen   San Blas   Guazapares   Villa Ocampo   Santa Maria

Santa Catalina   Ahome   El Fuerte   Guadalupe y Calvo   Bermejillo   La Camp

Ejido Insurgentes   Sierra de la Giganta   1162   Los Mochis   Guasave   Gómez Palacio   Lerdo   Torreón   Mata

25°N   Rocas Alijos   Los Burros   San José   Pericos   Topia   Santiago Papasquiaro   Rodeo   Nazas

Cape San Lázaro   San Carlos   La Paz   Espíritu Santo   Navolato   Culiacán   Canatlán   Miguel Auza   Cam

Quiñones   B.   Las Cruces   El Dorado   Cosalá   Guadalupe Victoria   Juan Aldama

La Paz   1250   Durango   1889   La Parilla

El Triunfo   Dimas   2778   El Salto

Tropic of Cancer   Todos Santos   Mezquital   Mazatlán   Villa Unión   3078

160°W   Cape San Lucas   San Lucas   Escuinapa   2073   Jerez

Haena   Kauai   1598   Tecuala   Acaponeta   Mesa del Nayar   Guar

Nihau   Mana   Lihue   Tres Marias Islands   Tuxpan   2995   Aguasca

Kaula   Oahu   Pearl City   Kaneohe   Maria Madre   Santiago Ixcuintla   Tlaltena

Hawaiian Islands   Waipahu   Honolulu   Molokai   Halawa   Maria Magdalena   Tepico   Ixtlán   Juchipila   San

Maunaloa   Wailuku   Maui   Maria Cleofas   Compostela   Etzatlán   Tepatitlán

Lanai   Kahului   3055   Banderas Bay   Puerto Vallarta   Ameca   Gua

Kahoolawe   Hawi   2740   Cocula   Chapala

20°N   Mauna Kea 4208   Hilo   San Benedicto   Tomatlán   Sayula   Cd. Guzmán

Kailua   Hawaii   Revilla Gigedo Islands   Autlán   Nev. de Colima 3860

Mauna Loa 4770   Roca Partida   Socorro   Tenacatita   Colima   Apatzi

Naalehu   Barra de Navidad   Mazahillo

These islands lie approximately 4000 kilometres to the west of here, in the Pacific Ocean.   Tecomán

160°W   Clarión   2764   Playa

P A C I F I C

15°N   115°W   110°W   105°W

O C E A N

n   o   p   q   r   s   t   u   v   w   x   y   z

16
a b c d e f g h i j k l m
100°W
95°W
90°W
85°W
35°N
30°N
25°N
20°N
15°N
STATES
OKLAHOMA
ARKANSAS
MISSISSIPPI
ALABAMA
GEORGIA
LOUISIANA
FLORIDA
TEXAS
Altus
Lawton
Ada
McAlester
Little Rock
Corinth
Florence
Huntsville
Decatur
Gainesville
Marietta
Atlanta
College Park
Wichita Falls
Red River
Paris
Sherman
Sulphur Springs
Texarkana
Arkadelphia
Pine Bluff
Arkansas
Clarksdale
Tupelo
Cullman
Gadsden
Winona
Columbus
Birmingham
Bessemer
Tuscaloosa
Greenville
El Dorado
Lake Providence
Fort Worth
Irving
Garland
Arlington
Dallas
Abilene
Sweetwater
Marshall
Minden
Shreveport
Monroe
Longview
Tyler
Vicksburg
Jackson
Meridian
Selma
Phenix City
Columbus
Montgomery
Opelika
Macon
Warner Robins
Eufaula
Dawson
Albany
Tifton
Valdosta
Thomasville
Chattahoochee
Tallahassee
Brownwood
Waco
Temple
Killeen
Brazos
Nacogdoches
Lufkin
Jasper
Natchitoches
Toledo Bend Reservoir
Alexandria
Red River
Mississippi
Brookhaven
McComb
Hattiesburg
Laurel
Tombigbee
Alabama
Greenville
Andalusia
Dothan
San Angelo
Edwards Plateau
Bryan
Huntsville
Austin
Kerrville
New Braunfels
Colorado
Houston
Beaumont
Lake Charles
Lafayette
New Iberia
Baton Rouge
Hammond
Slidell
Biloxi
Gulfport
Pascagoula
Mobile
Crestview
Pensacola
Fort Walton Beach
Marianna
Panama City
Kenner
New Orleans
Houma
Mississippi Delta
Cape San Blas
Apalachee Bay
Amistad Reservoir
Del Rio
Uvalde
San Antonio
Gonzales
Baytown
Pasadena
Texas City
Galveston
Lake Jackson
Pearsall
Victoria
Three Rivers
Piedras Negras
Allende
Nueva Rosita
Sabinas
Rio Grande
Corpus Christi
Kingsville
Laredo
Nuevo Laredo
Falcon Reservoir
Laguna Madre
Sabinas Hidalgo
Ciudad Mier
McAllen
Harlingen
Brownsville
Reynosa
Monterrey
China
Matamoros
Montemorelos
Rayones
Linares
Laguna Madre
La Carbonera
MEXICO
Sierra Madre Oriental
Aramberri
Jiménez
Ciudad Victoria
Jaumave
Llera
Tula
Ciudad Mante
Manuel
Charcas
Cerritos
San Luis Potosí
Ciudad Valles
Rio Verde
Cárdenas
Ciudad Madero
Tampico
Pánuco
Laguna Tamiahua
San Felipe
San Luis de la Paz
Verde
Moctezuma
Tamazunchale
Tuxpan
Zacualtipan
Poza Rica
Papantla
Querétaro
Salamanca
Celaya
Salvatierra
Acámbaro
Pachuca
Tula
Huauchinango
Martínez de la Torre
Tlapacoyan
Teziutlán
Perote
Jalapa
Mexico City
Toluca
Texcoco
Apizaco
Puebla
Citlaltépetl
Veracruz
Coscomatepec
Córdoba
Orizaba
Popocatépetl
Cuernavaca
Atlixco
Izúcar de Matamoros
Taxco
Iguala
Jojutla
Alvarado
Tlacotalpan
San Andrés Tuxtla
Tehuacán
Tierra Blanca
M. Alemán Reservoir
Acatlán
Ciudad Altamirano
Balsas
Tuxtepec
Acayucan
Coatzacoalcos
Minatitlán
Huajuapan de León
Huapanapan
Chilapa
Chilpancingo
Tlaxiaco
Nochixtlán
Oaxaca
Tierra Colorada
Atoyac
Acapulco
San Marcos
Southern Sierra Madre
Coixtlahuaca
Jesús Carranza
Paso Real
Mitla
Matías Romero
Ejutla
Miahuatlán
Juchatengo
Pinotepa Nacional
Ciudad Ixtepec
Juchitán
Tehuantepec
Salina Cruz
Puerto Escondido
Puerto Angel
Gulf of Tehuantepec
Mar Muerto
Arriaga
Tonalá
Isthmus of Tehuantepec
Villahermosa
Comalcalco
Frontera
Morelos
Mezcalapa
Macuspana
Tenosique
Palenque
Chichón
Balancán
Tuxtla Gutiérrez
San Cristóbal las Casas
Chiapa de Corzo
Comitán
Angostura Reservoir
Pijijiapan
Huixtla
Tapachula
Amatenango
Huehuetenango
Quezaltenango
Guatemala
GUATEMALA
Motagua
Usumacinta
Flores
Gulf of Mexico
Bay of Campeche
Ciudad del Carmen
Laguna de Términos
Mamantel
Champotón
Campeche
Sihochac
Chunhuhub
Bolonchén de Rejón
Calkiní
Maxcanú
Ticul
Tekax
Peto
Yucatán Peninsula
Mérida
Progreso
Motul
Izamal
Tizimín
Espita
Valladolid
Dzilam de Bravo
Rio Lagartos
Cape Catoche
Chiquilá
Puerto Juárez
Cancun
Puerto Morelos
Tulum
Cozumel
Ascensión Bay
Espiritu Santo Bay
Felipe Carrillo Puerto
Chetumal
Hondo
Altamira
BELIZE
Belize
Belmopan
Turneffe Islands
Desterrada
Pérez
Arenas
Nuevo
Triangulos
Arcas
CUBA
Pinar del Río
Guanahacabibes Peninsula
Straits of Yucatán
Isla de Pinos
Gulf of Honduras
Swan Island (Hond.)
Roatán
Guanaja
Utila
Bay Islands
Trujillo
Puerto Cortés
Puerto Barrios
Tela
La Ceiba
San Pedro Sula
HONDURAS
Patuca
Puerto Lempira
20
n o p q r s t u v w x y z
22
0 100 200 300 miles
Average linear scale
0 100 200 300 400 500 Km

a · b · c · d · e · f · g · h · i · j · k · l · m

Oklahoma City · Henryetta · 95°W · Clarksville · Newport · West Memphis · Memphis · 90°W · Jackson · TENNESSEE · Lawrenceburg · Fayetteville · Cleveland · Chattanooga · 85°W · Hendersonville · NORTH · Char

35°N · Ada · McAlester · Poteau · Fort Smith · Conway · 100· · Savannah · Florence · 879· · Huntsville · Dalton · Greenville · Spartanburg · Rock Hill · Rocki

OKLAHOMA · 722· · Arkadelphia · Pine Bluff · Arkansas · Corinth · 246· · Decatur · Cullman · Gadsden · Marietta · Gainesville · Anderson · Clinton · Camden · SOU

Paris · Sherman · ARKANSAS · Texarkana · El Dorado · Greenville · Clarksdale · Tupelo · MISSISSIPPI · 152· · Bessemer · Birmingham · ·734 · Atlanta · College Park · Athens · Columbia · CAROL

Fort Worth · Irving · Garland · Sulphur Springs · Marshall · Minden · Lake Providence · Monroe · Winona · Columbus · Tuscaloosa · 425· · Macon · Columbus · Warner Robins · Dublin · Statesboro · Walterboro

Arlington · Dallas · Tyler · UNITED STATES · 67· · 113· · Shreveport · Vicksburg · 149· · Jackson · Meridian · Selma · Montgomery · Opelika · Phenix City · Dawson · Tifton · Waycross · Savann

TEXAS · Waco · Nacogdoches · Red River · Toledo Bend Reservoir · Natchitoches · Alexandria · Brookhaven · Laurel · Jackson · Greenville · Eufaula · Albany · Thomasville · Chattahoochee · Valdosta · Brunswick · Fernandina B

Temple · Lufkin · Jasper · LOUISIANA · McComb · Hattiesburg · Andalusia · Dothan · Marianna · Live Oak · Perry · Jacksonville

Killeen · Huntsville · Bryan · Brazos · Hammond · Mobile · Crestview · Fort Walton Beach · Tallahassee · Lake City · St. Augustin

Austin · New Braunfels · Colorado · Houston · Baton Rouge · Lake Charles · Slidell · Biloxi · Gulfport · Pascagoula · Pensacola · Panama City · Apalachee Bay · Gainesville · Palatka

30°N · Gonzales · Beaumont · Baytown · Lafayette · New Iberia · New Orleans · Cape San Blas · Chiefland · Ocala · Daytor

Victoria · Texas City · Galveston · Houma · Mississippi Delta · Lake George · Crystal River · Leesburg · Altamonte Springs · Titusvi · Ca

Lake Jackson · Winter Garden · Orlando · Me

Three Rivers · 50· · Tampa · Lakeland

Corpus Christi · Largo · Brandon · Avon Park

Kingsville · St. Petersburg · Bradenton · FLORIDA

Laguna Madre · Gulf of · Sarasota · Lake Okeechobee

Mc Allen · Harlingen · Port Charlotte · Cape Coral · Fort Myers · Pa

Brownsville · Matamoros · Naples · Fort Lauderda

Laguna Madre · Mexico · Cape Romano · Everglade

19 · 25°N · Cape Sable · Florida Bay · La

La Carbonera · Key West

Ciudad Madero · Havana · Matanzas

Tampico · Güines · Colo

Pánuco · Pinar del Río · Guanahacabibes Peninsula · Yucatán Channel · Cienfuegos

Laguna de Tamiahua · Desterrada · Pérez · Isla de Pinos · G

Arenas · Río Lagartos · Cape Catoche · Chiquilá

Potrero del Llano · Nuevo · Dzilam de Bravo · Tizimín · Puerto Juárez

Tuxpan · Progreso · Motul · Cancún

Poza Rica · Papantla · Triangulos · Mérida · Izamal · Espita · Puerto Morelos

Huachinango · Martínez de la Torre · 8· · Valladolid · Cozumel

20°N · Tlapacoyan · Arcas · Maxcanú · Tulum

Teziutlán · Perote · Jalapa · Calkiní · Ticul · Tekax · 100· · Peto · Bolonchén de Rejón

Apizaco · 4110· · Bay of · Campeche · Yucatán · Ascensión Bay

Citlaltépetl(Orizaba) · Veracruz · Sihochac · Chunhuhub · Felipe Carrillo Puerto · Espíritu Santo Bay · Little Cayn · Cayma

Puebla · 5700· · Coscomatepec · Champotón · Peninsula · 310· · Georgetown · Grand Cayman · C

Orizaba · Córdoba · Alvarado · Tlacotalpan

Tehuacán · Tierra Blanca · Ciudad del Carmen · Laguna de Términos · Chetumal · Gulf of

Acatlán · San Andrés Tuxtla · 1879· · Frontera · Mamantel · Hondo

Huajuapan · Coatzacoalcos · Villahermosa · Balancán · Altamira · BELIZE

Huajuapan de León · Minatitlán · Macuspana · Tenosique · Belize · Turneffe Islands · Gulf of

Coixtlahuaca · Jesús Carranza · Palenque · Chichón · 2224· · Flores · Belmopan · Honduras

Nochixtlán · Isthmus · Morelos · MEXICO · Usumacinta · Roatán · Guanaja

Tlaxiaco · Oaxaca · Paso Real · 2727· · San Cristóbal de las Casas · 1122· · Bay Islands · Utila

1546· · Mitla · Tehuantepec · Matías Romero · Tuxtla Gutiérrez · Chiapa de Corzo

Miahuatlán · Ciudad Ixtepec · Juchitán · Arriaga · Comitán · Puerto Cortés · La Ceiba · Trujillo

Pinotepa Nacional · Juchitango · 1499· · Tehuantepec · Salina Cruz · Mar Muerto · Angostura-Reservoir · Tonalá · GUATEMALA · Puerto Barrios · San Pedro Sula · Puerto Lempira

Puerto Escondido · Gulf of · Pijijiapan · Lago de Izabal · Tela · HONDURAS

Puerto Angel · Tehuantepec · Amatenango · Motagua · 90°W · Patuca · Cape Gracias á Dios

15°N · Huixtla · 85°W

n · o · p · q · r · s · t · u · v · w · x · y · z

22

This map shows 1/60 of the earth's surface

75°W 70°W 65°W

35°N

N A
Goldsboro
New Bern
tteville
acksonville
Morehead City
rton
Wilmington
tle Beach
wn

Hamilton○ *Bermuda (U.K.)*

A T L A N T I C

30°N

Sargasso Sea

O C E A N

25°N

and
ama
and

Great Abaco Island

Nicholls Town
New Providence
Nassau
Eleuthera
dros
ands
Behring Point

Cat

San Salvador

BAHAMAS

Great Exuma Island
Rum Cay

Bahama Bank
Long Island

Crooked Island

Acklins

Mayaguana Island

Tropic of Cancer

Morón
iego de Avila

Grand Caicos

güey
Nuevitas

Victoria de las Tunas
Banes
Holguín

Great Inagua Island

Turks and Caicos Islands (U.K.)

Bayamo
Manzanillo
Palma Soriano
Baracoa
Niquero○ 2005
Santiago de Cuba
Guantánamo

Port-de-Paix

20°N

DOMINICAN
Cap-Haïtien
Puerto Plata
Mao
Santiago
REPUBLIC
Gonaïves
La Vega
San Francisco de Macorís
HAITI
St-Marc
3175
San Juan

A

Anse d'Hainault
Port-au-Prince

Puerto Rico (U.S.A.)
Virgin Islands (U.K.)

JAMAICA
Les Cayes
Jacmel
2680
Barahona
Santo Domingo
La Romana
Bayamón○ San Juan
Carolina
Mayagüez○
1398
Caguas
Virgin Islands (U.S.A.)
Anguilla (U.K.)
St. Martin
Philipsburg

ay
Montego

Spanish Town
May Pen○
Kingston
Ponce
St. Croix (U.S.A.)
Netherlands Antilles
Codrington○ *Barbuda*

A
n
t
i
l
l
e
s

Basseterre
ST KITTS
NEVIS
ANTIGUA AND BARBUDA
○**St. John's**
Antigua

B E A N

S E A

Montserrat○ Plymouth
(U.K.)

Guadeloupe (France)
Basse-Terre
○Pointe-à-Pitre

L e e w a r d   I s l a n d s

DOMINICA
Roseau

15°N

75°W 70°W 65°W

0 100 200 300 miles   Average linear scale   0 100 200 300 400 500 Km

MEXICO

90°W

GUATEMALA

HONDURAS

15°N

Amatenango

Huixtla

Huehuetenango

Tapachula

Quezaltenango

Mazatenango

Antigua 3752 1502 Guatemala

Ahuachapan 2386 Santa Ana

Sonsonate San Salvador

EL SALVADOR

Zacatecoluca

Escuintla

Puerto Barrios

Lago de Izabal

85°W

Tela La Ceiba Trujillo

San Pedro Sula

Puerto Cortés

Ulúa

Motagua

Santa Rosa

La Paz

Macaome

San Miguel

Estelí

Gulf of Fonseca

Chinandega

1745

León

Managua

Juticalpa

Tegucigalpa

Patuca

Puerto Lempira

Coco

Cabo Gracias á Dios

Cayos Miskitos

Puerto Cabezas

2435

2870

2438

Cordillera Isabella

NICARAGUA

Matagalpa

Grande

Mosquito Coast

Prinzapolca

Providencia (Col.)

C A R

San Andrés (Col.)

Granada

Lake Managua

Escondido

Rama

Bluefields

Rivas

Lake Nicaragua

1133

Cabo Santa Elena

Liberia 2020

San Carlos

San Juan

San Juan del Norte

10°N

COSTA

Alajuela Heredia 3432

Puntarenas San José

Nicoya Peninsula

Gulf of Nicoya

RICA

3820 Chirripó

Turrialba

Limón

Punta Manzanillo

Colón

Panama Canal

Ailigandi

Gulf of Darien

Barran

Ba

Cartagena

Arjona

Carm

Lorica

Almirante

Gulf of Mosquitos

Balboa

Panamá

2621

Puerto Cortés

3475

2826

David

P A N A M A

Penonomé

Perlas Archipelago

Rey

La Palma

Montería

Necoclí

Puerto Armuelles

Gulf of Chiriquí

Santiago

Azuero Peninsula

Coiba

1400

Pedasi

El Real

Gulf of Panama

Riosucio

Caucas

Chigorodó

Zar

3969

Cupica

Yarumal

4083 Bello

Medellín

Quibdó

PACIFIC

Cabo Corrientes

Cordillera

2140

Manizales 1424

Cartago

Armenia

Tuluá 4250

Punta Chirambirá

San Juan

Buenaventura

Palmira

Cali

OCEAN

Malpelo (Col.)

Santander

Nev. de Huila 5750

Nei

Gorgona

Popayán 4886

Garzón

Guapi

Patía

El Bordo

Tumaco

Cabo Manglares

San Lorenzo

Túquerres

Pasto

Mocoa

5°N

Darwin Wolf

Esmeraldas

Punta Galera

Rosa Zárate

4764

Ipiales

Tulcán

San Gabriel

Puerto As

Pinta

4930

Ibarra

Cayambe

Aguarico

Le

Marchena

Genovesa

1707

Esmeraldas

0° Equator

San Salvador

Fernandina

Santa Cruz

Galapagos Islands (Ecuador)

San Cristóbal

Isabela

Puerto Villamil

San María

Española

Bahía de Caráquez

Manta

Portoviejo

4794 Quito 2819

Machachi

5263 Cotopaxi

Latacunga

Ambato

Baeza

Coca

Tena

Cabo Pan

Napo

ECUADOR

Chimborazo 6272

Riobamba

Curaray

Babahoyo

Guayaquil

5230

Alausí

Macas

Tigre

Pastaza

La Puntilla Salinas

Azogues

Montalvo

80°W

Cuenca

90°W

85°W

80°W

This map shows 1/60 of the earth's surface

21
a b c d e f g h i j k l m
70°W
65°W
60°W
15°N
10°N
5°N
0°
DOMINICA
Roseau
Martinique-Passage
Fort-de-France
Martinique (France)
St.-Lucia-Passage
Castries
SAINT LUCIA
St.-Vincent-Passage
SAINT VINCENT AND GRENADINES
Kingstown
BARBADOS
Bridgetown
Saint George's
GRENADA
E A N
S E A
Lesser Antilles
Netherlands Antilles
Cabo Gallinas
Aruba (Neth.)
Curaçao
Willemstad
Bonaire
Guajira Peninsula
820
Paraguaná Peninsula
Punto Fijo
Puerto Cumarebo
Islas Los Roques (Ven.)
Blanquilla (Ven.)
ATLANTIC
OCEAN
Riohacha
Maicao
Gulf of Venezuela
Coro
Tortuga
Margarita
La Asunción
Tobago
Scarborough
TRINIDAD AND TOBAGO
Port of Spain
940
Trinidad
San Fernando
Serpent's Mouth
San Rafael
Churuguara
Tocuyo
Maiquetía
2765
Cabo Codera
Caracas
Cumaná
Carúpano
Güiria
Gulf of Paria
Maracaibo
La Concepción
Cabimas
1900
Carora
San Felipe
Puerto Cabello
Maracay
La Victoria
Valencia
Puerto La Cruz
Barcelona
2660
Caripito
Ciudad Ojeda
Barquisimeto
San Juan de los Morros
Píritu
Maturín
Machiques
3750
Lake Maracaibo
Acarigua
3652
Sierra de Perijá
Valera
Catatumbo
Boconó
El Sombrero
Valle de la Pascua
Cantaura
Zaraza
Anaco
Unare
Guanipa
Tigre
Manamo
Tucupita
Orinoco Delta
Grande
Boca Grande
Amacuro Delta
San José de Amacuro
Banco
San Carlos del Zulia
Mérida
5007
Cordillera de Mérida
Guanare
El Baúl
Calabozo
El Tigre
Pariaguán
Barrancas
Casigua
Barinas
Cojedes
Guárico
Suata
Orinoco
Ciudad Guayana
792
Ocaña
Cúcuta
San Cristóbal
Bruzual
Apure
San Fernando de Apure
Boca del Pao
Ciudad Bolívar
Upata
Serranía de Imataca
Hossororo
Mantecal
Caicara de Orinoco
Maripa
Lago de Guri
Pamplona
4100
El Canton
Arauca
VENEZUELA
1863
El Callao
Marlborough
Llanos
La Urbana
1839
Las Trincheras
La Paragua
Capanaparo
Cuyuni
Suddie
Georgetown
Málaga
5493
Socorro
El Dorado
Santa Maria
Sierra de Maigualida
Casanare
Cravo Norte
Meta
La Venturosa
Puerto Carreño
Sabana de Cardona
Caura
Paragua
Caroní
Mayupa
Angel Falls
2950
2100
1890
La Escalera
Mazaruni
Peters Mine
Bartica
New Amsterdam
26
Sogamoso
Puerto Nuevo
100
Rockstone
Linden
Totness
Nieuw Nickerie
Yopal
Trinidad
Tomo
Puerto Ayacucho
2285
Guiana
Puricama
Cavanayen
2040
Tumatumari
Apoera
Courantyne
Gran Sabana
2810
Roraima
Pakaraima
GUYANA
San Juan
Mesa del Cerro Jaua
2030
Ventuari
El Oso
Arabelo
Orocué
Santa Elena de Uairen
1240
Essequibo
Kabalebo-Reservoir
Meta
Sucuaro
Vichada
Maturuca
Depósito
SURINAME
Villavicencio
Puerto Lopez
San José de Ocuné
San Fernando de Atabapo
Catisimiña
Serra Pacaraima
Highlands
Apoteri
Juliana Top 1230
1026
Santa Barbara
Karanambo
Eilerts de Haan Geb.
Puerto Limón
Pavon
Santa Rosa
Guaviare
Arrecifal
2579
Uraricoera
882
OMBIA
Inírida
2396
La Esmeralda
Serra Parima
Lethem
Kanuku Mts.
Dadanawa
Victorino
Tacutu
Rupununi
Oronoque
Ariari
San Yanaro
Boa Vista
Serra do Apiaú
Guayabero
San José del Guaviare
San José
Casiquiare
Boca Mavaca
1047
Isherton
New
Papai
Morichal
Guainía
Catrimani
Biloku
Calamar
Uainambi
San Carlos
El Mango
Serra Curupira
Caracaraí
Kamoa Mts.
Serra Acaraí
Mesa de Yambí
Vista Alegre
Branco
734
Miraflores
Jibóia
Serra Tapirapeco
Demini
Mitú
Vaupés
Cucuí
3014
Pico da Neblina
Padauiri
São José do Anauá
Anauá
Maloca
Cuñaré
Apaporis
Iuaretê
Araca
Macuje
Içana
Negro
Catrimani
Mapuera
Trombetas
Taracuá
Uaupés
Uaupés
Lérida
Jauapari
Calanaque
Araracuara
São José
Tapurucuara
Paru de Oeste
BRAZIL
La Chorrera
Caquetá
100
Cuiuni
Barcelos
100
Tupanacca
La Pedrera
Moura
Puerto Miraña
El Encanto
Vila Bittencourt
Marcelino
Maraã
Unini
Santa Maria
Nhamunda
Oriximiná
Japurá
Airão
Uatumã
Faro
San Cristóbal
Arica
Jaú
Foz do Mamoriá
Santo Antonio
Santa Clotilde
Santa Clara
Tonantins
Amazon
Fonte Boa
Solimões
Negro
Urucará
Parintins
Amazon
n o p q r s t u v w x y z
25
26
0 100 200 300 miles
Average linear scale
0 100 200 300 400 500 Km

22

85°W 80°W 75°W

PACIFIC

OCEAN

0° Equator

5°S

10°S

15°S

COLOM

ECUADOR

Tumaco
Patía
Cabo Manglares
El Bordo
Florencia
Pasto
San Lorenzo
Túquerres
Mocoa
Buenos Aires
Esmeraldas
Punta Galera
Ipiales
Tulcán
Puerto Asís
Cuñ
Caguán
4754
4930
Ibarra
San Gabriel
Puerto Huitoto
Macu
Rosa Zárate
Otavalo
Cayambe
Aguarico
La Tagua
5843
La C
Quito
2818
4794
Bahía de Caráquez
Machachi
Cotopaxi
5896
Baeza
Coca
Napo
Puerto Leguizamo
Palermo
Manta
Tena
Cabo Pantoja
Putumayo
Portoviejo
Chimborazo
6272
Ambato
Curaray
Arica
Santa Maria
El Er
Jipijapa
Riobamba
Sa
Guayaquil
Babahoyo
5230
Montalvo
Marsella
La Puntilla
Alausí
Macas
Pastaza
Santa Clotilde
Salinas
Azogues
Vargas Guerra
Gulf of Guayaquil
Puná
Cuenca
4138
Santa Isabel
Santiago
Morona
Andoas
Mazán
Machala
Puerto Pardo
Sargento Lores
Iquitos
Zarumilla
Ta
Tumbes
Zorritos
Loja
Zamora
3810
Borja
Tigre
Corrientes
Nauta
Mancora
Cariamanga
Sta. Maria de Nieva
Concordia
S
Talara
Las Lomas
Orellana
Barranca
Bagazán
Cabo Pariñas
Sullana
San Ignacio
Marañón
Requena
Paita
Chulucanas
3139
Jeberos
Bretaña
Piura
Huancabamba
Piura
3779
Yurimaguas
Pacaya
Santa Isabel
Neuva Alejandria
Punta Aguja
Bayóvar
517
4153
Jaén
Bagua
3840
Rioja
Moyobamba
Dos de Mayo
Ucayali
Ro
Olmos
4193
Chachapoyas
Tarapoto
Saposoa
Orellana
609
Lobos Island
Santa Cruz
Ferreñafe
Bambamarca
Huallaga
Cruzei do S
Lambayeque
Cajamarca
4694
Juanjui
Contamaná
Chiclayo
Bolívar
Cajabamba
4467
Pacasmayo
4333
Tocache Nuevo
Tiruntán
San Pedro de Lloc
Chicama
Otuzco
4947
Pucallpa
Trujillo
Santiago de Chuco
Tayabamba
Masisea
To
Virú
Huacrachuco
Aguaytía
Santa
Marañón
Aguaytía
Tingo Maria
Puerto Inca
Puerto Portillo
Chimbote
Caraz
6768
Huascaran
Llata
Casma
Huaraz
4986
La Unión
Huánuco
Ambo
Bolognesi
Huarmey
Chiquián
Cajatambo
Yerupaja
6634
Oxapampa
5748
Atalaya
Pativilca
Cerro de Pasco
La Merced
Huacho
Huaral
La Oroya
Satipo
Puerto Rico
Chancay
Jauja
5334
Camisea
Callao
Matúcana
Huancayo
Lima
Yauyos
Pampas
Huancavelica
5291
Huanta
Quillabar
Pumasi
6246
San Vicente de Cañete
Huamanrazo
Castrovirreyna
Ayacucho
Chincha Alta
Chincheros
Huancapi
Chincha Islands
Pisco
Huancayo
5350
Andahuaylas
Ica
Chalhuanca
Palpa
Púquio
6185
Coracora
1725
Nazca
San Juán
Lampalla
5522
Caravelí
Chu
Chala
Ocoña
Atico
Ocoña
Camaná

This map shows 1/60 of the earth's surface

85°W 80°W 75°W

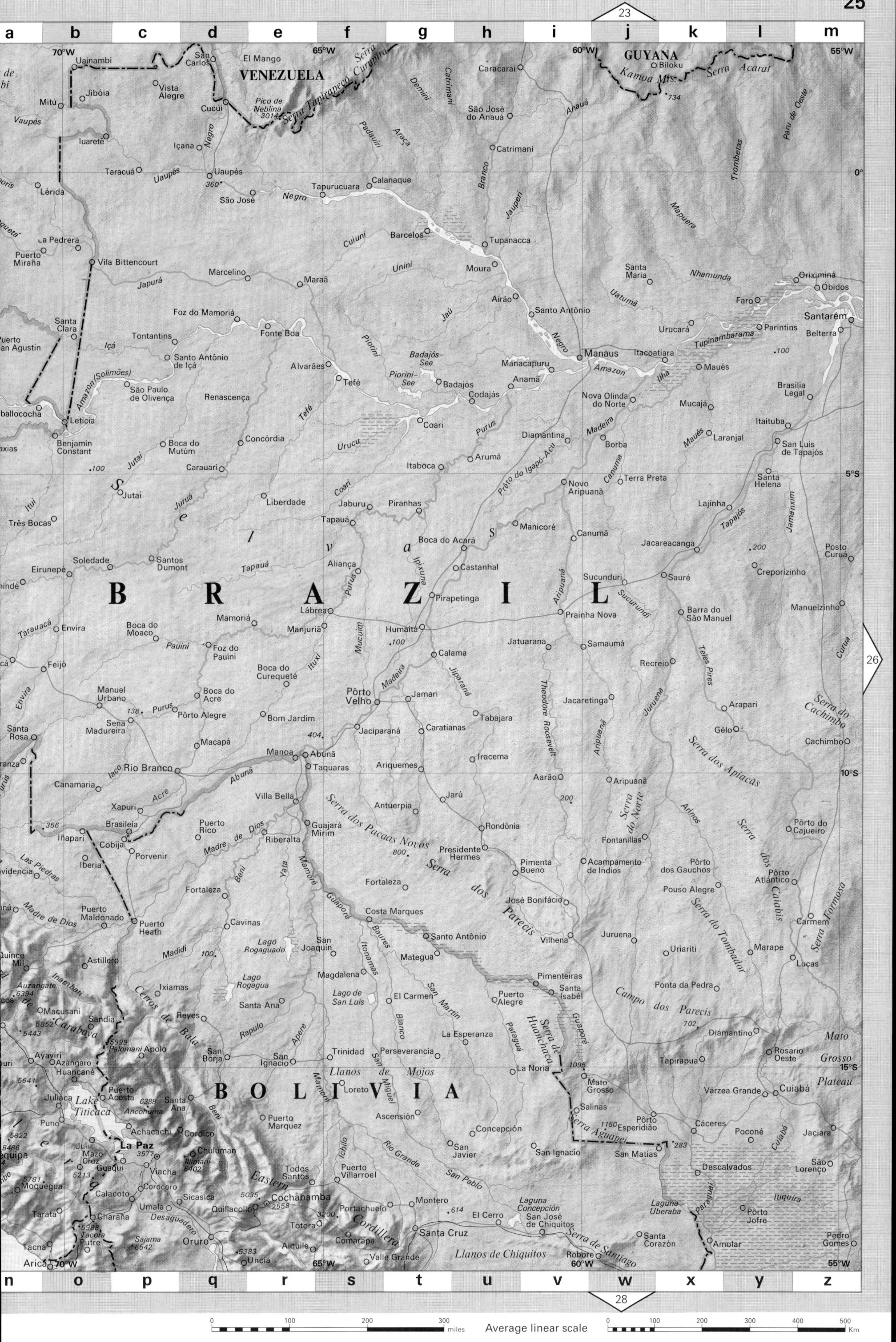
23
a b c d e f g h i j k l m
70°W
65°W
60°W
55°W
0°
5°S
10°S
15°S
VENEZUELA
GUYANA
BRAZIL
BOLIVIA
Uainambi
San Carlos
El Mango
Serra Tapirapecó
Serra Curupira
Caracaraí
Biloku
Kamoa Mts.
Serra Acaraí
734
Vista Alegre
Jibóia
Mitú
Vaupés
Cucuí
Pico de Neblina 3014
Demini
Catrimani
São José do Anauá
Anauá
Paru de Oeste
Iuaretê
Içana
Negro
Padauiri
Araça
Catrimani
Trombetas
Taracuá
Uaupés
Uaupés
360
Calanaque
Tapurucuara
São José
Negro
Lérida
Branco
Jauaperi
Mapuera
La Pedrera
Puerto Miraña
Barcelos
Cuiuni
Tupanacca
Vila Bittencourt
Marcelino
Japurá
Maraã
Unini
Moura
Santa Maria
Nhamundá
Oriximiná
Óbidos
Uatumã
Airão
Santo Antônio
Faro
Foz do Mamoriá
Jaú
Santa Clara
Fonte Boa
Urucará
Parintins
Santarém
Belterra
Tontantins
Içá
Piorini
Negro
Tupinambarama
Santo Antônio de Içá
Badajós-See
Manaus
Itacoatiara
100
Alvarães
Manacapuru
Amazon
Maués
Amazon (Solimões)
Tefé
Piorini-See
Badajós
Anamã
Ilha
São Paulo de Olivença
Renascença
Codajás
Nova Olinda do Norte
Mucajá
Brasília Legal
Leticia
Benjamin Constant
Tefé
Coari
Itaituba
Boca do Mutúm
Concórdia
Urucu
Purus
Diamantina
Madeira
Borba
Maués
Laranjal
São Luis de Tapajós
100
Jutaí
Carauari
Itaboca
Arumã
Preto do Igapó-Açu
Canumã
Terra Preta
Santa Helena
Jutaí
Coari
Novo Aripuanã
Itui
Juruá
Liberdade
Jaburu
Piranhas
Lajinha
Jamanxim
Três Bocas
Tapauá
Manicoré
Tapajós
Boca do Acará
Canumã
Jacareacanga
200
Posto Curuá
Soledade
Santos Dumont
Tapauá
Aliança
Castanhal
Eirunepé
Ipixuna
Aripuanã
Sucunduri
Sauré
Creporizinho
Purus
Pirapetinga
Lábrea
Mamoriá
Prainha Nova
Sucurundi
Barra do São Manuel
Manuelzinho
Tarauacá
Envira
Boca do Moaco
Manjuriã
Humaitá
Pauini
Foz do Pauini
Mucuim
100
Jatuarana
Samaumã
Calama
Recreio
Teles Pires
Curuá
26
Feijó
Boca do Curequeté
Ituxi
Jiparaná
Theodore Roosevelt
Envira
Manuel Urbano
Boca do Acre
Madeira
Pôrto Velho
Jamari
Jacaretinga
Juruena
Arapari
Serra do Cachimbo
138
Purus
Pôrto Alegre
Sena Madureira
Bom Jardim
Tabajara
Santa Rosa
Jaciparaná
Caratianas
Aripuanã
Gêlo
404
Macapá
Serra dos Apiacás
Cachimbo
Iaco
Rio Branco
Manoa
Abunã
Taquaras
Ariquemes
Iracema
Canamaria
Abunã
Aarão
Aripuanã
Acre
Xapuri
Villa Bella
Serra dos Pacaas Novos
Jarú
Antuerpia
200
Serra do Norte
Arinos
Brasileia
356
Iñapari
Puerto Rico
Guajará Mirim
Rondônia
Serra
Pôrto do Cajueiro
Cobija
Porvenir
Madre de Dios
Riberalta
800
Presidente Hermes
Fontanillas
Iberia
Las Piedras
Beni
Yata
Mamoré
Serra dos Pacaas Novos
Pimenta Bueno
Acampamento de Indios
Pôrto dos Gauchos
dos Caiabis
Pôrto Atlântico
Fortaleza
Fortaleza
Serra dos Parecis
Pouso Alegre
Madre de Dios
Puerto Maldonado
Guaporé
Costa Marques
José Bonifácio
Serra do Tombador
Serra Formosa
Carmem
Puerto Heath
Cavinas
Baures
Santo Antônio
Vilhena
Juruena
Quince Mil
Madidi
100
Lago Rogaguado
San Joaquín
Uriariti
Marape
Lucas
Astillero
Itonamas
Mategua
Inambari
Auzangate 6394
Ixiamas
Lago Rogagua
Magdalena
Pimenteiras
Cordillera de Carabaya
Cerros de Bala
Lago de San Luis
El Carmen
San Martin
Puerto Alegre
Santa Isabel
Ponta da Pedra
Macusani
Santa Ana
Campo dos Parecis
5852
Sandia
Reyes
Serra de Huanchaca
Guaporé
5443
Rapulo
Apere
Blanco
La Esperanza
Paraguá
702
Diamantino
Mato Grosso Plateau
5999
Palomani
Apolo
Ayaviri
Azángaro
San Borja
San Ignacio
Trinidad
Perseverancia
Rosario Oeste
Huancané
Tapirapua
La Noria
1095
5641
Llanos de Mojos
Mamoré
San Miguel
Mato Grosso
Várzea Grande
Cuiabá
Puerto Acosta
Loreto
Juliaca
6388
Ancohuma
Santa Ana
Lake Titicaca
Beni
Puerto Marquez
Ascensión
Salinas
Serra Aguapeí
1150
Esperidião
Pôrto
Cáceres
Poconé
Puno
Concepción
5822
Achacachi
Coroico
Jaciara
Cuiabá
5486
Juli
Mazo Cruz
La Paz
3577
Chuluman
Illimani 6402
San Javier
San Ignacio
San Matías
283
Moquegua
Guaqui
Ichilo
Rio Grande
5213
Viacha
Todos Santos
Puerto Villarroel
San Pablo
Descalvados
São Lourenço
5781
Moquegua
Corocoro
Eastern
Itiquira
Calacoto
Sicasica
5035
Cochabamba
Montero
Laguna Concepción
Laguna Uberaba
Paraguai
Pôrto Jofre
Tarata
Charaña
Umala
Desaguadero
Quillacollo
2558
Portachuelo
614
El Cerro
San José de Chiquitos
Cordillera
5988
Tacora
Putre
Sajama 6542
3200
Totora
Santa Cruz
Serra de Santiago
Santa Corazón
Pedro Gomes
Tacna
Oruro
5383
Aiquile
Comarapa
Amolar
Arica
Uncía
Valle Grande
Llanos de Chiquitos
Roboré
n o p q r s t u v w x y z
28
0 100 200 300 miles
Average linear scale
0 100 200 300 400 500 Km

VENEZUELA

Caura
Mayupa   2100
2950   1890
La Escalera
Cavanayen
Puricama
Arabelo
Santa Elena de Uairen
Paregua
Cerro Jaua
Macizo del
Catisimiña
Serra Parima
Serra Curupira
Serra Tapirapeco

Roraima
Gran Sabana
2810
2040
Tumatumari
Maturuca
1240
Depósito
1047

GUIANA HIGHLANDS
Pakaraima Mountains
Pacaraima

Rockstone
New Amsterdam
Linden
Nieuw Nickerie
Groningen
Paranam
Apoera
Brokopondo
Aurora
Prof. van Blommestein Lake
694
Totness
Paramaribo
Mana
Moengo
St. Laurent
Apatou
Montsinery
Kourou
Cayenne
Kaw
Régina
Grand Santi
710
Patience
Saul
Oyapock
St. Georges
Oiapoque
Vila Velha
Cunani

SURINAME
FRENCH GUIANA
Juliana Top 1230
1026
Bakrakondre
Tapanahoni
Eilerts-de-Haan Geb.
882
Intelewa
658
Quaqui
Kawatop
Orangegebergte
Camopi
635

Uraricoera
Boa Vista
Lethem
Dadanawa
Kanuku Mts.
Karanambo
Apoteri
New
Isherton
Oronoque
Papai
Biloku
734
Kamoa Mts.
Serra Acarai
Serra Maloca Velha
Tumucumaque
690
Serra Lombarda
Lorenço
Calçoene
Amapá
Cabo Orange
Maracá
Cabo Norte

Caracarai
São José do Anauá
Catrimani
Anauá
Trombetas
Maloca
Malaripó
315
Acampamento
Meriruma
Terezinha
Serra do Navio
Aporema
Ferreira Gomes
Pôrto Grande
Janaucú
Macapá
Caviana

Calanaque
Barcelos
Moura
Tupánacca
Santa Maria
Nhamunda
Faro
Óbidos
Oriximiná
Prainha
Mulata
305
Almeirim
Monte Dourado
228
Boca do Jari
Barraca da Boca
Jari
Pôrto Santana
Queimada
Canal do Norte
Afuá
Chaves
Mexiana
Marajó
Anajás
Cachoeira do Arari
Breves
Abaetetuba
Pará

Cuiuni
Unini
Airão
Santo Antônio
Urucará
Santarém
Parintins
Belterra
Alenquer
Monte Alegre
Curua-Una
Pacoval
Victoria
Belo Monte
Portel
Cametá
Mocajuba
Baião
Pindobal
Tucuruí

Tefé
Lago Badajós
Lago Piorini
Badajós
Anama
Manacapuru
Manaus
Itacoatiara
100
Tupinambarama
Maués
Ilha
Amazon
Brasilia Legal
Caima
229
Altamira
Tuerê
Jacundá
Jatobal
São Félix
Marabá

Jaburu
Piranhas
Tapauá
Coari
Itaboca
Codajós
Arumã
Diamantina
Nova Olinda do Norte
Borba
Terra Preta
Mucajá
Maués
Laranjal
Itaituba
Rurópolis
Sem-Tripa
Pôrto Alegre
Iriri
Lontra
Jatobá
Serra dos Carajás
399
Carajás
Itacaiúnas

BRAZIL

Novo Aripuanã
Manicoré
Canumã
Jacareacanga
Lajinha
Tapajós
Santa Helena
Paga-Conta
Jamanxim
Forte Veneza
São Sebastião
Posto Curuá
Araras
Cajueiro
José Rodrigues
Tucumã
Xinguara
Araguaia

Castanhal
Pirapetinga
Prainha Nova
Sucunduri
Sauré
Barra do São Manuel
500
Creporizinho
Manuelzinho
Jojoca
Posto Cocraimore
Gorotiré
Garimpo Cumaru
Redenção
Conceição do Araguaia

Lábrea
Humaitá
100
Calama
Jatuarana
Samaumá
Recreio
Teles Pires
Juruena
Arapari
Gêlo
Serra do Cachimbo
Cachimbo
Plara-Açu
Campo Alegre
Santana do Araguaia
Araguacema
Barreira do Campo
Miracema do Norte

Pôrto Velho
Jamari
Tabajara
Jaciparaná
Caratianas
Iracema
Aarão
Aripuanã
Serra do Norte
Theodore Roosevelt
Pôrto do Cajueiro
São José do Xingu
Santa Teresinha
Cristalandia
Fátima
Paraíso do Norte de Goiás

Ariquemes
Antuerpia
Jarú
Rondônia
242
Presidente Hermes
800
Pimenta Bueno
Fontanillas
Acampamento de Indios
Pôrto dos Gauchos
Pouso Alegre
Posto Alto Manissaua
Posto Alto Diauarum
Campo de Diauarum
Xingu
Pôrto Alegre
São Félix
Ilha do Bananal

Fortaleza
Costa Marques
San Joaquin
Magdalena
El Carmen
Mategua
Santo Antônio
Pimenta Bueno
José Bonifácio
Juruena
Vilhena
Uriariti
Marape
Carmem
Lucas
Pôrto Artur
Pôrto Atlântico
Serra do Tombador
Serra Formosa
São José do Xingu
Pôrto dos Meinacos
Garapu
São Miguel do Araguaia
Porangatu
Bandeirante
635
Peixe
Alvorada
Araguaçu
Gurupi

BOLIVIA
Lago de San Luis
Puerto Alegre
Santa Isabel
Ponta da Pedra
Campo dos Parecis
Mato Grosso Plateau
Serra do Roncador
Serra dos Parecis

This map shows 1/60 of the earth's surface

a
b
c
d
e
f
g
h
i
j
k
l
m
45°W
40°W
35°W
5°N
0°
Equator
5°S
10°S
A T L A N T I C
O C E A N
Fernando de Noronha
Atol das Rocas
Cabo São Roque
São Marcos Bay
São José do Ribamar
São Luís
Alcantara
Pinheiro
Maracaçumé
Turiaçu
Viseu
Bragança
Rosário
Tutóia
Parnaíba
Camocim
Acaraú
Itapipoca
Sobral
Tianguá
Fortaleza
Mecejana
Caponga
Maranguape
Canindé
Aracati
Quixadá
Russas
Mossoró
Macau
Ceará-Mirim
Natal
Açu
Lajes
Jaguaribe
Pau de Ferros
Currais Novos
Caicó
Canguaretama
Mamanguape
Guarabira
João Pessoa
Patos
Pombal
Cajàzeiras
Soledade
Campina Grande
São José do Egito
Goiána
Timbaúba
Olinda
Recife
Jaboatão
Limoeiro
Gravatá
Caruarú
Pesqueira
Arcoverde
Catende
Palmares
Barreiros
Garanhuns
União dos Palmares
Rio Largo
Maceió
Palmeira los Indios
Arapiraca
São Miguel dos Campos
Penedo
Propriá
Aracaju
Estancia
Conde
Alagoinhas
Santo Amaro
Camaçari
Candeias
Salvador
Nazaré
Valença
Gandu
Jequié
Contas
Santo Antônio de Jesus
Cruz das Almas
Cachoeira
Feira de Santana
Itaberaba
Paraguaçu
Iramaia
Contendas do Sincorá
Brumado
Caetité
Serrinha
Cipó
Itapicuru
Queimadas
Itabaiana
Jeremoabo
Senhor do Bonfim
Canudos
Vasa Barris
Juàzeiro
Petrolina
Casa Nova
Rajada
Sobradinho Reservoir
Remanso
Pilão Arcado
Xique-Xique
Serra São Francisco
1090
Jacobina
Gavião
Irece
Mundo Novo
Rui Barbosa
Seabra
Chapada Diamantina
1275
Ibotirama
Paramirim
Barra
Ibitunane
Boqueirão
Rio Grande
Pirajiba
Barreiras
Santana
Bom Jesus da Lapa
Santa Maria da Vitória
Corrente
São Francisco
Formoso
Correntina
Roda Velha
Campos Belos
Posse
Serra Geral de Goiás
Dianópolis
Formosa do Rio Preto
884
Serra das Mangabeiras
Corrente
Gilbués
Curimatá
Serra da Tabatinga
Lizárda
Alto Parnaiba
Santa Filomena
Serra do Penitente
Tasso Fragoso
Cristino Castro
Serra do Uruçuí
Caracol
Serra de Piauí
São Raimundo Nonato
Pausa
Eliseu Martins
Canto do Buriti
Piauí
São João do Piauí
Paulistana
Serra do Dois Irmãos
Cabrobó
Belem de São Francisco
Chorrocho
Paulo Alfonso
Santana do Ipanema
Aguas Belas
Parnamirim
Salgueiro
Ouricuri
Serra Talhada
Planalto da Borborema
1102
Paraíba
Itaporanga
Chapada do Araripe
Juazeiro do Norte
Crato
Campos Sales
Iguatu
Icó
Açudo Orós
Senador Pompeu
Tauá
Crateús
Nova Russas
Ipu
1066
Açude Araras
Serra da Ibiapaba
Piripiri
Piracuruca
Campo Major
Teresina
Timón
Poti
São Pedro do Piauí
Palmeirais
Amarante
Valença do Piauí
Serra da Batista
506
Oeiras
Picos
Jaicós
Canindé
Formosa
Floriano
Uruçuí
Gurguéia
495
Ribeiro Gonçalves
Parnaíba
Balsas
Boa Esperanca Reservoir
Pastos Bons
Serra do Valentim
Serra do Itapicuru
640
Colinas
Serra das Alpercatas
Barra do Corda
Itapicuru
Presidente Dutra
Caxias
Codó
Coroatá
União
Chapadinha
Urbano Santos
Itapicuru Mirim
Arari
Santa Inês
Cocalzinho
Bacabal
Pedreiras
Grajaú
Mearim
São Raimundo das Mangabeiras
Rio do Tiracambu
C á a t i n g a s
C a m p o s
I L
n
o
p
q
r
s
t
u
v
w
x
y
z
29
Average linear scale
miles
Km

25

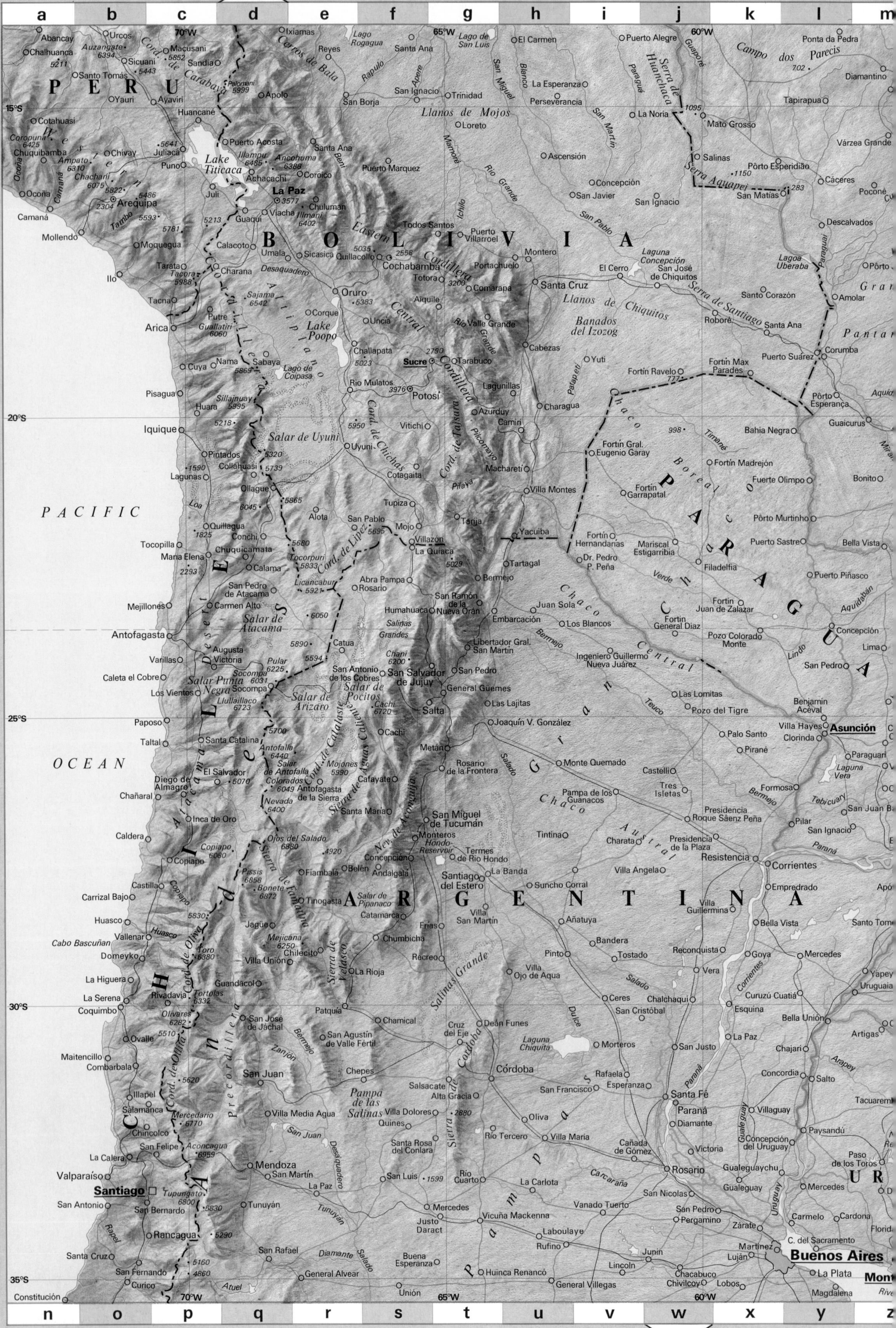
a b c d e f g h i j k l m
n o p q r s t u v w x y z
70°W
65°W
60°W
15°S
20°S
25°S
30°S
35°S
PERU
BOLIVIA
PARAGUA
ARGENTINA
CHILE
UR
PACIFIC
OCEAN
Abancay
Urcos
Chalhuanca
Auzangate 6394
Macusani
Sicuani
Sandia
Santo Tomás
Cord. de Carabaya
Palomani 5999
Apolo
Ixiamas
Cerros de Bala
Reyes
Lago Rogagua
Santa Ana
Lago de San Luis
El Carmen
Puerto Alegre
Ponta da Pedra
Campo dos Parecis
Diamantino
Yauri
Ayaviri
San Borja
San Ignacio
Trinidad
Llanos de Mojos
Loreto
La Esperanza
Perseverancia
La Noria
Serra de Huanchaca
Mato Grosso
Tapirapua
Cotahuasi
Coropuna 6425
Chuquibamba
Chivay
Juliaca
Puno
Huancané
Puerto Acosta
Lake Titicaca
Illampu 6485
Ancohuma 6388
Santa Ana
Puerto Marquez
Ascensión
Salinas
Pôrto Esperidião
Várzea Grande
Cáceres
Ampato 6310
Chachani 6075
Arequipa
Ocoña
Camaná
Mollendo
Achacachi
Coroico
La Paz
Chuluman
Illimani 6402
Viacha
Guaqui
Juli
Concepción
San Javier
San Ignacio
Serra Aquapei
San Matías
Poconé
Descalvados
Moquegua
Calacoto
Umala
Sicasica
Quillacollo
Cochabamba
Todos Santos
Puerto Villarroel
Montero
Portachuelo
El Cerro
Laguna Concepción
San José de Chiquitos
Lagoa Uberaba
Pôrto
Ilo
Tarata
Tacora 5988
Charana
Desaquadero
Totora
Comarapa
Santa Cruz
Llanos de Chiquitos
Serra de Santiago
Santo Corazón
Amolar
Tacna
Sajama 6542
Oruro
Corque
Aiquile
Valle Grande
Banados del Izozog
Roboré
Santa Ana
Arica
Putre
Guallatiri 6060
Lake Poopo
Uncia
Cabezas
Corumba
Puerto Suárez
Cuya
Nama
Sabaya
Lago de Coipasa
Challapata
Sucre
Tarabuco
Yuti
Fortín Ravelo
Fortín Max Parades
Pisagua
Huara
Sillajhuay 5995
Rio Mulatos
Potosí
Lagunillas
Charagua
Pôrto Esperança
Azurduy
Camiri
Iquique
Salar de Uyuni
Vitichi
Uyuni
Cord. de Chichas
Cord. de Tajsara
Pilcomayo
Bahia Negra
Guaicurus
Pintados
Collahuasi
Lagunas
Cotagaita
Macharetí
Fortín Gral. Eugenio Garay
Fortín Madrejón
Fuerte Olimpo
Bonito
Ollague
Villa Montes
Fortín Garrapatal
Chaco Boreal
Pôrto Murtinho
Quillagua
Alota
Tupiza
San Pablo
Mojo
Tarija
Yacuiba
Fortín Hernandarias
Mariscal Estigarribia
Puerto Sastre
Bella Vista
Tocopilla
María Elena
Chuquicamata
Conchi
Tocorpuri 5833
Cord. de Lipez
Villazón
La Quiaca
Tartagal
Dr. Pedro P. Peña
Filadelfia
Puerto Piñasco
Calama
Licancabur 5921
Abra Pampa
Rosario
Bermejo
San Pedro de Atacama
Mejillones
Carmen Alto
Salar de Atacama
Humahuaca
San Ramón de la Nueva Orán
Juan Sola
Los Blancos
Fortín Juan de Zalazar
Fortín General Diaz
Embarcación
Concepción
Antofagasta
Salinas Grandes
Pozo Colorado
Monte Lindo
Lima
Augusta Victoria
Catua
Libertador Gral. San Martín
Chani 6200
Ingeniero Guillermo Nueva Juárez
San Pedro
Varillas
Pular 6225
Socompa 6031
San Antonio de los Cobres
San Salvador de Jujuy
Caleta el Cobre
Salar Punta Negra
Los Vientos
Llullaillaco 6723
Salar de Arizaro
Salar de Pocitos
General Güemes
Las Lomitas
Pozo del Tigre
Benjamin Aceval
Salta
Las Lajitas
Cachi 6720
Paposo
Joaquín V. González
Villa Hayes
Asunción
Clorinda
Palo Santo
Pirané
Taltal
Santa Catalina
Antofalla 6440
Salar de Antofalla
Cachi
Metán
Paraguarí
Rosario de la Frontera
Monte Quemado
Castelli
Laguna Vera
Diego de Almagro
El Salvador
Mojones 5990
Cafayate
Tres Isletas
Formosa
Chañaral
Colorados 6049
Antofagasta de la Sierra
Pampa de los Guanacos
Chaco Austral
Nevada 6400
Santa María
San Miguel de Tucumán
Presidencia Roque Sáenz Peña
Pilar
San Ignacio
Inca de Oro
Caldera
Ojos del Salado 6880
Monteros
Hondo Reservoir
Termes de Rio Hondo
Tintina
Charata
Presidencia de la Plaza
Resistencia
Corrientes
Copiapo 6080
Copiapó
Belén
Fiambalá
Andalgalá
Concepción
Santiago del Estero
La Banda
Villa Angela
Suncho Corral
Emprdrado
Castilla
Pissis 6858
Bonete 6872
Tinogasta
Salar de Pipanaco
Villa San Martín
Villa Guillermina
Carrizal Bajo
Catamarca
Sierra de Famatina
Huasco
Vallenar
Cabo Bascuñan
Domeyko
Jagüe
Mejicana 6250
Chilecito
Frias
Añatuya
Bella Vista
Santo Tomé
Chumbicha
Bandera
Tostado
Reconquista
Goya
Mercedes
Toro 6380
Villa Unión
Recreo
Pinto
La Rioja
Sierra de Velasco
Vera
Yapey
La Higuera
La Serena
Coquimbo
Rivadavia
Tortolas 6332
Guandacol
Salinas Grandes
Villa Ojo de Aqua
Salado
Ceres
Chalchaqui
Curuzú Cuatiá
Uruguaia
San Cristóbal
Esquina
Olivares 6282
San José de Jáchal
Patquía
Chamical
Deán Funes
Cruz del Eje
Bella Unión
Ovalle
Precordillera
San Agustín de Valle Fértil
Laguna Chiquita
Morteros
San Justo
La Paz
Artigas
Maitencillo
Combarbalá
Chepes
Córdoba
Rafaela
Chajarí
Concordia
Salto
San Juan
Pampa de las Salinas
Salsacate
Alta Gracia
San Francisco
Esperanza
Santa Fé
Paraná
Diamante
Villaguay
Tacuarembó
Illapel
Salamanca
Mercedario 6770
Villa Media Agua
Villa Dolores
Quines
Sierra de Córdoba
Oliva
Chincolco
Aconcagua 6959
San Felipe
Santa Rosa del Conlara
Rio Tercero
Villa Maria
Cañada de Gómez
Victoria
Concepción del Uruguay
Paysandú
La Calera
Valparaíso
Mendoza
San Martín
Desaguadero
San Luis
Rio Cuarto
La Carlota
Rosario
Gualeguaychu
Paso de los Toros
Santiago
Tupungato 6800
La Paz
Carcarana
San Nicolas
Mercedes
Gualeguay
San Antonio
San Bernardo
Tunuyán
Mercedes
Justo Daract
Vicuña Mackenna
Vanado Tuerto
San Pedro
Pergamino
Zárate
Carmelo
Cardona
Rancagua
Laboulaye
C. del Sacramento
Santa Cruz
San Rafael
Diamante
Buena Esperanza
Rufino
Junín
Martinez
Luján
Buenos Aires
San Fernando
General Alvear
Huinca Renancó
Lincoln
Chacabuco
La Plata
Curicó
Constitución
Atuel
Unión
General Villegas
Chivilcoy
Lobos
Magdalena
Montevideo
Pampas
Gran Chaco
Cordillera Central
Altiplano
Eastern Cordillera
Cordillera Occidental
Atacama Desert
Cord. de Olivares
Cord. de Oliva
Sierra de Aguas Calientes
Cord. de Calalaste
Nev. de Aconquija
Western Cordillera

30

a b c d e f g h i j k l m

26 27

635 · Bandeirante 50°W Alto Paraíso de Goiás Posse Formoso Guanambi Contendas do Sincorá Jequié 40°W
Nova Crixas Guanambi Caetité Brumado Ipiau

o Grosso Chavantina Uruaçu Padre Bernardo Serra da Capivara Malhada Vitória da Conquista Itabuna Ilhéus
Aruaña Tocantins Januária Itapetinga 15°S

Plateau Vale do Sonho Ceres Goianésia Formosa Ceilândia Brasília Brazilian Janaúba Canavieiras
Batovi Jaçara Anápolis Arinos São Romão Taiobeiras Pedra Azul

Rondonópolis São Luis de Montes Belos Goiânia Cristalina Plateau Montes Claros Jequitinhonha Porto Seguro
Ponta Branca Caiapônia Indiara Pires do Rio Paracatu Brasilândia Coronel Murta Itaobim Almenara

Alto do Araguaia Mineiros Rio Verde Jatai Morrinhos Ipameri ·1020 Pirapora Minas Engenheiro Dolabela Nanuque Itamaraju
Pedro Gomes Placa Goiatuba Itumbiara Catalão Tres Marias Teófilo Otoni Caravelas Abrolhos Archipelago

Verde de o Grosso Paraíso Cassilandia Araguari Patos de Minas Tres Marias Reservoir Diamantina Gerais Governador Valadares Mantena São Mateus
Capim Verde Ituiutaba Uberlândia Patrocinio Abaeté Corinto Curvelo 20°S

Campo Grande Campina Verde Uberaba Araxá Bom Despacho Sete Lagoas Ipatinga Aimorés Linhares
Ribas do Rio Pardo Aqua Clara Véstia Fernandópolis Frutal Bambui Belo Horizonte Caratinga Colatina

R A Andradina São José do Rio Preto Barretos Z Franca Divinópolis João Monlevade Manhuaçu Vitória Vila Velha
Casa Verde Araçatuba Monte Alto Batatais Passos Oliveira Conselheiro Lafaiete Cachoeiro de Itapemirim

Nova Alvorada Dracena Osvaldo Cruz Lins Ribeirão Preto Boa Esperança Barbacena Muraé Bom Jesus de Itabapoana
Guaçu Presidente Prudente Marilia Araraquara Pocos de Caldas Tres Corações Juiz de Fora Campos

Navirai Paranaiba São Carlos Rio Claro Pouso Alegre Tres Rios Novo Friburgo Macaé
Pôrto São José Bauru Americana Campinas Guaratinguetá Volta Redonda Petrópolis

Cruzeiro do Oeste Maringá Londrina Ourinhos Avaré Taubaté Angra Niterói Cabo Frio Rio de Janeiro
Campo Mourão Apucarana Piraju Itapetininga Guarulhos São José dos Campos Grande

Guaira Ivaiporã Telemaco Borba Castro Capão Bonito São Paulo Sto. André Santos São Sebastião Tropic of Capricorn
Toledo Periquitos Ponta Grossa Itapeva Registro ·1350

Cascavel Guarapuava Curitiba Iporanga 25°S
Foz do Iguaçu Campo Largo Paranaguá

Francisco Beltrão União da Vitória Mafra Joinville São Francisco
Pato Branco Caçador Blumenau ATLANTIC

Chapeco Joaçaba Itajai
Irai Curitibanos Florianópolis

Erexim Lajes São José
Carazinho Lagoa Vermelha Vacaria 1808 OCEAN

Passo Fundo Criciúma Tubarão
Cruz Alta Lajeado Caxias do Sul Araranguá 1250

Santa Maria Novo Hamburgo
Cachoeira do Sul Butiá Canoas Pôrto Alegre Osório 30°S

Camaquã Lagoa dos Patos
Bagé Canguçu Pelotas

Rio Grande
Melo Jaguarão Lagoa Mirim

Rocha
35°S

n o p q r s t u v w x y z

31

50°W 45°W 40°W

0 100 200 300 miles Average linear scale 0 100 200 300 400 500 Km

a b c d e f g h i j k l m

80°W · 75°W · 70°W · 65°W

Juan Fernández Islands
(Chile)

Alejandro
Selkirk

Robinson
Crusoe

Valparaíso
Santiago
San Antonio

San Bernardo

Tupungeto
6800

San Martín

1599

Río
Cuarto

San Luis

La Ca

Vicuña
Macke

Rancagua

Santa
Cruz

San Fernando
Curicó

San Rafael

5290

5830

5160

4860

4090

Tunuyán

La Paz

Diamante

Mercedes

Justo
Daract

Labou

35°S

Constitución

Talca

Malargüe

4020

4800

Maule

Sierra del Nevado 3810

General
Alvear

Victorica

Santa
Isabel

Huinca
Renan

Eduardo
Castex

Riv

Santa
Rosa

Talcahuano

Chillán

3680

Barrancas

Algarroho
del Aguila

Bañados
del Atuel

Chacharramendi

General
Acha

Concepción

Punta Lavapié

Los Angeles

4115

Chos Malal

Colorado

2200

Catriel

Puelches

Villa Ir

Lebú

Victoria

2969

Las
Lajas

Cerros
Colorados
Reservoir

Plaza
Huincul

Neuquén

Curacó

PACIFIC

Temuco

Curacautín

3124

Zapala

Cutral-Có

General
Roca

Chelforó

Río Co

Villarrica

Limay

Picuún
Leufú

Choele
Choel

Col

Valdivia

3740

Junín
de los
Andes

San Martín
de los Andes

Ezequil Ramos
Mexia Reservoir

General
Conesa

Negro

40°S

Lago de Ranco

Osorno

Lago
Nahuel
Huapi

2660

Paso Limay

Sierra
Colorada

Los
Menucos

Valcheta

San Antonio
Oeste

Vie

Lago
Llanquihue

San Carlos
de Bariloche

Maquinchao

Mesa de Somuncura

Puerto
Lobos

Puerto
Montt

Ingeniero
Jacobacci

Gastre

San Matías
Gulf

Ancud

El
Maitén

Gangan

Telsen

Puerto
Madryn

Nuevo
Gulf

Chiloe

Castro

2440

Esquel

Cabo Quilán

Chaitén

Gulf of Guafo

2260

Tecka

José de
San Martín

Chubut

Las Plumas

Paso de los Indios

Chubut

Florentino
Ameghino
Reservoir

Trelew

Rawson

Gulf of Corcovado

2400

Gran
Laguna
Salada

Camarones

45°S

OCEAN

Chonos
Archipelago

2360

Puerto
Cisnes

Magdalena

Puerto
Aisén

Colhaique

Facundo

Lago
Mustars

Lago
Colhué
Huapi

Chico

Malaspina

Gulf of
San Jorge

Río Mayo

Sarmiento

Comodoro
Rivadavia

Taitao
Peninsula

San Valentín
4058

Lago
Buenos Aires

Chile
Chico

Perito
Moreno

Las Heras

Caleta
Olivia

Penas
Gulf

Lago Gen.
Carrera

Pico
Truncado

Jaramillo

Cabo Tres Puntas

Campana

3440

Cochrane

3700

San Lorenzo

Bajo Caracoles

Deseado

Puerto
Deseado

Lago
o Higgins

Lago
Cardiel

Gobernador
Gregores

El Salado

Puerto
San Julián

3375

Lago
Viedma

Tres Lagos

Chico

La
Julia

Piedrabuena

Murallón
3600

Lago Argentino

Santa Cruz

Puerto Santa
Cruz

50°S

2380

El Calafate

150

Esperanza

Bahía
Grande

Hanover

Lago del
Toro

Yacimiento

Río
Turbio

Gallegos

Río Gallegos

Nelson Strait

Puerto
Natales

1285

Punta Delgada

1750

Laguna
Blanca

Cerro
Sombrero

Magellan Str.

Desolación

Punta Arenas

Porvenir

Magellan Straits

Tierra del
Fuego

Río Grande

Cabo San Diego

Santa
Inés

Brunswick
Peninsula

Grande

Lago Fagnano

Staten Isla

Sarmiento Pen.

Ushuaia

55°S

Hoste

Cape Horn

n o p q r s t u v w x y z

80°W · 75°W · 70°W · 65°W

This map shows 1/60 of the earth's surface

60°W   55°W   50°W   45°W

Gualeguay

San Nicolas

nado
erto
San
Pedro
Pergamino

Mercedes

Duranzo

Treinta-y-
Tres

U R U G U A Y

Carmelo   Cardona

Florida

Zárate
Martinez
Luján

C. del
Sacramento

San Jose
de Mayo

Junín
Mercedes
Chacabuco

**Buenos
Aires**

Lanús

Canelones

Minas

Rocha

35°S

Chivilcoy
onte

Lobos

La Plata
Magdalena

Montevideo

Maldonado

9 de Julio

San Miguel
del Monte

Chascomús

Saladillo
ehuajó

*Samboronbón
Bay*

Salado

San Carlos
de Bolivar

Las Flores

Dolores

Punta Norte

Azúl

Rauch

Ayacucho

General Juan Madariaga

ni
Olavarría

Tandil

oronel
árez

Benito
Juárez

Coronel
Pringles

Loberia

Mar del Plata

Tres
Arroyos

Miramar

Blanca
Cnel. Dorrego

Necochea

*Bahía
Blanca*

A T L A N T I C

40°S

45°S

O C E A N

50°S

Falkland Islands / Islas Malvinas
(U.K.)

*West
Falkland*

*East
Falkland*

Stanley

South Georgia Islands
(U.K.)

55°S

60°W   55°W   50°W   45°W

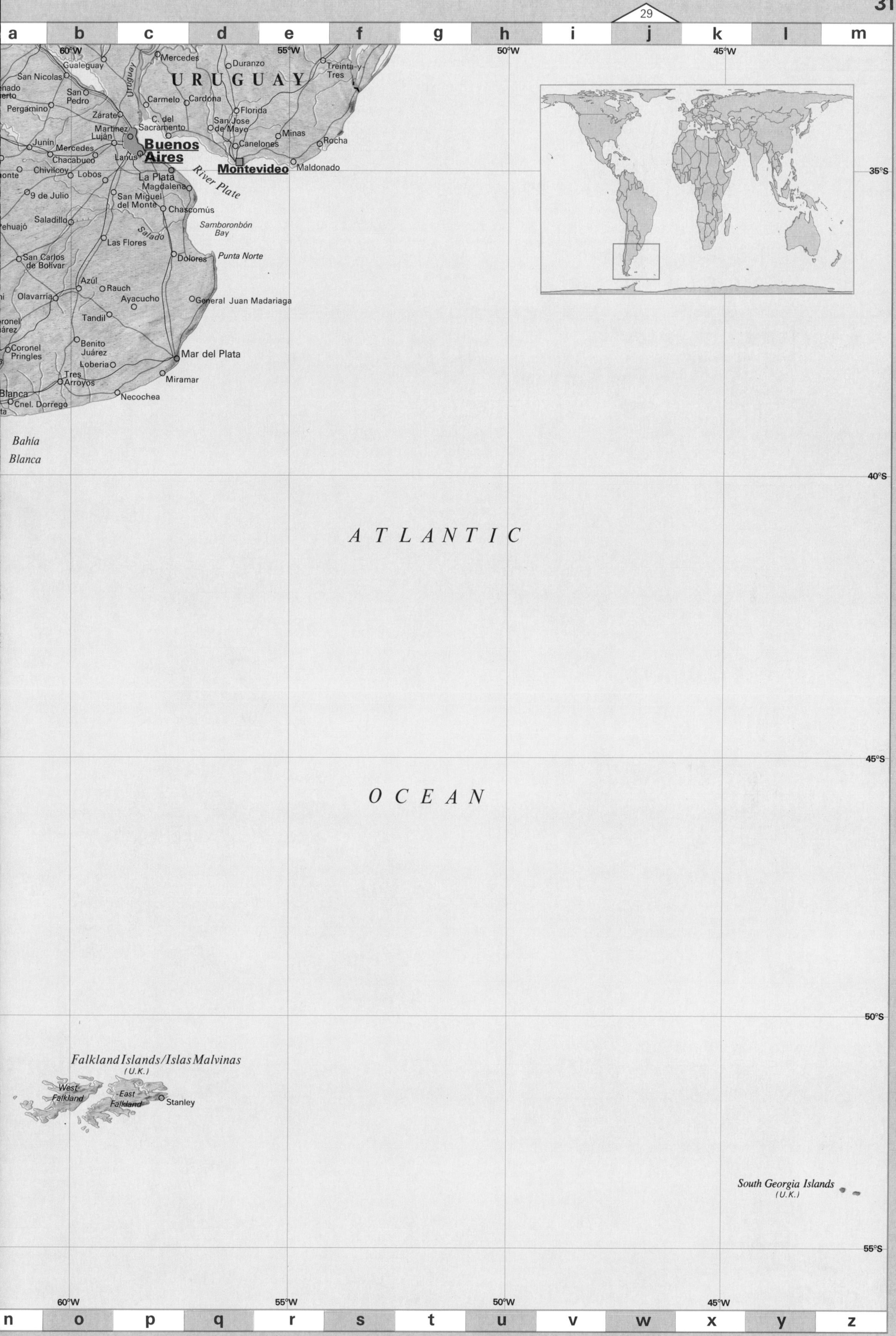

0   100   200   300 miles   Average linear scale   0 100 200 300 400 500 Km

Greenland
(Denmark)
Scoresby Sound
○ Scoresbysund

20°W   15°W   10°W   5°W   0°

Jan Mayen
(Norway)

70°N

A R C T

Denmark Strait

Cape Horn
Fontur
Arctic Circle

○ Isafjördur   Akureyri ○
Húna Bay

O C E

Breidhi Fjord
I C E L A N D   • 1765

65°N   1400   Vatnajökull
○ Djúpivogur
Akranes ○   2119 •
Faxa Bay   ● Reykjavik
Keflavik ○
Reykjanes

Faeroe Islands
(Denmark)

Shetland
Islands
Lerwick ○

60°N

A T L A N T I C

Orkney
Islands   N O

Cape
Wrath   Pentland Firth
Thurso

Hebrides   Lewis   Minch   Moray Firth
Skye   Inverness ○   Elgin ○
Loch   Highlands
Ness   • 1309   ○ Aberdeen
S C O T L A N D
Fort William ○ • 1343

90   Mull   Perth ○   Dundee ○
Stirling ○
Islay   Edinburgh ○   Berwick
Glasgow ○   upon
Ayr ○   Tweed
GREAT BRITAIN   Newcastle
North Channel   upon Tyne ○
Londonderry ○   **AND**   ○ Sunderland
55°N   NORTHERN   Carlisle ○
IRELAND   **NORTHERN IRELAND**   Middlesbrough ○
Donegal   Lough Neagh   ○ Belfast
Bay   Portadown ○   Isle of   S
Sligo ○   Man   York ○
Dundalk ○   ○ Douglas   Leeds ○   ○ Kingston upon Hull
IRISH   Irish   Blackpool ○   Manchester ○
Westport ○   Athlone ○   Sea   Liverpool ○   ○ Sheffield
Galway ○   Holyhead ○   Stoke-on- ○   ○ Nottingham
Dublin   Anglesey   Trent   Derby ○   Leicester ○   ○ Norwich
Shannon   886   • 1085   **Birmingham**   ○ Cambridge
Roscrea ○   ○ Arklow   ● WALES   ○ Coventry   ○ Ipswich
O C E A N   **REPUBLIC**   Wexford ○   Aberystwyth ○   Oxford ○   ○ Luton
Limerick ○   Waterford ○   Fishguard ○   Thames
Killarney ○   920   Swansea ○   Southend-
○ Cork   Cardiff ○   Reading ○   on-Sea
Bristol   ● **London**
St. George's   Channel   Bristol ○   ○ Dover
Cape Clear   Channel   Bournemouth ○   Southampton ○   Brighton ○   Calais
Exeter ○   Isle of   Strait of
Wight   Valenc
○ Plymouth
50°N   Land's End   ○ Penzance   English Channel   Abbeville ○
Amiens ○
Cherbourg ○   Rouen ○
Guernsey   Le Havre ○
Channel Islands   Caen ○   Evreux ○
(U.K.) Jersey   Seine
Gulf of St. Malo   Granville ○   ● **Paris**
Brest ○   St. Brieuc ○   Alençon ○   Chartres ○
Rennes ○   **F R A N**
Le Mans ○
Lorient ○   Angers ○   Orl
St. Nazaire ○   Nantes ○   0°   ○ Tours   Loire

20°W   15°W   10°W   5°W

This map shows 1/60 of the earth's surface

a b c d e f g h i j k l m

92

10°E   15°E   20°E   25°E   North Cape   30°E

Söröya   Cape Kiberg
Hammerfest   70°N
Senja   Tromsö   Alta   1139   Lakselv   Kirkenes   Tana
Vesterålen   Andöya   Skibotn   623   Lake Inari   Pečenga
Langöya   Narvik   1590   Ivalo   Lotta   Padunskoye
Lofoten Islands   Bognes   Kebnekaise   Kiruna   807   More
Vest Fjord   2117   Muonio   636   RUSSIA
Bodö   2090   Kolari   L a p p l a n d
1906   Sarek   Gällivare   Torne
Svartisen   Lönsdal   Kemijärvi
1599   Mo-i-Rana   1609   Hornavan   697   396   Kemi   Kuusamo
Mösjöen   1915   Arjeplog   Pite   211   Tornio   Kemi   Lake Pyaozero
Lake Udd   Luleå   Kalevala   263
Kvigtind   Oulu   65°N
Vikna   1703   Storuman   Skellefte   Luleå   Lake Oulu   Reboly
Grong   1390   Lycksele   Skellefteå   Kajaani   Lake Pielis
Steinkjer   Ume   Raahe   355
Kristiansund   Trondheim   Åre   Strömsund   Ångerman   Umeå   Kokkola   239   Kuopio   F I N L A N D
Molde   Åndalsnes   Oppdal   1796   Östersund   Örnsköldsvik   Jakobstad   Joensuu
Ålesund   Lake Stor   Kramfors   Vaasa   125   Kyyjärvi   279
Tynset   1009   Sundsvall   Jyväskylä   Lake Saimaa   Sortavala
Målöy   2038   2469   2183   Sveg   Ljungan   Hudiksvall   Pori   Parkano   Lake Näsi   Imatra
Galdhöpiggen   Särna   430   Söderhamn   Lake Päijänne   Lappeenranta   Lake Ladoga
Sognfjord   Övre Årdal   Lillehammer   Ljusnan   Tampere   Lahti   Vyborg
Gudvangen   1862   Gol   Hamar   774   Gävle   Åland Islands   Hämeenlinna
Hardangerfjord   Lake Mjösa   Lake Siljan   (Finland)   Vantaa   Kotka
Eidfjord   1660   Grungedal   Kongsvinger   Borlänge   Dal   Turku   Espoo   Helsinki   179
Drammen   Hönefoss   Uppsala   Mariehamn   62   (Helsingfors)   St. Petersburg   60°N
Oslo   Karlstad   Västerås   Hankö   Gulf of Finland   Kolpino
Evje   Larvik   Fredrikstad   Örebro   Lake Mälar   Norrtälje   Tallinn   Narva   Chudovo
Arendal   Oslofjord   Lake Vänern   279   Södertälje   Stockholm   Hiiumaa   Luga
Uddevalla   Lidköping   Linköping   Norrköping   ESTONIA   Tartu   Lake Peipus   Novgorod
Kristiansand   Cape Skagen   Lake Vättern   Saaremaa   Pärnu   145   (L. Chud)   Lake Pskov   Lake Ilmen
Skagerrak   Frederikshavn   Göteborg   Borås   Jönköping   Västervik   Visby   Gulf of Riga   Valga   Pskov   Staraja Russa
Ålborg   377   Gotland   Ventspils   Ostrov   RUSSIA   50
Holstebro   Randers   Kattegat   Växjö   Kalmar   Riga   311   Opochka
Jutland   173   Halmstad   Öland   LATVIA   Liepāja   Jekabpils   Velikije Luki
Århus   Helsingör   Helsingborg   Karlskrona   Dvina   Daugavpils   Nevel
DENMARK   Kristianstad   Klaipeda   Siauliai   259   Vitebsk
Copenhagen   207   228   Panevèžys   Polotsk   55°N
Kolding   (København)   Malmö   LITHUANIA   Postavy   Smolensk
Esbjerg   Odense   Zealand   Ystad   Neman   Molodetschno   Orsha
Fünen   The Sound   Bornholm   Kaliningrad   Sovetsk   Lida   342   Borisov
Svendborg   (Denmark)   BALTIC SEA   RUSSIA   Kaunas   Vilnius   Mogilev
Flensburg   Lolland   Falster   Cape Arkona   Gulf of Danzig   Chernyakhovsk   Grodno   Minsk   Krichev
Kiel Bay   Rügen   Gdynia   Suwałki   BELARUS   Dovsk
Kiel   Stralsund   Pomeranian Bay   Słupsk   Gdansk   Elblag   Olsztyn   Baranovichi   Bobruysk
Heligoland   Lübeck   56   Greifswald   Koszalin   Tczew   Grodno   Slonim   Slutsk   192   Klintsy
Bight   Bay   Rostock   Szczecinek   Vistula   312   Grudziądz   Łomza   Białystok   Gomel
Wilhelmshaven   Lübeck   Wismar   176   Szczecin   Bydgoszcz   Brest   Pinsk   Mozyr
Frisian Islands   Bremerhaven   Schwerin   Neubrandenburg   Stargard   Torun   P r i p e t
Groningen   Emden   Hamburg   Neuruppin   Gorzów-Wlkp   Włocławek   Warsaw   M a r s h e s   Chernigov
Leeuwarden   Bremen   Elbe   Wittenberge   Poznan   Kutno   (Warszawa)   Brest
Emmen   Oder   POLAND   Warta   Siedlce   Styr   Pripet
NETHERLANDS   Münster   Hannover   Potsdam   Berlin   Oder   Łódź   Bug   Kovel   Nézhin
Amsterdam   Osnabrück   (Hanover)   Magdeburg   Frankfurt   162   Leszno   Kalisz   289   Lublin   240
Utrecht   Dessau   Cottbus   Piotrkow   Korosten
Arnhem   Göttingen   Halle   Leipzig   Legnica   Radom   Kiev Reservoir
Rotterdam   Dortmund   GERMANY   Weimar   Dresden   Wrocław   Kielce   Zamość   Rovno   Novograd Volynskiy   252
Eindhoven   Essen   840   Kassel   Erfurt   Gera   Czestochowa   Lutsk   Kiev   (Kyyiv)
Brussels   Düsseldorf   Bad Hersfeld   983   Chemnitz   1603   Wałbrzych   Katowice   Radom   Zhitomir
Aachen   Cologne   Bonn   689   Plauen   Hradec Králové   Krakow   Rzeszow   Przemyśl   UKRAINE
Liège   (Köln)   774   Karlovy Vary   Kolin   Ostrava   L'viv   50°N
Charleroi   Koblenz   Wiesbaden   Frankfurt   244   Pilzen   Prague   1490   Bielsko-Biala   617   Ternopol'   Khmel'nitskiy   Belaya Tserkov
LUXEMBOURG   Trier   Main   Würzburg   Bamberg   (Praha)   CZECH   Olomouc   Žilina   1726   Vinnitsa
Luxembourg   Mannheim   České   REPUBLIC   Brno   Zakopane   Gerlachovsky   1346   Ivano-   Cherkassy
Metz   Saarbrücken   Nuremberg   Budějovice   Jihlava   Znojmo   2663   Prešov   Frankovsk   383
Nancy   Karlsruhe   (Nürnberg)   1457   Danube   SLOVAKIA   2045   Košice   Uzgorod   Kolomyya   Uman'
Strasbourg   Stuttgart   Regensburg   Zvolen   Mukachevo   Kamenets-Podol'skiy
Chaumont   Rhine   Augsburg   Passau   Linz   Morava   Zlín   Chernovtsy   Mogilev Podol'skiy
Freiburg   Memmingen   Munich   Vienna   Bratislava   Miskolc   Ivano-Frankovsk   Pervomaysk
Mulhouse   1493   (München)   (Wien)   Vác   Nyíregyháza   Botoşani   South Bug
Dijon   Salzburg   2075   Györ   Satu Mare   2305   Pietrosu   Bălti
Besançon   Basle   Zürich   Lake Constance   AUSTRIA   Leoben   Budapest   HUNGARY   Baia Mare   Suceava   MOLDOVA
Zugspitze   Zugspitze   Dachstein   2996   Debrecen   ROMANIA   Orgejev
SWITZERLAND   2963   Innsbruck   Inn   2713   Prut

n o p q r s t u v w x y z

35

0   100   200   300   miles   Average linear scale   0   100   200   300   400   500   Km

ATLANTIC

OCEAN

Bay of

Biscay

GREAT BRITAIN

English Channel

Plymouth
Penzance
Land's End
Exeter
Bournemouth
Southampton
Isle of Wight
Brighton
Dover
Strait of Dover
Calais
Ghent
Brussels (Bruxelles)
BELGIUM
Charleroi
Lille
Valenciennes
St Quentin
Amiens
Abbeville
LUXEM-BOURG
Luxembourg
Liège
Cologne (Köln)
Aachen
Bonn
Koblenz
Bad Hersfeld
Erfurt
Plauen
GERMANY
Wiesbaden
Frankfurt
Würzburg
Bamberg
Mannheim
Nuremberg (Nürnberg)
Reg
5°W
0°
5°E
10°E
50°N

Cherbourg
Le Havre
Rouen
Compiègne
Sedan
Thionville
Trier
Saarbrücken
Karlsruhe
Stuttgart
Augsburg
Munich (Münche)
Channel Islands (U.K.)
Guernsey
Jersey
Gulf of St. Malo
Granville
Caen
Évreux
Seine
Paris
Reims
Chaumont
Metz
Nancy
Strasbourg
Freiburg
Memmingen
Zugspitze 2963
Brest
St. Brieuc
Alençon
Chartres
Troyes
Mulhouse
Basle
Zürich
Liechten-stein
Landeck
St. Nazaire
Rennes
Le Mans
Orléans
Auxerre
Dijon
Besançon
Berne
Lucerne
Vaduz
Chur
FRANCE
Angers
Tours
Loire
Moulins
Chalons-sur-Saône
SWITZERLAND
Brig
Bernina
Dolomites
Nantes
288
Poitiers
Châteauroux
Allier
Mâcon
Geneva (Genève)
Lake Geneva
Mont Blanc 4807
Monte Rosa
Como
Bolzano
La Roche-sur-Yon
Aosta
Bergamo
Brescia
Verona
Padova
La Rochelle
Limoges
Clermont-Ferrand
1885
St. Étienne
Lyons
Annecy
Novara
Milan (Milano)
Vice
Saintes
Angoulême
Brive
Massif
Le Puy
Grenoble
Valence
Turin (Torino)
Piacenza
Parma
Gironde
Bordeaux
Dordogne
Aurillac
Central
Cévennes
Rhône
Pelvoux 4102
Alessandria
Cuneo
Genoa (Genova)
Modena
Ferrara
45°N
Lot
Cèvennes
Maritime Alps
Gulf of Genoa
La Spezia
Bologna
SAN MARIN
Landes
Agen
Garonne
Nîmes
Avignon
Aix-en-Provence
Nice
Imperia
Pisa
Florence (Firenze)
Livorno (Leghorn)
Adour
Bayonne
Toulouse
Montpellier
Arles
MONACO
Siena
Elba
San Sebastián
Pau
Tarbes
Carcassonne
Narbonne
Marseilles
Toulon
LIGURIAN SEA
Grosseto
Corunna
Gijón
Santander
Bilbao
1604
Gulf of Lion
Bastia
Viterbo
Cantabrian Mountains 2583
Vitoria
Pamplona
3404
Perpignan
Corsica (France)
Civitavecchia
Roma (Roma)
Cape Finisterre
Santiago de Compostela
Oviedo
León
Logroño
Pico de Aneto 2923
ANDORRA
Costa Brava
Gerona
Ajaccio
2710
Orense
Ponferrada
Burgos
Jaca
Huesca
Saragossa
Lérida
Bonifacio
Str. of Bonifacio
Olbia
Vigo
Braga
Miño
2142
Soria
Calatayud
Ebro
Tarragona
Barcelona
Sassari
Nuoro
Sardinia (Italy)
Zamora
Valladolid
Duero
Segovia
2430
Guadalajara
Tortosa
Oristano
1834
Oporto (Porto)
Douro
1382
Salamanca
Ávila 2592
Madrid
Teruel
Castellón
Cágliari
TYRR
Aveiro
Guarda
Coimbra
SPAIN
2020
Cape Teulada
40°N
Talavera de la Reina
Toledo
Tajo
La Almarcha
Valencia
Balearic Islands
Menorca
Alcudia
Palma
Mallorca
Leiria
Tagus
Cáceres
Trujillo
Ciudad Real
Guadiana
Albacete
Júcar
Gandia
Ibiza
Lisbon (Lisboa)
PORTUGAL
Mérida
Badajoz
Puertollano
Segura
Cabo de la Nao
Setúbal
Évora
Guadiana
Sierra Morena
Córdoba
Úbeda
2036
Murcia
Alicante
Costa Blanca
MEDITE
Sines
Beja
Mértola
Aracena
Jaén
Lorca
Cartagena
Tra
Odemira
Guadalquivir
Écija
Baza
Aguilas
Egai
Mars
Algarve
Lagos
Huelva
Sevilla
Granada 3478
Almería
Sierra Nevada
Motril
Binzert
Gulf of Tunis
Cape Bon
Sagres
Cape St. Vincent
Gulf of Cádiz
Antequera
Málaga
Annaba
Tabarka
TUNIS
Kélibia
Cádiz
Jerez de la Frontera
Costa del Sol
Algiers (Alger)
Dellys
Bejaia
Skikda
Beja
Taboursouk
Zaghouan
Algeciras
Gibraltar (U.K.)
Ceuta (Sp.)
Tangier
Tétouan
Ténès
Blida
Tizi Ouzou
Constantine
586
Souk Ahras
Le Kef
1357
Sousse
Pelagie (Sic.)
Lampedu
Str. of Gibraltar
Khemis Miliana
Medea
Bordj Bou-Arréridj
Setif
Aïn Beïda
Kairouan
Mahdia
Cape Kaboudia
Asilah
Chechaouen
Melilla (Sp.)
Beni Saf
Mostaganem
Oran
Mohammadia
1983
Cheliff
Tell Atlas
Relizane
Tiaret
Metlili Chaamba
Bou Saada
2326
Khenchela
Tebessa
Kasserine
Fériana
Sfax
Kerkenna Islands
MOROCCO
Ksar el Kebir
Aknoul
Sidi-bel-Abbès
Ouida
Al Hoceima
Chellala
767
Biskra
Gafsa
35°N
Ouettha
Marhoum
Tlemcen
Atlas
Hauts Plateaux
Monts des Ouled Nail
Atlas
Chott Melrhir
40
Tozeur
Gabès
Djerba
Chott ech Chergui
Djelfa
Ouled Djellal
Chott Djerid
Kebili
Médenine
Zarzis
Mecheria
Aflou
Messaad
Laghouat
El Meghaier
Diamaa
2236
Brézina
Saharan Atlas
1977
El Oued
Ben Guerdane
Aïn Sefra
Ghardaia
Chebka du Mzab
Guerara
Touggourt
238
Bordj Bourguiba
Remada
ALGERIA
Tilrhemt
Aïn Oussera
Ouargla
145
Hassi Messaoud
306
Great Eastern Erg
Bir Zar
Nalut 688
Jac
Great Western Erg
502
El Goléa
Kebili
Sinawan
834
5°W
0°
5°E
10°E

Safi

Essaouira
Amizmiz
Jebel Igdet 3615
Toubkal 4165
Rissani
Tagouz
Abadla

This map shows 1/60 of the earth's surface

a b c d e f g h i j k l m

15°E Wałbrzych Wrocław 20°E 25°E 30°E Nezhin 35°E Sumy
Czestochowa Kielce Lutsk Rovno Korosten Kiev Reservoir Priluki
Hradec Zamość Kiev Akhtyrka
Králové Katowice Kraków Rzeszów (Kyyiv) Lubny Khar'kov
1490 POLAND L'viv Novograd Zhitomir U K R A I N E Poltava Valki
CZECH REPUBLIC Ostrava Bielsko-Biala Przemyśl Volynskiy Belaya Kremenchugskoye
Olomouc 1725 Ternopol Tserkov Reservoir Pereshchepino
Jihlava Žilina Zakopane Stryy Khmel'nitskiy Vinnitsa Cherkassy Kremenchug Novomoskovsk
1552 Gerlachovsky Ivano Dnestr Kamenets Uman' Znamenka Dneprodzerzhinsk
Brno Znojmo 2043 Košice Prešov Frankovsk Podol'skiy Mogilev Kirovograd Dnepropetrovsk
Linz Danube Zvolen Uzgorod Mukachevo Kolomyya Chernovtsy Podol'skiy Pervomaysk Krivoy Rog Nikopol Zaporozh'ye
Vienna SLOVAKIA Miskolc Satu Baia Mare Suceava Botoşani Bălti South Bug Kakhovskoye
(Wien) Bratislava Györ Nyíregyháza Mare Piẹtrosu MOLDOVA Orgejev Nikolayev Reservoir
2075 Danube Vác Debrecen 2305 Iaşi Chişinău Tiraspol Kakhovka
Leoben Budapest Oradea Dej 2103 Prut Belgorod Novaya Melitopol
Graz Veszprém H U N G A R Y Cluj Napoca Tirgu Bacău Odessa Kherson Kakhovka
Balaton Békéscsaba Arad Mureş Siret Bolgrad Crimea Dzhankoy Sea of
Maribor Lake Szeged Timişoara Sibiu Braşov Galaţi Tulcea Mouths of Azov
Varaždin Nagykanizsa Mureş Deva R O M A N I A Bolgrad the Danube Simferopol Feodosiya
Ljubljana Pécs Subotica Tisza Negoiu 2509 Turnu Piteşti Ploieşti Danube 1259 45°N
SLOVENIA Zagreb Drava Osijek Zrenjanin Vršac 2546 Severin Sevastopol Jalda
CROATIA Sava Novisad Craiova Bucharest Constanţa BLACK
Karlovac Brod Belgrade Smederevo (Bucureşti)
Krk Bihać Banja Mitrovica (Beograd) Svetozarevo YUGO- Ruse SEA
Zadar Luka Tuzla Morava SLAVIA Vidin Rosiori Kolarovgrad Varna
Šibenik BOSNIA- Zenica Sarajevo Užice Niš Vraca Pleven Turnovo
Split HERZEGOVINA 2107 Priština Leskovac Pirot Balkan 2376 Sliven Burgas
Brac Jablanica Ivangrad Kumanovo Sofia Plovdiv Stara Zagora
Hvar Korčula Podgorica 2693 Prizren (Sofiya) BULGARIA Edirne Kürdžali
Pelješac Dubrovnik Shkodër Skopje Musala Blagoevgrad Rhodope Lüleburgaz
ADRIATIC Ohrid Veles MACEDONIA (F.Y.R.) 2925 Komotini 2191 Tekirdağ Istanbul Üsküdar Ereğli Sinop
SEA Lake Bitola Sérra Kavalla Sea of Marmara Izmit Bolu Karabük Kastamonu Samsun
Campobasso Tirana Prespa Edessa Thessaloniki Thasos Canakkale Bandırma Bursa Adapazari Gerede 2565 Çorum 2068
Foggia (Tiranë) Lake Chalkidike Imbros Troy Balikesir Bilecik 2543 Eskişehir Kızılırmak Turhal
Benevento Korça Kozáni Lemnos Ayvalik Ankara Kırıkkale 54
Bari Viore 2683 2911 Gulf of Thermai Lesbos Kütahya A n a t o l i a Yozgat 2345 40°N
Potenza Corfu Jánina Tríkala Lárisa AEGEAN Northern Chíos Manisa Afyon TURKEY Kayseri
Salerno Corfu Pindus Volos Sporades Akhisar 2446 Aksaray 3976
Sapri Capo Santa Maria Northern Izmir Alaşehir Lake Ereğli Kozan
di Leuca Lamía SEA Euboea Chalkis Sámos Aydin Egridir Konya Niğde 3488
Corigliano Delphi Levkas Agrinion Cephalonia Chalkis Menderes Denizli Lake Karaman Geyhan
Cosenza IONIAN Athens Ándros Beyşehir Mugla Adana
Lipari SEA (Athinai) Tinos Antalya Mersin
Islands Patras Piraeus Cyclades Southern Fethiye (Içel) Iskenderun
Messina 1965 (Pátrai) Korinth Sporades Alanya Silifke 1795
Reggio Zante 2224 Náxos Rhodes Gulf of Anamur Antakya
Etna Riposto Pyrgos Gulf of Corinth Milos 1215 Antalya Taurus Cape Anamur Cape
3340 Catania Tripolis Andros Rhodes CYPRUS Andreas
Gela Syracuse Kalamai Cape Akrítas Cape Maléa Nicosia Latakia
Noto (Siracusa) Cape Matapan Sea of Olympos Famagusta 1385
Kithira Crete 1951 Larnaca 35°N
Valletta Kánea Iráklion Cape Arnauti Paphos Limassol Tartus
Melambes Kárpathos Tripoli
2456 Crete 3089
LEBANON
Beirut Zahlé
Damascus
Al Bayda Darnah Sur Qunaitra
Al Marj 882 Golan Irbid
Al Jabal al Akhdar Haifa Heights Dar'ā
Benghazi Al Abyar Tobruk Hadera 2247
Al Adam ISRAEL WEST Zarqa
Qaminis 169 Tel-Aviv-Jaffa BANK
Gulf of Al Burdi Nile Delta Jerusalem Amman
Buerát el Hsun L I B Y A Sîdi Barrâni Rosetta Baltim GAZA Dead
Sirte Sallûm Mersa Damanhûr Dumyat Gaza Sea Beer
15°E Sirte 20°E Matruh Al Port Said Sheba Al Karak
EGYPT Alexandria 25°E Fuka Mansura Suez Ar Arish 35°E
30°E Canal

n o p q r s t u v w x y z

0 100 200 300 miles Average linear scale 0 100 200 300 400 500 Km

a   b   c   d   e   f   g   h   i   j   k   l   m

15°W   10°W   5°W   0°

PORTUGAL   SPAIN

Sines
Ourique
Odemira   Aljustrel   Aracena   Córdoba   Jaén   Huéscar   Lorca   Murcia
                                                        ·2036
Portimão   Sevilla   Lucena   Granada   Guadix   Baza   Aguilas   Cartagena
Sagres   Lagos   Faro   Tavira   Huelva   Marchena   ·3478   Almería
                Jerez de la   ·1554   Antequera   Sa. Nevada   Motril
            Gulf of   Frontera   Ronda   Málaga
            Cádiz   Cádiz   Algeciras   Gibraltar(U.K.)   Mostaganem
                        Str. of Gibraltar   Ceuta(Sp.)   Oran   Relizane
                    Tangier   Tetuan   Melilla(Sp.)   Sidi-   Masc
                Asilah   Chechaouen   Al Hoceima   Nador   bel-Abbes
                    El Arisch   Midar   Beni Saf   Mohammadia
                    Ksar el Kebir   Ouerrha   Aknoul   Ghazaouet   Tlemcen   Marhoum
                    Ouezzane   Midar   Oujda   Ras-al-Ma   Cho
                Mehdia   Sidi   Taza   Taourirt   El Aricha   Boug
            Salé   Kacem   Fès   Guercif   Hauts P   El Bay
        Rabat   Kenitra   Sefrou   ·3190   Debdou   Mêchéria
    Casablanca   Khemisset   Meknes   Azrou   Mouilouya   Outat-el-Hadj   Sa
        Azemmour   Rommani   Midelt   Missour   Tendrara   Aïn Sefra ·2236
    El Jadida   Berrechid   ·3741   Ksabi   Bou Arfa   Ben Benimathar
        Khouribga   Oued   Talsinnt   Mengoub   Figuig
    Oualidia   Settat   Zem.   Beni Mellal   Rich ·2670   Beni Cunif
    Sidi   Benguerir   ·4071   Goulmina   Ksar es Souk   Colomb
    Safi   Bennour   Demnate   Ighil   Tinerhir   Kenadsa   Béchar
        Tensift   Marrakech   Erfoud   Abadla   ·834
    Essaouira   Chichaoua   Tazzarine   Rissani   Taouz   Taghit
        Amizmiz   Agdz   Tinerhir   Taouz   Igli
    Jebel Igdet   Toubkal ·4165   Tazenakht   Zagora   Beni Abbès
    ·3615   Taroudannt   Tagounite   ·757
    Agadir   Inezgane   Tata   Kerzaz

30°N   Tiznit   ·2359
        Sidi Ifni   ·1250   Djebel   Bani   Hamada of Dra   Tabelbala   Erg er Raoui   Ksabi
        Bou Izakarene   Foum   Tinfouchy   ·890   Kahal Tabelbala   Tim
    Tantan   Dj. Ouarkziz   El Aassane   Bou Akba   Charouin
                    Ouahila   Gourara
    C. Yubi   Tindouf   ·437   ALGERIA
    Tarfaya   Erg   L   G   E
        Hagunia   Mcherrah   Bordj Flye   Adrar   Tamentit
        Daora   Iguidi   Sainte Marie   El Mansour   Titaf
    El Aaiún   Al Farcia   Aftout
            Smara   El Eglab   ·680   Chenachane   Sali
    Lemsid   Reggane
    C.Bojador   Tifariti
    Bojador   Amasin   Chech   Erg
        Aïn ben Tili
    WESTERN   Bir   ·701   Oum Greine   Chegga   a
        Guelta   Rhallamane   Aioun Abd   Tanezrouft
        Zemmur   Zemmour   Bir el Khzaim   el Malek
    Dakhla   Kreb en Naga
    Aargub   Bir   SAHARA   El   Hank   ·305   Erg el Ahmar ·315   Tanezrouft
    Rio de Oro   Enzarah   ·370   El Mreïti   Oukar   Tane
    Imilili   Karet
    G. de Cintra   ·639   Zedness   Hamada Safia
            Zouerate   500   Aguelt el Melah   Agueraktem   El Maia
    Cap   Fdérik   ·250   Taoudenit   Hamada el Haricha
    Barbas   Agailas   ·273   ·361
                Hammami   ·322
    Bir   Tichla   Zug   ·647   ·330   Er Mreyer   Ouarane   ·296   El   Khenachich
    Gandus   Maker   Ouarane   ·321   Bordj-M
    Nouâdhibou   Choûm   Ksar   Guelb er
    Güera   Torchane   Richat   El Djouf   Douaouir   ·450
    Cape   Atar   Ouadane   Jafene   ·284
    Nouâdhibou   Chinguetti
            MAURITANIA   Azaouad   Mabrouk
20°N   Tidra   Oujeft
    C. Timiris   Nouamrhar   Adafer   MALI   Timétrine   Aguelo
                ·501   ·750
        Akjoujt   Meraia   In Alay   Oudeïka   Ano
        Faye   Dahar Oualata
    Nouakchott   ·88   Dabar Tichitt   Agam
    Trarza   ·23   Tamassoumit   Tidjikja   Tichitt   Dahar Oualata
            ·554   Akreijit   Bamba   Niger   Bourem
            Moudjeria   Aouker
        Boutilimit   Tamchaket   ·318
        Aleg   Mal   Oudeïka

n   o   p   q   r   s   t   u   v   w   x   y   z

ATLANTIC   OCEAN

Madeira (Portugal)
Funchal   Desertas

Canary
Islands
(Spain)   Tenerife
Tenerife   Santa
Pico   Cruz
de Teide   Guia
·3718
Gomera   Las
Palmas
·1949

MOROCCO

Anti Atlas   High Atlas   Middle Atlas   Atlas

Lanzarote
Arrecife
Puerto del Rosario
Fuerteventura

This map shows 1/60 of the earth's surface

0 100 200 300 miles Average linear scale 0 100 200 300 400 500 Km

35
a b c d e f g h i j k l m
20°E
25°E
30°E
35°E
Kithira
Cape Maléa
GREECE
Sea of Crete
1215
Rhodes
Kárpathos
2540
Finike
Gulf of Antalya
TURKEY
Anamur
Cape Anamur
Silifke
CYPRUS
Cape Andreas
Cape Arnauti
Nicosia
Famagusta
Olympus 1951
Larnaca
Paphos
Limassol
1795
Antakya
Idlib
Latakia
Asi
1385
Hama
Tartus
Homs
Tripoli
Tall Kalakh
3087
Baalbek
Nabk
Zahlé
2659
Beirut
LEBANON
Damascus
Sur
Qunaitra
Golan Heights
Haifa
1735
Hadera
Irbid
Dar'a
Mafraq
WEST BANK
Tel-Aviv-Jaffa
Zarqa
Amman
Jerusalem
Gaza
GAZA
ISRAEL
Dead Sea
Al Karak
Beer Sheba
JORDAN
35°N
30°N
25°N
20°N
MEDITERRANEAN
SEA
Gulf of Sidra
Benghazi
Al Mekhily
Tobruk
Al Burdi
Al Adam
Qaminis
169
Sallûm
Sîdi Barrânî
Mersa Matruh
Marmarica
Cyrenaica
Ajdabiyah
Fuka
Al Alamein
Al Hammam
Alexandria
Rosetta
Nile Delta
Baltîm
Dumyat
Port Said
Damanhûr
Al Mansura
Suez Canal
Al Arish
Tanta
Zagazig
Ismâilîya
Lower Egypt
Great Bitter Lake
Shubra al Kheima
Cairo
Giza
Pyramids
Memphis
Helwân
Suez
Nakhl
Wadi al Arish
Libyan Plateau
Qattara Depression
-123
Qara
Wadi al Hamim
Fort Qarain
30
Al Jaghbub
113
Jaghbub Oasis
Siwa
Siwa Oasis
Awjilah
Jalu
Jalu Oasis
Ain Sukhna
Sudr
Al Faiyûm
Beni Suef
Nile
Gulf of Suez
Sinai
Peninsula
1626
Katherina 2637
Nuweiba
Dahab
Gulf of Aqaba
Elat
Aqaba
Al Mudauwara
850
Quseima
Wadi Araba
1641
1615
Ma'an
Petra
Bayir
Al Isaw
Al Mu
Al Bir
2580
Al Bad
Tabuk
Wadi al Akhdar
Ofira
Ash Sharmah
Bahariya Oasis
Bawîti
Beni Mazâr
Al Minyâ
Ras Ghârib
Gemsa
Ras Muhammad
1990
Duba
Dairût
Arabian
Desert
Hurghada
Asyût
Abu Tig
Farafra
Farafra Oasis
LIBYA
Libyan
Desert
EGYPT
Akhmîm
Sohâg
Wadi Qena
Port Safaga
Al Balyana
Qena
Qusair
Al Wajh
Qasr
Dakhla Oasis
Mût
Thebes
Qus
Karnak
Luxor
Al Khârga
Al Khârga Oasis
Isna
Upper Nile Egypt
Idfu
Marsa Alam
RED
Ras Abu Madd
184
Tazirbu
Zighan
Kufrah Oasis
Al Jawf
Rabyanah
625
Tropic of Cancer
Bâris
Kom Ombo
Wadi Garara
1st. Cataract
Aswân
1977
Berenice
Ras Banas
Gilf Kebir Plateau
Lake Nasser
Wadi Hadarba
Bir al Hasa
Wadi Allaqi
Abu Simbel
Wadi Ibib
Ras Abu Dara
Halaib
Ras Ha
1893
Uweinat
2nd. Cataract
Wadi Halfa
2217
Wadi Gabgaba
Wadi Oko
Dungunab
2218
Erba
Muhammad Qol
Kosha
Nubian Desert
2260
Oda
Delgo
Abu Hamed
Kerma
Ouninga Kebir
Erdi
Dongola
3rd. Cataract
Umm Mirdi
Amur
Sinkat
CHAD
SUDAN
Karima
4th. Cataract
5th. Cataract
Al Khandaq
Merowe
Musmar
Haiya
Debba
Korti
Berber
Atbara
Mourdi Depression
Fada
545
Ennedi
Baiyuda
Derudeb
Adarama
Archei
Howar
al Milk
Atbara
White Nile
Shendi
Haouach
Wadi Seidna
6th. Cataract
517
738
Mitatib
Omdurman
Khartoum North
n o p q r s t u v w x y z
42
37

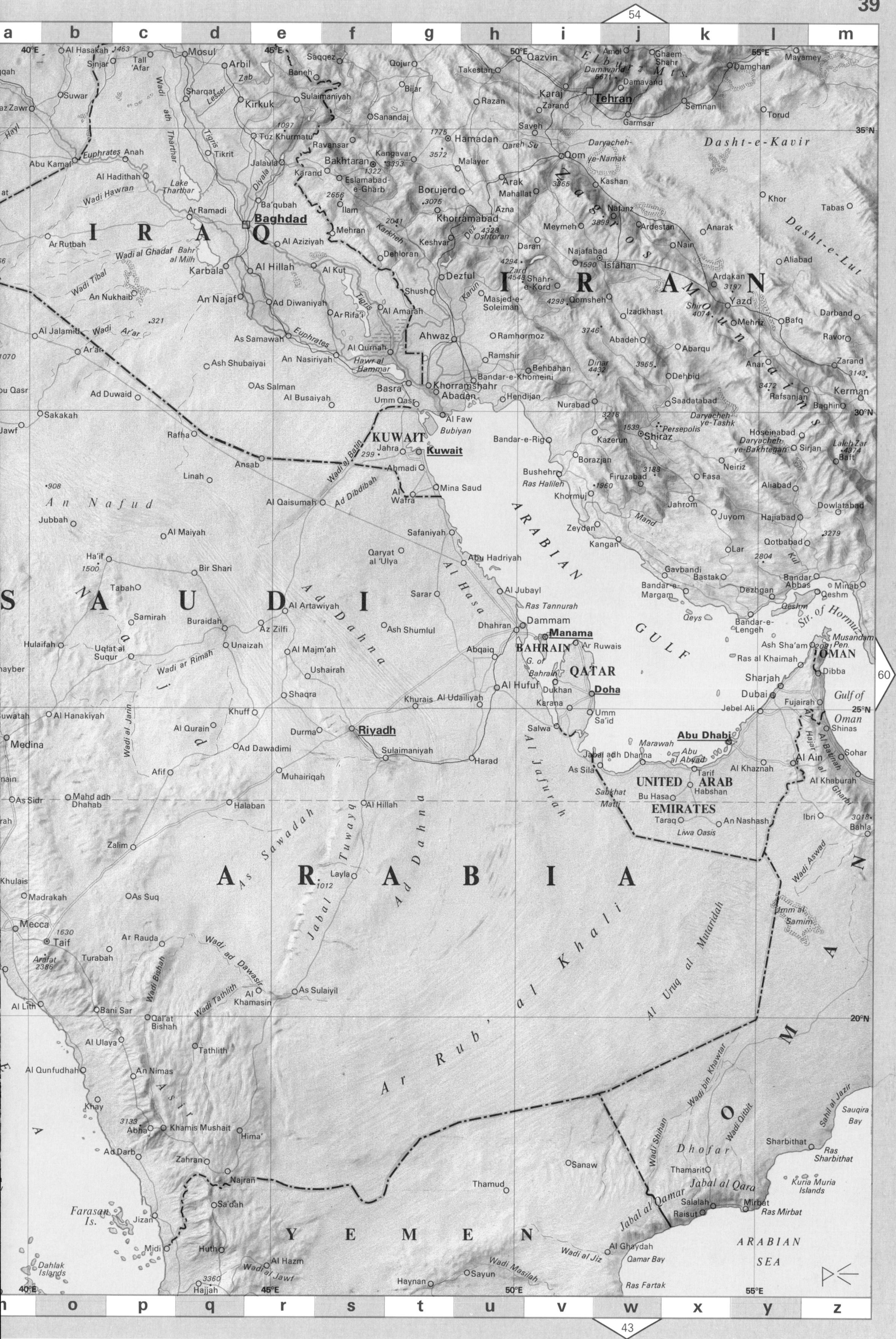

Average linear scale

0 100 200 300 miles

0 100 200 300 400 500 Km

a b c d e f g h i j k l m

54

IRAQ

IRAN

40°E 45°E 50°E 55°E

Al Hasakah 1463 Mosul Saqqez Qazvin Amol Ghaem-Shahr Mayamey Damghan

Sinjar Tall 'Afar Arbil Baneh Qojur Takestan Damavand Mts. 5671 Damavand

Suwar Sharqat Zab Kirkuk Qoiur Bijar Razan Karaj Zarand **Tehran** Semnan Torud

Abu Zawr Wadi ath Tharthar Lesser Sulaimaniyah 1097 Sanandaj 1775 Hamadan Saveh Garmsar

Euphrates Anah Tikrit Tuz Khurmatu Ravansar Kangavar 3572 Malayer Qareh Su Qom Daryacheh-ye-Namak **Dasht-e-Kavir** 35°N

Abu Kamal Al Hadithah Tigris Jalaula Bakhtaran 3393 1322 Arak Mahallat Najanz Kashan Khor Tabas

Wadi Hawran Diyala Karand Eslamabad-e-Gharb 2656 Borujerd Azna 3365 Ardestan Anarak Aliabad

Lake Tharthar Ba'qubah Ilam 2041 Khorramabad Meymeh 3895 Nain Najafabad Darband

Baghdad Mehran Keshvar Daran Najafabad 1590 Isfahan Yazd Ravor

Ar Rutbah Al Aziziyah Dehloran Zard 4294 4545 Shahr-e-Kord Qomsheh Nain Ardakan 3197 Aliabad Zarand 3143

Ar Ramadi Wadi al Ghadaf Bahr al Milh Al Hillah Shush Dezful Masjed-e-Soleiman 4298 Izadkhast 4074 Mehriz Bafq Kerman

Karbala Al Kut Karun Ahwaz 3746 Abadeh Abarqu 3472 Rafsanjan Baghin

An Nukhaib An Najaf Ad Diwaniyah Ar Rifa'i Ramhormoz Behbahan 3965 Dehbid Anar

Al Jalamid As Samawah An Nasiriyah Hawr al Hammar Basra Ramshir Bandar-e-Khomeini Dinar 4432 3218 Daryacheh-ye-Tashk Hoseinabad 30°N

1070 Ar'ar As Salman Al Busaiyah Umm Qasr Khorramshahr Abadan Hendijan Nurabad 1539 Persepolis Shiraz Daryacheh-ye-Bakhtegan Sirjan Laleh Zar 4374 Bait

Sakakah Rafha Al Qaisumah Ad Diwaniyah Al Faw Bubiyan Bandar-e-Rig Kazerun Neiriz Aliabad

Jawf 321 Linah Ansab **KUWAIT** 299 Jahra **Kuwait** Borazjan 3188 Fasa Dowlatabad

Ou Qasr Al Dibdibah Ahmadi Bushehr 1960 Firuzabad Jahrom 3279

An Nafud 908 Jubbah Al Maiyah Ad Dibdibah Al Wafra Mina Saud Ras Halileh Khormuj Zeydan Juyom Hajiabad Qotbabad

Ha'il 1500 Bir Shari Qaryat al 'Ulya Safaniyah Abu Hadriyah Kangan Lar 2804 Bandar-e-Lengeh

Tabah Samirah Al Artawiyah Sarar Al Jubayl Ras Tannurah Gavbandi Bastak Dezhgan Bandar Abbas Minab

SAUDI Buraidah Az Zilfi Ash Shumlul Dhahran Dammam Bandar-e-Margam Qeys Qeshm Qeshm

Hulaifah Uqlat al Suqur Unaizah Al Majm'ah **Manama** Ar Ruwais Ash Sha'am Musandam Pen. 2001 **OMAN**

Khayber Wadi ar Rimah Ushairah Khurais Al Udailiyah **BAHRAIN** G. of Bahrain **QATAR** Ras al Khaimah Dibba

Al Hanakiyah Shaqra Al Hufuf Dukhan **Doha** Sharjah Fujairah Al Ain Sohar

Medina Al Qurain Khuff Durma Karana Dubai Jebel Ali **Oman** Shinas

Afif Ad Dawadimi **Riyadh** Harad Umm Sa'id **Abu Dhabi** Al Khaznah Al Ain

As Sidr Mahd adh Dhahab Sulaimaniyah Salwa Marawah Abu al Abyad Tarif Habshan Al Khaburah Ibri

As Sidr Wadi al Jarin Halaban Al Hillah As Sila Jabal adh Dhanna **UNITED ARAB** An Nashash 3018 Bahla

As Suq Zalim Layla 1012 Sabkhat Matti Bu Hasa **EMIRATES** Taraq Liwa Oasis Umm al Samim

ARABIA As Sawadah Jabal Tuwayq Ad Dahna Al Uruq al Mutaridah OMAN

Madrakah As Suq Al Jafurah

Mecca Taif 1630 Ar Rauda Wadi ad Dawasir Wadi bin Khawtar Wadi Qitbit

Arafat 2386 Turabah As Sulaiyil **Ar Rub' al Khali** Wadi Aswad

Al Lith Bani Sar Al Khamasin 20°N

Al Ulaya Qal'at Bishah Dhofar Sharbithat Ras Sharbithat

Al Qunfudhah An Nimas Sanaw Thamarit Sauqira Bay

Khay 3133 Khamis Mushait Hima' Thamud Jabal al Qara Kuria Muria Islands

Abha Ad Darb Zahran Jabal al Qamar Salalah Mirbat

Farasan Is. Najran Huth Al Hazm Al Ghaydah Raisut Ras Mirbat

Jizan Sa'dah **YEMEN** Wadi Masilah Qamar Bay **ARABIAN SEA**

Midi 3360 Hajjah Wadi al Jawf Haynan Sayun Wadi al Jiz Ras Fartak

Dahlak Islands 40°E 45°E 50°E 55°E

n o p q r s t u v w x y z

43

60

25°N

Gulf of Oman

Str. of Hormuz

36

a b c d e f g h i j k l m
15°W
10°W
5°W
Moudjéria
Boûmdeïd
Tamchaket
Aoukâr
Trarza
Boutilimit
Mederdra
Aleg
Mâl
Montagnes de l'Afollé
600
Ayoûn el Atroûs
Oualâta
In Alay
Oudeika
Bamba
Tombouctou
Rosso
Senegal
Bogué
Dagana
Kiffa
MAURITANIA
Néma
Timbedgha
Irîgui
Lake Faguibine
Goundam
Tua
St. Louis
Kaédi
Mbout
Kankossa
Amourj
Niafounké
Louga
Kobenni
Bassikounou
Hamoud
Sahel
Matam
Maghama
Lac Débo
Linguère
Sélibabi
Nioro du Sahel
Nampala
Hombori
Fourdou
Ballé
Nara
1155
15°N
Dakar
Cape Verde
Thiès
Mbaké
Diourbel
Ferlo
Birou
Sokolo
Douentza
Macina
Kidira
Kayes
Koniakari
Diéma
Mopti
Mbour
Kaolack
SENEGAL
Malème-Hodar
Bandiagara
Bamba
MALI
Djibo
Diamou
Koumpentoum
Bafoulabé
Didiéni
Niger
Djenné
Tambacounda
Banjul
Karang
Georgetown
Ouahigouya
GAMBIA
Gambia
Kolokani
Banamba
Ségou
Sere Kunda
Brikama
Basse Santa Su
Dialakoto
Dialafara
Toukoto
Bani
San
BURKINA FASO
Yako
Bignona
Kolda
Niokolo Koba
Saraya
Kita
Kati
Koulikoro
Fana
Bla
Nouna
Casamance
Kédougou
Satadougou
Bamako
Dédougou
Farim
Ziguinchor
Koundara
Baguinéda
Mpessoba
GUINEA-BISSAU
1538
Koutiala
Koudougou
Ouagadougou
Mansôa
Bafatá
Bissau
Corubal
Gaoual
Ouéléssébougou
Koundougou
Toéssé
Fouta Djalon
Bafing
Siguiri
Bissagos Islands
Kogon
Tougué
Labé
Dinguiraye
Bougouni
Sikasso
Houndé
Bobo-Dioulasso
Léo
Po
Catió
1264
Pita
GUINEA
820
505
Télimélé
Garalo
Boké
1028
Tumu
Navrongo
Bolgatanga
Lawra
Fatala
Fria
Konkouré
Dabola
Kouroussa
Manankoro
Banfora
Dalaba
1015
Gaoua
Mamou
1094
Kankan
Pogo
1421
Kavendou
Sanouyah
Wa
Yala
Boffa
Kindia
Faranah
Samatiguila
10°N
Ouangolodougou
Ga
Bohodoyou
Black Volta
White Volta
Conakry
Forécariah
Odienné
Kabala
Little Scarcies
Boundiali
Ferkéssédougou
Rokel
Kissidougou
Kérouané
Loma Mts.
1948
Bouna
Kambia
Bako
Korhogo
Sawla
Makeni
Koidu
Morondo
Kong
Bole
SIERRA LEONE
Tibé
1504
430
Kanawolo
Maluwe
Koro
Koutouba
Freetown
Guéckédou
Macenta
Beyla
Kani
1656
1257
Bamboi
Pendembu
Touba
Kintampo
Katiola
Bondoukou
Bo
Nzérékoré
Séguéla
Goumeré
Sewa
Kenema
Zorzor
Biankouma
Kossou Reservoir
Techiman
Sherbro Island
1752
Man
Bouaké
700
Moa
Lofa
1189
Pujehun
Sanniquellie
CÔTE D'IVOIRE
GHANA
Berekum
Mano River
Bouaflé
Agnibilekrou
Sunyani
Bomi Hills
St. Paul
Gbarnga
Ganta
Danané
Yamoussoukro
Duékoué
Daloa
Bong
Mani
Guiglo
Dimbokro
Abengourou
Kumasi
Konongo
LIBERIA
Toulépleu
Komoé
Tano
Monrovia
Tapeta
Toumodi
Akoupé
Awaso
554
Obuasi
Tchien
Gagnoa
Soubré
Agboville
Dunkwa
Taï
Lakota
Buchanan
Cess
Sassandra
Bandama
Prestea
Juarzon
396
Niénokoué
Cavally
Abidjan
Tarkwa
Dabou
Grain Coast
Grand-Lahou
Grand-Bassam
Greenville
5°N
Sekondi-Takoradi
Grabo
Sassandra
San Pédro
Ivory Coast
Plibo
Tabou
Gold Coast
Harper
ATLANTIC OCEAN
Equator
0°
15°W
10°W
5°W
n o p q r s t u v w x y z

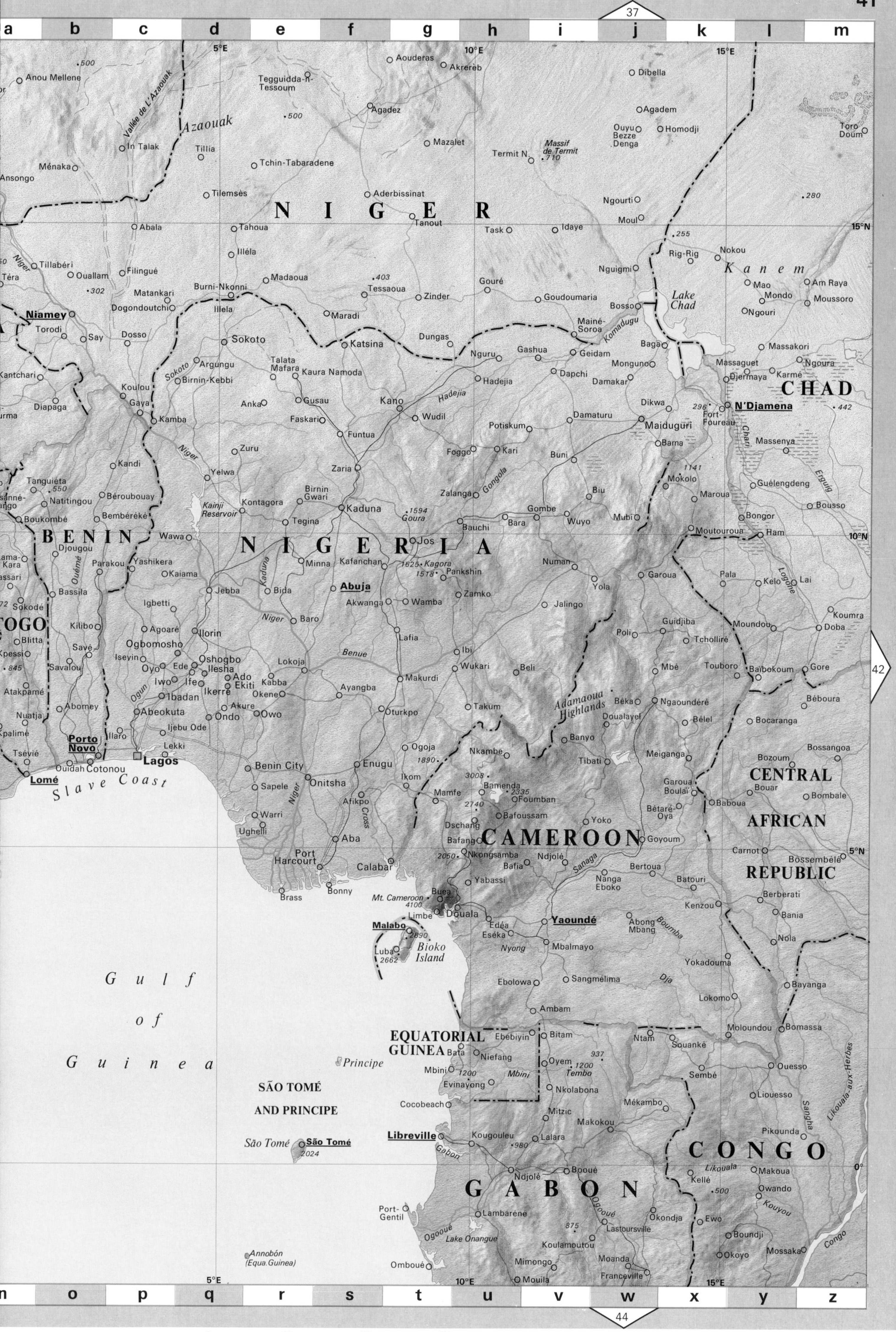
37
a b c d e f g h i j k l m
n o p q r s t u v w x y z
44
42
5°E
10°E
15°E
15°N
10°N
5°N
0°
NIGER
NIGERIA
BENIN
TOGO
CHAD
CAMEROON
CENTRAL AFRICAN REPUBLIC
EQUATORIAL GUINEA
SÃO TOMÉ AND PRINCIPE
GABON
CONGO
Gulf of Guinea
Slave Coast
Niamey
Abuja
N'Djamena
Porto Novo
Lomé
Malabo
Yaoundé
Libreville
São Tomé
Anou Mellene
Vallée de L'Azaouak
Azaouak
In Talak
Ménaka
Ansongo
Tillia
Tegguidda-n-Tessoum
Aouderas
Akrerèb
Agadez
Mazalet
Tchin-Tabaradene
Tilemsès
Aderbissinat
Tanout
Termit N.
Massif de Termit
Dibella
Agadem
Ouyu
Bezze Denga
Homodji
Toro Doum
Ngourti
Moul
Task
Idaye
Abala
Tahoua
Illéla
Tillabéri
Téra
Ouallam
Filingué
Madaoua
Burni-Nkonni
Illela
Tessaoua
Zinder
Maradi
Goudoumaria
Gouré
Matankari
Dogondoutchi
Torodi
Say
Dosso
Sokoto
Katsina
Dungas
Nguigmi
Bosso
Lake Chad
Mainé-Soroa
Komadugu
Rig-Rig
Nokou
Kanem
Mao
Am Raya
Mondo
Moussoro
Ngouri
Baga
Massakori
Nguru
Gashua
Geidam
Monguno
Damakar
Dapchi
Hadejia
Massaguet
Djermaya
Karmé
Ngoura
Argungu
Birnin-Kebbi
Talata Mafara
Kaura Namoda
Kantchari
Diapaga
Koulou
Gaya
Kamba
Anka
Gusau
Kano
Hadejia
Wudil
Faskari
Funtua
Dikwa
Maiduguri
Fort-Foureau
Damaturu
Potiskum
Foggo
Kari
Bama
Buni
Massenya
Chari
Zuru
Kandi
Yelwa
Zaria
Tanguiéta
Natitingou
Bérouboua
Bembéréké
Boukombé
Kainji Reservoir
Kontagora
Birnin Gwari
Kaduna
Goura
Tegina
Zalanga
Gongola
Biu
Mokolo
Maroua
Guélengdeng
Erguig
Bousso
Gombe
Bara
Bauchi
Wuyo
Mubi
Bongor
Moutouroua
Ham
Wawa
Djougou
Ouémé
Parakou
Yashikera
Kaiama
Minna
Kafanchan
Jos
Kagora
Pankshin
Numan
Yola
Garoua
Pala
Kelo
Lai
Logone
Bassila
Jebba
Bida
Kaduna
Zamko
Akwanga
Wamba
Jalingo
Igbetti
Sokodé
Kilibo
Agoaré
Ilorin
Niger
Baro
Lafia
Poli
Guidjiba
Tcholliré
Moundou
Doba
Koumra
Blitta
Savé
Ogbomosho
Iseyin
Oyo
Ede
Oshogbo
Ilesha
Ado Ekiti
Benue
Lokoja
Ibi
Wukari
Beli
Mbé
Touboro
Baïbokoum
Gore
Savalou
Iwo
Ife
Ibadan
Ikerre
Kabba
Okene
Makurdi
Ayangba
Atakpamé
Abomey
Abeokuta
Akure
Ondo
Owo
Oturkpo
Takum
Adamaoua Highlands
Béka
Ngaoundéré
Béboura
Bocaranga
Nuatja
Palimé
Tsévié
Ilaro
Ijebu Ode
Lekki
Lagos
Ouidah
Cotonou
Dounlayel
Bélel
Banyo
Meiganga
Tibati
Bossangoa
Bozoum
Bouar
Bombale
Ogoja
Nkambe
Enugu
Benin City
Sapele
Onitsha
Ikom
Bamenda
Foumban
Garoua Boulaï
Baboua
Mamfe
Afikpo
Cross
Warri
Ughelli
Bafoussam
Dschang
Bafang
Nkongsamba
Bétaré Oya
Yoko
Goyoum
Aba
Port Harcourt
Calabar
Bonny
Brass
Carnot
Bossembélé
Bafia
Ndjolé
Sanaga
Bertoua
Nanga Eboko
Batouri
Yabassi
Mt. Cameroon
Buea
Limbe
Douala
Edéa
Eséka
Kenzou
Berberati
Bania
Abong Mbang
Boumba
Nola
Bioko Island
Luba
Nyong
Mbalmayo
Yokadouma
Ebolowa
Sangmélima
Dja
Bayanga
Lokomo
Ambam
Moloundou
Bomassa
Ebebiyin
Bitam
Ntam
Souanké
Bata
Niefang
Mbini
Evinayong
Oyem
Tembo
Nkolabona
Principe
Sembé
Ouesso
Liouesso
Cocobeach
Mitzic
Mékambo
Makokou
Sangha
Likouala-aux-Herbes
Kougouleu
Lalara
Pikounda
Gabon
Ndjolé
Booué
Likouala
Makoua
Kellé
Owando
Kouyou
Port-Gentil
Lambaréné
Ogooué
Okondja
Lastoursville
Ewo
Boundji
Mossaka
Congo
Lake Onangue
Koulamoutou
Okoyo
Annobón (Equa.Guinea)
Mimongo
Moanda
Franceville
Omboué
Mouila
500
403
302
550
845
1594
1625
1518
1890
3008
2335
2740
2050
4100
2890
2662
1200
937
980
875
2024
255
280
296
442
1141
710
72
0 100 200 300 miles
Average linear scale
0 100 200 300 400 500 Km

20°E   25°E   30°E

Fada   *Ennedi*   Nile   Shendi
Bodélé   Archei   6th Cataract
Koro Toro   Haouach   Wadi Howar   Wadi Seidna   Omdurman   Khartoum North
Ouagat   Kapka •1220   Umm Saggat   Sindi   Magtur   Wadi al Milk   *517   **Khartoum**   Umm Inderaba
15°N   Salal   Maba   Triné   Haraza •1127   Umm Saiyala   al Dueim
S a h e l   Haddad   Hamrat al Shaikh   *K o r d o f a n*   El Hasahei
al Ouaday   Biltine   Sodiri   Umm   El Gezira
Rime   Abéché   Adré   al Junayna   Kebkabiya   El Fasher   Umm Keddada   Saiyala   Wad M
Ati   Oum Hadjer   Zalingei •3071   *Jebel Marra*   Dam Gamad   Bara   al Dueim   Senna
C H A D   *Batha*   Batha   Menawashei   Wad Banda   El Obeid   Tendelti   Kosti   Singa
Guedi •1506   Mangalmé   Goz Beida   Kass   Kirim •640   al Nahûd   Abu Zabad   Umm Ruwaba   Rabak   El Jebelein
1613   Bitkine   Mongo   Nyala   Ghubeish   al Udaiya   Dilling   *Nuba Mountains* •1325   Renk   Ed Damazin
Abou Deïa   'Idd al Ghanam   al Da'ain   Babanusa   •842   Kadugli   Turum •1122   Lake Roseir
Mélfi   Zakouma   Am Timan   Rahad al Berdi   al Muglad   Talodi   Kurmuk
Ibra   **S U D A N**   •1093   Tungaru   Paloich
Erguig   *Salamat*   Kendégué   Háraze   Birao   Dango •790   *Bahr al Arab*   Sumaih   •1325   Bam
10°N   *S u d a n*   Sumaih   Malakal
Chari   Sarh   Ouandja   Tiroungoulou   Bentiu   Tonga   Sobat   Nasir
Koumra   Aouk   Tété   Toussoro •1330   Bora   Raga   *Bahr al Ghazel*   Aweil   Akobo   Gam
Maro   Bamingui   Ndélé   *Massif des Bongos*   Sopo   Wau   Toni   Kongor   Pibor Post
Kabo   Gribingui   •850   Ouadda   •1050   Pongo   Busseri   Rumbek   *White Nile*   Bor
41   Batangafo   Ouandago   Bozoum   *Haute Kotto*   Yalinga   Maridi   Mvolo   Ngangala   Kend
Kaga Bandoro   Mbrès   Bria   *Kotto*   Ndji   Angeleri •838   Mundri   Mongalla   Swa
Bossangoa   Bouca   Dékoa   Sibut   **C E N T R A L   A F R I C A N**   Vovodo   Ouara   Tambura   Medi   Juba
Bambari   Chinko   Obo   Li Yuba   Ibba   Doruma   Garmabe   Kapoe
Bogangolo   Kouango   Alindao   **R E P U B L I C**   Mbari   Dembia   Zémio   Yambio •1067   Maridi   •1940
5°N   Damara   Bossémbélé   Kongbo   Gambo   Rafai   M'bomou   Doruma   •1065   Yei   Aba   Torit   Kinyeti •3187
Bangui   Bimbo   Zongo   Gbadolite   Mobaye   Matundu   Monga   Bili   Ango   Ese   Niangara   Dungu   Faradje   Garmabe   Lalyo   Kajo-Kaji
Mbaïki   Zinga   Bosobolo   Mobayi-Mbongo   Yakoma   *Uele*   Bondo   Api   Bambili   Baranga   Rungu   Watsa   Arua •1310   Nimule   Kaabong •2381
Boyabo   Libenge   Businga   *Ebola*   Abumonbazi   Bili   Api   Bambesa   Poko   Isiro   Gombari   Aru   Gulu   Anaka   Kitgum   Loyor
CONGO   Lobaye   Gemena   *Dua*   Bodala   Dulia   Buta   Titule   Medje   Nepoko   Wamba   Mahagi •2448   Pajule   Lira   **U G A N D A**
Dongou   Kungu   Budjala   Modjamboli   Aketi   *Tele*   Ibembo   Zambeke   Kole   *Ituri*   Bomili   Nia Nia   Mambasa   Fataki   Lake Albert   Masindi   Soro
Mobeka   Mongola   Lisala   Bumba   *Izimbiri*   Bomili   Bunia   Hoima   Nakasongola   Kamuli
Impfondo   Makanza   Busu-Djanoa   *Lopori*   Basoko   Aruwimi   Banalia   *Lindi*   Bafwabalinga   Batama   Komanda   Hoyo •1450   Kaliro   Iganga
Enyélé   Bongandanga   Basankusu   Yahuma   Yambuya   Bengamisa   Yangambi   Ntoroko   Fort Portal   Kyanjojo   Mubende   Kayunga   Jinja
Lulonga   Waka   Lingomo   Djolu   Isangi   Kisangani   *Maiko*   Opienge   Butembo   Margherita Peak •5109   Kasese   **Kampala**
Bolomba   Befale   Samba   Befori   Yatolema   Madula   *Boyoma Falls*   Lake Edward •2197   Masaka   Entebbe
0°   Mbandaka   Ruki   Ingende   **D E M O C R A T I C**   Yali   Watsi   Yekana   Pene Tungu   Ubundu   Lubero   Bushenyi   *Sese Islands*
Bikoro   *Busira*   Kalamba   Boende   Wema   *Tshuapa*   Ekoli   Opala   Kirundu   Lubutu   •956   Ishasha River   Mbarara   Kikagati   Bukoba
Yandja   *Lake Tumba*   Bolia   Watsi-Kengo   Busanga   Ikela   Likoto   Yolombo   *Lomani*   Punia   Walikale   Masisi   Karisimbi •4507   Kyaka   Lake   Musoma
R E P U B L I C   O F   C O N G O   Yalifafu   Monkoto   Kabunga   Goma   Gisenyi   Kayonza   *Victoria*   **T A N Z A N I**
Ihongo   Kiri   *Lake Mai-Ndombe*   Rutshuru   Kabale   Ruhengeri   Ukerewe Island   Nansio
Ntademele   Yandja   *Lake Kivu*   Kavumu   **Kigali**   **R W A N D A**   30°E   Tarim

20°E   25°E   30°E

This map shows 1/60 of the earth's surface

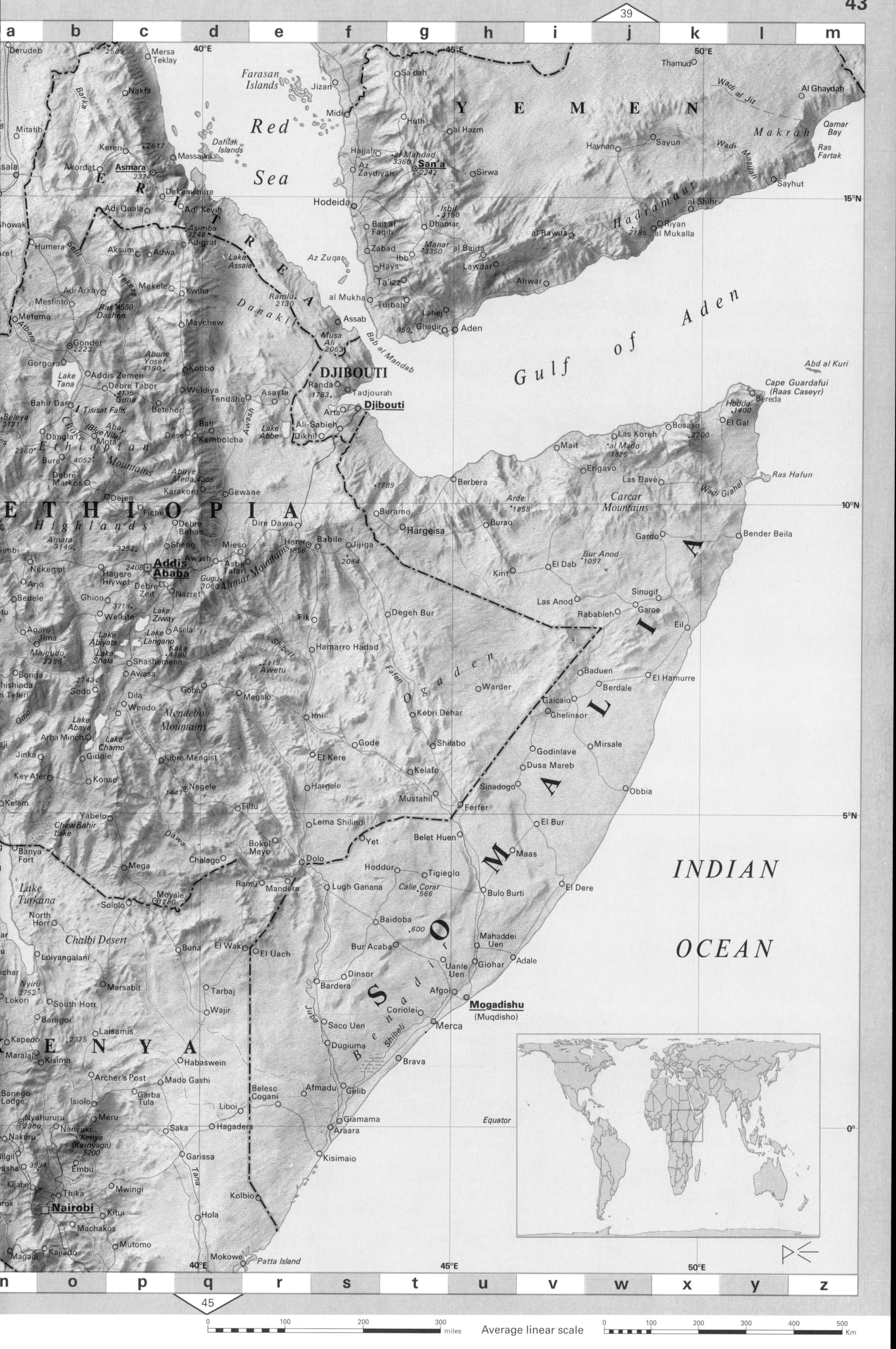
39
a b c d e f g h i j k l m
Red Sea
Farasan Islands
Dahlak Islands
YEMEN
Gulf of Aden
ERITREA
DJIBOUTI
ETHIOPIA
SOMALIA
KENYA
INDIAN OCEAN
Ethiopian Highlands
Ethiopian Mountains
Danakil
Ogaden
Ahmar Mountains
Mendebo Mountains
Carcar Mountains
Chalbi Desert
Benadir
Hadramaut
Makrah
Asmara
2374
Massawa
Keren
Nakfa
Mersa Teklay
Derudeb
Mitatib
Akordat
Dekemehare
Adi Quala
Adi Keyih
Asimba 3248
Adigrat
Humera
Aksum
Adwa
Mekele
Kwiha
Adi Arkay
Ras Dashen 4550
Mesfinto
Metema
Gonder 2223
Gorgora
Lake Tana
Addis Zemen
Debre Tabor
Guna 4135
Abune Yosef 4190
Kobbo
Weldiya
Bahir Dar
Tisisat Falls
Dangla
Mota
Abay (Blue Nile)
Bure
4052
Debre Markos
Dejen
Fiche
Debre Birhan
Shewa
Amara 3146
3292
Addis Ababa
2408
Nekempt
Arjo
Bedele
Hagere Hiywot
Debre Zeit
Nazret
Ghion
Welkite
Lake Ziway
Asela
Lake Abiyata
Lake Langano
Kaka 4190
Lake Shala
Shashemene
Agaro
Jima
Maigudo 2386
Bonga
Awasa
Sodo
2743
Dila
Wendo
Lake Abaya
Arba Minch
Lake Chamo
Gidole
Jinka
Konso
Key Afer
Kelem
Yabelo
Chew Bahir Lake
Banya Fort
Mega
Moyale
Sololo
Lake Turkana
North Horr
Loiyangalani
Marsabit
Nyiru 2752
South Horr
Baragoi
Laisamis
Kapedo
Maralal
Kisima
2375
Archer's Post
Baringo Lodge
Isiolo
Nyahururu 2360
Nanyuki
Meru
Kenya (Kirinyaga) 5200
Nakuru
Embu
Thika
Mwingi
Nairobi
Kitui
Machakos
Mutomo
Kajiado
Magadi
Habaswein
Mado Gashi
Garba Tula
Saka
Garissa
Tana
Hola
Kolbio
Mokowe
Patta Island
Liboi
Hagadera
Belesc Cogani
Wajir
Tarbaj
Buna
El Wak
El Uach
Mandera
Ramu
Chalago
Bokol Mayo
Dolo
Filtu
Negele
Kibre Mengist
Goba
Megalo
Dawa
Kembolcha
Dese
Bati
Tendaho
Asayta
Lake Abbe
Awash
Abuye Meda 4305
Karakore
Gewane
Dire Dawa
Harer 1856
Babile
Jijiga
2064
Mieso
Asbe Tafari
Gugu 3060
Lake Assale
Ramlu 2130
Musa Ali 2063
Assab
Bab al Mandab
Randa 1783
Tadjourah
Djibouti
Arta
Ali-Sabieh
Dikhil
Fik
Hamarro Hadad
Shibeli
Awetu 2119
Fafen
Degeh Bur
Imi
Gode
El Kere
Hargele
Kebri Dehar
Shilabo
Kelafo
Mustahil
Lema Shilindi
Yet
Ferfer
Belet Huen
Warder
Buramo
Hargeisa
Burao
Berbera
1789
Arde 1858
Maït
Las Koreh
al Mado 1826
Erigavo
Bosaso
2200
Las Davé
Hodda 1400
El Gal
Bereda
Cape Guardafui (Raas Caseyr)
Abd al Kuri
Ras Hafun
Wadi Giahel
Bender Beila
Gardo
Bur Anod 1097
El Dab
Kirit
Las Anod
Sinugif
Garoe
Rabableh
Eil
Baduen
Berdale
El Hamurre
Galcaio
Ghelinsor
Mirsale
Godinlave
Dusa Mareb
Sinadogo
Obbia
El Bur
Maas
El Dere
Hoddur
Tigieglo
Lugh Ganana
Calie Corar 566
Bulo Burti
Baidoba
600
Mahaddei Uen
Bur Acaba
Uanle Uen
Giohar
Adale
Dinsor
Bardera
Afgoi
Mogadishu (Muqdisho)
Coriolei
Merca
Juba
Saco Uen
Dugiuma
Brava
Afmadu
Gelib
Giamama
Araara
Kisimaio
Jizan
Midi
Sa'dah
Huth
al Hazm
Hajjah
al Mahdad 3360
San'a 2242
Az Zaydiyah
Sirwa
Hodeida
Bait al Faqih
Isbil 3190
Dhamar
Zabad
Manar 3350
al Baida
Ibb
Hays
Lawdar
Ta'izz
Az Zuqar
al Mukha
Turbah
Lahej
850
Ghadir
Aden
Ahwar
al Rawda
Thamud
Wadi al Jiz
Al Ghaydah
Qamar Bay
Ras Fartak
Haynan
Sayun
Wadi Masilah
Sayhut
al Shihr
Riyan
2185
al Mukalla
40°E
45°E
50°E
15°N
10°N
5°N
0°
Equator
n o p q r s t u v w x y z
45
Average linear scale
0 100 200 300 miles
0 100 200 300 400 500 Km

41
42
48
a b c d e f g h i j k l m
n o p q r s t u v w x y z
10°E
15°E
20°E
0°
Equator
5°S
10°S
15°S
SÃO TOMÉ AND PRINCIPE
São Tome
2024
GABON
CONGO
DEMOCRATIC
REPUBLIC
CONGO
CABINDA
(Angola)
ANGOLA
NAMIBIA
BOTSWANA
ATLANTIC
OCEAN
Cocobeach
Mitzic
Mékambo
Makokou
Libreville
Kougouleu
Lalara
980
Gabon
Ndjolé
Booué
Port-Gentil
Lambaréné
Ogooué
Lake Onangué
Okondja
Bonda (Lastoursville)
875
Koulamoutou
Omboué
Mimongo
Moanda
Franceville
820
Mouila
975
Boumango
Ndendé
Mayoko
Bambama
Tchibanga
Mossendjo
Kibangou
834
Mayumba
Mapati
Sibiti
Kouilou
Sounda
Loubomo
Madingou
Bas-Kouilou
Pointe-Noire
Brazzaville
Kinkala
Boko
Kinshasa
Luozi
Tshela
798
Lândana
Cabinda
Lukula
Seke Banza
Isangila Falls
Boma
Matadi
Muanda
Soyo
M'Pala
M'Banza-Congo
Maquela do Zombo
Tombôco
Damba
Bembe
N'Zeto
Mussera
Ambriz
Uíge
Quitexe
Negage
Nambuangongo
Camabatela
Caxito
Quibaxe
Samba Caju
Luanda
Catete
Lucala
Kalandula
N'Dalatando
Muxima
Dondo
Cuanza
Malange
Calulo
Mussende
Porto Amboim
Quibala
Gabela
Sumbe
Waco-Kungo
Andulo
Lobito
Benguela
Alto Hama
Bailundo
Balombo
Camacupa
Kuito
Cuanza
Catengue
Ganda
Caala
Cachingues
Chitembo
Mumbué
Lucira
Caconda
Negola
Cacula
Gambos
Capelongo
Menongue
Cuchi
Longa
Lubango
Chibia
Cassinga
Chianje
Mulundo
Cuvelai
Caiundo
Quiteve
1265
Cubango
1190
Oncócua
Roçadas
Savate
Rito
Cunene
Naulila
N'Giva
Ruacana
Cuangar
Oshakati
Ondangwa
Obombo
1096
Opuwa
1784
Cape Frio
Purros
Etosha Pan
Namutoni
Keibeb
Numkaub
Rundu
Shakamku
Mékambo
Likouala
Kéllé
Makoua
Kouyou
500
Owando
Ewo
Boundji
Okoyo
Gamboma
Bouanga
Nsah
Ngo
Inoni
Pikounda
Sangha
Oubangui
Mossaka
Lukolela
Irebu
Bikoro
Lake Tumba
Mbandaka
Ruki
Ingende
Kalamba
Lulonga
Bolomba
Waka
Befale
Yekana
Lingomo
Djolu
Samba
Maringa
Befori
Yali
Busira
Boende
Watsi
Wema
Tshuapa
Lomela
Momboyo
Watsi Kengo
Busanga
Ikela
Yalifafu
Monkoto
Yolon
Lome
Bolia
Kiri
Inongo
Lake Mai-Ndombe
Yandja
Ntadembele
Nioki
Kutu
Bandundu
Oshwe
Lukenie
Dekese
Lodja
Masia-Mbio
Bagata
Kasai
Cuango
Fatunda
Kwilu
Kapia
Ilebo
Bena Dibele
Sankuru
Kenge
Bulungu
Mayamba
Madimba
Masi-Manimba
Kikwit
Idiofa
Mpata
Mweka
Bena-Tshadi
Kakenge
Inkisi-Kisantu
Mbanza-Ngungu
Ngidinga
Kimpese
Kimvula
Popokabaka
Banda
Luebo
Demba
Dimbel
Feshi
Gungu
Kilembe
Kananga
Kazumba
Kasongo-Lunda
Quimbele
Tshikapa
Kamiji
Sanza Pombo
Wamba
Luiza
Kahemba
Luachimo
Forte Carumbo
Cuango
1150
Verissimo Sarmento
Kapanga
Luremo
Caungula
Camaxilo
Lucapa
Chicapa
Cuango
Xá-Muteba
Xinge
Saurimo
Sandoa
Nova Gala
Quitapa
Cacolo
Mona-Quimbundo
Muriege
Kasai
Muconda
Luau
Dilolo
Dala
Buçaco
Cassai
Luena
Moxico
Cuemba
Chicala
Cazombo
Luena
Lucusse
Lumbala
Zambezi
Cassamba
Luzi
Luvuei
Lutembo
Zambesi
Lungué-Bungu
Sessa
Lumbala N'Guimbo
Lukulu
Cuito Cuanavale
Chiume
Mongu
Mavinga
Rivungo
Cuando
Luengué
1160
Cuito
Chibaranda
Luiana
Mucusso
Kongo
Shakawe
Sepopa

43
a b c d e f g h i j k l m
UGANDA
KENYA
RWANDA
BURUNDI
TANZANIA
MALAWI
MOZAMBIQUE
ZIMBABWE
ZAMBIA
SOMALIA
INDIAN
OCEAN
Lake Victoria
Lake Tanganyika
Lake Malawi (Lake Nyasa)
Lake Rukwa
Lake Mweru
Lake Bangweulu
Lake Edward
Lake George
Lake Kivu
Lake Natron
Lake Chilwa
Lake Upemba
Kariba Reservoir
Cabora Bassa Reservoir
Kampala
Entebbe
Jinja
Tororo
Kaliro
Iganga
Kayunga
Mubende
Fort Portal
Kyanjojo
Kasese
Beni
Margherita Peak
5109
Butembo
Kasindi
Lubero
Bushenyi
Masaka
Mbarara
Kikagati
Ishasha River
Sese Islands
Rutshuru
Kabale
Karisimbi 4507
Masisi
Goma
Gisenyi
Ruhengeri
Kigali
Kibuye
Gitarama
Kayonza
Kavumu
Bukavu
Cibitoke
Kayanza
Bujumbura
Kibondo
Kisangani
Madula
Opienge
Pene-Tungu
Kirundu
Lubutu
Mitumba Mountains
Walikale
Punia
Kabunga
Kalima
Pangi
Kasambule
Kampene
Kingombe
Kipaka
Kasongo
Samba
Mwenga
Kitutu
Kalole
Kindu
Lindi
Maiko
Lowa
Ulindi
Congo
Kisumu
Kakamega
Eldoret
Kapsabet
Kericho
Kisii
Kilkoris
Nakuru
Gilgil
Naivasha
Nyahururu
Nanyuki
Kenya (Kirinyaga) 5200
Meru
Embu
Baringo Lodge
Loruk
Archer's Post
Isiolo
Garba Tula
Mado Gashi
Liboi
Hagadera
Saka
Garissa
Mwingi
Thika
Kijabe
Nairobi
Kitui
Machakos
Narok
Mutomo
Kajiado
Magadi
Nyiri Desert
Tsavo
Mtito Andei
Tsavo National Park
Kilimanjaro 5895
Meru 4566
Oloitokitok
Moshi
Arusha
Manyami
Mwatate
Malindi
Kilifi
Mombasa
Kwale
Same
Lushoto
Tanga
Pemba Island
Mkomazi
Korogwe
Handeni
Segera
Hola
Tana
Mokowe
Patta Island
Kolbio
Kisimaio
Afmadu
Belesc Cogani
Equator
Rift Valley
Serengeti Plain
Tarime
Mara
Musoma
Bukoba
Kyaka
Ukerewe Islands
Nansio
Banagi
Mwanza
Geita
Nyakanazi
Ngudu
Shinyanga
Manonga
Kahama
Nzega
Ibologero
Igombe
Kasulu
Kigoma
Uvinza
Malagarasi
Tabora
Singida
Ndareda 3420
Katesh
Babati
Mbulu
Oldeani
Makuyuni
Namanga
Masai Steppe
Kondoa Irangi
Sikonge
Ugalla
Itigi
Manyoni
Dodoma
Kongwa
Gairo
Mpwapwa
Mvomero
Msata
Chalinze
Bagamoyo
Zanzibar
Zanzibar Island
Dar-es-Salaam
Kisarawe
Morogoro
Kilosa
Mikumi
Mbuyuni
Iringa
Kibiti
Rufiji
Mafia Island
Kilindoni
Mohoro
Ifakara
Sao Hill
Mahenge
Luhombero
Nangurukuru
Makambako
Njombe
Chimala
Mbeya
Chunya
Makongolosi
Uyole
Rungwe
Tunduma
Itungi
Livingstone Mountains
Lukumburu
Kitunda
Rungwa
Kisigu
Kipembawe
Sumbawanga
Namanyere
Mpanda
Katemie
Kabalo
Lukuga
Nyunzu
Niemba
Katompi
Kaloko
Luvua
Sange
Moba
Kapona
Manono
Kiambi
Mulongo
Malemba Nkulu
Kikondja
Pidi
Marungu Mountains
Pweto
Chiengi
Sumbu
Kasanga
Mpulungu
Mbala
Nakonde
Mitwaba
Kabondo Dianda
Mukana
Nchelenge
Mporokoso
Kasembe
Kawambwa
Kapatu
Kasama
Isoka
Kasenga
Bunkeya
Busanga
Luambo
Kambove
Likasi
Lubumbashi
Kipushi
Solwezi
Munungu
Luwingu
Minga
Mansa
Samfya
Luapula
Chambeshi
Mbesuma
Chinsali
Luangwa
Muchinga Mountains
Karonga
Chilumba
Livingstonia
Rumphi
Mzuzu
Nkhata Bay
Mzimba
Chama
Chisoso
Mpika
Chikwa
Lundazi
Chilonga
Chembe
Mokambo
Mukuku
Kapalala
Chililabombwe
Chingola
Mufulira
Kitwe
Ndola
Luanshya
Chibembe
Jenda
Dwangwa
Nkhotakota
Kasungu
Serenje
Kanona
Chifwefwe
Kapiri Mposhi
Kabwe
Lubungu
Landless Corner
Mumbwa
Rufunsa
Lusaka
Kafue
Namwala
Mazabuka
Zambezi
Chipata
Mchinji
Lilongwe
Salima
Katete
Petauke
Nyimba
Kachalola
Dedza
Chitunde
Bene
Fingoè
Zumbo
Songo
Chiúta
Tete
Mangochi
Balaka
Mandimba
Massangulo
Zomba
Limbe
Blantyre
Mulanje
Nsanje
Chikwawa
Kariba
Choma
Kalomo
Karoi
Sanyati
Mhangura
Mkumbura
Mvurwi
Mount Darwin
Nyamapanda
Bindura
Mutoko
Banket
Harare
Binga
Livingstone
Victoria Falls
Hwange
Gokwe
Chegutu
Kadoma
Gwai River
Dete
Inyanga
Rusape
Catandica
Guro
Changara
Tambara
Sena
Caia
Mopeia
Inhaminga
Gorongosa
Chinde
Quelimane
Namacurra
Pebane
Mucubela
Mocuba
Moma
Erego
Gurué
Alto Molócuè
Nametil
Angoche
Liupo
Namialo
Monapo
Nampula
Ribauè
Mutuali
Cuamba
Lúrio
Nacaroa
Nacala
Lumbo
Moçambique
Namapa
Metoro
Pemba
Montepuez
Marrupa
Maúa
Nungo
Malanga
Lichinga
Litunde
Maniamba
Lugenda
Messalo
Nantulo
Macomia
Mocimboa da Praia
Diaca
Mueda
Masuguru
Ruvuma
Newala
Nangomba
Masasi
Nachingwea
Mingoyo
Lindi
Mtwara
Cape Delgado
Tunduru
Chamba
Songea
Gumbiro
46
30°E
35°E
40°E
0°
5°S
10°S
15°S
n o p q r s t u v w x y z
49
0 100 200 300 miles
Average linear scale
0 100 200 300 400 500 Km

a b c d e f g h i j k l m

25°E   30°E   35°E   40°E

Kaloko
Luvua
Kilosa
Bagamoyo
Chalinze
Dar-es-Salaam
Kisarawe

Kaniama
Kabongo
Manono
Sange
Kiambi
Kapona
Moba
Lake Tanganyika
Mpanda
Kitunda
Rungwa
Morogoro
.2287
Kibiti

.1060
Pidi
Mulongo
Marungu Mountains
.2460
Namanyere
Mbuyuni
Mikumi
.2646
Mafia Island

Kikondja
Malemba Nkulu
Lake Rukwa
Sumbawanga
.2418
Kipembawe
Iringa
.2576
Ifakara
Kilindoni
Mohoro

DEMOCRATIC
Pweto
Sumbu
Kasanga
Makongolosi
Chunya
Sao Hill
Mahenge
Luhombero
Nangurukuru

REPUBLIC
.1139
Mitwaba
Lake Mweru
Chiengi
Mpulungu
Mbala
Mbeya
Uyole
.2072
Makambako

Kamina
Kabondo Dianda
Mukana
Nchelenge
Mporokoso
Nakonde
Tunduma
Itungi
Njombe

OF
Luena
Kawambwa
Kapatu
Karonga
Lukumburu

CONGO
Busanga
Bunkeya
Kasenga
Kasama
Mbesuma
Isoka
Chilumba
Livingstonia
Gumbiro
Songea
Nachingwea
Lindi
Mingoyo
Mtwara

10°S
Kolwezi
Luambo
Mununga
Luwingu
Chinsali
.2606
Rumphi
Mzuzu
TANZANIA
Masasi
Nangomba
Newala

Kambove
Likasi
Minga
Mansa
Samfya
Lake Bangweulu
.1475
Chisoso
Chama
Mzimba
Nkhata Bay
Chamba
Ruvuma
Mueda
Mocimboa

Mwinilunga
Chisasa
Kipushi
Lubumbashi
Chembe
Mpika
Chikwa
Jenda
Maniamba
.1836
Marrupa
Nantulo
Macomia
Diaca

Chililabombwe
Mokambo
Kapalala
Mukuku
Chilonga
Lundazi
Dwangwa
Lake Malawi (Lake Nyasa)
Litunde
Malanga
Montepuez
Metoro
Pemba

Solwezi
Chingola
Kitwe
.1350
Ndola
.1261
Kanona
Serenje
Chibembe
Nkhotakota
Lichinga
Messalo
Mãua
Nungo
Namapa

Mufulira
Luanshya
Chifwefwe
Kasungu
.1836
Massangulo
Nacaroa
Naca

ZAMBIA
Kasempa
Kapiri Mposhi
Chipata
Mchinji
Lilongwe
Salima
Mandimba
Cuamba
Ribauè
Namialo
Monapo
Moç

Kabompo
Lunga
Kabwe
Petauke
Katete
MALAWI
Dedza
.2035
Mangochi
Mutuali
Gurué
Nampula
Lumbo
Moç

15°S
Kaoma
Lubungu
Mumbwa
Landless Corner
Kachalola
Nyimba
Chitunde
Bene
Balaka
Zomba
Molócuè
.200
Liupo
Nametil

.1220
Namwala
Lusaka
.1279
Rufunsa
Zumbo
Cabora-Bassa Reservoir
Songo
Chiúta
Blantyre
Limbe
.3000
Errego
.760
Angoche

Mazabuka
Kafue
Zambezi
.560
Tete
Mulanje
.2054
Gurué
Mocuba
Mucubela
Moma

Kariba Reservoir
Mkumbura
Hunyani
.1204
Changara
Tambara
Nsanje
Pebane

Sesheke
Choma
Karoi
Mhangura
Mount Darwin
Nyamapanda
Guro
Vila de Sena
MOZAMBIQUE
Namacurra

45
Katima Mulilo
Kalomo
Karoi
Mvurwi
Bindura
Mutoko
.2592
Catandica
.1862
Inhaminga
Quelimane
Mopeia

Kazungula
Livingstone
Binga
Gokwe
Harare
Chegutu
Inyanga
Guro
Gorongosa
.105
Chinde

.1108
Kataba
Victoria Falls
Zambezi
Kadoma
Rusape
Chimoio
Donde

Pandamatenga
Hwange
Deti
Gwai River
Kenmaur
.1472
Kwe Kwe
.1447
Chivhu
Dorowa
Mutare
Chimanimani
.2436
Beira

ZIMBABWE
Gwai
Nkayi
Gweru
Chatsworth
Nyanyadzi
Donde
Sofala Bay

20°S
Kanyu
Nata
Bulawayo
.1345
Zvishavane
Masvingo
Chipinge
Nova Golegã
Rupisi
Espungabera

Tsoe
Mosetse
.1028
Plumtree
Tuli
Gwanda
∴Zimbabwe
.502
Chiredzi
Macane
Jofane
Inhassoro
Bazaruto

Makgadikgadi Pans
Antelope Mine
Mvenezi
Rutenga
.500
Massangena
.167
Pambarra
Mabote
Mapinhane

Xhumo
.974
Letlhakane
Tlalamabele
Francistown
Selebi-Phikwe
.1000
Tuli
Bubye
Tswiza
Chicualacuala
Machaila

BOTSWANA
Serule
Beitbridge
Mazunga
Chigubo
Funhalouro
Massinga

Metsiamonong
Serowe
Palapye
Pontdrift
Messina
Pafuri
.438
Mapai
Guijá
Massingir
Panda
Inhambane

Kikao
Shoshong
Groblersbrug
Louis Trichardt
Shingwedzi
Limpopo
.132
Quissico

Mahalapye
Marken
Pietersburg
.2128
Tzaneen
Phalaborwa
Massingir
.169
Massinga

Molepolole
Jwaneng
Soje
Mosomane
Letlhakeng
Mahalapye
Potgietersrus
.1856
Safara
Macia
Xai-Xai

Gaborone
Thabazimbi
.2085
Nylstroom
Steelport
Sabie
Skukuza
Manjacaze

Kanye
Dwarsberg
Warmbad
Lydenburg
Witrivier
Magude

Lobatse
Zeerust
Rustenburg
.1833
Witbank
Middelburg
Carolina
Nelspruit
.575
Komatipoort
Maputo

25°S
Delareyville
Mmabatho
Pretoria
Benoni
SOUTH AFRICA
Ermelo
Waterval Boven
Mbabane
Namaacha

Lichtenburg
Potchefstroom
Johannesburg
.1661
Germiston
Springs
Bethal
SWAZILAND
Manzini
Bela Vista

Klerksdorp
.1263
Vereeniging
Standerton
.1440
Catuane

25°E   30°E   35°E   40°E

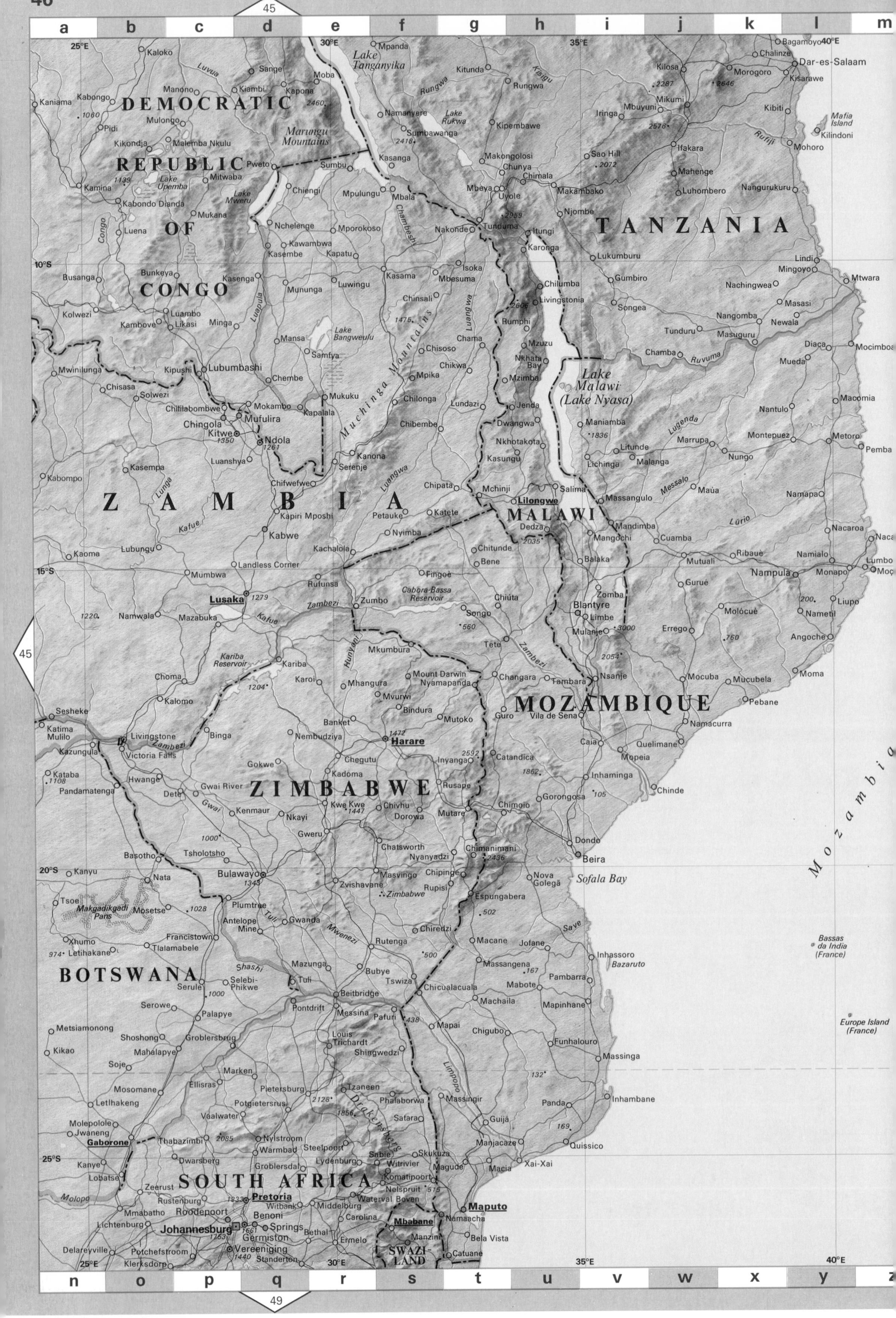

This map shows 1/60 of the earth's surface

a b c d e f g h i j k l m
45°E
50°E
55°E
60°E
10°S
15°S
20°S
25°S
Aldabra Island
I N D I A N   O C E A N
Moroni
COMOROS
Moheli
Anjouan
Comoros Islands
Dzaoudzi
Mayotte (France)
Antsiranana
Ambilobe
Nosy-Bé
Hell-Ville
Iharaña
Tsaratanana Mountains
2876
Sambava
Andapa
Antalaha
Antsohihy
Befandriana Av.
1218
Maroantsetra
Ambohitralanana
Mahalevona
Mahajanga
Port-Bergé-Vaovao
Mandritsara
Marovoay
Mampikony
Mananara
1301
Betsiboka
Mahavavy
Miarinarivo
Nosy Boraha
1325
Maevatanana
Andriamena
MADAGASCAR
1545
Morafenobe
Vohidiala
Toamasina
Ankazobe
Antsalova
Tsiroanomandidy
Antananarivo
1387
Manambolo
2643
Mandoto
Betafo
Antsirabe
Mahanoro
Tsimafana
Tsiribihina
2140
Fandriana
Morondava
Mahabo
Ambositra
Mandabe
Mananjary
Fianarantsoa
Irondro
Mangoky
Ambalavao
Manakara
2658
Ankazoabo
1348
Ihosy
Ivohibe
Isalo Mountains
Menarana
Farafangana
Toliara
Andranovory
Betroka
1824
Vangaindrano
Tropic of Capricorn
Betioky
Ampanihy
1957
Antanimora
Taolañaro
Tsihombe
Ambovombe
Port Louis
MAURITIUS
Saint-Denis
3069
Réunion
(France)
n o p q r s t u v w x y z
0 100 200 300 miles
Average linear scale
0 100 200 300 400 500 Km

44

a b c d e f g h i j k l m

10°E

Namibe

Tômbua
(Porto Alexandre)

Chibia
Chianje
Mulundo
Cassinga
Cuito Cuanavale
Chiume

15°E
20°E

Cuvelai
Caiundo
Rivungo

·900
Tambor
Quiteve
Roçadas
·1265
A N G O L A
·1190
Rito
Luengué
·1160
Chibaranda
Luia

Oncócua
Savate
Xamavera
Mucusso

Iona
N'Giva

Foz do Cunene
Cunene
Naulila
Cuangar
Rundu
Okavango

·2195
Ruacana
Ondangwa
Shakamku
Shakawe

Orupembe
Obombo
Oshakati
O v a m b o l a n d
Sepopa

Opuwa
·1096
Numkaub
·950

Cape Frio
·1784
Etosha
Pan
Namutoni
Keibeb
Gumare
Oka
D

Purros
·1093
Mount Aha
·1070
Tsau

Kowares
Okaukuejo
Tsumeb
Tsumkwe

Kamanjab
Otavi
·2149
Grootfontein

·869
20°S

Terrace Bay
Goreis
Outjo

Khorixas
Otjiwarongo
Okakarara
Dekar

·1932
Ghanzi

Brandberg
2579
Kalkfeld
N A M I B I A
Hochfeld

Uis Mine
Omaruru
Steinhausen

Cape Kruis
2350
Okahandja
·1537
Buitepos
Kalkfontein
B O

Henties Bay
Usakos
Witvlei
Gobabis
Takatshw

Swakopmund
Anschluss
Windhoek
Dordabis
Kule
Kalah

·160
1654

Walvis Bay
Leonardville
Ukwi
·1000
Kang

Tropic of Capricorn
2334
Rehoboth
Derm

A T L A N T I C
Abbabis
Kalkrand
Aranos
Tshane

Stampriet
Mariental

Sesriem
Gochas
·1046
Mpaathutlwa
Pan
Mak

25°S
Naribis
Zaris
Maltahöhe
Asanib
Nossob

Asab
Twee
Rivier
Koës
Tshabong

Helmeringhausen
·1185

Great Tiráz
1867
Bethanie
Twee Rivieren

Lüderitz
Aus
Keetmanshoop
Aroab
Gemsbok
·1000
K
Sish
183

Goageb
Narubis
Gr. Karasberge
2202

Pomona
Witpütz
·1107
K

Grünau
Karasburg

Orange
1341·
Ariamsvlei
·903
Upington

Alexander Bay
Augrabies
Falls
Keimoes
Orange
Postm

Vioolsdrif
Onseepkans
Kakamas
Groblershoop
Grie

O C E A N
Port Nolloth
Steinkopf
Pofadder
Kenhardt

Nababeep
Namies
Marydale

Springbok

30°S
Platbakkies
Van Wyksvlei
Coppert

Garies
Brandvlei
Vosbur

Loeriesfontein
Carnarvon

Bitterfontein
Nieuwoudtville
Williston
Loxton

Calvinia

Vanrhynsdorp
Fraserburg

Clanwilliam
Sutherland
Komsberg
·1721

Citrusdal
Prince Albert Road
Grea

Slippers Bay
·1040
Laingsburg
Little Swartberge
2325
W

Vredenburg
Gr. Winterhoek
2078

Saldanha
Touws River
Oudtshoorn

Malmesbury
Wellington
Little Karoo
George

Cape Town
Worcester
Swellendam
Mosselb

Strand
Caledon
Witsand
Stilbaai

Cape of
Good Hope
Agulhas

Cape Agulhas

35°S

This map shows 1/60 of the earth's surface

n o p q r s t u v w x y z

10°E
15°E
20°E

0 100 200 300 miles Average linear scale 0 100 200 300 400 500 Km

85°N

35°E 40°E 45°E 50°E 55°E 60°E 65°E

A R

80°N

Alexandra Land · George Land · Salisbury I. · Jackson I. · Rudolf I. · Yeva-Liv
Luidzhi · Karla-Aleksandra · La Rons'yer
Hooker I. · McClintock I. · Hall I. · Wilczek Land · Gra
Isl
Sal'm
Zem

F r a n z   J o s e f   L a n d

Russkaya Gavan

N o v a y a   Z e m l y a

Smidovich

75°N

Sedova
1115
Stolbovoy

B A R E N T S   S E A

Litke

K A R A   SE

· 260

Krasino

Proliv Karskiye Vorota

Cape

· 162
Vaigač

70°N

Pechora Sea

Amderma

Bar

Kolgujev
166

Cape Kanin Nos

Chernaya

Pay-Kho

Ust'-Kara
Yangarey

· 242

*Kanin
Peninsula*
*Češa
Bay*

Dresvyanka
· 201

Tundr

Khal'mer-Yu

Volonga

Nar'yan
Mar

Bol'shezemel'skaya

Koreyver

Vorkuta

Malozemel'skaya Tundra

Velikovisochnoye
· 106

Kolva

Yeletsk

Murmansk

Mončegorsk
· 1191

*Mezen'
Gulf*

Mezen'

Stafonovo

Nonburg

Makarikha

Adzva

Abez
U Y
Pay-yer
1495

Kirovsk

397

Usa

K o l a

Arctic Circle

Azopol'ye

Ust'Tsil'ma

Trosh

Inta

La

Kandalakša

Politovo

Izhma

· 155

Pechora

Kosyu

Kandalaksa Gulf

*White
Sea*

Pinega

Mezen'

· 463

Kadzherom

Narodnaya
1894

Saranpaul'

65°N

Dvina Bay

Severodvinsk
Archangel

Pinega

Shomvukva

Kedva
· 164
Voyvozh

Kyrta *1617*

Patrasuy

Berezovo·

Belomorsk

Onega Bay

Onega

Dvina

Vendenga

Pinega

Ukhta

Pechora

Muligort

Segeža

· 417

North Dvina

· 259

Loptyuga

Zheleznodorozhnyy

Vey Vozh
· 324

Troisko-Pechorsk

Northern

Nyaksimvol

Serg

Medvežjegors

Onega

Verkhnyaya
Toyma

Mikun

R

Puzla

1108

U

Tajsur

Khal

S

Petrozavodsk

*Lake
Onega*

Kargopol

Vaga

Irta

Vyčegda

Porog

Suyevatpaul

· 1027

Sovets

Sukhona

Sukhona

Syktyvkar

Ust'Kulom

Kur'ya
303

Kolva

Kaminsomol

Pionerskiy

Podporoze

Konoša

Vel

Velsk

Kizema

239

Kotlas

Vizinga

Noshul'

· 213

Kazhim

U v a l y

Cherdyn

Polunochnoye

· 1493

Ivdel

Tichvin

Velikiy
Ustyug

Pyatigory

Kama

· 162

60°N

Čerepovec

*Rybinsker
Reservoir*

Totma

Nizhniy
Yenangsk

Nikol'sk

Murashi

Kirs

Northern

Kudymkar

Krasnoturin'sk

Solikamsk
Berezniki

Sos'va

Vologda

· 292

Vetluga

Vetluzhskiy

Kirov
Novo-Vyatsk

*Kamskoje
Reservoir*

· 883

Gubakha

Dobryanka

Lobva

Rybinsk

Bui

Kotel'nich

Glazov

Krasnokamsk

Verkhniy Tura

Turinsk

Vyšni Voloček

Jaroslavl

Kostroma

Kinešma

Volga

Pizhma

Uren

Yaransk

Nolinsk

Igra

Kez

Perm'

· 321

Nizhniy Tagil

Ostashkov
· 343

Kalyazin

Iwanovo

Krasnyye-Baki

Votkinsk

Kungur

Artemovskiy

Torzhok

Tver

Dubna

Klin Dmitrov

Volga

Kil'mez

Izhevsk

Krasnoufimsk

Pervoural'sk

Yekaterinburg

Talitsa

Nelidovo

Staritsa

Rzev

Volokolamsk

Sergiyev Posad

Kovrov

Yoshkar
Ola

· 115

Malmyzh
217·

Agryz

Sarapul

Bogdanovich

Dubna

Nizhniy
Novgorod

Volga

Arsk

Yalut

Moscow
(Moskva)

Mytišč

Noginsk
Orechovo
Zujevo

Vladimir

Dzerzhinsk

Yadrin

Cheboksary

Neftekamsk

Nyazepetrovsk

Degtyarsk
Sysert'

Kamensk-
Ural'skiy

35°E

Odintsovo

Elektrostal

Balashikha

Oka

Kovrov

Murom

235·

45°E

Kazan'

Mamadysh

Naberezhnyje
Čelny

Ufa

50°E

Kasli

Shadrinsk

55°E

65°

33

This map shows 1/60 of the earth's surface

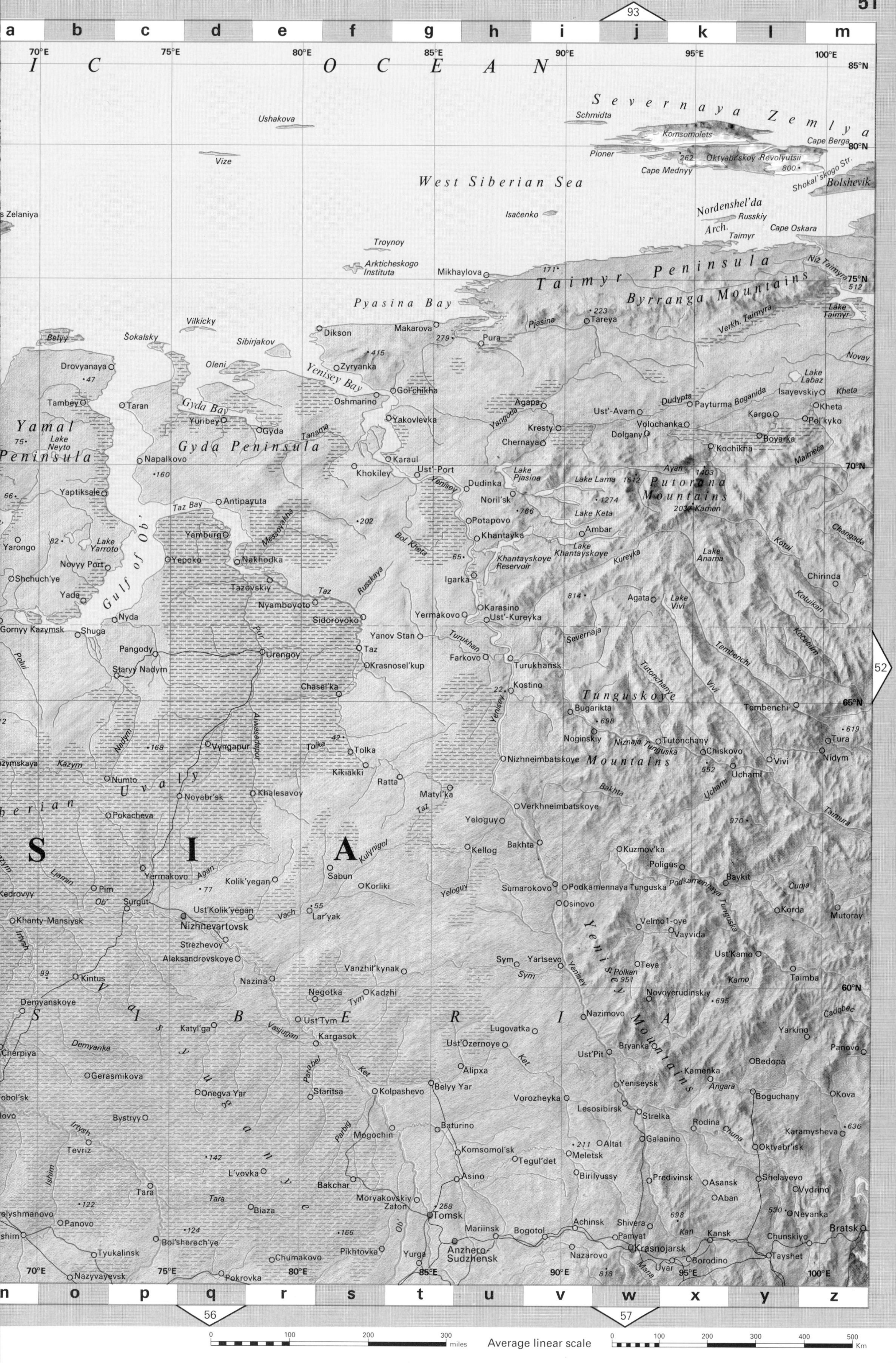

a b c d e f g h i j k l m
93
70°E 75°E 80°E 85°E 90°E 95°E 100°E
85°N
I C O C E A N
Severnaya Zemlya
Schmidta
Komsomolets
Pioner
262
Oktyabr'skoy Revolyutsii
800
Cape Berga
80°N
Cape Mednyy
Shokal'skogo Str.
Bolshevik
Ushakova
Vize
West Siberian Sea
Isačenko
s Zelaniya
Nordenshel'da Arch.
Russkiy
Taimyr
Cape Oskara
Troynoy
Arkticheskogo Instituta
Mikhaylova
171
Taimyr Peninsula
Byrranga Mountains
Niz Taimyra
75°N
512
Lake Taimyr
Pyasina Bay
Makarova
279
Pura
Pjasina
223
Tareya
Verkh. Taimyra
Novay
Vilkicky
Šokalsky
Belyy
Sibirjakov
Dikson
415
Zyryanka
Yenisey Bay
Drovyanaya
47
Oleni
Lake Labaz
Isayevskiy
Kheta
Gol'chikha
Oshmarino
Tambey
Taran
Gyda Bay
Yuribey
Gyda
Yakovlevka
Agapa
Yangoda
Ust'-Avam
Dudypta
Payturma
Boganida
Kheta
Kargo
Pol'kyko
Yamal Peninsula
Lake Neyto
75
Gyda Peninsula
Tanama
Kresty
Chernaya
Volochanka
Dolgany
Boyarka
Kochikha
Napalkovo
160
Karaul
Khokiley
Ust'-Port
Yenisey
Dudinka
Lake Pjasina
Lake Lama
1612
Ayan
1403
Putorana Mountains
Maimeča
70°N
Yaptiksale
66
Taz Bay
Antipayuta
Noril'sk
766
1274
2037
Kamen
Lake Keta
Potapovo
202
Messoyakha
Changada
Yarongo
82
Lake Yarroto
Yamburg
Khantayka
Ambar
Lake Khantayskoye
Khantayskoye Reservoir
Kureyka
Lake Anama
Kotui
Gulf of Ob'
Yepoko
Nakhodka
Bol. Kheta
Novyy Port
65
Shchuch'ye
Tazovskiy
Igarka
Chirinda
Yada
Taz
Russkaya
Nyamboyoto
814
Agata
Lake Vivi
Kotuikan
Nyda
Sidorovoko
Karasino
Ust'-Kureyka
Yermakovo
Gornyy Kazymsk
Shuga
Yanov Stan
Turukhan
Severnaja
Kočečum
52
Pangody
Pur
Urengoy
Taz
Farkovo
Turukhansk
Tembenchi
Poluj
Staryy Nadym
Krasnosel'kup
Tutonchanye
Chasel'ka
Kostino
22
Vivi
Tunguskoye Mountains
65°N
Tembenchi
Bugarikta
698
619
Nadym
Aivasedapur
Yenisey
Tura
168
Vyngapur
Tolka
42
Tolka
Noginskiy
Niznaja Tunguska
Tutonchany
Chiskovo
Nidym
azymskaya
Kazym
Nizhneimbatskoye
552
Uchami
Vivi
Numto
Kikiakki
Uvaly
Ratta
Bakhta
Noyabr'sk
Khalesavoy
Matyl'ka
Uchami
Taimura
berian
Verkhneimbatskoye
Pokacheva
Taz
970
Yeloguy
S I A
Kulynigol
Kellog
Bakhta
Kuzmov'ka
Yermakovo
Agan
Sabun
Poligus
Ljamin
Kolik'yegan
Baykit
Pim
77
Korliki
Yeloguy
Sumarokovo
Podkamennaya Tunguska
Čunja
Kedrovyy
Ob'
Surgut
Osinovo
Korda
Ust'Kolik'yegan
55
Vach
Lar'yak
Podkamennaya Tunguska
Mutoray
Khanty-Mansiysk
Nizhnevartovsk
Velmo 1-oye
Vayvida
Irtysh
Strezhevoy
Yenisey Mountains
Aleksandrovskoye
Ust'Kamo
Sym
Yartsevo
Sym
Polkan
951
Teya
Vanzhil'kynak
Taimba
99
Kintus
Nazina
Kamo
Negotka
Kadzhi
60°N
Vasyugan'ye
Tym
Novoyerudinskiy
695
Demyanskoye
S I B E R I A
Katyl'ga
Ust'Tym
Nazimovo
Čadobec
Vasjugan
Lugovatka
Kargasok
Yarkino
Demyanka
Cherpiya
Ust'Ozernoye
Bryanka
Ust'Pit
Panovo
Parabel
Ket
Ket
Gerasmikova
Alipxa
Bedopa
Kamenka
Ket
Yeniseysk
Angara
obol'sk
Onegva Yar
Staritsa
Kolpashevo
Belyy Yar
Boguchany
Vorozheyka
Kova
lovo
Bystryy
Lesosibirsk
Strelka
Parbig
Baturino
Rodina
Chuna
636
Irtysh
Mogochin
Galanino
Karamysheva
Tevriz
211
Altat
142
Komsomol'sk
Meletsk
Oktyabr'sk
Ishim
Tegul'det
L'vovka
Birilyussy
Asino
Predivinsk
Asansk
Shelayevo
Tara
Bakchar
Vydrino
122
Tara
Moryakovskiy Zaton
258
Aban
elyshmanovo
Biaza
Tomsk
698
530
Nevanka
Panovo
124
166
Kan
shim
Mariinsk
Bogotol
Achinsk
Shivera
Pamyat
Kansk
Chunskiyo
Bratsk
Tyukalinsk
Bol'sherech'ye
Ob'
Pikhtovka
Anzhero-Sudzhensk
Krasnojarsk
Chumakovo
Yurga
Nazarovo
Uyar
Borodino
Tayshet
Mana
818
Nazyvayevsk
Pokrovka
n o p q r s t u v w x y z
56
57
0 100 200 300 miles
Average linear scale
0 100 200 300 400 500 Km

This map shows 1/60 of the earth's surface

94
59
10
a b c d e f g h i j k l m
n o p q r s t u v w x y z
135°E
140°E
145°E
150°E
155°E
160°E
75°N
70°N
65°N
60°N
55°N
New Siberian Islands
Bel'kovskiy
Kotel'nyy
Kotel'nyy
320
Ambardakh
Stolbovoy
Mal. Lyakhovskiy
Fedorovskiy
Bol. Lyakhovskiy
Kigilyakh
Laptev Strait
Chay-Povarnaya
420
Bennetta
Bol'shoye Zimov'ye
Novaya Sibir'
East Siberian Sea
Cape Buorkhaya
Kharstan
Chikhacheva
Uyëdey
Star.Dom
Kokuora
Kiseleva
Tabor
Kuogastakh
Balagannakh
Khroma
Kolesovo
Kular
Kazach'ye
Yana
Boru
Ukta
Indigirka
Chokurdakh
Ulovo
Tumat
Tenkeli
Ust'-Kuyga
Byyangnyr
Alekseyevo
Kondakovo
914
Oyun-Yurege
Uyandi
1221
Kolymskiy Plain
Oyun-Kyuyel'
Deputatskiy
Lake Ozhogino
Ozhogino
Tenalr
Ilimniir
Khara-Tala
Chukochye
Lake Nerpich'ye
Tirekhtyakh
Uyandina
Balagannakh
Mys
Cherskiy
Saydy
Kyrbana
Bytantay
Orto-Kyuyel'
Chibagalakh
Syagannakh
Druzhina
Shestakova
Urdakh
Konzaboy
Bagata
Oysurdakh
Volochsk
Batagay
Gorelova
Malaya
Suordakh
Bertes
Chernyy Mys
Khongsey
Srednekolymsk
Zhirkova
1919
Tuostakh
Mayor-Krest
1726
Khobolchan
Pastakh
Omolon
Tokuma
Tyugyuren
Ust' Charky
Tuostakh
Cherskogo Mountains
Ozhogina
Sededema
Berezovka
Etykan
Arga
Arctic Circle
1926
Khastakh
SIA
Khonu
Mama
Kusagan-Olokh
Nel'gese
Astakh
Cheulik
Chibagalakh
Udanna
Kycham-Kyuyel'
Erozionnyy
Yugo-Tala
Zatish'ye
721
Zyryanka
Khara-Tas
2703
Tyubelyakh
3147
Rassokha
Bulun
Shcherbakovo
Adycha
Alyaskitovyy
Oroyek
1627
Korkodon
Korkodon
Ust'-Nera
Kolymskiy Mountains
Marshal'skiy
Suglan
Tirgelir
Nera
Artyk
2558
Ust'-Sugoy
Abkit
2341
Tompo
Sugoy
Munugudzhak
Omolon
Khongo
Razdolnoye
Kysyl-Suluo
Oymyakon
Khuzdzhakh
2038
Kolyma
1550
Khara-Aldan
Dal'stroy
Tomtor
Sordongnokh
Arkagala
im Chapayeva
1347
Dyalinnya
Seymchan
Byuchennyakh
Adygalakh
Omsukchan
Khandyga
Tyry
Burkhala
Debin
Galimyy
1714
2933
1830
Gizhiga
Sayylyk
Gvardeyets
Khatyngnakh
Orotutkan
Okhotskiy-Perevoz
Kennya
Pik Aborigen
2586
Strelka
Nayakhan
Vetrenyy
Viliga-Kushka
Kolyma
Allakh-Yun'
im Gastello
Myakit
Zolotoy
Burgakhchan
Ust'Omchug
El'dikan
Ancha
Atka
Tumany
Kencha
Inya
1585
Kandychan
Cape Taygonos
Ust'-Maya
Chertovo-Ulovo
Ynykchanskiy
2350
Ugulan
Gulf of Shelekhova
Ayaya
Yudoma
Arka
Neter
Palatka
Yugorenok
Yudoma-Krestovskaya
Bulun
Star. Kheydzhan
Kuntuk
Talon
Arman
Magadan
Malkachan
Yama
Ulukuut
Balagannoye
Lesnaya
Ust'-Mil'
Shilkan
Yamsk
Sordongnokh
Maya
Urak
Okhotsk
Inya
Motykleyka
Nyurchan
Sredniy
Palana
Aim
Amka
Cape Tolstoy
1549
Kurun Uryak
Ul'ya
Cape Alevina
Sivuch
Ingili
Omnya
Kaval'kan
Alachakh
Khanyangda
Ust'-Tigil'
Chigul'bach
Tigil'
Khakhar
Nel'kan
Enkan
Utkholok
Dzhugdzhur Mountains
Chasovnya-Uchurskaya
Topko
1906
2531
Kemkara
Ust'-Belogolovoye
Batomga
Uchur
Kekuk
Maymakan
Ayan
Sea of Okhotsk
Ust'-Sopochnoye
Klyuchi
Esso
Sredinnyy Mountains
Nemuy
Icha
3621
Atlasovo
4750
Oblukovino
Tvayan
Ichinskaya Sopka
Kamchatka
Maya
1500
Shantar
Mil'kovo
Chumikan
Cape Yelizavety
Kronok
Udskoye
Burandzha
Kamchatka
Nyvrovo
Kirovskiy
Pushchino
Shevli
602
Zhupanovskiy
Litke
Tugur
Usal'gin
Okha
Pymta
Baladek
Lake Orel'
Bol. Vlas'evo
1870
Tugur
Malka
Nalychevo
Ekimchan
Nikolayevsk na-Amure
Paratunka
2295
Petropavlovsk-Kamchatskiy
Tyr
Paromay
Guga
Oktyabr'skiy
Yashkino
Gaktsynka
Bogorodskoye
Sofiysk
Boatasyn
Bol'sheretsk
Lake Chukchagirskoye
Sakhalin
1462
Mariinskoye
Duki
Nysh
Ust' Niman
Sofiysk
Bolodzhak
Kondon
De Kastruskoye
Urgal
Boktor
Aleksandrovsk-Sakhalinskiy
1609
2010
Amur
Novoilinovka
Tymovskoye
Gornyy
Siziman
Paramušir
Mogdy
Komsomol'sk-na-Amure
0 100 200 300 miles
Average linear scale
0 100 200 300 400 500 Km

This map shows 1/60 of the earth's surface

51
a b c d e f g h i j k l m
n o p q r s t u v w x y z
60
56
60°E
65°E
70°E
75°E
55°N
50°N
45°N
40°N
KAZAKSTAN
ASIA
UZBEKISTAN
TURKMENISTAN
KYRGYZSTAN
TAJIKISTAN
AFGHANISTAN
PAKISTAN
CHINA
Yekaterinburg
Chelyabinsk
Omsk
Astana
Karaganda
Pavlodar
Almaty
Bishkek
Tashkent
Dushanbe
Ashgabat
Kungur
Pervoural'sk
Talitsa
Krasnoufimsk
Bogdanovich
Kamensk-Ural'skiy
Nyazepetrovsk
Degtyarsk
Sysert'
Kasli
Shadrinsk
Yalutorovsk
Golyshmanovo
Ishim
Panovo
Tevriz
Tara
Biaza
Bol'sherech'ye
Tyukalinsk
Kurgan
Makushino
Nazyvayevsk
Pokrovka
Tatarsk
Barabinsk
Zlatoust
Min'yar
Asha
Suleya
Ufa
Chernikovsk
Ust'-Kata
Shumikha
Kurtamysh
Petukhovo
Petropavlovsk
Lyubinskiy
Isil'kul
Kalachinsk
Chistoozernoye
Lake Chany
Kupino
Chudinovo
Plast
Troitsk
Ust'-Uyskoye
Presnovka
Presnogor'kovka
Petrovka
Lake Ul'kenkaroy
Cherlak
Beloretsk
Krasnousol'skiy
Verkhneural'sk
Komsomolets
Borovskoye
Dem'yanovka
Mar'yevka
Krasnoarmeyesk
Kzyltu
Zhelezinka
Karasuk
Sterlitamak
Magnitogorsk
Kaga
Varna
Kartaly
Kustanay
Uritskiy
Peski
Volodarskoye
Kokchetav
Lake Selety-Tengiz
Lake Azhbulat
Kachiry
Stavropolka
Ruzayevka
Stepnyak
Aydabul'
Makinsk
Aksu
Bestobe
Shuga
Meleuz
Baymak
Tobol
Bredy
Kushmurun
Troitskoye
Dznetygara
Saraktash
Krasnoyarskiy
Dzhaksy
Yesil
Atbasar
Alekseyevka
Tortkuduk
Yermak
Jamyševo
Orsk
Terensay
Akkarga
Dzhambul
Naurzum
Zhaltyr
Zholymbet
Yermentau
Ekibastuz
Maykain
Mednogorsk
Novoishimskiy
Novodolinka
Mar'tuk
Dombarovskiy
Derzhavinsk
Sabyndy
Karashoky
Aktyubinsk
Tolybay
Aksuat
Arkalyk
Lake Tengiz
Kurgal'dzhino
Aktau
Ajryk
Khrom-Tau
Karabutak
Temirtau
Ul'yanovskoye
Alga
Akkabak
Turgay
Shenber
Saran
Sonaly
Abay
Korobovskiy
Kiikkaškan
Temir
Emba
Saga
Zahksykan
Dar'inskiy
Karagayly
Kajnar
Kaulkeldy
Irgiz
Brali
Ulutau
Atasu
Uspenskiy
Myylybulak
Shakhty
Nura
Kyzyl-Dzhar
Agadyr
Kyzyluy
Nikol'skiy
Baykonyr
Dzhezkazgan
Ayshirak
Zharkamys
Chelkar
Togyz
Zhamshi
Kiik
Mointy
Chushakyl'
Akespe
Beleutty
Sajak
Sokyrbulak
Aral'sk
Karazhingil
Balkhash
Kokaral
Betpak-Dala Steppe
Bet-Pak-Dala
Tomar
Karabas
Kulanoy
Bugun
Lake Arys
Kashkanteniz
Karoy
Barsa-Kel'mes
Kazalinsk
Leninsk
Dzhusaly
Aral Sea
Vozrozhdeniya
Zhanay
Mynaral
Kuyygan
Burylbaytal
Uštobe
Taldy-Kurgan
Kyzyl-Orda
Kamkaly
Uzynkair
Erimbet
Aksumbe
Algatart
Furmanovka
Aktogaj
Saryozek
Chilli
Khantau
Šatlyk
Yany-Kurgan
Uyuk
Kapčagajskoje Reservoir
Kapčagaj
Urga
Muinak
Čilik
Lake Sudočje
Kazakdarya
Kentau
Čemolgan
Karaozek
Turkestan
Kara Tau
Tatty
Kaskalen
Chimbay
Kyzyl Kum
Džambul
Lugovoi
Kara-Balta
Ananjevo
Kungrad
Arys'
Issyk-Kul'
Lake Issyk-Kul'
Prževal'sk
Lake Sarykamyškoje
Chodzeili
Bolševik
Kun'a-Urgenč
Mynbulak
Uchkuduk
Čimkent
Ottuk
Tašauz
Turtkul'
Zarafshan
Toktogul Res.
Toktogul
Čajek
Urgenč
Circik
Naryn
Taragay
Karasaj
Lebap
Cardara
Jangijul'
Namangan
Taš-Kumyr
Pik Dankowa
Cardarinskoje Reservoir
Angren
Kok-Jangak
Čatyrtaš
Toxkan
Amudarja
Syrdarja
Kokand
Margilan
Andižan
Lake Catyrk'ol
Sari Bulak
Akqi
Gulistan
Oš
Darvaza
Gorel'de
Gizhduvan
Navoi
Khujand
Kajrakkumskoje Reservoir
Fergana
Gul'ča
Bukhara
Dzizak
Bekabad
Sugun
Sanchakou
Kagan
Kattakurgan
Samarkand
Ura-Tjube
Daraut-Kurgan
Irkeštam
Kabakly
Jerbent
Kara Kum
Alat
Mubarek
Ajni
Alai
Dzirgatal
Lenina
Kashgar
Yopurga
Čardžou
Šachrisabz
Mt. Communism
Lake Karakul
Opal
Markit
Kizyl-Arvat
Bachardok
Karši
Novabad
Bulunkol
Yarkant
Repetek
Denau
Vischary
Arkbajtal
Kungur
Shache
Arčman
Tezejet
Kul'ab
Murgab
Pamir
Mamazair
Yecheng
Hasalbag
Karakumskiy Canal
Mary
Bajram Ali
Keriči
Kurgan-T'ube
Artyk
Tedžen
Nička
Iolotan
Dusti
Chorog
Muji
Bojnurd
Termez
Faidzabad
Quchan
Dušak
Andkhoy
Aqcha
Khulm
Kunduz
Qala Panja
Misgar
Mazar-i-Sharif
Sheberghan
Taliqan
Zebak
Kunar
Mazar
Sarakhs
Tirich Mir
Mastuj
Yasin
Rakaposhi
Sabzevar
Neishabur
Mashhad
Sar-i-Pul
Baghlan
Hindu Kush
Karakoram Range
Takhta Bazar
Maimana
Aibak
Chitral
Gilgit
Doshi
K2
Qaisar
Bala Murghab
Balkhab
Doab-i Mikhe Zarin
Drosh
Indus
Chilas
Ronda
Kopet Dag
Khorasan
South Urals
Mugodzhary
Turgay Valley
Turgayskaya Steppe
Ulu Tau
Kazak Uplands
Lake Balkhash
Tien Shan
Ala-Tau
Saraysu
Sarysu
Degandely
Karatal
Ču
Irtysh
Tobol
Ishim
Kabyrga
Murgab
Vakhsh
Yarkant
Ural
Lake Tengiz
Averge linear scale
0 100 200 300 miles
0 100 200 300 400 500 Km

51

55

This map shows 1/60 of the earth's surface

61

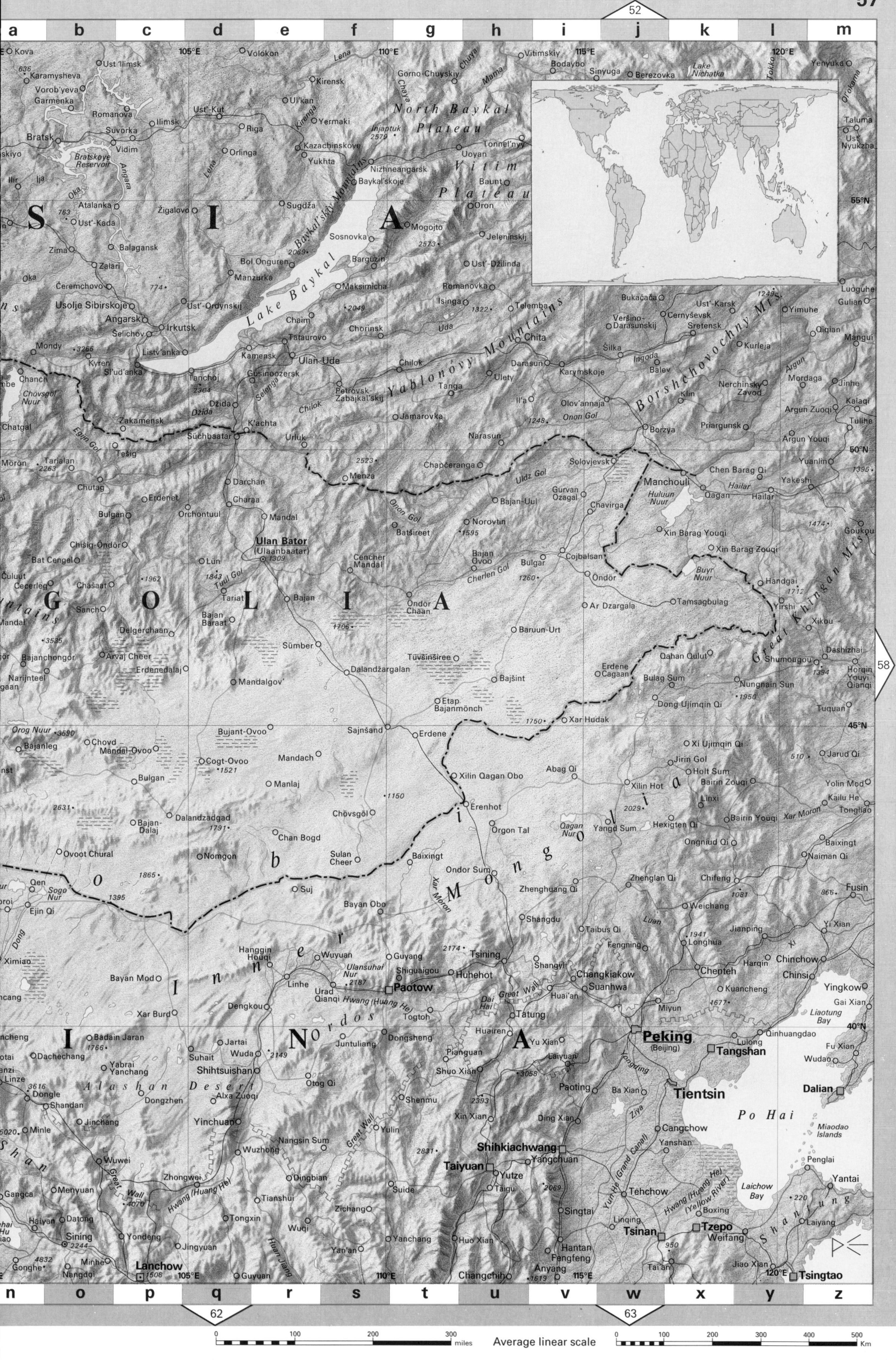
52
a
b
c
d
e
f
g
h
i
j
k
l
m
Kova
Ust' Ilimsk
105°E
Volokon
Lena
110°E
Vitimskiy
115°E
Bodaybo
120°E
Yenyuka
Karamysheva
Vorob'yeva
Garmenka
Kirensk
Gorno-Chuyskiy
Chuya
Mama
Sinyuga
Berezovka
Lake Nichatka
Tokko
Olekma
Romanova
Ul'kan
North Baykal Plateau
Ilimsk
Ust'-Kut
Riga
Kirenga
Yermaki
Injaptuk
2579
Bratsk
Suvorka
Vidim
Kazachinskoye
Tonnel'nyy
Taluma
Ust'Nyukzha
Bratskoye Reservoir
Angara
Orlinga
Yukhta
Uoyan
Vitim
Plateau
Nizhneangarsk
Baykal'skoje
Baunt
Ilir
Lena
Oka
Atalanka
Sugdža
Oron
55°N
S
I
A
763
Ust'-Kada
Žigalovo
Baykal'skiy Mountains
Mogojto
Sosnovka
Jeleninskij
Balagansk
2573
Zima
2069
Zalari
Bol Onguren
Barguzin
Ust'-Džilinda
Manzurka
Lake Baykal
Oka
Čeremchovo
774
Maksimicha
Romanovka
Luoguhe
Usolje Sibirskoje
Ust'-Ordynskij
2049
Isinga
1322
Telemba
Bukačača
Ust'-Karsk
1249
Gulian
Yimuhe
Angarsk
Chaim
Uda
Veršino-Darasunskij
Černyševsk
Sretensk
Qiqian
Šelichov
Irkutsk
Chorinsk
Chita
Mangui
Mondy
3266
Listv'anka
Tataurovo
Yablonovy Mountains
Šilka
Kurleja
Kyren
Kamensk
Ulan-Ude
Ingoda
Borshchovochny Mts
Sl'ud'anka
Gusinoozersk
Chilok
Darasun
Karymskoje
Balev
Argun
Mordaga
Chanch
Tanchoj
Selenga
Petrovsk-Zabajkal'skij
Ulety
Nerchinsky Zavod
Jinhe
Chövsgöl Nuur
2304
Chilok
Tanga
Il'a
Klin
Kalaqi
Džida
Olov'annaja
Argun Zuoqi
Chatgal
Zakamensk
Džida
Jamarovka
1248
Onon Gol
Borzya
Priargunsk
Tulihe
K'achta
Egiin Gol
Süchbaatar
Urluk
Narasun
Argun Youqi
Tešig
Mörön
Tarialan
2263
2523
Čapčeranga
Solovjevsk
50°N
Yuanlin
Menza
Chen Barag Qi
1395
Chutag
Darchan
Uldz Gol
Manchouli
Hailar
Yakeshi
Erdenet
Charaa
Gurvan Ozagal
Bajan-Uul
Huluun Nuur
Qagan
Hailar
Bulgan
Orchontuul
Mandal
Onon Gol
Chavirga
Norovtin
1474
Goukou
Batsireet
1595
Xin Barag Youqi
Chišig-Öndör
Ulan Bator
(Ulaanbaatar)
Xin Barag Zouqi
Bat Cengel
Lün
1309
Cencher Mandal
Bajan Ovoo
Bulgar
Cojbalsan
Čuluut
1843
Tuul Gol
Buyr Nuur
Cecerleg
Chašaat
1962
Cherlen Gol
1260
Öndör
Handgai
Tariat
Bajan
Ondor Chaan
1712
Great Khingan Mts
G
O
L
I
A
Tamsagbulag
Sanch
Ar Dzargala
Yirshi
Mandal
Bajan Baraat
1706
Xikou
Delgerchaan
Baruun-Urt
3535
Sümber
Dashizhai
Bajanchongor
Arvaj Cheer
Tuvšinširee
Qahan Qulut
Shumougou
Horqin Youyi Qianqi
1394
58
Narijnteel
Erdenedalaj
Dalandžargalan
Erdene Cagaan
Mandalgov'
Bajšint
Bulag Sum
Nungnain Sun
1950
Etap Bajanmönch
Dong Ujimqin Qi
Tuquan
Orog Nuur
3690
Sajnšand
1750
Xar Hudak
45°N
Bujant-Ovoo
Erdene
Bajanleg
Chovd
Mandal-Ovoo
Xi Ujimqin Qi
Jarud Qi
Mandach
510
Cogt-Ovoo
Jirin Gol
1521
Abag Qi
Holt Sum
Bulgan
Manlaj
Xilin Qagan Obo
Xilin Hot
Bairin Zouqi
Yolin Mod
Kailu He
2631
1150
Erenhot
2029
Linxi
Tongliao
Bajan-Dalaj
Dalandzadgad
Chövsgöl
Orgon Tal
Qagan Nur
Yangd Sum
Hexigten Qi
Bairin Youqi
Xar Moron
1791
Chan Bogd
Ongniud Qi
Baixingt
Ovoot Chural
Nomgon
Sulan Cheer
Baixingt
Naiman Qi
1865
Ondor Sum
Zhenglan Qi
Chifeng
Qen
Sogo Nur
Suj
Zhenghuang Qi
1081
866
Fusin
1395
Xar Moron
Ejin Qi
Bayan Obo
Weichang
Dong
Shangdu
Taibus Qi
Luan
Jianping
Yi Xian
1941
Xi
Ximiao
Hanggin Houqi
Wuyuan
Guyang
2174
Tsining
Fengning
Longhua
Ulansuhai Nur
Shiguaigou
Huhehot
Shangyi
Changkiakow
Harqin
Chinchow
Bayan Mod
2187
Chepteh
Chinsi
Linhe
Urad Qianqi
Paotow
Great Wall
Suanhwa
Kuancheng
Yingkow
Dengkou
Hwang (Huang He)
Dai Hai
Huai'an
1677
Gai Xian
Xar Burd
Togtoh
Tatung
Miyun
Liaotung Bay
Badain Jaran
Jartai
Nordos
Huairen
Yu Xian
Peking
(Beijing)
Qinhuangdao
40°N
1766
Suhait
Wuda
2149
Juntuliang
Dongsheng
Pianguan
Laiyuan
Tangshan
Lulong
Fu Xian
Dachechang
Yabrai Yanchang
Shihtsuishan
Shuo Xian
Yongding
Wudao
3616
Alashan Desert
Otog Qi
3058
Paoting
Ba Xian
Tientsin
Dalian
Dongle
Alxa Zuoqi
Dongzhen
Shenmu
Shandan
2393
Po Hai
Jinchang
Yinchuan
Xin Xian
Ding Xian
Ziya
Miaodao Islands
5020
Minle
Yulin
Cangchow
Great Wall
Nangsin Sum
Wuzhong
2831
Shihkiachwang
Yanshan
Wuwei
Taiyuan
Yangchuan
Penglai
Yun He (Grand Canal)
Dingbian
Yutze
Laichow Bay
Yantai
Zhongwei
Great Wall
Hwang (Huang He)
Hwang (Huang He) (Yellow River)
Gangca
Menyuan
4070
Tianshui
Suide
Taigu
2069
Tehchow
220
Tongxin
Zichang
Singtai
Linqing
Boxing
Haiyan
Datong
Shantung
Sining
Yondeng
Wuqi
Yanchang
Huo Xian
Tsinan
Tzepo
Laiyang
2244
Jingyuan
Huan Jiang
Yan'an
Hantan
Weifang
4832
Gonghe
Minhe
Nangdoi
Lanchow
1508
105°E
Guyuan
110°E
Changchih
Fengfeng
Anyang
1619
115°E
950
Tai'an
Jiao Xian
120°E
Tsingtao
n
o
p
q
r
s
t
u
v
w
x
y
z
62
63
0
100
200
300
miles
Average linear scale
0
100
200
300
400
500
Km

52

57

a b c d e f g h i j k l m
n o p q r s t u v w x y z
120°E 125°E 130°E 135°E
50°N 45°N 40°N 35°N
RUSSIA
MONGOLIA
CHINA
Manchuria
Inner Mongolia
Gobi
NORTH KOREA
SOUTH KOREA
SEA OF JAPAN
Yellow Sea
East China Sea
Po Hai
Korea Bay
Liaotung Bay
Laichow Bay
Korea Strait
Inland Sea
Great Khingan Mts.
Little Khingan
Khingan Mts.
Changpai Shan
Paektu-san 2744
Shantung
Kyushu
Shikoku
Great Wall
Grand Canal
Amur
Sungari
Nen Jiang
Ussuri
Yalu
Tumen
Liao He
Xar Moron
Xinkai He
Dongliao He
Muling He
Luan He
Xi He
Yongding He
Ziya He
Hwang (Huang He)
Yangtze (Chang Jiang)
Hailar
Argun He
Ingoda
Zeya
Bureya
Lake Khanka
Hulun-Nur
Buyr-Nur
Lake Hungtze
Lake Kaoyu
Lake Tai
Miaodao Islands
Zhoushan Islands
Cape Chengshan
Quelpart Island (Cheju)
Tsushima (Japan)
Oki
Tanega
Yaku
Ōsumi Channel
Bungo Channel
Kii Strait
Baley
Nerchinsky Zavod
Klin
Borzya
Priargunsk
Mordaga
Argun Zuoqi
Jinhe
Kalaqi
Tulihe
Argun Youqi
Oroqen Zizhiqi
Linhai
Huma
Shisanzhan
Shimanovsk
Svobodnyy
Novokiyevskiy Uval
Belogorsk
Blagoveshchensk
Heihe
Zavitinsk
Bureya
Raychikhinsk
Xunke
Arkhara
Talandzha
Izvestkovyy
Birobidzhan
Kukan
Ust'Niman
Urgal
Chegdomyn
Chekunda
Ust'Tyrma
Tyrma
Mogdy
Bolodzhak
Duki
Kondon
Komsomolsk-na-Amure
Bolon
Litovka
Sarapulskoye
Khabarovsk
Kruglikovo
Fuyuan
Khor
Manchouli
Qagan
Chen Barag Qi
Hailar
Yakeshi
Yuanlin
Xiao'ergou
Dayangshu
Huolongmen
Sunwu
Nenjiang
Morin Dawa
Goukou
Xin Barag Youqi
Xin Barag Zuoqi
Arun Qi
Nehe
Zalantun
Fuyu
Yi'an
Bei'an
Longzhen
Jiayin
Wuyiling
Wuying
Yichun
Luobei
Tongjiang
Fujin
Handgai
Yirshi
Tamsagbulag
Longjiang
Tsitsihar (Qiqihar)
Baiquan
Suileng
Hokang
Nancha
Jalaid Qi
Dorbod
Qing'an
Suihua
Kiamusze
Schwangyashan
Kotikova
Bikin
Xikou
Dashizhai
Tailai
Daqing
Anda
Lanxi
Qagan Qulut
Shumugou
Horqin Youyi Qianqi
Dongfanghong
Luchegorsk
Svetlovodnaya
Glubinnoye
Bulag Sum
Nungnain Sum
Baicheng
Harbin
Fangzheng
Qitaihe
Hulin
Dal'nerechensk
Dong Ujimqin Qi
Tuquan
Tao'an
Zhaoyuan
Shuangcheng
Lalin He
Shangzhi
Linkou
Kisi
Lesozavodsk
Velikaya
Sidatun
Kirovskiy
Qian Gorlos
Tongyu
Dehui
Yushu
Mutankiang
Xiachengzi
Spassk Dal'niy
Rudnaya
Xi Ujimqin Qi
Jarud Qi
Jirin Gol
Holt Sum
Ning'an
Suifenhe
Arsen'yev
Dongjingcheng
Kavalerovo
Xilin Hot
Bairin Zuoqi
Yolin Mod
Horqin Zuoyi Zhongqi
Changchun
Kirin (Jilin)
Emu
Ussuriysk
Linxi
Kailu He
Jiaohe
Bairin Youqi
Tongliao
Shwangliao
Dunhua
Wangqing
Artem
Vangou
Margaritovo
Hexigten Qi
Szeping
Liaoyuan
Huadian
Hunchun
Vladivostok
Nakhodka
Ongniud Qi
Baixingt
Naiman Qi
Kaiyuan
Huinan
Yenki
Hoeryong
Zhenglan Qi
Chifeng
Fusin
Jingyu
Liuhe
Najin
Weichang
Xinmin
Fushun
Qingyuan
Linkiang
Ch'ongjin
Chuuronjang
Mukden (Shenyang)
Tunghwa
Jianping
Yi Xian
Penki
Liaoyang
Hyesanjin
Longhua
Huanren
Fengning
Harqin
Chinchow
Anshan
Manp'ojin
Kapsan
Chengteh
Chinsi
Kuandian
Yingkow
Kimchaek
Kuancheng
Miyun
Gai Xian
Hŭich'ŏn
Pukch'ong
Antung (Dandong)
Sinŭiju
Peking (Beijing)
Lulong
Qinhuangdao
Gushan
Hamhung
Tangshan
Wudao
Fu Xian
Anju
Tientsin
Ba Xian
Dalian
Pyŏngyang
Wŏnsan
Chinnamp'o
Hwangju
Ich'ŏn
Cangchow
Sokch'o
Yanshan
Haeju
Kaesŏng
Ch'unch'ŏn
Kangnŭng
Ongjin
Penglai
Yantai
Inch'ŏn
Seoul
Wŏnju
Tonghae
Tehchow
Boxing
Laiyang
Ch'ungju
Tzepo
Tsinan
Weifang
Ch'ŏngju
Andong
Tai'an
Jiao Xian
Tsingtao
Taejŏn
Kunsan
Chŏnju
Taegu
Ulsan
Yanzhou
Tsining
Liangcheng
Masan
Pusan
Junan
Kwangju
Chinju
Mokp'o
Yŏsu
Tsaochuang
Lienyunkang
Suchow
Huaibei
Binhai
Suhsien
Huaiyin
Hongze
Cheju
Pengpu
Hwainan
Yangchow
Taichow
Chu Xian
Nanking
Nantung
Changshu
Hefei
Wuhsi
Suchow
Shanghai
Lujiang
Wuhu
Xuancheng
Kashing
Tonkling
Anking
Hangchow
Kanazawa
Fukui
Tottori
Matsue
Kyōto
Ōsaka
Kobe
Nishinomiya
Himeji
Okayama
Fukuyama
Hiroshima
Takamatsu
Tokushima
Sakai
Matsusaka
Wakayama
Tanabe
Masuda
Yamaguchi
Shimonoseki
Kita-Kyūshū
Ube
Matsuyama
Kōchi
Nakamura
Fukuoka
Ōita
Sasebo
Kumamoto
Nagasaki
Yatsushiro
Miyazaki
Kagoshima

63

53
a b c d e f g h i j k l m
140°E
145°E
150°E
155°E
50°N
45°N
40°N
35°N
SEA OF
OKHOTSK
PACIFIC
OCEAN
JAPAN
Kamchatka
Paramušir
Onekotan
Kuril Islands
Simušir
Urup
Iturup
Kunašir
Sofiysk
Mariinskoye
De Kastruskoye
Novoilinovka
Nysh
1609
Aleksandrovsk-Sakhalinskiy
Tymovskoye
Siziman
1628
Koto
Sakhalin
(Russia)
1324
Poronaysk
Makarov
Gavan
Gulf of Tartary
Adzhima
Samarga
Kholmsk
Yuzhno-Sakhalinsk
Korsakov
La Pérouse Strait
Wakkanai
1129
Asahikawa
2290
Asahi-dake
Kitami
Hokkaido
Nemuro
Otaru
Sapporo
Obihiro
Kushiro
2052
Muroran
Uchiura Bay
Erimo
Hakodate
Tsugaru Channel
Ōma
Aomori
1625
Akita
Morioka
1914
Sakata
Kesen
Ishinomaki
Yamagata
Sendai
Niigata
2105
Fukushima
Kashiwazaki
Kōriyama
Iwaki
Honshū
Utsunomiya
Maebashi
Mito
Tokyo
Chōshi
Kawasaki
Chiba
Yokohama
Yokosuka
Shizuoka
n o p q r s t u v w x y z
0 100 200 300 miles
Average linear scale
0 100 200 300 400 500 Km

55

This map shows 1/60 of the earth's surface

39

64

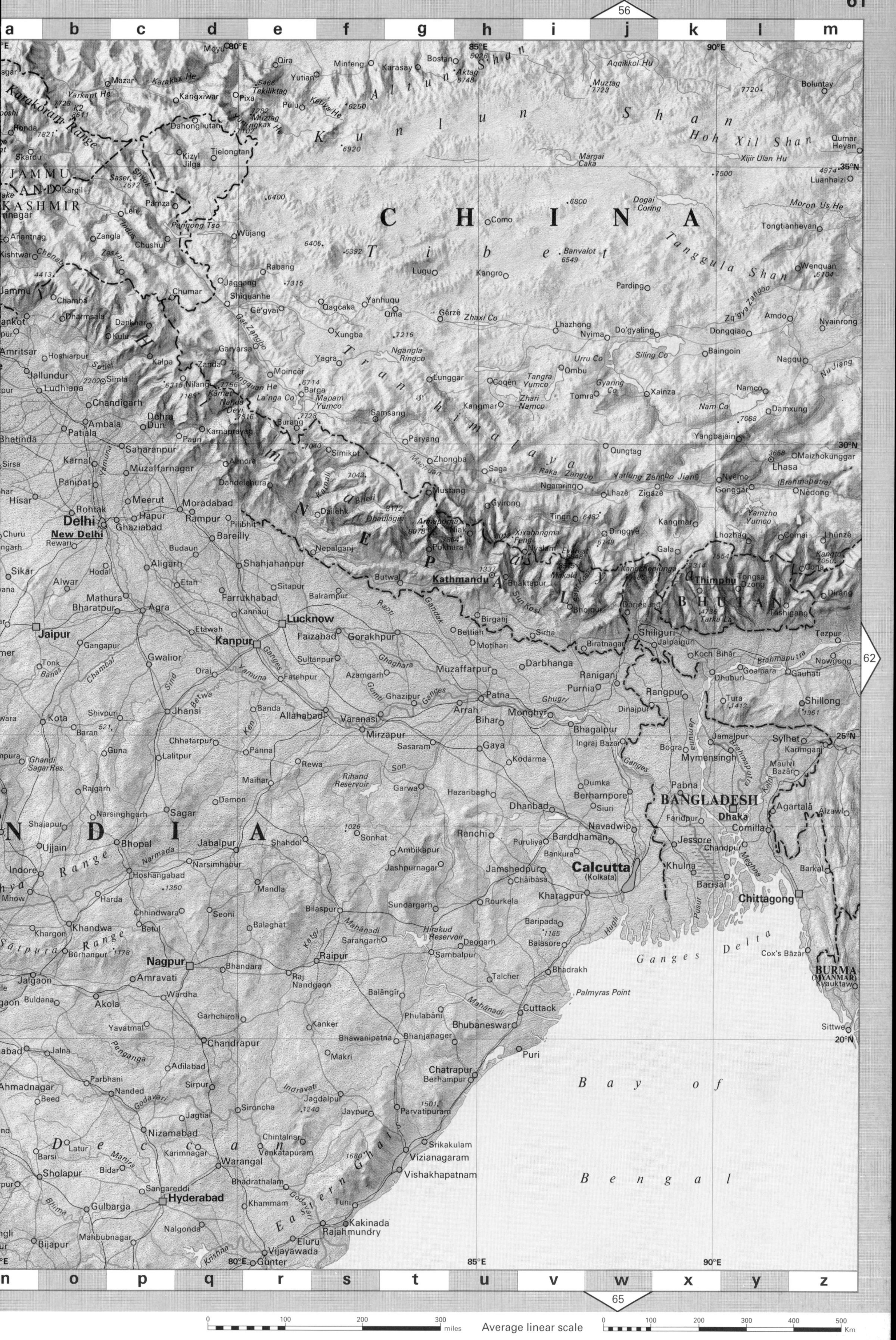
56
a b c d e f g h i j k l m
n o p q r s t u v w x y z
62
65
80°E
85°E
90°E
35°N
30°N
25°N
20°N
CHINA
Tibet
Kunlun Shan
Altun Shan
Hoh Xil Shan
Tanggula Shan
Transhimalaya
Himalaya
Karakoram Range
JAMMU AND KASHMIR
NEPAL
BHUTAN
BANGLADESH
BURMA (MYANMAR)
INDIA
Deccan
Eastern Ghats
Satpura Range
Ganges Delta
Bay of Bengal
Palmyras Point
Ganges
Yamuna
Brahmaputra
Yarlung Zangbo Jiang
Mahanadi
Godavari
Krishna
Narmada
Chambal
Son
Gandak
Kosi
Indus
Chenab
Sutlej
Pangong Tso
Nam Co
Siling Co
Delhi
New Delhi
Kathmandu
Thimphu
Dhaka
Calcutta
(Kolkata)
Lucknow
Kanpur
Jaipur
Agra
Patna
Varanasi
Allahabad
Gorakhpur
Nagpur
Hyderabad
Bhopal
Jabalpur
Raipur
Cuttack
Bhubaneswar
Puri
Chittagong
Lhasa
Shigatse
Shiliguri
Darjeeling
Gauhati
Shillong
Sylhet
Comilla
Khulna
Jessore
Rangpur
Mymensingh
Vishakhapatnam
Vizianagaram
Srikakulam
Kakinada
Rajahmundry
Vijayawada
Guntur
Warangal
Nizamabad
Chandrapur
Amravati
Akola
Jhansi
Gwalior
Sagar
Ranchi
Jamshedpur
Gaya
Dhanbad
Kota
Ujjain
Indore
Meerut
Moradabad
Bareilly
Aligarh
Mathura
Saharanpur
Chandigarh
Ambala
Ludhiana
Amritsar
Jammu
Srinagar
Leh
Kargil
Skardu
K2
8611
Everest
8848
Kangchenjunga
8586
Annapurna
8078
Dhaulagiri
8172
Nanda Devi
7816
Xixabangma Feng
8012
Sittwe
Cox's Bāzār
Kyauktaw
Average linear scale
0 100 200 300 miles
0 100 200 300 400 500 Km

56
57
a b c d e f g h i j k l m
n o p q r s t u v w x y z
66
61
95°E
100°E
105°E
35°N
30°N
25°N
20°N
C H I
INDIA
BHUTAN
BANGLA-
DESH
BURMA
(MYANMAR)
VIETNAM
LAOS
THAILAND
INDIAN
OCEAN
Gulf
of
Tongking
Kunlun Shan
Qing Zang
Gaoyuan
Bayan Har Shan
Nyainqêntanglha Shan
Ningjing Shan
Hengduan Shan
Sichuan
Pendi
Dalou Shan
Tsinling Shan
Wuliang Shan
Arakan Mountains
Patkai
Tongking
Great Wall
Qinghai Hu
Hwang (Huang He)
Yulongxue Shan
Jiuding Shan
Minya Konka
Namjagbarwa Feng
Takpa Shiri
Kangto
Saikhoa Ghat
Fan si Pan
Doi Inthanon
Phu Soai Dao
Brahmaputra
Yarlung Zangbo Jiang
Nu Jiang
Salween
Irrawaddy
Chindwin
Sittang
Mekong
Lancang Jiang
Jinsha Jiang
Yalong Jiang
Min Jiang
Jialing Jiang
Wu Jiang
Hongshui
Yu Jiang
Nanpang Jiang
Hong Ha
Da
Wei He
Tongtian He
Moron Us He
Dam Qu
Za Qu
Nan Hulsan Hu
Dabsan Hu
Suli Hu
Gyaring Hu
Dian Chi
Mangnai
Shaliangzi
Da Qaidam
Golmud
Xitieshan
Delingha
Tianjun
Gangca
Menyuan
Wuwei
Zhongwei
Dingbian
Tianshui
Sining
Lanchow
Linsia
Lintao
Dingxi
Guyuan
Pingliang
Qingyang
Tungchuan
Paoki
Sian
Tienshui
Hanzhong
Wudu
Guangyuan
Wanyuan
Chengtu
Mianyang
Nanchung
Chungking
Wanhsien
Daxian
Neikiang
Tzekung
Ipin
Luchou
Kweiyang
Anshun
Kunming
Qujing
Zhaotong
Xichang
Dechang
Lijiang
Dali
Siakwan
Baoshan
Tengchong
Lincang
Jinghong
Simao
Pu'er
Kokiu
Gejiu
Wenshan
Nanning
Bose
Hechi
Lashio
Myitkyina
Bhamo
Mandalay
Monywa
Myingyan
Meiktila
Magwe
Pyinmana
Toungoo
Prome
Pyu
Pegu
Henzada
Rangoon
(Yangon)
Insein
Thaton
Kyaikto
Sittwe
Kyaukpyu
Sandoway
Gwa
Chittagong
Cox's Bāzār
Imphal
Kohima
Shillong
Silchar
Agartala
Comilla
Aizawl
Tezpur
Jorhat
Dibrugarh
Tinsukia
Itanagar
Guwahati
Nowgong
Chiang Mai
Chiang Rai
Lampang
Phrae
Nan
Phayao
Phitsanulok
Udon Thani
Vientiane
Nong Khai
Louangphrabang
Xam Nua
Sayaboury
Vang Vieng
Pak Sane
Thakhek
Hanoi
Haiphong
Nam Dinh
Thanh Hoa
Vinh
Ha Tinh
Dong Hoi
Lang Son
Lai Chau
Ha Giang
Cao Bang
Lhasa
Nagqu
Qamdo
Garzê
Kangding
Ya'an
Litang
Batang
Dêgê
Jomda
Zayü
Bomi
Nyingchi
Nêdong
Tongtianheyan
Wenquan
Amdo
Madoi
Maqên
Darlag
Chindu
Yushu
Sêrxu
Zhag'yab
Markam
Dêqên
Gongshan
This map shows 1/60 of the earth's surface

58
a
b
c
d
e
f
g
h
i
j
k
l
m
Taiyuan
Yutze
Taigu
Yangchuan
115°E
Tehchow
120°E
Penglai
Yantai
Cape Chengshan
125°E
Ongjin
Kangnung
Inch'ŏn
Seoul
Wŏnju
Ch'ungju
Singtai
Linqing
Boxing
Tzepo
Tsinan
Laiyang
Huo Xian
Fengfeng
Hantan
Weifang
Shantung
Yellow
Ch'ŏngju
SOUTH
Andong
Taejŏn
Changchih
Anyang
Tai'an
Jiao Xian
Tsingtao
Hohpi
Kunsan
Chŏnju
Taegu
Houma
Heze
Yanzhou
Liangcheng
Sea
KOREA
Jiaozuo
Sinsiang
Tsining
Junan
Masan
Kwangju
Chinju
35°N
Sanmenhsia
Chengchow
Kaifeng
Tsaochuang
Mokp'o
Yŏsu
Loyang
Qi Xian
Shangkiu
Lienyunkang
Suchow
Grand Canal
Binhai
Hsuchang
Zhecheng
Huaibei
Pingtingshan
Bo Xian
Suhsien
Huaiyin
Nanzhao
Luohe
Shangshui
Hongze
Cheju
Lake Hungtze
Great
Quelpart Island (Cheju)
Zhenping
Nanyang
Pengpu
Lake Kaoyu
Tanghe
Xincai
Fuyang
Hwainan
Yangchow
Taichow
Huai He
Chu Xian
Xinyang
Lueshan
Huangchuan
Nantung
Nanking
Siangfan
Sui Xian
Hefei
Changshu
Nanzhang
N
A
Wuhsi
E A S T   C H I N A
Han Shui
Macheng
Lujiang
Wuhu
Lake Tai
Suchow
Shanghai
Yunmeng
Xuancheng
Chang Jiang
Yangtze
Plain
Tonkling
S E A
Wuhan
Anking
Kashing
Yidu
Shasi
Mianyang
Hwangshih
Hangchow
Zhoushan Islands
Tongshan
Tunxi
Shaohing
30°N
Li Xian
Ningpo
Guoju
Kiukiang
Xingzi
Kingtehchen
Xin'anjiang
Changteh
Yueyang
Lake Tungting
Lake Poyang
Kinhwa
Xiushui
Nanchang
Quzhou
Linhai
Yiyang
Gao'an
Shangjao
Lishui
Changsha
Cuixi
Siangtan
Chuchow
Xinyu
Fuzhou
Yunhe
Wenchow
Pingsiang
Pucheng
Lianyuan
Gongxi
Nanfeng
Shaowu
Zhenghe
Fuding
Shaoyang
Gan Jiang
Ryūkyū Islands
Hengyang
Ningde
Ji'an
Nanping
Okinawa
Xiang Jiang
Leiyang
Ningdu
Wuyi Shan
Min Jiang
Sanming
(Japan)
Naha
Minqing
Foochow
Kanchow
Ruijin
Yong'an
Quanzhou
Chen Xian
Ningyuan
Putian
Nanxiong
Chilung
Taoyüan
Longyan
Taipei
Hsinchu
25°N
Lian Xian
Shaokwan
Ilan
Miyako
Changchow
Amoy (Xiamen)
Mei Xian
Taiwan Strait
Xueweng
Yingde
Iriomote
Zhangpu
Taichung
Qiuling
Changhua
Hualien
Dong Jiang
Longchuan
Huaiji
Zhao'an
Wuchow
Jieyang
Chiai
TAIWAN
Tropic of Cancer
Swatow
Si Xiang
Chaoyang
Canton (Guangzhou)
Foshan
Huizhou
Tainan
Luoding
Lufeng
Shun-te
Kaohsiung
Pingtung
Kongmoon (Jiangmen)
Kowloon
Fangshan
Chuhoi
Hong Kong
Macao
Hengchun
Yangjiang
Mowming
PACIFIC
Bashi Channel
Luzon Strait
Batan Islands
20°N
OCEAN
Hainan
Babuyan Islands
Cape Bojeador
Cape Engaño
Aparri
Laoag
Luzon
Cordillera Central
Sierra Madre
Bangued
Tuguegarao
Vigan
PHILIPPINES
Ilagan
Pulog
115°E
120°E
125°E
n
o
p
q
r
s
t
u
v
w
x
y
z
67
0
100
200
300
miles
Average linear scale
0
100
200
300
400
500
Km

a b c d e f g h i j k l m

61

Puri

Jawhar

75°E

Jalna

Pengang

Chandrapur

80°E

Makri

Berhampur

85°E

Aurangabad

Adilabad

Sirpur

Indravati

Jagdalpur

Jaypur

Parvatipuram

1646

Thane

Ahmadnagar

Parbhani

Nanded

1240

1501

Bombay

(Mumbai)

Pune

Dhond

Beed

Godavari

Jagtial

Chintalnar

Srikakulam

1680

Janjira

Bhor

Barsi

Latur

Nizamabad

Karimnagar

Bhadrachalam

Vizianagaram

Satara

Pandharpur

Bidar

Venkatapuram

Godavari

Vishakhapatnam

Koyna Res.

Sangareddi

Manjra

Warangal

Tuni

Chiplun

INDIA

Gulbarga

Hyderabad

Khammam

Ratnagiri

Sangli

Bhima

Mahbubnagar

Nalgonda

Rajahmundry

Kakinada

Kolhapur

Bijapur

Krishna

Raichur

Nagarjuna Res.

Guntur

Vijayawada

Lingsugur

Krishna

Tenali

Machilipatnam

Belgaum

Ramdurg

Kurnool

Markapur

Ongole

ARABIAN

Goa

Gadag

Adoni

Panaji

Dharwar

Tungabhadra Res.

Hospet

Bellary

Banganapalli

Gooty

Kavali

15°N

Karwar

Savanur

.1100

Davangere

Kotturu

Anantapur

Penner

Nellore

Sagar

Chitradurga

Cuddapah

Gudur

Linganamakki Res.

Penukonda

Kadiri

1151

Coondapoor

Bhadravati

Bhadra Res.

1323

Chik Ballapur

Vayalpad

Tirupati

Chikmagalur

Tumkur

Kolar

Chittoor

Madras (Chennai)

Mangalore

Hassan

Mandya

Bangalore

Vellore

Kanchipuram

Madikeri

Mysore

Krishnagiri

Polur

SEA

1745

Dharmapuri

Pondicherry

Cannanore

Ootacamund

(Udagamandalam)

Salem

1627

Cuddalore

Amindivi Islands

2636

Erode

Parambalur

Doda Betta

Calicut

(Kozhikode)

Coimbatore

Cauvery

Mayuram

Lakshadweep

(India)

Tiruchchirappalli

Thanjavur

Trichur

Palghat

Pudukkottai

Cannanore Islands

Anai Mudi

Dindigul

10°N

Ernakulam

2695

Palk Strait

Cochin

Madurai

Jaffna

Nine Degree Channel

Alleppey

Virudunagar

Rameswaram

Mullaittivu

2019

Ramanathapuram

Adam's Br.

Mannar

Minicoy

Quilon

Tenkasi

Tuticorin

Trincomalee

Tirunelveli

Gulf of Mannar

Anuradhapura

Eight Degree Channel

Trivandrum

(Thiruvananthapuram)

1654

Puttalam

Nagercoil

Cape Comorin

Dambulla

Batticaloa

Kurunegala

SRI LANKA

Kandy

Pidurutalagala

2518

Colombo

Badulla

Pottuvil

2243

Hambantota

Male

Galle

Dondra Head

Equator

BA

B

MALDIVES

INDI

75°E

80°E

85°E

n o p q r s t u v w x y z

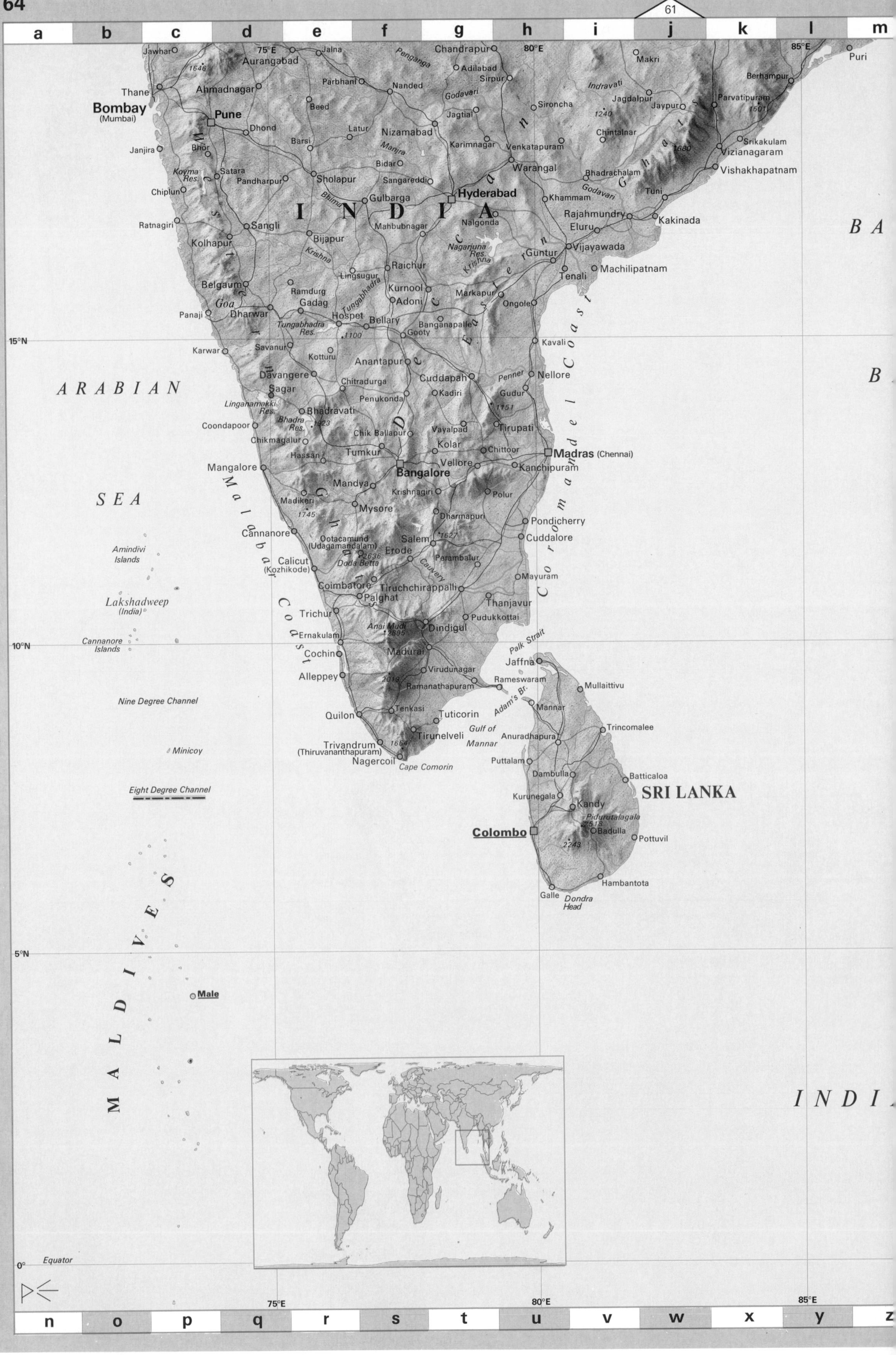

This map shows 1/60 of the earth's surface

62
a
b
c
d
e
f
g
h
i
j
k
l
m
90°E
95°E
100°E
Loikaw
Pyinmana
Muang Chiang Rai
1854
Mekong
Luang Prabang
Ban Ban
Thayetmyo
Ramree
Salween
Phayao
Sayaboury
Vang Vieng
2820
Xieng Khouang
Toungoo
Cheduba
Prome
1056
Inthanon 2590
Chiang Mai
Nan
LAOS
Bia
Pak Sane
Pyu
Sittang
Kham Keut
Myanaung
Irrawaddy
Lampang
Phrae
Soai Dao 2102
Vientiane
Mekong
BURMA
(MYANMAR)
Henzada
Nong Khai
Thakhek
Pegu
Kyaikto
Wang Saphung
Miang 2316
Udon Thani
Sakon Nakhon
OF
Insein
Thingangyun
Rangoon
(Yangon)
Thaton
Mae Sot
Tak
Phitsanulok
Bassein
Kanbe
Gulf of Martaban
Moulmein
Chum Phae
Khon Kaen
Kalasin
Phetchabun
Pyapon
Maha Sarakham
Roi Et
Mouths of the Irrawaddy
Chaiyaphum
Yasothon
Nakhon Sawan
THAILAND
Ubon Ratchathani
Ye
Chao Phraya
Nakhon Ratchasima
Si Sa Ket
15°N
Preparis
Sing Buri
Lop Buri
Buriram
Surin
Suphan Buri
Chai Si
Khiaw 1282
L
Kanchanaburi
Prachin Buri
849
Samrong
Cocos Islands (Burma)
Tavoy
Nakhon Pathom
Ban Pong
Bangkok
(Krung Thep)
Thon Buri
Sisophon
North Andaman
Angkor
Chon Buri
Phetchaburi
Battambang
Tonle Sap
Siracha
Andaman Islands (India)
Tenasserim
Tenasserim
1633
CAMBODIA
Klaeng
Mergui Archipelago
Kadan
Rayong
Middle Andaman
Mergui
Hua Hin
Chantaburi
Pursat
Kompong Chhnang
Laem Ngop
Chang
1813
South Andaman
Kut
1251
Prachuap Khiri Khan
Hat Lek
Phnom Penh
Andaman
Letsok-Aw
Gulf
Little Andaman
758
Lanbi
of
Chumphon
Kompong Som
Ranong
Isthmus of Kra
Thailand
Phu Quoc
Ten Degree Channel
Sea
St. Matthew's
10°N
Phangan
Samui
66
Car Nicobar
Surat Thani
Ban Takua Pa
Ban Na San
Khao Luang 1835
Nakhon Si Thammarat
Cape Mau
Thap Put
Nicobar Islands (India)
Krabi
Katchall
Phuket
Phatthalung
Little Nicobar
Thale Luang
Trang
Great Nicobar
Songkhla
Hat Yai
Pattani
Terutao
Satun
Sai Buri
Yala
Narathiwat
Langkawi
Alor Setar
Kota Baharu
Sungai Ko-lok
Malay Peninsula
Sungai Petani
Banda Aceh
Sigli
Pinang (George Town)
Pinang
Butterworth
2171
Chamah
Kelantan
Kuala Terengganu
Lhokseumawe
Bireuen
Lhoksukon
Idi
5°N
2855 Geureudong
Peureulak
Taiping
Perak
Sungai Siput Utara
Dungun
Calang
Ipoh
MALAYA
Langsa
Kampar
2131
Kuala Lipis
Meulaboh
Pangkalanbrandan
Tapis 1512
Tanjungpura
Raub
Kuantan
Leuser 3404
Medan
Sumatra
Kuala Kubu Baharu
Bentong
Kutacane
Tebingtinggi
MALAYSIA
(WESTERN)
Tapaktuan
Petaling Jaya
Kuala Lumpur
Kabanjahe
Tanjungbalai
Kelang
Putrajaya
Pematangsiantar
Seremban
Tioman
OCEAN
Lake Toba
Strait of Malacca
Simeulue
Singkilbaru
Malacca
Segamat
2300 Sihabuhabu
Rantauprapat
Blumut 1010
Muar
Johor
Tuangku
Tarutung
Rupat
Keluang
Sibolga
Barumun
Dumai
Kulai
Johor Baharu
Duri
Padangsidimpuan
Singapore
Balaipungut
Nias
Panyabungan
Riau Islands
INDONESIA
Hutanopan
Pakanbaru
Kampar
Pini
Ophir 2912
Lubuksikaping
0°
Payakumbuh
Lingga Islands
Bukittinggi
Padangpanjang
Rengat
Tanahbala
Indragiri
Singkep
n
o
p
q
r
s
t
u
v
w
x
y
z
68
0
100
200
300
miles
Average linear scale
0
100
200
300
400
500
Km

Hainan

Dongfang

Yaxian

Gulf of Tongking

Toungoo
Pyu
Prome
Myanaung
Henzada
Pegu
Kyaikto
Insein Thingangyun
Rangoon (Yangon)
Kanbe
Thaton
Moulmein
Pyapon
Gulf of Martaban

BURMA (MYANMAR)

Inthanon 2590
Chiang Mai
Phayao
Nan
Sayaboury
Vang Vieng 2520
Bia
Xieng Khouang
Quynh Luu
Vinh
Ha Tinh

Lampang
Phrae
Soai Dao 2102
Nong Khai
Vientiane
Pak Sane
Napé 2286
Kham Keut
Rao Go
Dong Hoi

Tak
Mae Sot
Phitsanulok
Miang 2316
Wang Saphung
Udon Thani
Sakon Nakhon
Thakhek
V I E T N A M

Ye
Nakhon Sawan
Chum Phae
Phetchabun
Khon Kaen
Kalasin
Maha Sarakham
Roi Et
Khemarat
Savannakhet
Sepone
Hue

THAILAND
Chaiyaphum
Nakhon Ratchasima
Yasothon
Ubon Ratchathani
B.Thateng
2500 Atouat
Da Nang

15°N
Tavoy
Sing Buri
Lop Buri
Buriram
Surin
Si Sa Ket
Warin Chamrap
Pakse
2009
Phiafay
Attopeu

Suphan Buri
Kanchanaburi
Nakhon Pathom
Khiaw 1282
Prachin Buri 849
Samrong
Det Udom
Khong
Kontum

Ban Pong
Thon Buri
Bangkok (Krung Thep)
Chon Buri
Sisophon
Angkor
Stung Treng
Pleiku 1570
An Tuc

Mergui Archipelago
Kadan
Mergui
Phetchaburi
Siracha
1633
Chantaburi
Battambang
Tonle Sap
Kompong Chhnang
Ban Pu Kroy
1544
Mdrak
Qui Nhon

Letsok-Aw
1251
Khiri Khan Prachuap
Klaeng
Rayong
Pursat
Kompong Cham
Kratie
Nha Trang

Lanbi
758
Chumphon
Laem Ngop
Chang
1813
Kut
Hat Lek
Phnom Penh
Basac
Kompong Som
Bao Loc
Di Linh 1532
Da Lat
Cam Ranh

A n d a m a n

Gulf of Thailand

Kompong Som
Chau Phu
My Tho
Phu Chong
Bien Hoa
Saigon (Ho Chi Minh)

10°N
St Matthew's
Ranong
Isthmus of Kra
Phangan
Long Xuyen
Rach Gia
Can-Tho
Vung Tau

S e a
65
Ban Takua Pa
Samui
Surat Thani
Ban Na San
Luang 1835
Khanh Hung
Mekong Delta

Nakhon Si Thammarat
Nam Can
Cape Mau

Spratly Islands

Thap Put
Krabi
Phuket
Trang
Thale Luang
Phatthalung
Songkhla

S O U T H

A n d a m a n

Hat Yai
Pattani
Sai Buri

Terutao
Satun
Yala
Narathiwat

Langkawi
Alor Setar
Sungai Ko-lok
Kota Baharu

Sungai Petani
Pinang (George Town)
Pinang
Butterworth
Kuala Terengganu

5°N
Banda Aceh
Sigli
Lhokseumawe
Choksukon
2171 Chamah
MALAYA
Dungun

Bireuen
Idi
Peureulak
Taiping
Sungai Siput Utara
Ipoh
Kampar
Kuantan
North Natuna

Calang
Langsa
2131
Kuala Lipis
Tapis 1512
S O U T H

Geureudong 2855

Meulaboh
Pangkalanbrandan
Tanjungpura
Raub
Kuala Kubu Baharu

Leuser 3404
Medan
Bentong
Kelang
Kuala Lumpur
Petaling Jaya
Putrajaya
Natuna

Kutacane
Tebingtinggi
MALAYSIA (WESTERN)
Natuna Islands (Indonesia)

Tapaktuan
Kabanjahe
Pematangsiantar
Tanjungbalai
Seremban
Tioman
Anambas Islands (Indonesia)
South Natuna Islands

Simeulue
Lake Toba
Sihabuhabu 2300
Rantauprapat
Segamat
Malacca
Blumut 1010
Muar
Keluang

Nias
Singkilbaru
Sibolga
Tarutung
Rupat
Kulai
Cape Datu
Binatang
Sarik

Tuangku
Barumun
Dumai
Johor Baharu
Datuk Bay
Kuching
Bau
Sri

Padangsidimpuan
Duri
SINGAPORE
Sambas
Singkawang
Lupar

Panyabungan
Balaipungut
Riau Islands
Pamangkat
Kapuas

INDIAN
Hutanopan
Pakanbaru
Tambelan Islands
Pinang
Ngabang
Sanggau

Equator
Pini
2912
Lubuksikaping
Kampar
Lingga Islands
Pontianak

OCEAN
Bukittinggi
Payakumbuh
Rengat
Singkep
Berhala Strait
Cape Jabung
Bengkolan Bay
Kapuas

Tanahbala
Padangpanjang
Solok
Indragiri
Singkep
Maya
Nanga Sokan

Siberut
Padang

100°E
105°E
110°E

This map shows 1/60 of the earth's surface

a b c d e f g h i j k l m
63
115°E
120°E
125°E
Babuyan Islands
Cape Bojeador
Laoag
Aparri
Cape Engaño
Bangued
Vigan
Tuguegarao
Cordillera Central
Sierra Madre
Luzon
Ilagan
Pulog 2934
Bayombong
Lingayen Gulf
Baguio
Lingayen
Dagupan
San Carlos
San Jose
San Ildefonso Peninsula
Masinloc
Tarlac
Cabanatuan
Iba
Angeles
San Fernando
Olongapo
Caloocan
Polillo Islands
Manila
Quezon
Pasig
Manila Bay
Laguna de Bay
Lamon Bay
San Pablo
Lipa
Batangas
Lucena
Lopez
Daet
Catanduanes
Virac
Naga
Lubang
Calapan
Boac
Marinduque
Halcon 2582
Mayon 2462
Legazpi
Sorsogon
Bulan
Burias
Mindoro
Baco 2363
San Jose
Mindoro Strait
Sibuyan
Tablas
Masbate
Laoang
Catarman
Calbayog
Catbalogan
Calamian Group
Roxas
Biliran
Samar
Tacloban
Nangtud 2117
Panay
Cadiz
Bogo
Ormoc
Iloilo
Silay
Cebu
San Jose de Buenavista
Bacolod
Abuyog
Leyte
Bago
San Carlos
Guimaras
Mandaue
Toledo
Cebu
Dinagat
2465
Maasin
Binalbagan
Cleopatra Needle 1602
Palawan
Honda Bay
Puerto Princesa
Negros
Bais
Bohol
Siargao
Surigao
Tagbilaran
Bayawan
Dumaguete
Camiguin
Siquijor
Mantalingajan 2085
Butuan
Dapitan
Dipolog
Gingoog
Oroquieta
Cagayan de Oro
Ozamiz
Tangub
Iligan
Malaybalay
Bislig
Marawi
Pagadian
Bugsuk
Balabac
Balabac Strait
Banggi
Tagum
Moro Gulf
Cotabato
Cagayan Sulu
Davao
Apo 2954
Zamboanga
Jambongan
Basilan
Basilan
Davao Gulf
Digos
Koronadal
Mindanao
Kota Kinabalu
Kinabalu 4175
Labuk Bay
Sandakan
Jolo
General Santos
Sulu Archipelago
Beaufort
SABAH
Lahad Datu
Tawitawi
Sarangani Islands
Brunei Bay
Bandar Seri Begawan
Kuala Belait
Darvel Bay
Tawitawi Group
Miri
BRUNEI
Baram
Mulu 2371
Tawau
Sebuku Bay
Kawio Islands
Talaud Islands
Sesayap
Tarakan
Sangihe
Sangihe Islands
2550
Kayan
Guguang 2467
Tanjungredeb
Morotai
Tobelo
Manado
2202
Tondano
Akelamo
Sulawesi (Celebes)
Jailolo
Buol
Paleleh
2240
Liangpran
Menyapa 2000
Rapak
Dondo Bay
2217
Kuandang
Ternate
Halmahera
Kotamobagu
2913
Moutong
Tilamuta
Gorontalo
Weda
Weda Bay
Mahakam
Dongkalang
Gebe
Gulf of Tomini
Mapaga
Muarabadak
Samarinda
Togian Is.
Malik
Labuha
Donggala
Palu
Uebonti
2400
Teku
Bacan
Makassar Strait
PHILIPPINES
PACIFIC OCEAN
Sulu Sea
Celébes Sea
Molucca Sea
Malayan Sea
SOUTH CHINA SEA
Zhongye Islands
MALAYSIA (EASTERN)
SARAWAK
Borneo
KALIMANTAN
INDONESIA
15°N
10°N
5°N
0°
70
69
n o p q r s t u v w x y z
0 100 200 300 miles
Average linear scale
0 100 200 300 400 500 Km

This map shows 1/60 of the earth's surface

95°E

SOUTH

100°E

105°E

110°E

Phatthalung
Thale Luang
Trang
Songkhla
THAILAND
Hat Yai
Pattani
Terutao   Satun
Sai Buri
Yala
Narathiwat
Langkawi
Alor Setar
Sungai Ko-lok
Kota Baharu
Kuala Terengganu

S   E   A

Sungai Petani
Butterworth
Pinang (George Town)
Pinang

Banda Aceh
Sigli
Lhokseumawe
Bireuen   Lhoksukon
Calang   Idi
2855   Peureulak
Geureudong
Langsa
Meulaboh   Pangkalanbrandan

Perak   2171
Chamah

5°N

Taiping
Sungai Siput Utara
Dungun

North Natuna

Leuser   Tanjungpura
3404
Medan
Tebingtinggi
Kutacane
Kabanjahe   Pematangsiantar
Tapaktuan
Tanjungbalai

Ipoh
Kampar   2131
Raub
Kelantan

Kuala Lipis
Tapis   1512

MALAYA

Kuantan

Natuna
(Bunguran)

Natuna Islands
(Indonesia)
South Natuna

Kuala Kubu Baharu
Bentong

Simeulue

Lake Toba
Sihabuhabu
2300
Rantauprapat
Tarutung
Singkilbaru
Sibolga

Kuala Lumpur
Petaling Jaya
Kelang   **Putrajaya**
Seremban

**MALAYSIA
(WESTERN)**

Tioman

*Anambas
Islands*
(Indonesia)

Segamat

Cape Datu
Datuk Bay
Kuc

Tuangku

Padangsidimpuan
Panyabungan

Muar   Malacca
*Keluang
1010*
Blumut

Sambas
Pamangkat
Singkawang

Nias

Hutanopan

Dumai
Rupat

Kulai
Johor Baharu
□**SINGAPORE**

Riau Islands

Pinang   Ngabang

Equator

Pini

Lubuksikaping
Ophir   Duri
2912   Balaipungut
Payakumbuh
Bukittinggi   Padangpanjang
Pakanbaru

Kampar

Tambelan Islands

Pontianak

Sa

0°

Tanahbala

Rengat
Indragiri

Lingga Islands

Singkep

Bengkolan Bay

Siberut

Padang
Solok

Muarabungo
Hari
Jambi

Berhala Strait
Cape Jabung

Maya

Karimata
Ketapang

Nan

*Kerinci
3805*
Sungaipenuh
Sipora

Sarolangun

Muntok
Pangkalpinang
Bangka

Karimata Strait

65

North Pagai

Palembang
Tanjungpandan
Belitung

*South
Pagai*

Lubuklinggau
Sungaigerung
Perabumulih

Gaspar Strait

Bengkulu
Lahat
*Dempo
3159*

I

Bintuhan
Kotabumi
*Pesagi
2231*

N

D

5°S

Enggano

Tanjungkarang
Telukbetung
(Bandarlampung)

J

Merak   **Jakarta**

Krakatau

*Cape
Cangkuang*

Bogor
Cirebon
Pekalongan

a

Sukabumi
Bandung   *J*   Tegal
*Slamet
3418*
Sem

I   N   D   I   A   N

Tasik Malaya   Purwokerto
Magelang
Cilacap
Yog

a

O   C   E   A   N

10°S

Christmas Island
(Australia)

95°E

100°E

105°E

110°E

67
a b c d e f g h i j k l m
115°E
120°E
125°E
PHILIPPINES
Sulu Sea
Balabac Strait
Banggi
Cagayan Sulu
Jambongan
I N A
Malayan Sea
Kota Kinabalu
Kinabalu 4175
Labuk Bay
Sandakan
SABAH
Beaufort
Brunei Bay
Lahad Datu
Darvel Bay
Bandar Seri Begawan
Kuala Belait
BRUNEI
Miri
Mulu 2371
Baram
Tawau
Sebuku Bay
MALAYSIA (EASTERN)
Sesayap
Tarakan
Bintulu
SARAWAK
2550
Kayan
Rajang
Guguang 2467
Tanjungredeb
Liangpran 2240
Menyapa 2000
Rapak
Kapuas
Borneo
Mahakam
KALIMANTAN
Pinoh
Raya 2278
Muarabadak
Samarinda
Barito
Balikpapan
Tumbangsamba
Buntok
Sarempaka 1380
Palangkaraya
Tanjung
Meratus Mountains
Sampit
Kandangan
Besar 1892
Kotabaru
Banjarmasin
Laut
Batakan
Cape Selatan
Pagadian
Zamboanga
Moro Gulf
Cotabato
Davao
Apo 2954
Tagum
Digos
Davao Gulf
Mindanao
Basilan
Basilan
Koronadal
General Santos
Pangutaran Group
Jolo
Sulu Archipelago
Sarangani
Tawitawi
Tawitawi Group
5°N
Kawio
Talaud Islands
Celebes Sea
Sangihe
Sangihe Islands
Morotai
Tobelo
Akelamo
Manado
Klabat 2022
Tondano
Dondo Bay
Buol
Paleleh
2217
Jailolo
Ternate
Saolat 1508
Halmahera
Ogoamas 2913
Kuandang
Kotamobagu
Moutong
Tilamuta
Gorontalo
Molucca Sea
Weda
Weda Bay
Dongkalang
0°
Makassar Strait
Mapaga
Gulf of Tomini
Togian Islands
Bacan Islands
Labuha
Donggala
Malik
Teku
Palu
Uebonti
2400
Batui
Peleng
Pasangkayu
Poso
Obi
Banggai Islands
Gulf of Tolo
Taliabu
Mangole
Sula Islands
Moluccas
Lumu
Sulawesi (Celebes)
Ceram Sea
70
Gandadiwata 3074
Masamba
Wotu
Palopo
Strait of Manipa
Ceram
Namlea
Buru
Gulf of Bone
Rantekombola 3455
Majene
Mekongga 2799
Ambon
Kendari
Parepare
Kolaka
Kolono
NESIA
Watampone
Jatisiri
Raha
Muna
Butung
5°S
Ujung Pandang
Sinjai
2871
Kabaena
Baubau
Sea
Masalembo
Bawean
Tukangbesi Islands
Banda Sea
Salajar
Madura
Kangean
Tanahjampea
Kalao
Barat Daya Islands
Surabaya
Madura Strait
Bali Sea
Flores Sea
Lesser Sunda Islands
Wetar
Probolinggo
Semeru 3676
Jember
Banyuwangi
2276
Bali
Denpasar
3726
Lombok
Mataram
Sumbawa Besar
Raba
Sumbawa
Ruteng
2400
Flores
Ende
Maumere
Solor Islands
Alor
Dili
EAST TIMOR
2960
Leti Islands
Atambua
Timor
Besikama
Waikabubak
Waingapu
Sumba
Sawu Sea
10°S
Kupang
Sawu
Roti
Timor Sea
n o p q r s t u v w x y z
72
0 100 200 300 miles
Average linear scale
0 100 200 300 400 500 Km

a b c d e f g h i j k l m
130°E
135°E
140°E
Yap Islands
Faraulep Atoll
Ngulu Atoll
Sorol Atoll
M I C
PALAU
Babel Thuap
Koror
Woleai Atoll
Ifalik Atoll
Eauripik Atoll
Caroline
Sonsorol
5°N
Pulo Anna
Merir
P A C I
Tobi
Helen Reef
Morotai
Akelamo
Halmahera
Mapia Islands
Ayu Islands
O C E
Waigeo
0°
69
Dampier Strait
Sorong
Kwoko 3000
Manokwari
Peg Ariak 2939
Biak
Cenderawasih
Yapen
Misool
990
Sarmi
Steenkool
C e r a m S e a
INDONESIA
Babo
Gulf of Cenderawasih
Jayapura
Vanimo
Van Rees Mountains
Ceram
3019
Bula
Fakfak
Bomberai
WEST
Memberamo
Aitape
Tobo
Ambon
Kaimana
Maoke Mountains
Wamena
Lumi
Dreikikir
Wewak
Jaya 5029
Sepik
PAPUA
New
Kokonau
Mandala 4702
5°S
Telefomin
Kai Islands
Guinea
Wabag
Banda Sea
Kopiago
Aru Islands
Strickland
Mendi
Tanahmerah
2895
Digul
Lake Murray
Mappi
NEW
Damar
Kikori
Tanimbar Islands
Dolak Island
Fly
Babar
Sermata
Selaru
Cape Vals
Merauke
Daru
ARAFURA SEA
Torres Strait
10°S
Badu
Moa
Prince of Wales Island
Cape York
130°E
135°E
140°E
n o p q r s t u v w x y z
73

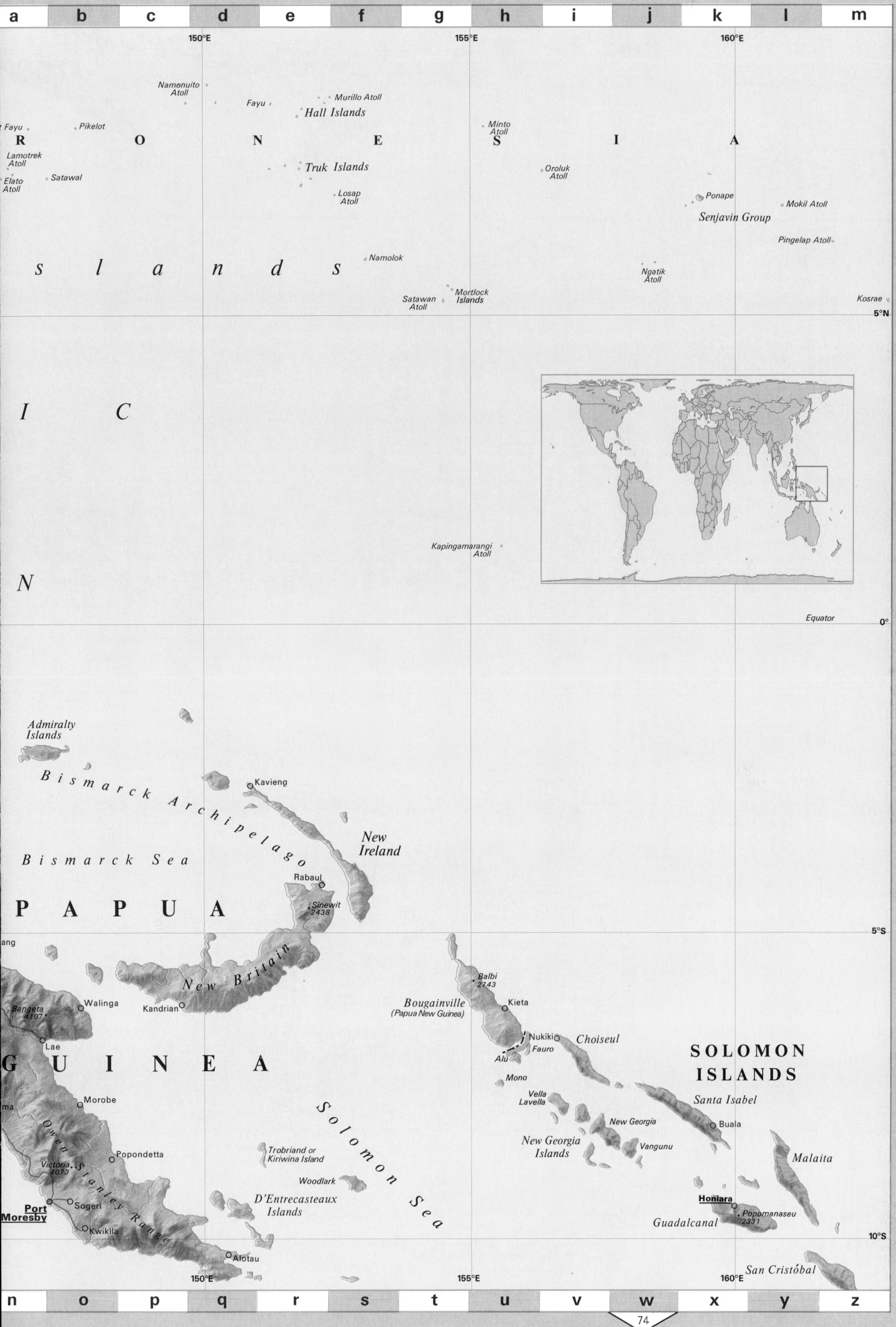

150°E   155°E   160°E

Namonuito Atoll

Fayu   *Murillo Atoll*

Fayu   Hall Islands

Pikelot

R   O   N   E   S   I   A

Lamotrek Atoll

Minto Atoll

Elato Atoll   *Satawal*   Truk Islands   *Oroluk Atoll*

Losap Atoll   *Ponape*   *Mokil Atoll*

Senjavin Group

Pingelap Atoll

s   l   a   n   d   s

Namolok

Ngatik Atoll

Satawan Atoll   *Mortlock Islands*   *Kosrae*

5°N

I   C

N

Kapingamarangi Atoll

Equator   0°

Admiralty Islands

Bismarck   Archipelago   Kavieng

New Ireland

Bismarck Sea   Rabaul

Sinewit 2438

P A P U A   5°S

ang

Bangeta 4107   Walinga   Kandrian   New Britain

Balbi 2743   Kieta

Bougainville (Papua New Guinea)

Lae   Nukiki   *Choiseul*   Fauro

G U I N E A   *Alu*

Mono   SOLOMON ISLANDS

Morobe   *Vella Lavella*   *Santa Isabel*

ma   *New Georgia*   Buala

Popondetta   S o l o m o n   *New Georgia Islands*   *Vangunu*

Trobriand or Kiriwina Island   *Malaita*

Victoria 4073   *Woodlark*

Sogeri   S e a   *D'Entrecasteaux Islands*   **Honiara**   *Popomanaseu 2331*

Port Moresby   *Kwikila*   *Guadalcanal*

Alotau   *San Cristóbal*   10°S

150°E   155°E   160°E

0   100   200   300 miles   Average linear scale   0   100   200   300   400   500 Km

69

76

This map shows 1/60 of the earth's surface

Map labels

Java
Bali
Denpasar
Mataram
Lombok
Sumbawa
Besar
1400
Sumbawa
3726
Raba
Ruteng *2400*
Maumere
Ende
Flores
Solor
Alor
Dili
EA
TIM
Atambua *2960*
Timor
Besikama

INDONESIA

Sawu
Waingapu
Waikabubak
Sea
Sumba *1175*
Kupang
Sawu
Roti

T i m
S

Cartier

I N D I A N

15°S

Cape
Bougainville
Ka
Theda
Kuri Bay
Kimb
Mount Hann *778*
Pl
Collier
Bay
Panter
Downs
Gi
Riv
Beverley
Springs
Mount Hous
Mount Ord *836*
Tablet
9271
Mt.
Broome
Glenor

O C E A N

Cape
Lévêque
Lombardina
Oobagooma
King Leopold Ranges
King Sound
Beagle
Bay
Dampier
Land
Derby
Kimberley
Downs
Camballin
Fitzroy
Fitzroy
Crossing
Coulomb
Point
Broome
Roebuck
Plains
Myroodah
Nerrima
Moun
522 Huxle
Mar
R
Dampier
Downs
Lagrange
Frazier Downs
247
Christmas
Creek
Boh
Dov
Anna Plains

Eighty Mile Beach
Wallal Downs

20°S
Port
Hedland
Goldsworthy
Shay Gap
Yarrie
Warrawagine
Great Sandy Desert
Mount
Elliott
Barrow
Island
Dampier
Roebourne
Whim
Creek
Kangan
Marble
Bar
Bamboo
Creek
Cooya
Pooya
Yule
W E S T E R N
Percival Lakes
Yarraloola
Millstream
Mount Florance
Nullagine
Lake
Dora
Lake
Auld
North West Cape
Onslow
Pannawonica
Wittenoom
Exmouth
Hamersley
Mount
Minnie
Lake
Blanche
Tabletop
427
Learmonth
Yanrey
Forescue
A U S
S
Wyloo
Tom Price
Mount Tom
Price *1075*
Range
Talawana
Uaroo
1251
Mount
Meharry
Mount
Newman
1053
Lake
Disappointment
Winning
Mount
Palgrave
704
Ashburton
Downs
Paraburdoo
Newman
Gibson Deser
Ullawarra
Tropic of Capricorn
Lyndon
Ashburton
Turee
Creek
Bulloo Downs
Cape
Cuvier
Lake
McLeod
Minnie Creek
Augustus
Mount
Vernon
Kumarina
Lyons
Mount
Augustus
1105
A U S T R A L I
Waldburg Range
Three
Rivers
Mount
Essendon
906
Glenayle
25°S
Carnarvon
Gascoyne
Junction
Dairy
Creek
Gascoyne
Milgun
Carnarvon Range
Neds Creek *738*
Granite Peak
Shark Bay
Cape
Inscription
Mount
Seabrook
552
Peak Hill
Lake
Nabberu
Carnegie
Denham
Byro
Karalundi
Wiluna
Yelma
Warburton
Useless Loop
Curbur
732 Mount Hale
Mileura
Meekatharra
Lake
Carnegie
Hamelin Pool
Tamala
Kalli
Wonganoo
Wannoo
Yallalong
530
Big
Bell
Cue
Tuckanarra
Gidgee
Kalbarri
Billabalong
Murgoo
Sandstone
Agnew
Booylgoo
Springs
594
Gr

110°E   115°E   120°E   125°E

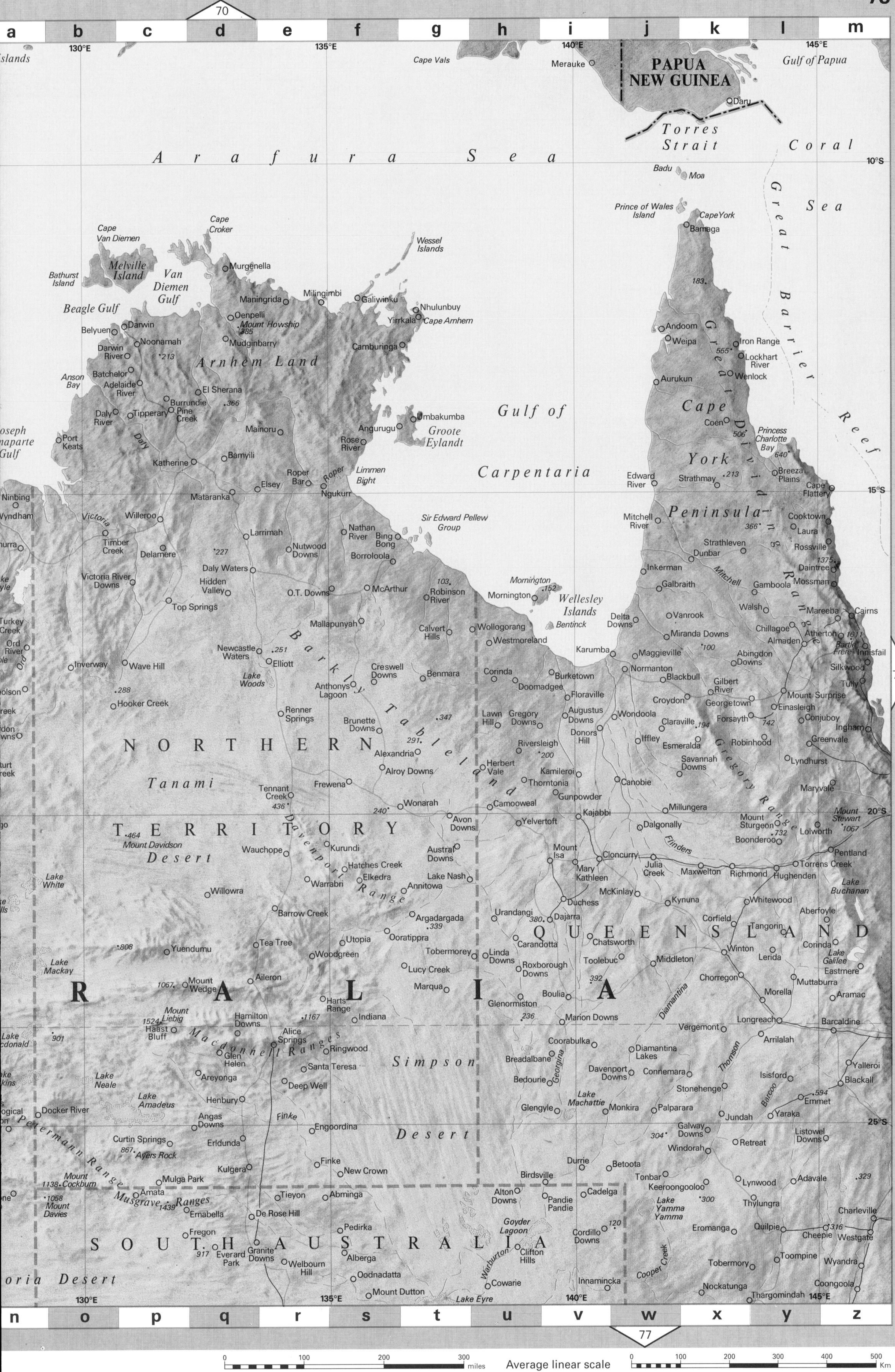
70
a b c d e f g h i j k l m
130°E
135°E
140°E
145°E
Islands
Cape Vals
Merauke
PAPUA NEW GUINEA
Gulf of Papua
Daru
Torres Strait
Coral Sea
10°S
Arafura Sea
Badu
Moa
Prince of Wales Island
Cape York
Bamaga
Cape Van Diemen
Cape Croker
Wessel Islands
Bathurst Island
Melville Island
Van Diemen Gulf
Murgenella
Beagle Gulf
Maningrida
Milingimbi
Galiwinku
Nhulunbuy
Yirrkala
Cape Arnhem
Oenpelli
Mount Howship
385
Belyuen
Darwin
Noonamah
Mudginbarry
Camburinga
Darwin River
213
Arnhem Land
Anson Bay
Batchelor
Adelaide River
El Sherana
Burrundie
366
Daly River
Tipperary
Pine Creek
Umbakumba
Joseph Bonaparte Gulf
Port Keats
Daly
Mainoru
Angurugu
Groote Eylandt
Rose River
Gulf of Carpentaria
Katherine
Bamyili
Limmen Bight
Roper Bar
Roper
Elsey
Ngukurr
Mataranka
Ninbing
Wyndham
Victoria
Willeroo
Timber Creek
Delamere
Larrimah
Nutwood Downs
Nathan River
Bing Bong
Borroloola
Sir Edward Pellew Group
227
Daly Waters
Victoria River Downs
Hidden Valley
O.T. Downs
McArthur
103
Robinson River
Mornington
152
Wellesley Islands
Bentinck
Top Springs
Mallapunyah
Calvert Hills
Wollogorang
Westmoreland
Turkey Creek
Ord River
Ord
Newcastle Waters
251
Elliott
Barkly Tableland
Inverway
Wave Hill
Lake Woods
Creswell Downs
Benmara
Anthony's Lagoon
Corinda
Burketown
Doomadgee
Floraville
288
Hooker Creek
Renner Springs
Brunette Downs
347
291
Alexandria
Lawn Hill
Gregory Downs
Augustus Downs
Donors Hill
Riversleigh
200
NORTHERN TERRITORY
Tanami
Alroy Downs
Herbert Vale
Kamileroi
Thorntonia
Frewena
Tennant Creek
436
Gunpowder
240
Wonarah
Camooweal
Avon Downs
Yelvertoft
Kajabbi
464
Mount Davidson Desert
Davenport Range
Kurundi
Wauchope
Hatches Creek
Elkedra
Warrabri
Austral Downs
Lake Nash
Annitowa
Mount Isa
Mary Kathleen
Cloncurry
Lake White
Willowra
Barrow Creek
Argadargada
339
Urandangi
380
Dajarra
Duchess
Tea Tree
Utopia
Ooratippra
Tobermorey
Linda Downs
Carandotta
Chatsworth
808
Yuendumu
Woodgreen
Lucy Creek
Roxborough Downs
Lake Mackay
1067
Mount Wedge
Aileron
Marqua
RALIA
Boulia
Harts Range
1167
Indiana
Glenormiston
236
Marion Downs
Mount Liebig
1524
Haast Bluff
Hamilton Downs
Alice Springs
Macdonnell Ranges
Ringwood
901
Lake Macdonald
Glen Helen
Santa Teresa
Simpson Desert
Areyonga
Deep Well
Lake Neale
Henbury
Lake Amadeus
Docker River
Petermann Range
Angas Downs
Finke
Engoordina
Curtin Springs
867
Ayers Rock
Erldunda
Kulgera
Finke
New Crown
Mount Cockburn
1138
Mulga Park
Amata
Musgrave Ranges
1439
1058
Mount Davies
Tieyon
Abminga
Ernabella
De Rose Hill
Fregon
SOUTH AUSTRALIA
917
Everard Park
Granite Downs
Welbourn Hill
Pedirka
Alberga
Oodnadatta
Mount Dutton
Lake Eyre
Victoria Desert
Birdsville
Alton Downs
Pandie Pandie
Cadelga
Goyder Lagoon
Cordillo Downs
120
Clifton Hills
Warburton
Cowarie
Innamincka
Durrie
Betootta
Andoom
Weipa
Iron Range
555
Lockhart River
Wenlock
Aurukun
Great Dividing Range
Great Barrier Reef
Cape York Peninsula
Coen
506
Princess Charlotte Bay
640
183
Edward River
Strathmay
213
Breeza Plains
Cape Flattery
15°S
Mitchell River
366
Cooktown
Laura
Strathleven
Dunbar
Rossville
1375
Daintree
Inkerman
Mitchell
Galbraith
Gamboola
Mossman
Walsh
Mareeba
Cairns
Delta Downs
Vanrook
Chillagoe
Atherton
Almaden
Bartle Frere
1611
Innisfail
Miranda Downs
Karumba
Maggieville
100
Abingdon Downs
Silkwood
Normanton
Blackbull
Tully
74
Gilbert River
Croydon
Georgetown
Mount Surprise
Einasleigh
Wondoola
Claraville
194
Forsayth
742
Conjuboy
Iffley
Esmeralda
Robinhood
Ingham
Greenvale
Savannah Downs
Gregory Range
Lyndhurst
Canobie
Maryvale
Millungera
Mount Sturgeon
Mount Stewart
1067
20°S
Dalgonally
732
Boonderoo
Lolworth
Flinders
Pentland
Julia Creek
Maxwelton
Richmond
Hughenden
Torrens Creek
McKinlay
Lake Buchanan
Kynuna
Whitewood
Corfield
Aberfoyle
Tangorin
QUEENSLAND
Winton
Lerida
Corinda
Lake Galilee
Toolebuc
392
Middleton
Chorregon
Eastmere
Muttaburra
Diamantina
Morella
Aramac
Longreach
Barcaldine
Vergemont
Arrilalah
Coorabulka
Breadalbane
Georgina
Diamantina Lakes
Thomson
Yalleroi
Bedourie
Davenport Downs
Connemara
Isisford
Blackall
Stonehenge
Barcoo
594
Emmet
Glengyle
Lake Machattie
Monkira
Palparara
Jundah
Yaraka
25°S
304
Galway Downs
Windorah
Retreat
Listowel Downs
Tonbar
Keeroongooloo
Lynwood
Adavale
329
Lake Yamma Yamma
300
Thylungra
Charleville
Eromanga
Quilpie
316
Cheepie
Westgate
Cooper Creek
Toompine
Tobermory
Wyandra
Nockatunga
Coongoola
Thargomindah
145°E
n o p q r s t u v w x y z
77
0 100 200 300 miles
Average linear scale
0 100 200 300 400 500 Km

145°E 150°E 155°E 160°E

PAPUA
NEW GUINEA
**Port
Moresby**
Owen
Stanley
Range
Mount
Suckling 3676
3129
1925
Kwikila
Robinson
River
Baniara
D'Entrecasteaux
Islands
Normanby
Alotau
Louisiade Archipelago
Honia
Guadalca
4233
SOLOMON
ISLAN

10°S

M
e
l
a

SOLOMON

SEA

*Cape
York*

G
r
e
a
t

183

Cape

York

Peninsula

Iron
Range
Lockhart
River
Wenlock
Coen
506
Princess
Charlotte
640
Breeza
Plains
Cape
Flattery
Cooktown
Rossville
Daintree
Laura
Strathleven
366
1375
Gamboola
Mossman
Walsh
Mareeba
Cairns
Chillagoe
Atherton
Bartle
Frere
1611
Innisfail
Silkwood
Tully
Abingdon
Downs
Almaden
Gilbert
River
Georgetown
Mount
Surprise
Forsayth
742
Einasleigh
Esmeralda
Greenvale
Robinhood
Lyndhurst
Ingham
Townsville
Ayr
Mount Elliot
1234
Bowen

*G
r
e
g
o
r
y*

*R
a
n
g
e*

Mitchell

Gregory

Burdekin

PA

CORAL

Willis Islands

SEA

E A

Chesterfield
Islands
(France)

P
A

O

15°S

20°S

*B
a
r
r
i
e
r*

*R
e
e
f*

Mount
Sturgeon
Richmond
Lolworth
732
Mount
Stewart
1076
Charters
Towers
Torrens
Creek
Pentland
Hughenden
Whitewood
Aberfoyle
Tangorin
Winton
Chorregon
Muttaburra
Morella
Longreach
Arrilalah
Barcaldine
Alpha
Bogantungan
Lake
Buchanan
Mount
Coolon
Mount
Douglas
Lake
Galilee
Eastmere
Blair
Athol
Clermont
Peak
Downs
Capella
Emerald
Proserpine
Collinsville
Mount
Dalrymple
1260
Finch
Hatton
Mackay
Sarina
Nebo
Carmila
St. Lawrence
Marlborough
Yeppoon
Rockhampton
Mount Morgan
Cato

Suttor

*D
i
v
i
d
i
n
g*

Thomson

Fitzroy

QUEENSLAND

AUSTRALIA

Barcoo

Range

Yalleroi
Isisford
Stonehenge
594
Blackall
Emmet
Yaraka
Retreat
Windorah
Lynwood
Adavale
Augathella
329
Tambo
Consuelo Peak
1219
806
Theodore
Monto
Bundaberg
Hervey
Bay
Childers
Fraser
Island
Maryborough
Gayndah
Gympie
Gladstone
Wowan
Baralaba
Banana
Biloela
Miriam Vale
Duaringa
Springsure
Rolleston
Mundubbera
Wandoan
Murgon
Nambour
Maroochydore
Moreton
Island
Caboolture
Thargomindah
Tobermory
Thylungra
Quilpie
Eromanga
Cheepie
Charleville
Westgate
Morven
Mitchell
Roma
Miles
Chinchilla
Kingaroy
Yarraman
Dalby
Esk
Gatton
Ipswich
Brisbane
Gold Coast
Murwillumbah
Lismore
Casino
Stanthorpe
Warwick
Inglewood
Talwood
Goondiwindi
Nindigully
Thallon
Hebel
Dirranbandi
St. George
Bollon
Westmar
Moonie
Glenmorgan
Surat
Albany
Downs
Wyandra
Coongoola
Cunnamulla
Eulo
Bulloo
Downs
Toowoomba
Clifton

Warrego

Paroo

Bulloo

Chesterton Range

Carnarvon Range

25°S

145°E 150°E 155°E 160°E

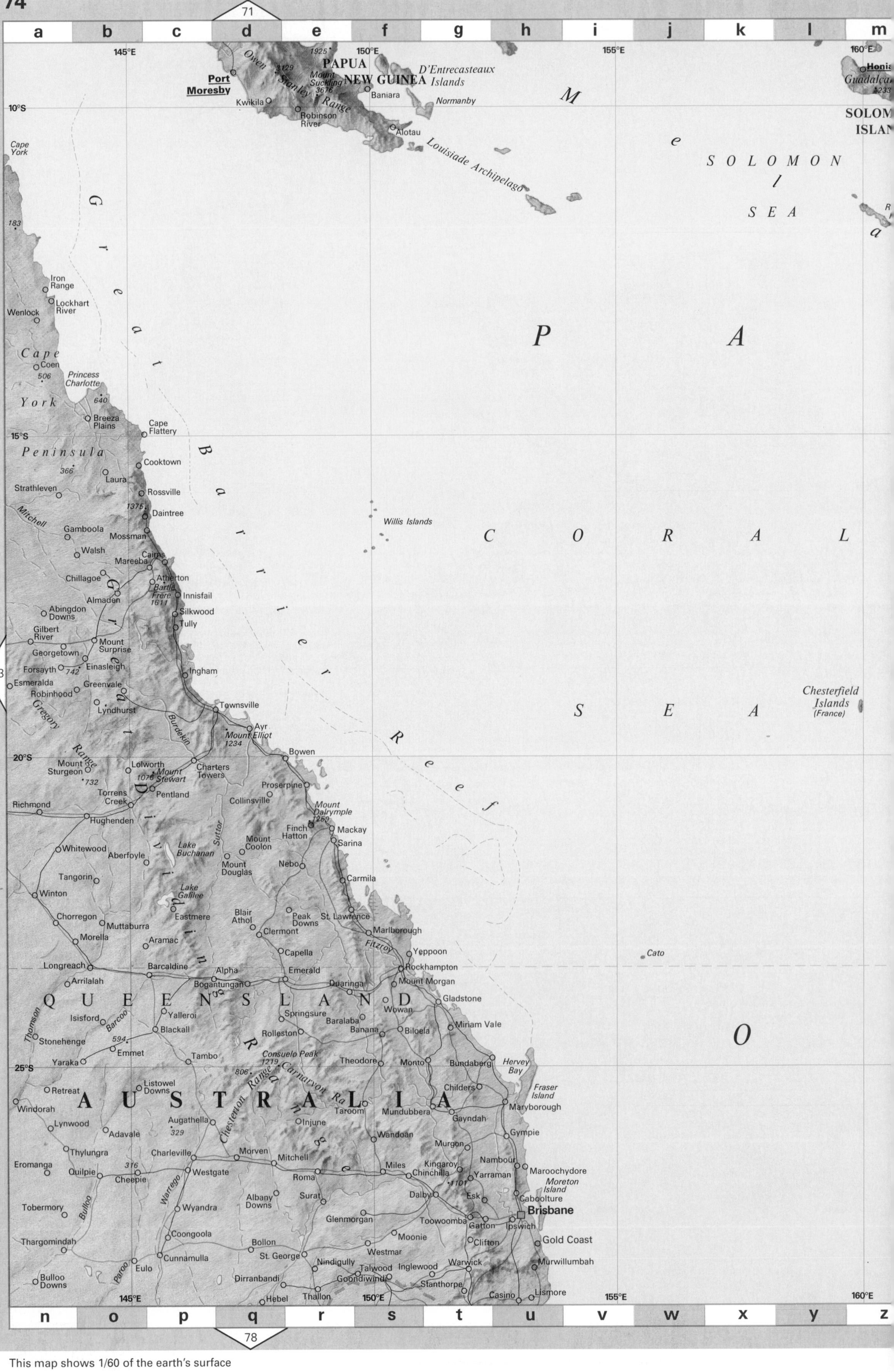

This map shows 1/60 of the earth's surface

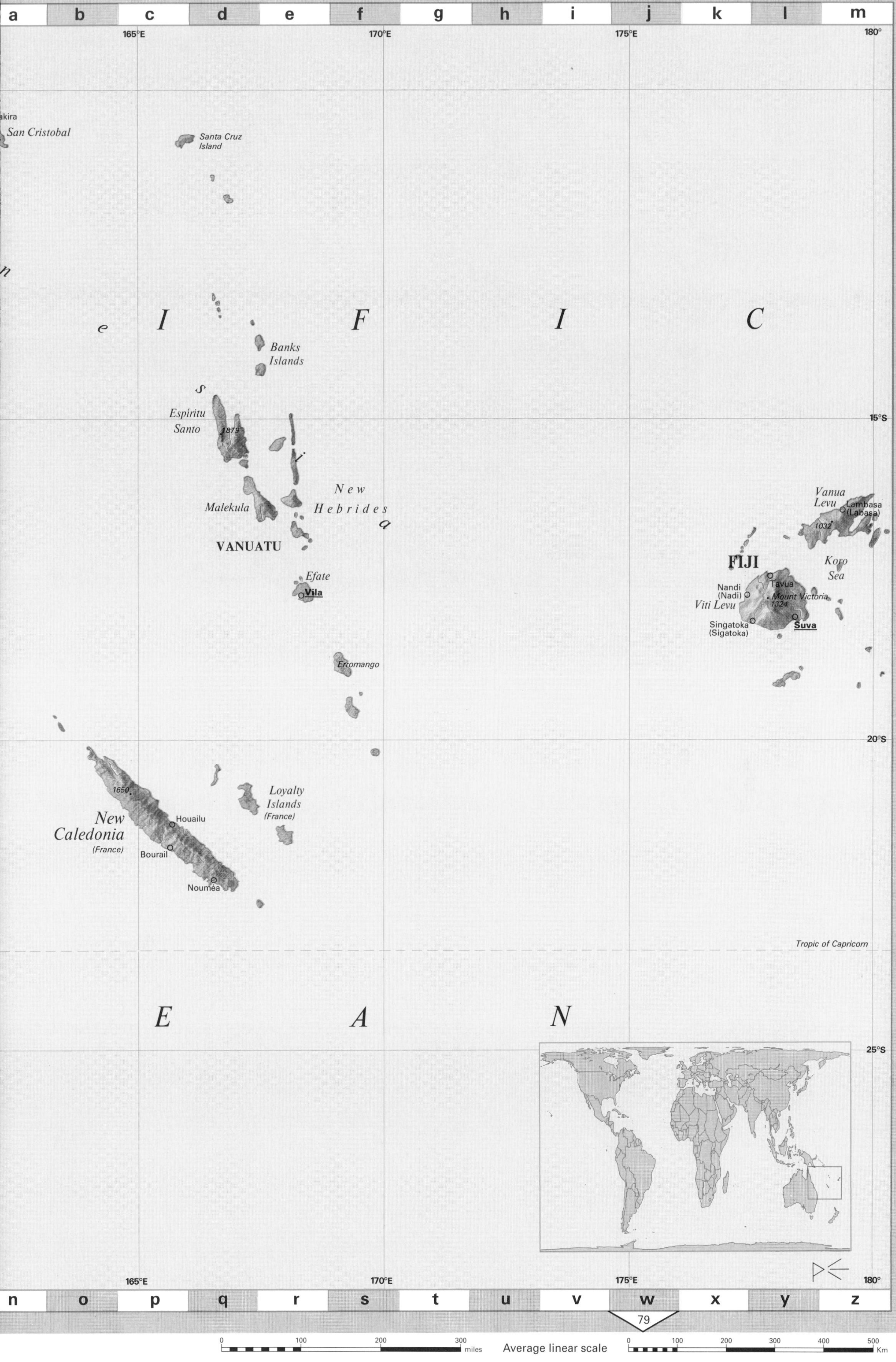
a b c d e f g h i j k l m
165°E
170°E
175°E
180°
15°S
20°S
25°S
San Cristobal
Santa Cruz Island
Banks Islands
Espíritu Santo
1879
Malekula
New Hebrides
VANUATU
Efate
Vila
Erromango
New Caledonia
(France)
1650
Houailu
Bourail
Noumea
Loyalty Islands
(France)
Vanua Levu
Lambasa (Labasa)
1032
FIJI
Koro Sea
Tavua
Nandi (Nadi)
Mount Victoria 1324
Viti Levu
Singatoka (Sigatoka)
Suva
Tropic of Capricorn
P A C I F I C
O C E A N
n o p q r s t u v w x y z
79
0 100 200 300 miles
Average linear scale
0 100 200 300 400 500 Km

72

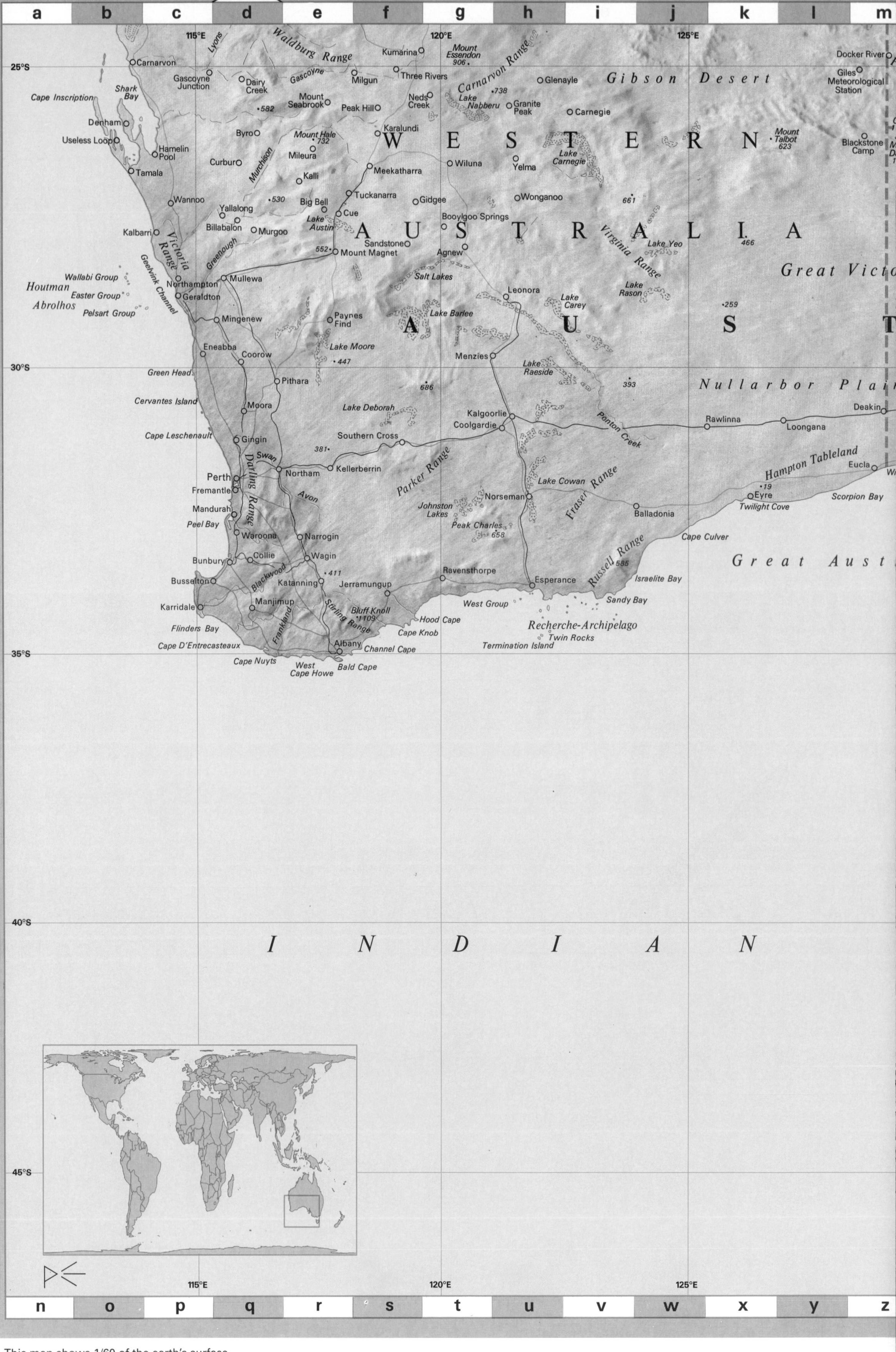
a
b
c
d
e
f
g
h
i
j
k
l
m
115°E
120°E
125°E
25°S
30°S
35°S
40°S
45°S
Carnarvon
Lyons
Waldburg Range
Kumarina
Mount Essendon 906
Carnarvon Range
Docker River
Giles Meteorological Station
Gascoyne Junction
Dairy Creek
Gascoyne
Milgun
Three Rivers
Glenayle
Gibson Desert
Cape Inscription
Shark Bay
Mount Seabrook
Neds Creek
Lake Nabberu
738
Granite Peak
Carnegie
Denham
582
Peak Hill
Useless Loop
Byro
Mount Hale 732
Karalundi
WESTERN
Mount Talbot 623
Blackstone Camp
Hamelin Pool
Murchison
Mileura
Curbur
Meekatharra
Wiluna
Yelma
Lake Carnegie
Tamala
Kalli
Wannoo
530
Big Bell
Tuckanarra
Gidgee
Wonganoo
661
Yallalong
Cue
Booylgoo Springs
Kalbarri
Billabalong
Murgoo
Lake Austin
AUSTRALIA
Victoria Range
Greenough
Sandstone
Virginia Range
Lake Yeo
466
552
Mount Magnet
Agnew
Geelvink Channel
Wallabi Group
Houtman Abrolhos
Easter Group
Pelsart Group
Northampton
Mullewa
Salt Lakes
Great Victo
Geraldton
Leonora
Lake Rason
Lake Carey
259
Mingenew
Paynes Find
Lake Barlee
AUST
Eneabba
Coorow
Lake Moore
447
Menzies
Green Head
Lake Raeside
Pithara
686
393
Nullarbor Plai
Cervantes Island
Moora
Lake Deborah
Kalgoorlie
Ponton Creek
Rawlinna
Deakin
Coolgardie
Loongana
Cape Leschenault
Gingin
Southern Cross
381
Swan
Darling Range
Hampton Tableland
Parker Range
Eucla
Perth
Northam
Kellerberrin
Fremantle
Lake Cowan
Fraser Range
Avon
Eyre
19
Scorpion Bay
Mandurah
Norseman
Twilight Cove
Peel Bay
Johnston Lakes
Balladonia
Peak Charles
658
Waroona
Narrogin
Cape Culver
Russell Range
Bunbury
Collie
Wagin
Great Aust
585
Blackwood
Busselton
Katanning
411
Ravensthorpe
Israelite Bay
Jerramungup
Esperance
Karridale
Manjimup
West Group
Sandy Bay
Bluff Knoll 1109
Stirling Range
Hood Cape
Flinders Bay
Frankland
Cape Knob
Recherche-Archipelago
Twin Rocks
Cape D'Entrecasteaux
Albany
Channel Cape
Termination Island
Cape Nuyts
West Cape Howe
Bald Cape
INDIAN
n
o
p
q
r
s
t
u
v
w
x
y
z

73
78
a b c d e f g h i j k l m
n o p q r s t u v w x y z
135°E
140°E
145°E
25°S
30°S
35°S
40°S
45°S
NORTHERN TERRITORY
QUEENSLAND
SOUTH AUSTRALIA
NEW SOUTH WALES
VICTORIA
AUST. CAPITAL TERRITORY
TASMANIA
OCEAN
Bight
Simpson Desert
Sturt Desert
Lake Amadeus
Henbury
Angas Downs
Erldunda
Finke
Engoordina
Kulgera
Mulga Park
Musgrave Ranges
Ernabella
Tieyon
Abminga
New Crown
Fregon
Everard Park
917
Granite Downs
Pedirka
Alberga
Welbourn Hill
Oodnadatta
Mount Dutton
181
Coober Pedy
216
Lake Maurice
205
Lake Eyre
-16
11
Cowarie
Cooper
Marree
91
951
Leigh Creek
Lake Frome
Lake Torrens
Woomera
Tarcoola
Kingoonya
1186
Lake Everard
Ooldea
Yalata
Head of Bight
Penong
168
Ceduna
Fowler's Bay
Nuyts Arch.
Streaky Bay
Gawler Ranges
Lake Gairdner
Island Lagoon
472
307
Iron Knob
Wudinna
Anxious Bay
250
Eyre Peninsula
Cowell
Whyalla
Investigator Group
Pearson Island
Whidby Point
Port Lincoln
Sir Joseph Banks Group
Thistle I.
Cape Spencer
Spencer Gulf
Wallaroo
Kadina
Yorke Peninsula
St. Vincent Gulf
Investigator Strait
Kangaroo Island
Quorn
Port Augusta
Port Pirie
Peterborough
Flinders Ranges
1189
Wilpena
Passmore
934
Burra
Morgan
Murray
Gawler
Adelaide
Murray Bridge
Victor Harbor
Encounter Bay
Lake Alexandra
The Coorong
Lacepede Bay
Naracoorte
Millicent
220
Mount Gambier
Discovery Bay
Glengyle
Lake Machattie
Monkira
Diamantina
Durrie
Betoota
Birdsville
Alton Downs
Pandie Pandie
Cadelga
Warburton
Goyder's Lagoon
Clifton Hills
Cordillo Downs
120
Innamincka
142
Gidgelpa
Eurinilla
Barrier Ra.
Mount Robe
474
Cockburn
Broken Hill
Benda Ra.
Renmark
Pinnaroo
Stonehenge
Palparara
Thomson
Jundah
Galway Downs
304
Windorah
Retreat
Tanbar
Keeroongooloo
300
Lake Yamma Yamma
Thylungra
Grey Range
Eromanga
Quilpie
Toompine
Bulloo
Nockatunga
Thargomindah
Paroo
Emmet
Blackall
725
Yaraka
Tambo
Chesterton Range
Listowel Downs
Adavale
Charleville
Moven
Mitchell
914
316
Cheepie
Westgate
Wyandra
Coongoola
Cunnamulla
Maranoa
251
St. George
Bollon
Dirranbandi
Hebel
Thallon
427
Milparinka
Wanaaring
Warrego
Bourke
Brewarrina
Walgett
White Cliffs
221
Wilcannia
Cobar
419
Crowl
Nyngan
Coonamble
1372
Narromine
Dubbo
Darling
Ivanhoe
Condobolin
Parkes
Forbes
Wentworth
Mildura
Balranald
Lachlan
Hay
Murrumbidgee
West Wyalong
732
Griffith
Leeton
Narrandera
Cocoparra Range
Cootamundra
Junee
Wagga Wagga
Billabong
101
Ouyen
Swan Hill
Lake Hindmarsh
Nhill
Loddon
Deniliquin
Corowa
Albury
Hume Res.
Lake Eucumbene
Mt. Kosciuszko
2228
Snowy
Donald
Shepparton
Wangaratta
Horsham
Glenelg
Maryborough
Bendigo
Seymour
Buller
1804
1922
1742
Omeo
Great Dividing Range
Mitchell
1320
Orbost
Ararat
1011
Hamilton
Emu
Ballarat
Healesville
Melbourne
Geelong
Port Philip Bay
Warrnambool
Portland
Cape Otway
Apollo Bay
Moe
Traralgon
Sale
Ninety Mile Beach
Wonthaggi
Port Albert
Waratah Bay
Wilson's Promontory
Kent Group
Bass Strait
Currie
King Island
Flinders I.
Furneaux Group
Banks Strait
Hunter Island
Three Hummock Island
Smithton
Arthur
Burnie
Sandy Cape
Devonport
Herrick
Mt. Ossa
1617
1573
St. Marys
Launceston
Coles Bay
Queenstown
Macquarie Harbour
Strahan
1444
Derwent
Oatlands
Swansea
Point Hibbs
Gordon
New Norfolk
1327
Hobart
Frankland Ra.
Elliot Bay
Storm Bay
Port Arthur
Port Davey
Maatsuyker Islands
South East Cape
0 100 200 300 miles
Average linear scale
0 100 200 300 400 500 Km

a b c d e f g h i j k l m

145°E   150°E   155°E   160°E

Bulloo
Adavale   Taroom   Mundubbera   Maryborough
                 Augathella   Gaynдah
                       914   Murgon   Gympie
316.   Charleville   Morven   Mitchell   Roma   Wandoan   Nambour
Quilpie Cheepie   Westgate   Miles   Kingaroy   Yarraman   Caboolture
Toompine   Wyandra   Dalby   Esk   Moreton
         Coongoola   251   Toowoomba   Island
Eulo Cunnamulla   St. George   Surat   Moonie   Brisbane
              Bollon   Glenmorgan   Clifton
         Dirranbandi   Talwood   Inglewood Warwick   Gold Coast
              Thallon   Goondiwindi   Stanthorpe   Murwillumbah
         Hebel   Mungindi   Casino   Lismore
                              Tenterfield
QUEENSLAND

Wanaaring   Brewarrina   Moree   Inverell   Grafton   Middleton Reef
30°S   Bourke   Walgett   Namoi   Glen   Elisabeth Reef
                        Narrabri   Innes
AUSTRALIA   Round
                  Coonamble   Armidale   1608   P   A
         Cobar   Gunnedah   Tamworth
NEW SOUTH WALES   1372 Coonabarabran   1494   Kempsey
                     Coolah   Port Macquarie
         Narromine Dubbo   Mudgee   Taree   Lord Howe
Ivanhoe   Wellington   Macquarie Barrington Muswellbrook   Island
                           1585 Tops   (N.S.W.)
         Forbes Orange Coricudgy
                     1274
              Parkes   Newcastle
Hay Griffith West Wyalong Bathurst Lithgow Gosford
         Cowra 732 Katoomba Sydney
Leeton   1298 Wollongong
Narrandera Cootamundra
35°S   Junee   Goulburn Nowra
Deniliquin   Canberra
              Queanbeyan   O
         Corowa   AUST. CAPITAL
                     TERRITORY
Shepparton Albury Hume Lake
         Wangaratta Reservoir Eucumbene
Bendigo   Mt. Cooma
Seymour Buller Kosciuszko
         1804 2228 Snowy
VICTORIA Omeo 1320
Healesville Orbost
Melbourne   Cape Howe
Geelong Moe Sale
Port Philip Traralgon Ninety Mile Beach
Bay
Wonthaggi Port Albert
Waratah Bay Wilsons Promontory

Bass Strait   Kent Group

King Island   Flinders Island
40°S   Furneaux   T A S M A N
Hunter Three Hummock Group
Island Island   Banks Strait
Smithton   Herrick
         Burnie
Arthur Devonport Launceston
         Ossa 1573 St. Marys
         1617
Strahan Queenstown   Coles Bay
Macquarie   Oaklands Swansea
Harbour 1444 Derwent New
                  Norfolk TASMANIA
Elliot Bay Frankland Range Hobart
Port Davey Storm Bay Port Arthur
Maatsuyker South East
Islands   Cape

45°S

145°E   150°E   155°E   160°E

n o p q r s t u v w x y z

This map shows 1/60 of the earth's surface

75
a b c d e f g h i j k l m
165°E
170°E
175°E
180°E
Norfolk Island (Australia)
30°S
Macauley Island
Kermadec Islands (N.Z.)
Curtis Island
C I F I C
E A N
A
Three Kings Island
North Cape
Ninety Mile Beach
35°S
Kaitaia
Bay of Islands
774
Whangarei
Dargaville
Great Barrier Island
Hauraki Gulf
Auckland
Waikato
Bay of Plenty
Te Araroa
East Cape
Tauranga
Hamilton
NORTH ISLAND
Whakatane
1478
Tokoroa
Rotorua
Taupo
Taumarunui
Gisborne
New Plymouth
Lake Taupo
Wairoa
Egmont 2518
Wanganui
Ngauruhoe 2291
Ruapehu 2797
Hawke Bay
Napier
Hastings
Hawera
Ruahine Range
NEW ZEALAND
Wanganui
40°S
Palmerston North
Paraparaumu
Tararua Range
1571
Masterton
Collingwood
Tasman Bay
Cook Strait
Picton
Lower Hutt
Wellington
Karamea Bight
Nelson
Blenheim
Cape Palliser
Richmond Range
Westport
Travers 2337
Greymouth
Kaikoura
Hokitika
Arthurs Pass
SOUTH ISLAND
Southern Alps
Waipara
Mt. Cook (Aoraki) 3764
Arrowsmith 2795
Canterbury Plains
Christchurch
Haast
Lake Pukaki
Ashburton
Banks Peninsula
Canterbury Bight
Twizel
Timaru
Aspiring 3027
Waitaki
Milford Sound
Queenstown
45°S
Lake Wakatipu
Oamaru
Alexandra
Te Anau
2035 Jane Peak
Clutha
Lumsden
West Cape
Dunedin
Gore
Invercargill
Foveaux Strait
Stewart Island
Southwest Cape
Bounty Islands (N.Z.)
Snares Islands
n o p q r s t u v w x y z
0 100 200 300 miles
Average linear scale
0 100 200 300 400 500 Km

West of Greenwich

60°S

65°S

Antarctic Circle

70°S

80°W

85°W

90°W

95°W

100°W

105°W

110°W

115°W

55°S

120°W

60°S

125°W

130°W

B E L L I N G S H A U S E N

S E A

Smyley Island

Eltanin Bay

Farewell Island

Abbott

Thurston Island

Peter Island

S O U T H E R N   O C E A N

P A C I F I C

O C E A N

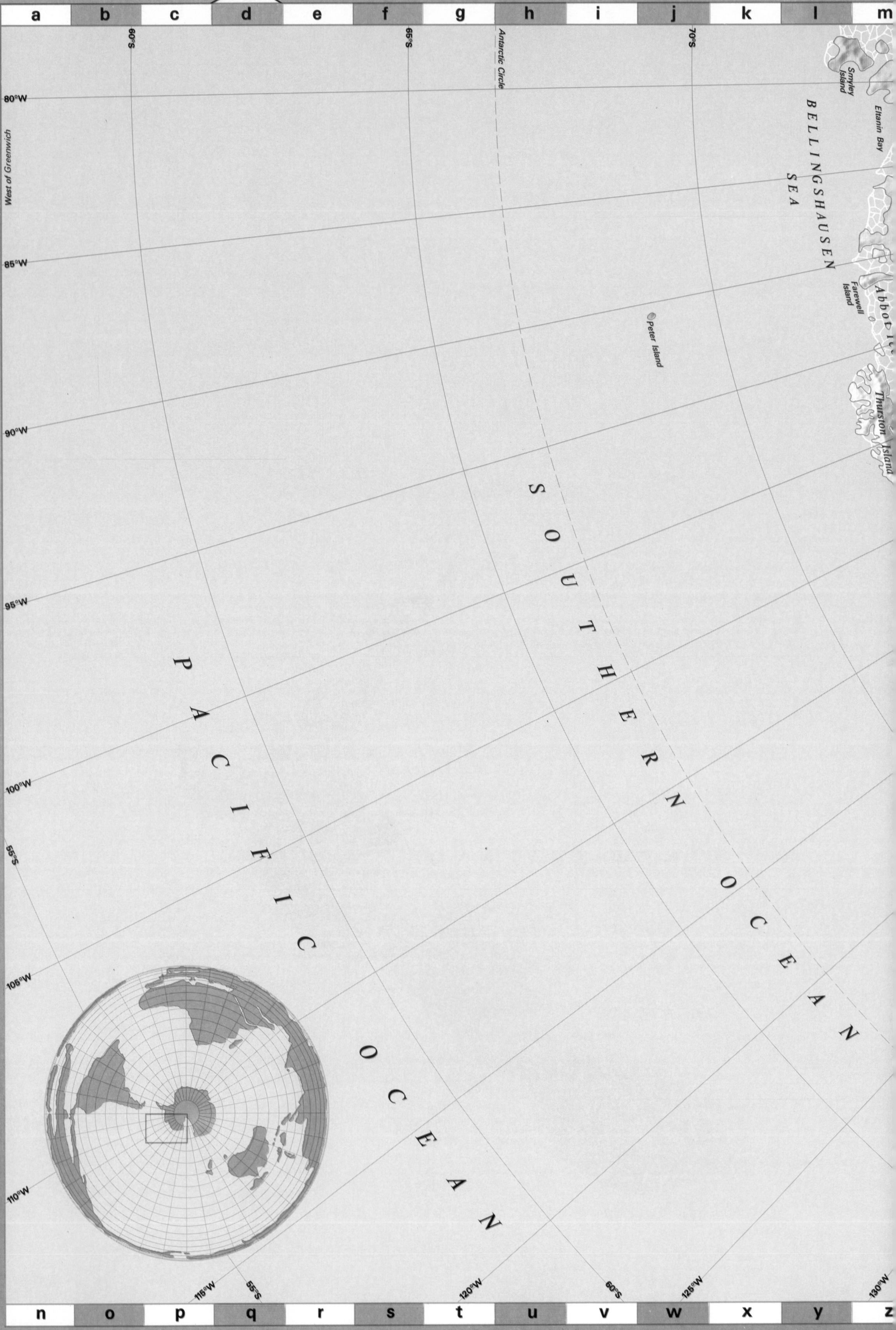

This map shows 1/60 of the earth's surface

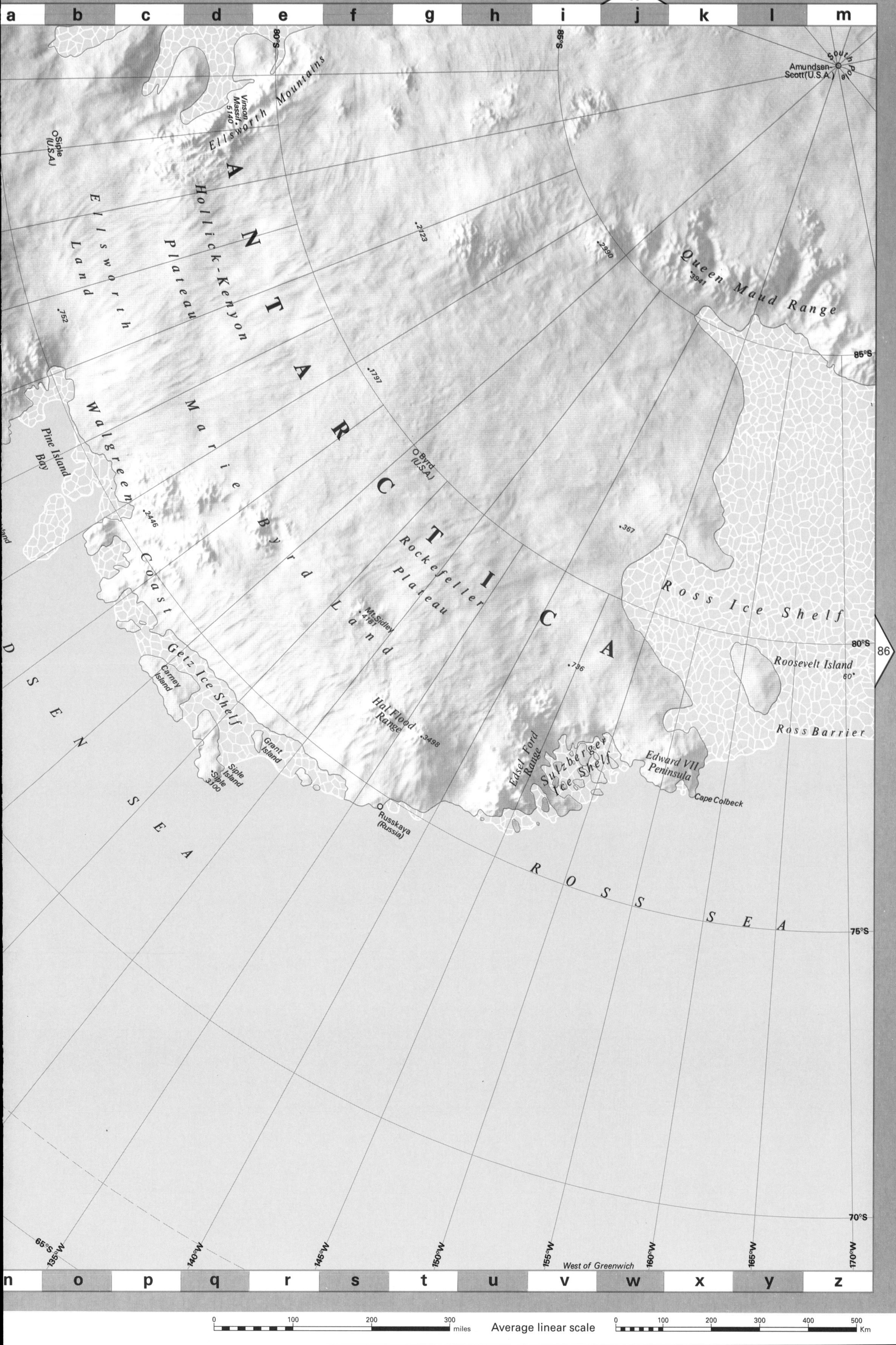
83
86
ANTARCTICA
Ellsworth Mountains
Vinson Massif 5140
Siple (U.S.A.)
Hollick-Kenyon Plateau
Ellsworth Land
Marie Byrd Land
Walgreen Coast
Pine Island Bay
Getz Ice Shelf
Carney Island
Siple Island
Siple 3100
Grant Island
Rockefeller Plateau
Mt. Sidley 4181
Byrd (U.S.A.)
Hal Flood Range
3498
Edsel Ford Range
Sulzberger Ice Shelf
Edward VII Peninsula
Cape Colbeck
Russkaya (Russia)
Queen Maud Range
3941
2990
2123
1797
752
2446
367
736
Ross Ice Shelf
Roosevelt Island
60
Ross Barrier
ROSS SEA
DSEN SEA
Amundsen-Scott (U.S.A.)
South Pole
85°S
80°S
75°S
70°S
65°S
135°W
140°W
145°W
150°W
155°W
160°W
165°W
170°W
West of Greenwich
a b c d e f g h i j k l m
n o p q r s t u v w x y z
0 100 200 300 miles
Average linear scale
0 100 200 300 400 500 Km

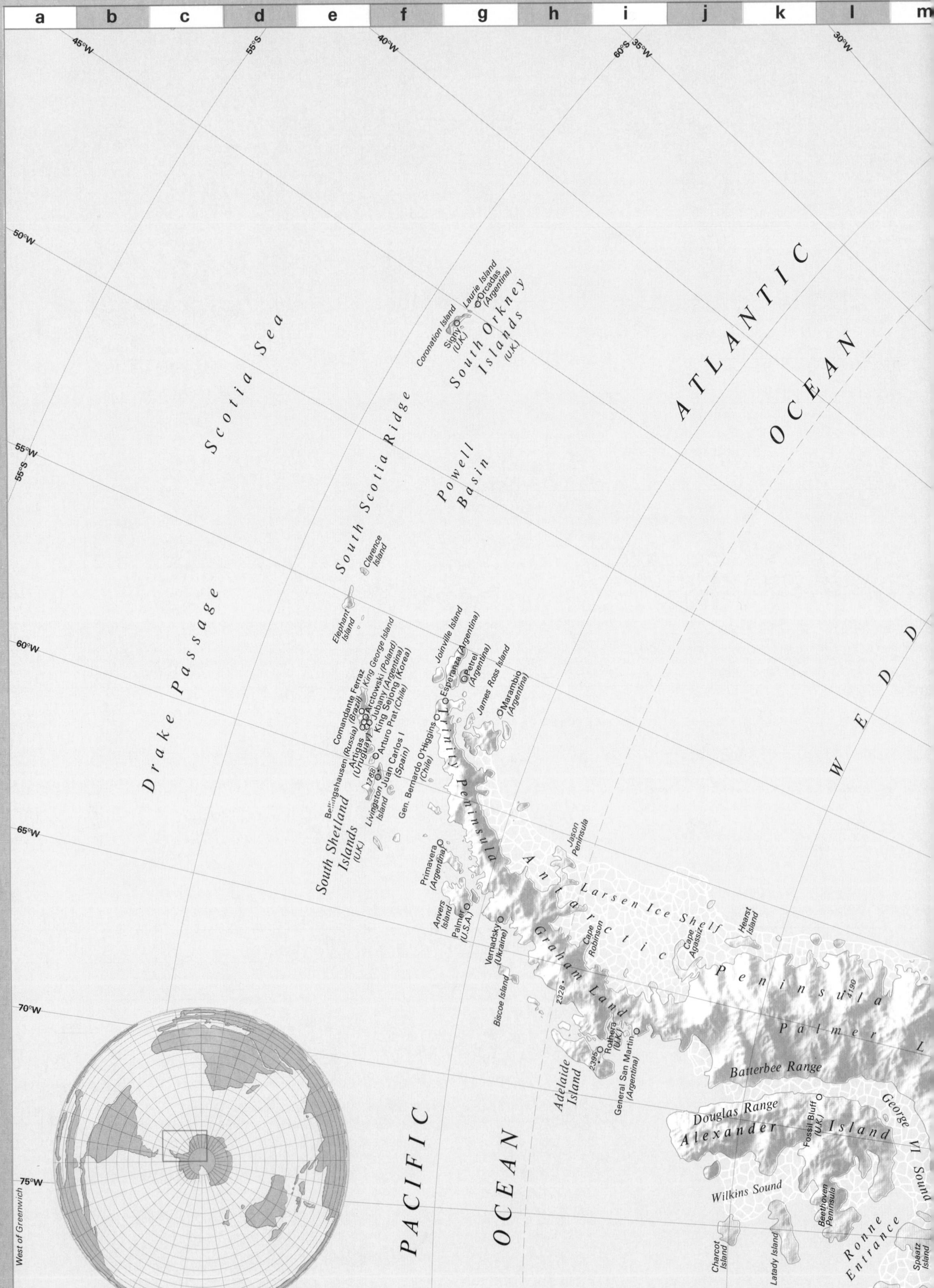
Scotia Sea
Drake Passage
South Scotia Ridge
Powell Basin
ATLANTIC OCEAN
PACIFIC OCEAN
South Orkney Islands (U.K.)
Coronation Island
Laurie Island
Orcadas (Argentina)
Signy (U.K.)
Clarence Island
Elephant Island
King George Island
Comandante Ferraz (Brazil)
Bellingshausen (Russia)
Artigas (Uruguay)
Arctowski (Poland)
Jubany (Argentina)
King Sejong (Korea)
Arturo Prat (Chile)
Juan Carlos I (Spain)
Livingston Island
Gen. Bernardo O'Higgins (Chile)
South Shetland Islands (U.K.)
Joinville Island
Esperanza (Argentina)
Petrel (Argentina)
James Ross Island
Marambio (Argentina)
Trinity Peninsula
Jason Peninsula
Primavera (Argentina)
Anvers Island
Palmer (U.S.A.)
Vernadsky (Ukraine)
Biscoe Islands
Antarctic Peninsula
Larsen Ice Shelf
Cape Robinson
Cape Agassiz
Hearst Island
Graham Land
Palmer Land
Rothera (U.K.)
General San Martin (Argentina)
Adelaide Island
Batterbee Range
Douglas Range
Alexander Island
Fossil Bluff (U.K.)
George VI Sound
Wilkins Sound
Charcot Island
Latady Island
Beethoven Peninsula
Ronne Entrance
Spaatz Island
Smyley Island
W E D D
West of Greenwich
80

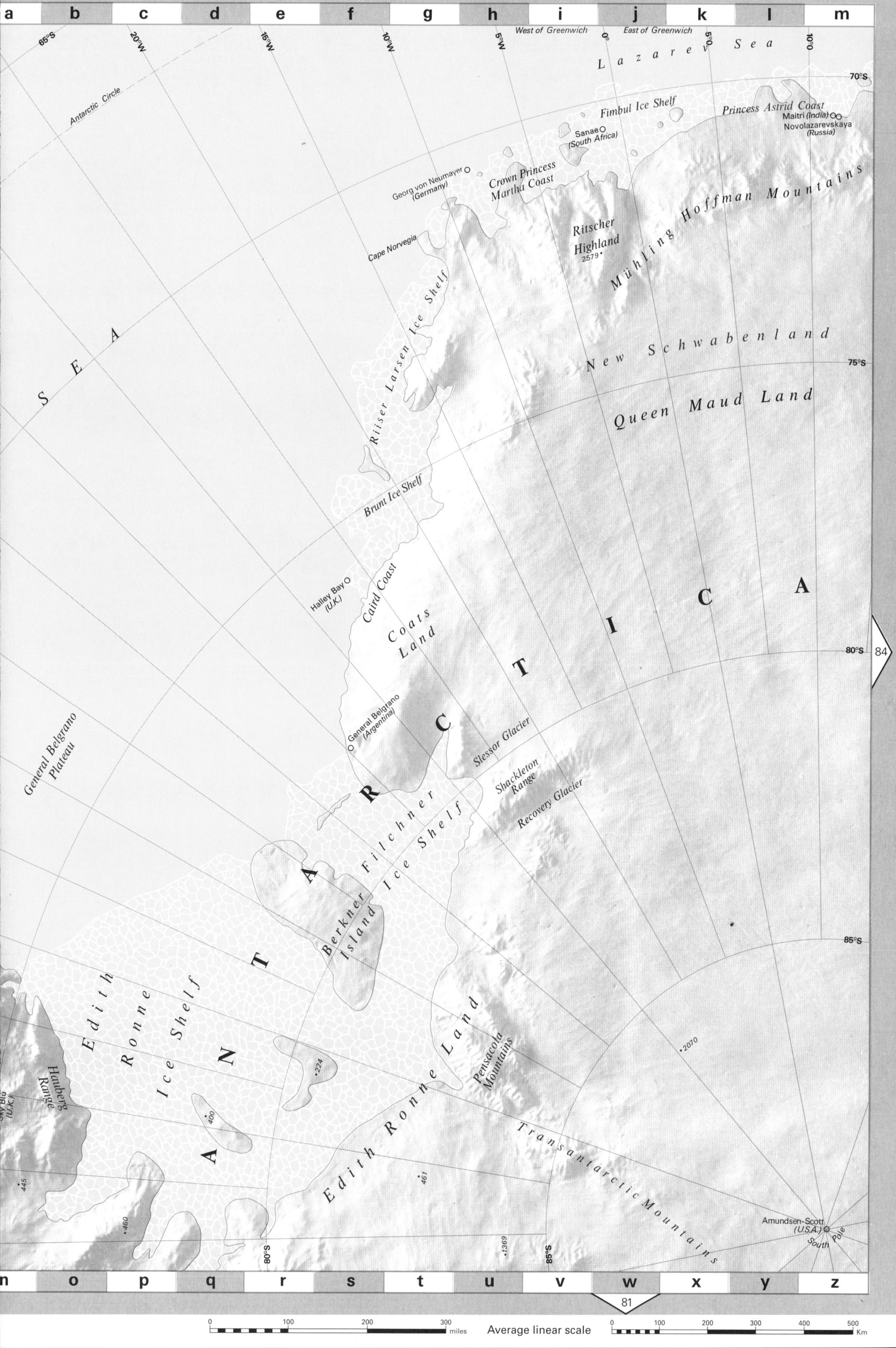
a
b
c
d
e
f
g
h
i
j
k
l
m
West of Greenwich
East of Greenwich
65°S
20°W
15°W
10°W
5°W
0°
5°E
10°E
70°S
75°S
80°S
85°S
Antarctic Circle
Lazarev Sea
Fimbul Ice Shelf
Princess Astrid Coast
Maitri (India)
Novolazarevskaya
(Russia)
Sanae
(South Africa)
Georg von Neumayer
(Germany)
Crown Princess
Martha Coast
Ritscher
Highland
2579
Mühling Hoffman Mountains
Cape Norvegia
Riiser Larsen Ice Shelf
New Schwabenland
Queen Maud Land
SEA
Brunt Ice Shelf
Halley Bay
(U.K.)
Caird Coast
Coats
Land
ANTARCTICA
General Belgrano
(Argentina)
Slessor Glacier
Shackleton
Range
Recovery Glacier
General Belgrano
Plateau
Filchner Ice Shelf
Berkner
Island
Edith
Ronne
Ice Shelf
Hauberg
Range
Sky Blu
(U.K.)
224
400
445
460
461
1369
2070
Edith Ronne Land
Pensacola
Mountains
Transantarctic Mountains
Amundsen-Scott
(U.S.A.)
South Pole
80°S
85°S
84
n
o
p
q
r
s
t
u
v
w
x
y
z
81
0
100
200
300
miles
Average linear scale
0
100
200
300
400
500
Km

Lazarev Sea

East of Greenwich

70°S

Princess Astrid Coast

Riiser Larsen Sea

Maitri
(India)

Novolazarevskaya
(Russia)

Princess Ragnhild Coast

Asuka
(Japan)

Princess Ragnhild
Land

*Riiser Larsen
Peninsula*

Lützow Holm
Bight

Prince Harald
Coast

Cosmonaut
Sea

Antarctic Circle

Syowa
(Japan)

Crown Prince Olaf Coast

Molodezhnaya
(Russia)

Casey Bay

Amundsen
Bay

Christensen
Mountains

Enderby L

•2470

•2588

•2900

75°S

Queen Maud Land

•3602

A

N

T

A

R

Dome Fuji
(Japan)

•3365

80°S

83

Lambert Glacier

C

T

85°S

I

•3732

•3106

C

Sovetskaya
(Russia)

A

South Pole

Amundsen-Scott
(U.S.A.)

85°S

80°S

This map shows 1/60 of the earth's surface

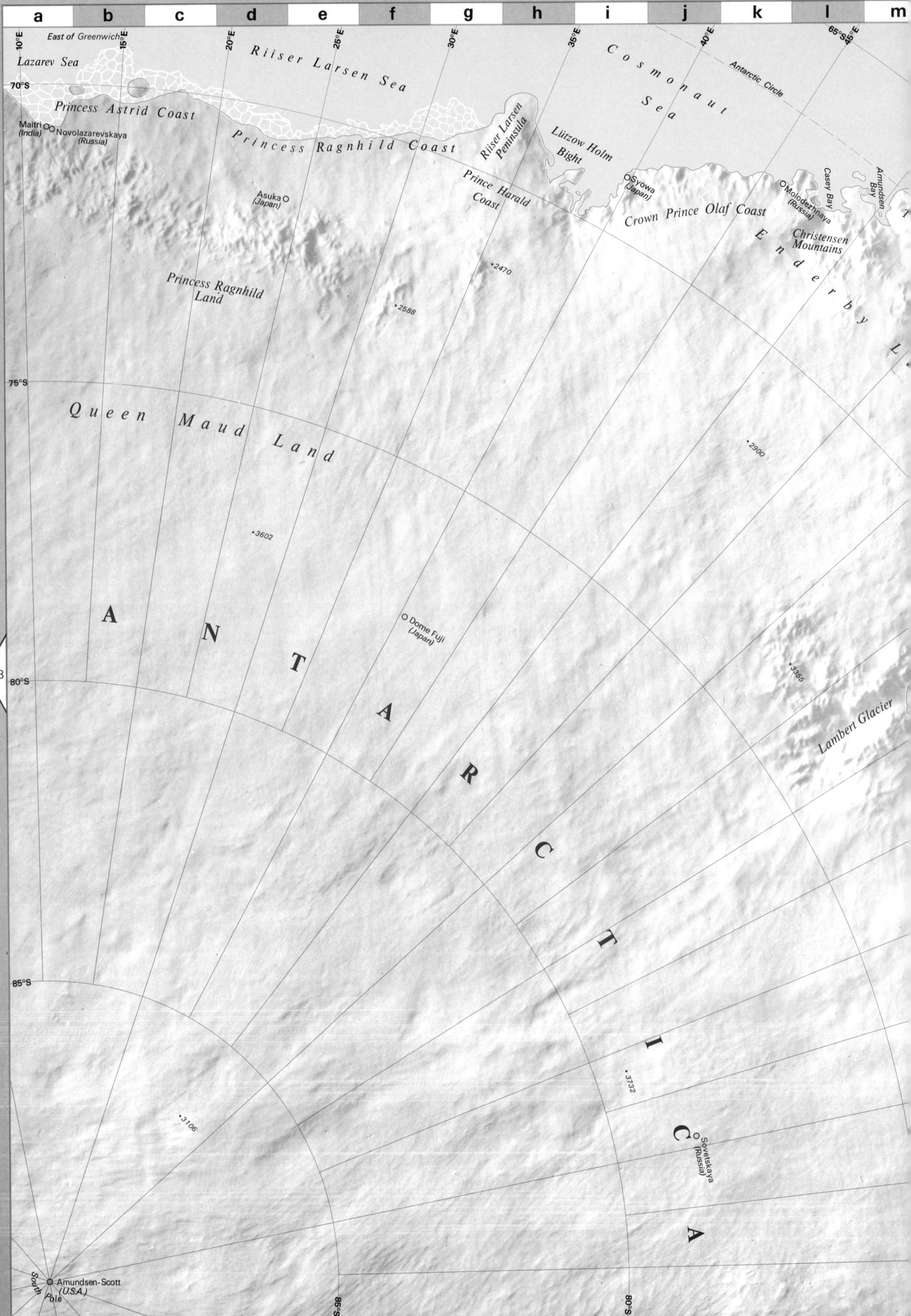

a b c d e f g h i j k l m
INDIAN OCEAN
Cooperation Sea
Amery Basin
Davis Sea
Cape Boothby
Mac Robertson Land
Mawson (Australia)
Cape Darnley
Mackenzie Bay
Amery Ice Shelf
Zhongshan (China)
Ingrid Christensen Coast
Davis (Australia)
Princess Elizabeth Land
West Ice Shelf
King Leopold and Queen Astrid Coast
King Wilhelm II Land
Mirny (Russia)
Drygalski Island
Shackleton Ice Shelf
Queen Mary Land
Denman Glacier
Pionerskaya (Russia)
Vostok 1 (Russia)
2070
2992
1380
East of Greenwich
50°E
55°E
60°E
65°E
70°E
75°E
80°E
85°E
90°E
95°E
100°E
55°S
60°S
65°S
70°S
n o p q r s t u v w x y z
87

Average linear scale 0 100 200 300 miles; 0 100 200 300 400 500 Km

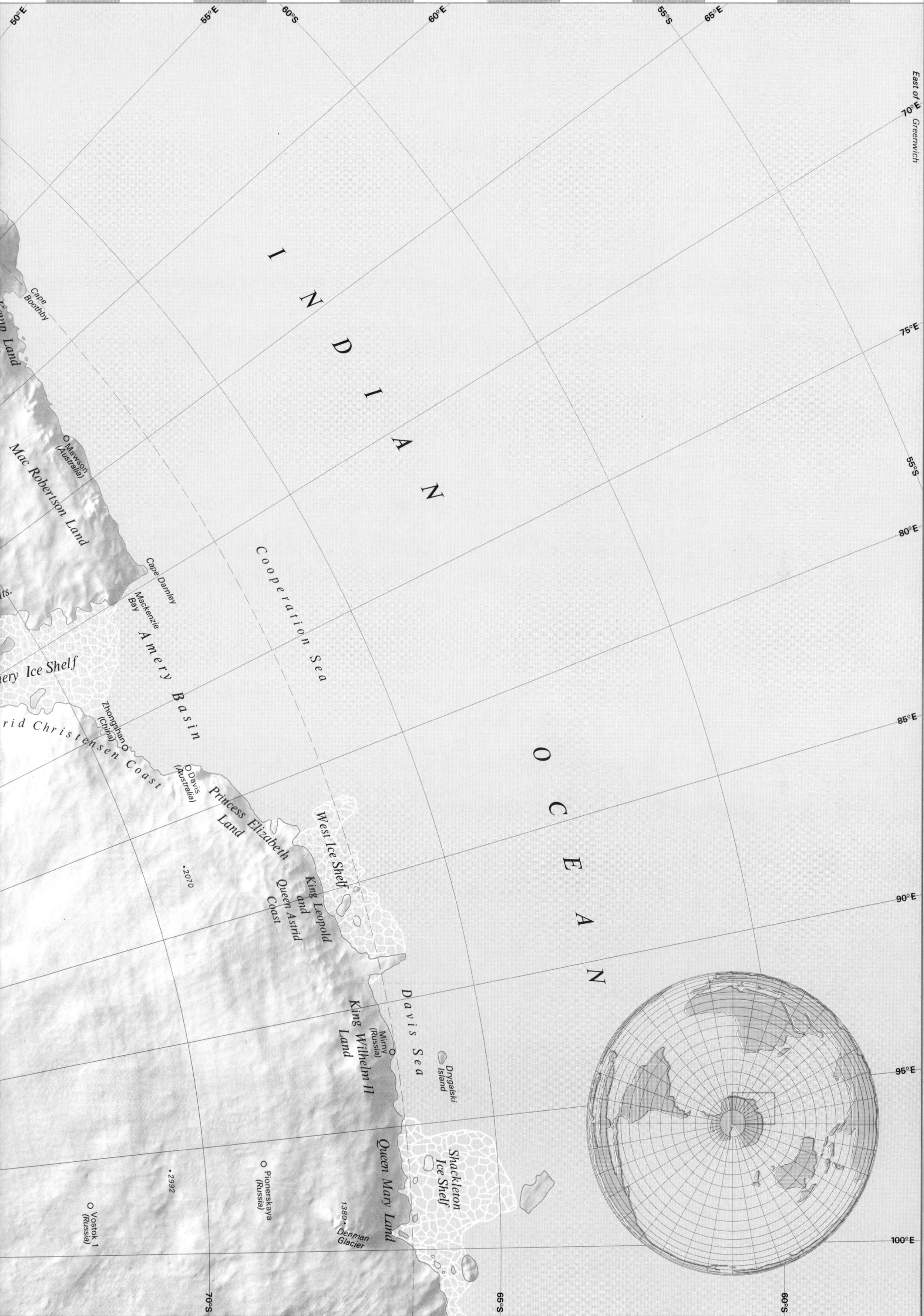

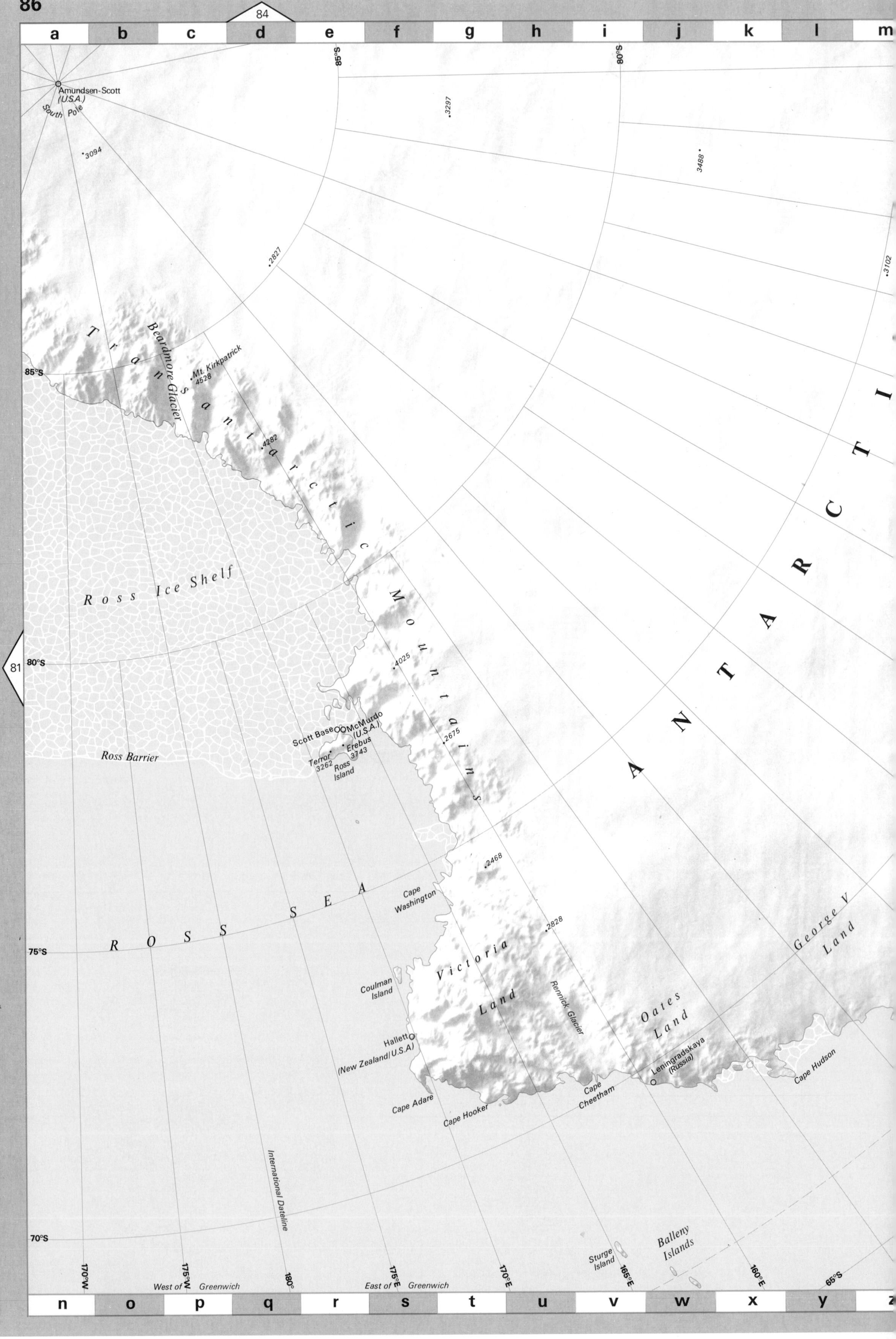
84
a
b
c
d
e
f
g
h
i
j
k
l
m
Amundsen-Scott
(U.S.A.)
South Pole
3094
3297
3488
3102
2827
85°S
80°S
T r a n s a n t a r c t i c M o u n t a i n s
Beardmore Glacier
Mt. Kirkpatrick
4528
4282
Ross Ice Shelf
81
4025
Scott Base
McMurdo
(U.S.A.)
Erebus
3743
Terror
3262
Ross
Island
2675
Ross Barrier
A N T A R C T I C A
2468
Cape
Washington
R O S S S E A
2828
75°S
Victoria
Land
Coulman
Island
Rennick Glacier
Oates
Land
George V
Land
Hallett
(New Zealand/U.S.A)
Leningradskaya
(Russia)
Cape Hudson
Cape Adare
Cape Hooker
Cape
Cheetham
International Dateline
70°S
Sturge
Island
Balleny
Islands
170°W
175°W
180°
175°E
170°E
165°E
160°E
65°S
West of Greenwich
East of Greenwich
n
o
p
q
r
s
t
u
v
w
x
y
z

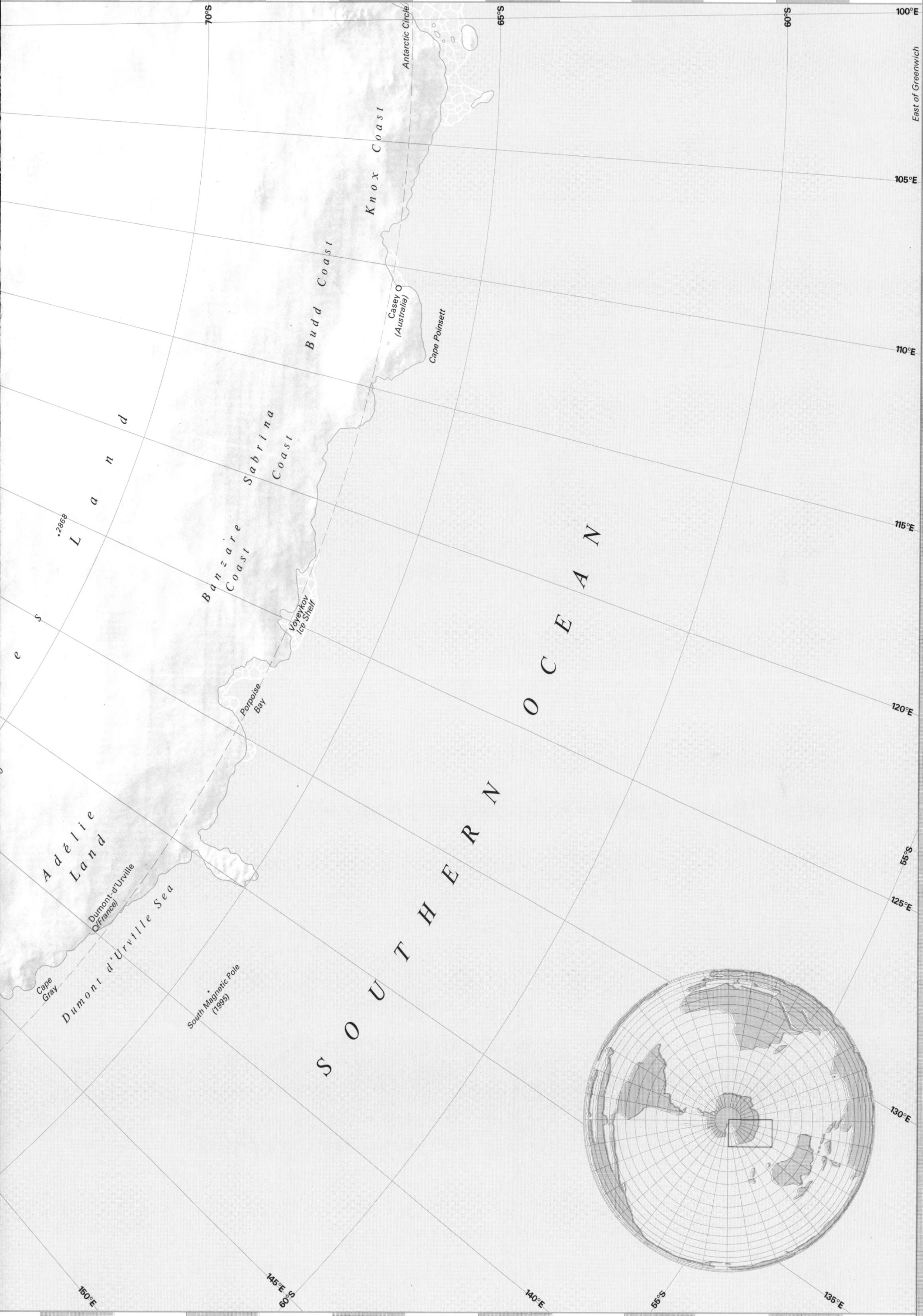
85
a
b
c
d
e
f
g
h
i
j
k
l
m
70°S
65°S
60°S
55°S
100°E
105°E
110°E
115°E
120°E
125°E
130°E
135°E
140°E
145°E
150°E
East of Greenwich
Antarctic Circle
Knox Coast
Budd Coast
Casey (Australia)
Cape Poinsett
Sabrina Coast
Banzare Coast
Voyeykov Ice Shelf
Porpoise Bay
2868
Land
Adélie Land
Dumont-d'Urville (France)
Dumont d'Urville Sea
Cape Gray
South Magnetic Pole (1995)
SOUTHERN OCEAN
n
o
p
q
r
s
t
u
v
w
x
y
z

a   b   c   d   e   f   g   h   i   j   k   l   m

Mackenzie Mou

Keele Peak
2975

Hanna ○
914

Wetaskiwin ○
Wainwright ○
Barrhead ○
115°W
55°N
Peace River ○
Manning ○
120°W
Fort Liard ○
60°N
125°W
130°W

Lloydminster ○
Vegreville ○
Leduc ○
Edmonton ○
Westlock ○
Slave Lake ○
Lesser Slave Lake
High Level ○
Nahanni Butte ○
1548
Wrigley ○
Fort Norman (Tulita)
216?

100°W
North Battleford ○
North Saskatchewan
Grand Centre ○
676
Athabasca ○
Smith ○
Slave Lake
A L B E R T A
Peace
859
Hay
Fort Simpson ○
Mackenzie
1572
Franklin
Mou

Meadow Lake ○
Beaver
Fort McMurray ○
Athabasca
Caribou Mountains
1036
Enterprise ○
Fort Providence ○
Fort Rae ○Edzo
Lac La Martre ○
Rae Lakes ○
Fort Franklin (Déline) ○

747
Lac La Ronge ○
Fort Black ○
553
Churchill
Frobisher Lake
Fort Chipewyan ○
236
Slave
Dawson Landing ○
Fort Resolution ○
Great Slave Lake
Yellowknife ○
Snare River ○
704
Great Bear Lake
Port Radium (Echo Bay) ○
518

105°W
Island Falls ○
Flin Flon ○
S A S K A T C H E W A N
Cree Lake
674
Wollaston Lake ○
Eldorado ○Uranium City
594
N O R T H - W E S T E R R I T O R I E S
Nonacho Lake
394
Snowdrift (Lutsekle) ○
Reliance ○
Whitefish Lake
Artillery Lake
Hatter Lake
823
Takijuq Lake
Coppermine (Kugluktuk) ○
Dolphin and Union
Blue

100°W
Lynn Lake ○
Kinoosao ○
Reindeer Lake
Southend ○
Rabbit Lake ○
99°
Wholdaia Lake
Clinton Colden Lake
Aylmer Lake
Contwoyto Lake
C A N A D A
Bathurst Inlet ○
Coronation Gulf
Read Island ○
Wollaston Pen

95°W
13
251
M A N I T O B A
Southern Indian Lake
Caribou ○
140
Kasba Lake
Nueltin Lake
349
Ennadai Lake
Dubawnt Lake
413
Thelon
MacAlpine Lake
244
221
Dease Strait
Cambridge Bay ○
Victoria Is

90°W
Nelson ○
York Factory ○
Fort Nelson ○
McClintock ○
Churchill
Churchill
Cape Churchill
Eskimo Point (Arviat) ○
Whale Cove ○
Rankin Inlet ○
Thlewiaza
Yathkyed Lake
Baker Lake ○
122
Baker Lake
Chesterfield Inlet ○
Aberdeen Lake
503
Back
Garry Lake
Perry Island ○
Sherman Basin
Adelaide Peninsula
King William Island
St. Roch Basin
Queen Maud Gulf
Victoria Strait
McClintock Chan
Franklin Strait
Prince

Hudson Bay
Chesterfield Inlet (Igluligaarjuk) ○
Wager Bay
Repulse Bay ○
Rae Isthmus
Gjoa Haven ○
229
Hayes
Spence Bay (Taloyoak) ○
Pelly Bay
Simpson Peninsula
Gulf of Boothia
572
Boothia Peninsula
Bernier Bay
Prince Regent

85°W
Coral Harbour ○
Southampton Island
Roes Welcome Sound
Committee Bay
Wales I.
Brodeur Peninsula
Admiralty Inlet
244
549
Arctic

80°W
Inukjuak ○
Akulivik ○
Ivujivik ○
60°N
Bell Peninsula
625
Foxe Channel
Foxe Basin
65°N
Arctic Circle
Lyon Inlet
Vansittart I.
Melville Peninsula
Hall Beach ○
Jens Munk
Rowley I.
381
558
Fury and Hecla Strait
70°N
518
Gifford
Bylot I.
Eclipse Sound
Baffin Island
2134
1199
Borden Pen

This map shows 1/60 of the earth's surface

n   o   p   q   r   s   t   u   v   w   x   y   z

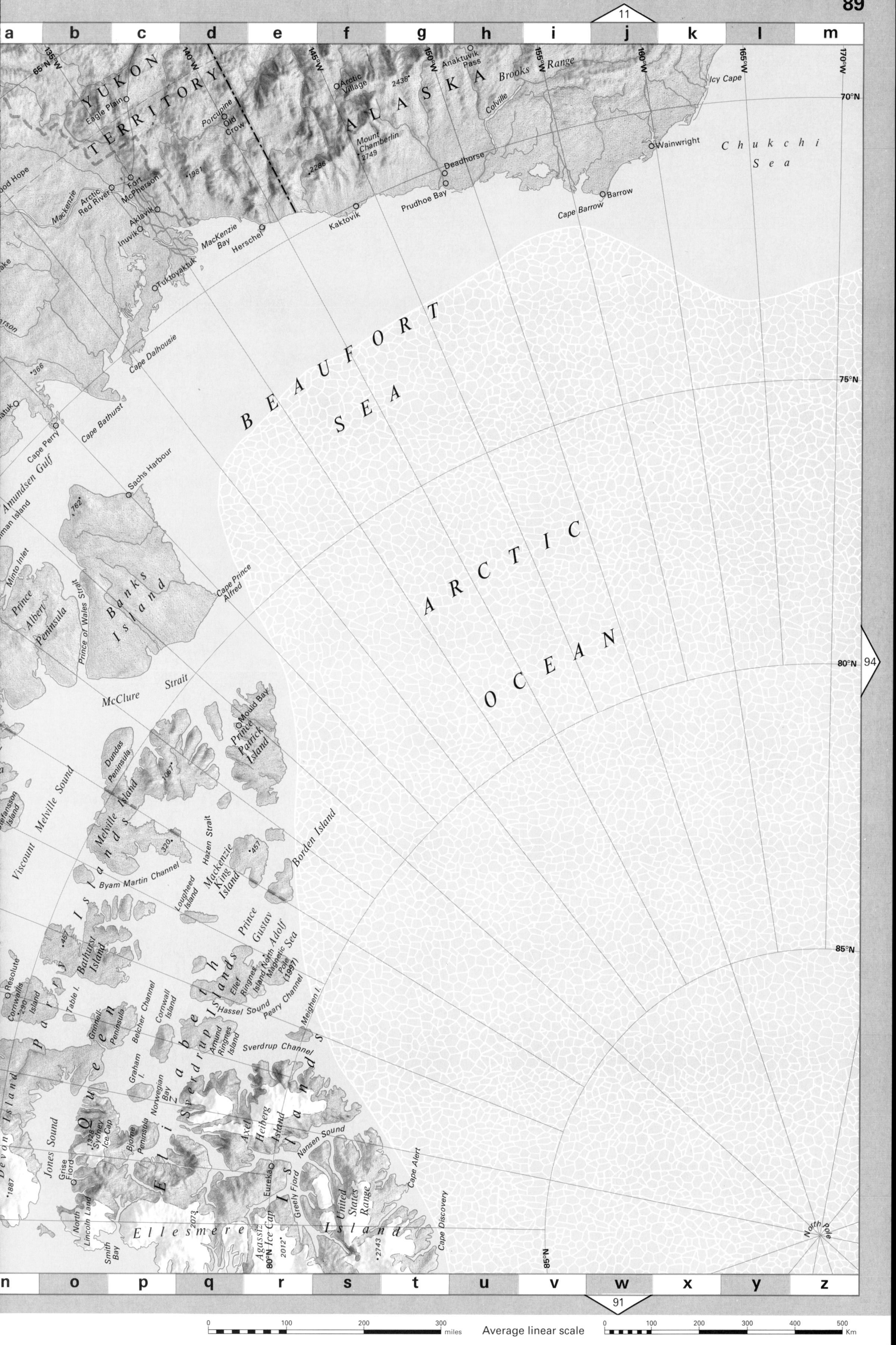
11
a b c d e f g h i j k l m
135°W 140°W 145°W 150°W 155°W 160°W 165°W 170°W
65°N 70°N 75°N 80°N 85°N
94
YUKON TERRITORY
ALASKA
Eagle Plain
Porcupine
Old Crow
Arctic Village
2438
Anaktuvik Pass
Brooks Range
Colville
Icy Cape
Mount Chamberlin
2749
2286
1981
Wainwright
Chukchi Sea
Deadhorse
Prudhoe Bay
Barrow
Cape Barrow
Kaktovik
Herschel
MacKenzie Bay
Fort McPherson
Arctic Red River
Mackenzie
Aklavik
Inuvik
Tuktoyaktuk
Cape Dalhousie
366
Cape Bathurst
Cape Perry
Amundsen Gulf
Sachs Harbour
762
BEAUFORT SEA
ARCTIC OCEAN
Minto Inlet
Prince Albert Peninsula
Prince of Wales Strait
Banks Island
Cape Prince Alfred
McClure Strait
Mould Bay
Prince Patrick Island
Dundas Peninsula
Melville Island
1067
Melville Sound
Viscount Melville Sound
320
Hazen Strait
Mackenzie King Island
457
Borden Island
Byam Martin Channel
Lougheed Island
Prince Gustav Adolf Sea
Bathurst Island
Parry Islands
North Magnetic Pole (1997)
Ellef Ringnes Island
Resolute
Cornwallis Island
290
Table I.
Grinnell Peninsula
Belcher Channel
Cornwall Island
Hassel Sound
Peary Channel
Meighen I.
Amund Ringnes Island
Sverdrup Islands
Sverdrup Channel
Queen Elizabeth Islands
Graham I.
Norwegian Bay
Axel Heiberg Island
Nansen Sound
Devon Island
Jones Sound
1528
Sydney Ice Cap
Bjorne Peninsula
Grise Fiord
1887
North Lincoln Land
Smith Bay
Ellesmere Island
2073
Eureka
Agassiz Ice Cap
2012
Greely Fiord
United States Range
2743
Cape Alert
Cape Discovery
80°N
85°N
North Pole
n o p q r s t u v w x y z
91
Average linear scale
0 100 200 300 miles
0 100 200 300 400 500 Km

a b c d e f g h i j k l m

80°W
60°N
65°N
Arctic Circle
70°N
75°W
70°W
65°W
60°W
55°N
55°W
50°W
45°W
50°N
35°N
40°W
60°W
35°W
30°W

13

n o p q r s t u v w x y z

Bay

Hudson

Bay

Inukjuak○

Akulivik○

Ivujivik○

Povungnituk○

Salluit○
661

Mansel
Island

Ungava Peninsula

QUEBEC

Labrador

aux Feuilles

39°

Koksoak
Kuujjuaq○

Nain○
·1076
Nutak○

Ramah○

Fraser

Kangiqsualujjuaq○
1621·

NEWFOUNDLAND

Purtuniq○
Kangiqsujuaq○

Hudson Strait

540·

Nottingham
Island

Salisbury
Island

·305

Cape
Dorset○

Foxe
Peninsula

·411

Nabukjuak○

Foxe
Channel

Foxe
Basin

CANADA

Prince
Charles
Island

Rowley
Island○

Foley
Island○

Jens Munk
Island○

NUNAVUT

Koukdjuak

Netilling
Lake

Amadjuak
Lake

Hall
Peninsula

·1148

Kigna○

Nunatak○

Arnaaluk
Lake

Penny
Ice Cap
·2591

Cumberland
Peninsula

○Pangnirtung
·2134

Cape Dyer

Exeter
Sound

Baffin

Island

Ice Cap
·1250

Barnes

·1554·

Henry Kater
Pen.

Home
Bay

Clyde○

Buchan Gulf

Kivitoo○

Broughton Island○

Eclipse
Sound

Bylot
Island·2134

Pond Inlet

·518·

Rowley

B a y

Cape Hopes
Advance○

Akpatok
Island

Ungava
Bay

Big
Island

Hudson
Strait

Lake
Harbour○

Frobisher Bay
(Iqaluit)○

Meta Incognita
Peninsula

Frobisher
Bay

Harper
Island

Resolution
Island

Port
Burwell○
Cape
Chidley

Cumberland
Sound

Hoare
Bay

L a b r a d o r   S e a

D a v i s

S t r a i t

A T L A N T I C

O C E A N

Sisimiut○

Maniitsoq○

Søndre Strømfjord
·1440

Nuuk
(Godthåb)○

○Søndrestrømfjord

Qeqertarsuaq
(Godhavn)○

Disko Bay

Qeqertarsuaq

Uummannaq○
·2231

Nuussuaq Halvø

Karrats Fj.

Svarte

·740

·1147

·4760

Paamiut○

Ivittuut○
·1643

Qaqortoq○

Nanortalik○

Narsarsuaq○
·2140

Kerasassuaq○

Danells Fj.

Cape Farewell
(Nunap Isua)

King Frederick VI Coast

King Frederick VI Coast

Bernstorff's Isfjord

Cape Mosting

Gyldenløves Fj.

K. Løvenørn

Dannebrog Island

Cape Dan

Ammassalik○

Kronprins Frederi
·2268

Mt. Forel
·3360

G r e (Kal

King C

This map shows 1/60 of the earth's surface

North
Pole

A R C T I C

O C E A N

85°N

ARCTIC OCEAN

Devon Island
•1887 North Lincoln Land
Smith Bay
•2073
80°N Greely Fjord
Island
Agassiz Ice Cap
Elle smere
United States Range •2743
Cape Discovery
Alert O

Nares Strait

Lincoln Sea

Nansen Land
•1920
Peary Land
1910
•1070
Frederick E. Hyde Fjord
Melville Land
Independence Fjord
Wandels Sea
Danmark Fjord
Crown Prince Christian Land •760
Nordostrundingen

Ingolf Fjord

Knud Rasmussens Land

•945

Inglefield Land
Hayes Halvø
Dundas Cape Athol
OQaanaaq (Thule)
•7500
Prudhoe Land
Washington Land
Hall Land
Nyeboe Land
Kane Basin
•796

Cape York
Melville Bay
Cape Seddon
Holm I.
Steenstrup Glacier

Halvø

n

d
a
n
l
a
n
(Nunaat)
t
(Denmark)

King Frederick VIII Land

•1100 Lambert Land

Île de France

Greenland

80°N
92

Spitsbergen •1454
Svalbard (Norway)
Prince Karls Foreland
Isa Fjord

Dronning Louise Land

King
Germania Land •550
Skær Fjord
Dove Bay
Store Koldewey
Shannon

Sea

Christian X
Land

Andrées Land
Hudson Land
•1604
Ardencaple Fjord
•1832
Clavering I.
Wollaston Foreland
Hold with Hope Pen.

Scoresby Land
Renland
Milne Land
1900•
Kaiser Franz Josephs Fjord
Geographical Society I.
Traill I.
King Oscars Fjord
•1740
Jameson Land
Liverpool Land

75°N

Gunnbjørn Fjeld

Kangerlussuaq

Scoresby Sound
Ittoqqortoormiit
Cape Brewster

Cape Dalton

D e n m a r k   S t r a i t

Jan Mayen (Norway)

70°N

Isafjördur O
Cape Horn
Breidhi Fjord •961
I C E L A N D
Húna Bay
65°N

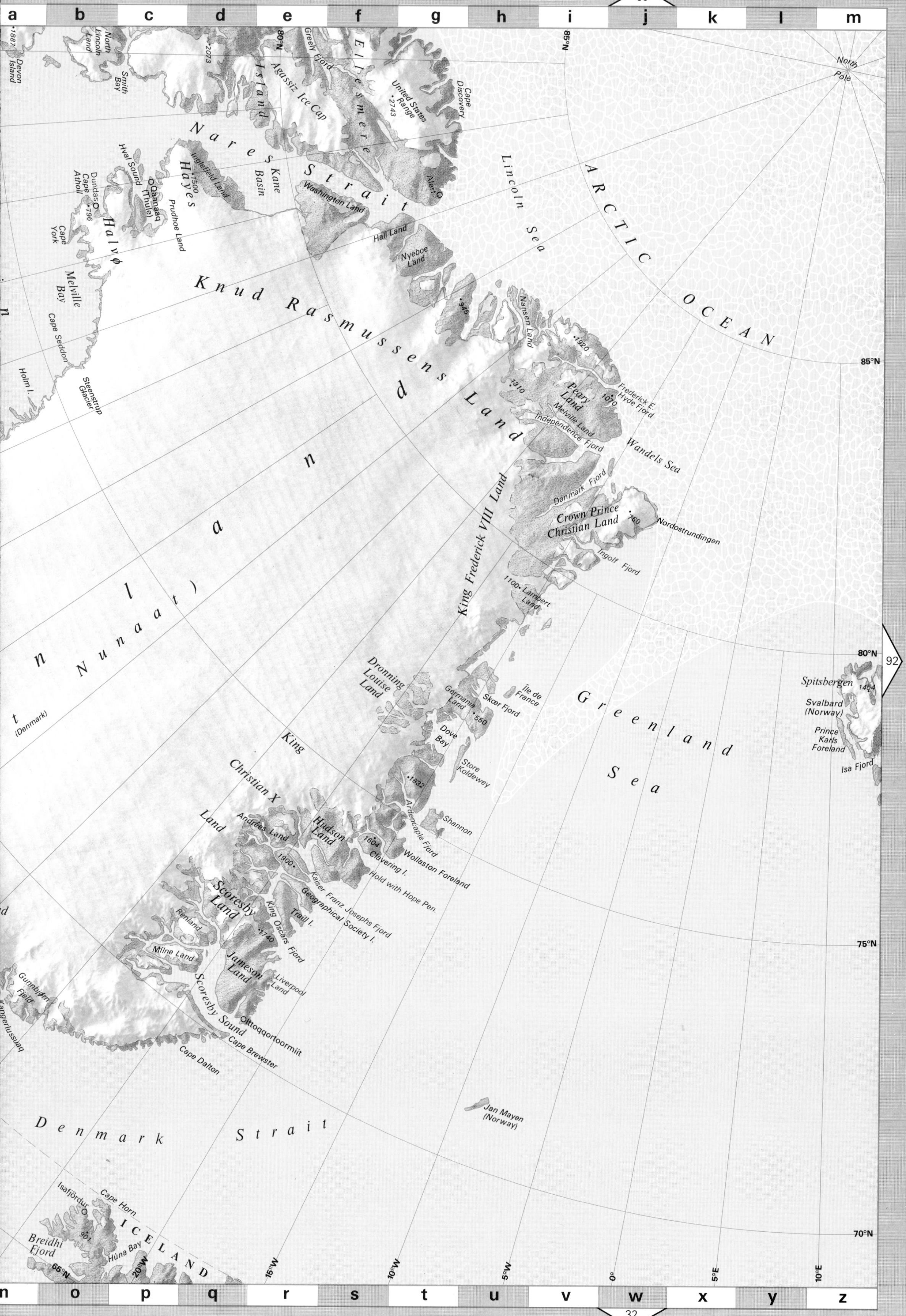

0   100   200   300 miles   Average linear scale   0 100 200 300 400 500 Km

94

a b c d e f g h i j k l m
n o p q r s t u v w x y
North Pole
85°N
80°N
75°N
70°N
10°E
15°E
20°E
25°E
30°E
35°E
40°E
45°E
ARCTIC OCEAN
Severnaya Zemlya
Komsomolets
Oktyabr'skaya Revolyutsii
Bolshevik
Pioner
Shmidta
Cape Berga
Cape Peschanyy
Cape Mednyy
Shokal'skogo Str.
Vilkitskogo Strait
Russkiy
Nordenshel'da Arch.
Cape Oskara
Taimyr
Ushakova
Isačenko
West Siberian Sea
Vize
Troynoy
Arkticheskogo Instituta
Mikhaylova
Yeva-Liv
Graham Bell Island
Rudolf I.
Karla-Aleksandra
Jackson I.
La Ronsʼyer
Wilczek Land
Salisbury I.
Luidzhi
Hall
Salʼm
Hooker I.
McClintock I.
Alexandra Land
George Land
Franz Josef Land
White Island
Mys Zelaniya
Russkaya Gavan
Novaya Zemlya
Smidovich
Sedova
Stolbovoy
Litke
Krasino
Belyy
KARA SEA
Proliv Karskiye Vorota
Pechora
North East Land
Hinlopenstr.
Spitsbergen
Barents Island
Edge Island
Isa Fjord
Longyearbyen
Barentsburg
Svalbard (Norway)
BARENTS SEA
Bear Island (Norway)
Kolguiev
Malozemel'skaya Tundra
Cape Kanin Nos
Kanin
Česa Bay
Volonga
Velikovisoch
Mezen' Gulf
Mezen'
Azopol'ye
North Cape
Cape Kiberg
Söröy
Hammerfest
Tana
NORWAY
Lakselv
Kirkenes
Pečenga
Alta
Murmansk
Lake Inari
Lapland
Padunskoye More
Kola
NORWEGIAN SEA
Tromsö
Skibotn
Senja
Ivalo
FINLAND
Lotta
Mončegorsk
Kirovsk
Arctic Circle

91

33

95
a b c d e f g h i j k l m
n o p q r s t u v w x y z
50
R U S S I A
Central Siberian Uplands
Putorana Mountains
Tunguskoye Mountains
Yenisey Mountains
Siberian Uvaly
Vasyugan'ye
Northern Ural Mountains
Gyda Peninsula
Yenisey Bay
Gyda Bay
Gulf of Ob'
Baidarata Bay
Bol'shezemel'skaya Tundra
Timan Ridge
Khatanga
Kheta
Lake Labaz
Popigay
Kotuy
Dudypta
Payturma
Volochanka
Kochikha
Boyarka
Kargo
Ust'Avam
Dolgany
Pyasina
Kresty
Agapa
Yangoda
Chernaya
Lake Pyasina
Noril'sk
Dudinka
Talnakh
Potapovo
Khantayka
Khantayskoye Reservoir
Lake Khantayskoye
Ambar
Lake Keta
Lake Lama
Ayan
Kamen 2037
Maimecha
Tukalan
Yessey
Changada
Murukta
Chirinda
Kotui
Kotuikan
Kočečum
Lake Anama
Lake Vivi
Agata
Severnaja
Kureyka
Igarka
Karasino
Ust'-Kureyka
Turukhansk
Kostino
Yenisey
Bugarikta
Noginskiy
Tutonchany
Tembenchi
Tura
Nidym
Vivi
Chiskovo
Uchami
Taimura
Mutoray
Vanavara
Cunja
Korda
Taimba
Baykit
Podkamennaya Tunguska
Ust'Kamo
Kamo
Vayvida
Polygus
Kuzmovka
Yelmo I-oye
Teya
Novoyeruдinskiy
Bryanka
Yarkino
Badopa
Boguchany
Kamanka
Angara
Rodina
Cuna
Panovo
Kova
Strelka
Galanino
Lesosibirsk
Yeniseysk
Nazimovo
Ust'Pit
Altat
Melletsk
Podkamennaya Tunguska
Osinovo
Sumarokovo
Verkhneimbatskoye
Nizhneimbatskoye
Bakhta
Yartsevo
Sym
Lugovatka
Ust'Ozernoye
Ket
Tegul'det
Chulym
Komsomol'sk
Yorozheyka
Turukhan
Farkovo
Yermakovo
Sidorovo
Yanov Stan
Taz
Krasnosel'kup
Bol. Kheta
Tanama
Messoyakha
Khokiley
Karaul
Ust'-Port
Gol'chikha
Yakovlevka
Zhyryanka
Oshmarino
Gyda
Yumbey
Taran
Napalkovo
Antipayuta
Nakhodka
Tazovskiy
Nyamboyoto
Taz Bay
Yamburg
Yeporko
Pur
Urengoy
Chaselka
Tolka
Kikiakki
Ratta
Matyl'ka
Yeloguy
Kellog
Sabun
Korliki
Vanzhil'kynak
Kadzhi
Tym
Lar'yak
Vach
Khalesavoy
Aiwasedapur
Kolik'yegan
Ust'Kolik'yegan
Strezhevoy
Nazina
Negotka
Ust'Tym
Kargosok
Vasyugan
Parabel
Kolpashevo
Mogochin
Belyy Yar
Alipka
Baturino
Asino
Tomsk
Moryakovskiy Zaton
Starica
Parbig
Bakchar
Pikhtovka
Lake Neyto
Yaptiksale
Lake Yarroto
Novyy Port
Yada
Nyda
Pangody
Staryy Nadym
Nadym
Vyngapur
Noyabrsk
Agan
Nizhnevartovsk
Aleksandrovskoye
Katyl'ga
Nizhniy Sugut
Marresale
Yarongo
Shuga
Gornyy Kazymsk
Shchuch'ye
Labytnangi
Salekhard
Polui
Kazym
Numto
Pokacheva
Yermakovo
Surgut
Pim
Ob'
Ljamin
Ust'-Kara
Khoy
Khal'mer-Yu
Vorkuta
Yeletskiy
Abez'
Pay-Yer
Adzva
Kashgert
Feduki
Vanzevat
Kazymskaya
Symya
Nazym
Khanty-Mansiysk
Irtysh
Kintus
Demyanka
Demyanskoye
Gerasimkova
Bystryy
Onega Yar
L'vovka
Biaza
Chumakovo
Pokrovka
Tatarsk
Lake Chany
Kalachinsk
Chistoozernoye
Omsk
Cherlak
Lake Ulkenkaroy
Kzyltu
Tara
Bol'sheretch'ye
Koreyver
Inta
Usa
Makarikha
Kosvu
Pechora
Saranpaul
Narodnaja
Berezovo
North Sosva
Sergino
Muligort
Patrasuy
Khangokurt
Sovetskiy
Komsomol'skiy
Pionerskiy
Mulymya
Konda
Cherpiva
Tapsui
Nyaksimvol
Kyrta
Kadzherom
Izhma
Voyvozh
Kedva
Ukhta
Vey Vozh
Troitsko-Pechorsk
Porog
Suyevatpaul
Polunochnoye
Ivdel'
Tavda
Sos'va
Tura
Turinsk
Tyumen
Talitsa
Denezhkin
Krasnotur'insk
Lobva
Verkhniy Tura
Nizhniy Tagil
Artemovskiy
Bogdanovich
Shadrinsk
Kurgan
Kurtamysh
Dem'yanovka
Peski
Stavropolka
Ruzayevka
Dzhaksy
Atbasar
Aydabul
Makinsk
Kur'ya
Kolva
Cherdyn
Ust'Kulom
Puzla
Zheleznodorozhnyy
Shomvukva
Vym'
Trosh
70°N
65°N
60°N
55°N
50°E
55°E
60°E
65°E
70°E
75°E
80°E
90°E
100°E
1403
1612
1274
766
814
698
619
552
970
2037
202
160
75
66
82
168
112
1499
1218
1894
1617
1108
1027
1493
324
303
155
164
321
100
78
39
77
55
142
124
186
258
211
636
887
22
42
65
Average linear scale
0 100 200 300 miles
0 100 200 300 400 500 Km

This map shows 1/60 of the earth's surface

a b c d e f g h i j k l m

10

170°W 175°W 180° 175°E 170°E 165°E 160°E 65°N

Chukchi

Mys
Shmidta

Sea

Illirney

Krasnoarmeyskiy

Retkucha

Southern Anyuskiy Mountains

Bol'Anyuy

Korkodon

Korkorn

Bulun

Zatishye

Kolymskiy Mountains

Yug

Sededen

Pastakh

L o n g   S t r a i t

70°N

1097

Wrangel Island

Pevek

1641

Oscrovnoy

Mal. Anyuy

Cherskiy

Mal.
Baranikha

Ambarchik

Northern Anyuskiy Mountains

Gorelova

Volochsk

Mys

Konzaboy

Chernyy

Mys

Zhirkova

Berezovka

Srednekolymsk

Khongsevo

Oysurdakh

Kyrbana

Malaya

Shestako

Lake
Nerpich'ye

Balagannakh

Khara-
Tala

Illimlir

Urdakh

Trenah

Ozhogino

Chukochye

K o l y m s k i y

Ulovo

Kondakovo

914

E a s t   S i b e r i a n

P l a i n

75°N

S e a

Indigirka

Alekseyevo

Bryangnyf

Lake
Ozhogino

Kolesovo

Chokurdakh

Ukta

Boru

Tabor

Kiseleva

Khroma

Chikhacheva

Kokuora

Kharstan

Star-Dom

Balgant

New Siberian Islands

Novaya
Sibir'

Bol'shoye
Zimov'ye

Laptev Str.

Bol'
Lyakhovskiy

Chay-Povarnaya

Kigilyakh

Bennetta

Fedorovskiy

Mal.
Lyakhovskiy

Stolbovoy

89

80°N

A R C T I C

Kotel'nyy

320

Ambardakh

Kotel'nyy

Berkovskiy

Antipinskiy

L a p t e v   S e a

85°N

O C E A N

Mal.Taimyr

313

Verezdekhodnaya

B y r r a n g a   M o u n t a i n s

North Pole

Komsomolets

Cape
Peschanyy

Shokal'skogo Str.

Bolshevik

Vil'kicki Str.

900

Oktyabr'skoy
Revolyutsii

Cape
Oskara

Cape
Berga

80°N

85°N

Niz Taimyra

n o p q r s t u v w x y z

92

53
52
51
93
a b c d e f g h i j k l m
n o p q r s t u v w x y z
R U S S I A
Dzhugdzhur Mountains
Cherskogo Mountains
Verkhoyanskiy Mountains
Stanovoy Mountains
Patomskoye Plateau
Vilyuy Mountains
Central Siberian Uplands
Yakutsk
Okhotsk
Ayan
Neryungri
Aldan
Lensk
Mirnyy
Olekminsk
Vilyuysk
Verkhoyansk
Tiksi
Khatanga
Zhigansk
Nyurba
Suntar
Udachnyy
Chernyshevskiy
Vilyuyskoye Reservoir
Lena
Aldan
Amga
Vilyuy
Olenëk
Vitim
Olekma
Maya
Uchur
Timpton
Tokko
Markha
Muna
Linde
Moyero
Kotuy
Angara
Bol. Shantar
Arctic Circle
55°N
60°N
65°N
70°N
100°E
105°E
110°E
115°E
120°E
125°E
130°E
135°E
140°E
145°E
150°E
0 100 200 300 miles
Average linear scale
0 100 200 300 400 500 Km

Principal sources for the thematic maps: Amnesty International Report 2001. * www.ancientscripts.com 2001. * Buch und Buchhandel in Zahlen. Frankfurt 1987. * British Geological Survey, Natural Environment Research Council: World Mineral Statistics 1979-1983. 1995-1999. * Brown, Louise: Sex Slaves: The Trafficking of Women in Asia. London 2000. * CIA World Factbook 2000. * Dathe, Heinrich und Paul Schöps (eds.): Pelztieratlas. Jena 1986. * Deutsche Gesellschaft für Luft und Raumfahrt: Astronautische Start-Verzeichnisse und Raumflugkörper-Statistiken 1957-1987. * Diercke Länderlexikon. Braunschweig 1983. * Durrell, Lee: State of the Ark. London 1986. * www.eia.doe.gov 2001. * Encyclopedia Britannica. 15th ed. 32 vls. 1985. * Encyclopedia Britannica Book of the Year 1986. 1987. 1988. * www.ethnologue.com 2001. * Fischer Weltalmanach 1986. 1987. 1988. 2001. 2002. * Food and Agricultural Organization of the United Nations (FAO) Rome: FAO Production Yearbook 1985. 1986. FAO Food Balance Sheets 1975-1977. 1979-1981. FAO Yearbook of Fishery Statistics 1983. FAO Trade Yearbook 1986. www.fao.org 2001. * Haack. Atlas zur Zeitgeschichte. Gotha 1985. * Herre. Wolf und Manfred Röhrs: Haustiere - zoologisch gesehen. Stuttgart 1973. * www.infoplease.com 2001. * Institut für Seeverkehrwirtschaft und Logistik, Bremen: Shipping Statistics Yearbook 2000. * The International Institute of Strategic Studies (ILSS): The Military Balance 1986-1987. 1995/1996. 2000. * International Labour Organization (ILO) Geneva: Yearbook of Labour Statistics 1978. 1979. 1980. 1981. 1982. 1983. 1984. 1985. 1986. 1987. Income Distribution and Economic Development. An Analytical Survey. Geneva 1984. Sixth African Regional Conference. Application of the Declaration of Principles and Programme of Action of the World Employment Conference. Geneva 1983. STAT Working papers, Bureau of Statistics 1950-2010. Geneva 1997. www.ilo.org 2001. * International Road Transport Union: World Transport Data. Geneva 1985. * International Telecommunication Union: Table of International Telex Relations and Traffic. Geneva 1987. * Inter-Parliamentary Union (IPU): Women in Parliament 1988. Participation of Women in Political Life and in Decision-Making Process. Geneva 1988. Distribution of Seats Between Men and Women in National Assemblies. Geneva 1987. www.ipu.org 2001. * Jain, Shail: Size Distribution of Income. Compilation of Data. World Bank Staff Working Paper No.190. Nov. 1974. Washington 1975. * Kidron, Michael and Ronald Segal: The State of the World Atlas. London 1981. The New State of the World Atlas (revised ed.). London 1987. * Kurian, George Thomas: The New Book of World Rankings. New York 1984. * Länder der Erde. Berlin 1985. * McDowell, Jonathan: Harvard-Smithsonian Center for Astrophysics. * Meyers Enzyklopädie der Erde (8 vls.). Mannheim 1982. * Moroney, John R.: Income Inequality. Trends and International Comparisons. Toronto 1979. * Myers, Norman (ed.): GAIA - Der Öko-Atlas unserer Erde. Frankfurt 1985. * www.nasa.gov 2001. * Nohlen, Dieter and Franz Nuscheler (eds.): Handbuch der Dritten Welt. 8 vls. Hamburg 1981-1983. * Ökumene Lexikon. Edited by Hanfried Krüger, Werner Löser et al. Frankfurt 1983. * Peters, Arno: Synchronoptische Weltgeschichte. 2 vls. Munchen 1980. * Saeger, Joni and Ann Olson: Der Frauenatlas. Frankfurt 1986. * Serryn, Pierre: Le Monde d'aujourd'hui. Atlas économique. social, politique, stratégique. Paris 1981. * South: South Diary 1987. 1988. * Statistisches Bundesamt, Wiesbaden: Statistisches Jahrbuch 1999. Statistik des Auslandes. Vierteljahreshefte zur Auslandsstatistik. 1985-1987. Statistik des Auslandes. Länderberichte. * Stockholm International Peace Research Institute (SIPRI): SIPRI Yearbook 1987. World Armaments and Disarmament. New York 1987. * Taylor, Charles Lewis and David A. Jodice: World Handbook of Political and Social Indicators. New Haven. London 1983. * UNESCO: Statistical Yearbook 1974. 1975. 1976. 1977. 1978. 1979. 1980. 1981. 1982. 1983. 1984. 1985. 1986. 1987. * UNICEF: The State of the World's Children 1987. * The United Nations (UN): UN Statistical Yearbook 1983/84. 1999. UN Demographic Yearbook 1972. 1979. 1984. 1985. 1986. National Accounts Statistics. Compendium of Income Distribution Statistics. New York 1985. UN Energy Statistics Yearbook 1984. UN Yearbook of International Trade Statistics 1982. 1983. 1984. 1986. 1998. Selected Indicators of the Situation of Women 1985. UN Industrial Statistics Yearbook 1983. 1984. World Conference of the United Nations Decade for Women: Equality, Development and Peace. Copenhagen 1980. World Culture Report 2000. World Education Report 2000. World Health Report 2000. The World's Women 2000. Activities for the Advancement of Women: Equality, Development and Peace. Report of Jean Fernand-Laurent. 1983. UNCTAD Handbook of Statistics 2000. UNIDO International Yearbook of Industrial Statistics 1995. 1996. 1997. 1998. 1999. 2000. 2001. www.un.org 2001. * University of Stellenbosch, Department of Development Administration and the Institute for Cartographic Analysis: The Third World in Maps. 1985. * Westermann Lexikon der Geographic. Edited by Wolf Tietze. Braunschweig 1968. * World Almanac & Book of Facts 1985. 1986. 1987. * The World Bank: World Development Report 1980. 1981. 1982. 1983. 1984. 1985. 1986. 1987. 1999/2000. 2000/2001. World Labour Report 1984. World Tables 1984. World Atlas of the Child 1979. Social Indicators of Development 1987. The World Bank Atlas 1987. World Economic and Social Indicators. Document of the World Bank. 1980. World Development Indicators 2001. www.worldbank.org 2001 * World Energy Resources 1985-2020, Renewable Energy Resources. The Full Reports to the Conservation Commission of the World Energy Conference. Published for the WEC by IPC Science and Technology Press 1978. * The World in Figures. Editorial information compiled by the Economist. London 1987. * World Health Organization (WHO), Geneva: World Health Statistics. Annual. * Völker der Erde. Bern 1982. * Voous, K.H.: Atlas of European Birds. New York 1960.

NATURE, HUMANKIND AND SOCIETY IN 246 THEMATIC MAPS

Each map presents a single subject. As a result, it is possible to dispense with symbols and allow the information to be expressed entirely in terms of colour: dark colours for high values, light for low ones. This makes it easy to see and assimilate the content of the maps - an important feature, since up to 16 maps can be dedicated to a single subject.

The individual subject should not be considered in isolation. The mutual interaction between all spheres of life, the intricacies of nature and culture, of economics, nations and society, mean that each of the subjects can be understood only in connection with the other 45 double-page spreads.

This richness and multiplicity of facts and insights is however the minimum which someone of our time must have in mind if they wish to form their own opinion on the current situation in the world and in their own country. Without this effort, their own view of the world can never be clear and reliable.

Over 40,000 individual pieces of factual information have been compiled for these 246 thematic world maps. They were obtained almost exclusively from published materials of the United Nations and other international organisations. There reliability is presumed, and an average of annual data available from 1980 onwards has been calculated. Where official figures were not available, estimates were made in consultation with the leading experts in the various fields concerned. No indication is given of these estimates, since their reliability is no less than that of the official figures.

The names of countries appear also on the small world maps. These can be read with the aid of a magnifying glass or by reference to the large whole-page maps such as that of "States" on pages 112-113.

Brief texts on each subject are intended to aid mental categorisation and to make historical connections plain. In addition, they contain the figures of extreme cases which cannot be extracted from the average values given by the colour-coding.

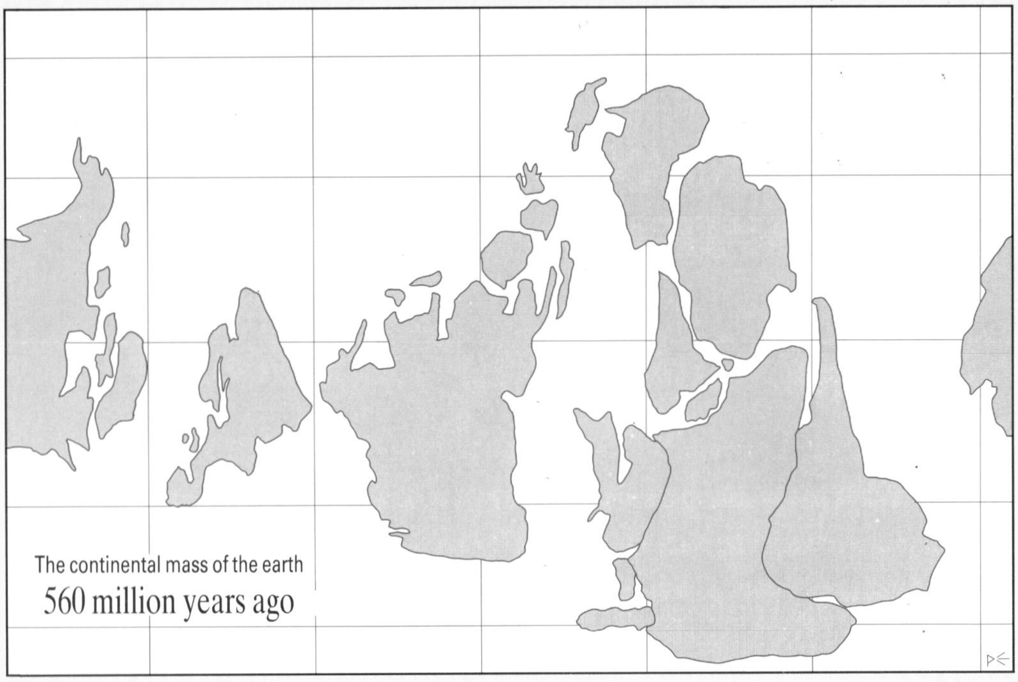

The continental mass of the earth
560 million years ago

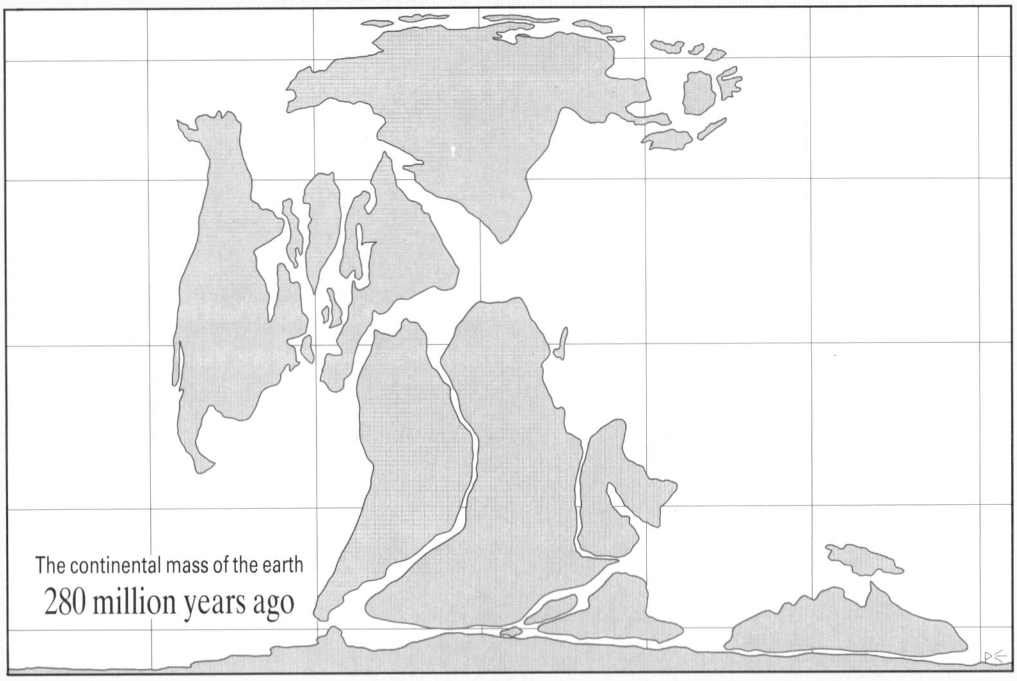

The continental mass of the earth
280 million years ago

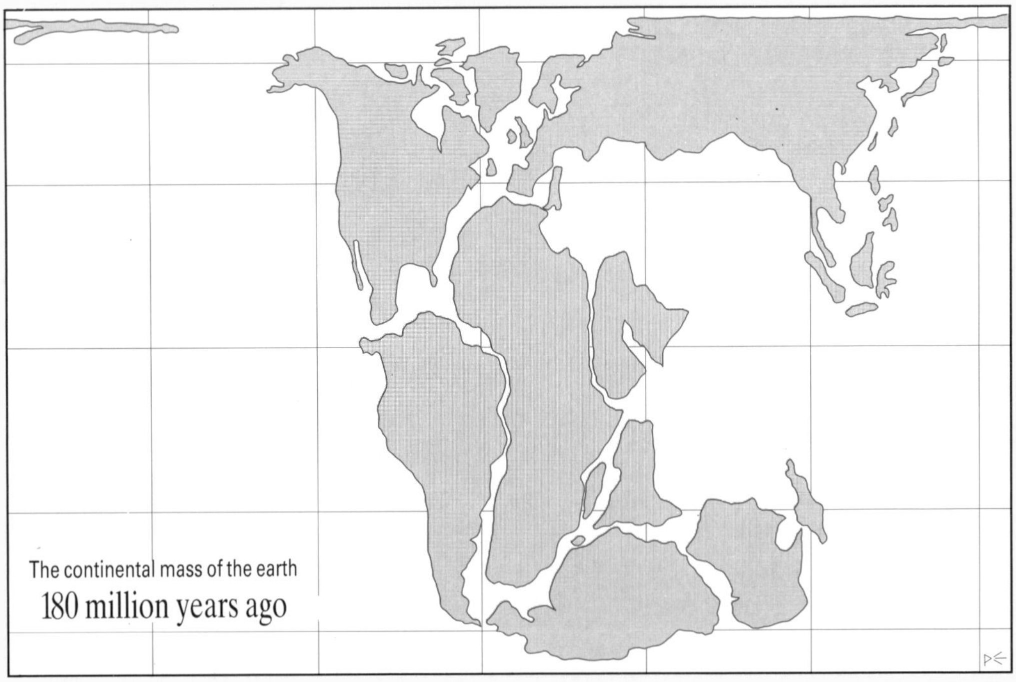

The continental mass of the earth
180 million years ago

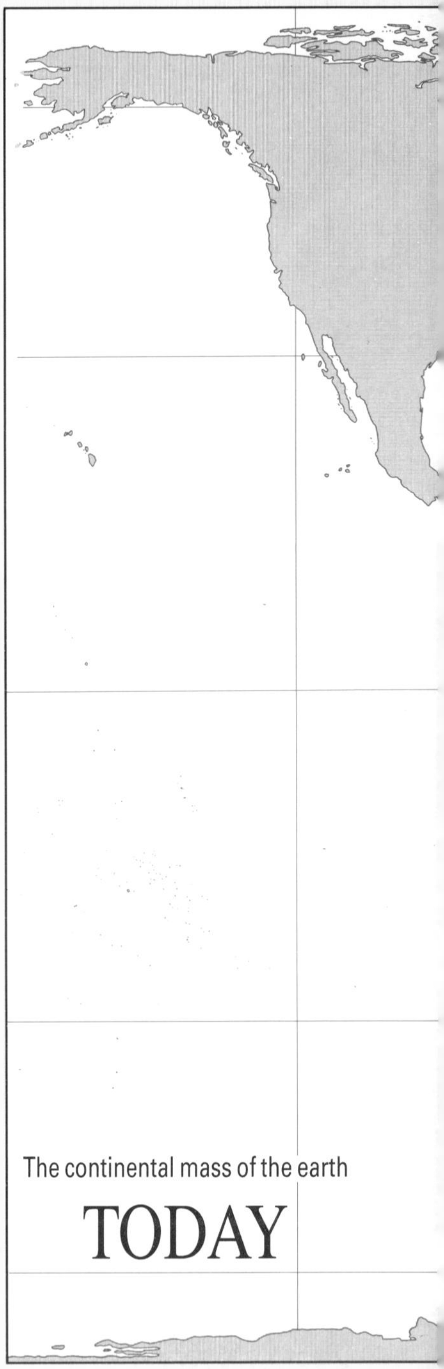

The continental mass of the earth
TODAY

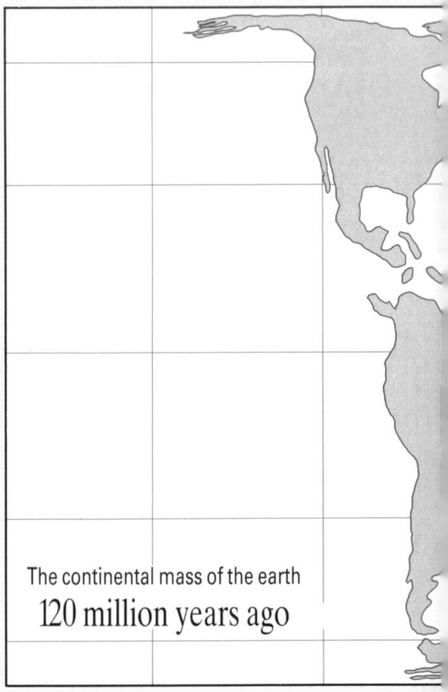

The continental mass of the earth
120 million years ago

The continents of the earth are in constant movement. The cause of this *DRIFT* is the displacement of half a dozen gigantic sheets of the earth's crust. These change their position by an average of three metres in the course of one human generation. There are however great differences in the speed of this movement; in the Atlantic area it is only one to two centimetres a year, but in the Pacific it is up to fifty centimetres annually.

THE CO

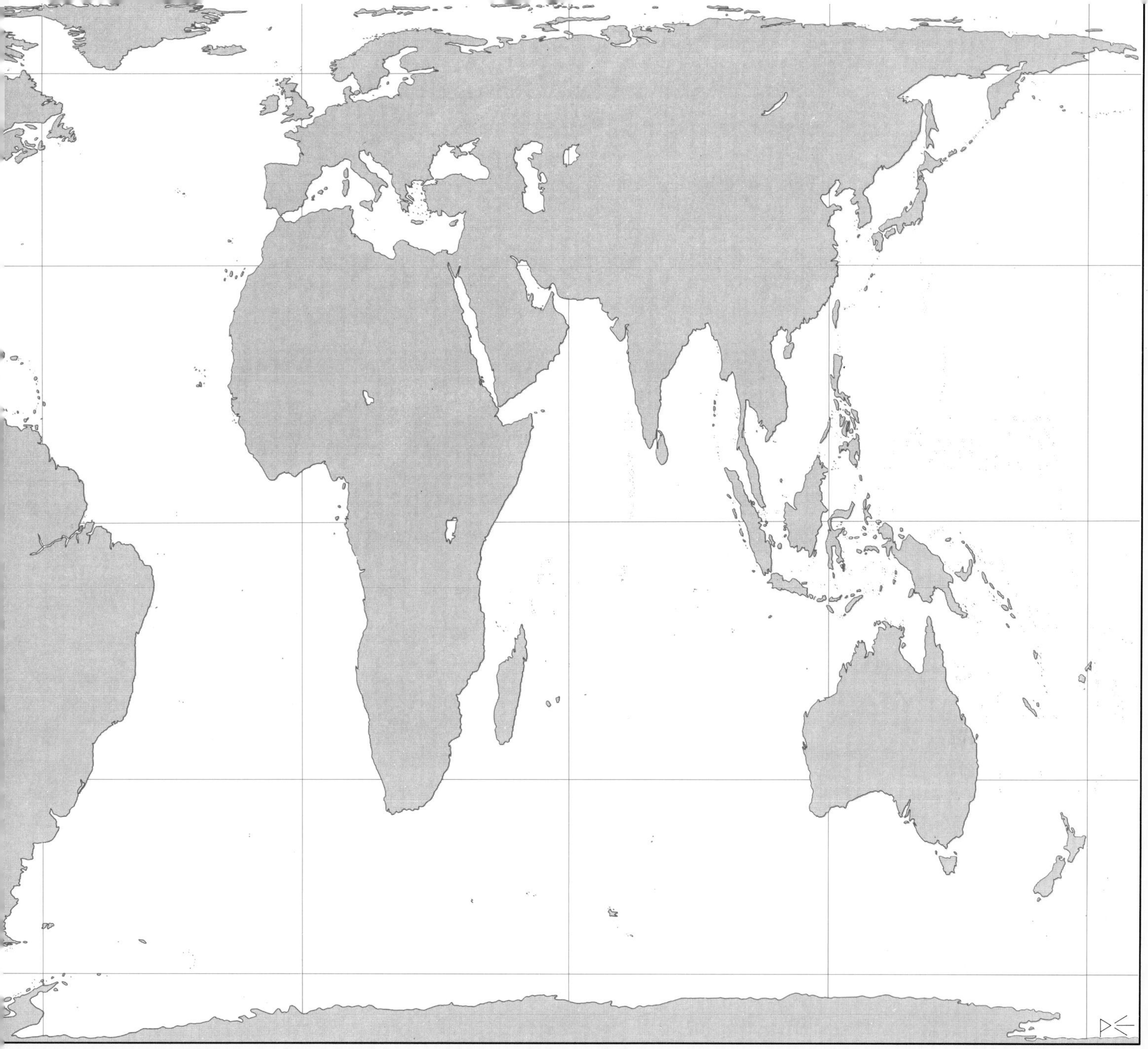

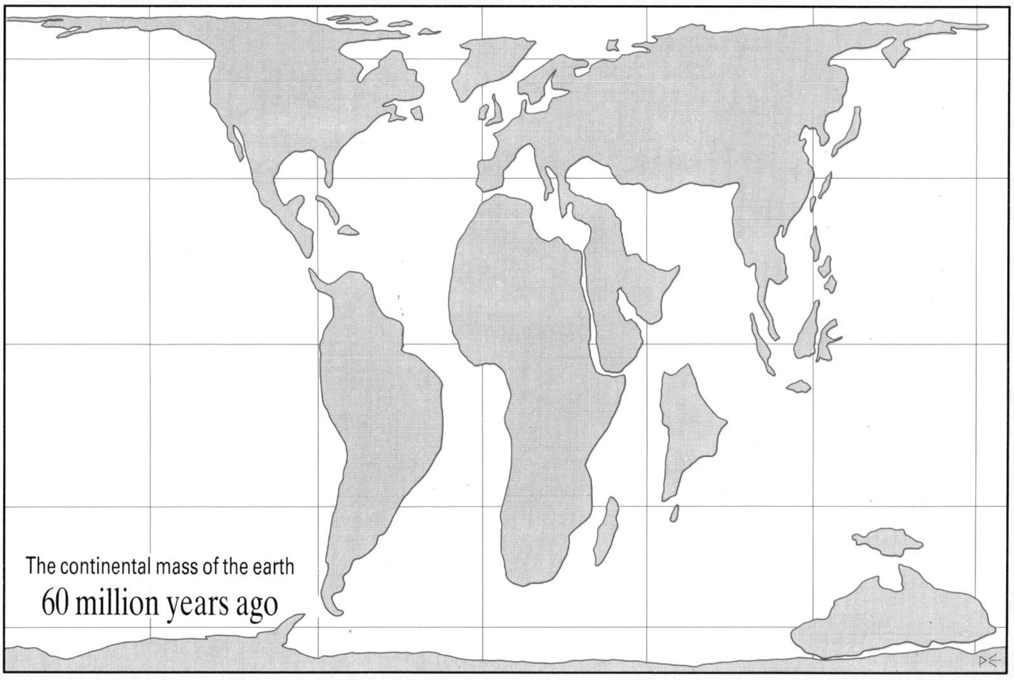

The continental mass of the earth
60 million years ago

TINENTS

Some 280 million years ago Europe was a separate land mass which could be regarded as a continent in its own right. By 200 million years ago Europe had combined with Asia into a single large continent. Later, Arabia, India and Africa joined onto it, while North and South America had also united into a single continent. In comparison with these two real continents of *AMERICA* and *EURASIA*, Australia, Greenland and Antarctica are only enormous islands.

Most mountain ranges were formed by the displacement of the continental land masses. When these collided, they forced up folds which became the high ranges (Alps, Andes, Himalaya). Then, over millions of years, parts of them were worn away by glaciers and erosion into highlands and tablelands. Where mountains are of volcanic origin (Iceland, Java, Hawaii) new lava bursting out of the earth counteracts this natural erosion. Periods of major earth movement alternate with quieter periods, but in general it can be said that the mountains are still constantly changing.

MOU

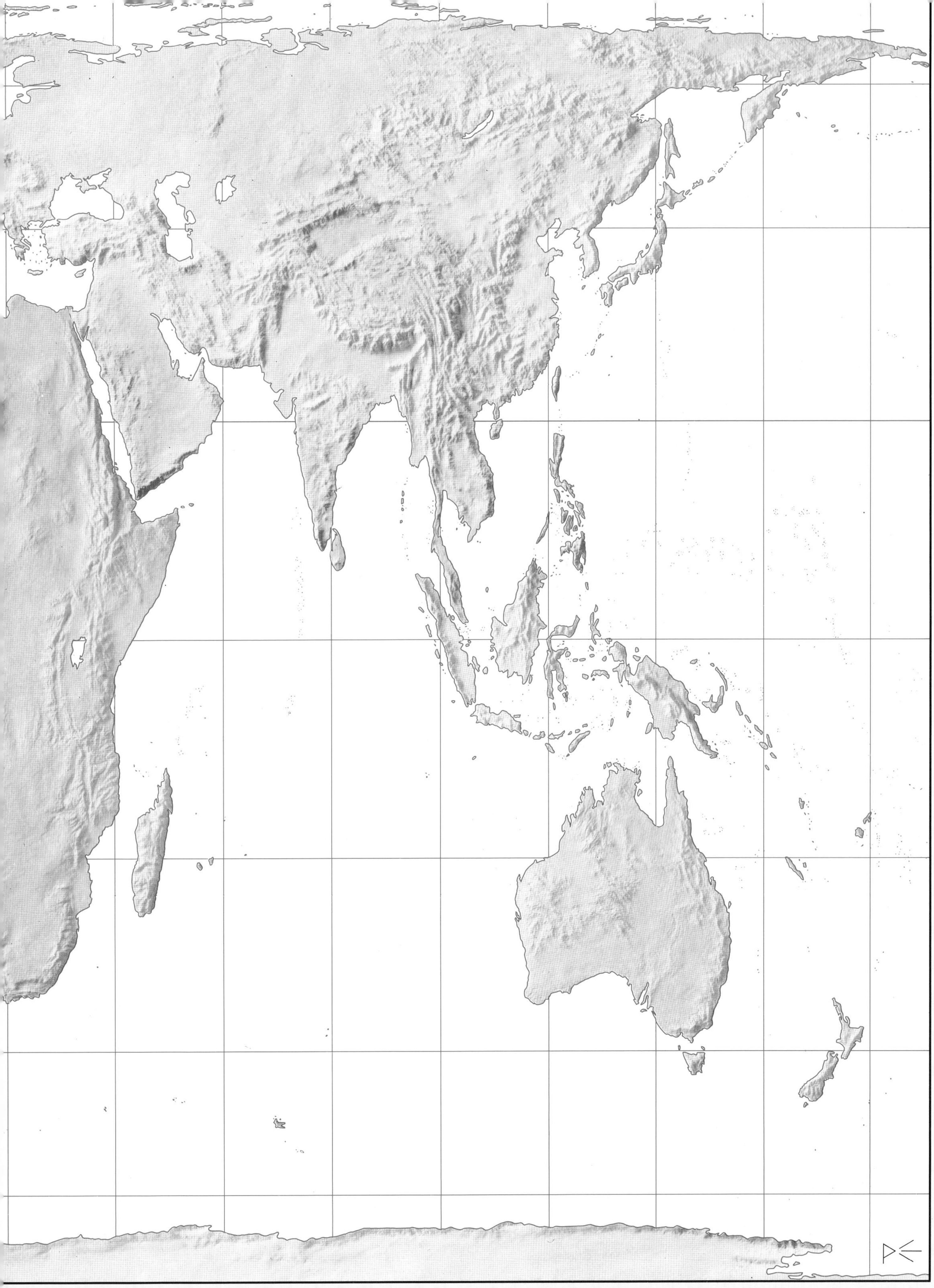

TAINS

Mountains are natural barriers and therefore often form the boundaries between countries. Up to the 20th century, mountainous regions were often isolated from the rest of the world and people there followed their own traditional ways of life. In recent decades, however, these regions, especially in Europe, have been opened up to tourist traffic. Mountains and valleys have thus lost much of their individual character. Tourism has become a major source of income and ski-lifts, hotels and motorways are increasingly changing their appearance.

Depth of sea less than 200 metres

Depth of sea 200 to 2000 metres

Depth of sea 2000 to 4000 metres

Depth of sea 4000 to 6000 metres

Depth of sea more than 6000 metres

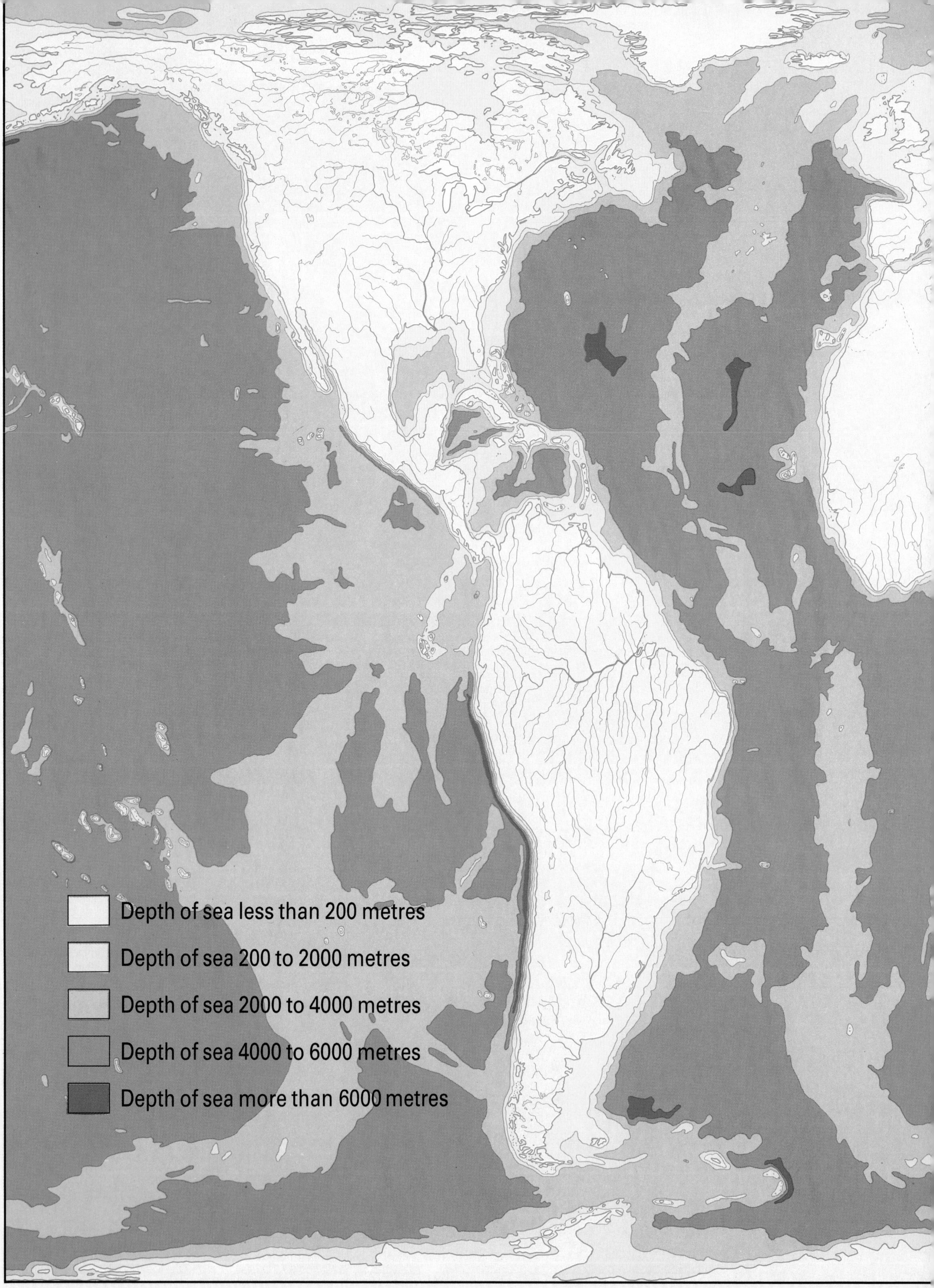

Every second, the earth's rivers carry more than a million cubic metres of water down to the oceans, where it evaporates and returns to the interior of the land masses as rain or snow. It runs into the rivers and is again carried down to the sea. This eternal water cycle, which involves less than one-hundredth of 1% of all the earth's water, is the essential basis for life and human existence. Two-thirds of our body consists of water.

RIVERS

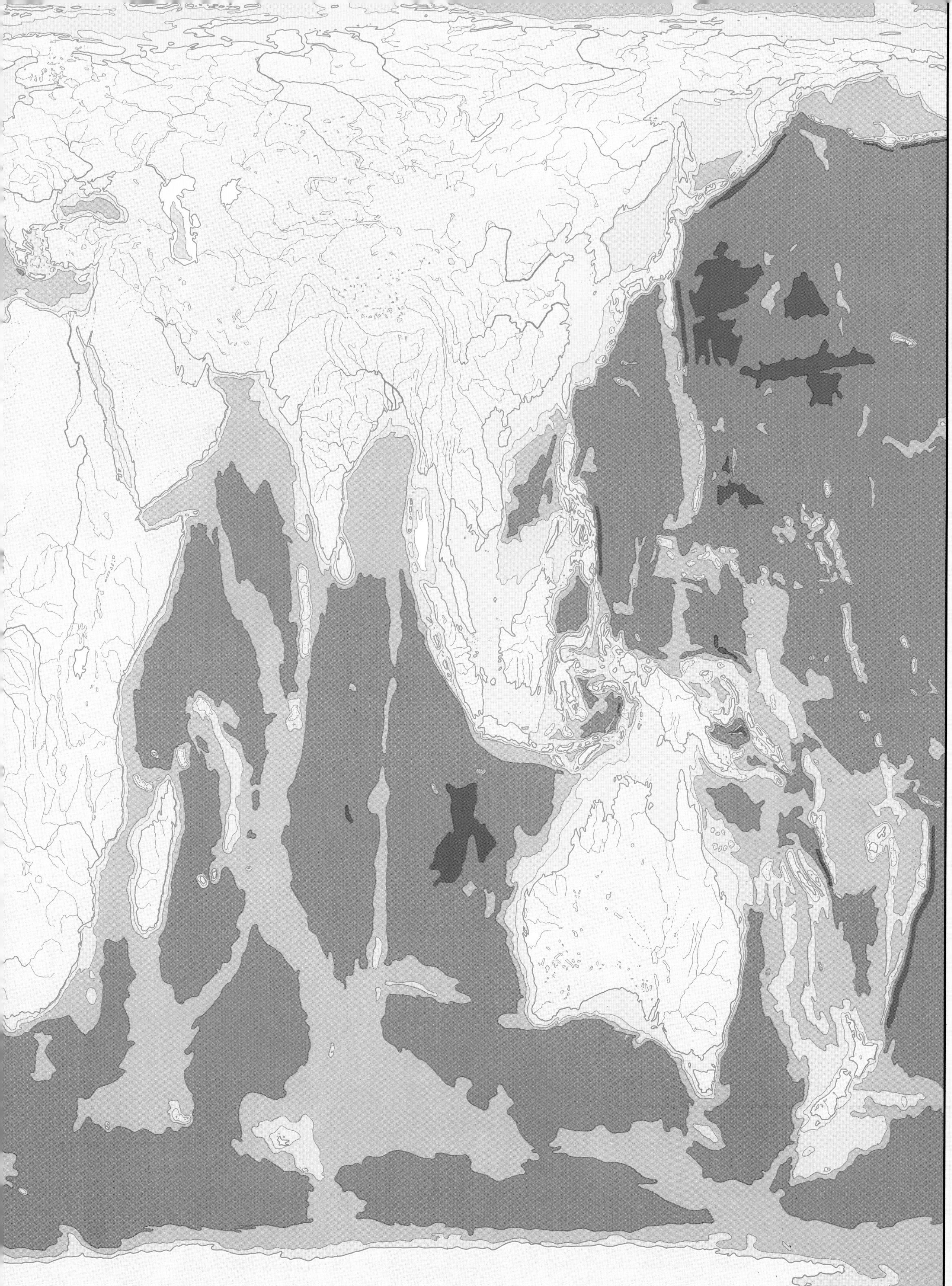

ND SEAS

The first human civilisations rose beside great rivers such as the Euphrates, Tigris, Nile, Indus and Huang He. The first city-states emerged there because people found drinking water and fish to provide nourishment. Rivers became their traffic routes, irrigated their fields and provided energy. The oceans, which covered more than 70% of the Earth's surface, limited the movement of early people until they learnt to conquer them with ships and thus make the Earth a single living space.

HOURS OF SUNSHINE

Fewer than 1600
hours of sunshine annually

1600 to 2400
hours of sunshine annually

2400 to 3200
hours of sunshine annually

3200 to 4000
hours of sunshine annually

over 4000
hours of sunshine annually

PRECIPITATION

Less than 100

100 to 500

500 to 1000

1000 to 2000

over 2000
millimetres annually

Less than 400

400 to 800

800 to 1500

1500 to 2000

over 2000
millimetres annually

EV

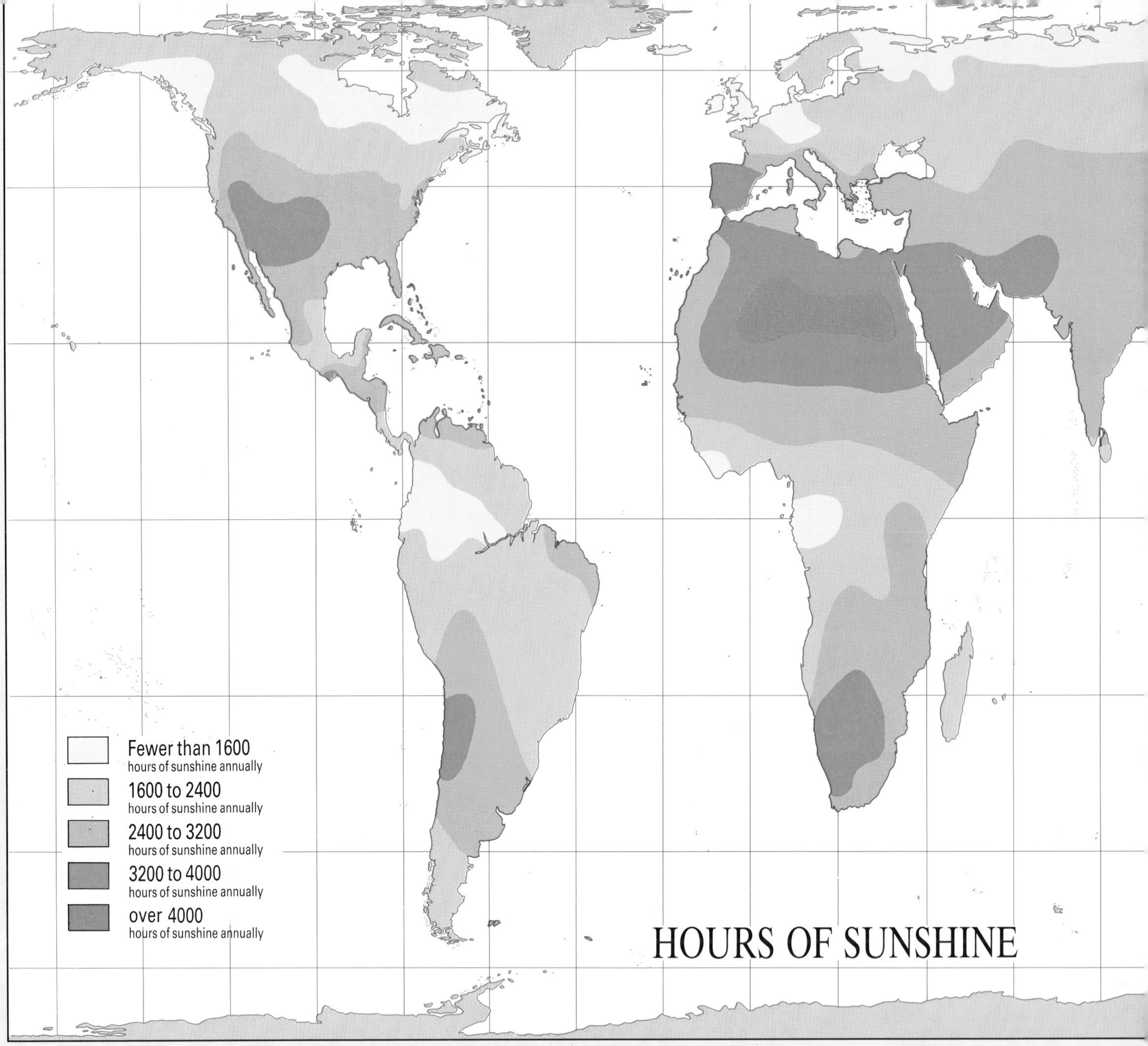

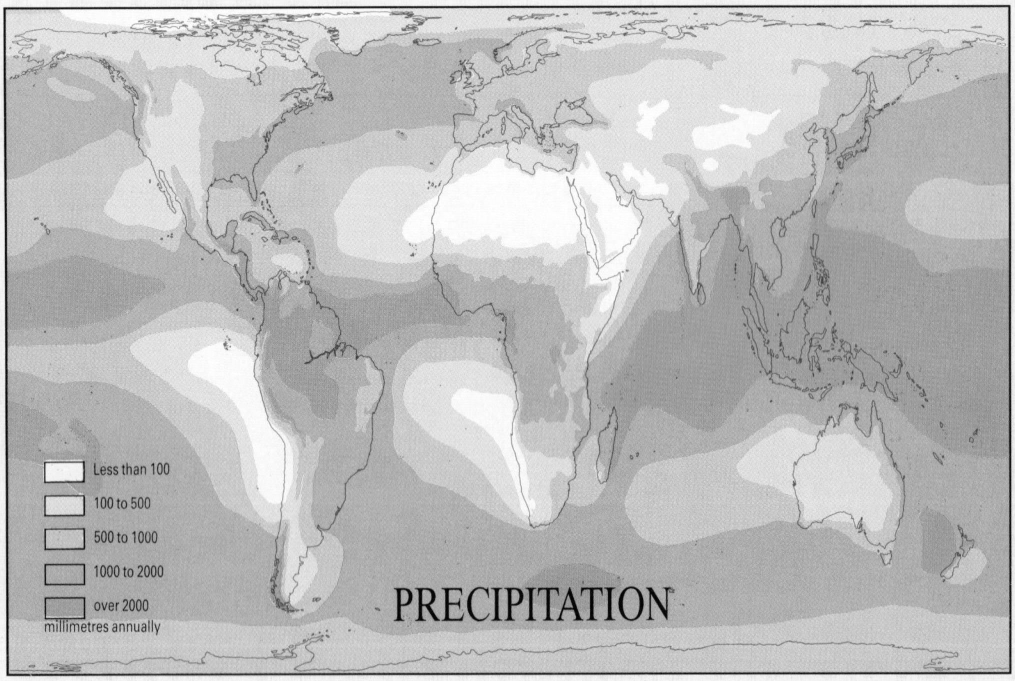

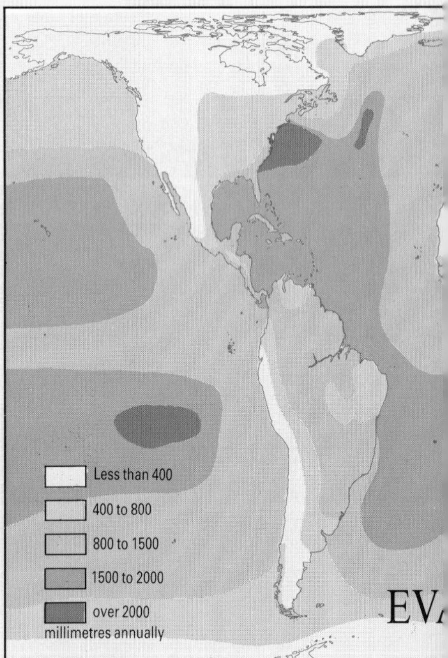

Like the rest of nature, people depend for their existence on weather factors, which together make up the climate. No matter how adaptable we may be, we cannot live everywhere on the earth's surface. 20% of it is covered by snow and ice and is uninhabitable. Another 20% is inhospitable desert, and a further 25% either consists of steep mountains, has insufficient soil, or is marshy or flooded land. Thus only about one-third of the earth's surface possesses suitable conditions for human habitation.

SUN AND

TEMPERATURE

Below minus 10 degrees Celsius
minus 10 to 0 degrees Celsius
0 to plus 20 degrees Celsius
20 to 30 degrees Celsius
above 30 degrees Celsius
mean annual temperature

TEMPERATURE VARIATION

Less than 2.5 degrees Celsius
2.5 to 10 degrees Celsius
10 to 20 degrees Celsius
20 to 40 degrees Celsius
more than 40 degrees Celsius
mean annual temperature variation

TION

INCIDENCE OF RAYS

Fewer than 100
100 to 140
140 to 180
180 to 200
over 200
kilocalories per square centimetre annually

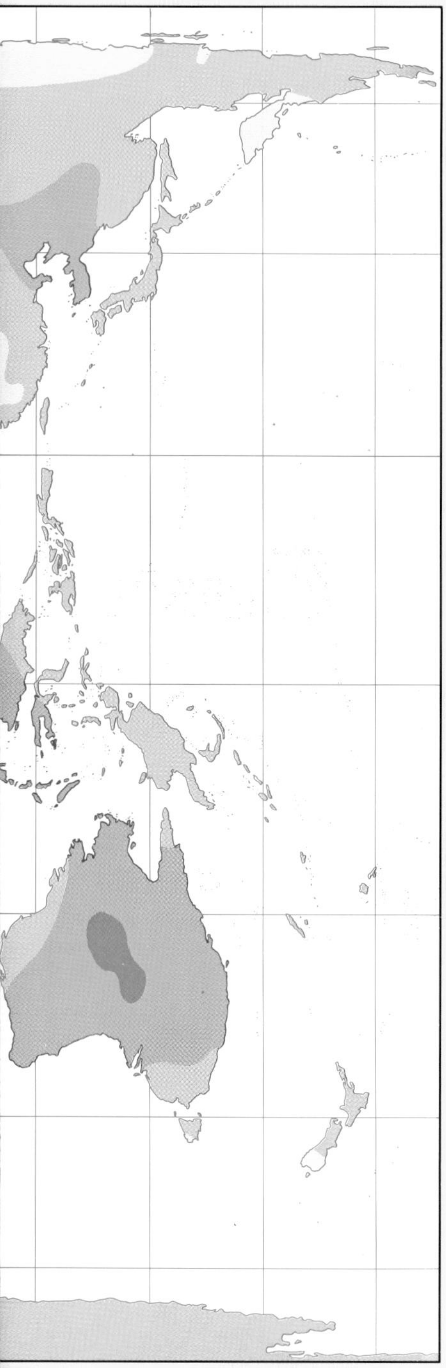

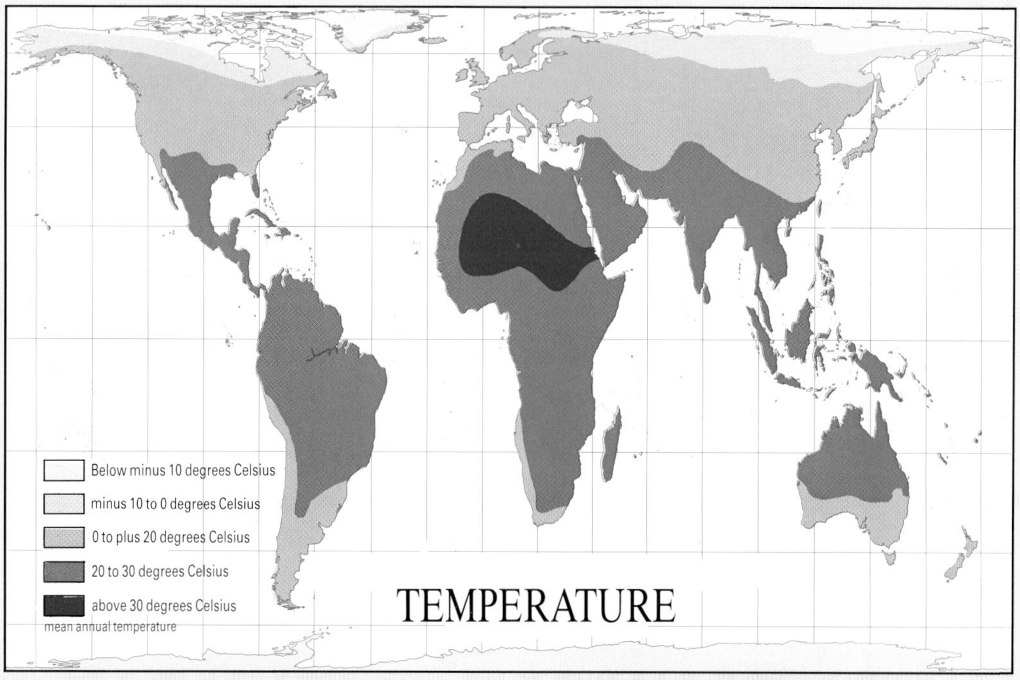

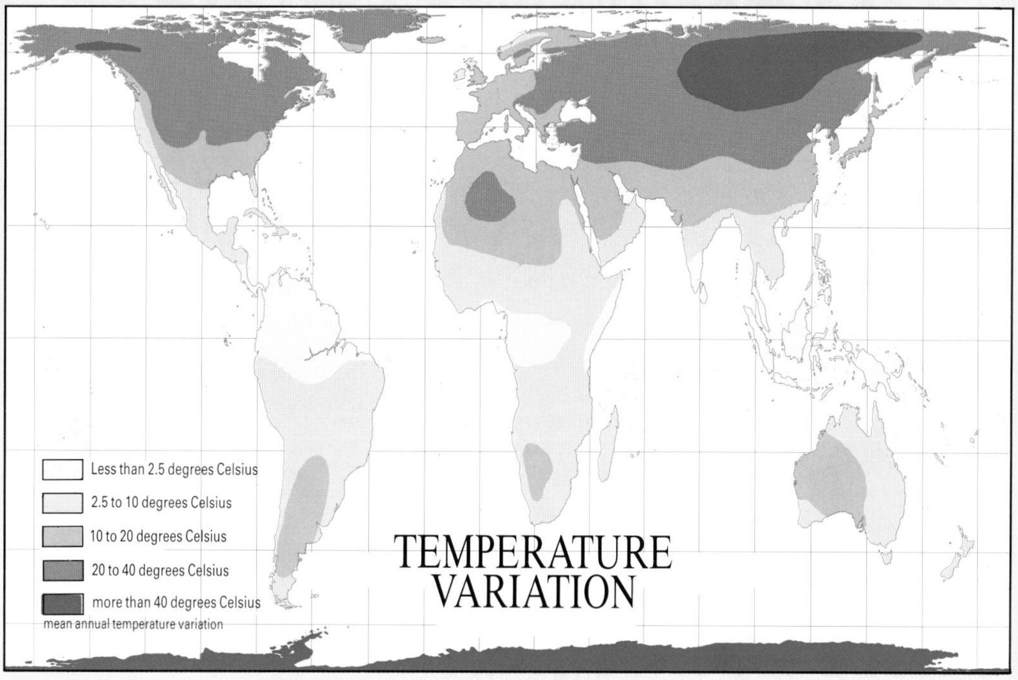

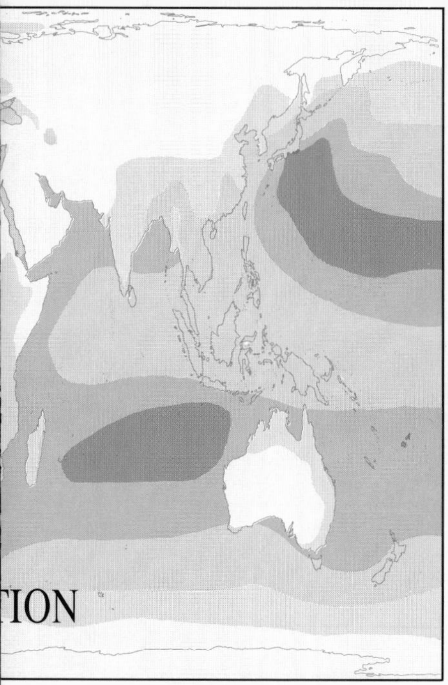

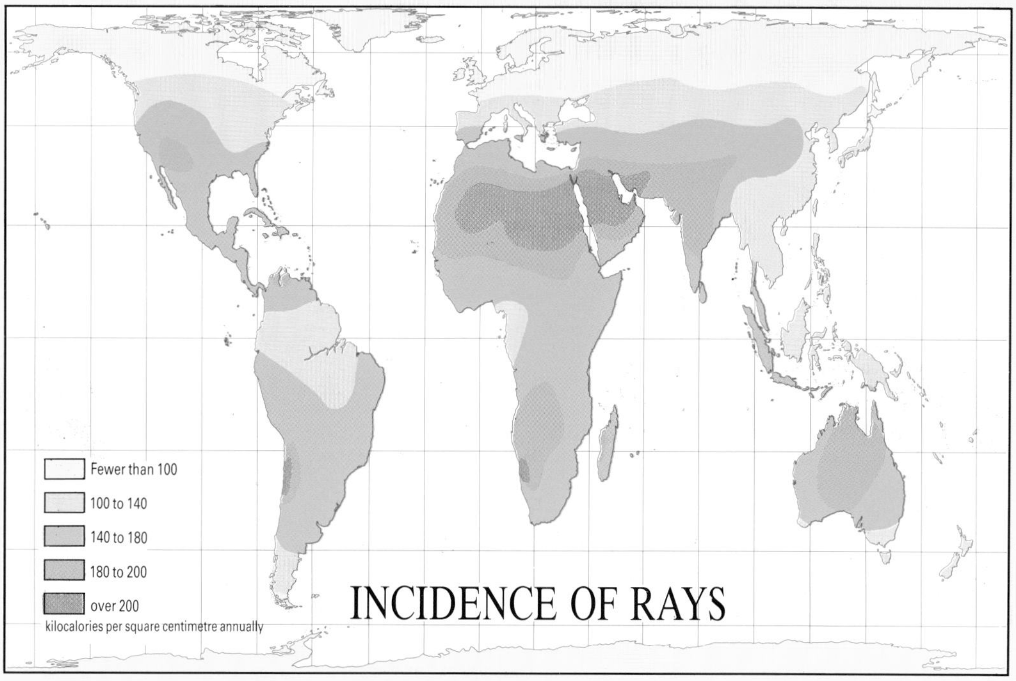

CLIMATE

A hundred years ago people began scientific research into weather in all its aspects—atmospheric pressure, temperature, humidity, hours of sunshine, amount of precipitation, cloud formation and wind. The origin of all weather conditions is the sun. This ball of fiery gas around which we travel once a year and whose diameter is about one hundred times greater than that of the earth, is one of the smallest of the over 200 billion fixed stars in the Milky Way. But it is our sun's light and warmth which make life on earth possible.

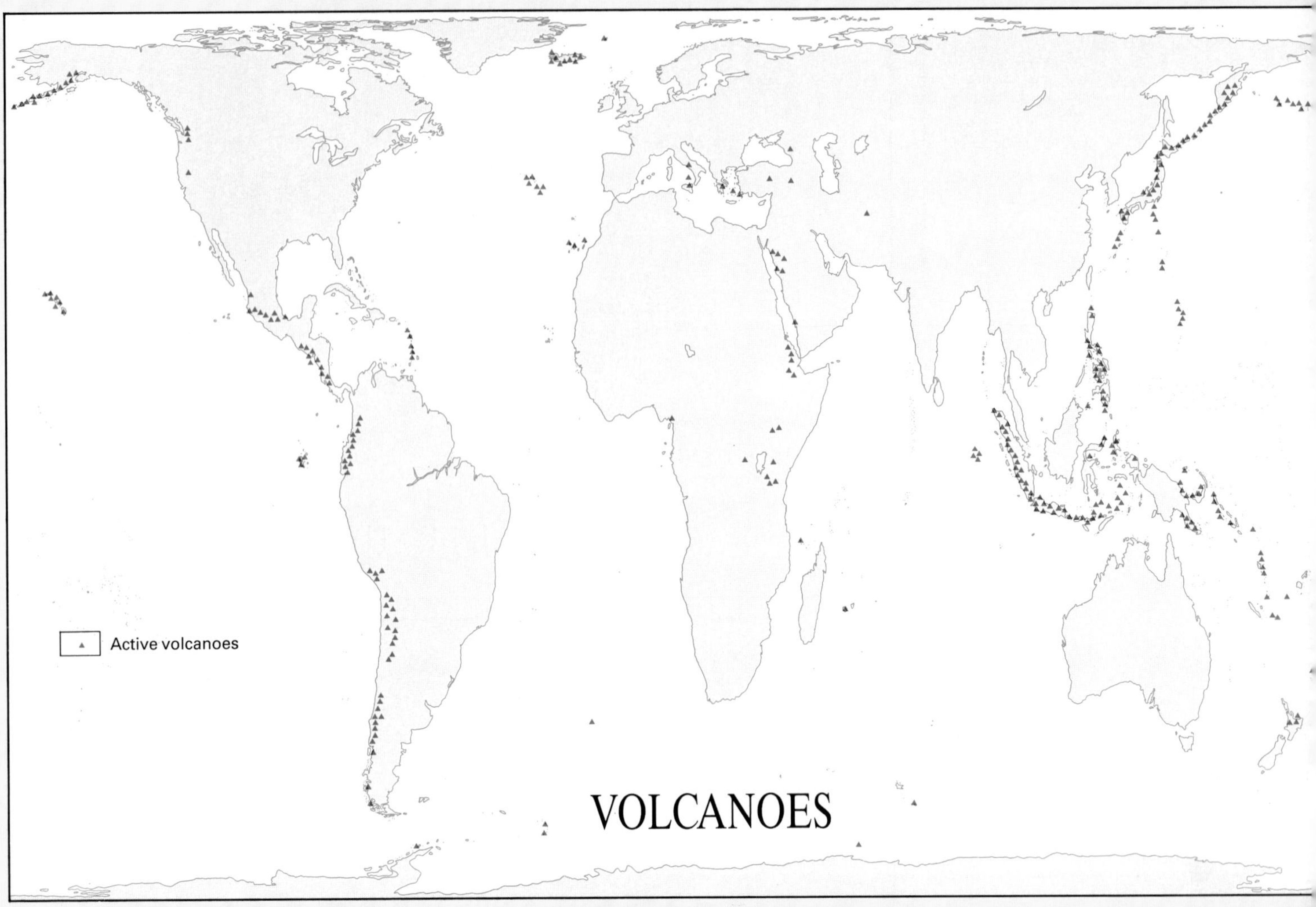

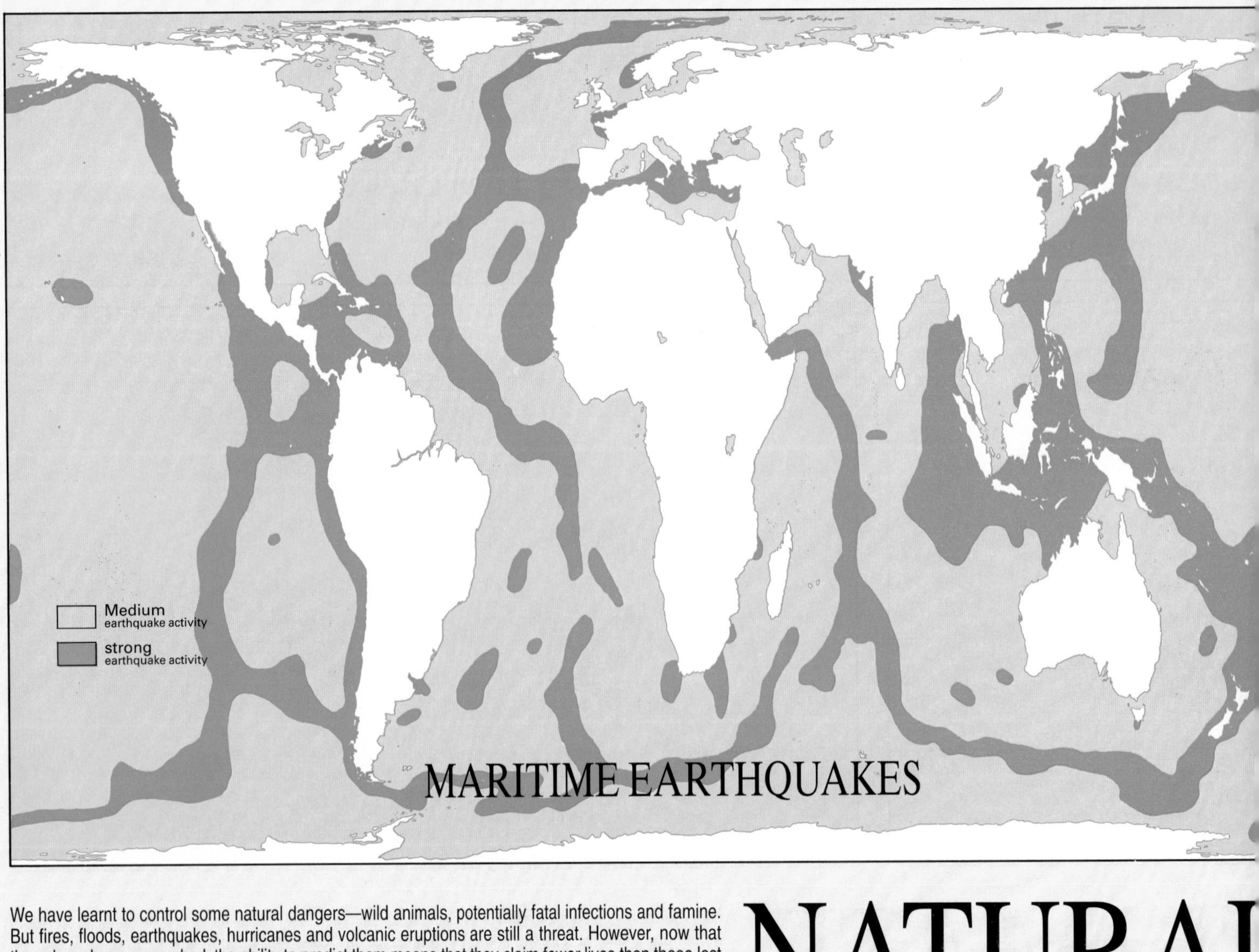

We have learnt to control some natural dangers—wild animals, potentially fatal infections and famine. But fires, floods, earthquakes, hurricanes and volcanic eruptions are still a threat. However, now that these have been researched, the ability to predict them means that they claim fewer lives than those lost through traffic accidents. Earthquake research, new building methods, the prediction of volcanic eruptions and worldwide hurricane and flood warning systems have made natural occurrences less perilous.

NATURAL

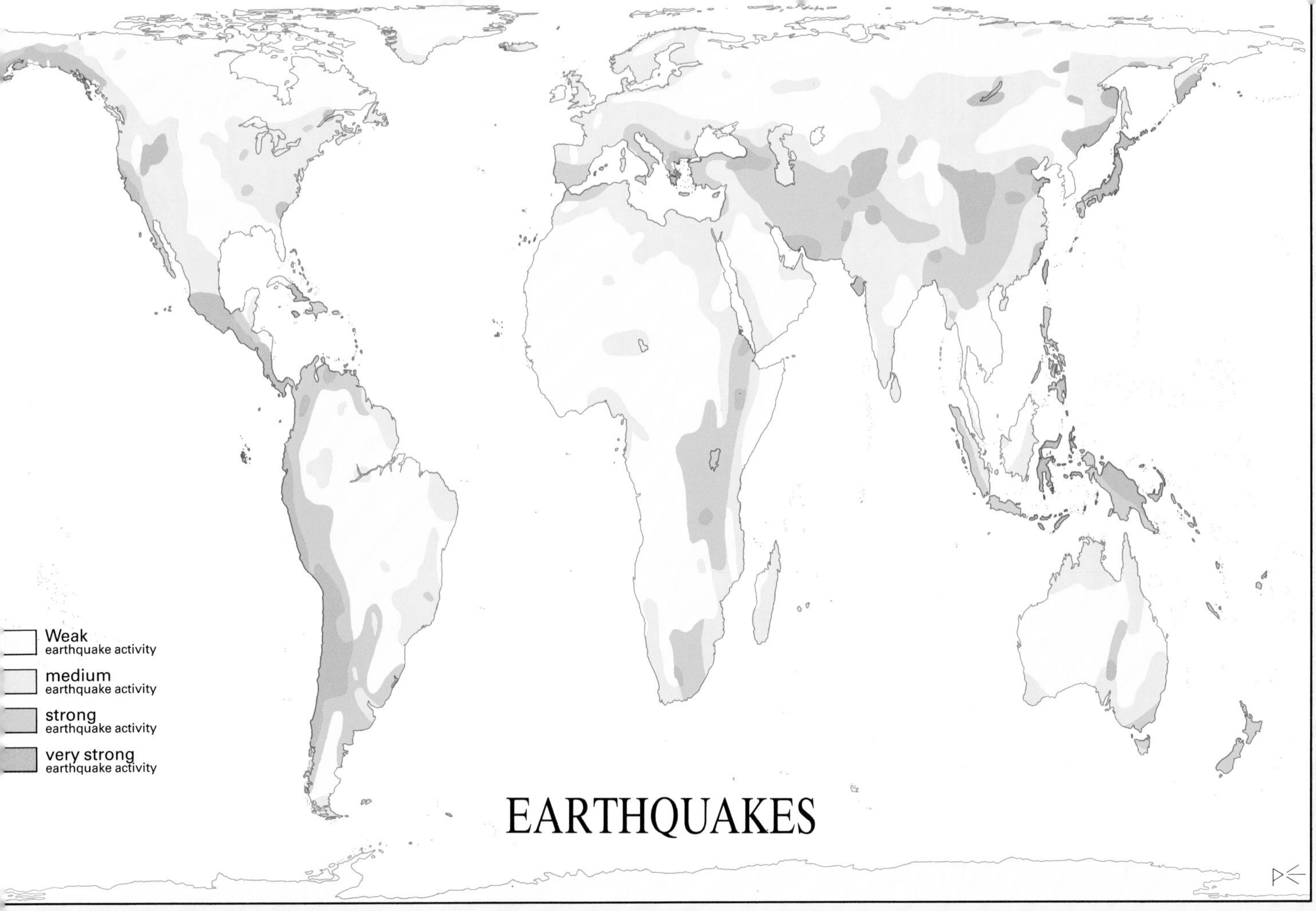

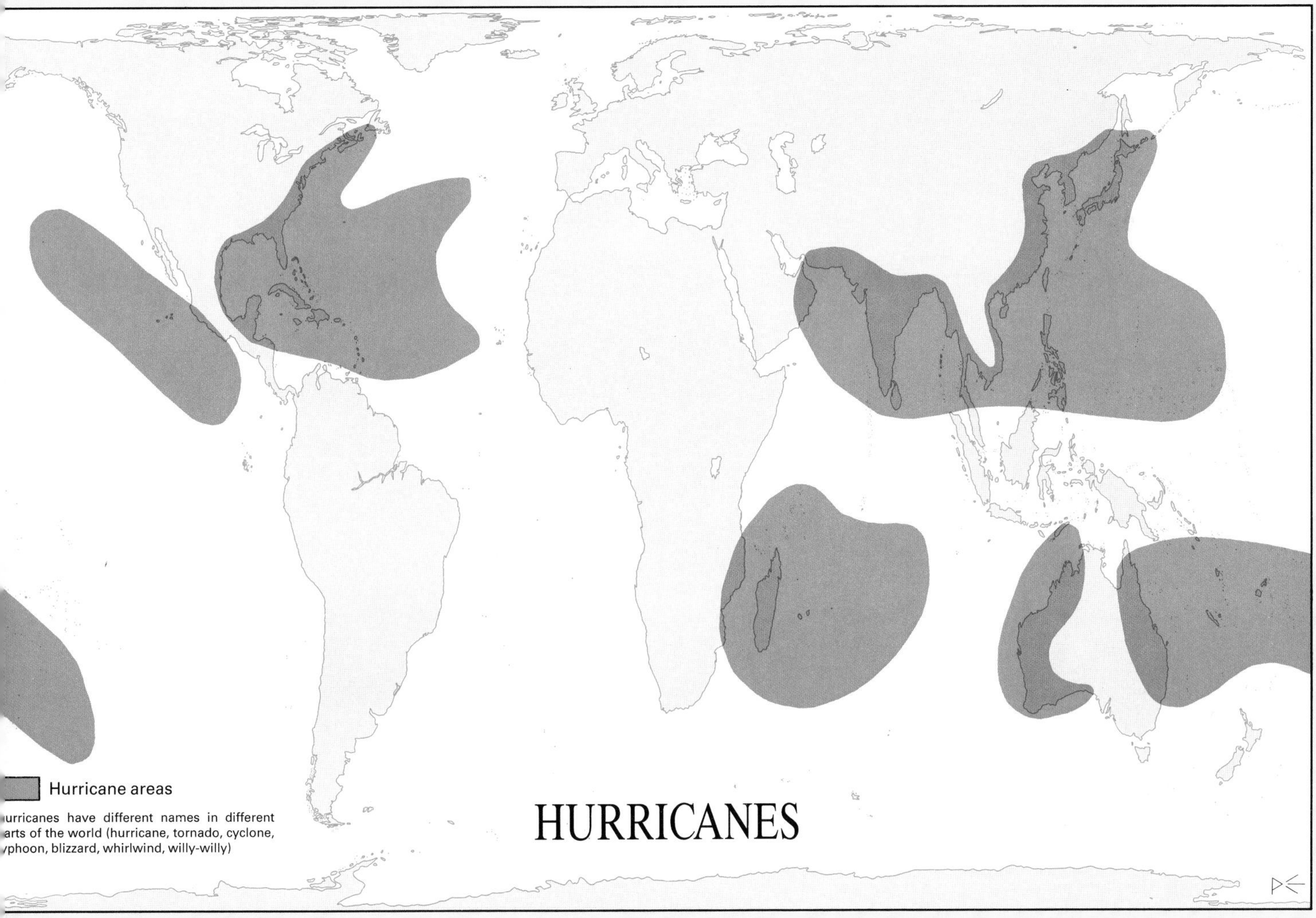

DANGERS

Greed for profit has led to the ruthless exploitation of natural resources and resulted in the emergence of new dangers in our day—deforestation, exhaustion of the soil, the pollution of air and water, the rapid spread of deserts, the poisoning of rivers and seas, the extermination of plant and animal species and the destruction of the ozone layer. These changes in the natural environment can threaten life and today they pose a greater danger to our existence than all the natural perils confronting us.

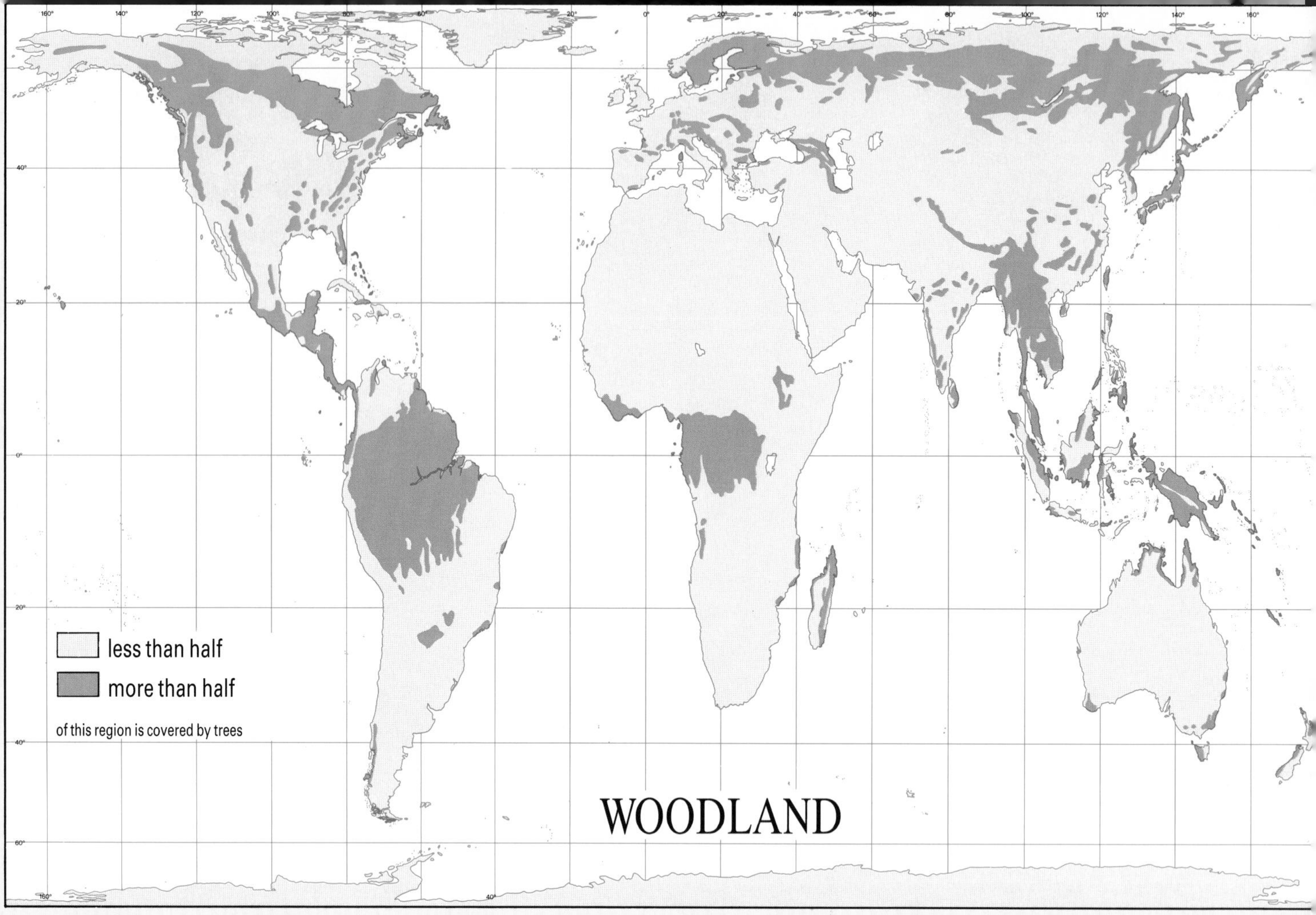

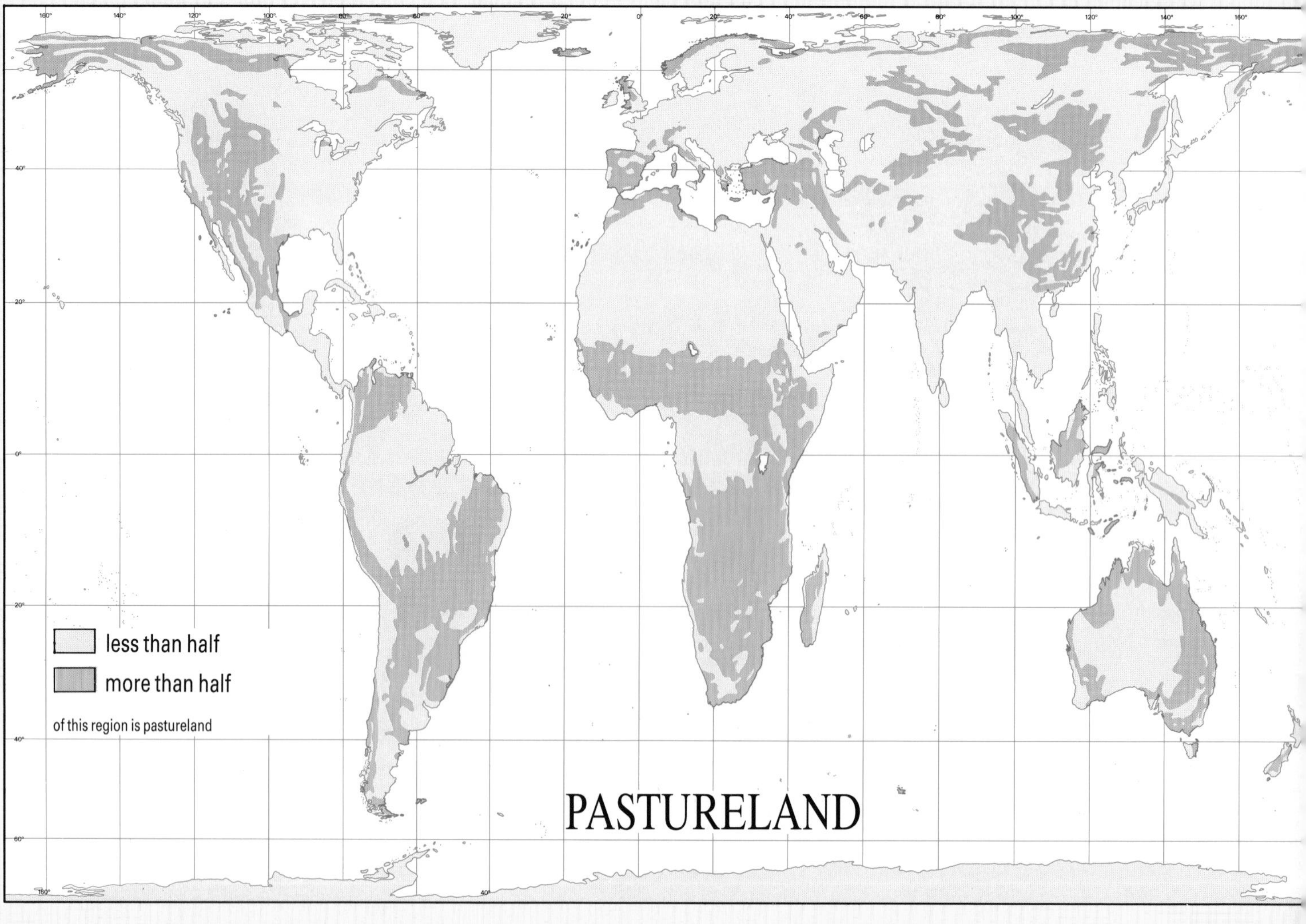

less than half

more than half

of this region is covered by trees

WOODLAND

less than half

more than half

of this region is pastureland

PASTURELAND

When life first appeared on earth two billion years ago, there was no oxygen. Only through plant life did the atmosphere become enriched with oxygen and thus make animal life possible. All higher life forms today, exist only because of the oxygen continually produced by plants. In addition, a sufficient quantity and quality of plant life are necessary as the basis to feed both people and animals. Yet every day some of the 25,000-odd higher types of plant life on the earth are exterminated by humans.

VEGE

less than half
more than half

this region is arable land

ARABLE LAND

less than half
more than half

this region is wasteland or desert

BARREN LAND

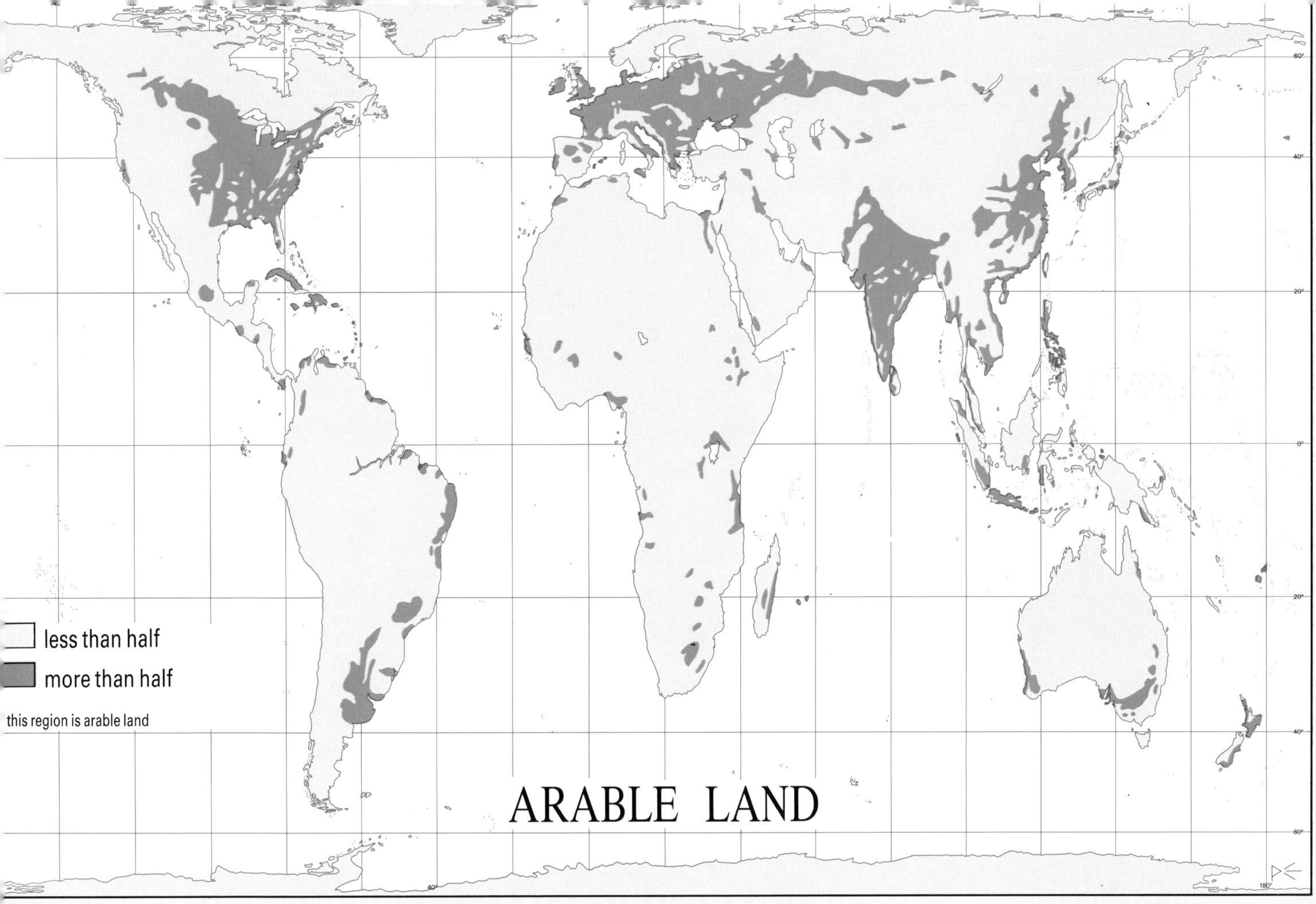

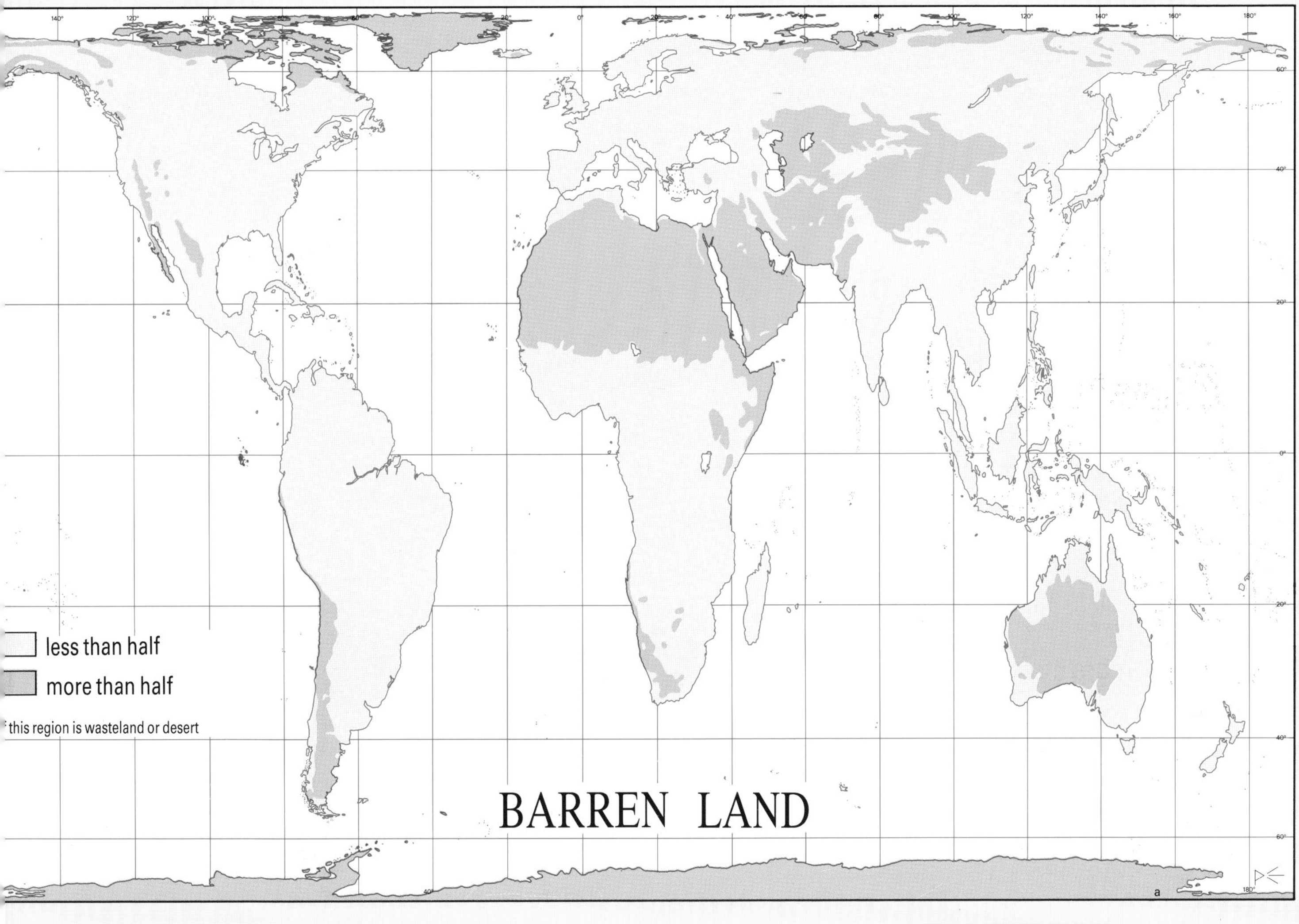

ATION

Plants are less demanding than people. They flourish in regions where permanent human settlement is impossible—steppes, tundra, prairies, karst, savannahs, taiga. Grass and moss grow almost everywhere in these regions and provide food for most animals. If we include the fertile fields and meadows of the temperate zones, about 50% of the land surface of the earth is pastureland. The other half consists of woodland (26%), arable (11%) and desert (13%).

Greenland

Alaska
(U.S.A.)

C A N A D A

UNITED STATES OF AMERICA
(U.S.A.)

M E X I C O

BAHAMAS

CUBA

DOMINICAN
REPUBLIC
HAITI

BELIZE

JAMAICA

ST. KITTS &
NEVIS

ANTIGUA & BARBUDA

DOMINICA

GUATEMALA HONDURAS

EL SALVADOR

NICARAGUA

ST VINCENT &
THE GRENADINES

ST LUCIA
BARBADOS

GRENADA

TRINIDAD & TOBAGO

COSTA RICA

PANAMA

VENEZUELA

GUYANA

SURINAME

French
Guiana

COLOMBIA

ECUADOR

P
E
R
U

B R A Z I L

BOLIVIA

C
H
I
L
E

PARAGUAY

A
R
G
E
N
T
I
N
A

URUGUAY

ICELAND

REPUBLIC
OF IRELAND

UNITED
KINGDOM

SPAIN

PORTUGAL

MOROCCO

ALG

WESTERN
SAHARA

MAURITANIA

SENEGAL

GAMBIA

GUINEA-BISSAU

GUINEA

SIERRA LEONE

CÔTE
D'IVOIRE

LIBERIA

MALI

BURKINA
FASO

GHANA

CAPE VERDE

Fewer than 1 inhabitant
per square kilometre

1 to 10 inhabitants
per square kilometre

10 to 100 inhabitants
per square kilometre

100 to 1000 inhabitants
per square kilometre

more than 1000 inhabitants
per square kilometre. The symbols mean
· 500,000 to 1 million inhabitants
● 1 million to 10 million inhabitants
■ more than 10 million inhabitants

Some 50,000 years ago humans began to build shelters. At first they made constructions
of branches and skins, which could be transported. Soon mud and clay began to be
used to cover the framework of branches. This was the beginning of our settled existence.
People started to tame animals and cultivate the soil. The first towns were built about
6,000 years ago, and the first city of a million inhabitants appeared 2,000 years ago.

PEOPLE A

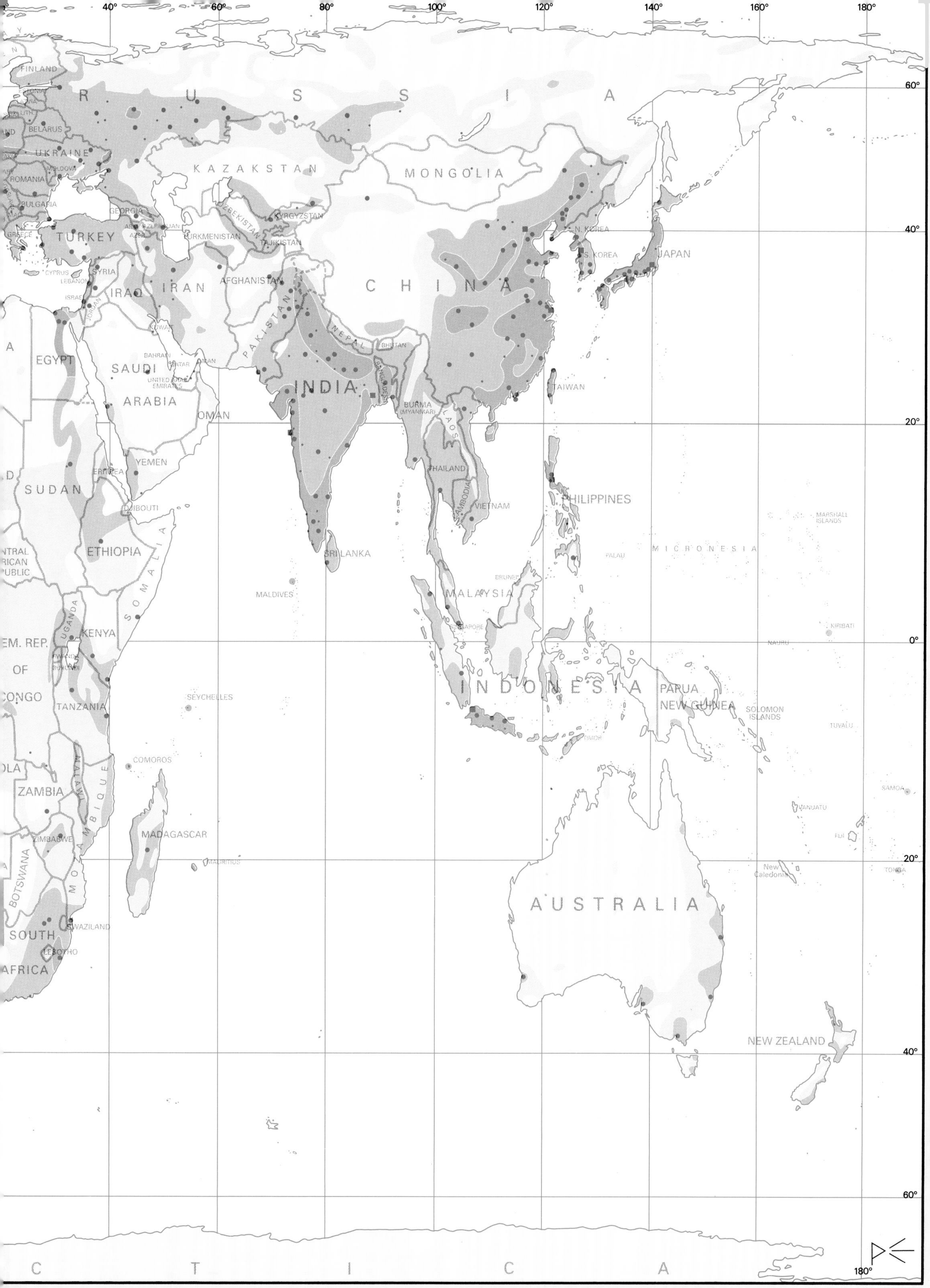

D CITIES

In about 1840 the world's population was one billion. One hundred years later it had doubled. Since then it has been growing by a further billion every 10 to 20 years. Today the average population density is about 25 people per square kilometre. Some countries however have over 500 inhabitants per square kilometre and in two hundred major cities there are over 10,000 to a square kilometre. In North Africa, Siberia, Canada, South America and Australia, however, vast areas are completely unpopulated.

With the earliest city-states 5,000 years ago came the first communities that saw themselves as political entities within territorially defined areas. As a result of the drive of the rich and powerful to subjugate and exploit other peoples these states grew into great empires that expanded and asserted themselves by force. The latest expression of this conception of the state was the Europeanisation of the world in the past five centuries. Its culmination in our epoch opened the way for all peoples to live together in solidarity in a world state.

STA

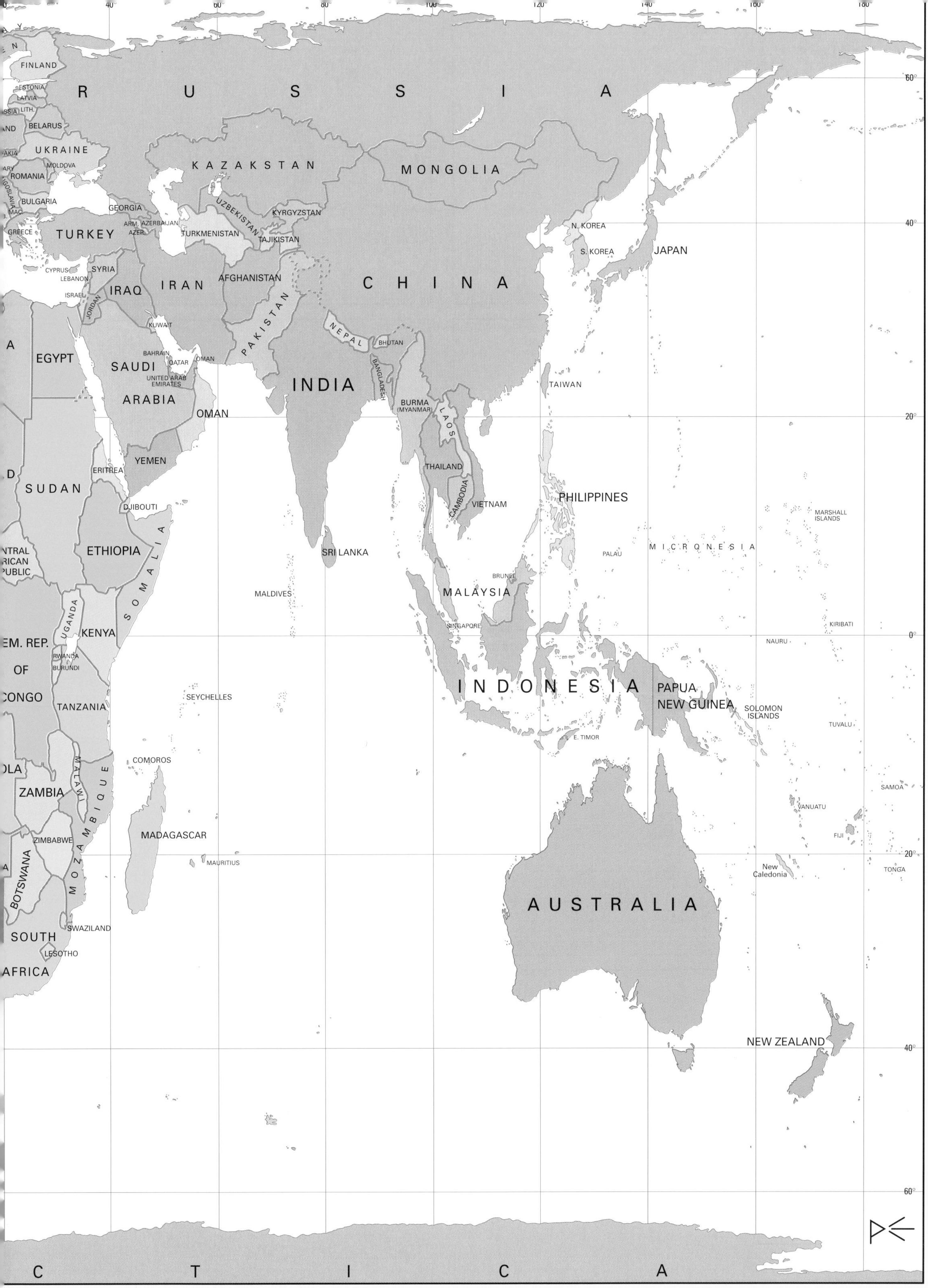

N
FINLAND
ESTONIA
LATVIA
SSIA LITH.
BELARUS

R   U   S   S   I   A

60°

AKIA
UKRAINE
ROMANIA
MOLDOVA

KAZAKSTAN

MONGOLIA

BULGARIA
GREECE
GEORGIA
ARM. AZERBAIJAN
AZER.
UZBEKISTAN
KYRGYZSTAN

40°

TURKEY
TURKMENISTAN
TAJIKISTAN

CYPRUS
LEBANON
SYRIA
ISRAEL
JORDAN
IRAQ
IRAN
AFGHANISTAN

N. KOREA
S. KOREA
JAPAN

CHINA

KUWAIT

EGYPT
SAUDI
BAHRAIN
QATAR
OMAN
UNITED ARAB
EMIRATES

PAKISTAN
NEPAL
BHUTAN

TAIWAN

20°

ARABIA
OMAN
INDIA
BANGLADESH
BURMA
(MYANMAR)

YEMEN
ERITREA

LAOS

SUDAN
DJIBOUTI

THAILAND

PHILIPPINES

ETHIOPIA
SOMALIA

CAMBODIA
VIETNAM

MARSHALL
ISLANDS

NTRAL
RICAN
PUBLIC

SRI LANKA

PALAU

M I C R O N E S I A

UGANDA
EM. REP.
KENYA
RWANDA
BURUNDI

MALDIVES

MALAYSIA
BRUNEI

KIRIBATI

OF
CONGO
TANZANIA

SINGAPORE

NAURU

0°

SEYCHELLES

I N D O N E S I A
PAPUA
NEW GUINEA
SOLOMON
ISLANDS

TUVALU

COMOROS
E. TIMOR

OLA
ZAMBIA

SAMOA

ZIMBABWE
MADAGASCAR

VANUATU

BOTSWANA
MOZAMBIQUE
MALAWI

MAURITIUS

FIJI

20°

New
Caledonia

TONGA

SOUTH
SWAZILAND
LESOTHO

AUSTRALIA

AFRICA

NEW ZEALAND

40°

60°

Most of today's states have come into existence in the past 60 years. After the Second World War there were 70 independent states in the world; today there are nearly 200. And there are still a few colonies struggling for their political independence. In many independent states, dependence on the new superpowers has intensified to such an extent that their sovereignty is only nominal. In addition, an ever-growing number of linguistic, ethnic and cultural groups are seeking independence from the states in which they find themselves.

FRENCH

Mother tongue and/or official language
Foreign language given preference in the country

SPANISH

Mother tongue and/or official language
Foreign language given preference in the country

GERMAN

Mother tongue and/or official language
Foreign language given preference in the country

RUSSIAN

Mother tongue and/or official language
Foreign language given preference in the country

MALAY

Mother tongue and/or official language

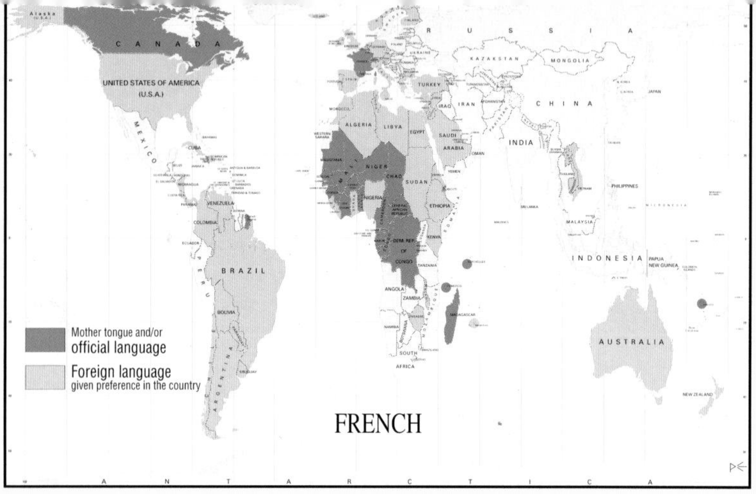

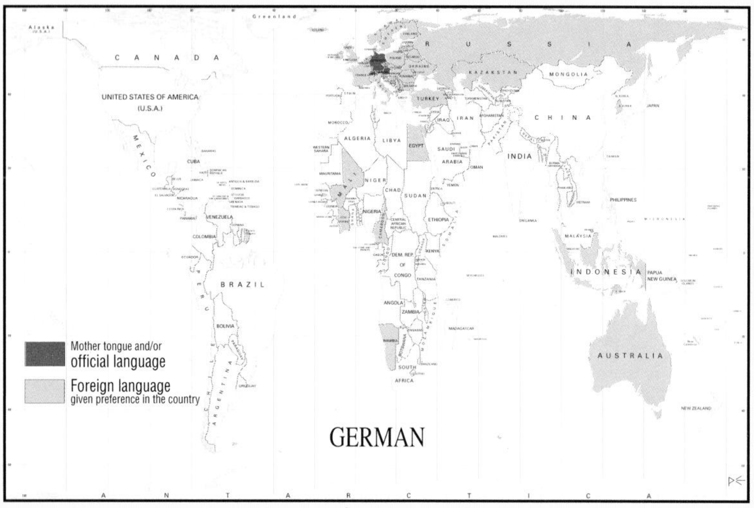

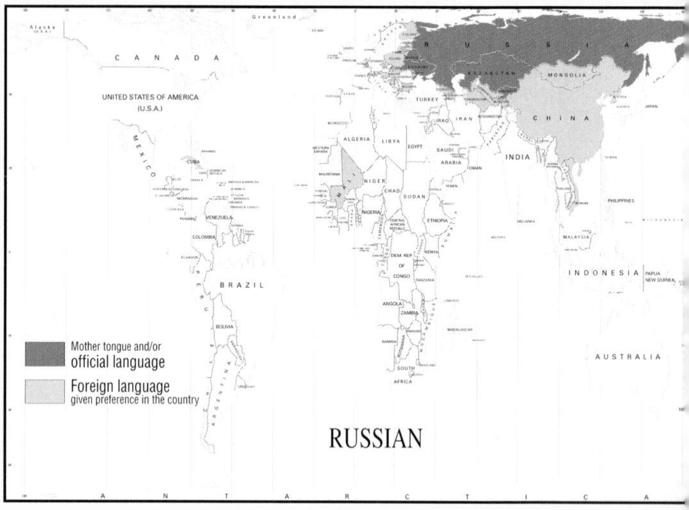

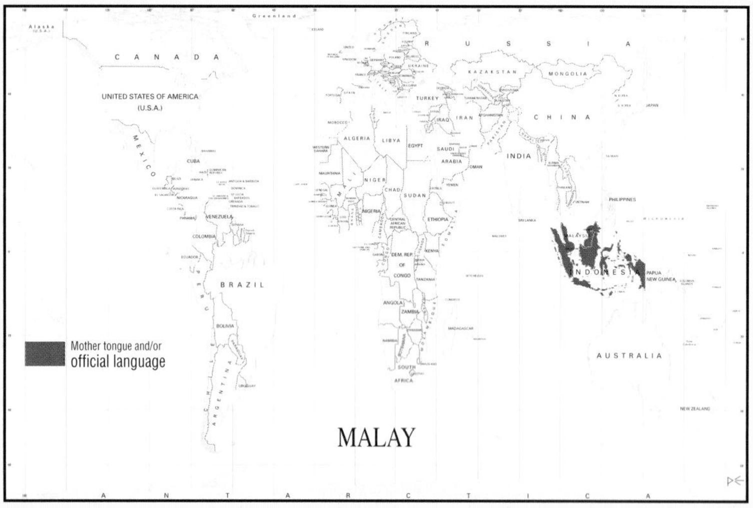

PROPORTION OF THE WORLD'S POPULATION SPEA OF THESE MAJOR LANGUAGES AS THE MOTHER

French	Spanish	Portuguese	English	German	Russian
1.2%	5.6%	2.8%	5.4%	1.6%	2.8%

CHINESE

Mother tongue and/or official language
Foreign language given preference in the country

JAPANESE

Mother tongue and/or official language
Foreign language given preference in the country

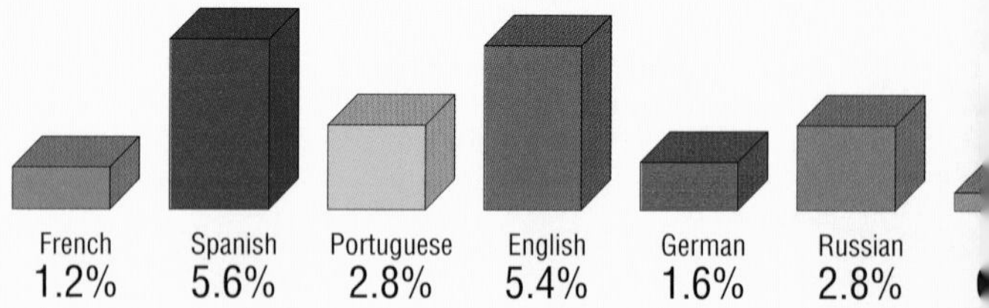

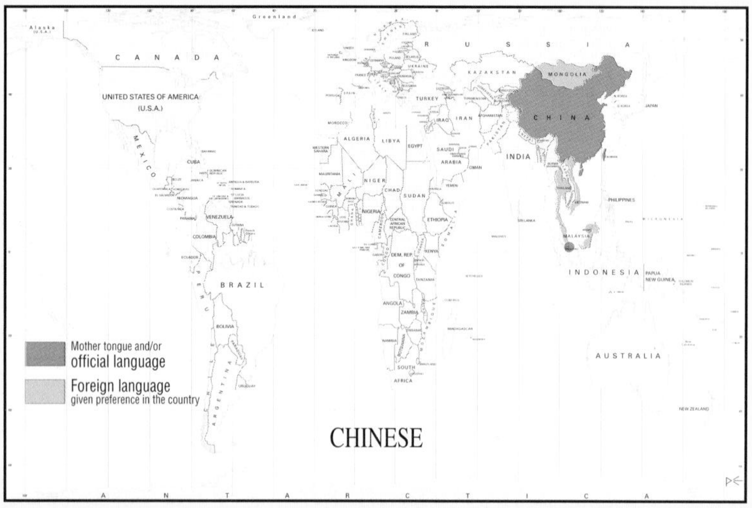

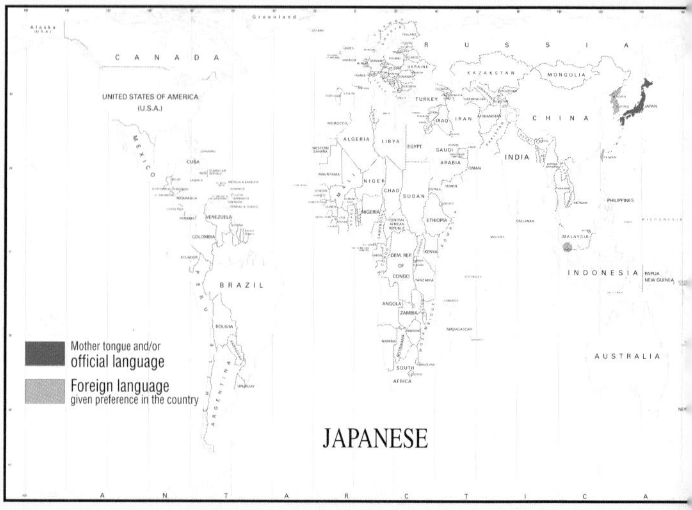

After attaining an upright stance some 20 million years ago, humans began to improve their verbal expression. But only after the creation and use of tools less than 1 million years ago did development towards articulate speech begin. In constant interaction with the growth of our mental ability, human language has since become more and more elaborate. The process is still going on, and every human being is contributing to it. By increasing our own vocabulary we contribute to the general growth of comprehension. Exactitude of the spoken language is both the expression and the origin of clear thinking, and makes possible a true and comprehensive view of the world.

PORTUGUESE

ENGLISH

Mother tongue and/or official language

Foreign language given preference in the country

ITALIAN

Mother tongue and/or official language

Foreign language given preference in the country

BENGALI

Mother tongue and/or official language

| Malay 0.3% | Arabic 2.9% | Chinese 20.5% | Japanese 2.0% | Hindi 3.0% | Swahili 2% |

ARABIC

Mother tongue and/or official language

Foreign language given preference in the country

HINDI

Mother tongue and/or official language

Foreign language given preference in the country

SWAHILI

Mother tongue and/or official language

Foreign language given preference in the country

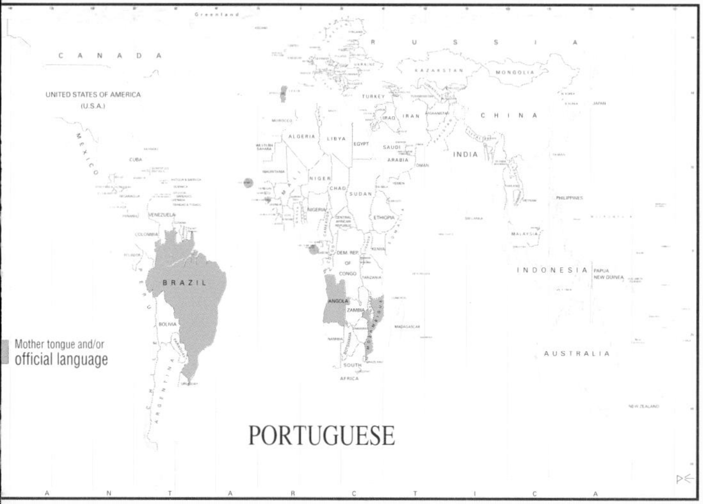

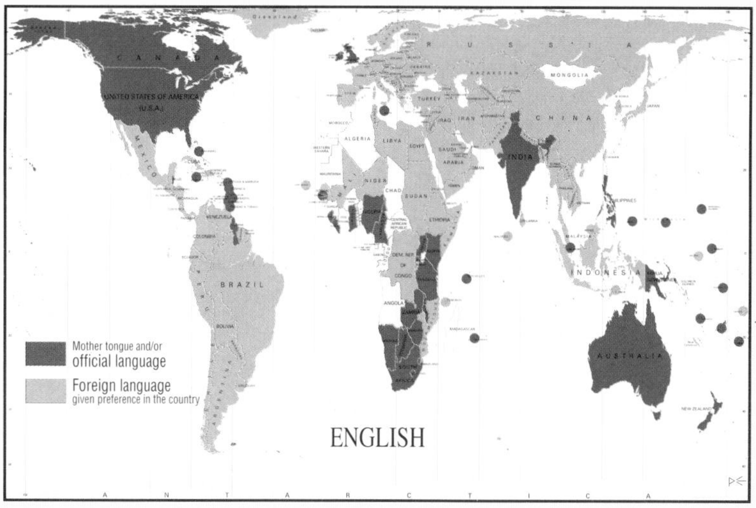

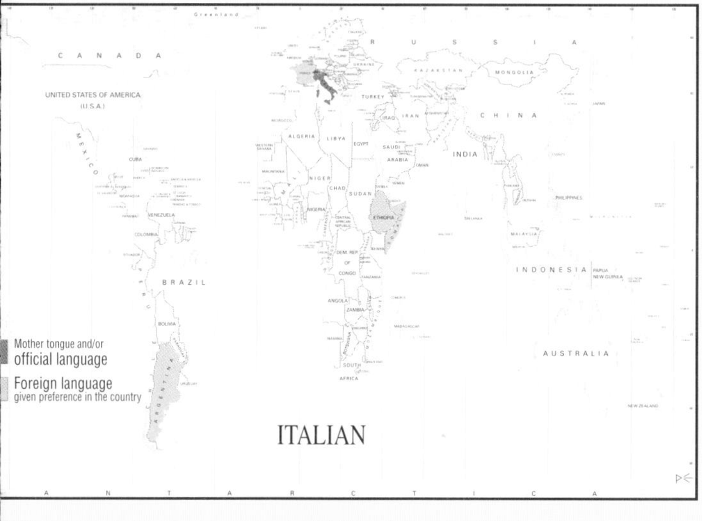

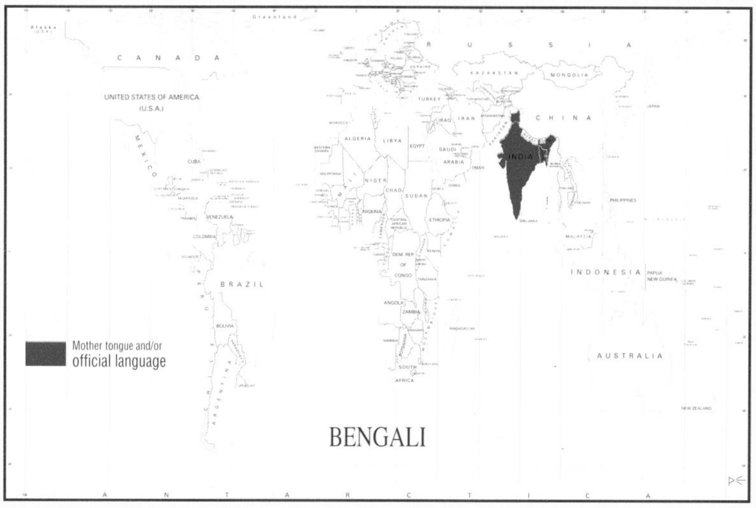

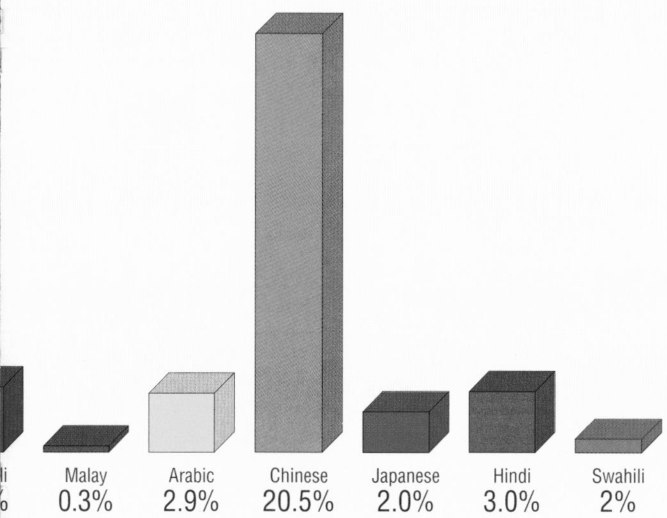

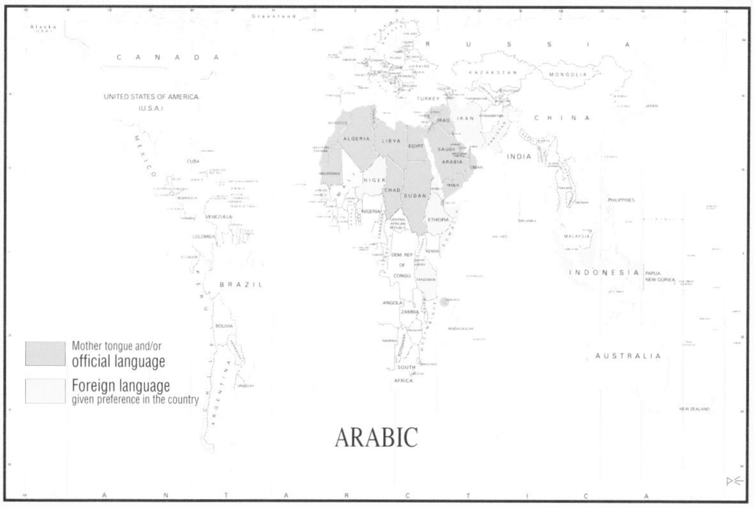

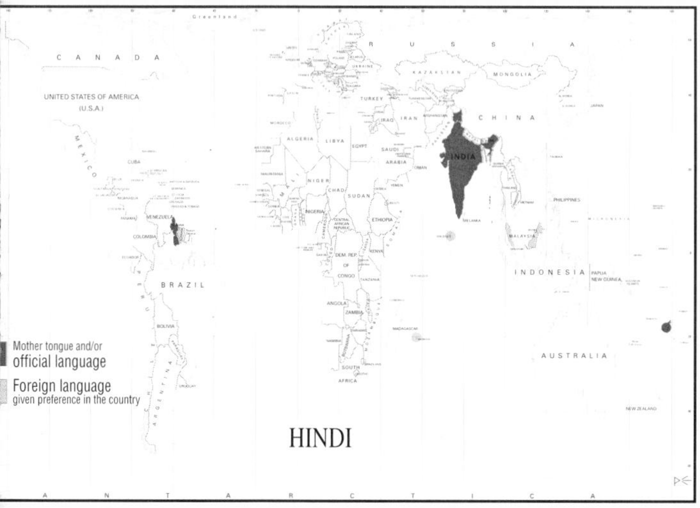

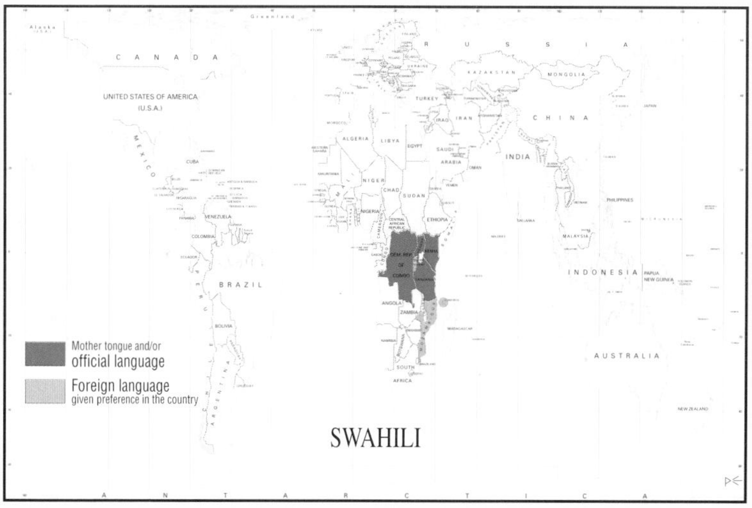

AGES

Although the world's various cultures are drawing closer together, there are still thousands of different languages in existence. But only fourteen of these are spoken as a mother tongue by more than 1% of humankind. After the 500 years of Europeanisation of the world, half of these major languages are European in origin. It also seems probable that English, spoken 500 years ago by only 1% of the world's population, will become the world language used by all peoples of the world. But at the same time the multiplicity of languages will remain as long as the peoples of the earth retain their cultural identities.

SCRIPTS OF
CHINESE ORIGIN

SCRIPTS OF
INDIAN ORIGIN

SCRIPTS OF
GREEK ORIGIN

From left to right
From right to left
From top to bottom

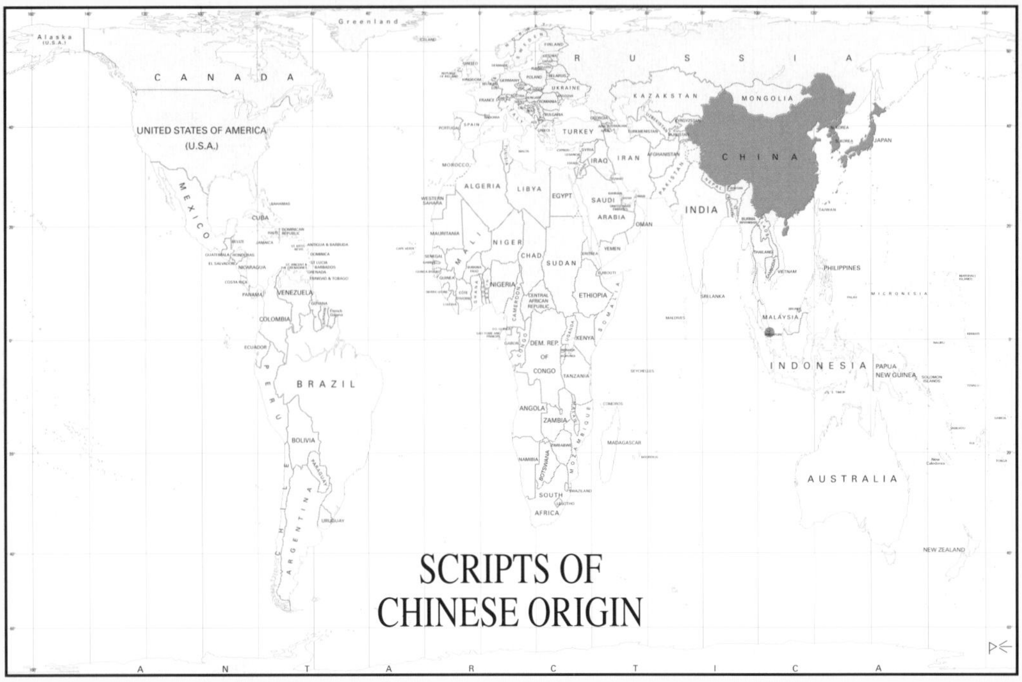

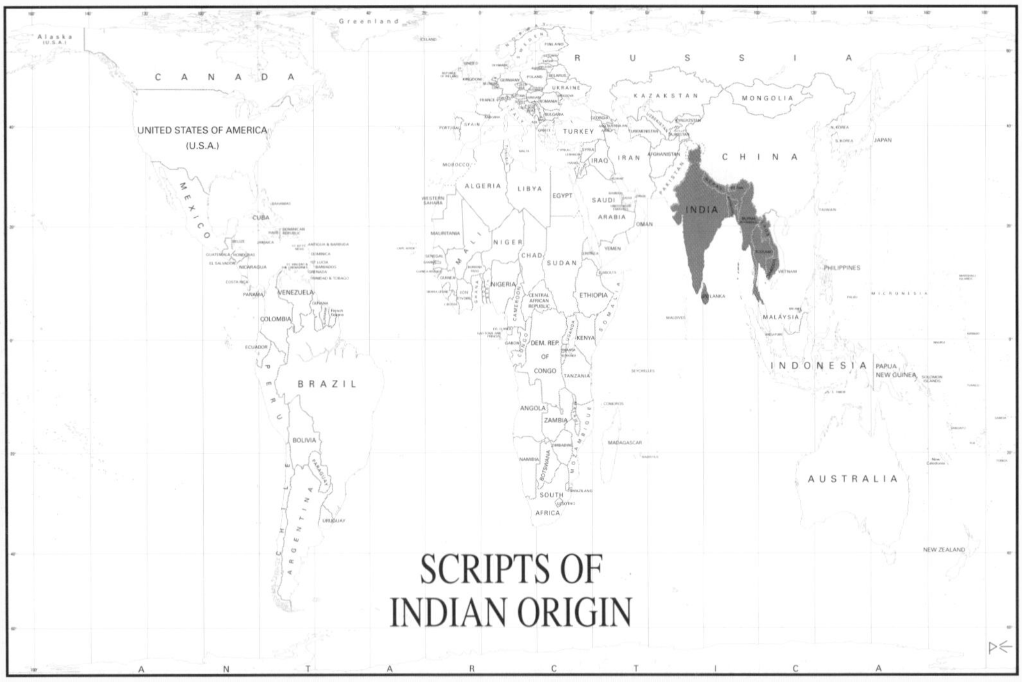

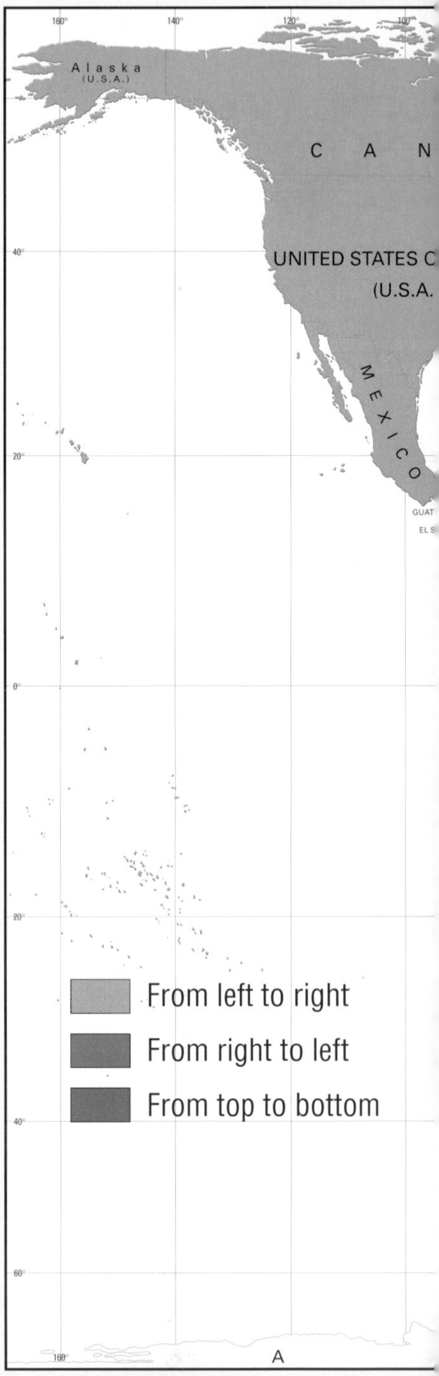

Pictures of their environment drawn by people developed 6,000 years ago into pictorial writing. This meant that language could be used to communicate over a distance or to pass information on to later generations. It created the essential precondition for the emergence of human culture. Pictorial writing turned into the use of word-symbols, then of symbols denoting syllables, and finally into scripts using the letters of an alphabet, the method employed by most people today in the Greek-Cyrillic, Latin, Indian or Arabic versions. Writing makes the creative achievements of humankind immortal, but it also widens the gap between rich and poor, since for thousands of years it was regarded as a privilege.

SCF

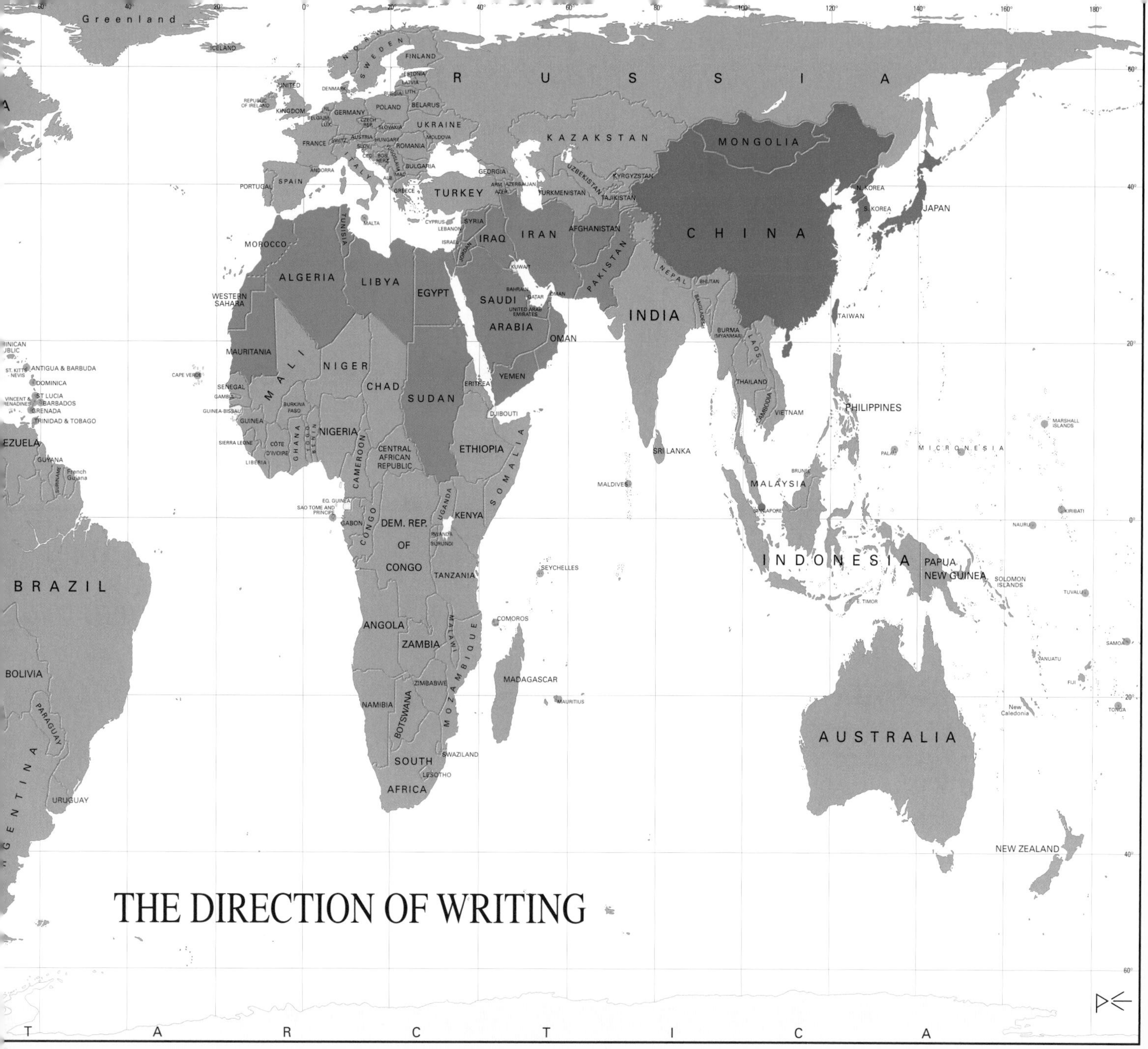

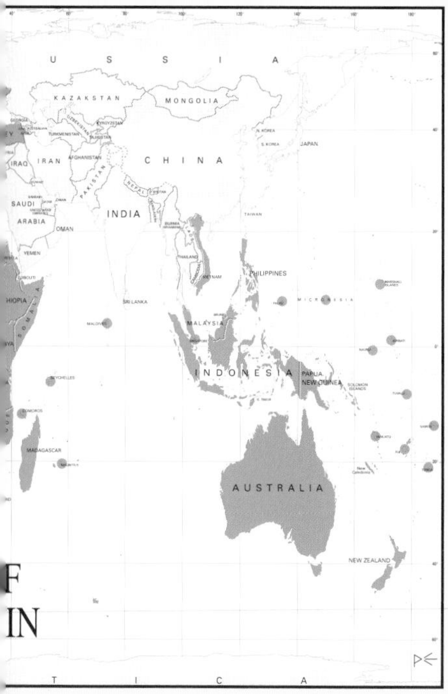

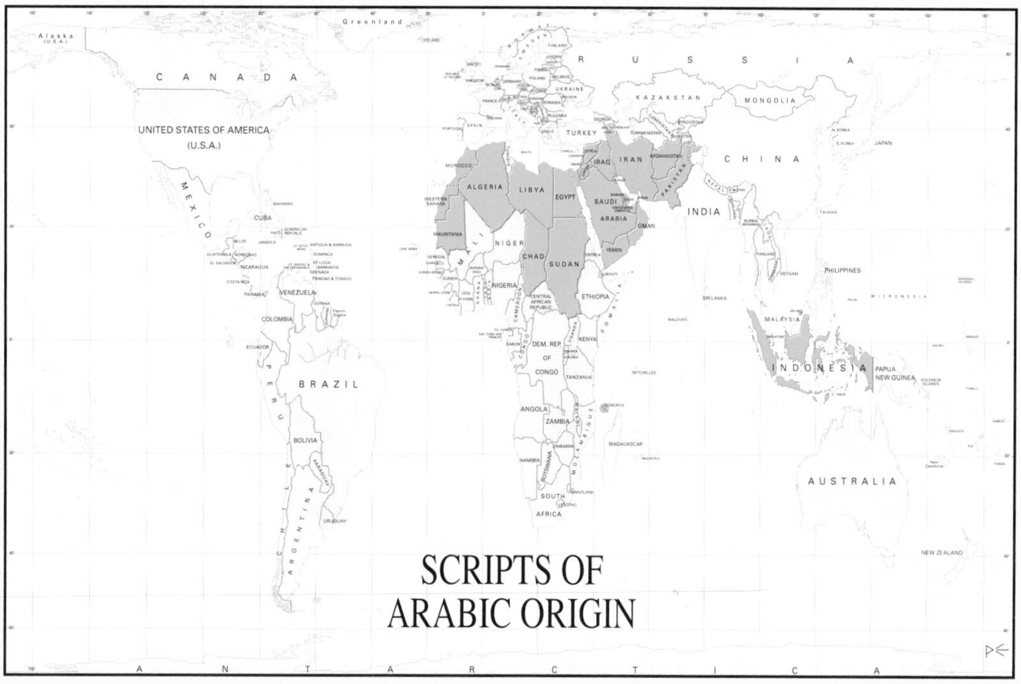

PTS

In contrast to the spoken language, writing is not in itself a direct expression of the cultural identity of a people. Turkey, Indonesia, Vietnam and other countries have in our century adopted the Latin alphabet without losing their own cultural basis. Shortly after the revolution, China also attempted to do the same, but then decided to retain the 50,000 ideograms of its traditional script, whose richness and beauty it was feared could suffer from a transcription into the 26 letters of the Latin alphabet. China and its neighbours are however in process of changing from the top-to-bottom way of writing to the Indo-European left-to-right direction. But writing is losing its prime importance in the age of radio and television.

NATURAL RELIGIONS

Less than 10%
10 to 50%
More than 50%
of the population

ISLAM

Less than 10%
10 to 50%
More than 50%
of the population

BUDDHISM

Less than 10%
10 to 50%
More than 50%
of the population

Less than 10%
10 to 50%
More than 50%
of the population

Less than 10%
10 to 50%
of the population

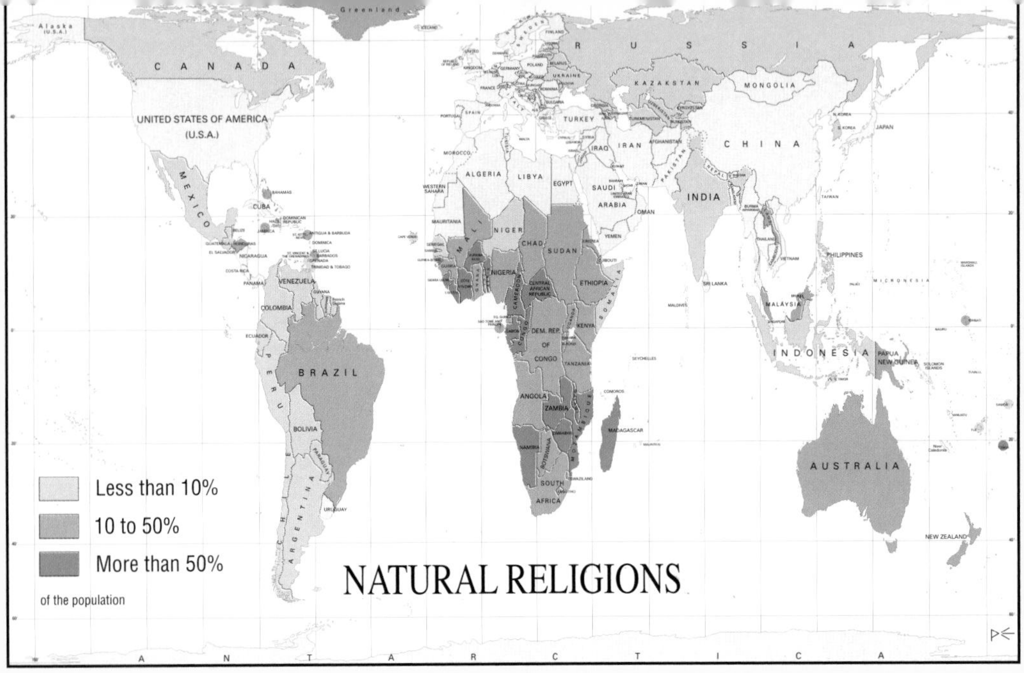

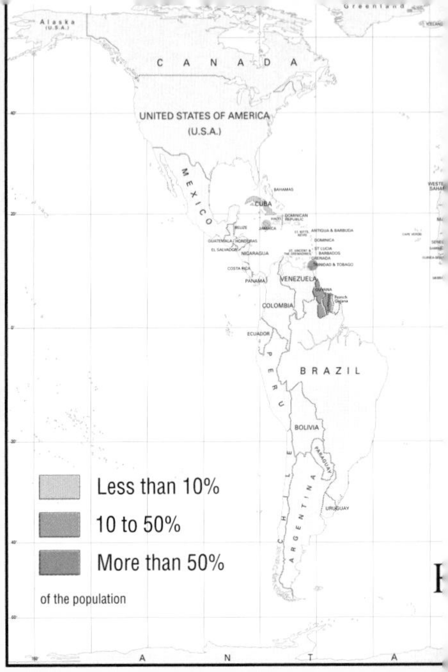

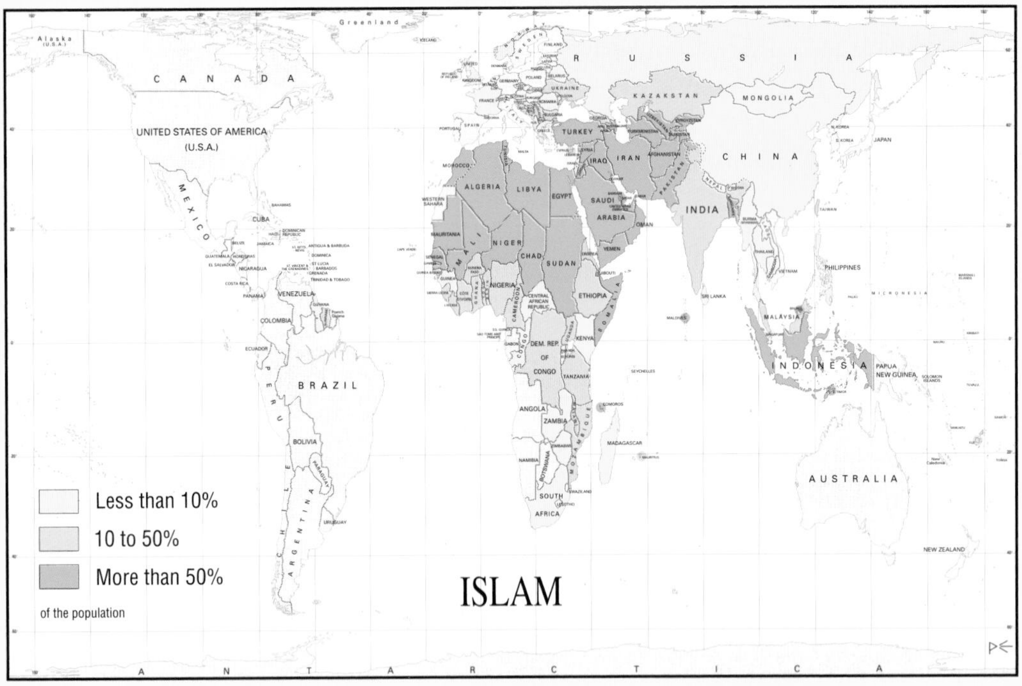

ONLY RELIGIONS WHOSE AD
OVER 1% OF THE WORLD'S P
INCLUDED ON THESE TWO P.

| Natural | Hinduism | Christianity | I: |
| 4% | 10% | 22% | 1 |

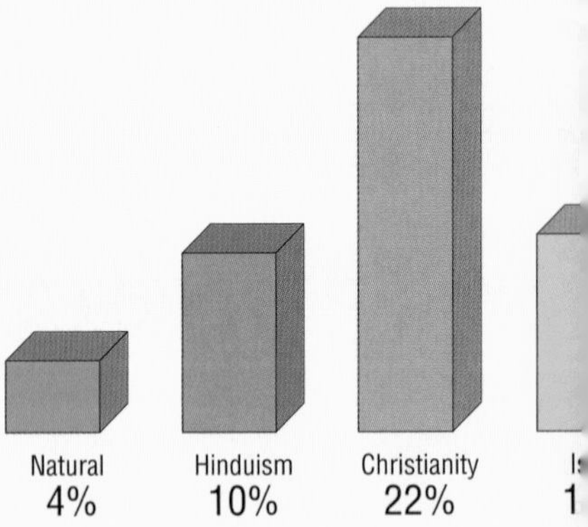

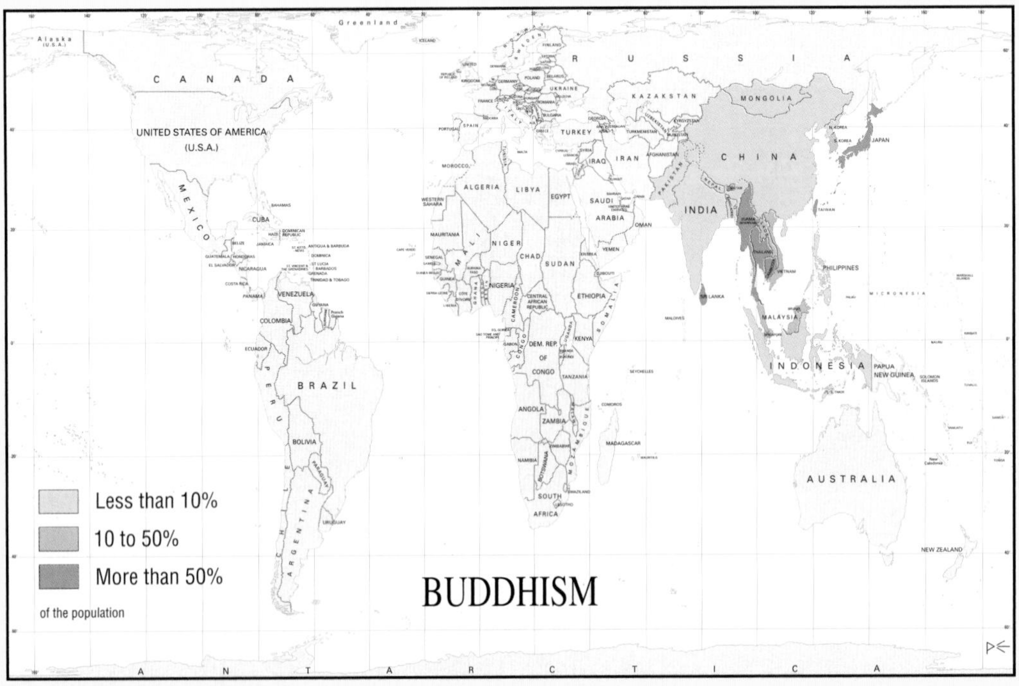

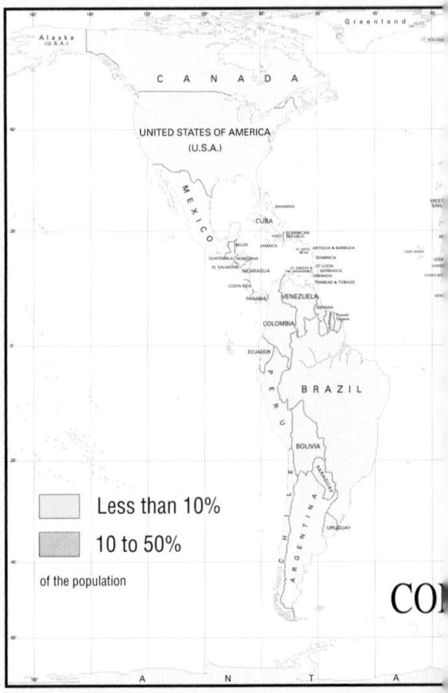

For over two million years, humans lived without religion. A few thousand years ago people started to try to influence the powers of nature by means of prayers and sacrifices. These nature-oriented religions were followed by world religions that tried to remove the fear of mortality by promising the continuation of life after death. In the past few hundred years science has harnessed the powers of nature and brought humanity back to nature, reconciling us to our mortality. As a result, only 40% of the world's population now subscribe to one of the world religions.

RELI

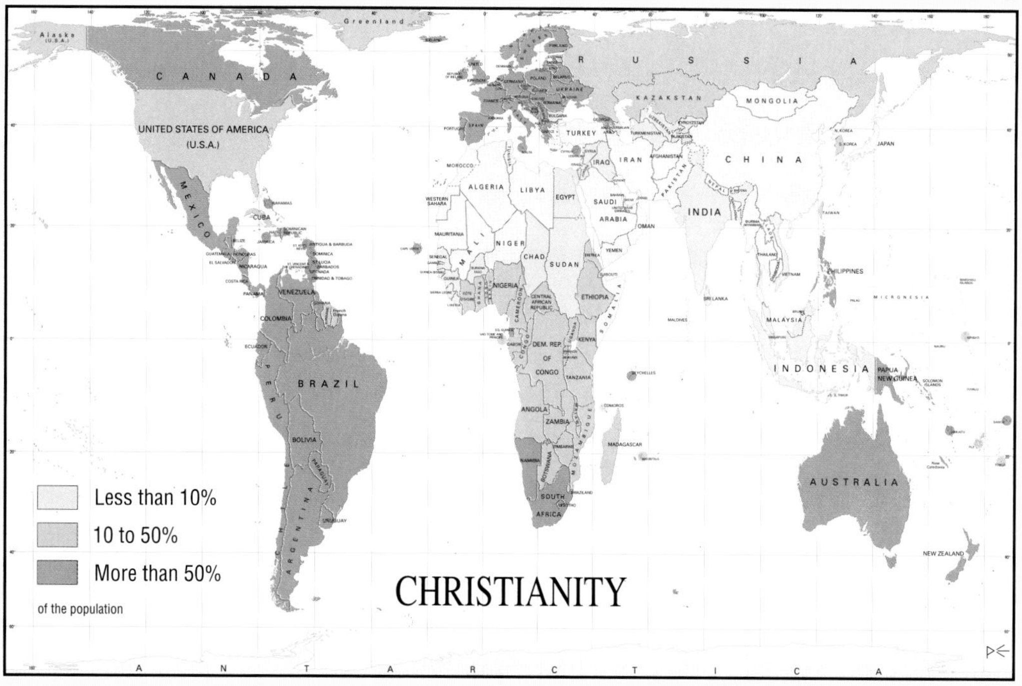

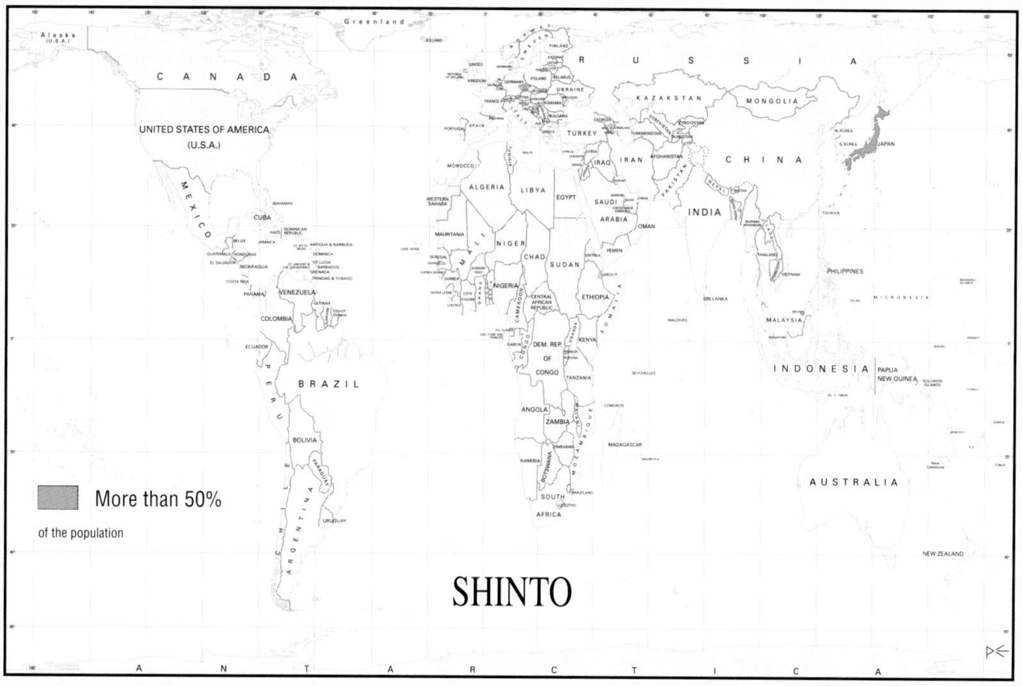

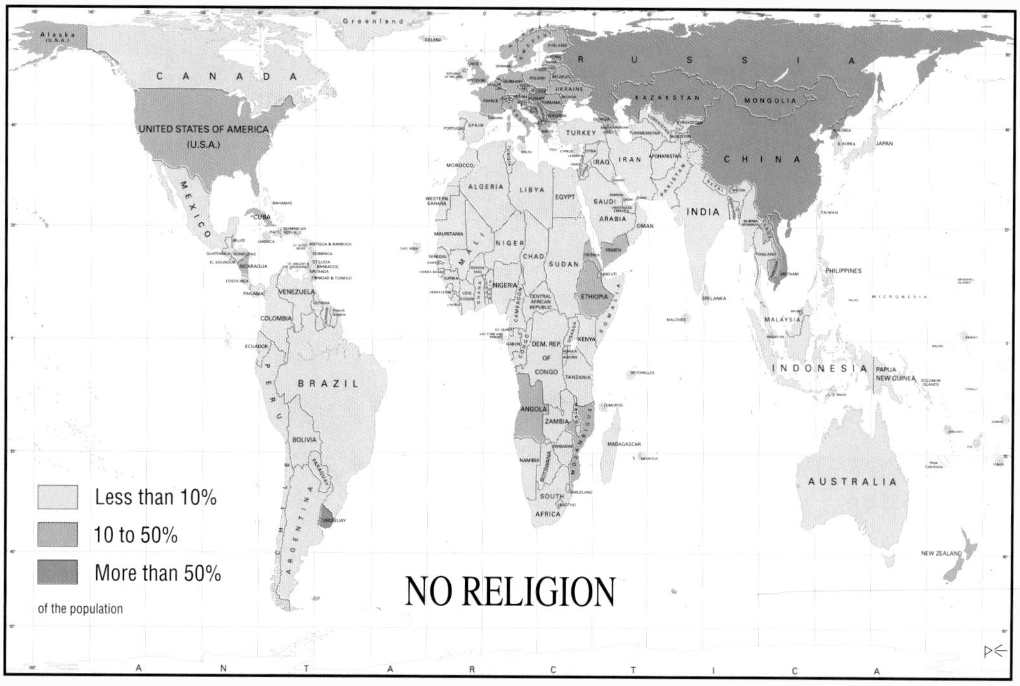

IONS

If we define religion as belief in a God, only three of the six world religions qualify. These are Hinduism, Christianity and Islam. Shintoism is about the veneration of nature, Confucianism teaches ethics without a hereafter and Buddhism also has no concept of God. A significant element of the three major world religions is about domination. Hinduism divides the classes into castes as God's commandment, Islam has been used to justify Arab and Ottoman Turkish military and political expansion, and Christianity became the ideological basis for the Europeanisation of the world in the age of discovery.

ILLITERACY

Less than 1%

1 to 5%

5 to 20%

20 to 50%

50 to 80%

More than 80%

of the total population

PRIMARY EDUCATION

Less than 40%

40 to 60%

60 to 80%

More than 80%

of the appropriate age group

SECOND

Less than 40%

40 to 60%

60 to 80%

More than 80%

of the appropriate age group

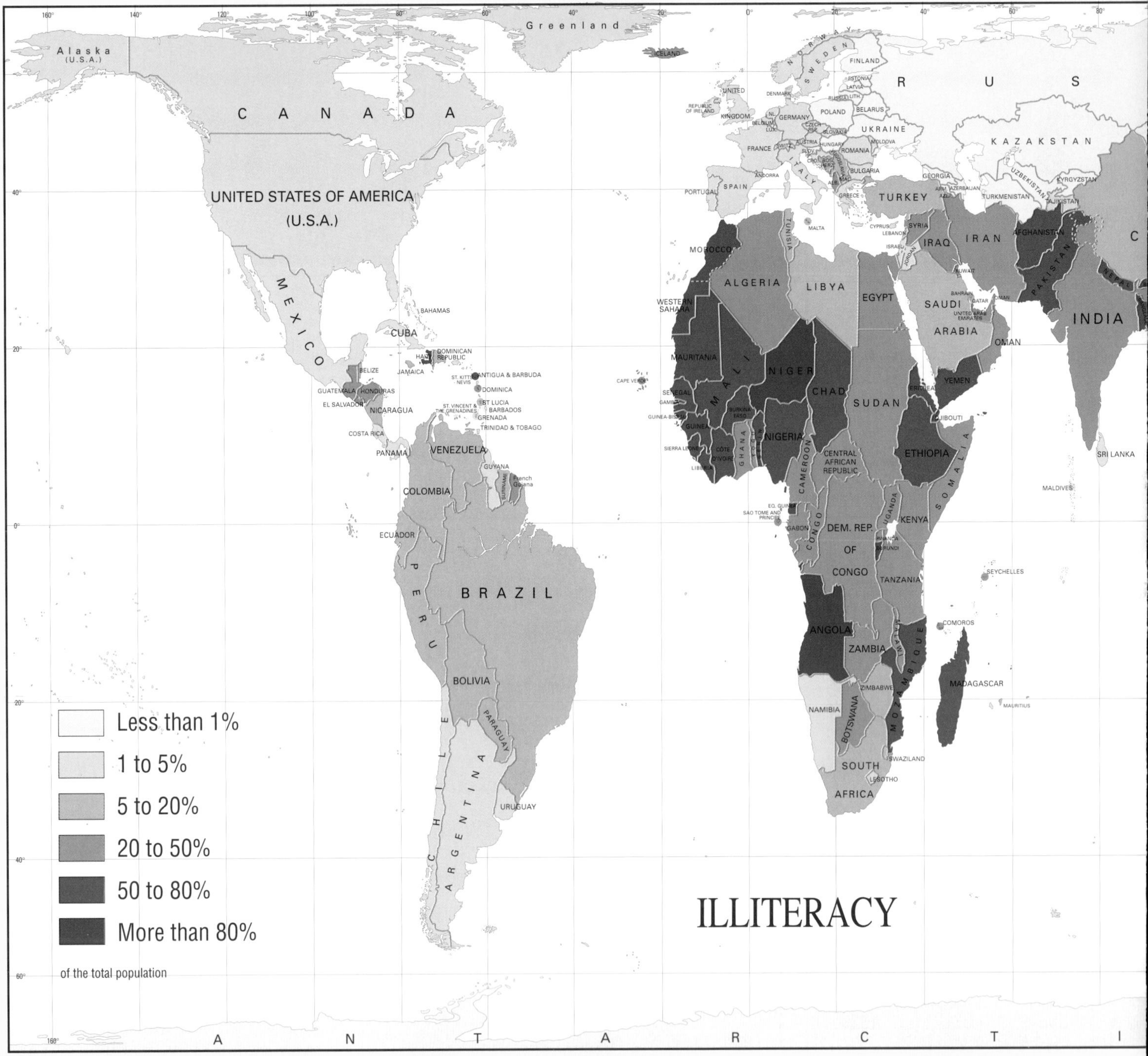

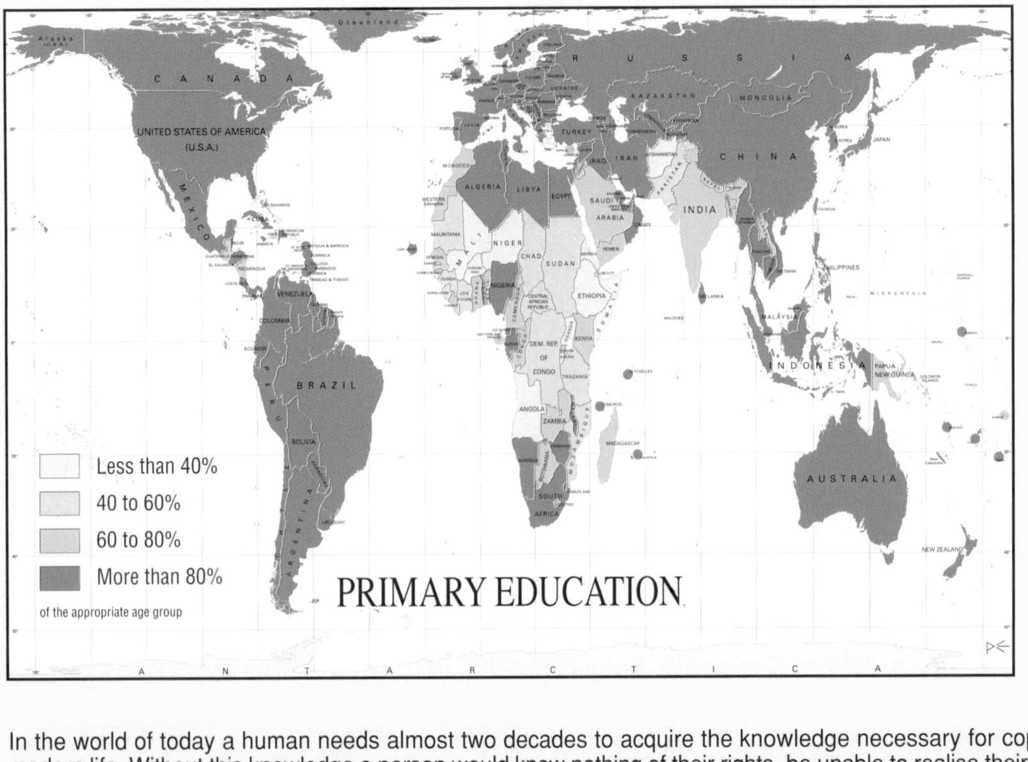

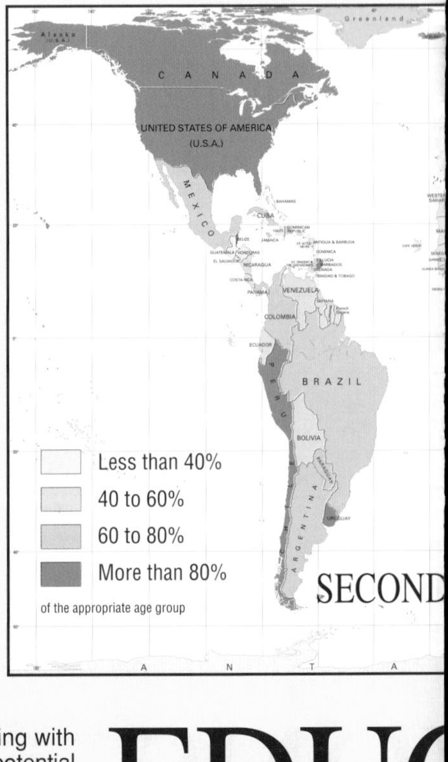

In the world of today a human needs almost two decades to acquire the knowledge necessary for coping with modern life. Without this knowledge a person would know nothing of their rights, be unable to realise their potential and could not comprehend the dangers which confront them. Without education they have no chance of controlling their own lives, but become mere pawns in the hands of those who possess education and will use such people for their own ends. The acquisition of education is therefore a means of participating in today's world.

EDUC

PUPIL / TEACHER RATIO

	Less than 20
	20 to 30
	30 to 40
	More than 40

pupils per teacher

UNIVERSITY

	Less than 100
	100 to 500
	500 to 1,000
	1,000 to 2,000
	More than 2,000

students per 100,000 of population

CATION

EXPENDITURE ON EDUCATION

	Less than 3%
	3 to 4%
	4 to 5%
	5 to 6%
	More than 6%

of the Gross National Product

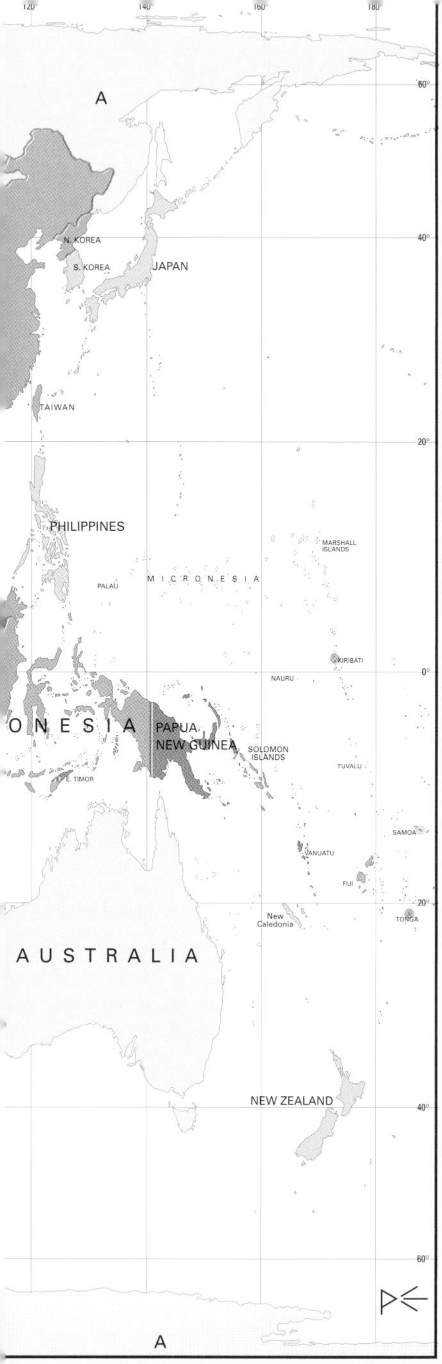

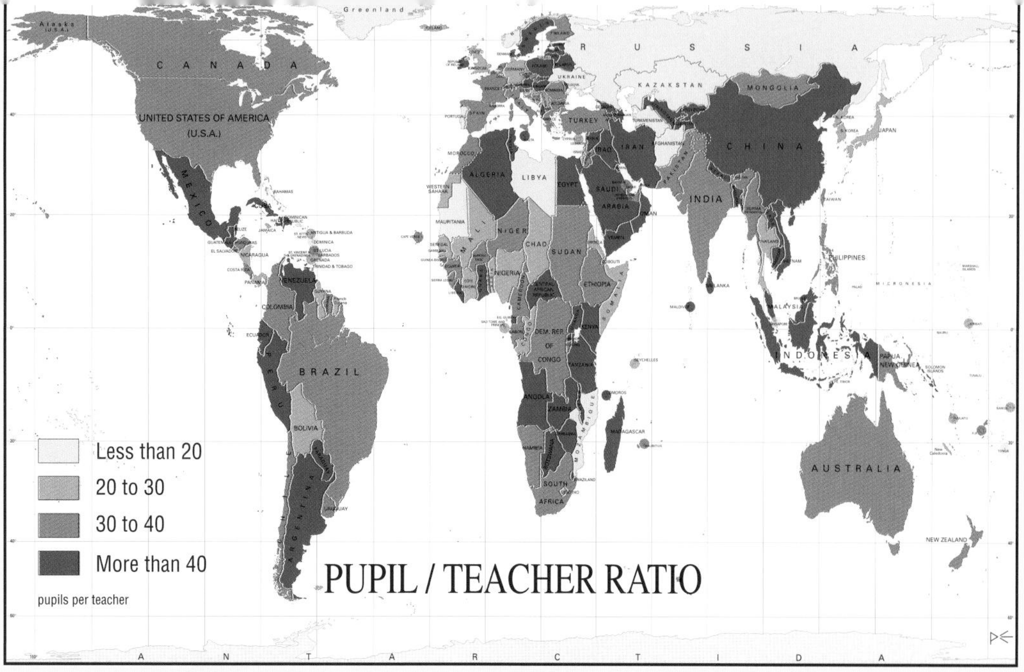

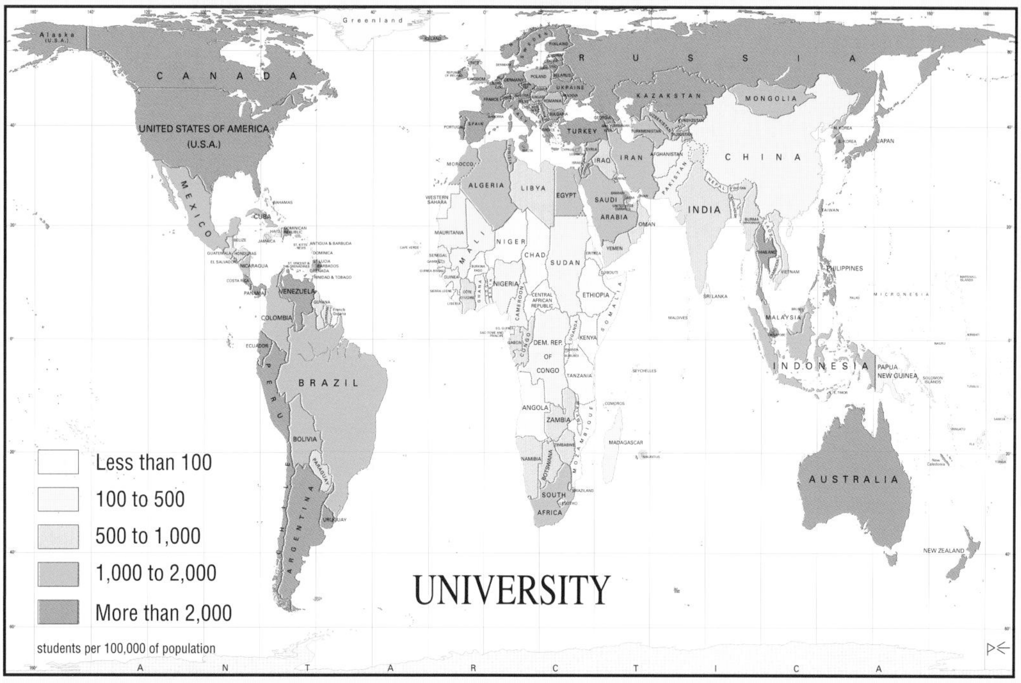

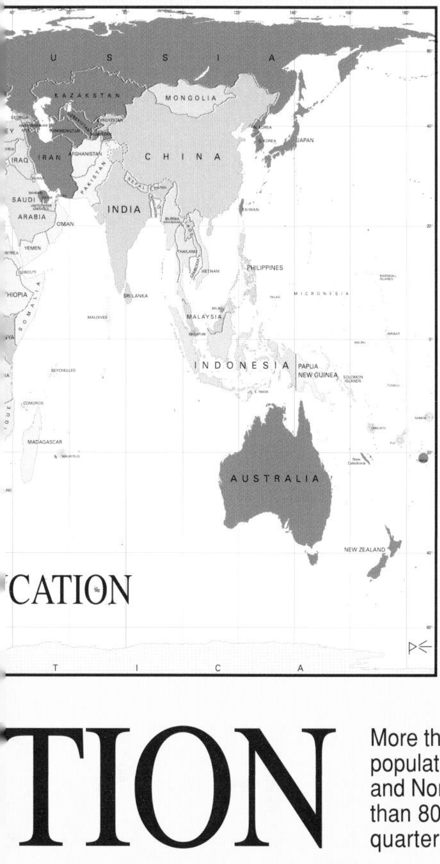

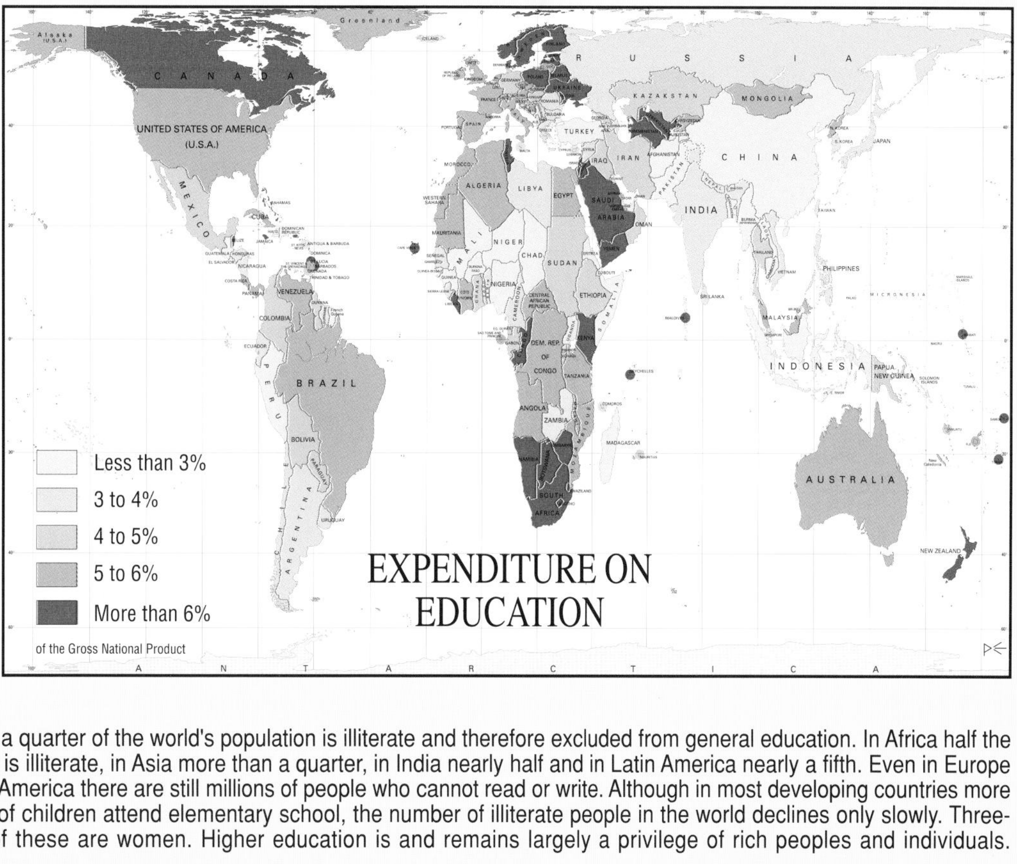

TION

More than a quarter of the world's population is illiterate and therefore excluded from general education. In Africa half the population is illiterate, in Asia more than a quarter, in India nearly half and in Latin America nearly a fifth. Even in Europe and North America there are still millions of people who cannot read or write. Although in most developing countries more than 80% of children attend elementary school, the number of illiterate people in the world declines only slowly. Three-quarters of these are women. Higher education is and remains largely a privilege of rich peoples and individuals.

UNIVERSITY TEACHERS

Very few
less than 50 per million of population

Few
50 to 100 per million of population

Average
100 to 500 per million of population

Many
500 to 1,000 per million of population

Very many
more than 1,000 per million of population

RESEARCHERS AND ENGINEERS

Very few
less than 100 per million of population

Few
100 to 500 per million of population

Average
500 to 1,000 per million of population

Many
1,000 to 5,000 per million of population

Very many
more than 5,000 per million of population

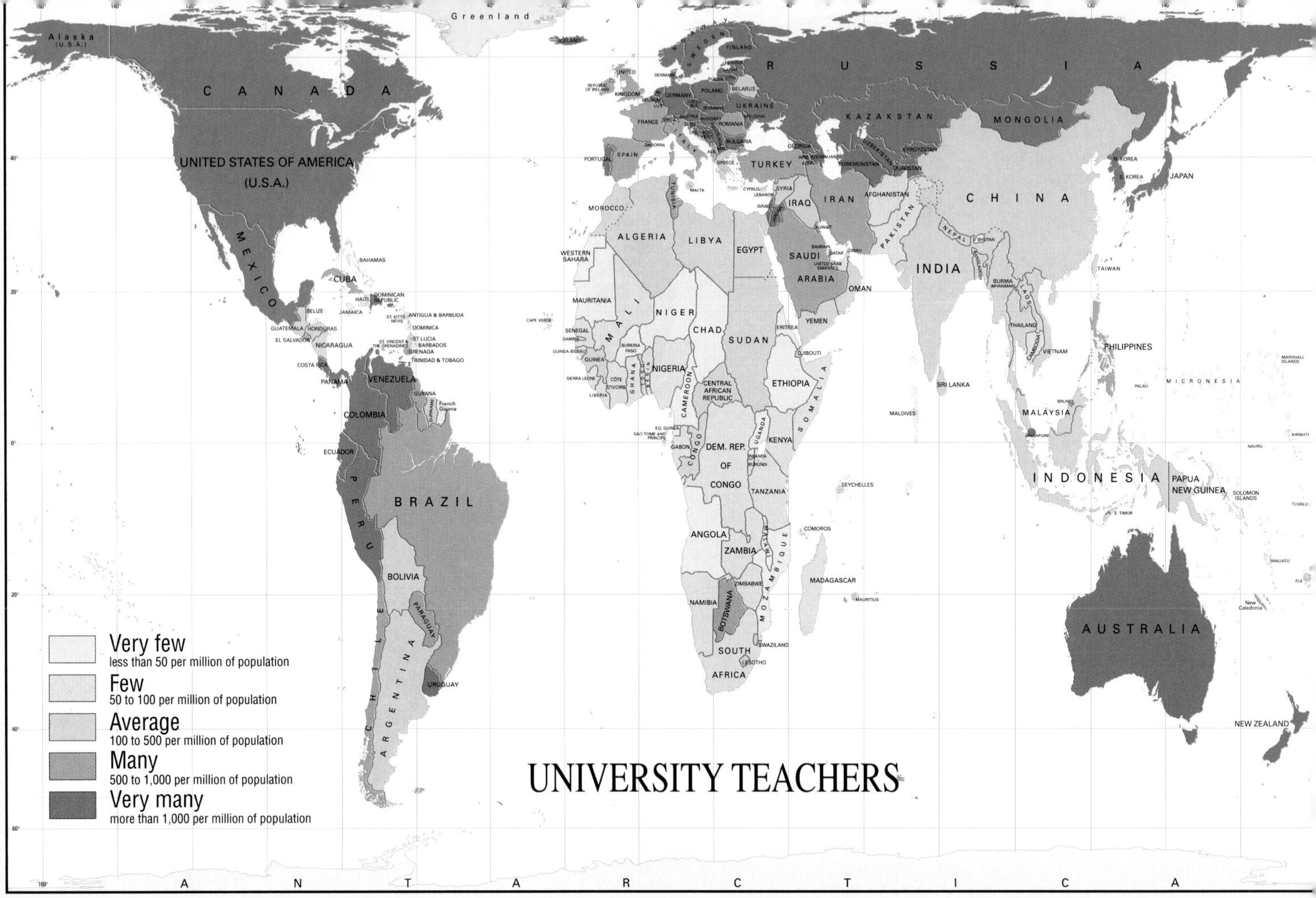

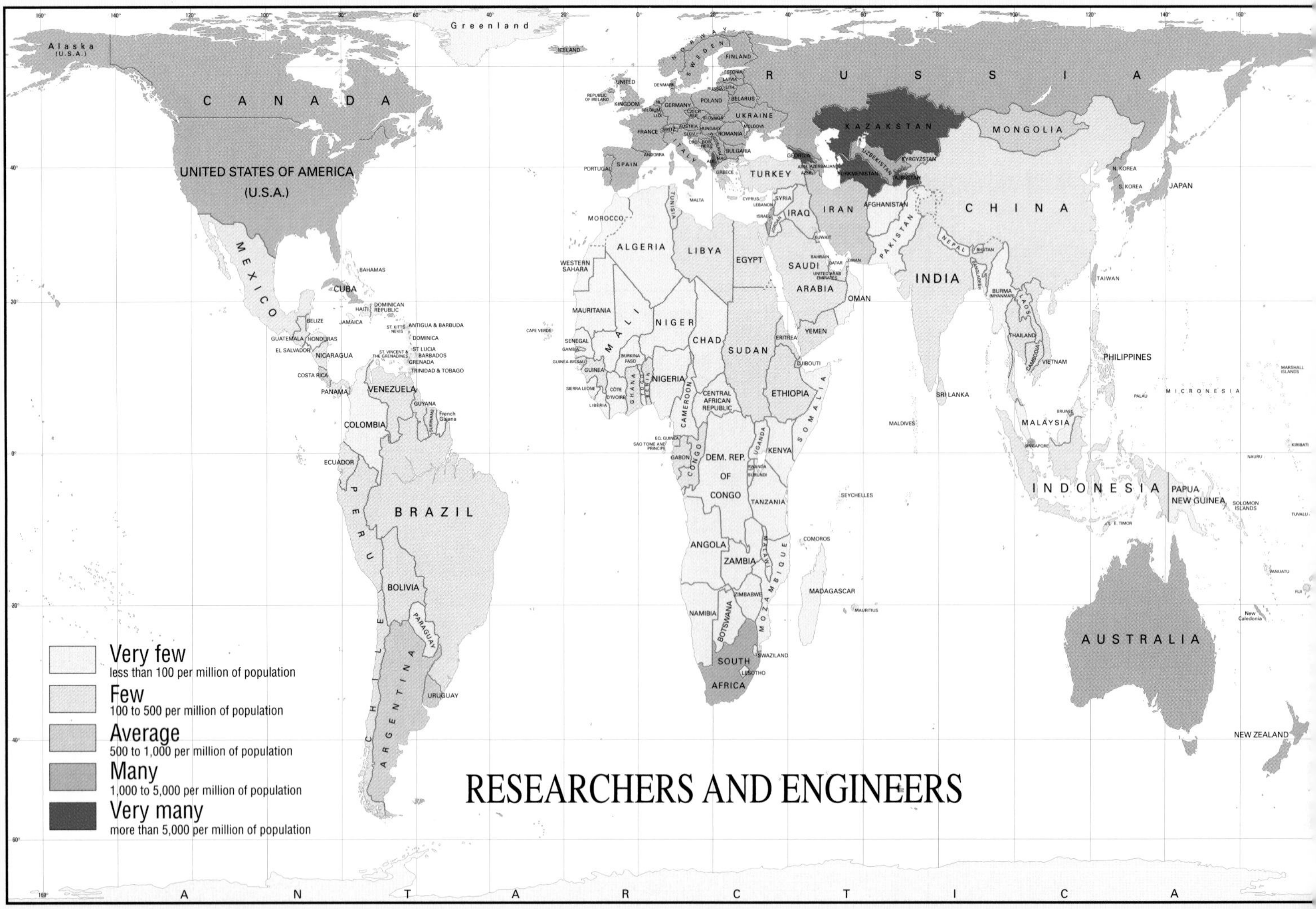

Today we regard ourselves more and more as living in the Age of Science. Detailed research into nature has given impetus to technical progress, and each day hundreds of new inventions add new dimensions to our lives. This technical revolution, which was set in train by science, has increased production on all levels to such an extent that it would be possible to assure sufficient and humane living standards for everyone in the world.

THE SC

Very few
less than 10 titles annually per million of population

Few
10 to 50 titles annually per million of population

Average
50 to 100 titles annually per million of population

Many
100 to 500 titles annually per million of population

Very many
more than 500 titles annually per million of population

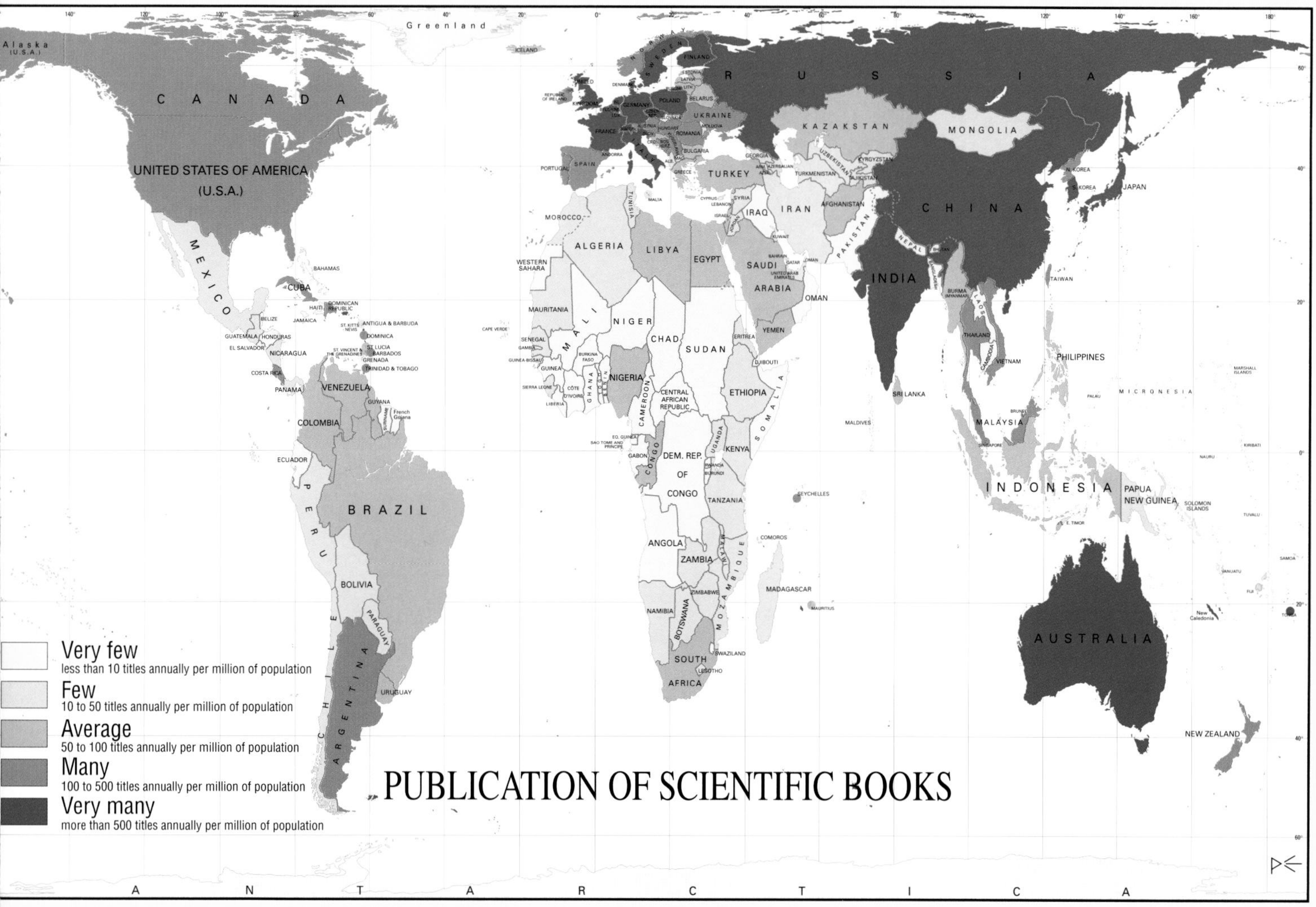

PUBLICATION OF SCIENTIFIC BOOKS

Very little
less than 0.5% of the Gross National Product

Little
0.5% to 1% of the Gross National Product

Average
1% to 2% of the Gross National Product

Much
2% to 3% of the Gross National Product

Very much
more than 3% of the Gross National Product

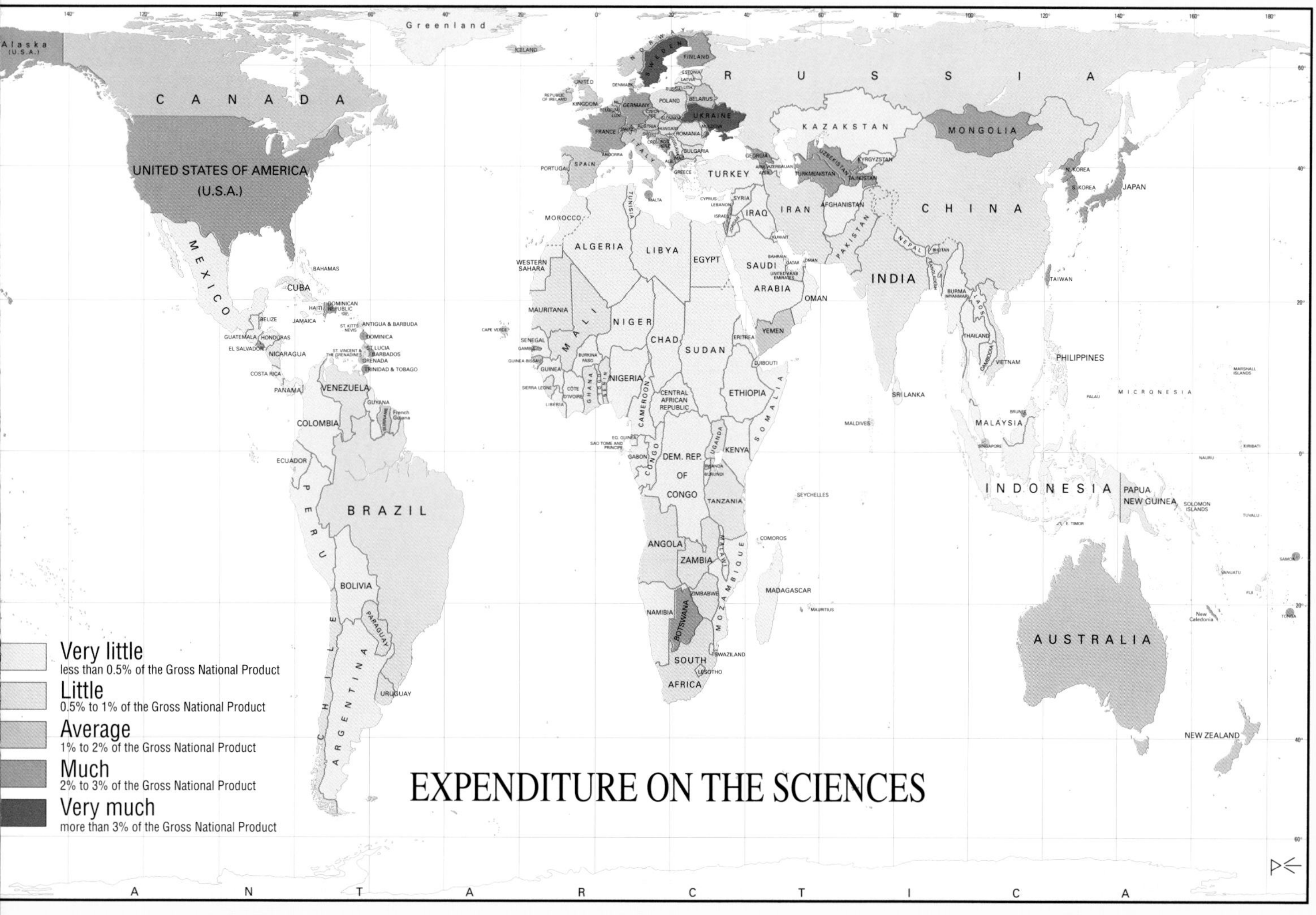

EXPENDITURE ON THE SCIENCES

Recent advances in science and mathematics have resulted in the development of computers. Scientific progress has furthered co-operation and revolutionised the production and distribution of goods. People's ability to share in scientific progress however still varies greatly. The poorer peoples of Africa, Asia and Latin America do not yet have the means to participate in the university-orientated scientific process.

NEWSPAPERS

Less than 10 newspapers
10 to 50 newspapers
50 to 100 newspapers
100 to 250 newspapers
250 to 500 newspapers
More than 500 newspapers

per 1,000 of population

TELEVISION

Less than 10 sets
10 to 100 sets
100 to 300 sets
300 to 500 sets
More than 500 sets

per 1,000 of population

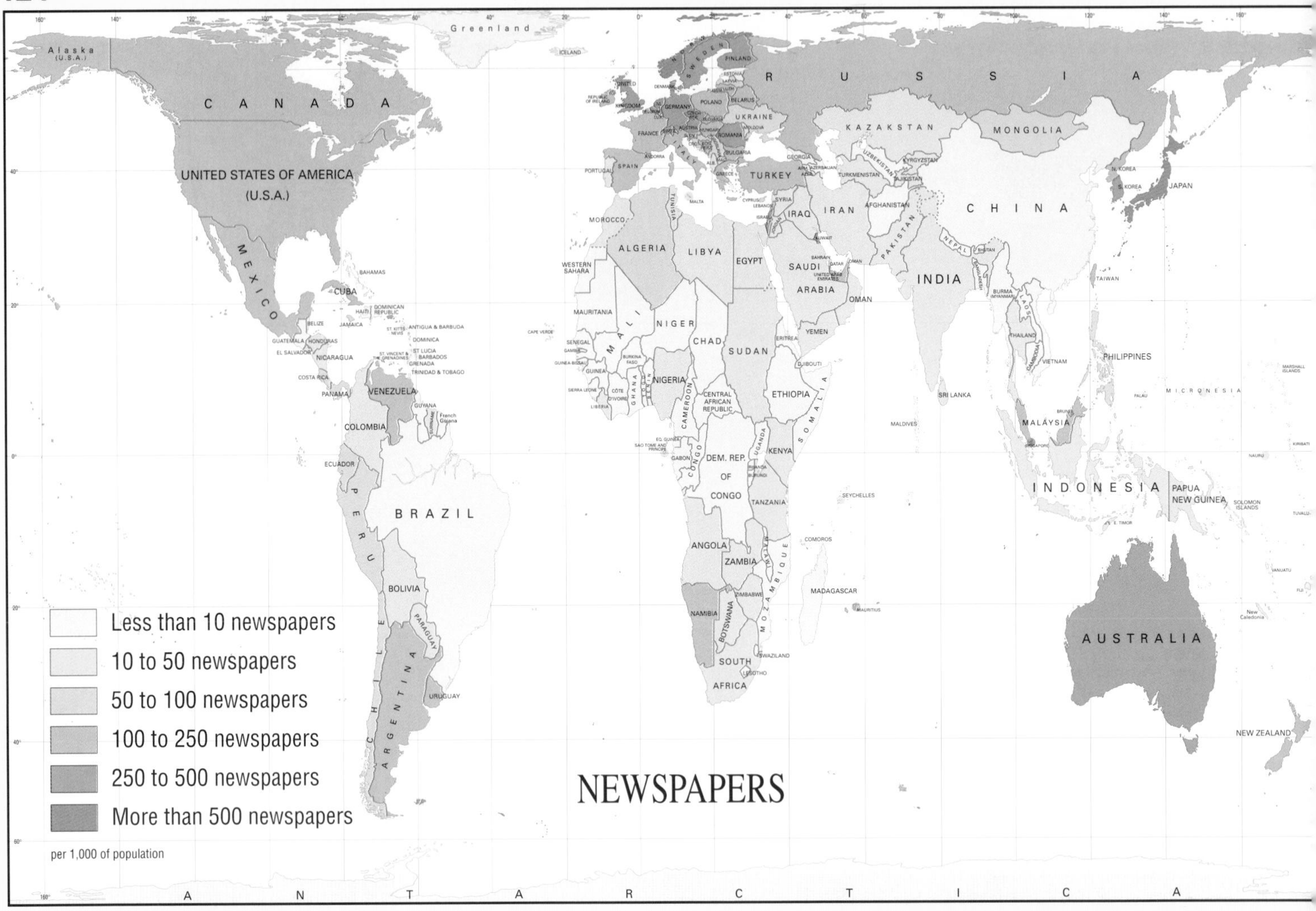

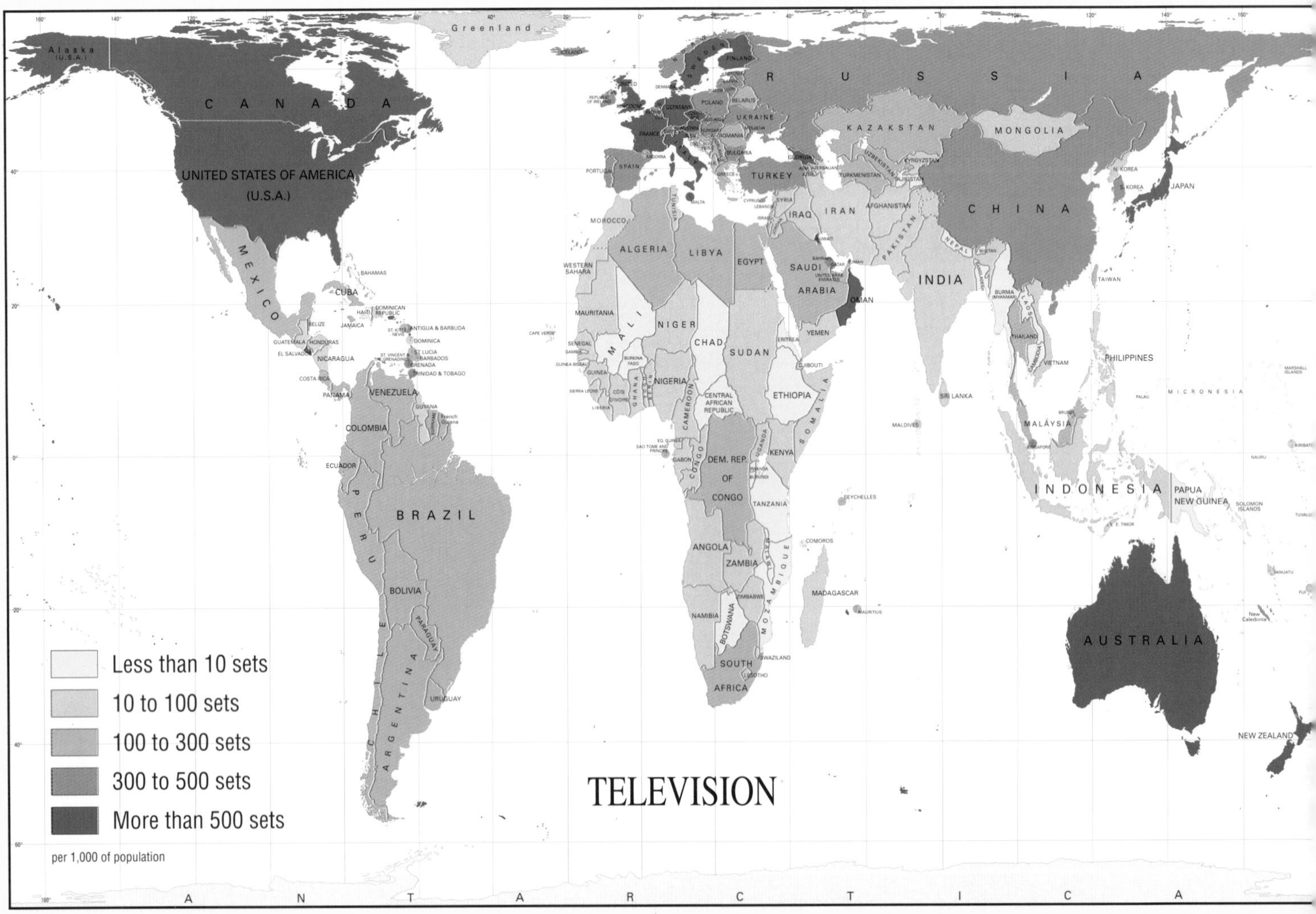

Access to information about events of general significance is increasingly a vital precondition for people's work and their ability to cope with their own ever more complicated personal lives. Often the information media are the only source for the lifelong process of further education for adults, which has become essential because of the rapidly changing world. The northern hemisphere, which has only one-quarter of the world's population, uses up three-quarters of the paper available for newspapers and books, that is, ten times as much per inhabitant as in the south.

INFOR

RADIO

Less than 50 sets
50 to 100 sets
100 to 500 sets
500 to 1,000 sets
More than 1,000 sets

er 1,000 of population

BOOKS

Less than 100
100 to 1,000
1,000 to 5,000
5,000 to 10,000
More than 10,000

ew titles annually

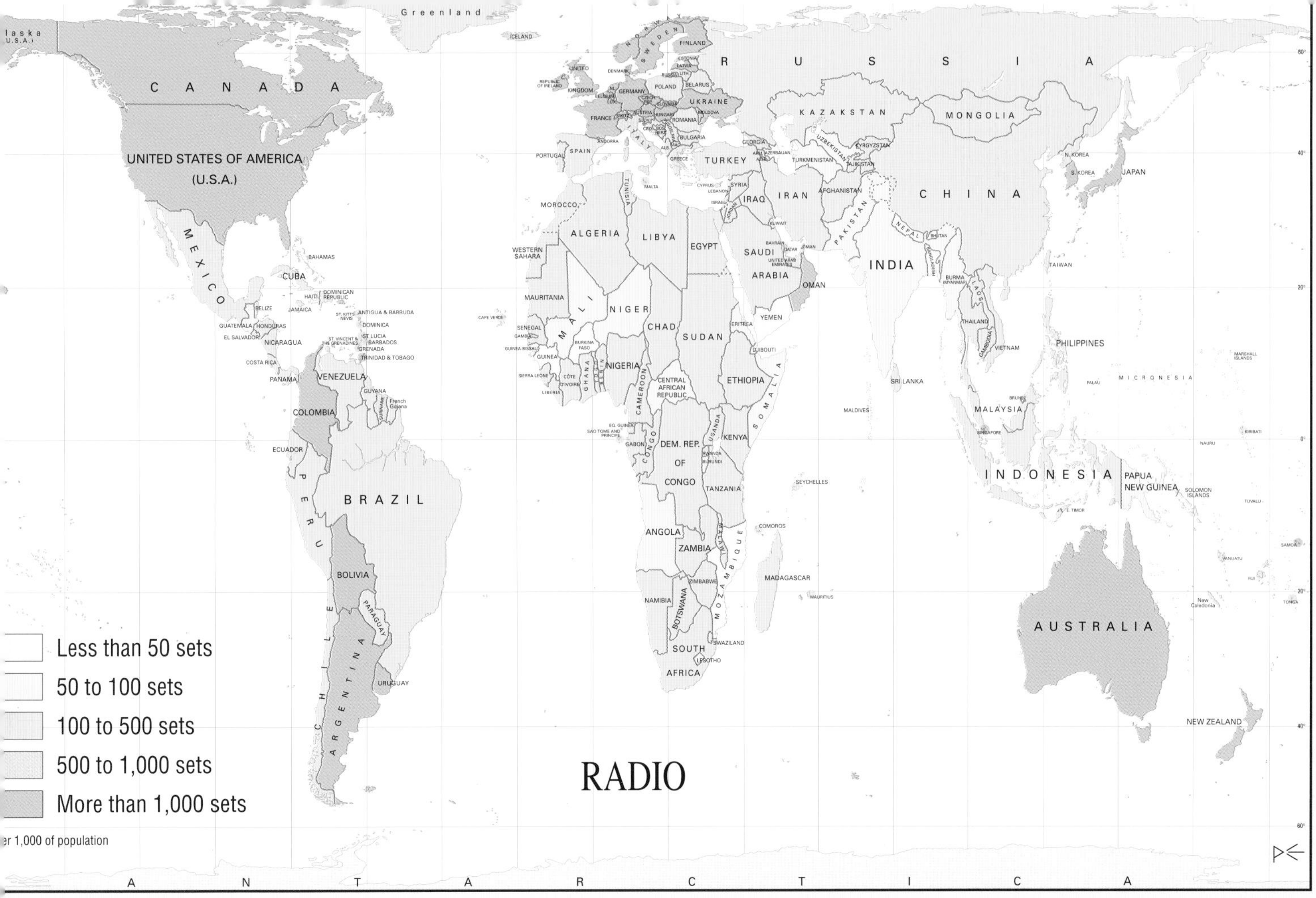

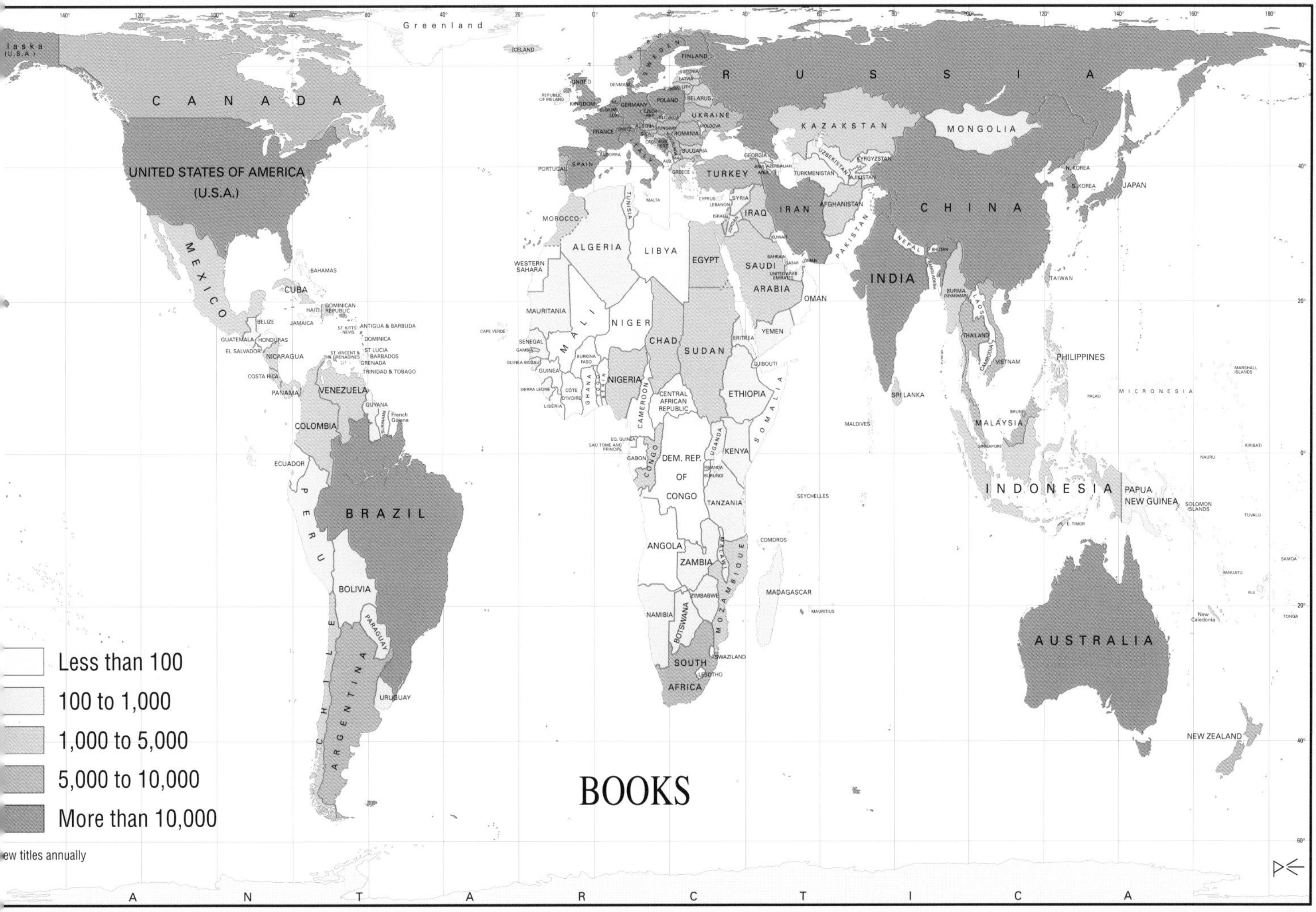

ATION

Radio and television are particularly important in the southern hemisphere because with their help even illiterate people can gain access to information. But while in the northern hemisphere at least every other person has either television or radio, in the southern hemisphere only 10% are in this position. There is only one newspaper per thousand of the population in Mali, Niger and Burkina Faso while in Norway and Japan there is one for every two people. In Malawi 500 people effectively share one television set, while in France and the United States there is one for every two people.

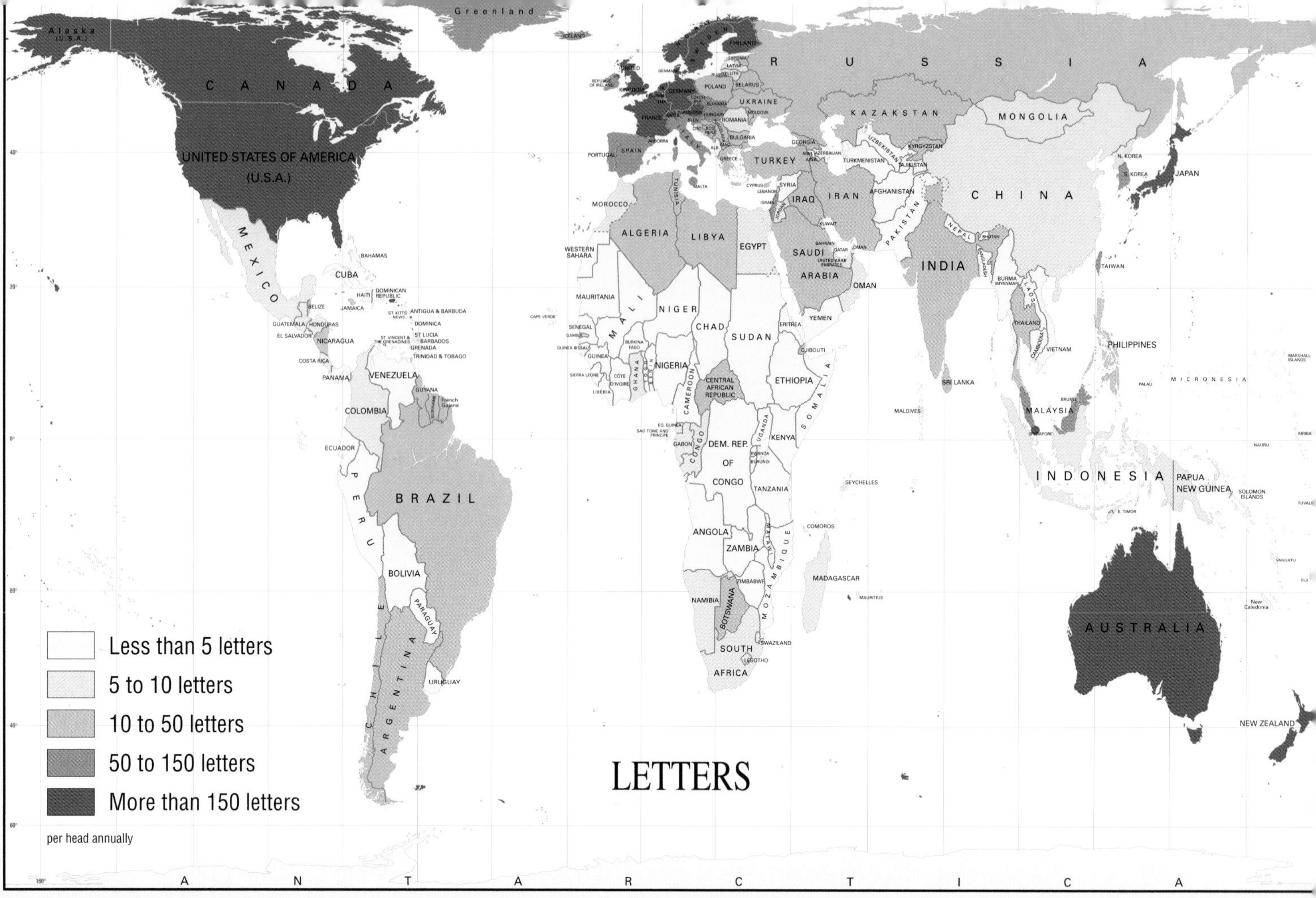

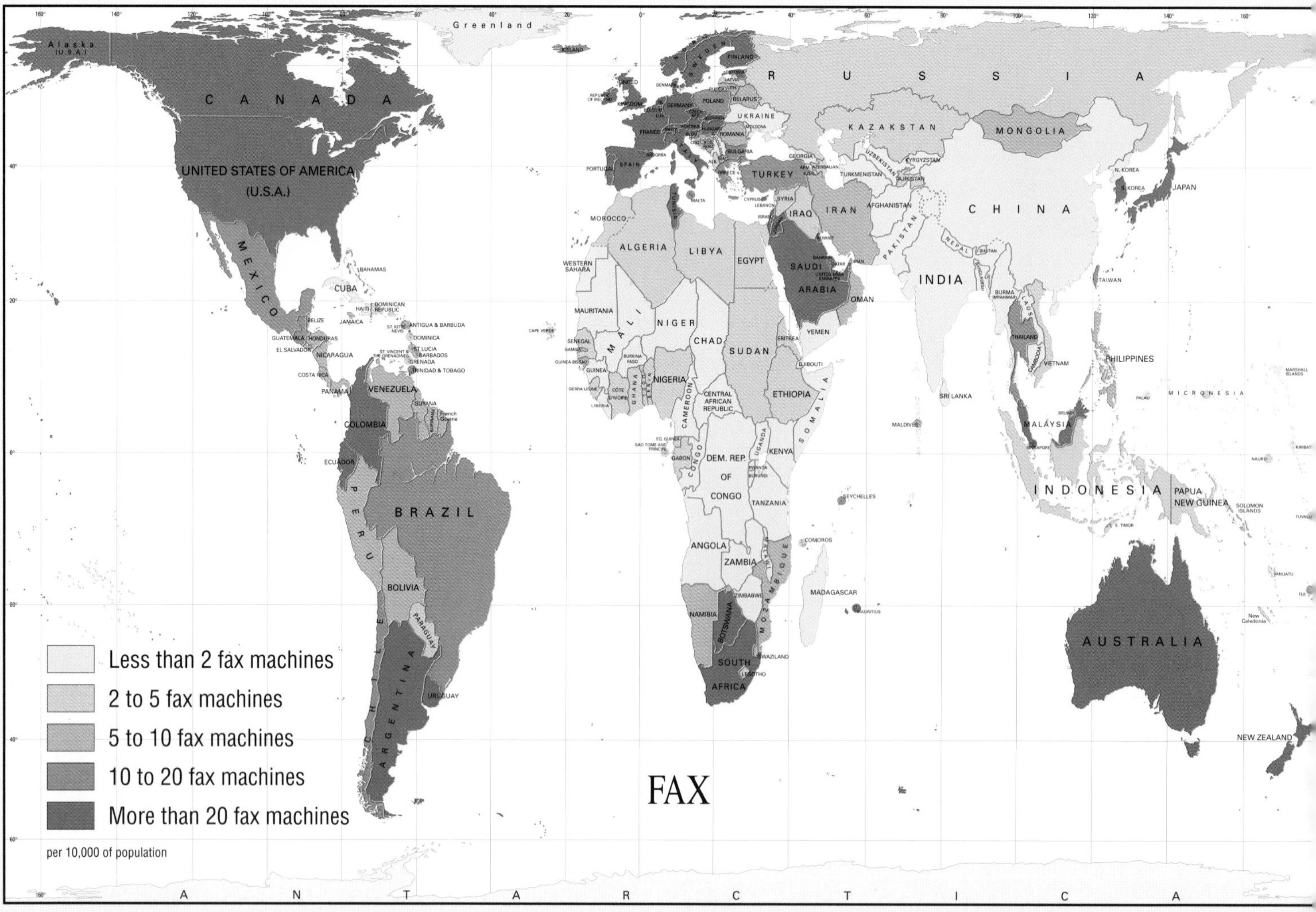

LETTERS

Less than 5 letters
5 to 10 letters
10 to 50 letters
50 to 150 letters
More than 150 letters

per head annually

FAX

Less than 2 fax machines
2 to 5 fax machines
5 to 10 fax machines
10 to 20 fax machines
More than 20 fax machines

per 10,000 of population

Today an essential part of world communication is the sending and receiving of personal information. Every person in every country could, theoretically, connect directly with everyone in the world. But the ability to do so is still a privilege which the rich states and peoples can use to bolster their position because communicating with text presupposes knowledge of reading and writing, which means it is denied to the poorest third of the world's people, those who are illiterate.

COMMUI

TELEPHONES

Less than 10 telephones
10 to 100 telephones
100 to 300 telephones
300 to 500 telephones
More than 500 telephones

r 1,000 of population

INTERNET

Less than 1 connection
1 to 10 connections
10 to 100 connections
100 to 500 connections
More than 500 connections

r 10,000 of population

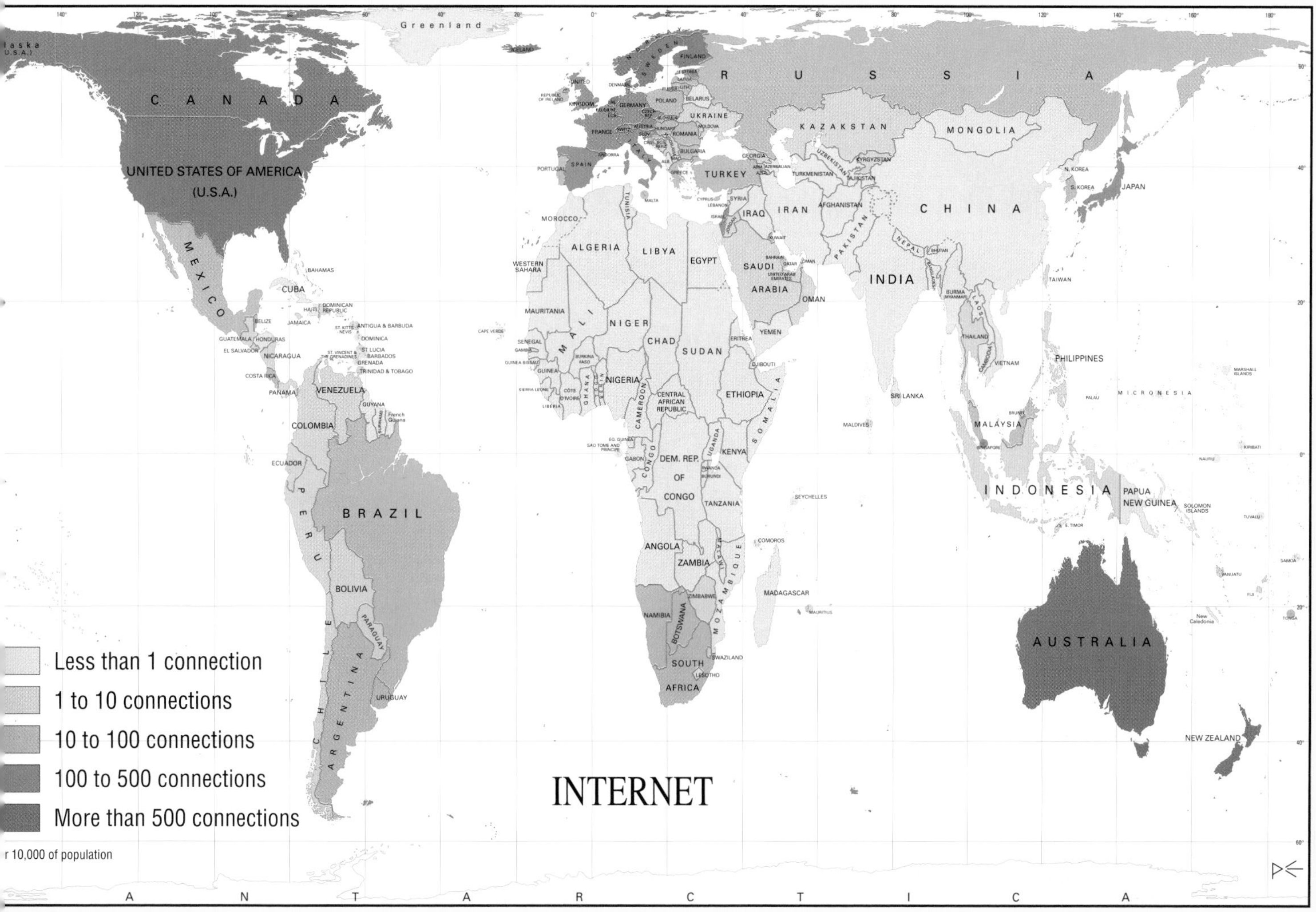

CATIONS

Telephone communication is not available world-wide. In the rich industrial states there are 500 telephones per 1,000 inhabitants (US 630, Canada 610, France 570, Monaco 1015). Poor developing countries like Mauritania have only one telephone per 1,000 of the population. The transmission of documents (fax) is also still a privilege of the rich industrial states, as is the computer, which is revolutionising communication.

RAILWAYS

Less than 5 km of rail
5 to 10 km of rail
10 to 20 km of rail
20 to 50 km of rail
More than 50 km of rail

per 1,000 km^2

CARS

Less than 10 cars
10 to 100 cars
100 to 300 cars
300 to 500 cars
More than 500 cars

per 1,000 of population

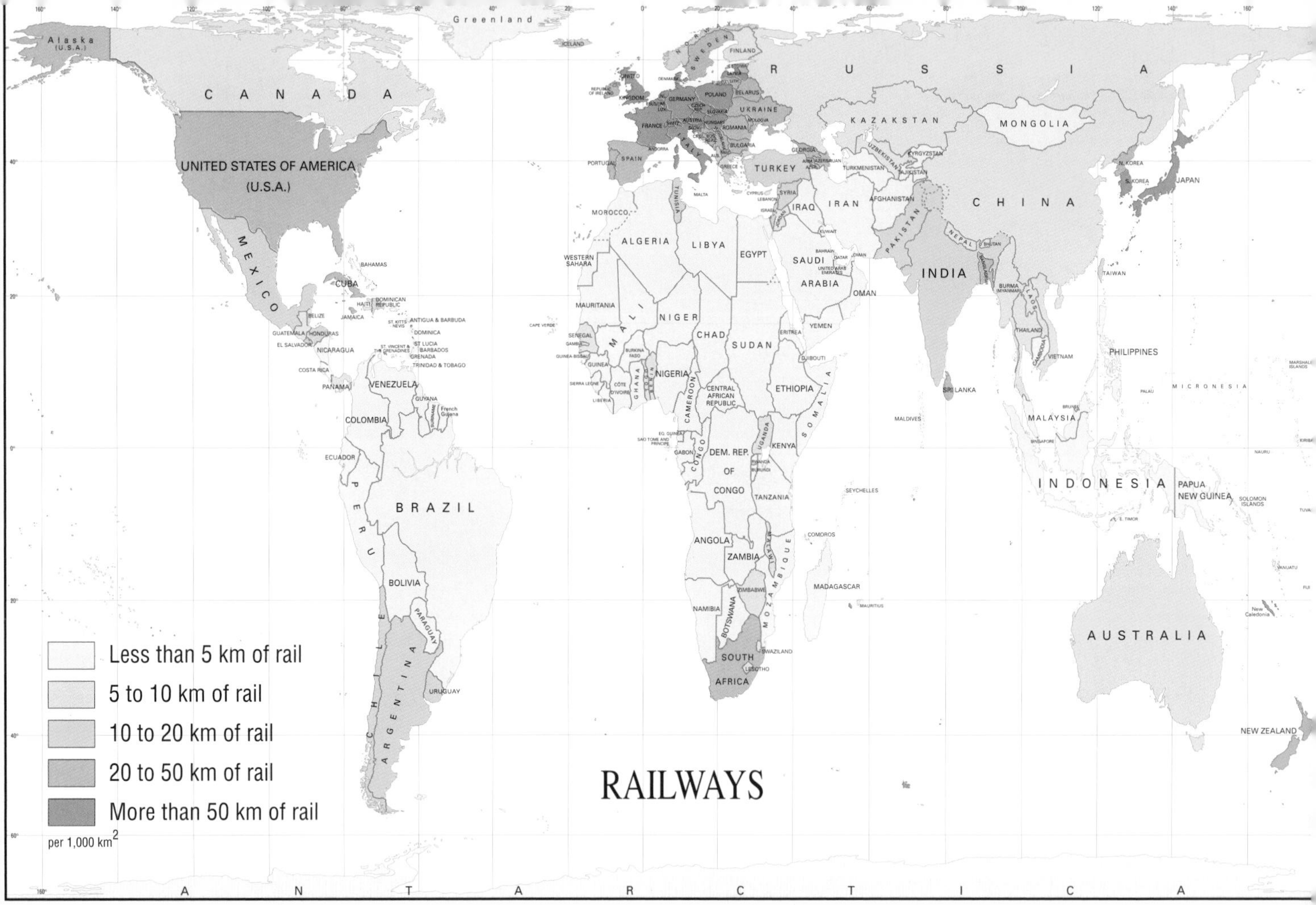

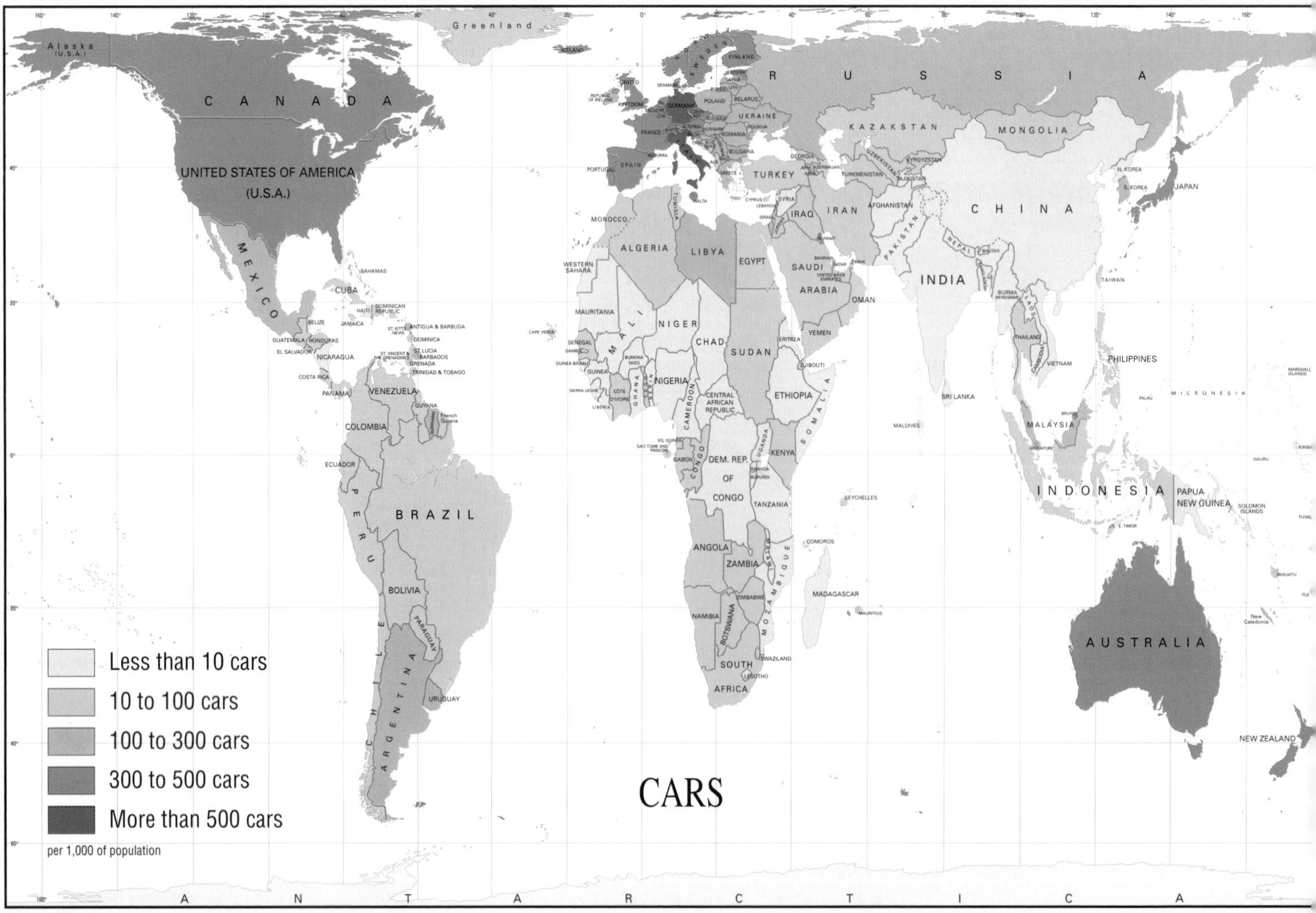

For centuries people were limited to travel within their own localities because only horses, donkeys, mules, ox-carts and horse-drawn vehicles were available. The use of ships and later, cars and planes meant that the movement of people and goods rapidly developed into global traffic. In our age of closely woven contacts it is possible to participate in world events at all levels.

TRAFFIC

AIR TRAFFIC

Less than 50 passengers
50 to 100 passengers
100 to 300 passengers
300 to 500 passengers
More than 500 passengers

er 1,000 of population annually

SHIPPING

Less than 1 million tonnes
1 to 10 million tonnes
10 to 100 million tonnes
100 to 500 million tonnes
More than 500 million tonnes

go turnover annually

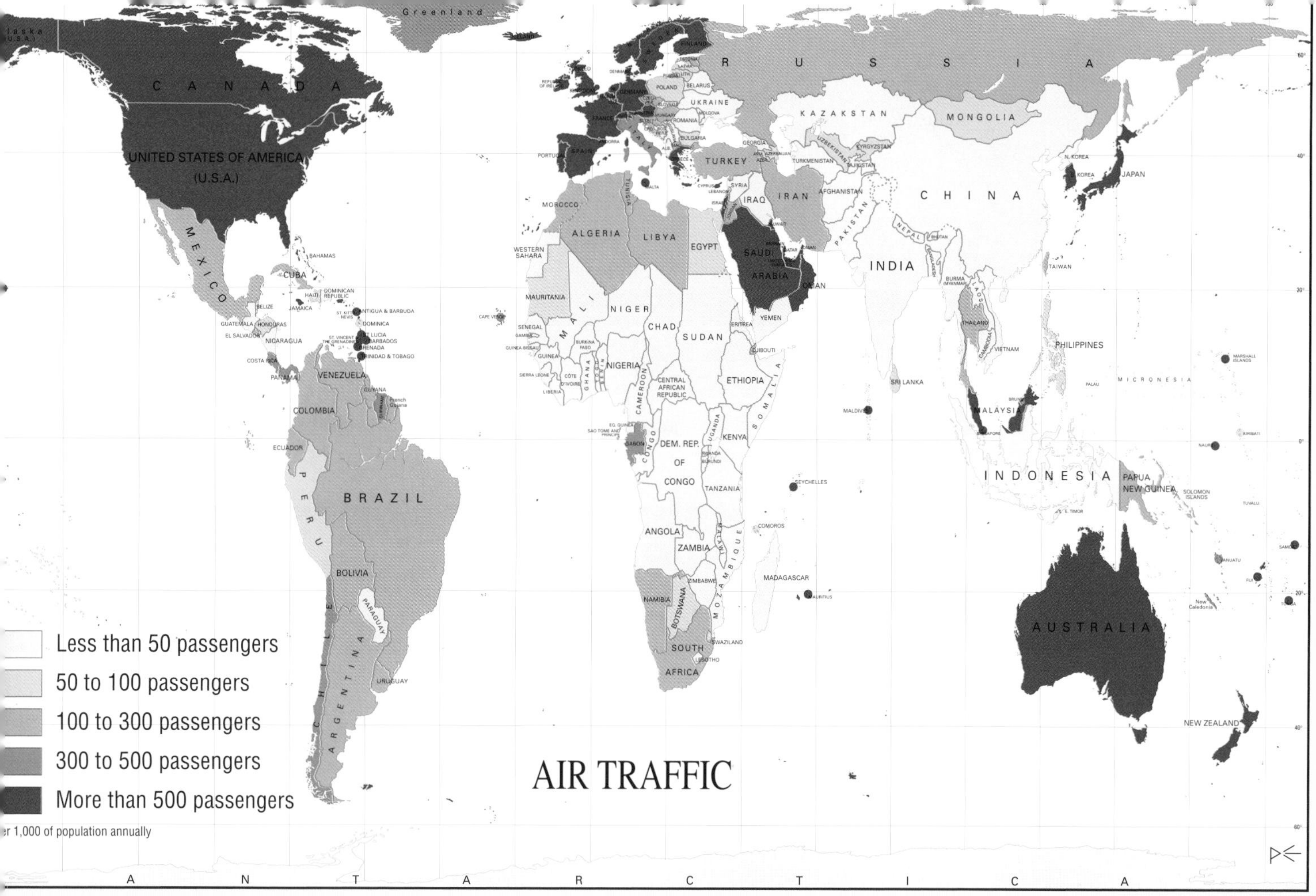

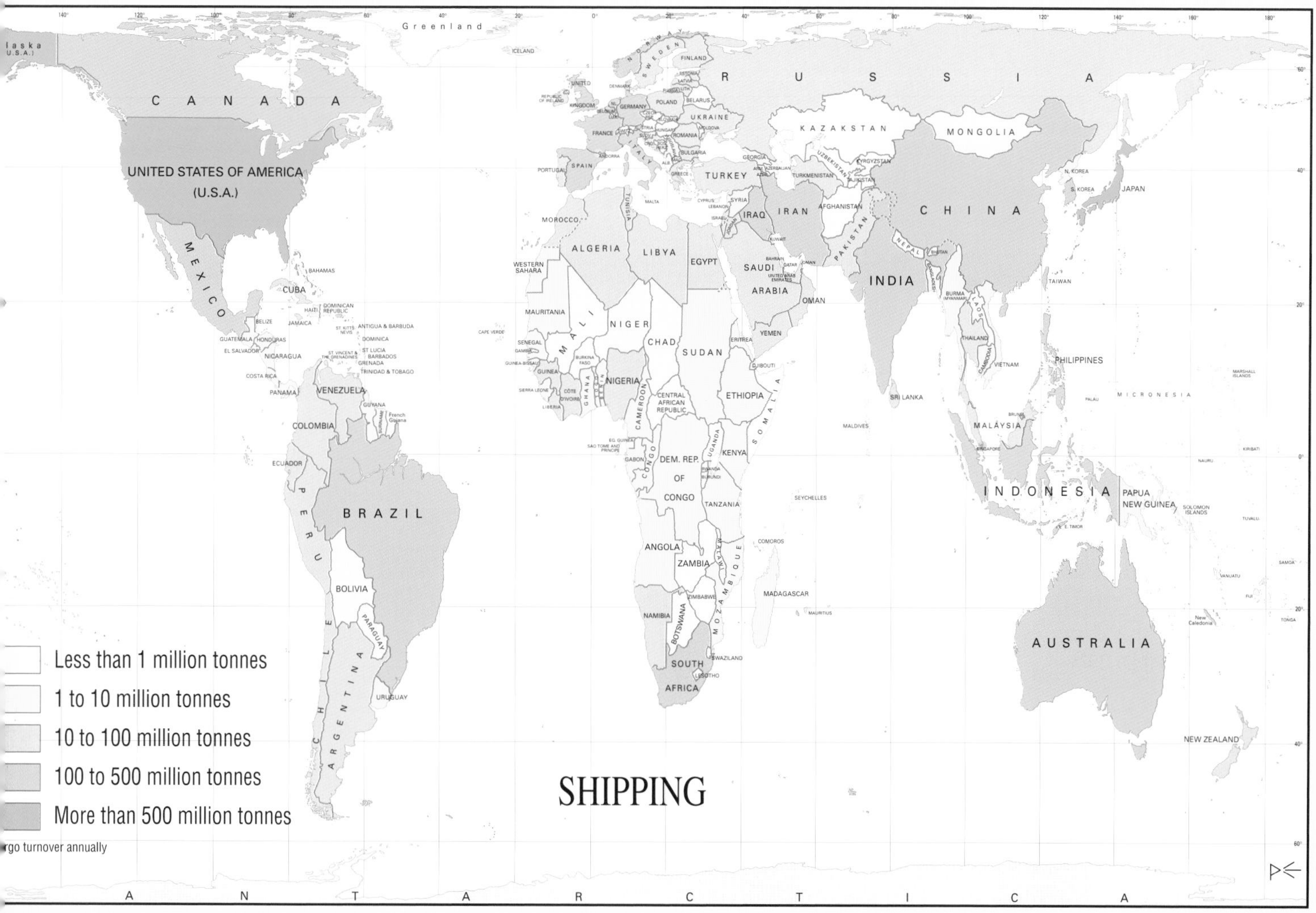

DENSITY

Half of the world's people live in countries with fewer than one car per 1,000 inhabitants (for example in Burma, Bangladesh, Mozambique, Afghanistan, Somalia). In most of these developing countries railways, air travel and shipping are still only slightly developed. While Japan ships nearly 700 million tonnes of goods a year, much bigger developing countries in general, ship well under one million tonnes each.

POPULATION DENSITY

Less than 10 inhabitants
10 to 25 inhabitants
25 to 100 inhabitants
100 to 200 inhabitants
More than 200 inhabitants

per km²

ADULTS / CHILDREN RATIO

Less than 20%
20 to 30%
30 to 40%
40 to 50%
More than 50%

of population is less than 15 years old

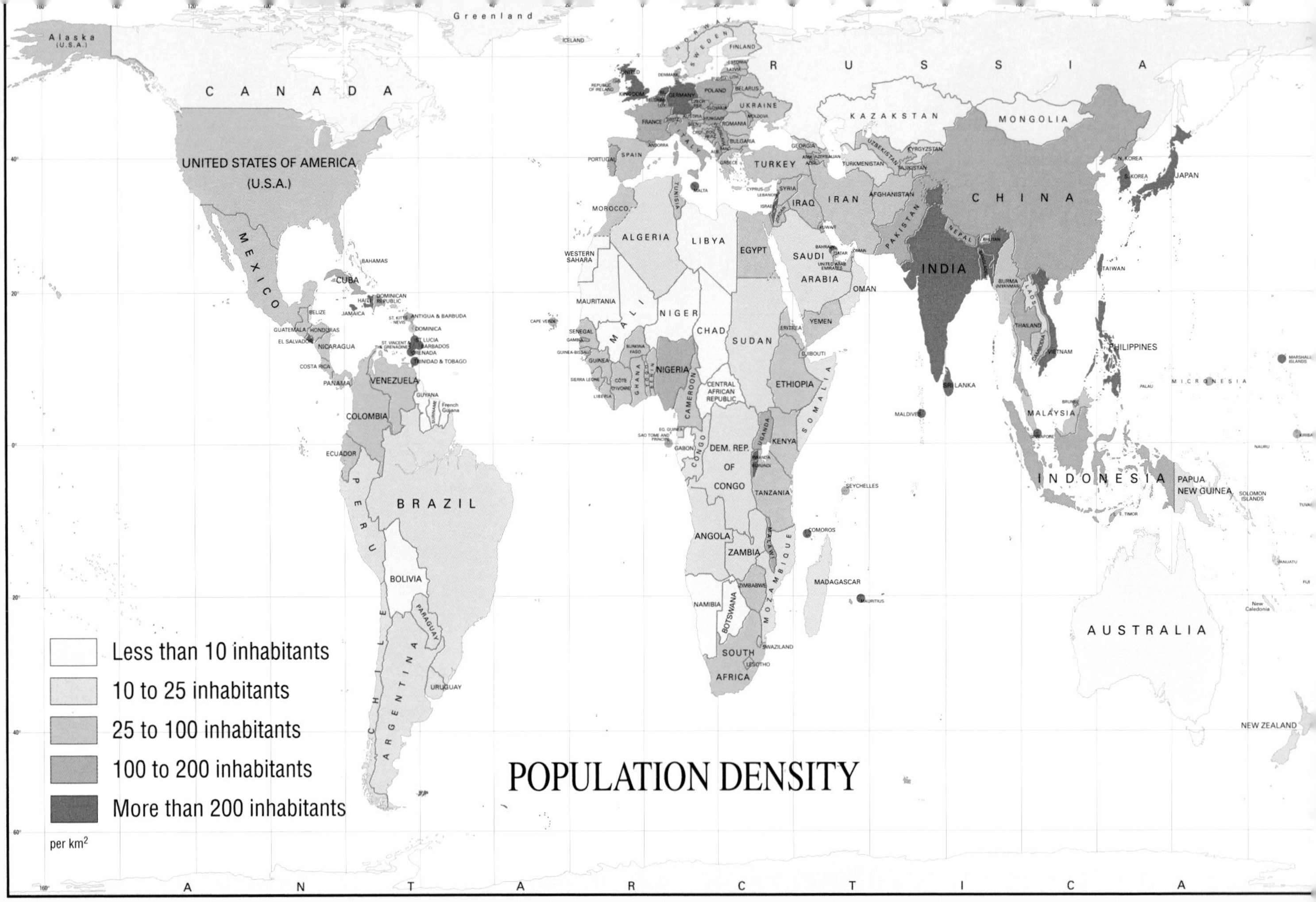

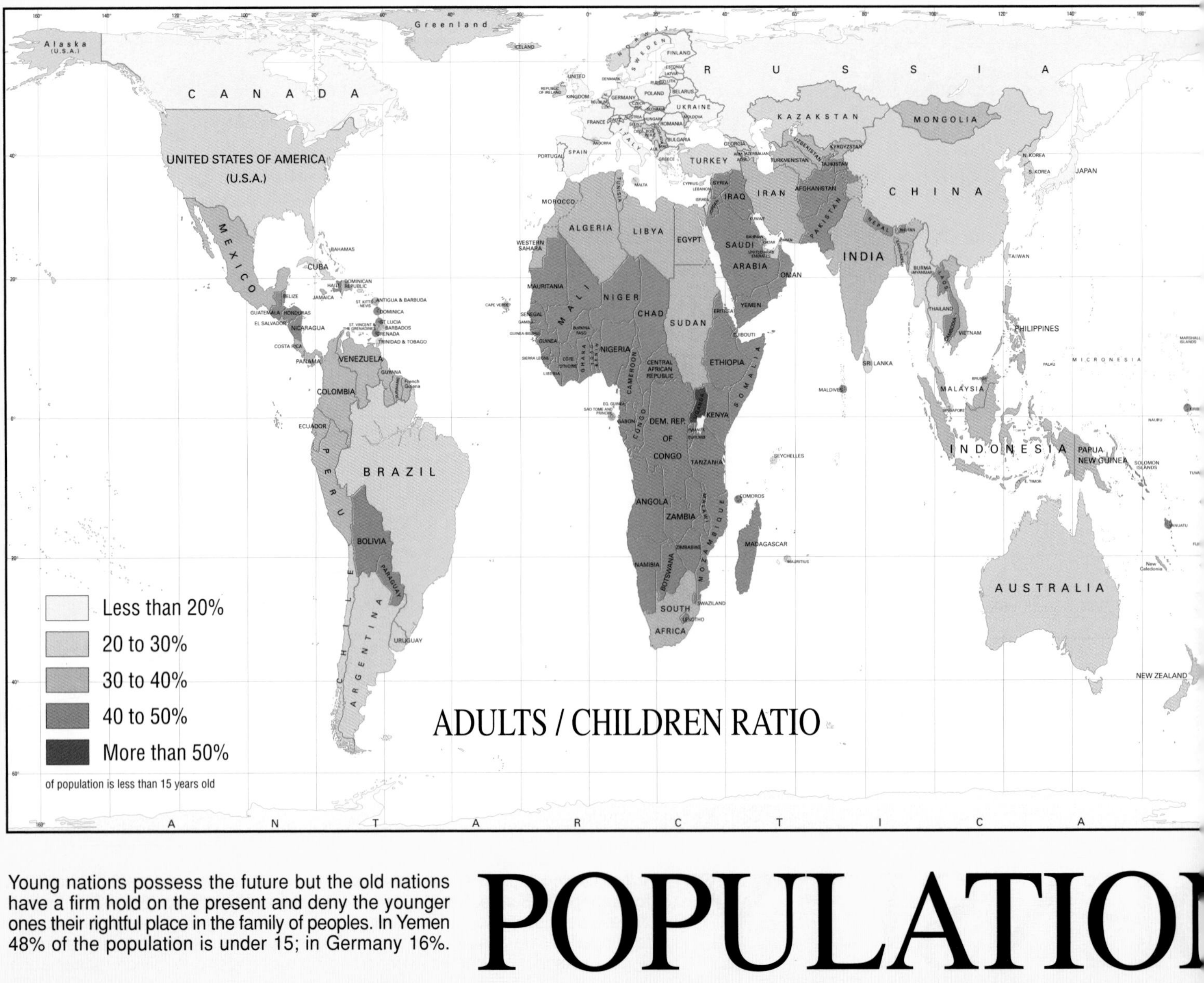

Young nations possess the future but the old nations have a firm hold on the present and deny the younger ones their rightful place in the family of peoples. In Yemen 48% of the population is under 15; in Germany 16%.

POPULATIO

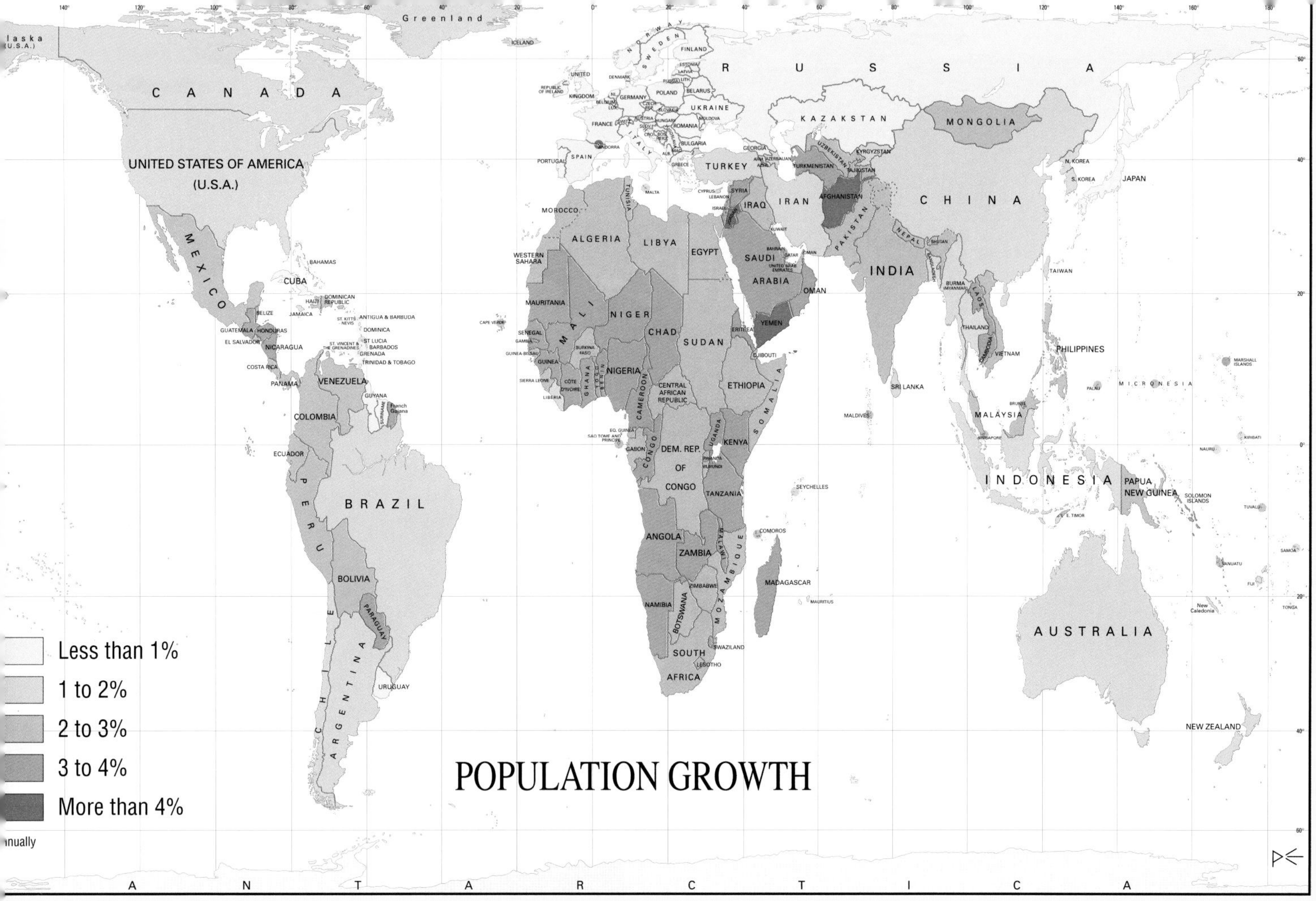

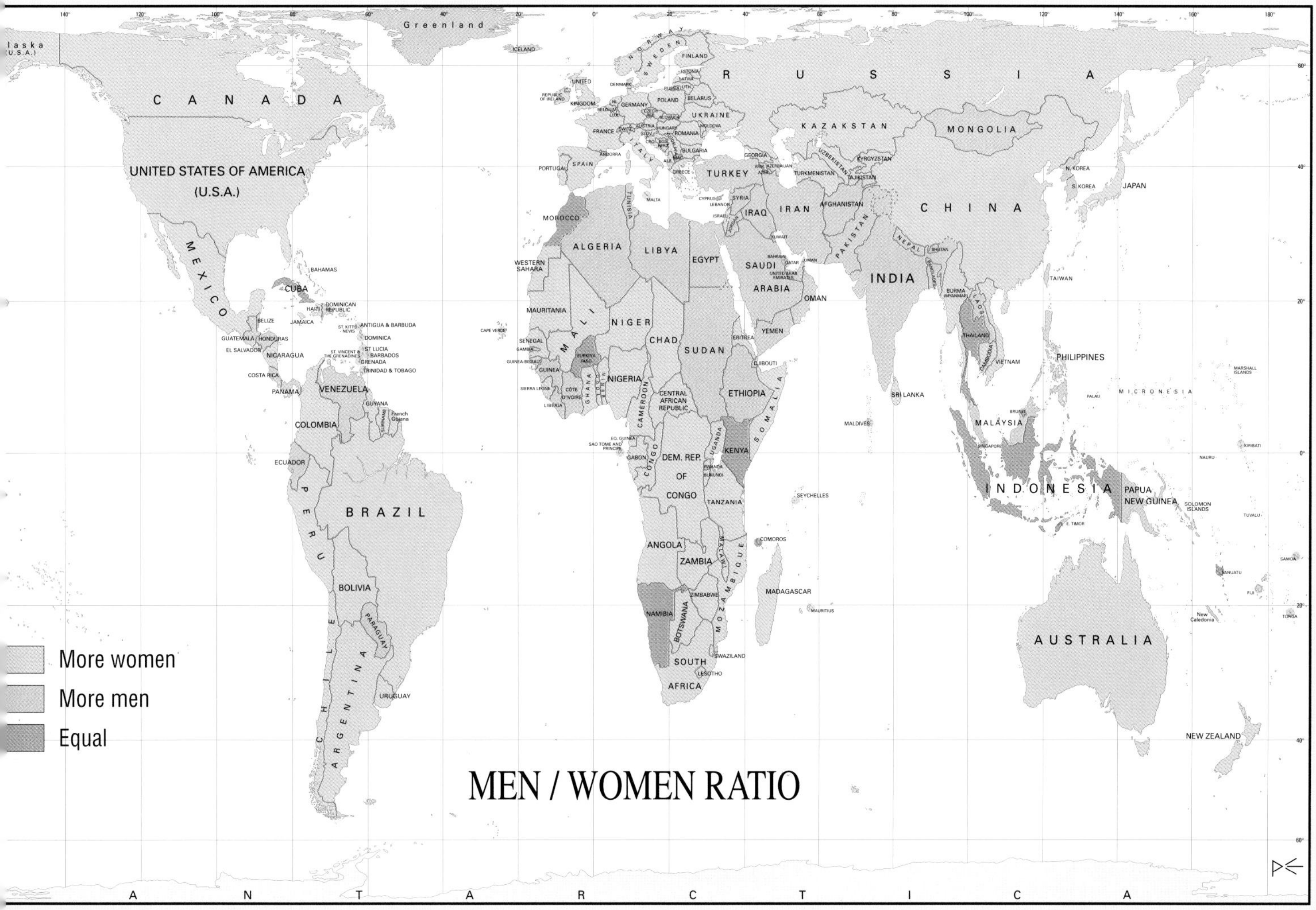

STRUCTURE

The increase in population amongst poor nations and recent population decline in rich nations also reflect the uneven distribution of wealth inherited from 500 years of colonial exploitation. As the affluence of the rich industrial nations in the North has increased, so has the population in the poor countries of the South.

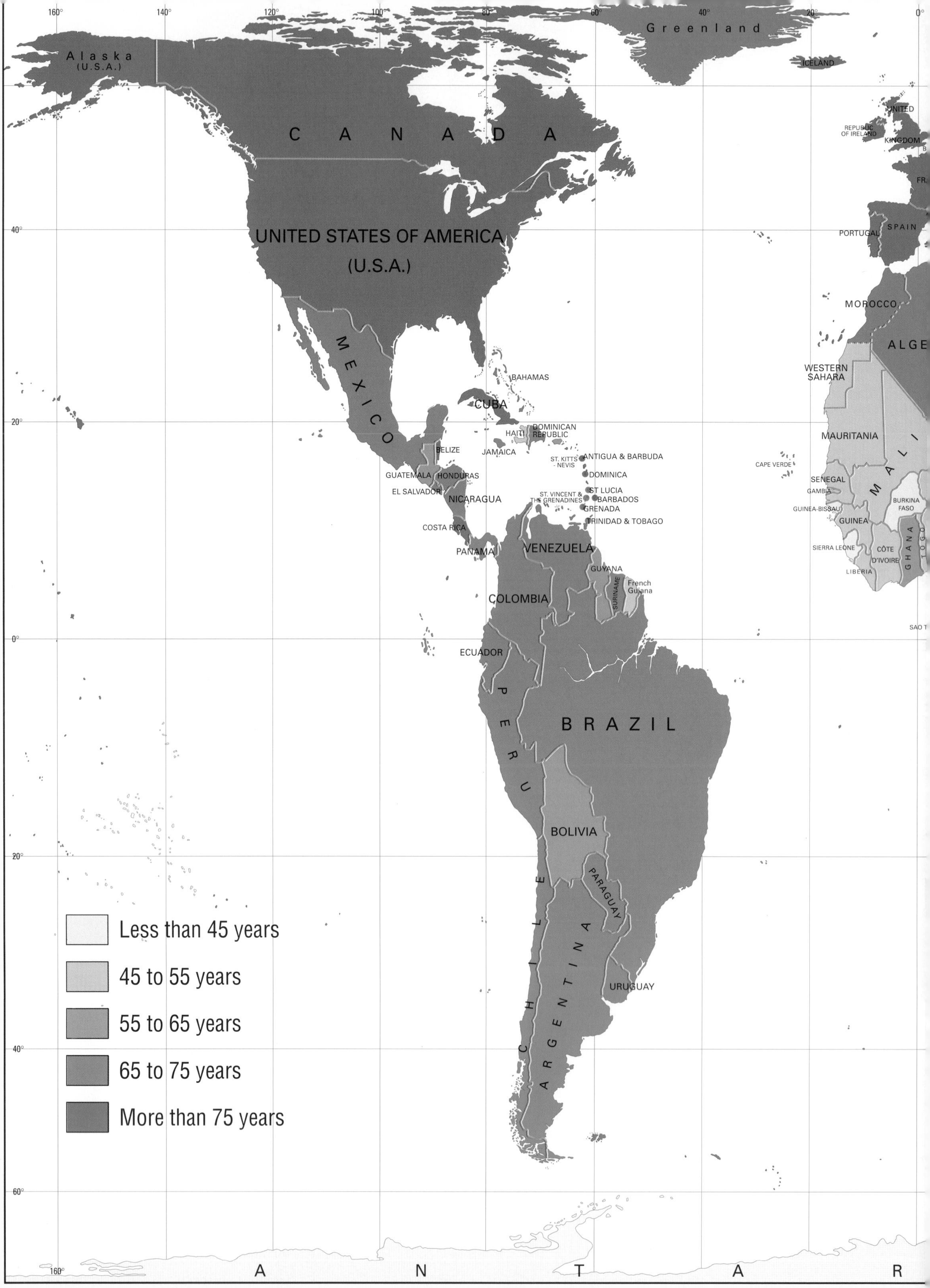

Advances in civilisation on all levels are expressed by an increase in life expectancy. Five thousand years ago the average length of life was about 20 years, 500 years ago people lived on average to 30 and 100 years ago to barely 40. Nowadays life expectancy in the rich world is around 70 and in some countries to almost 80.

LIFE EX

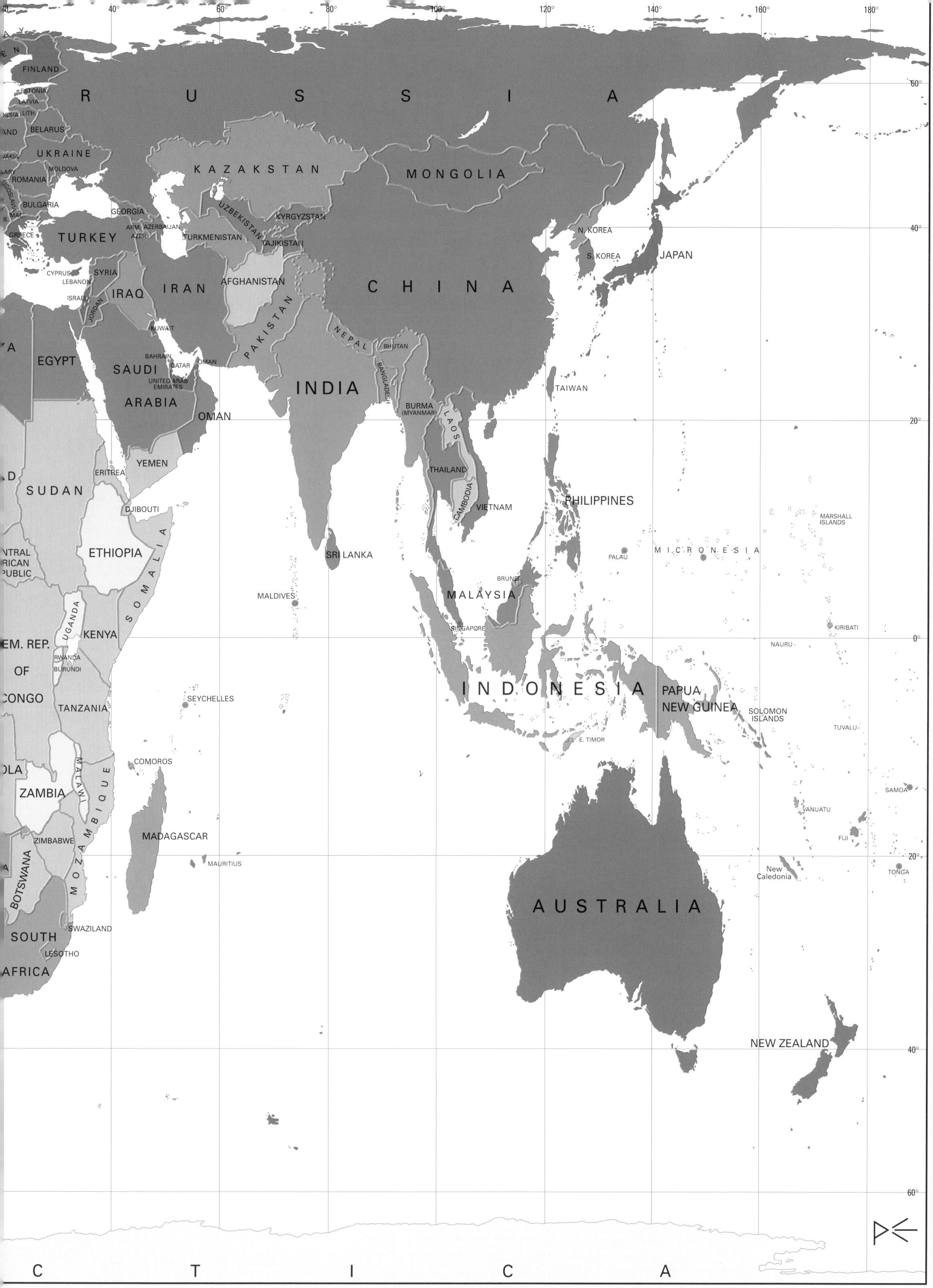

CTANCY

Life expectancy varies greatly in different countries of the world. A person born in Uganda or Ethiopia has a life expectancy today of about 40 years, while in rich industrial countries like France, England, Germany, Canada and Japan life expectancy is about twice as long.

MEDICAL ATTENTION

Very bad
less than 5 doctors per 100,000 people

Bad
5 to 20 doctors per 100,000 people

Adequate
20 to 100 doctors per 100,000 people

Very good
more than 100 doctors per 100,000 people

DRINKING WATER SUPPLIES

Very bad
less than 25% have access to clean water

Bad
25 to 50% have access to clean water

Average
50 to 75% have access to clean water

Good
more than 75% have access to clean water

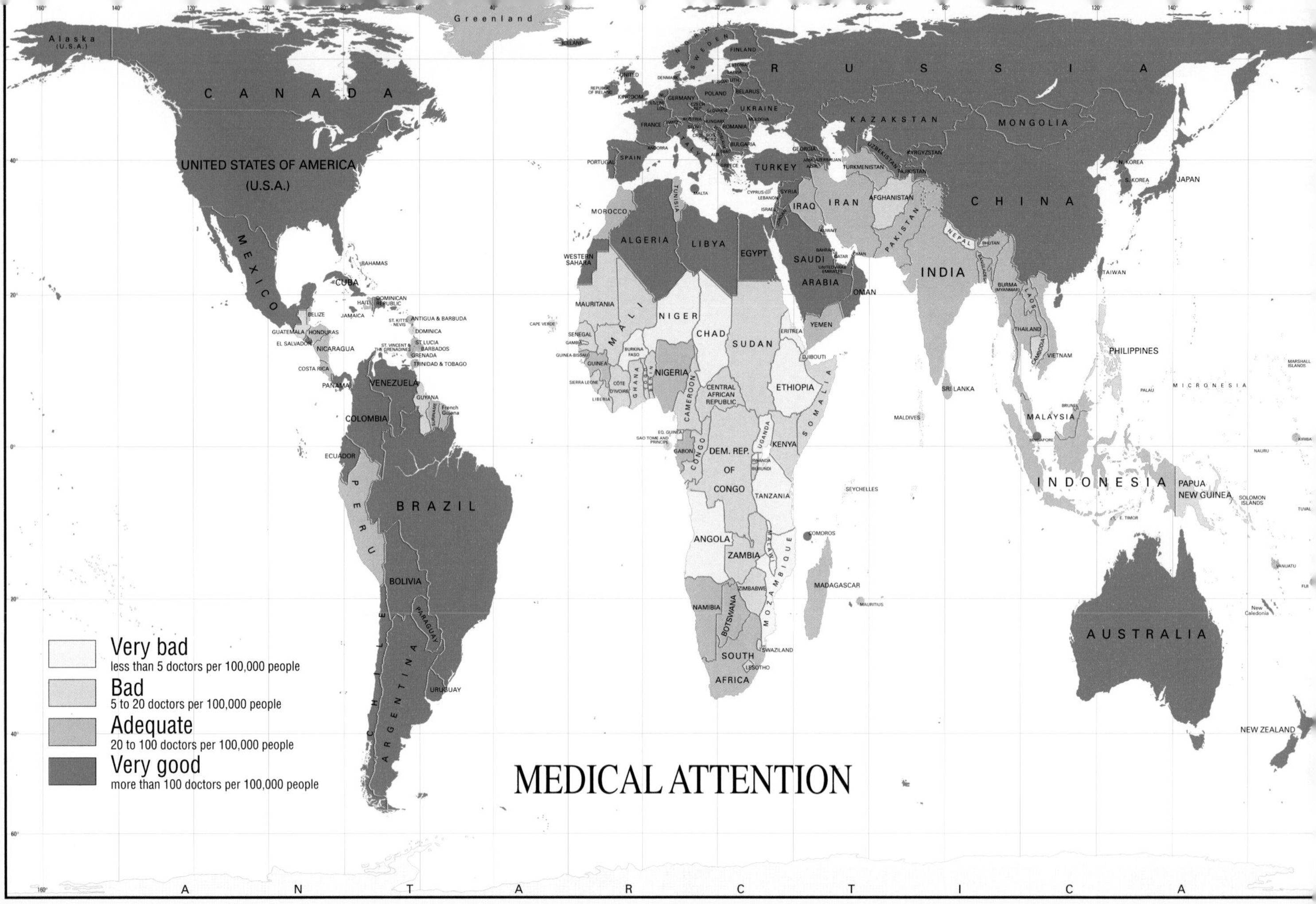

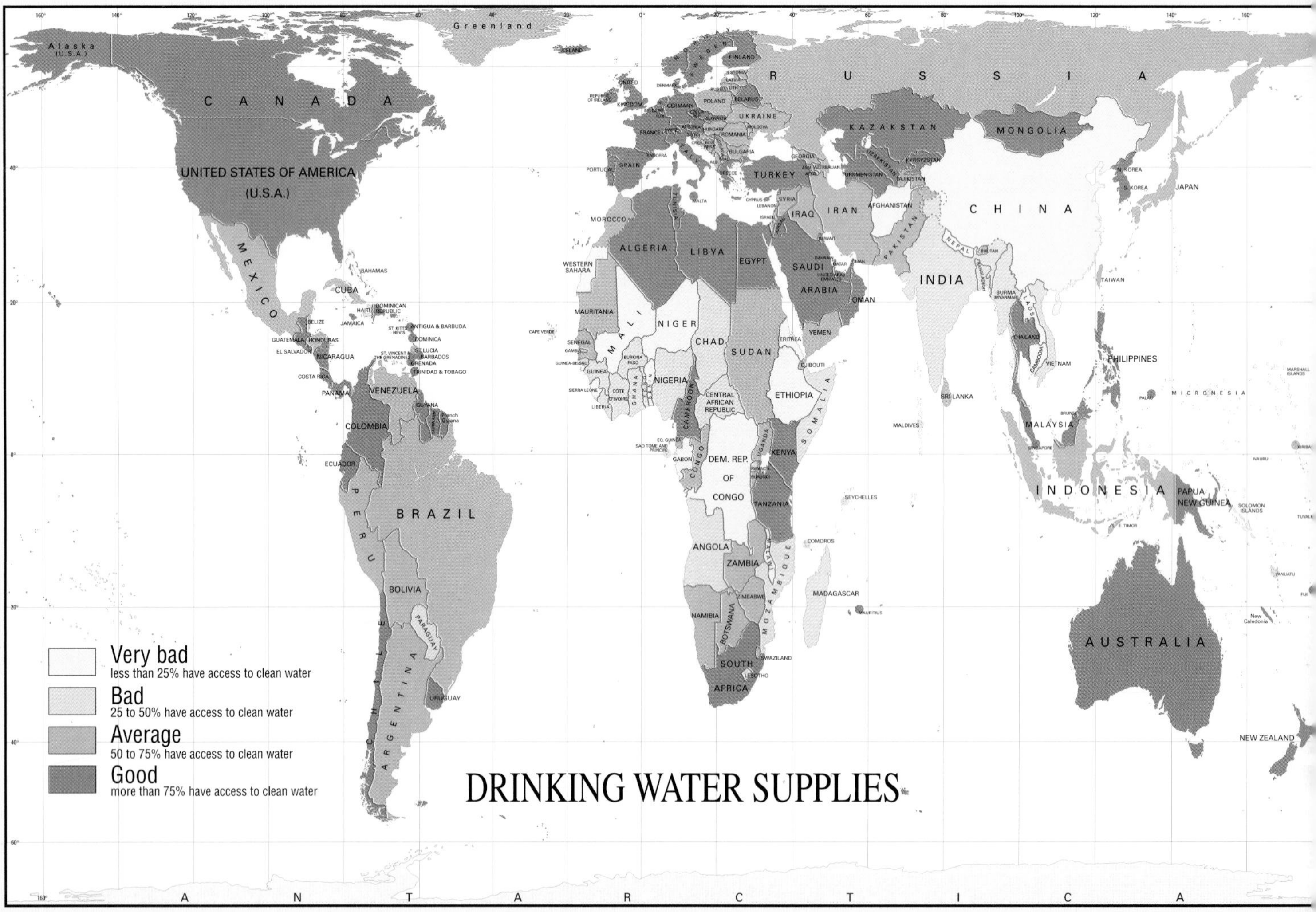

To remain healthy a person needs sufficient food and clean drinking water. Today both could be secured for everyone. But health depends on other factors: pollution-free air to breathe, regular and sufficient sleep, enough exercise, avoidance of toxins and toxic stimulants, bodily cleanliness, adequate living space, natural diet and clothing, sunny and calm living conditions, and harmony with the rhythms of nature.

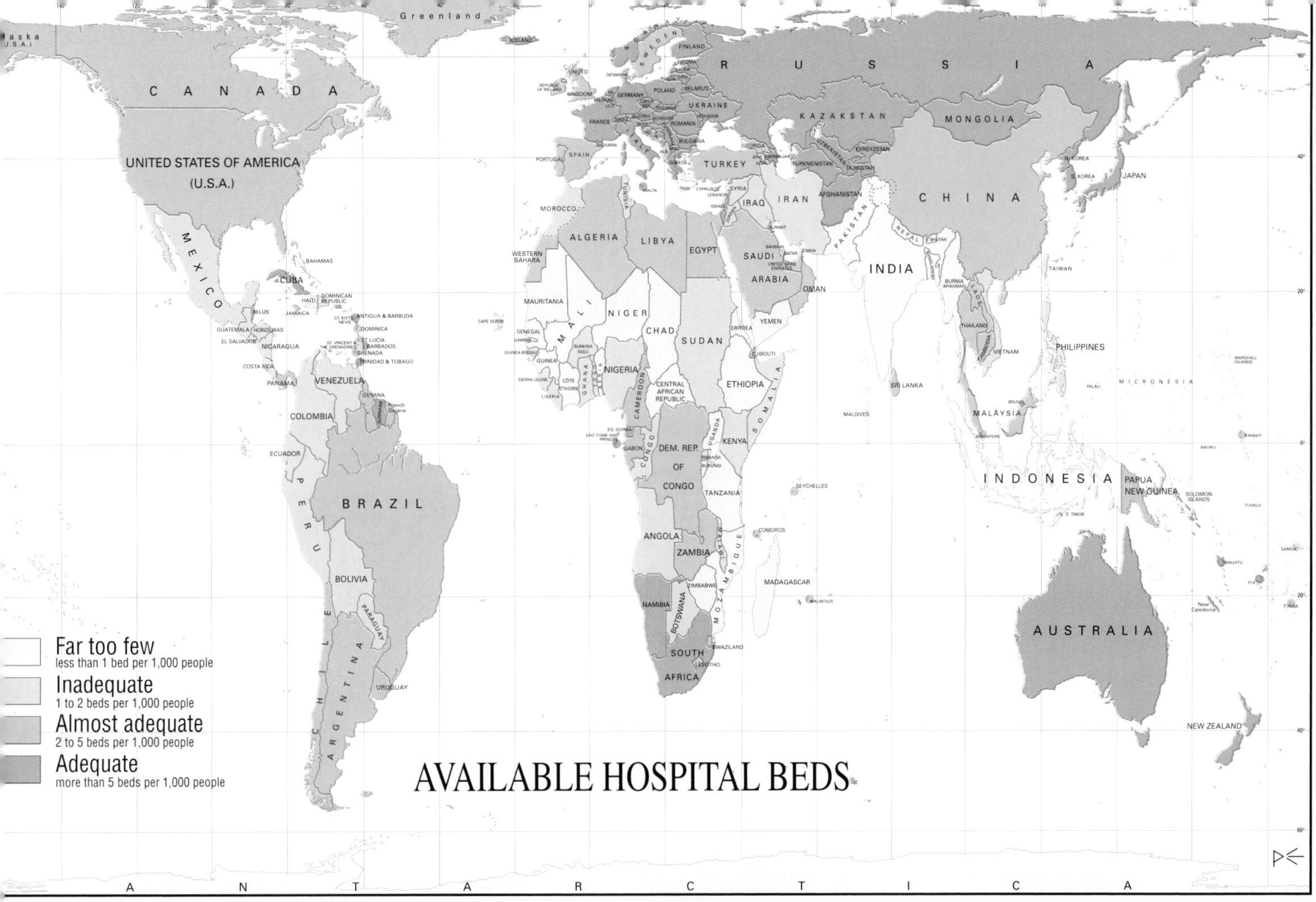

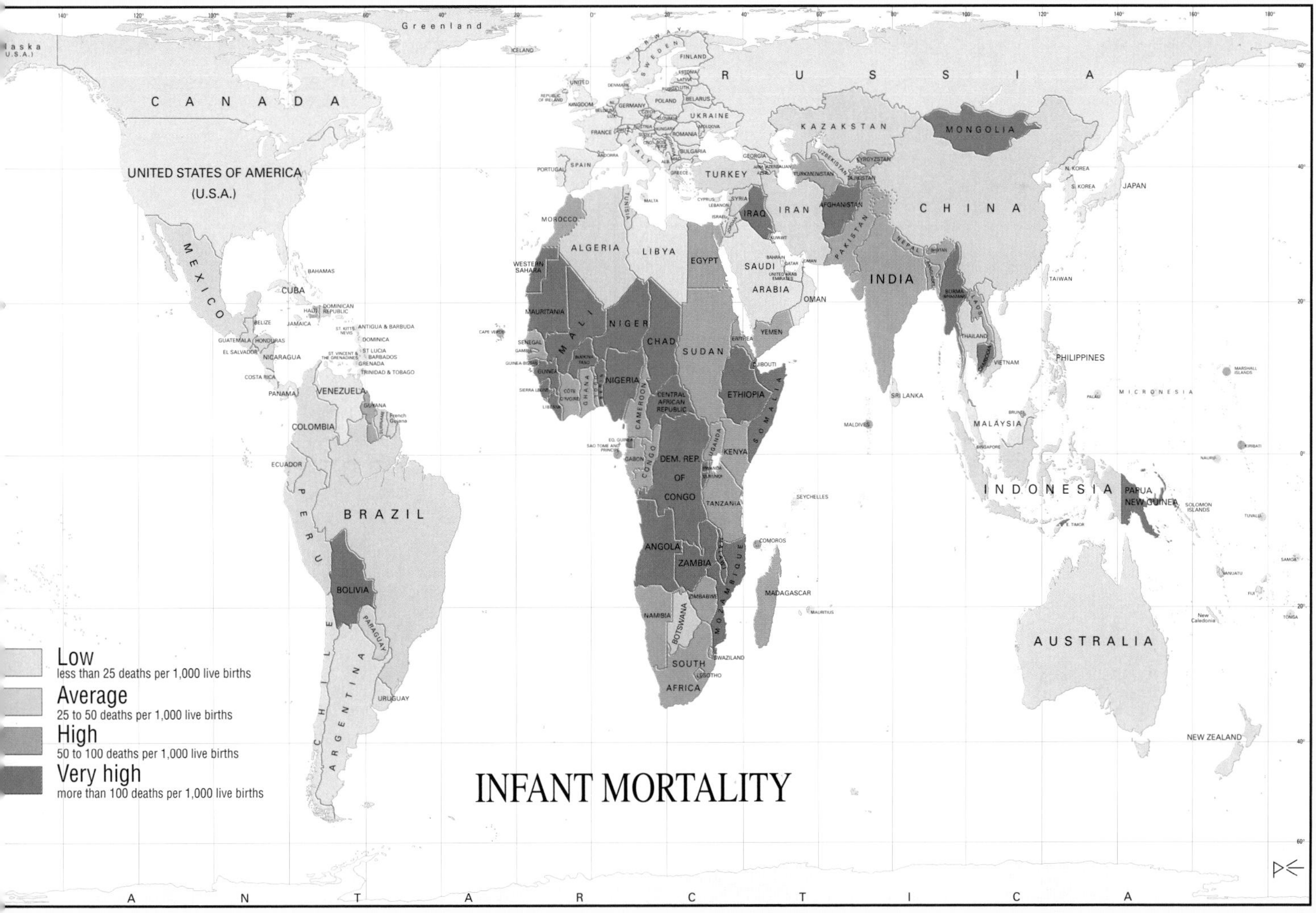

AVAILABLE HOSPITAL BEDS

Far too few
less than 1 bed per 1,000 people

Inadequate
1 to 2 beds per 1,000 people

Almost adequate
2 to 5 beds per 1,000 people

Adequate
more than 5 beds per 1,000 people

INFANT MORTALITY

Low
less than 25 deaths per 1,000 live births

Average
25 to 50 deaths per 1,000 live births

High
50 to 100 deaths per 1,000 live births

Very high
more than 100 deaths per 1,000 live births

When illness strikes the availability of a doctor can mean the difference between life and death. Where there is one doctor for every 300 people, as in Belgium, Bulgaria or Austria, the provision of medical care is assured. Where there are a hundred times more people per doctor (as in Chad with 30,000 or Burkina Faso with 32,000) people mostly have to rely on themselves. The same applies to the provision of hospitals: in Switzerland there are 55 inhabitants per hospital bed, in Niger 10,000. Thus health is today the privilege of the wealthier peoples.

RUNNING EVENTS

Participated
1 to 10 medals
10 to 50 medals
More than 50 medals

in Olympic Games since 1896

JUMPING EVENTS

Participated
1 to 10 medals
10 to 50 medals
More than 50 medals

in Olympic Games since 1896

SKIING

Participated
1 to 10 medals
10 to 50 medals
More than 50 medals

in Olympic Games since 1896

SKI JUMPING

Participated
1 to 10 medals
10 to 50 medals

in Olympic Games since 1896

SWIMMING EVENTS

Participated
1 to 10 medals
10 to 50 medals
More than 50 medals

in Olympic Games since 1896

ROWING EVENTS

Participated
1 to 10 medals
10 to 50 medals
More than 50 medals

in Olympic Games since 1896

CYCLING EVENTS

Participated
1 to 10 medals
10 to 50 medals
More than 50 medals

in Olympic Games since 1896

EQUESTRIAN EVENTS

Participated
1 to 10 medals
10 to 50 medals
More than 50 medals

in Olympic Games since 1896

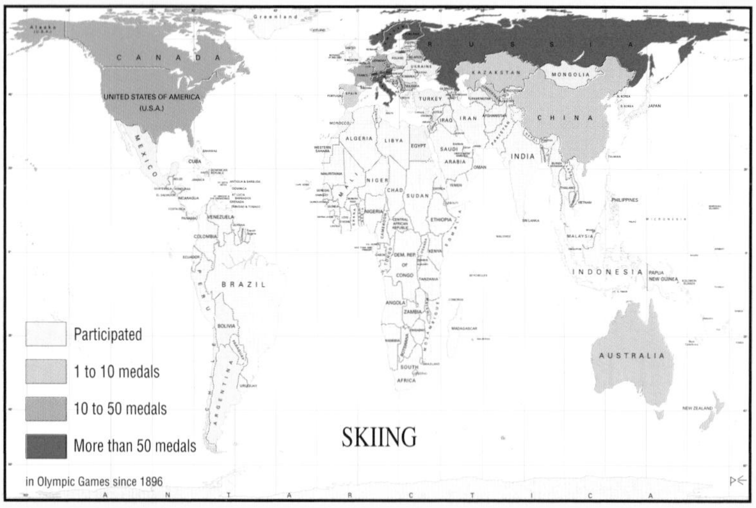

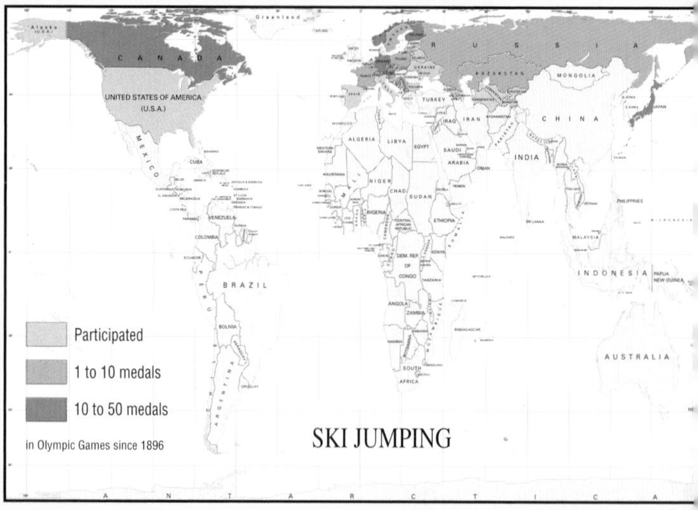

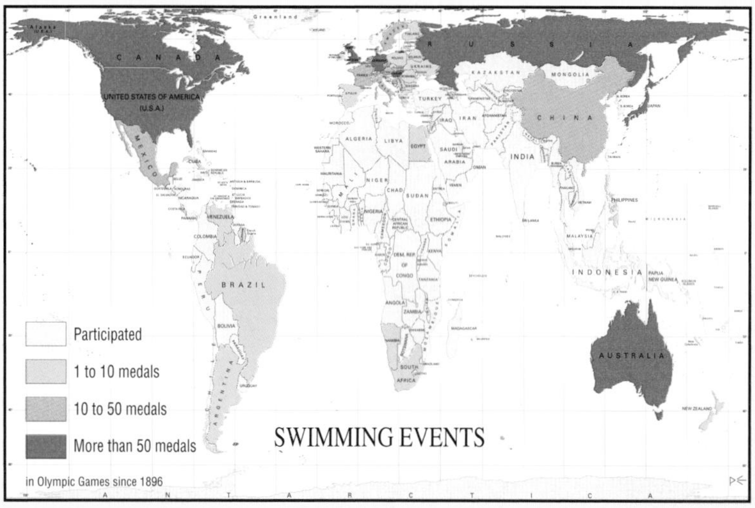

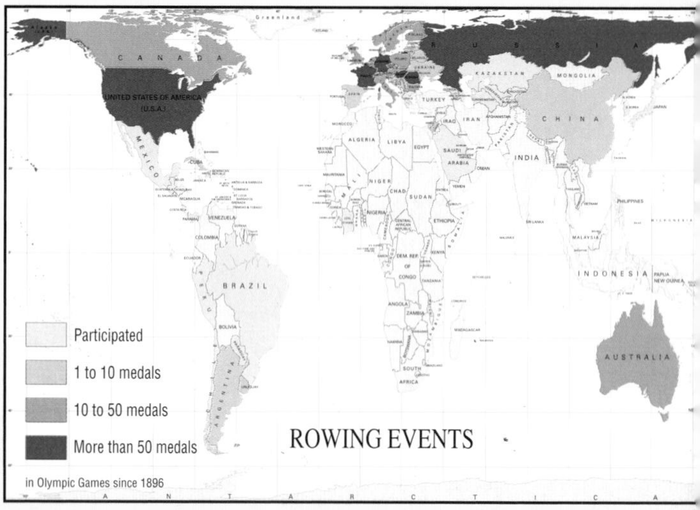

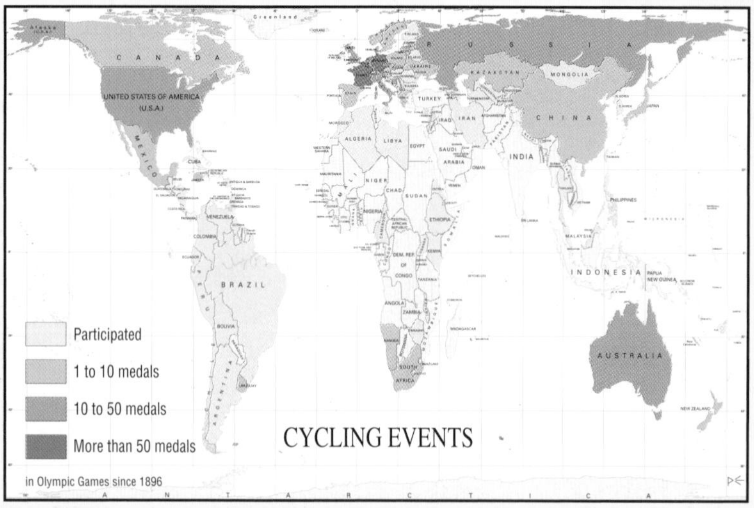

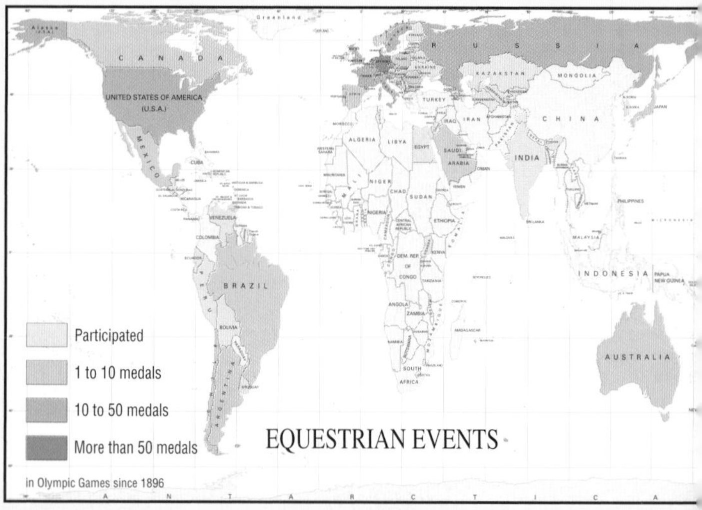

Movement in the form of games is natural to both people and animals. Exercise keeps body and mind fit. Sport is the playing of games according to set rules. It is based on competition and offers those taking part both a challenge and satisfaction. All people at all times have played games and with the growth of urban living and the decrease in the natural movement provided by physical work, sport has become increasingly important in our modern industrial society to safeguard health. Now that the peoples of the world have grown closer together, the top sportsmen and women from all over the world compete every four years in the Olympic Games.

SP

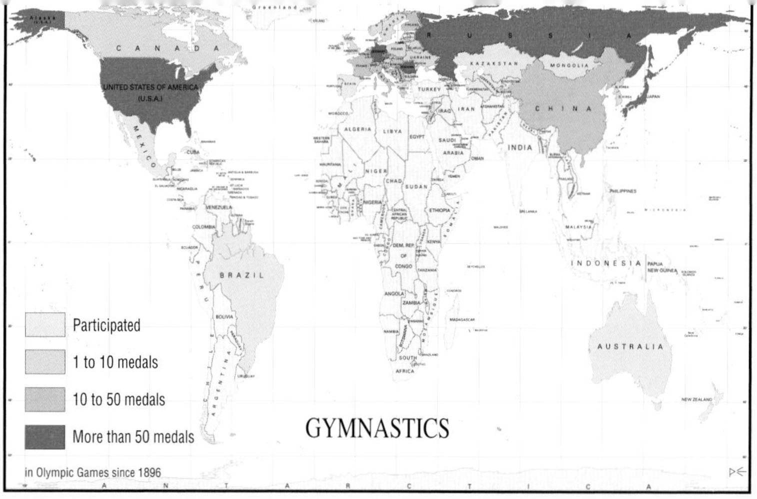

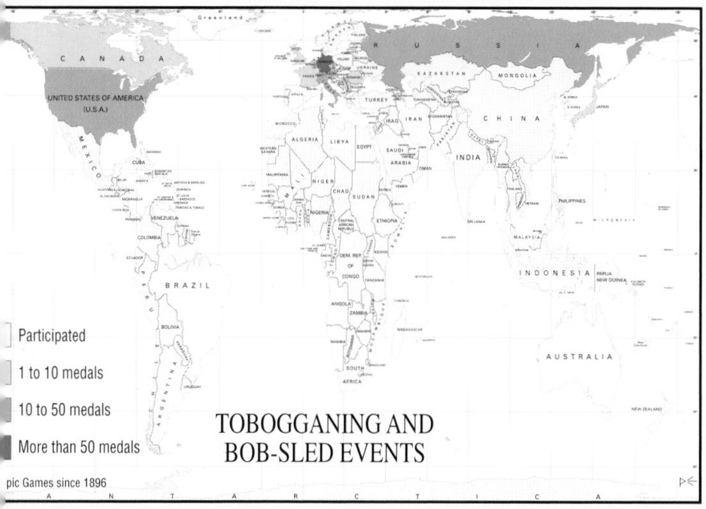

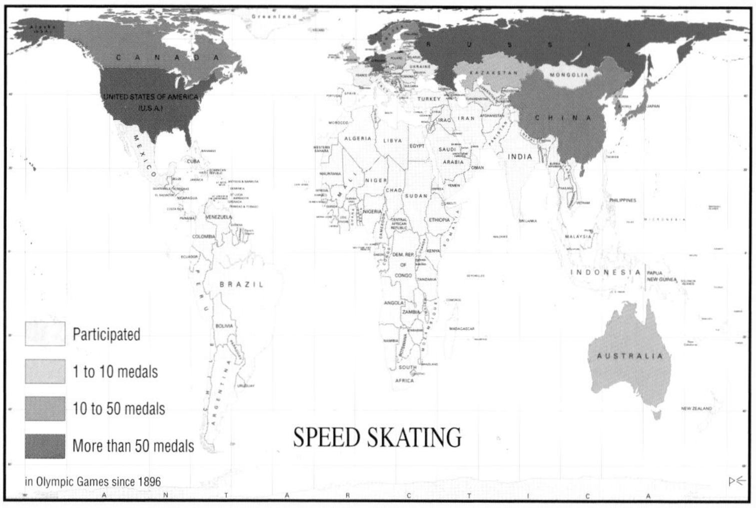

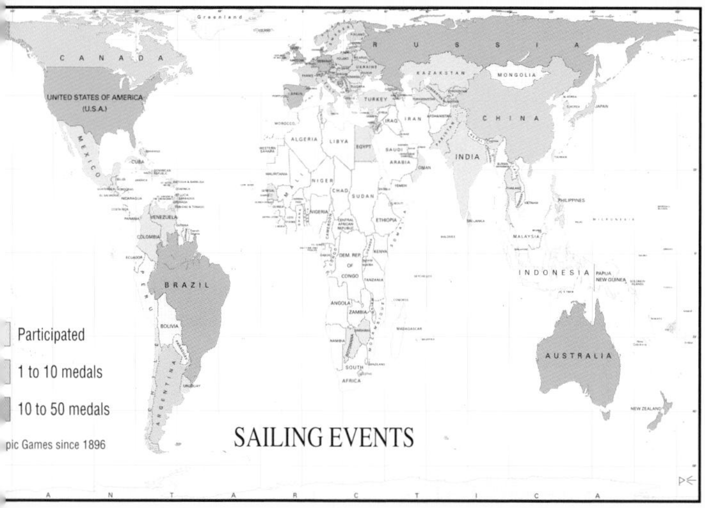

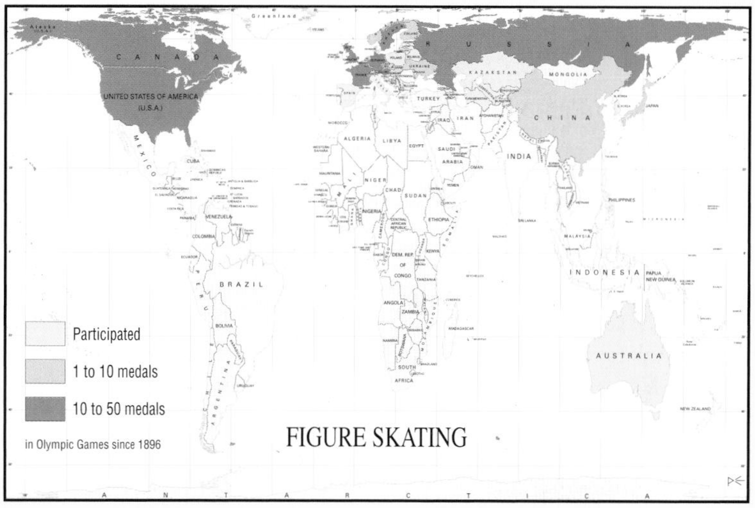

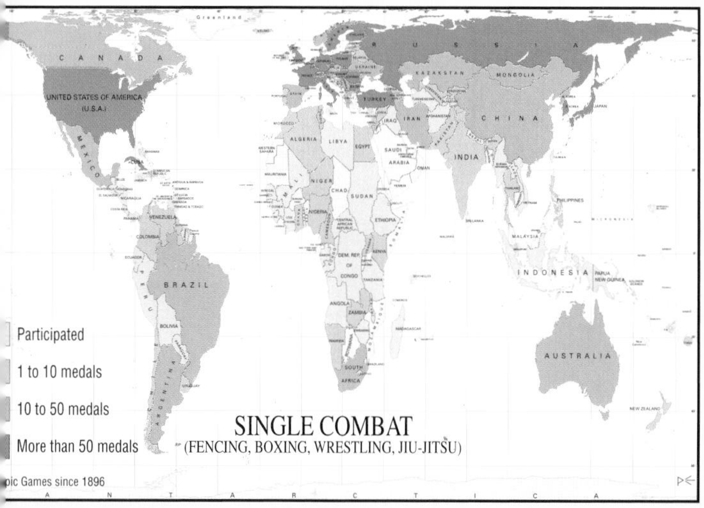

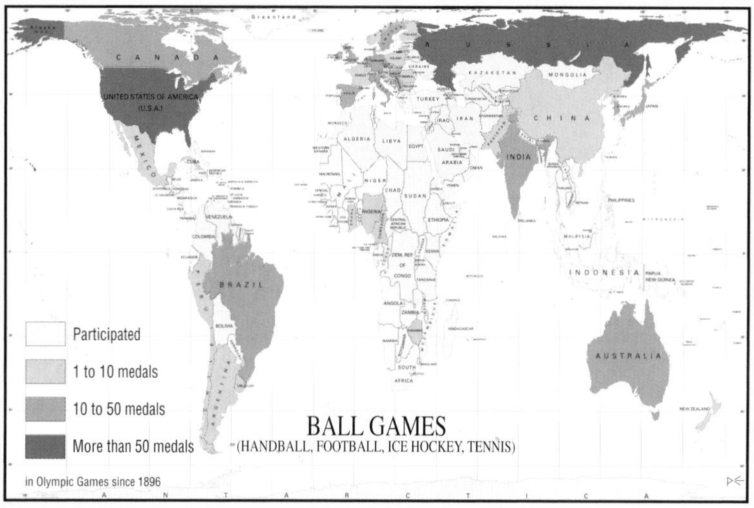

THROWING EVENTS

Participated
1 to 10 medals
10 to 50 medals
More than 50 medals

pic Games since 1896

GYMNASTICS

Participated
1 to 10 medals
10 to 50 medals
More than 50 medals

in Olympic Games since 1896

TOBOGGANING AND BOB-SLED EVENTS

Participated
1 to 10 medals
10 to 50 medals
More than 50 medals

pic Games since 1896

SPEED SKATING

Participated
1 to 10 medals
10 to 50 medals
More than 50 medals

in Olympic Games since 1896

SAILING EVENTS

Participated
1 to 10 medals
10 to 50 medals

pic Games since 1896

FIGURE SKATING

Participated
1 to 10 medals
10 to 50 medals

in Olympic Games since 1896

SINGLE COMBAT
(FENCING, BOXING, WRESTLING, JIU-JITSU)

Participated
1 to 10 medals
10 to 50 medals
More than 50 medals

pic Games since 1896

BALL GAMES
(HANDBALL, FOOTBALL, ICE HOCKEY, TENNIS)

Participated
1 to 10 medals
10 to 50 medals
More than 50 medals

in Olympic Games since 1896

In ancient Greece sport was reserved for free citizens. Later knightly tournaments were confined to the nobility. Modern sport, which originated in England, was for the ruling classes. Even at the Olympic Games of 1928, manual workers were excluded from some competitions and until 1948 equestrian events were for officers only. Sport for the workers developed as a means of promoting general physical fitness, while middle class sport became increasingly commercialised and competitive. The socialist countries, after holding their own sporting events, such as "workers' Olympics", now take part in the Olympic Games.

CALORIE CONSUMPTION

Undernourished
less than 2,000 calories daily

Badly nourished
2,000 to 2,500 calories daily

Adequately nourished
2,500 to 3,000 calories daily

Well nourished
3,000 to 3,500 calories daily

Overnourished
more than 3,500 calories daily

MEAT

Small proportion
less than 10%

Adequate proportion
10 to 20%

Good proportion
20 to 30%

Too much
more than 30%

percentage of total calories consumed

V

Small proportion
less than 70%

Adequate proportion
70 to 80%

Good proportion
80 to 90%

Large proportion
more than 90%

percentage of total calories consumed

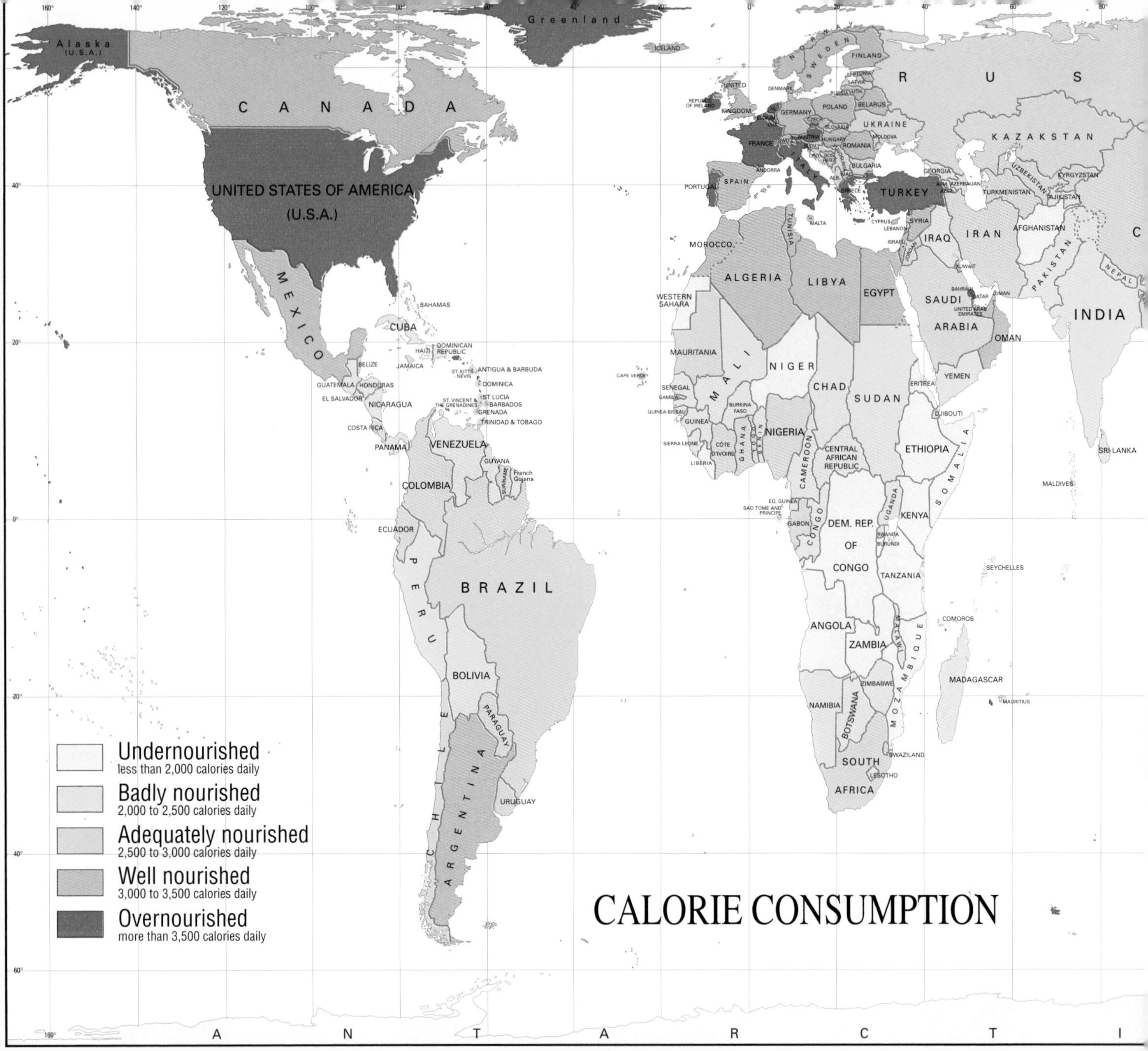

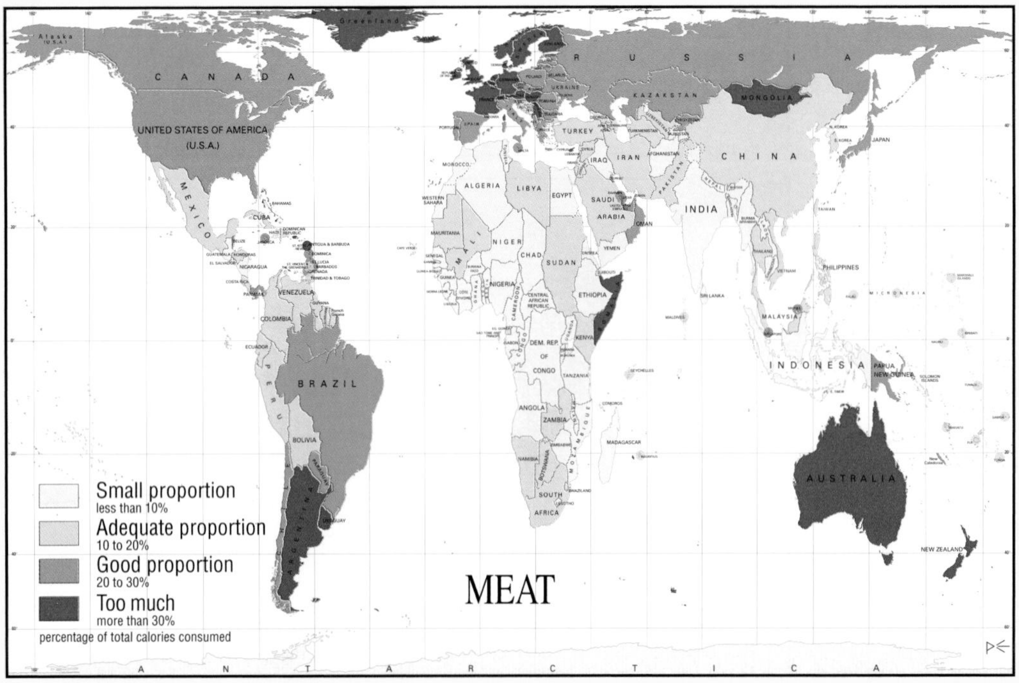

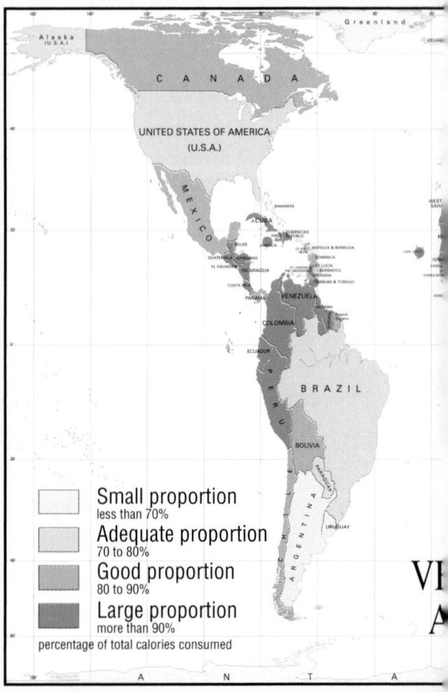

Life processes require constant energy, which all animals must renew through food. After people had begun to produce their own food through agriculture and animal husbandry, the human diet became better and more regular. Most of the world's people normally have enough to eat. Food production is increasing faster than the rise in the world's population. Today therefore, nutrition is only a question of distribution. The superfluous food of richer people and nations could supply the needs of the poor and hungry.

NUTR

CARBOHYDRATES

Insufficient
less than 50%

Sufficient
50 to 75%

Too many
more than 75%

percentage of total calories consumed

FAT

Insufficient
less than 20%

Sufficient
20 to 40%

Too much
more than 40%

percentage of total calories consumed

PROTEIN

Insufficient
less than 9%

Sufficient
9 to 11%

Large proportion
more than 11%

percentage of total calories consumed

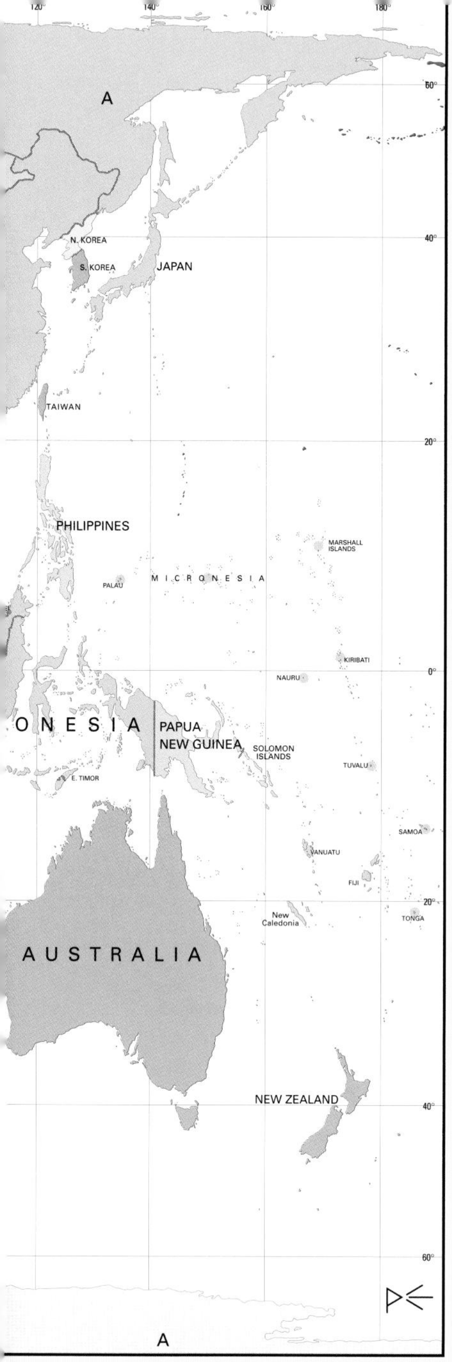

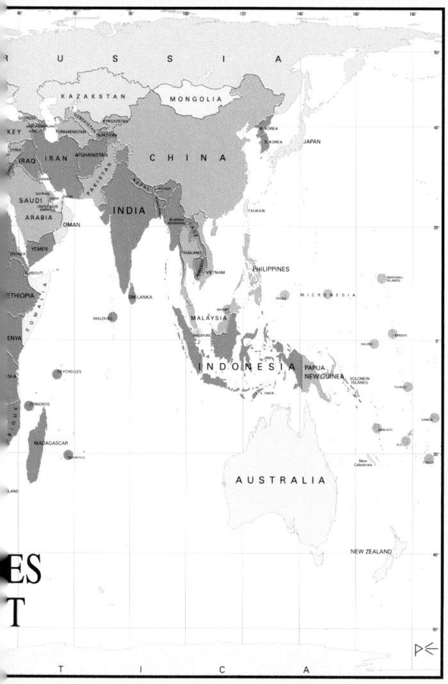

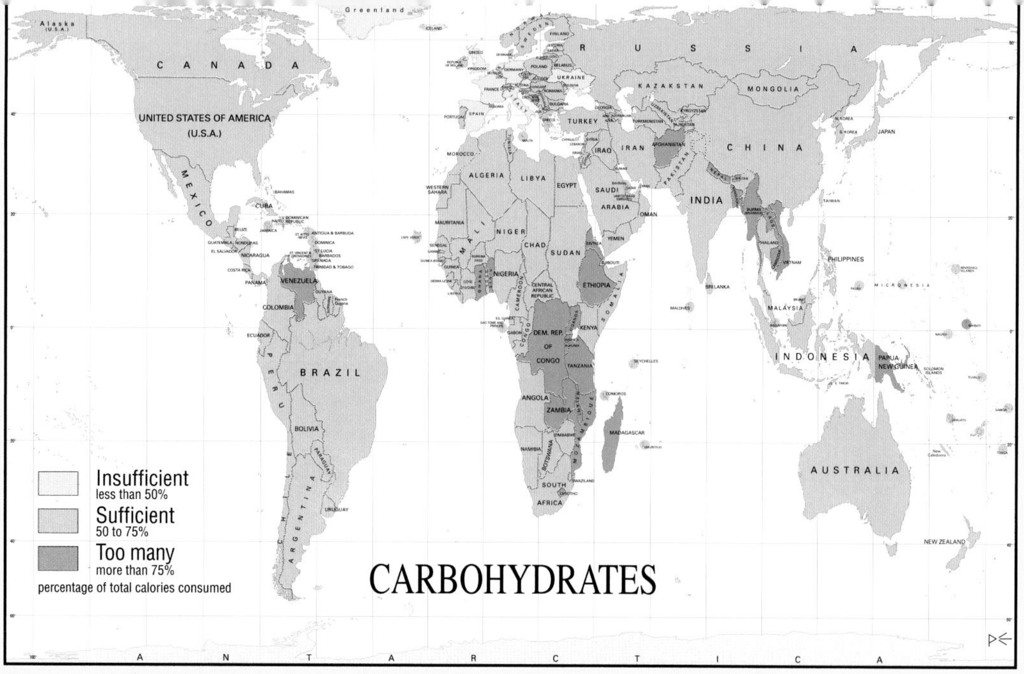

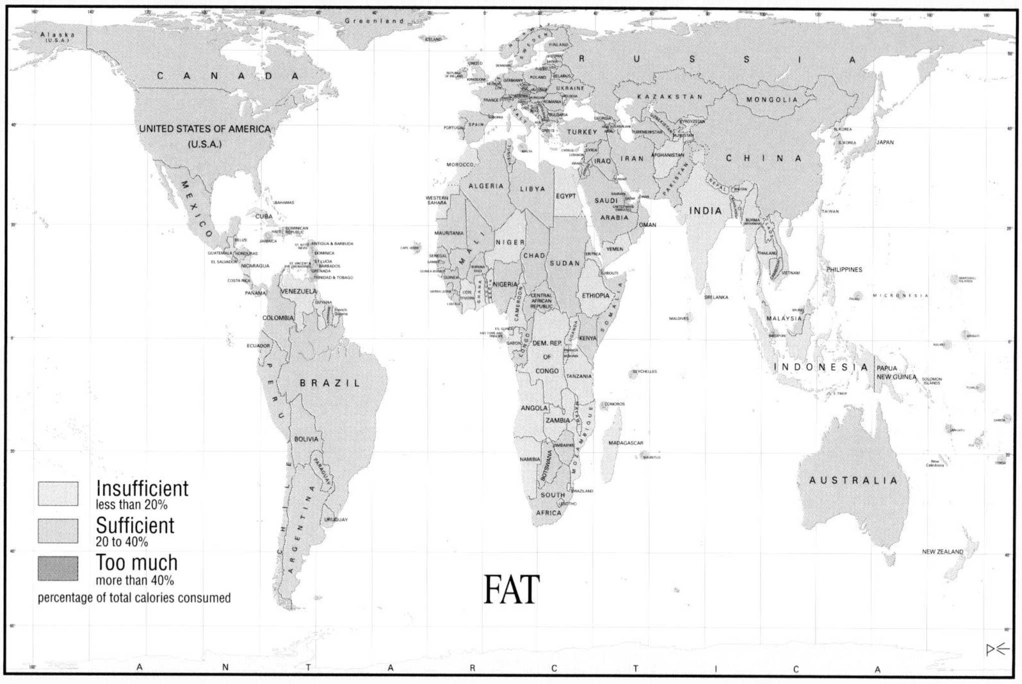

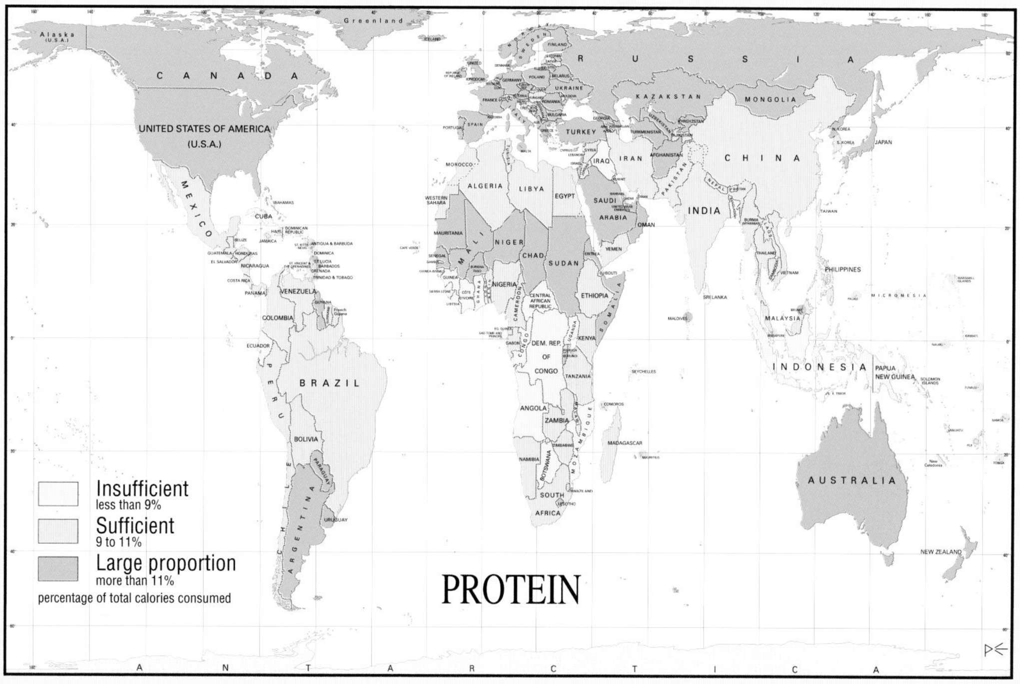

TION

The composition of our diet is no less important than the amount of energy (calories) which it provides. Protein, carbohydrates and fat must be present in balanced proportions. We eat a mixed diet and need both plant and animal foods, the former being essential. Although those doing heavy physical work require a larger amount of calorie-rich foods, intake worldwide is usually less than adequate in these.

Less than 10%
of the soil is cultivated

10 to 20%
of the soil is cultivated

20 to 30%
of the soil is cultivated

30 to 40%
of the soil is cultivated

40 to 50%
of the soil is cultivated

More than 50%
of the soil is cultivated

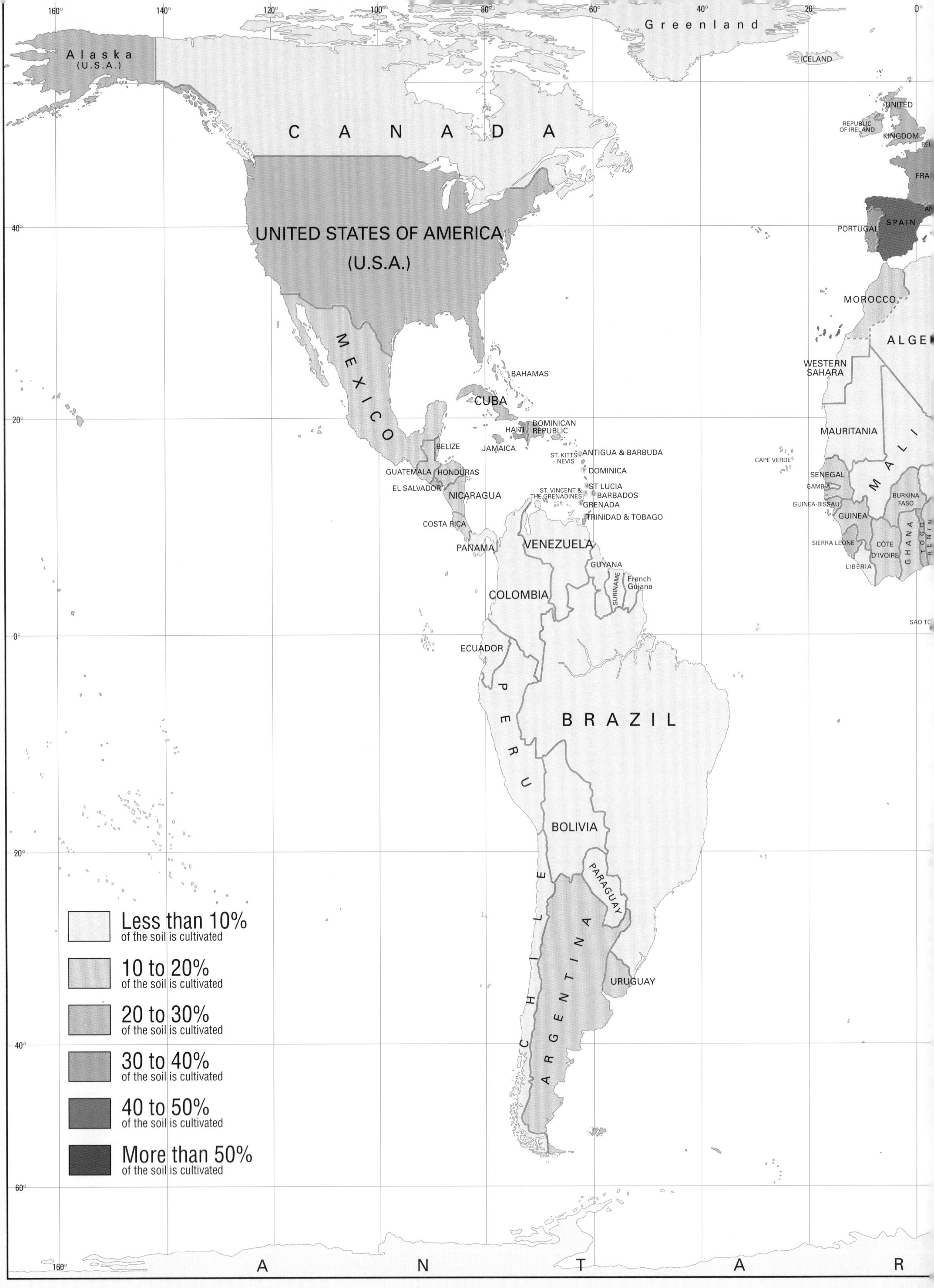

For thousands of years people lived without cultivating the soil. Even today large groups of the world's population do not practise agriculture but live on wild plants, fruit and roots plus meat from animals which they hunt or breed. But cultivation of the soil was a precondition for human settlement and therefore for the development of culture. Today the agricultural use of land is a safeguard for our existence.

SOIL CUL

TIVATION

Less than 10% of land is used for agriculture. Many conditions have to be met before cultivation can be undertaken - not only human ability but also sufficient sunshine, an adequate water supply and good drainage, moderate temperatures and of course, suitable soil. The proportion of land used for cultivation varies between 1% (Libya, Angola) and 63% (Denmark).

Greenland

ICELAND

Alaska
(U.S.A.)

C A N A D A

UNITED STATES OF AMERICA
(U.S.A.)

UNITED
KINGDOM

REPUBLIC
OF IRELAND

FRA

PORTUGAL   SPAIN

MOROCCO

WESTERN
SAHARA

ALGE

M
E
X
I
C
O

BAHAMAS

CUBA

DOMINICAN
REPUBLIC

HAITI

JAMAICA

BELIZE

GUATEMALA HONDURAS

EL SALVADOR

NICARAGUA

COSTA RICA

PANAMA

ST. KITTS -
NEVIS

ANTIGUA & BARBUDA

DOMINICA

ST LUCIA

ST VINCENT &
THE GRENADINES

BARBADOS

GRENADA

TRINIDAD & TOBAGO

VENEZUELA

GUYANA

French
Guiana

COLOMBIA

S
U
R
I
N
A
M
E

ECUADOR

MAURITANIA

MALI

CAPE VERDE

SENEGAL

GAMBIA

GUINEA-BISSAU

GUINEA

SIERRA LEONE

LIBERIA

BURKINA
FASO

CÔTE
D'IVOIRE

GHANA

BENIN

SAO TO
PRIN

P
E
R
U

B R A Z I L

BOLIVIA

PARAGUAY

C
H
I
L
E

A
R
G
E
N
T
I
N
A

URUGUAY

Less than 100 tonnes
per km² of cultivated land

100 to 200 tonnes
per km² of cultivated land

200 to 300 tonnes
per km² of cultivated land

300 to 400 tonnes
per km² of cultivated land

More than 400 tonnes
per km² of cultivated land

A N T A R

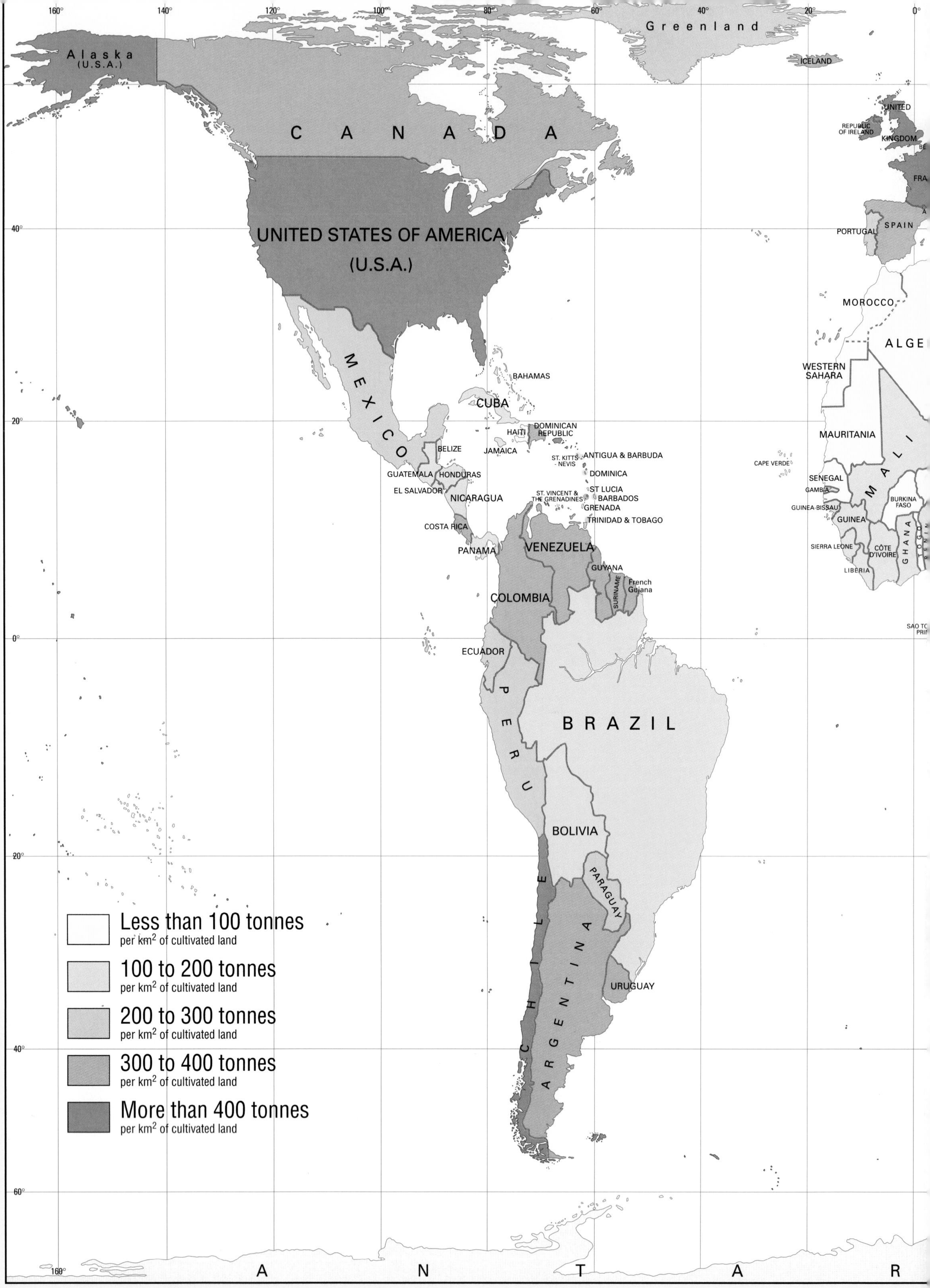

With the breakthrough of industrialisation in the mid-19th century, agriculture too benefited from improvements.
Before this Green Revolution, three farmers were required to produce enough to feed one town-dweller
over and above their own requirements. Nowadays one farmer can produce enough food for thirty town-
dwellers. Agricultural production has thus increased almost a hundredfold over the past hundred years.

CROP

FINLAND
ESTONIA
LATVIA
USSIA LITH.
AND BELARUS
R U S S I A
UKRAINE
GARY MOLDOVA
ROMANIA
KAZAKSTAN
MONGOLIA
BULGARIA
MAC
GEORGIA
GREECE
TURKEY
CYPRUS SYRIA
LEBANON
ISRAEL IRAQ
JORDAN
ARM. AZERBAIJAN
AZER.
TURKMENISTAN
UZBEKISTAN
KYRGYZSTAN
TAJIKISTAN
AFGHANISTAN
IRAN
N. KOREA
S. KOREA
JAPAN
KUWAIT
EGYPT
BAHRAIN
QATAR
UNITED ARAB
EMIRATES
OMAN
SAUDI
ARABIA
OMAN
PAKISTAN
NEPAL
BHUTAN
BANGLADESH
C H I N A
TAIWAN
YA
YEMEN
INDIA
BURMA
(MYANMAR)
SUDAN
ERITREA
DJIBOUTI
LAOS
THAILAND
NTRAL
FRICAN
PUBLIC
ETHIOPIA
SOMALIA
CAMBODIA
VIETNAM
PHILIPPINES
MARSHALL
ISLANDS
SRI LANKA
MALDIVES
M I C R O N E S I A
PALAU
UGANDA
KENYA
MALAYSIA
BRUNEI
EM. REP.
OF
CONGO
RWANDA
BURUNDI
TANZANIA
SINGAPORE
SEYCHELLES
I N D O N E S I A
PAPUA
NEW GUINEA
SOLOMON
ISLANDS
KIRIBATI
NAURU
TUVALU
E. TIMOR
COMOROS
VANUATU
SAMOA
OLA
ZAMBIA
MALAWI
MOZAMBIQUE
MADAGASCAR
MAURITIUS
FIJI
IA
ZIMBABWE
New
Caledonia
TONGA
A U S T R A L I A
BOTSWANA
SWAZILAND
SOUTH
LESOTHO
AFRICA
NEW ZEALAND
C T I C A

50°
40°
20°
0°
20°
40°
60°

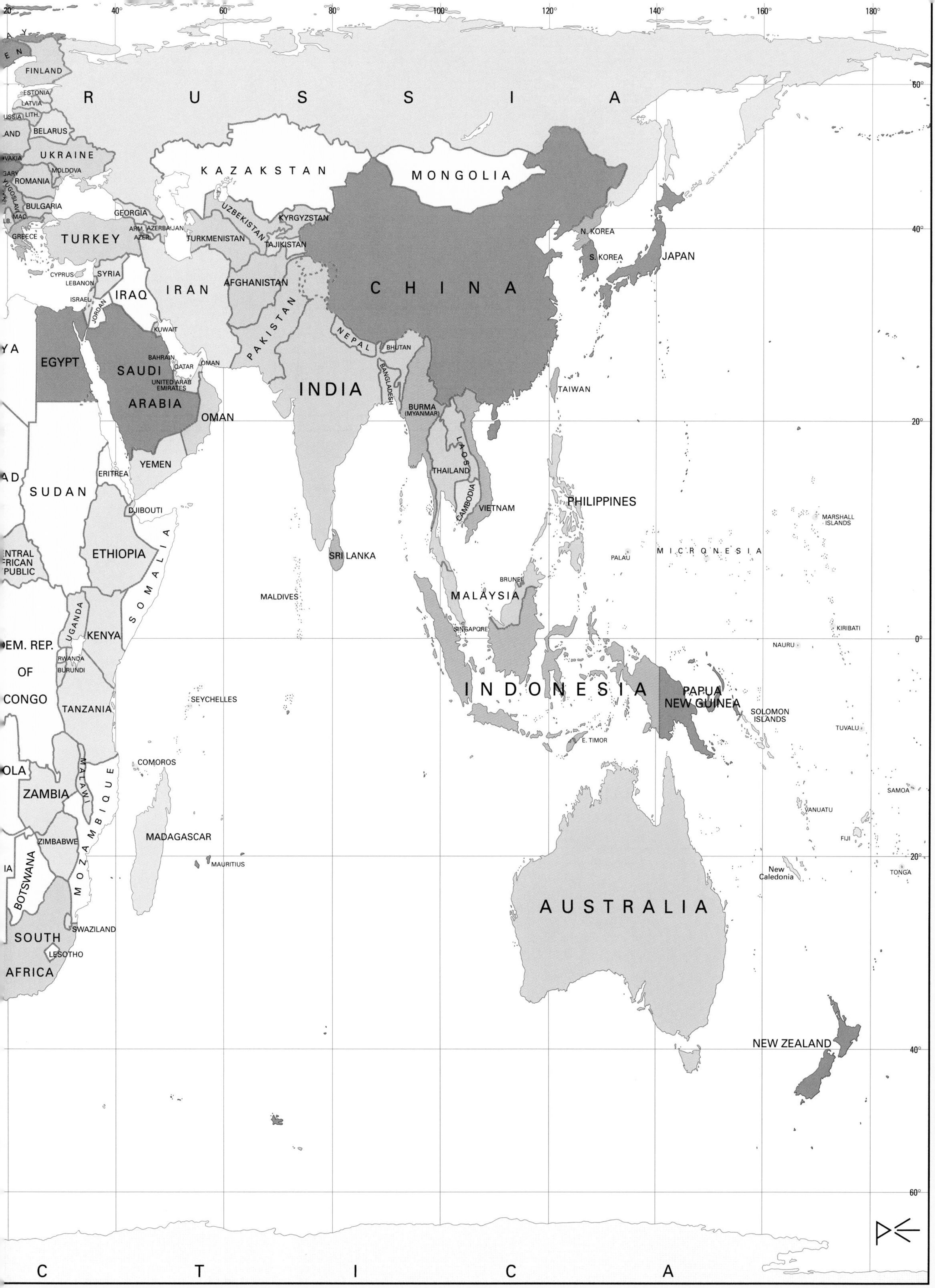

YIELD

The enormous increase in farming yields was achieved by the mechanisation of farming, artificial fertilisers and pesticides as well as the breeding of more productive animals. Because of the high costs involved, the poor countries can make only limited use of these methods. Thus farmers in Niger produce only 38 tonnes per square kilometre while French farmers produce 730 tonnes and the Japanese 600 - that is, over fifteen times as much.

WHEAT

Less than 100 grams
100 to 200 grams
200 to 300 grams
300 to 400 grams
More than 400 grams

consumption per head daily

Less than 1 gram
1 to 10 grams
10 to 50 grams
More than 50 grams

consumption per head daily

OATS

Less than 1 gram
1 to 5 grams
5 to 10 grams
More than 10 grams

consumption per head daily

Less than 10 grams
10 to 100 grams
100 to 200 grams
200 to 300 grams
More than 300 grams

consumption per head daily

MAIZE

Less than 10 grams
10 to 100 grams
100 to 200 grams
200 to 300 grams
More than 300 grams

consumption per head daily

Less than 1 gram
1 to 10 grams
10 to 50 grams
50 to 100 grams
More than 100 grams

consumption per head daily

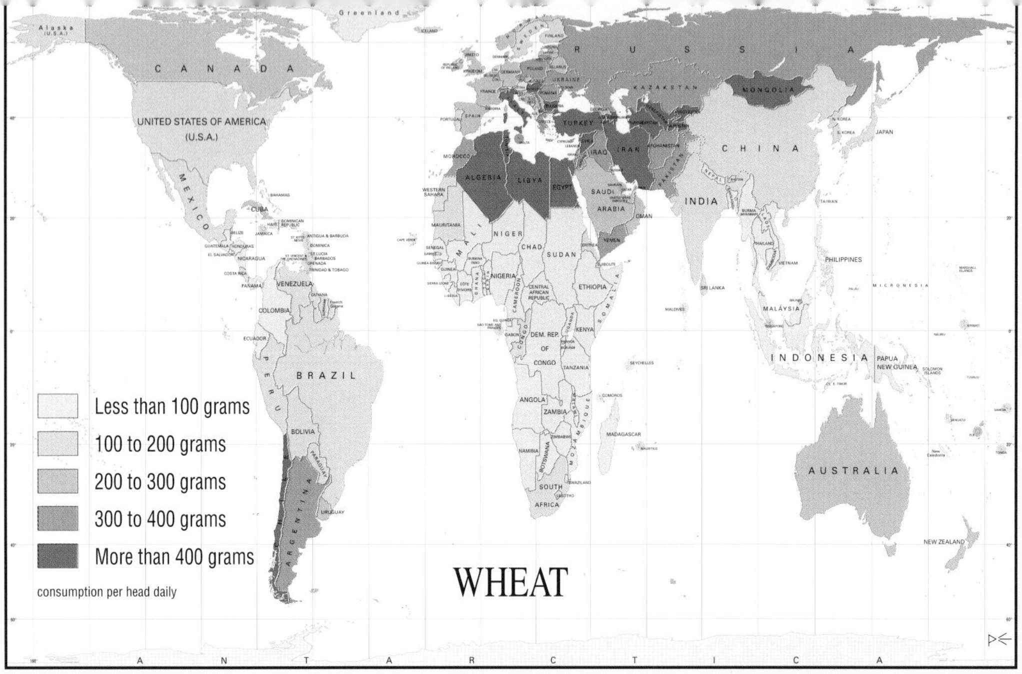

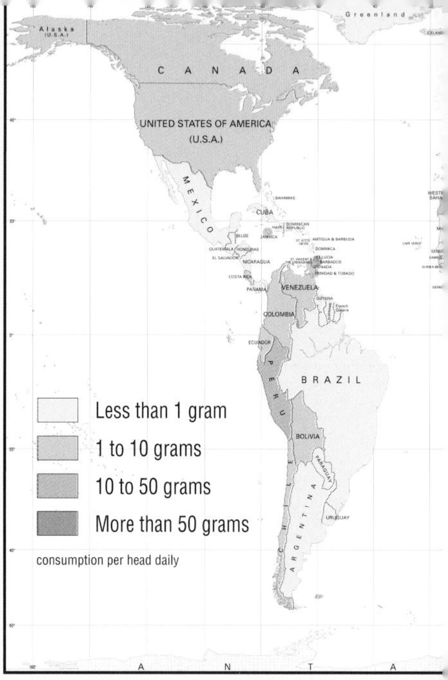

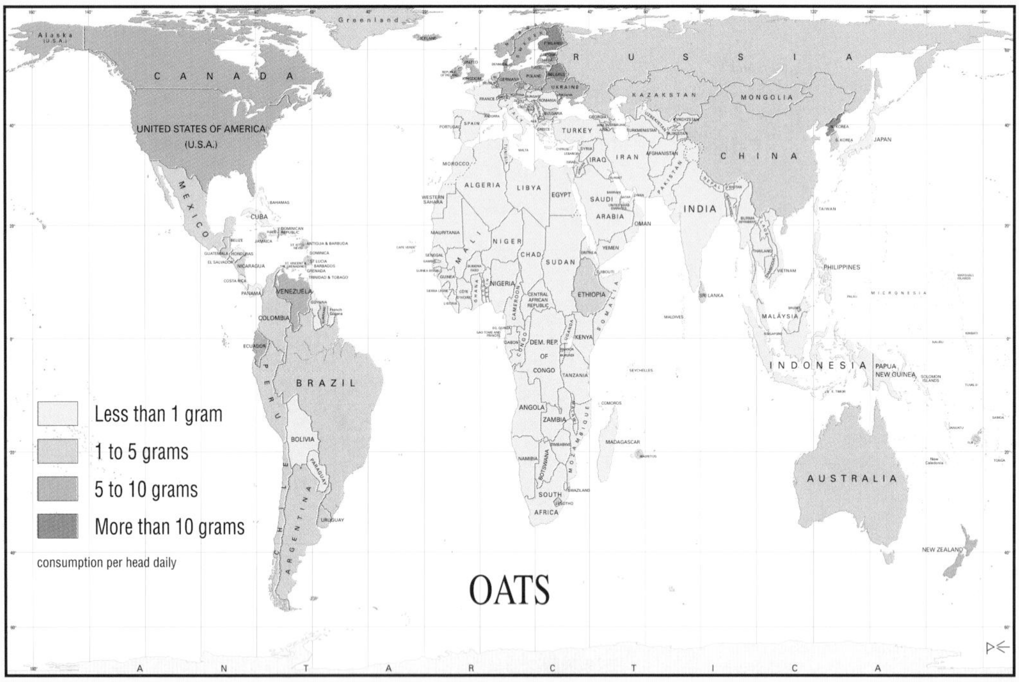

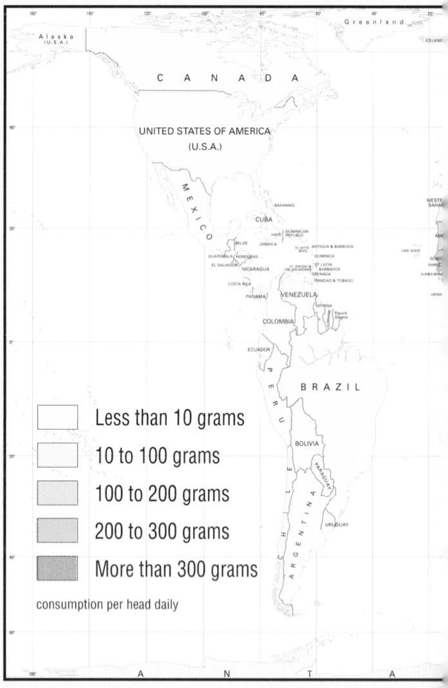

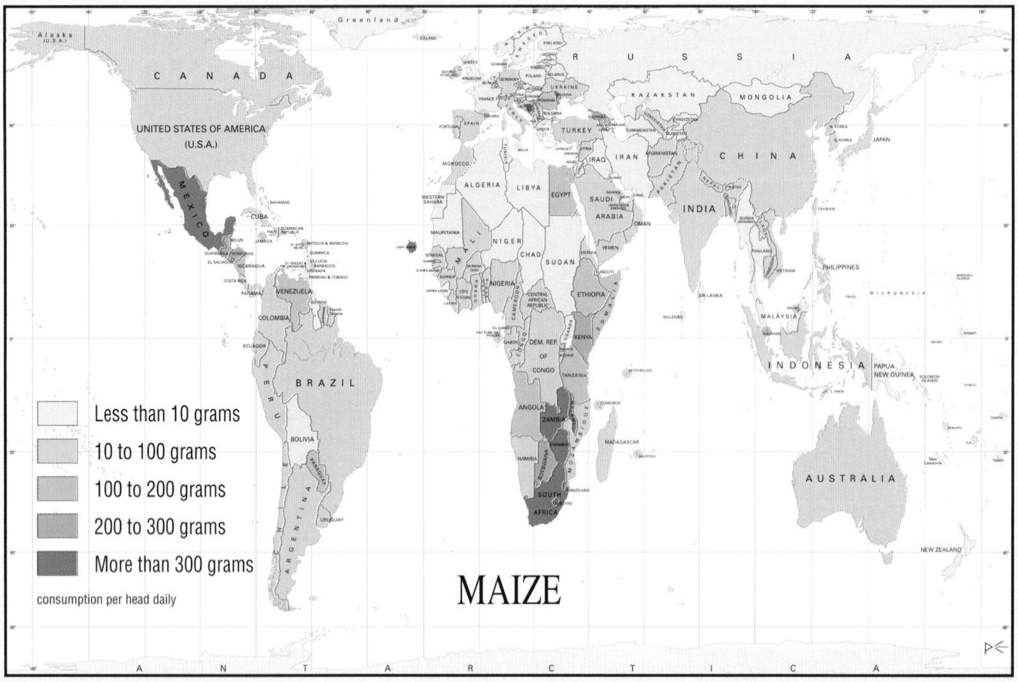

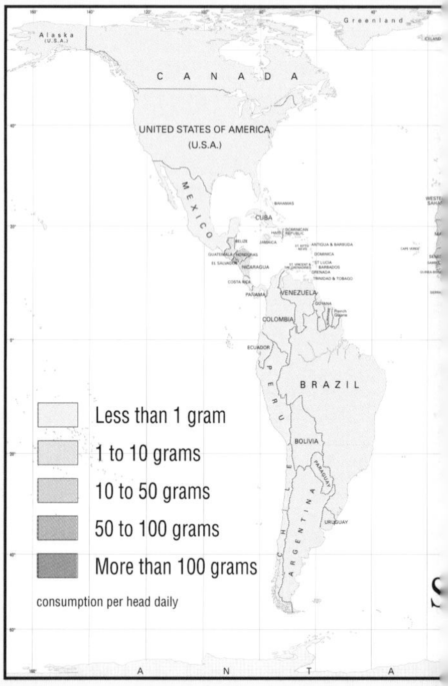

More than half of arable land worldwide is used to grow grain, which represents 56% of the calories consumed by people. Grain is a complete foodstuff containing not only carbohydrates, protein and fat but also the most important minerals and vitamins. In various forms it is still the staple food of the human race.

STAPLE FO

RYE

Less than 10 grams
10 to 50 grams
50 to 100 grams
More than 100 grams

consumption per head daily

SOYA

Less than 1 gram
1 to 10 grams
10 to 20 grams
More than 20 grams

consumption per head daily

RICE

Less than 100 grams
100 to 200 grams
200 to 300 grams
300 to 400 grams
More than 400 grams

consumption per head daily

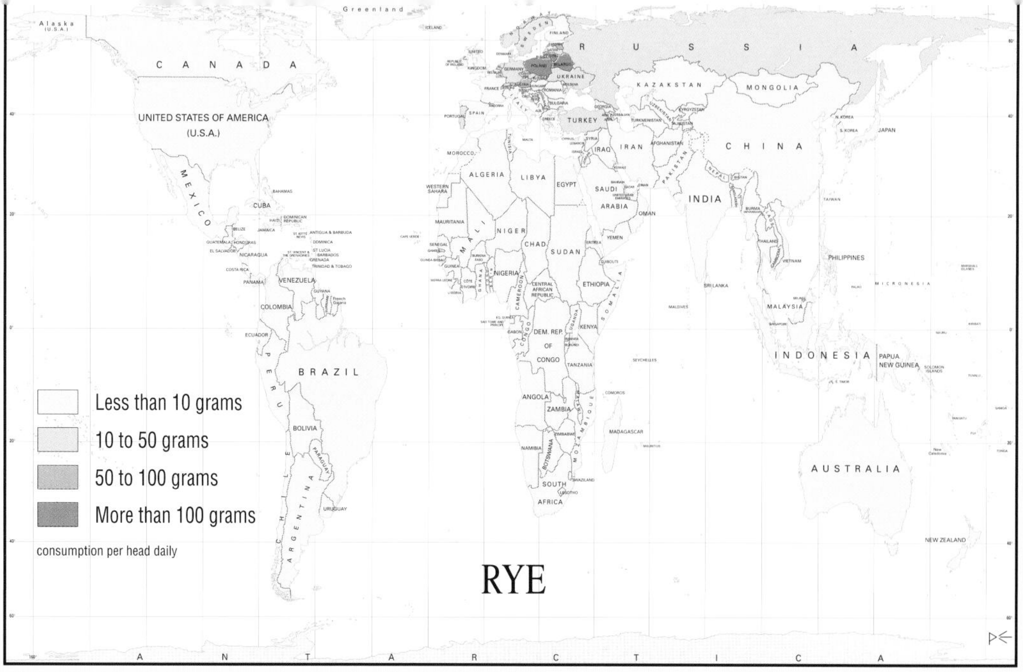

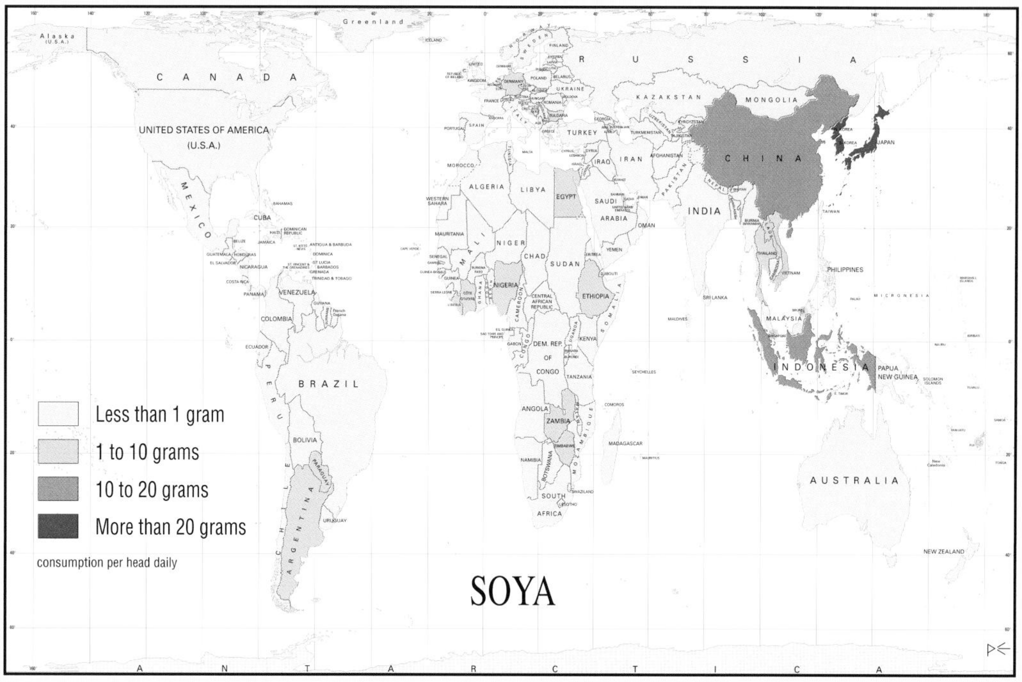

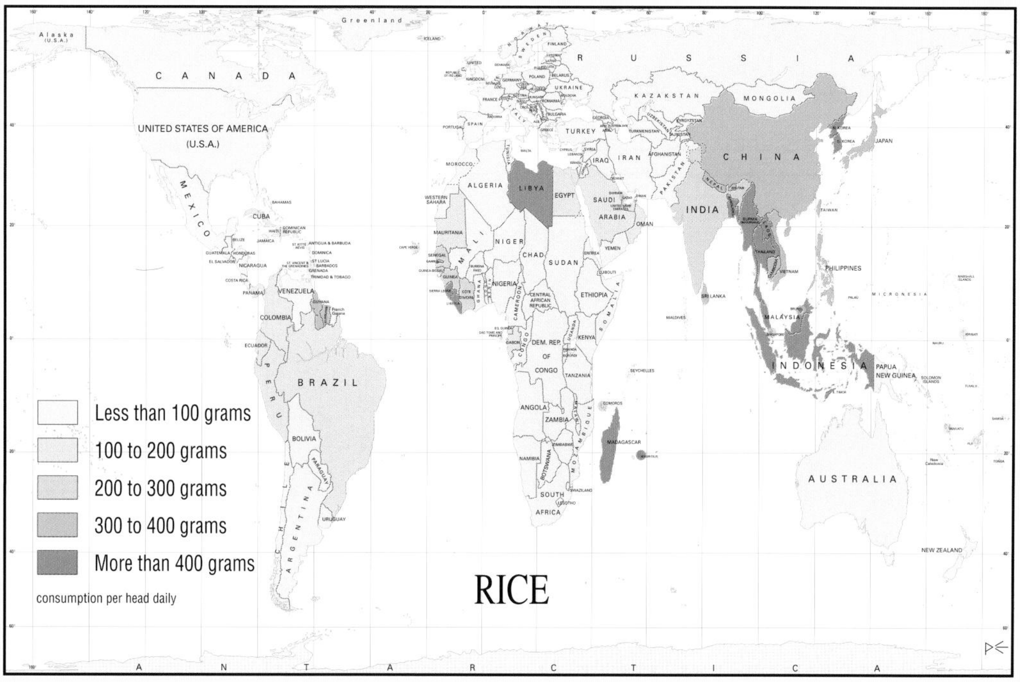

ODSTUFFS

The percentage of grain in the diets of different countries varies considerably. In the developing countries of Asia, Africa and Latin America nearly three-quarters of calories consumed come from grain, compared with a little over a quarter in the rich industrial nations. In the rich world, most of the grain is used as fodder for animals.

CATTLE

100 to 1,000
More than 1,000
per 1,000 of population

HORSES

5 to 50
More than 50
per 1,000 of population

CAMELS

5 to 50
More than 50
per 1,000 of population

BUFFALO

5 to 50
More than 50
per 1,000 of population

SHEEP

100 to 1,000
More than 1,000
per 1,000 of population

PIGS

10 to 100
More than 100
per 1,000 of population

CHICKENS

100 to 1,000
More than 1,000
per 1,000 of population

DUCKS

10 to 100
More than 100
per 1,000 of population

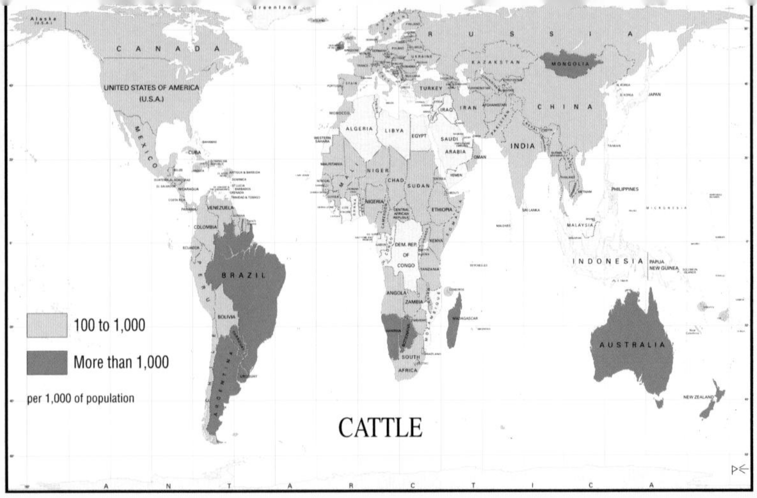

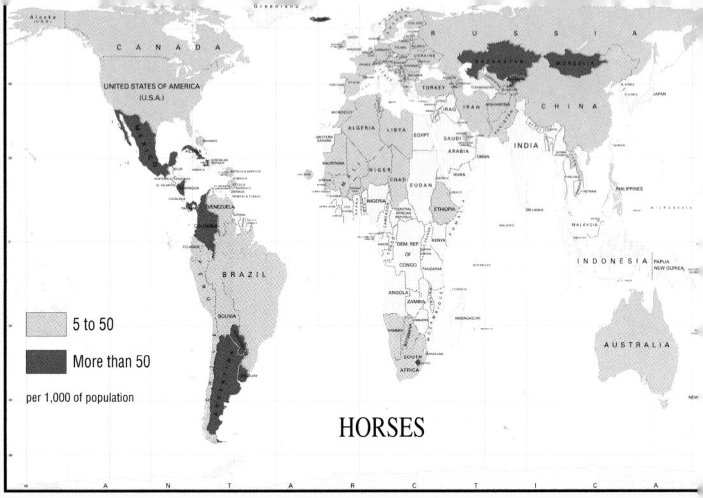

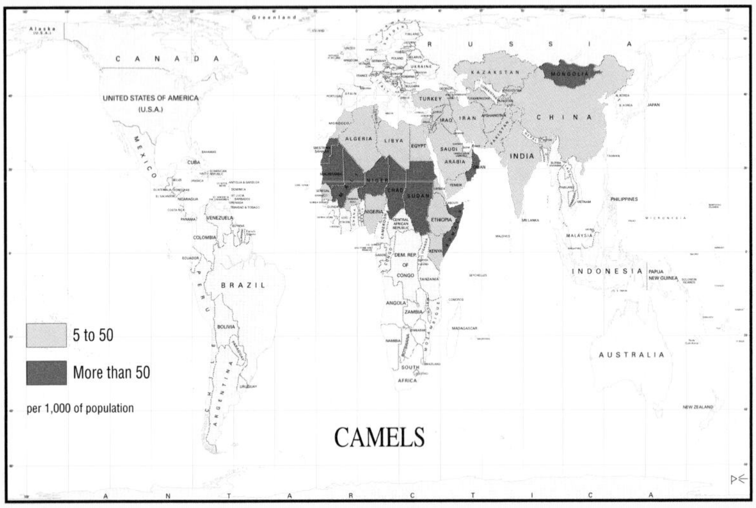

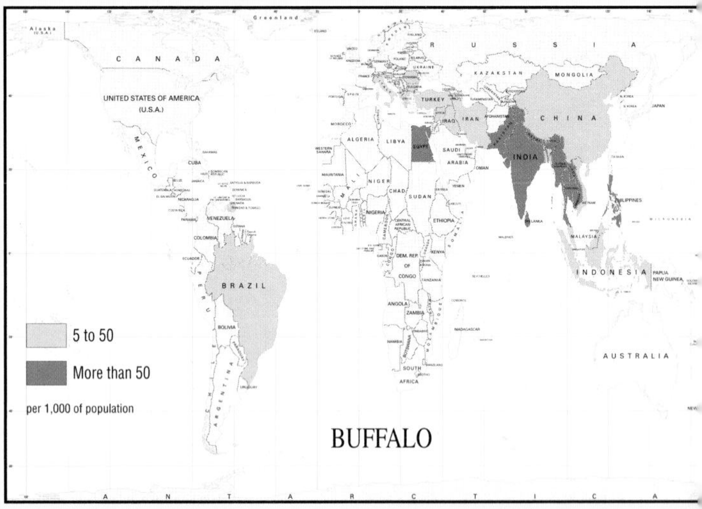

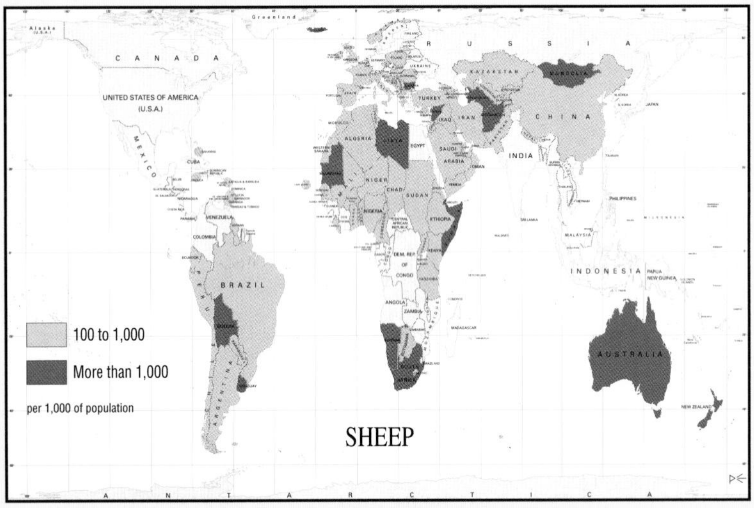

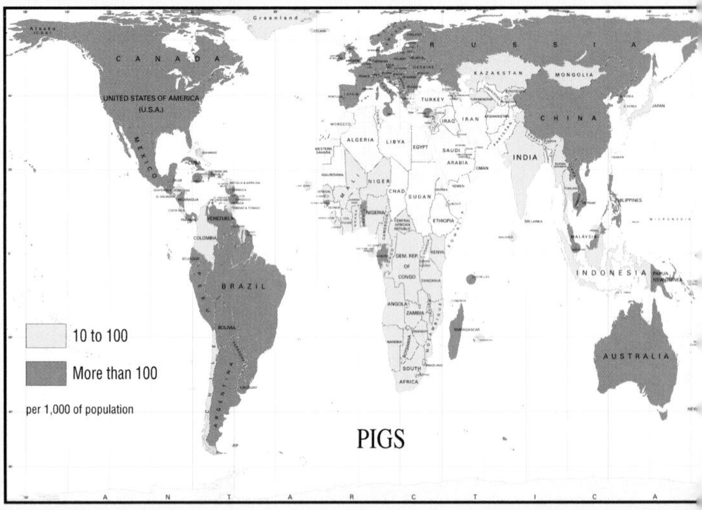

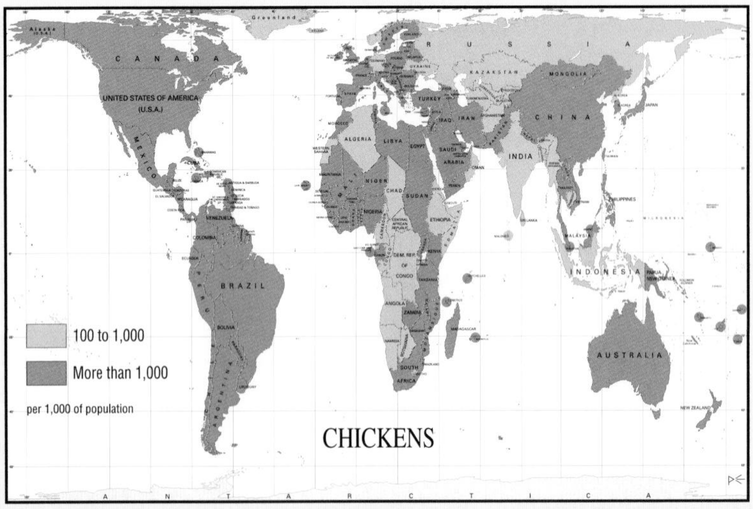

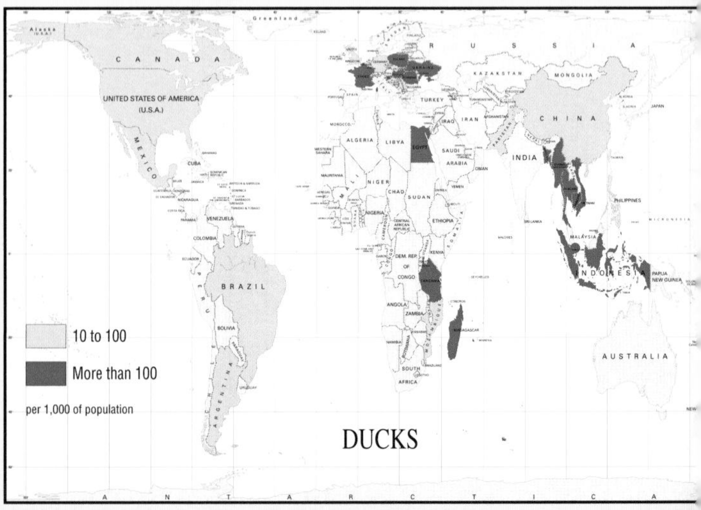

Only a dozen of the 6,000 species of wild mammals and a few birds and insects have been domesticated by humans. With these they developed a close link; they kept them in or near their own home, provided for their needs, and protected them from predators. With the rapid industrialisation of animal husbandry, this relationship has however deteriorated into a merely financial interest.

ANIMAL H

MULES

1 to 5
More than 5

0 of population

DONKEYS

5 to 50
More than 50

per 1,000 of population

ELEPHANT (INDIAN)

1 to 100
More than 100

on of population

REINDEER

1 to 10
More than 10

per 1,000 of population

GOATS

100 to 1,000
More than 1,000

0 of population

BEES

1 to 10 communities
More than 10 communities

per 1,000 of population

TURKEYS

10 to 100
More than 100

0 of population

SILKWORM

1,000 to 10,000
More than 10,000

per 1,000 of population

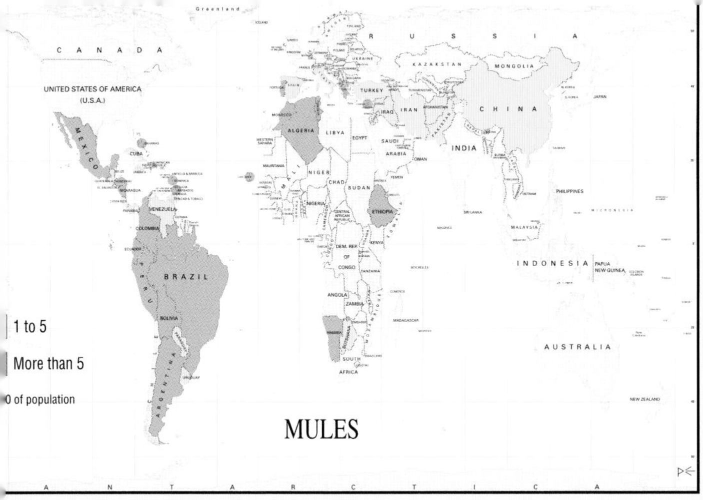

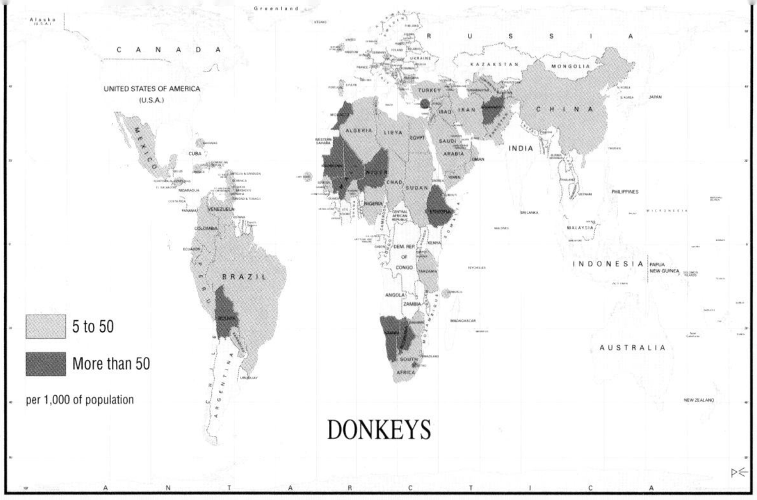

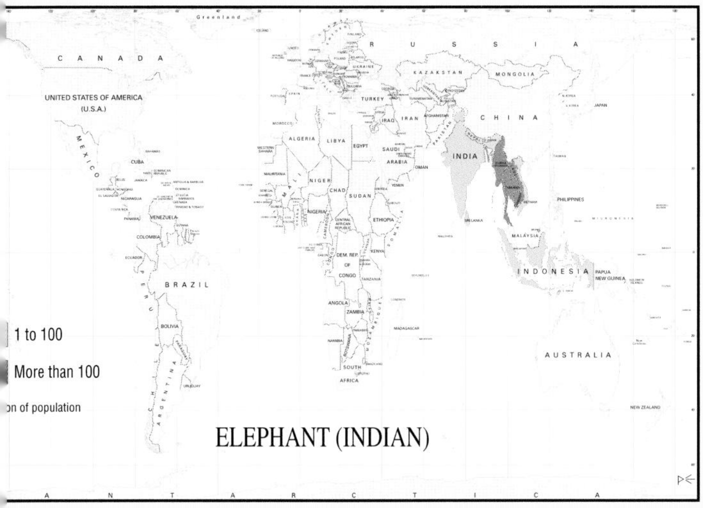

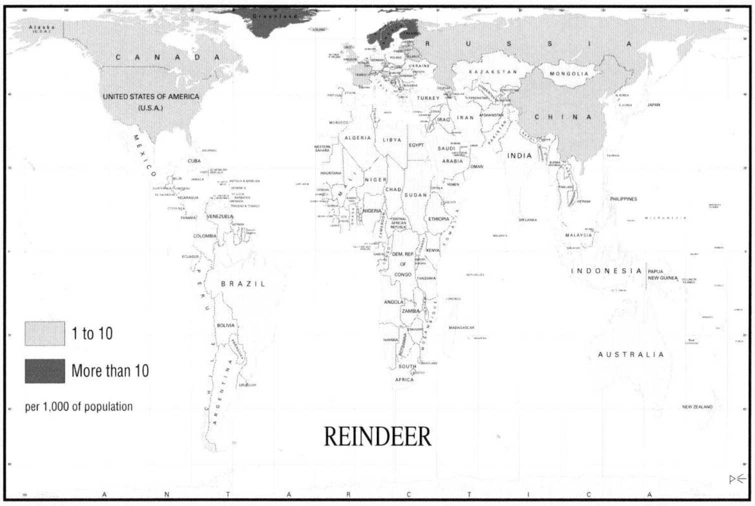

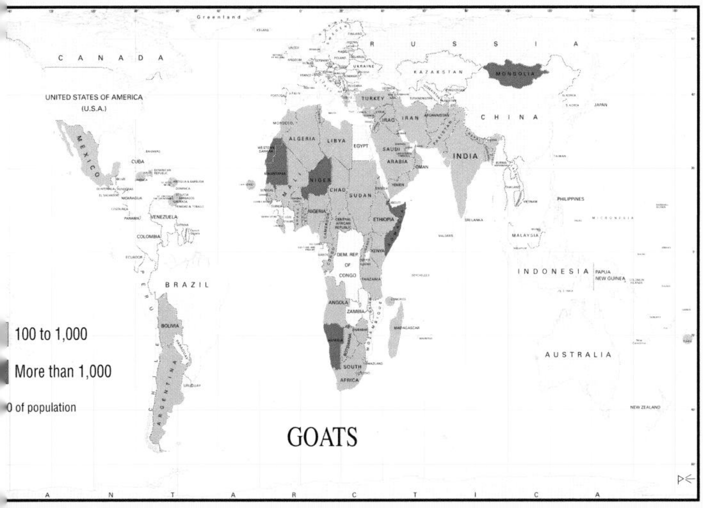

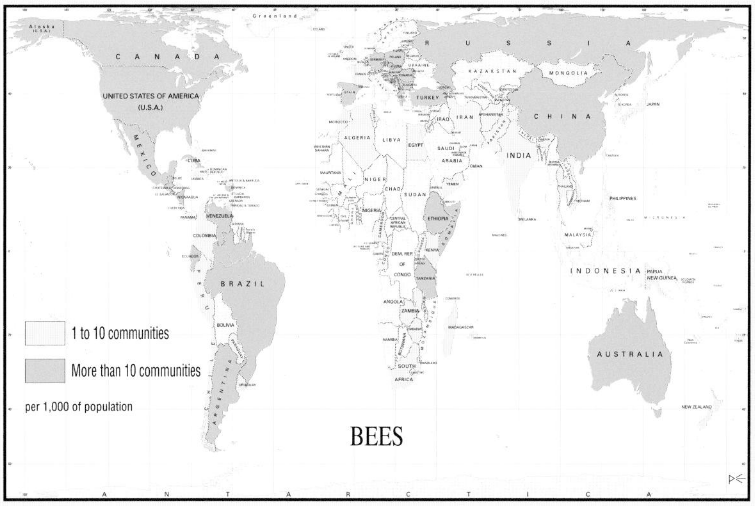

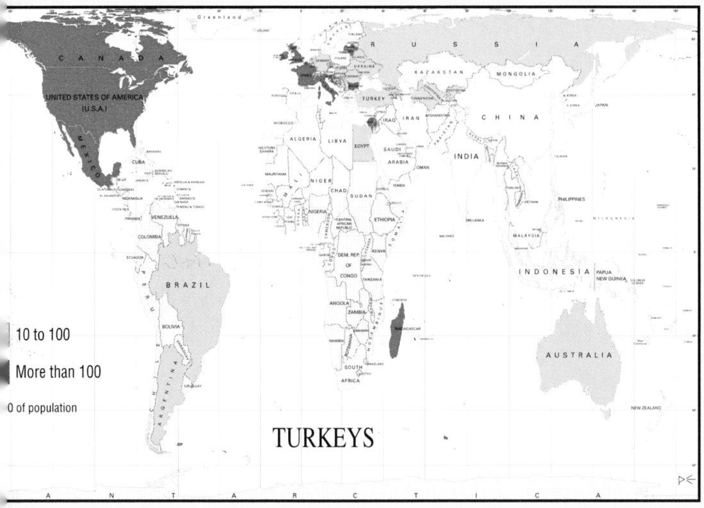

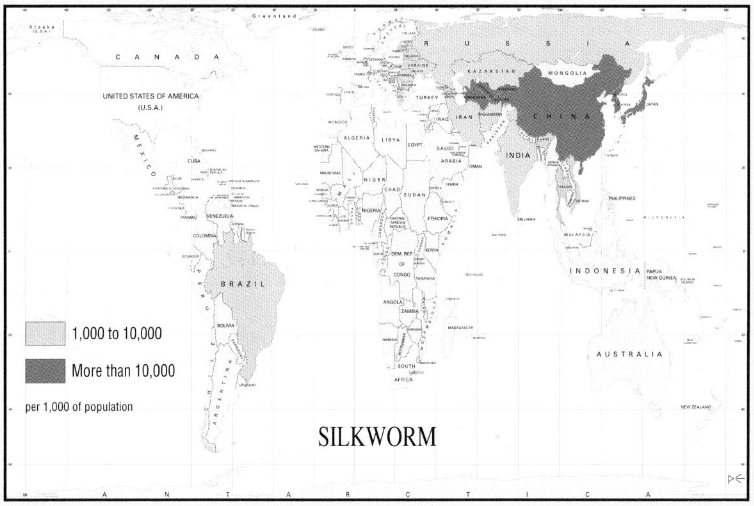

SBANDRY

The successful subjugation of animals almost 10,000 years ago served as a model for human exploitation of other people. Slavery was first limited to people of foreign tribes but 5,000 years ago it was extended to members of the same people as serfdom and wage work. At the same time the gap between rich and poor widened immeasurably. But this polarisation also had its origin in animal husbandry because increased ownership of animals in the hands of a few made a big social difference even 5,000 years ago.

SIZE OF CATCHES

Less than 10,000 tonnes
10,000 to 100,000 tonnes
100,000 to 1million tonnes
1 to 10 million tonnes
More than 10 million tonnes

annual catch

HERRING

Less than 3 tonnes
3 to 10 tonnes
10 to 30 tonnes
30 to 100 tonnes
More than 100 tonnes

per 1,000 km² annually

Less than 3 tonnes
3 to 30 tonnes
30 to 100 tonnes
More than 100 tonnes

per 1,000 km² annually

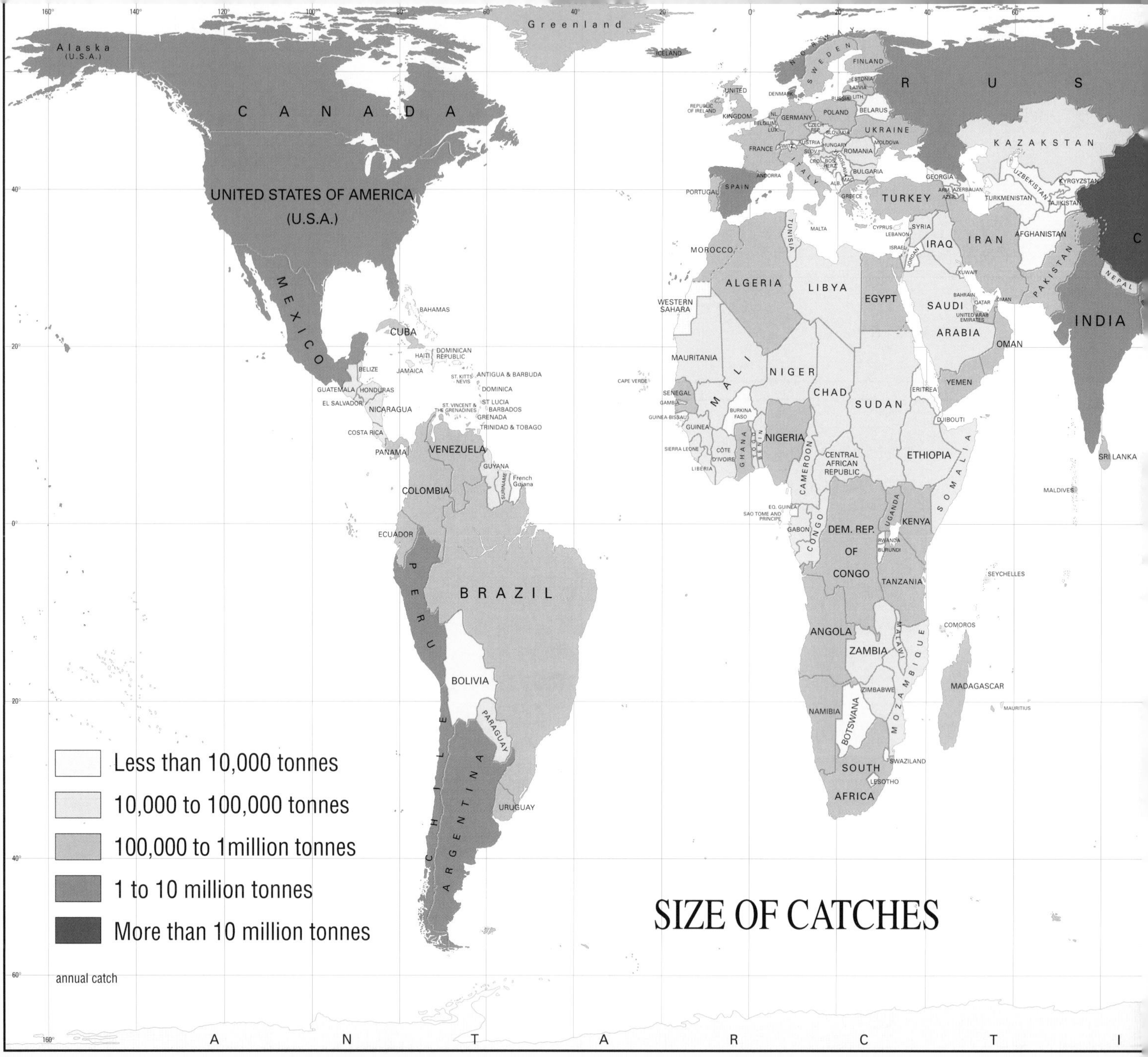

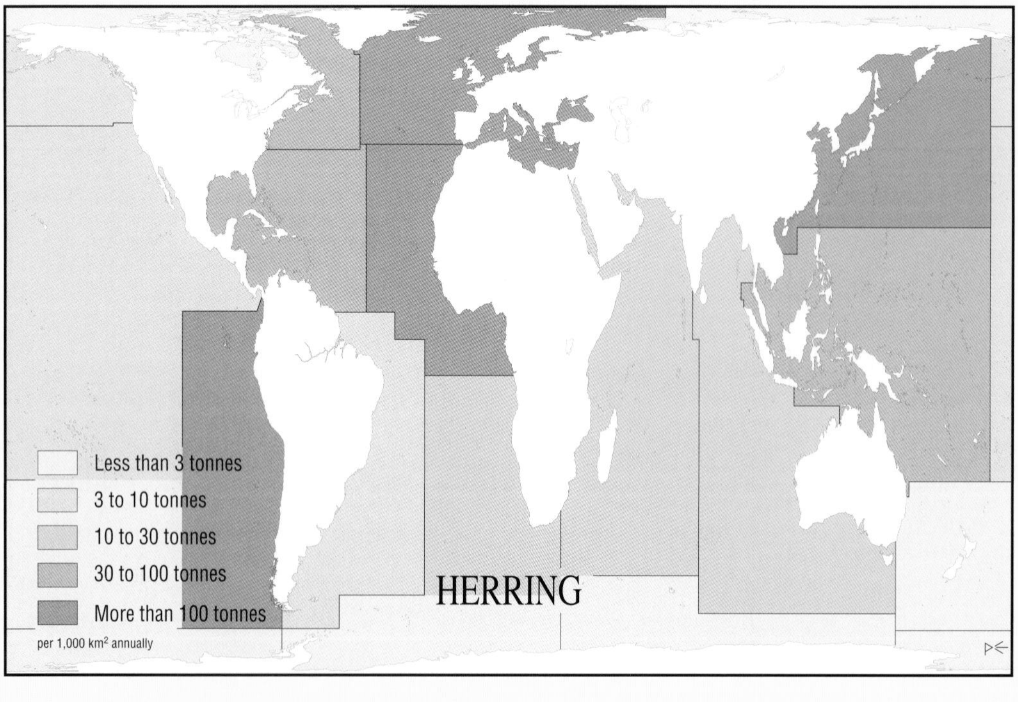

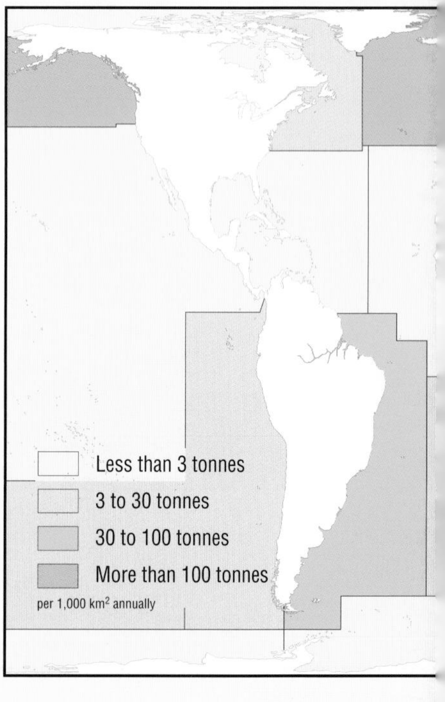

Before people learnt about farming and breeding animals they lived by hunting, gathering and fishing. Fish may originally have been caught by hand but later hunted by spear and finally with nets or hooks and lines. Fishing was limited initially to inland and coastal waters but was extended to the ocean with the introduction of factory ships and trawl nets. The size of the catch trebled in the second half of the 20th century as a result of onboard processing, refrigerated transport and commercialisation. Scientific research, international agreements and increased fish breeding have made for a further growth in production and lower prices so that fishing has become even more important.

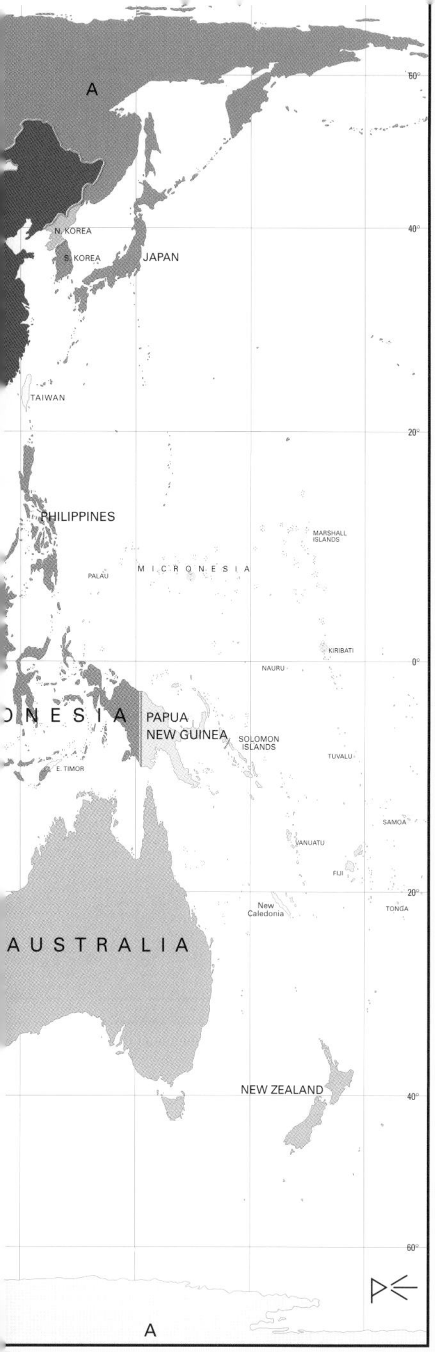

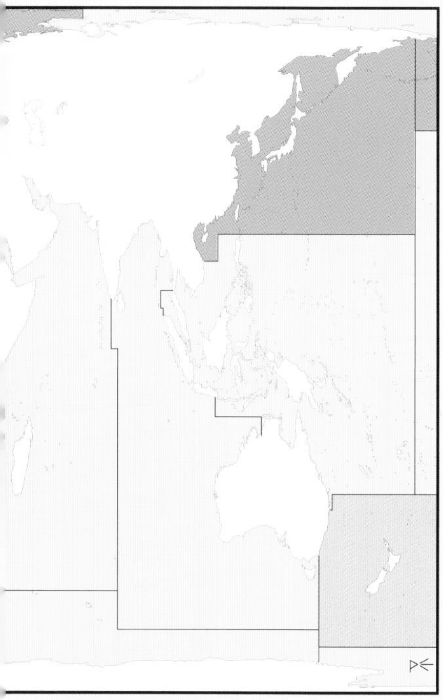

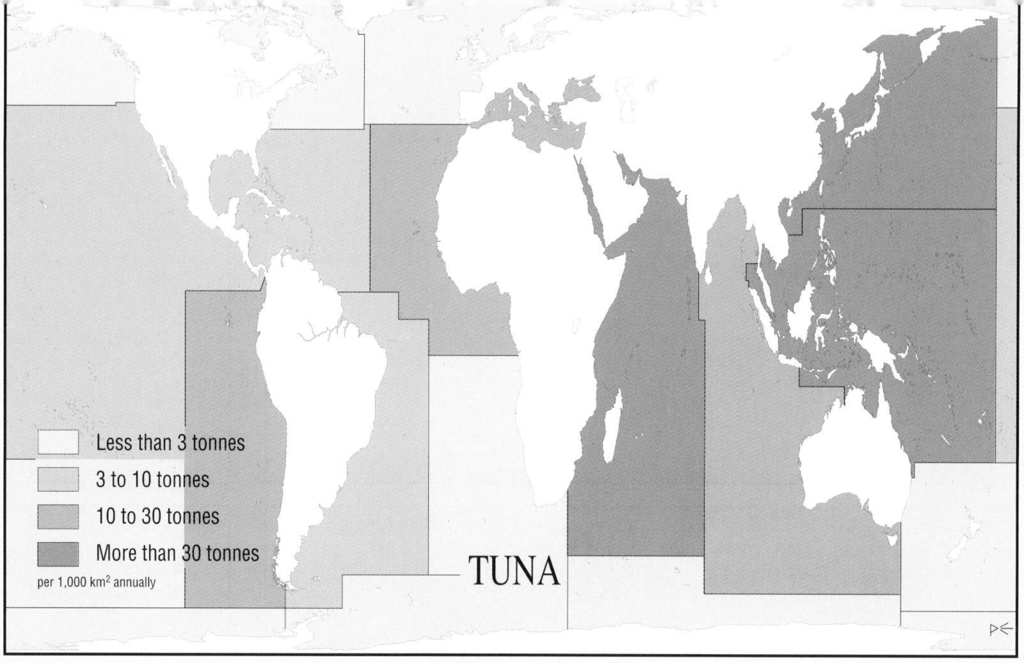

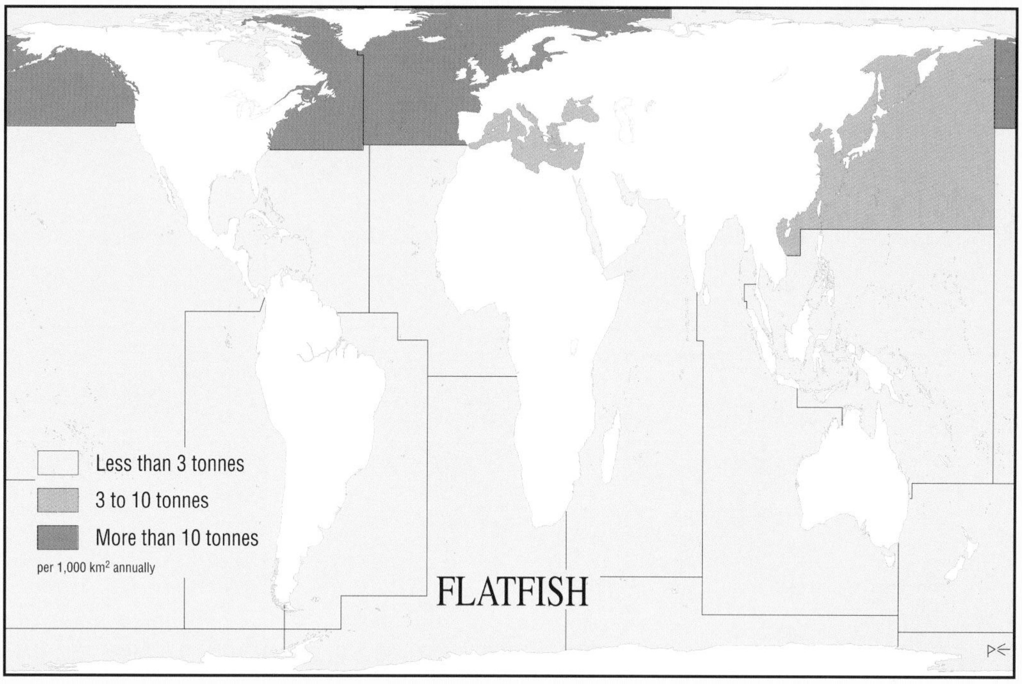

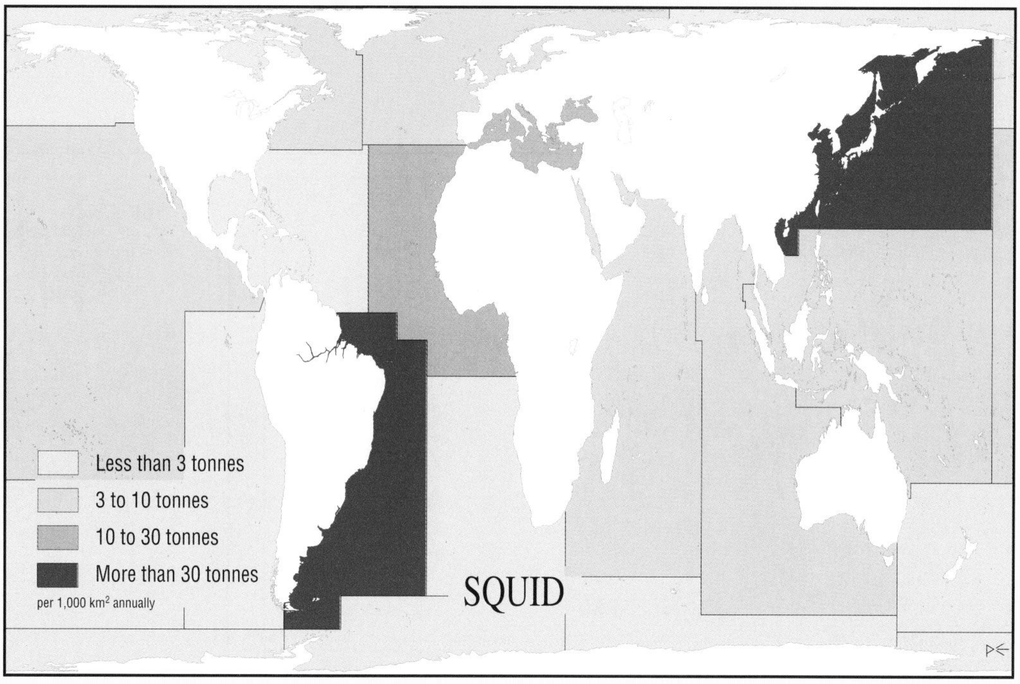

TUNA

Less than 3 tonnes
3 to 10 tonnes
10 to 30 tonnes
More than 30 tonnes

per 1,000 km² annually

FLATFISH

Less than 3 tonnes
3 to 10 tonnes
More than 10 tonnes

per 1,000 km² annually

SQUID

Less than 3 tonnes
3 to 10 tonnes
10 to 30 tonnes
More than 30 tonnes

per 1,000 km² annually

Barely one-third of the global catch of fish is eaten as fresh fish. 40% are frozen, smoked or preserved by other methods. 30% are processed into fish oil, margarine and fish meal or delivered to industry for use in cosmetics, medicaments and soap. A larger number of species of both fresh-water and sea fish are eaten in the hotter countries than in regions nearer the poles, where consumption is increasingly limited to fewer kinds. Almost half the fish caught today are varieties of herring or cod. Fish are cold-blooded and are being eaten more and more in preference to the more expensive flesh of warm-blooded animals by health and money-conscious consumers.

HARE, RABBIT

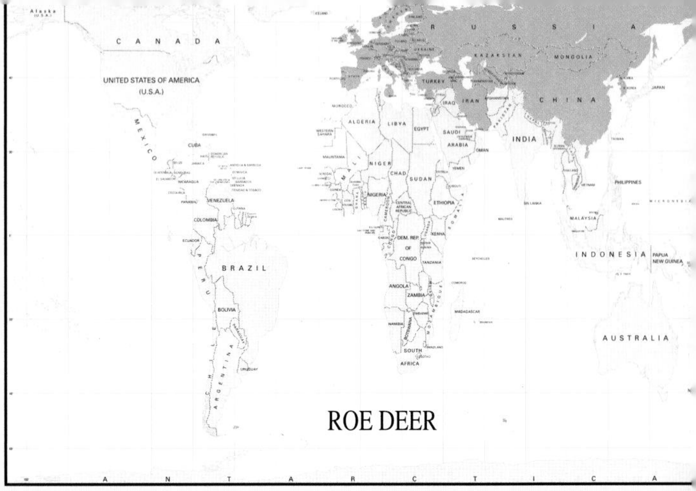

ROE DEER

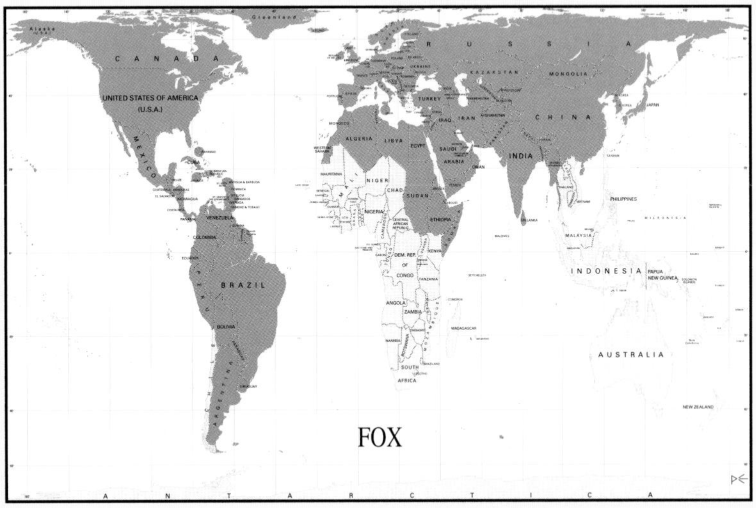

FOX

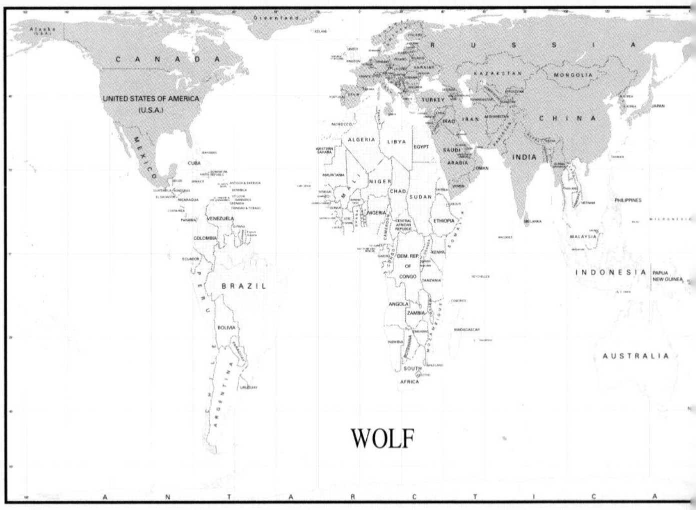

WOLF

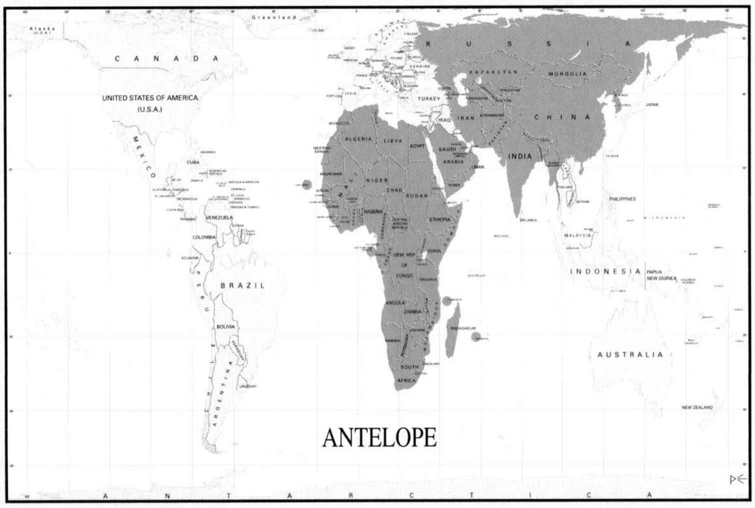

ANTELOPE

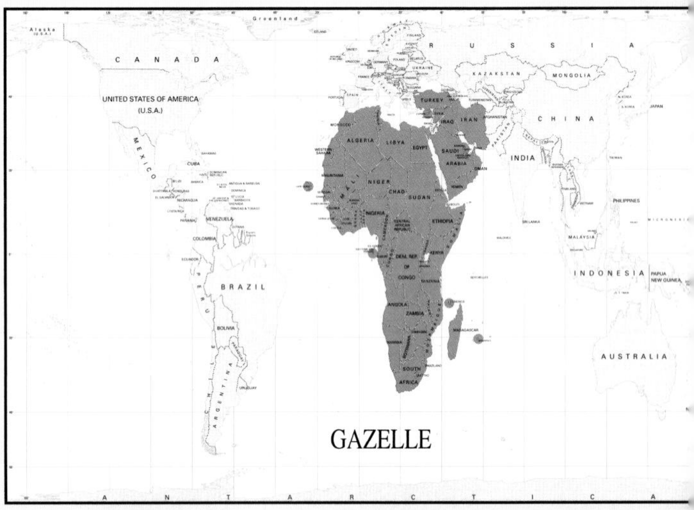

GAZELLE

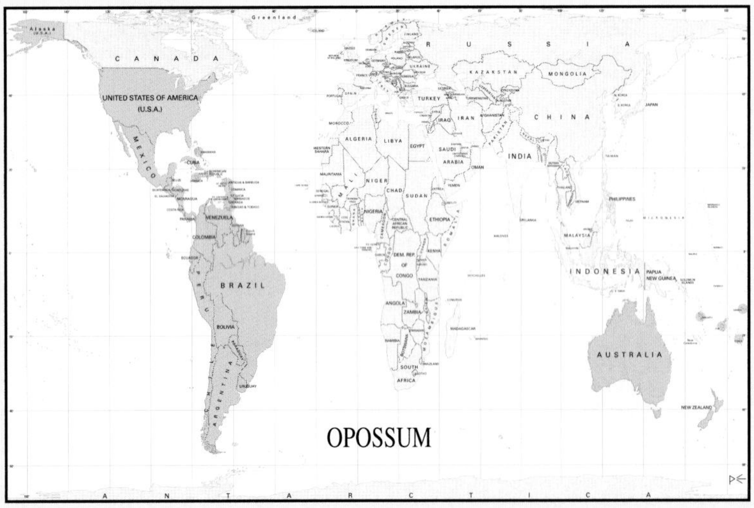

OPOSSUM

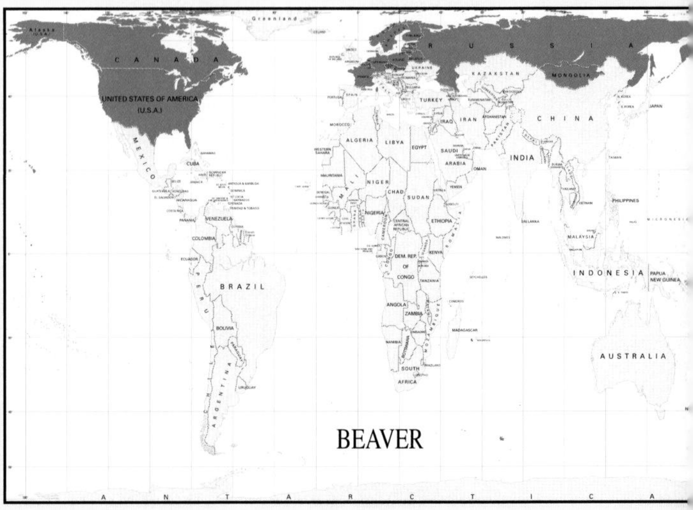

BEAVER

From the very beginning humans killed the animals in their surroundings. Meat from these and from those they kept, together with fish, plants and fruit, made up their diet. They also hunted those predatory animals whose prey they themselves would have become had they not killed them. They provided them too with skins which were used for shelter and clothing. Hunting required courage, strength and skill, and people developed these qualities. They also strengthened their sense of community, for hunting was undertaken as a co-operative activity. For all peoples at all times hunting was the responsibility of the men, whose character had essentially been influenced by it.

HUN

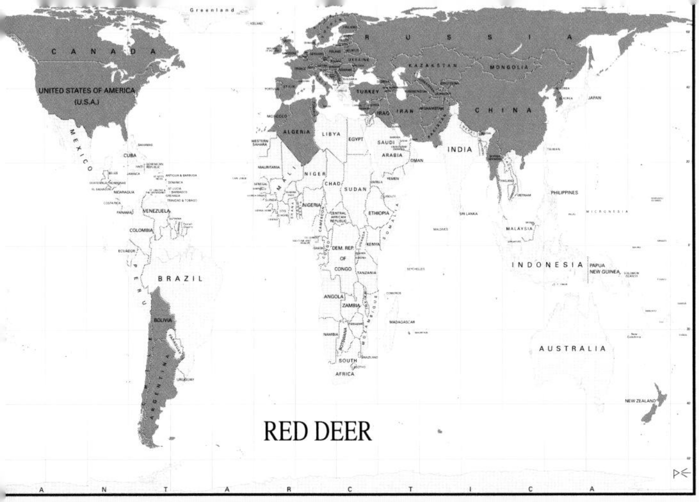

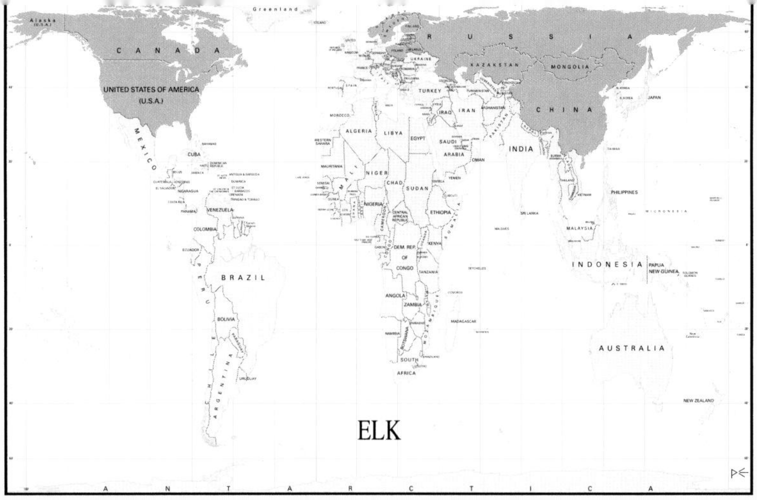

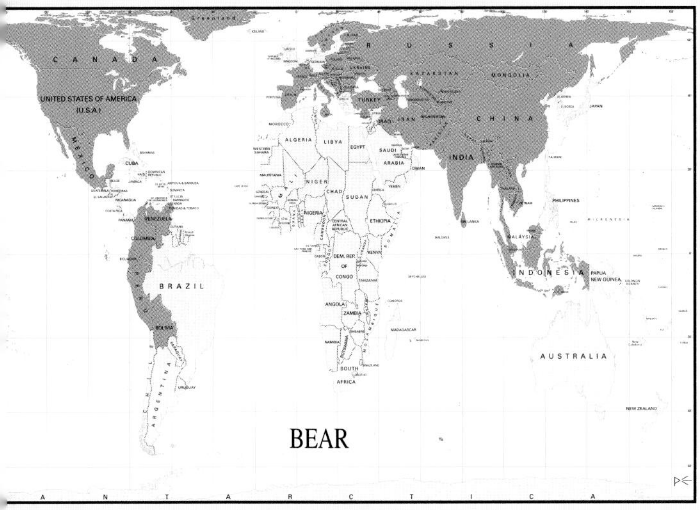

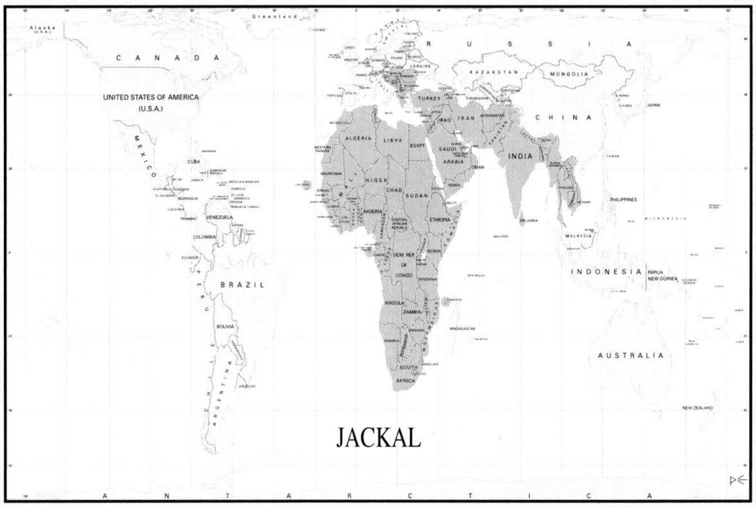

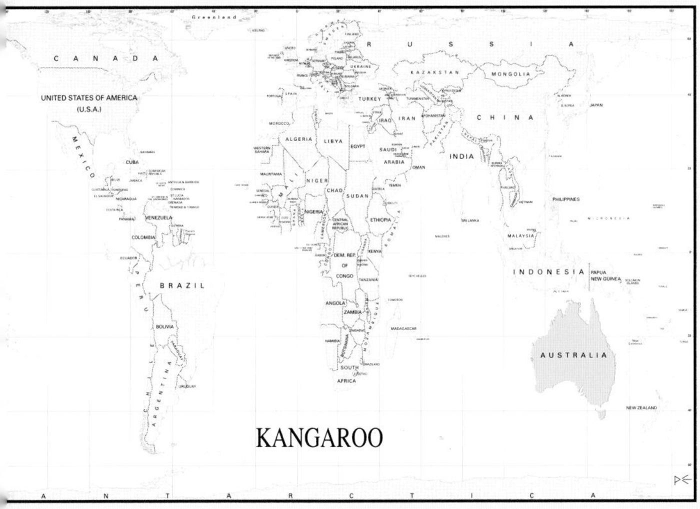

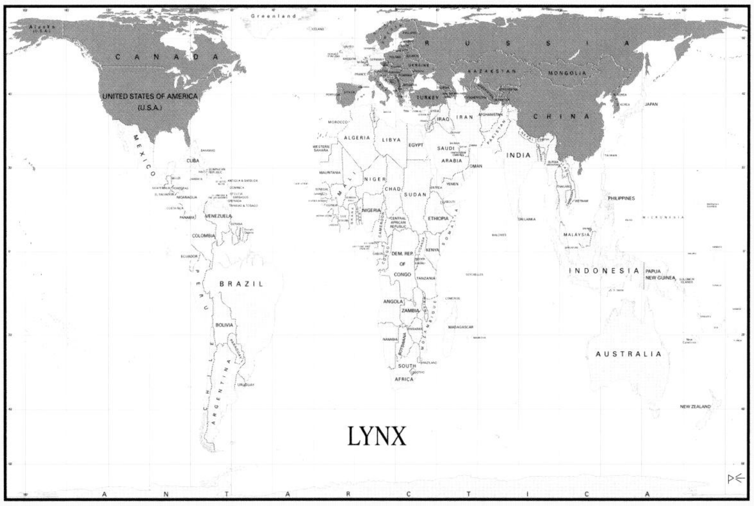

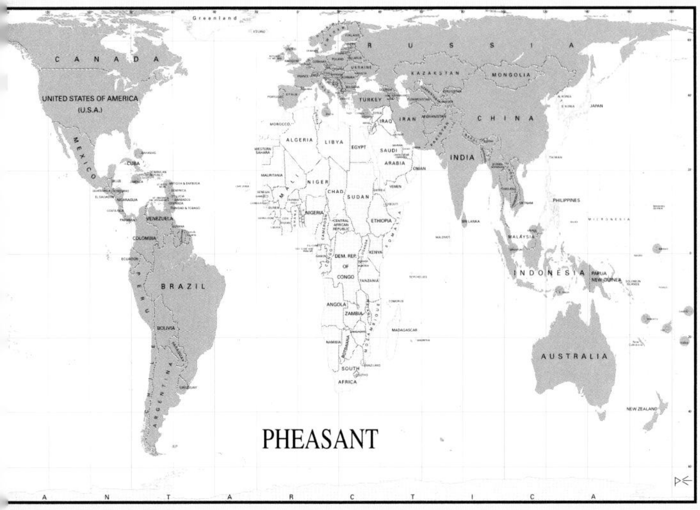

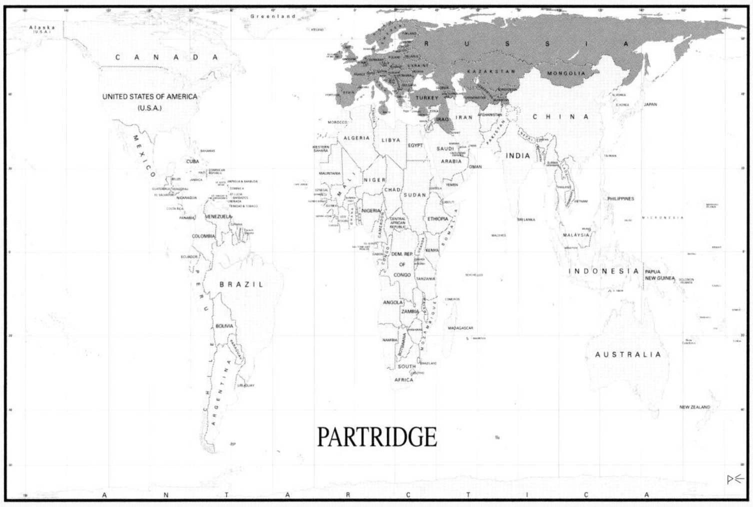

ING

With the emergence of farming and animal husbandry and because of the elimination of predators, hunting lost its original importance in most parts of the world. Food and clothes were available without it. With the invention of firearms hunting lost its danger. Therefore nearly everywhere it became just a sport for the wealthy. Parallel to this was the increasingly commercialised slaughter of wild animals whose skins or horns commanded high prices. In this way the equilibrium between the last hunting peoples and their natural environment has been destroyed.

WOOD
Less than 1,000,000 m³
More than 1,000,000 m³
production annually
per head of population

RUBBER
Less than 5 kg
More than 5 kg
production annually
per head of population

WOOL
Less than 10 kg
More than 10 kg
production annually
per head of population

SKINS
Less than 10 kg
More than 10 kg
production annually
per head of population

HONEY
Less than 1 kg
More than 1 kg
production annually
per head of population

EGGS
Less than 10 kg
More than 10 kg
production annually
per head of population

VEGETABLES
Less than 100 kg
More than 100 kg
production annually
per head of population

FRUIT
Less than 100 kg
More than 100 kg
production annually
per head of population

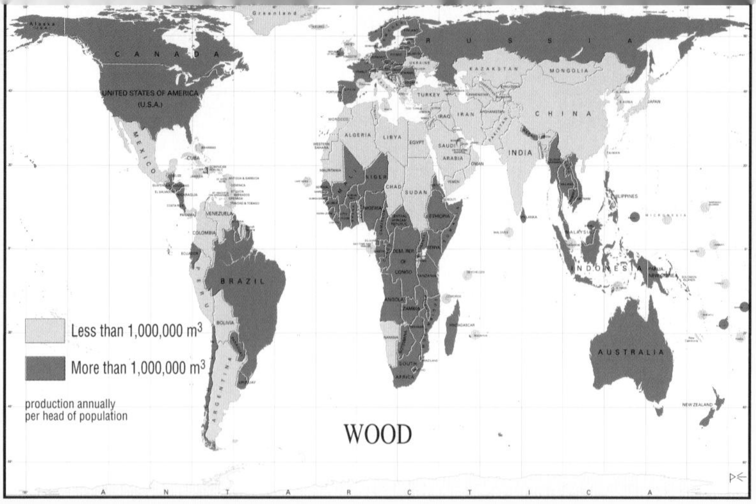

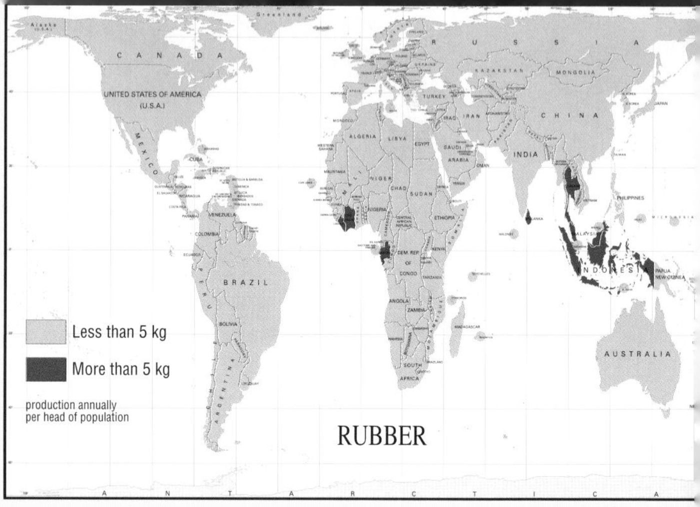

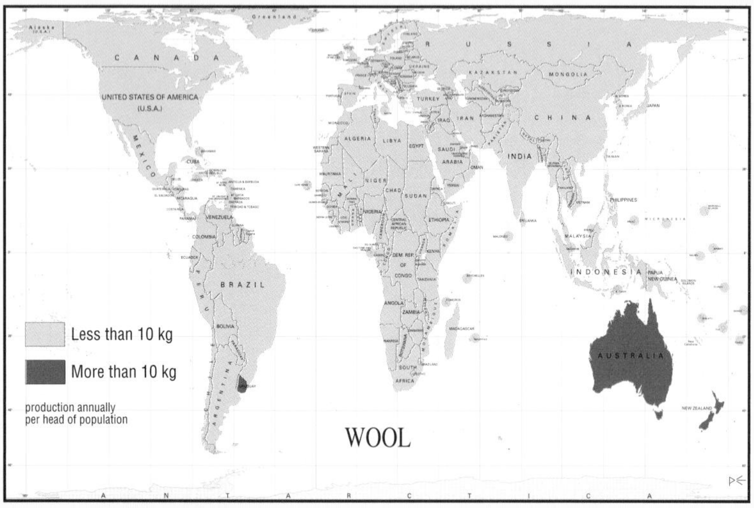

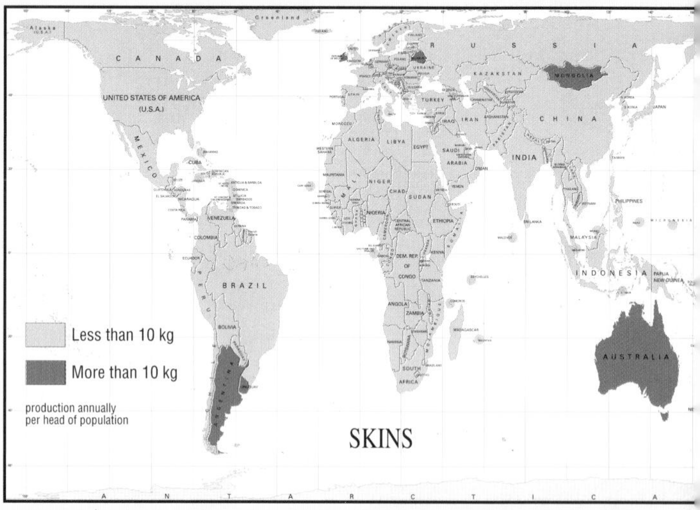

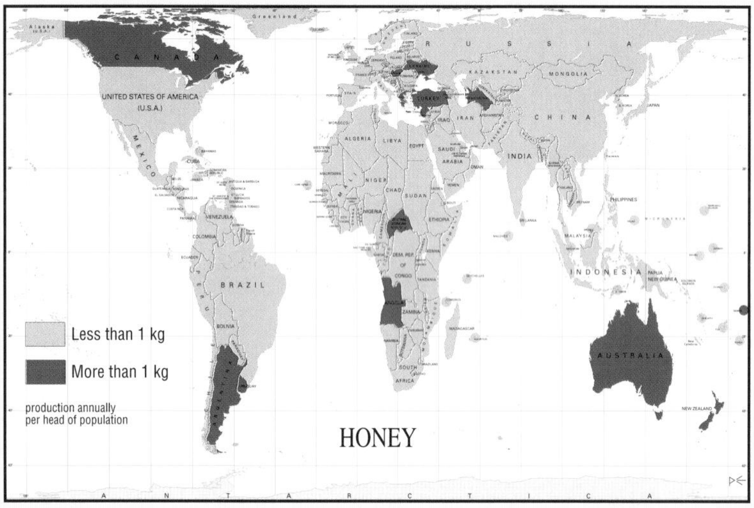

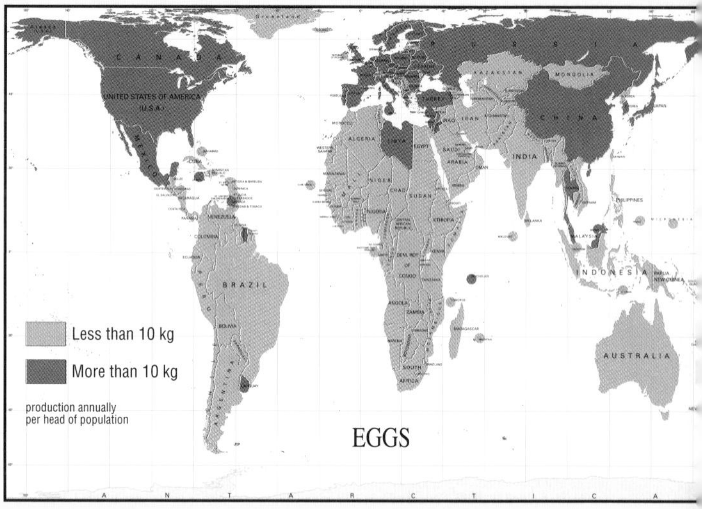

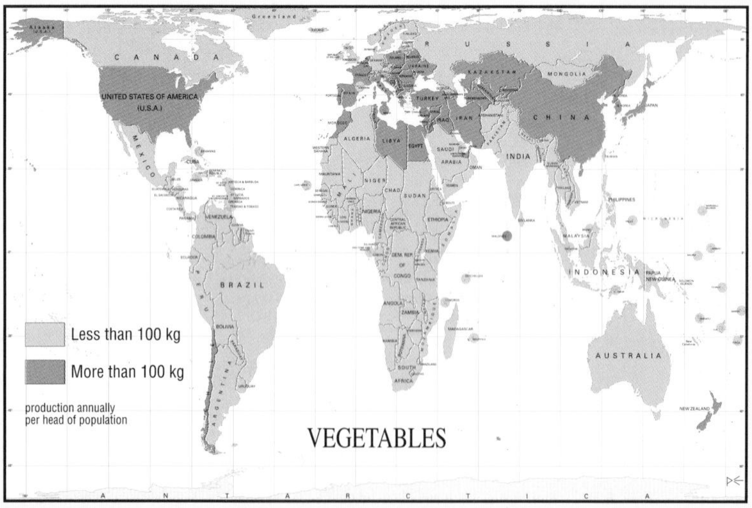

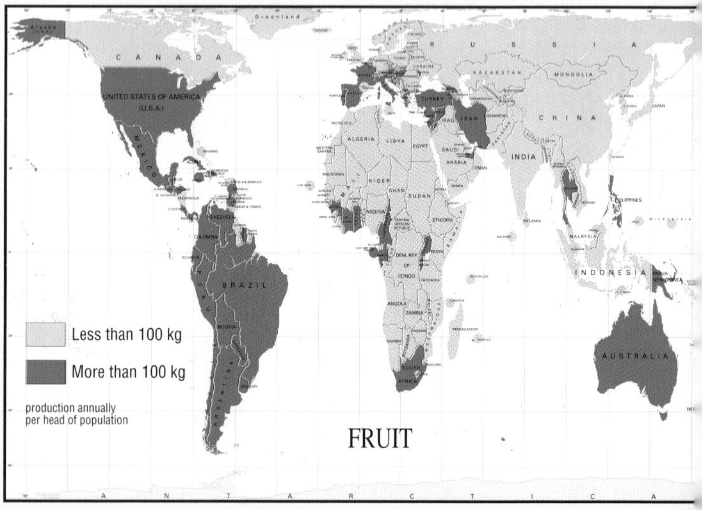

Like all other creatures, humans were for millions of years quite content with the plants and fruits provided by nature and the meat of the animals they kept or hunted. A few thousand years ago we began to improve upon nature's work, in order to satisfy our needs for food, clothing or shelter. Natural products are the essential basis for life and are therefore produced almost everywhere in the world. In addition they are also being produced in ever greater quantities to serve as raw materials for industry to process further.

NATURAL

SILK

Less than 10 g

More than 10 g

production annually
per head of population

COTTON

Less than 10 kg

More than 10 kg

production annually
per head of population

HEMP

Less than 100 g

More than 100 g

production annually
per head of population

FLAX

Less than 1 kg

More than 1 kg

production annually
per head of population

GRAIN

Less than 1,000 kg

More than 1,000 kg

production annually
per head of population

MEAT

Less than 100 kg

More than 100 kg

production annually
per head of population

SUGAR

Less than 100 kg

More than 100 kg

production annually
per head of population

MILK

Less than 100 kg

More than 100 kg

production annually
per head of population

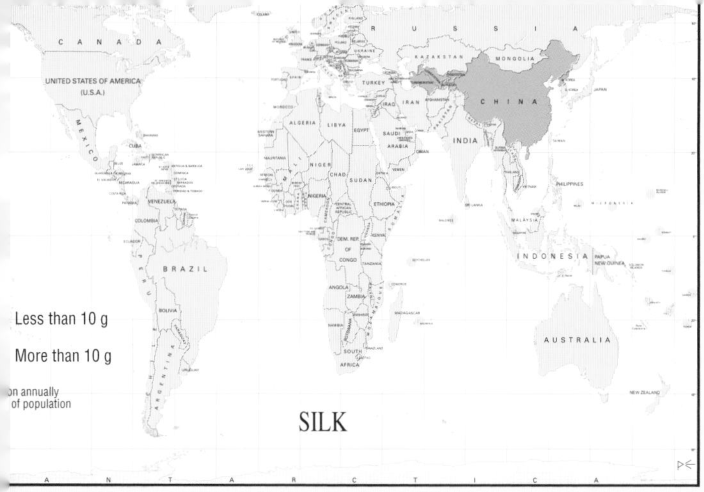

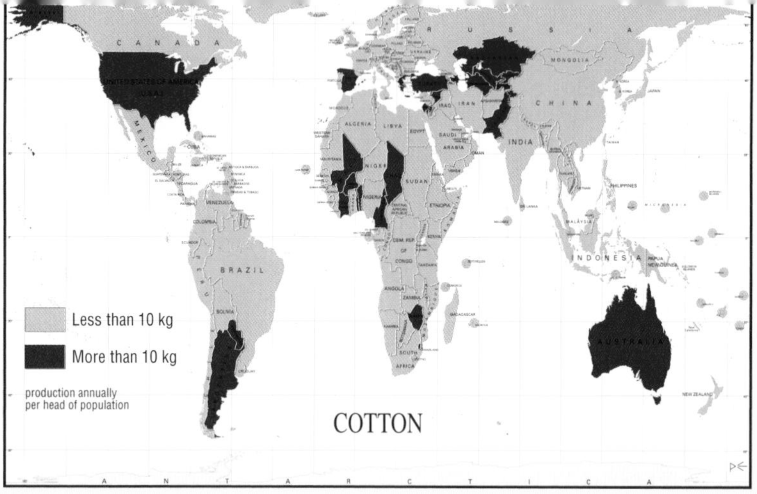

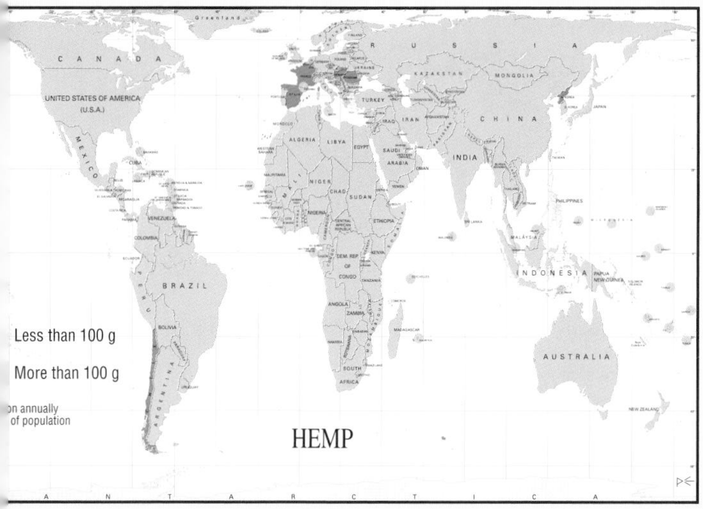

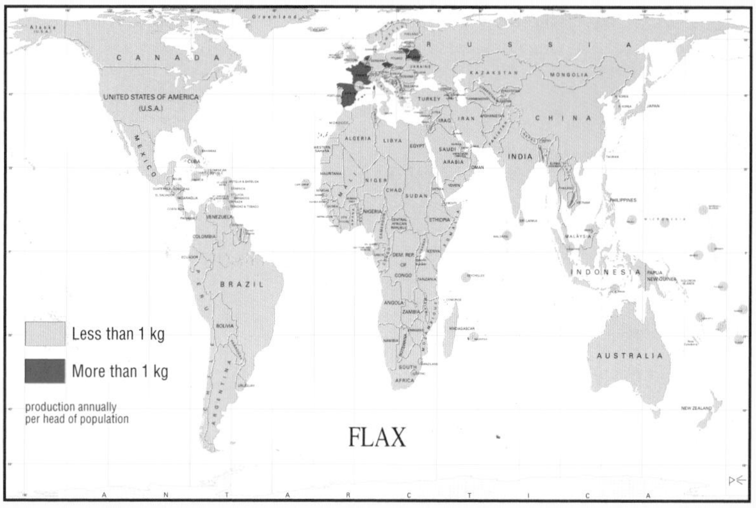

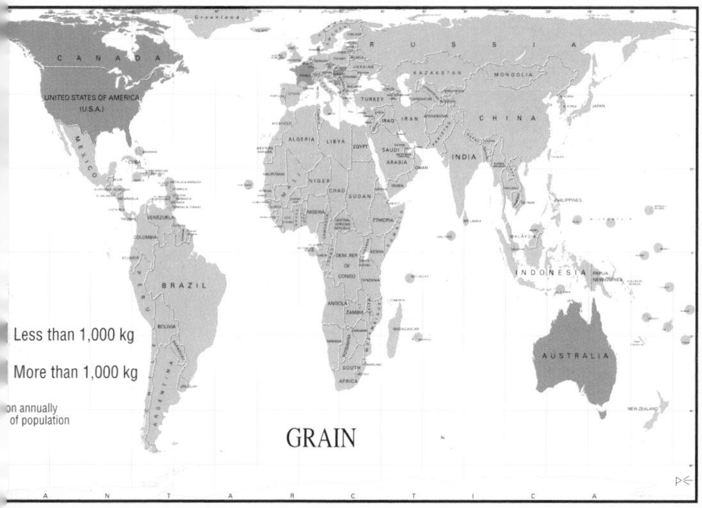

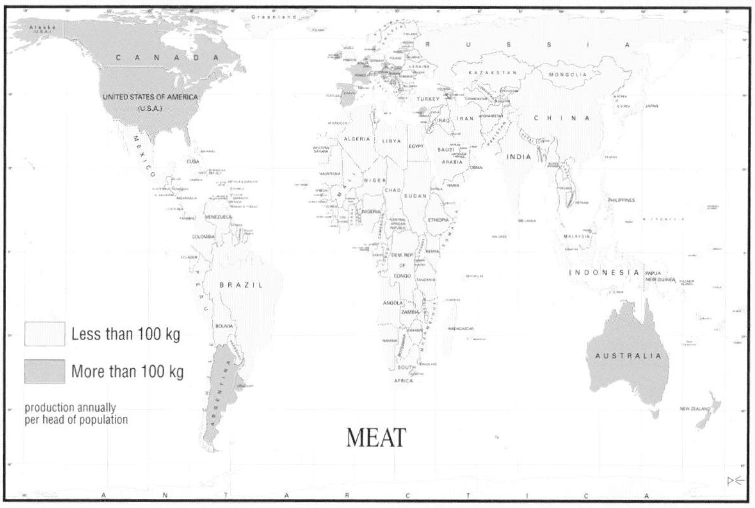

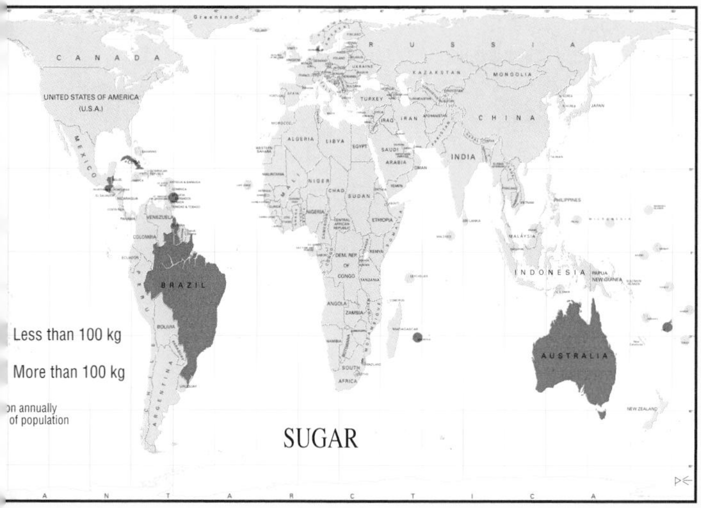

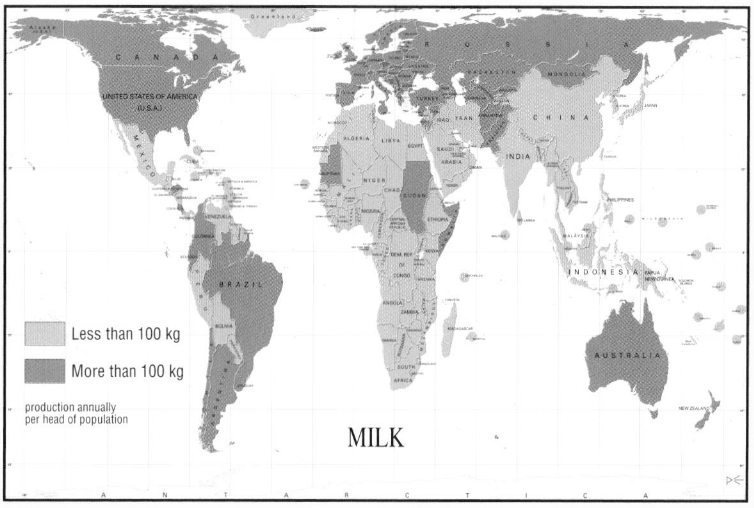

RODUCTS

Food, furs and wood are produced nearly everywhere in the world, and increasingly wool and cotton too. Rarer goods like silk, rubber, flax and hemp are produced in only a dozen countries. So much silk is produced in a single country, China, that it meets more than half the world's demand. Since natural products are available nearly everywhere in abundance their world market prices are low, particularly now that the rich industrial states, with their superior technology, biology and chemistry, dominate their production.

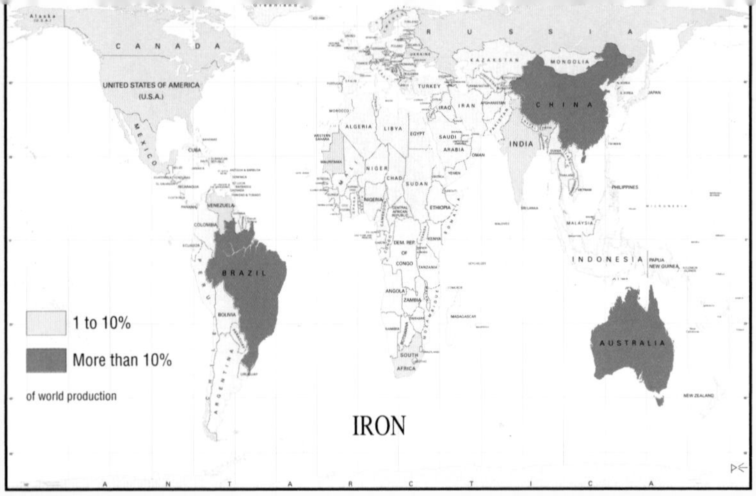

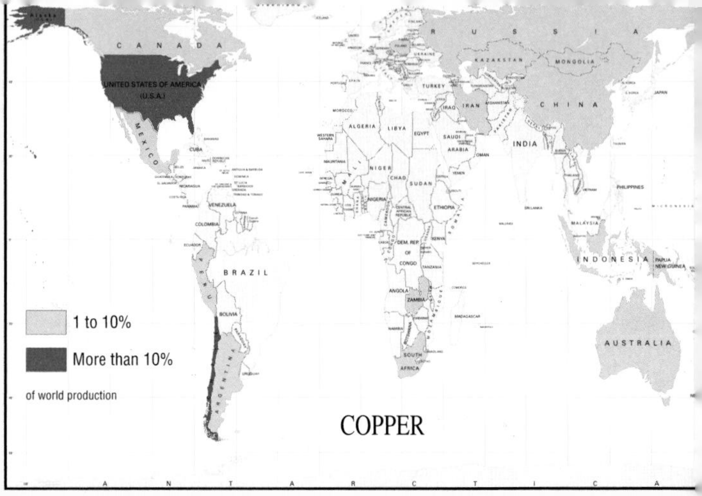

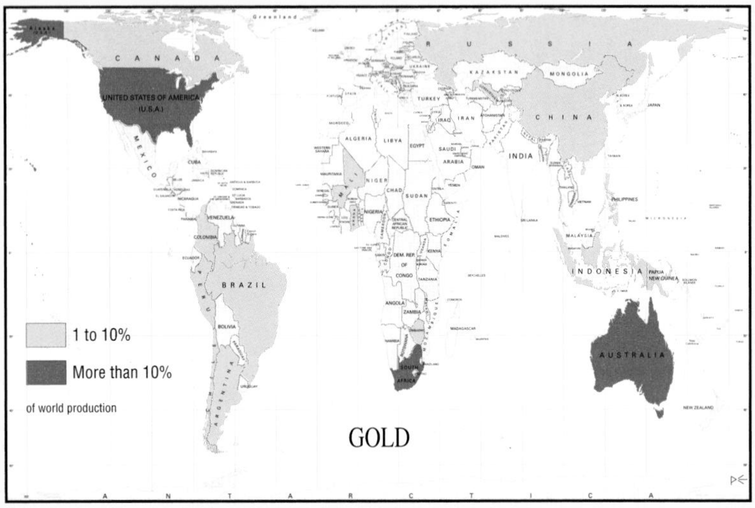

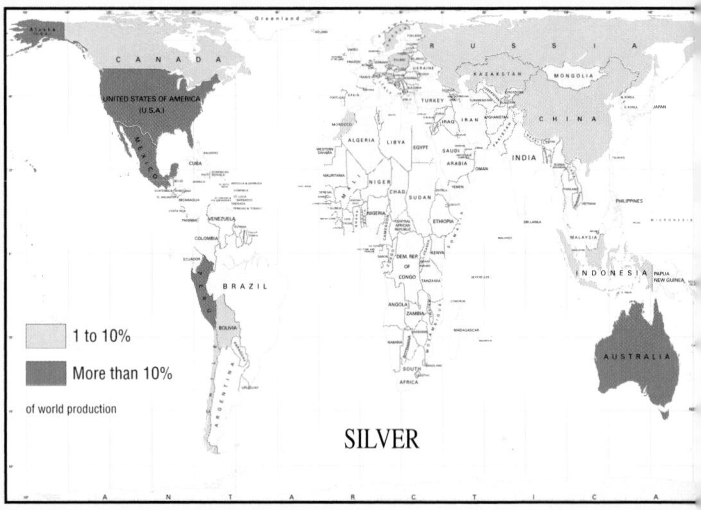

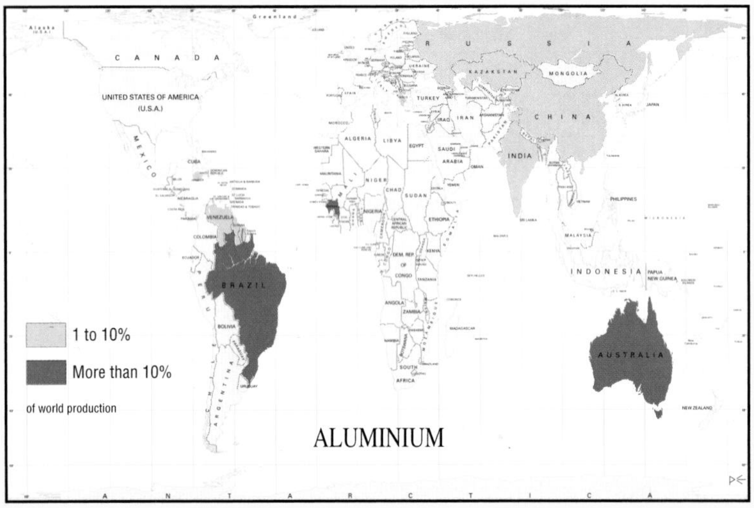

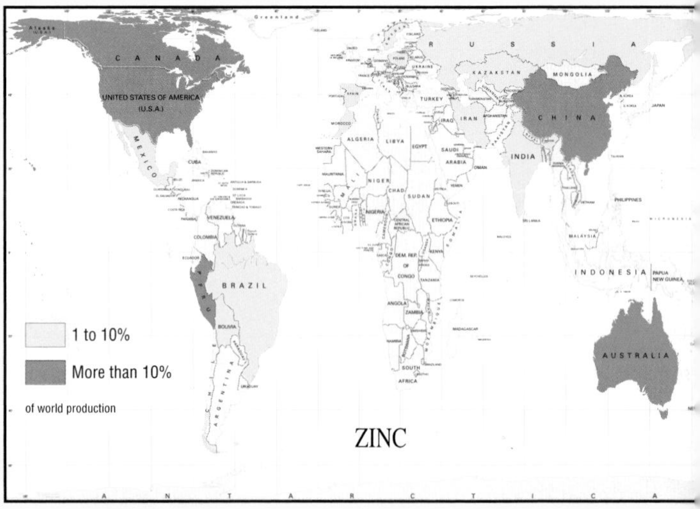

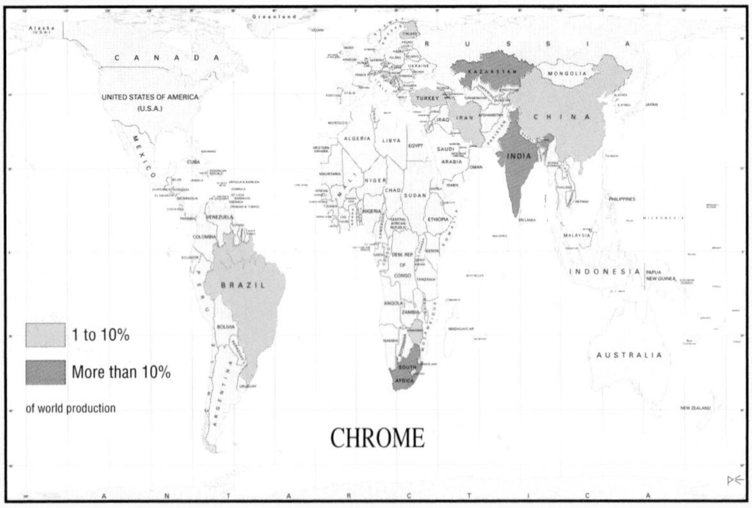

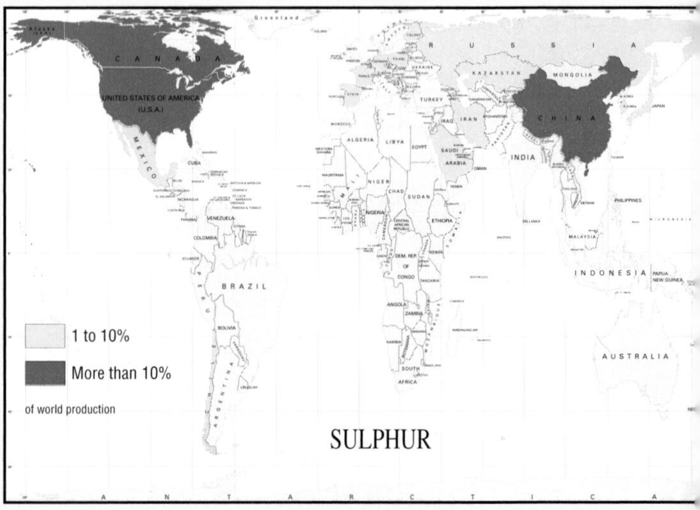

IRON

1 to 10%
More than 10%
of world production

COPPER

1 to 10%
More than 10%
of world production

GOLD

1 to 10%
More than 10%
of world production

SILVER

1 to 10%
More than 10%
of world production

ALUMINIUM

1 to 10%
More than 10%
of world production

ZINC

1 to 10%
More than 10%
of world production

CHROME

1 to 10%
More than 10%
of world production

SULPHUR

1 to 10%
More than 10%
of world production

Of the inorganic components found everywhere in the earth's crust, minerals have been used since time immemorial for the manufacture of tools (copper, iron) and the possession of gold, silver and diamonds has always been regarded as a sign of wealth. Throughout the course of history the desire to possess the source of these raw materials has often been the reason for invading and conquering another country. Even today each country is concerned to secure its own access to the minerals it needs for its economy and the production of weapons.

MINERAL

1 to 10%

More than 10%

production

TIN

1 to 10%

More than 10%

of world production

LEAD

1 to 10%

More than 10%

production

PLATINUM

1 to 10%

More than 10%

of world production

DIAMONDS

1 to 10%

More than 10%

production

MANGANESE

1 to 10%

More than 10%

of world production

NICKEL

1 to 10%

More than 10%

production

POTASSIUM

1 to 10%

More than 10%

of world production

PHOSPHATE

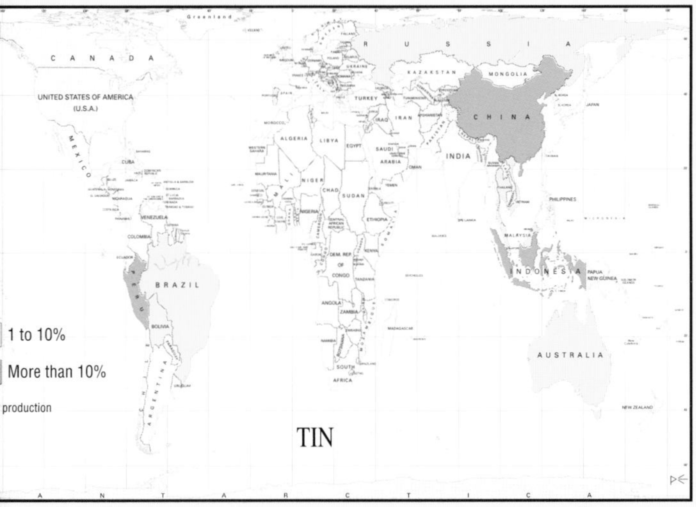

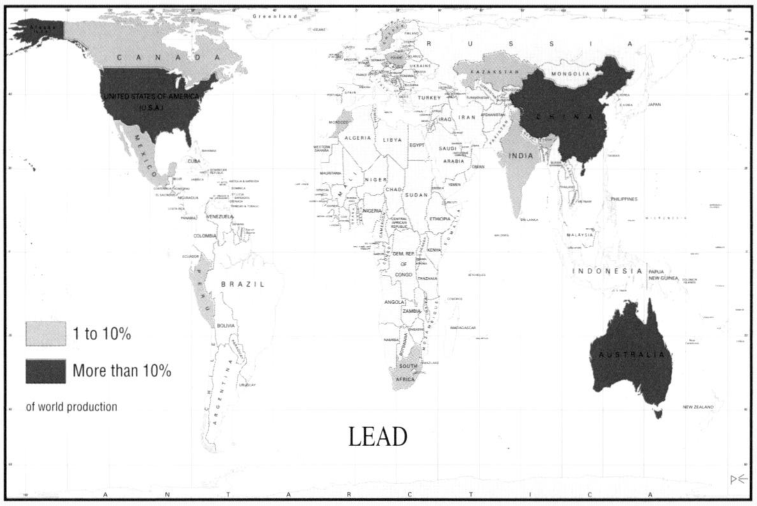

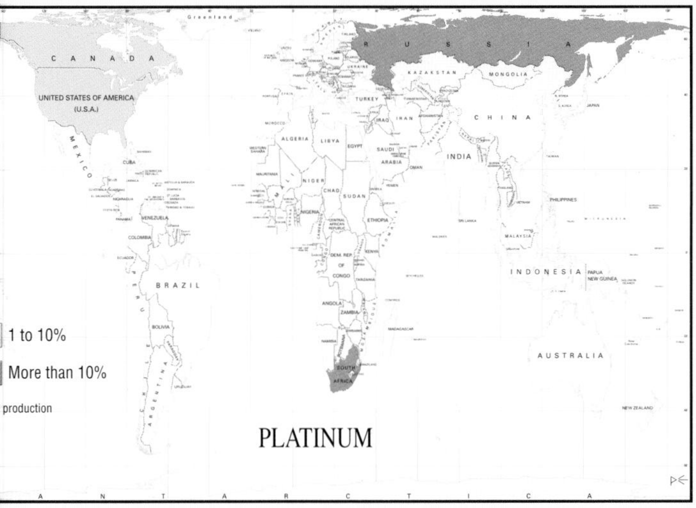

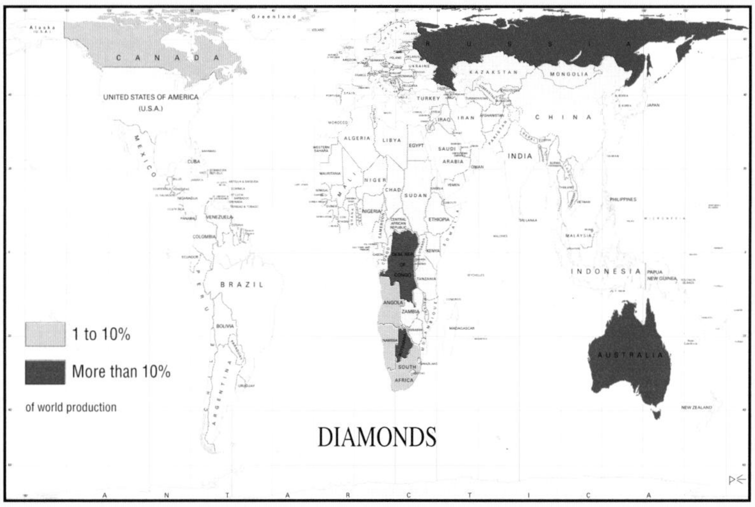

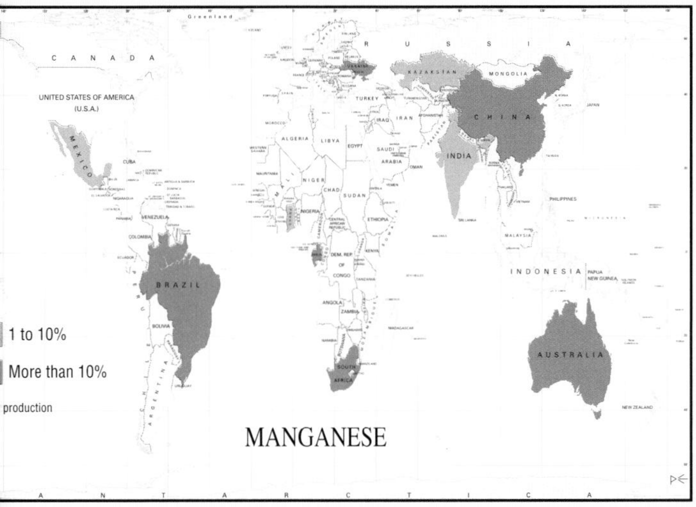

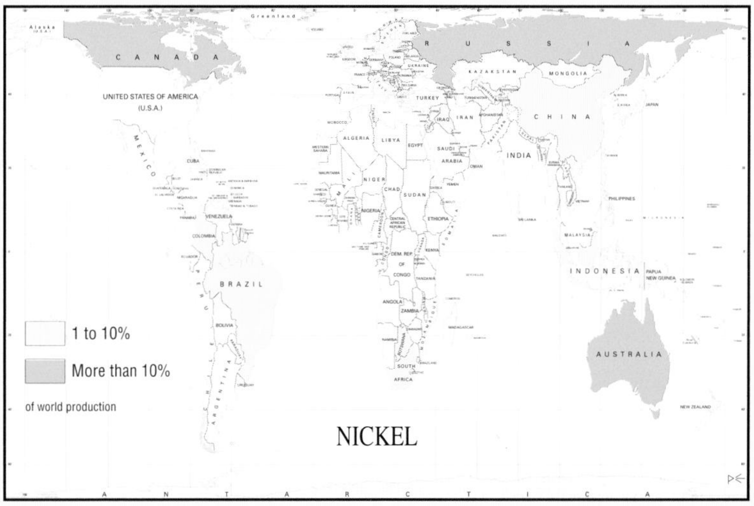

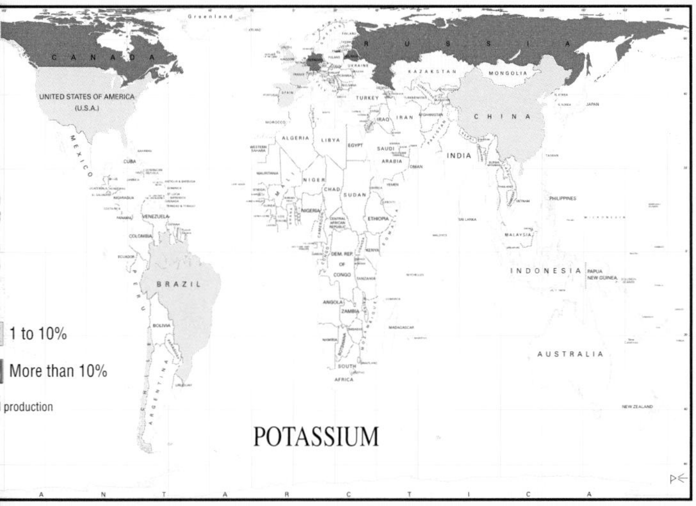

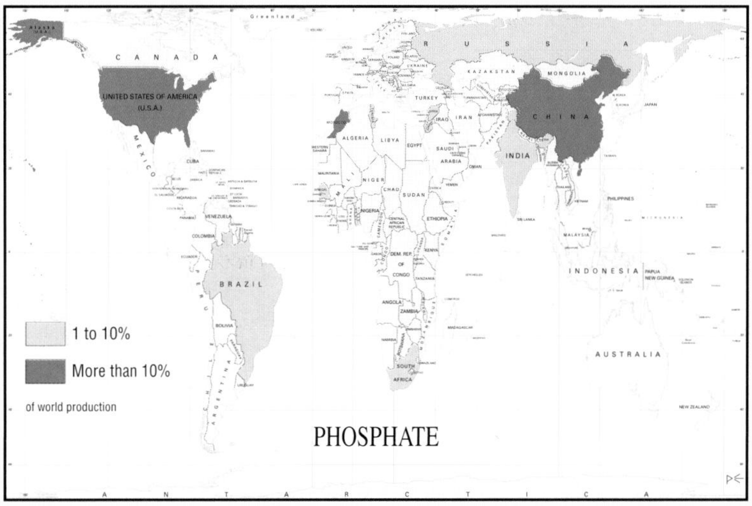

ESOURCES

The countries of the North seek to decrease their dependence on the mineral resources of the poor countries of the South for economic and strategic reasons. They buy or occupy large areas of foreign states and stockpile large amounts of minerals that they do not have themselves. Increasingly, the rich countries are looking to recover minerals from scrap or to replace with synthetic products. Despite this, most industrial nations are still heavily dependent on the South's mineral resources.

TOTAL CONSUMPTION

Very low:
less than 100 kWh per person annually

Low:
100 to 1,000 kWh per person annually

Average:
1,000 to 5,000 kWh per person annually

High:
5,000 to 10,000 kWh per person annually

Very high:
More than 10,000 kWh per person annually

OIL

Less than 10,000

10,000 to 100,000

More than 100,000

units of 1,000 t annually

NA

Less than 10,000

10,000 to 100,000

100,000 to 500,000

More than 500,000

units of 1 million m³ annually

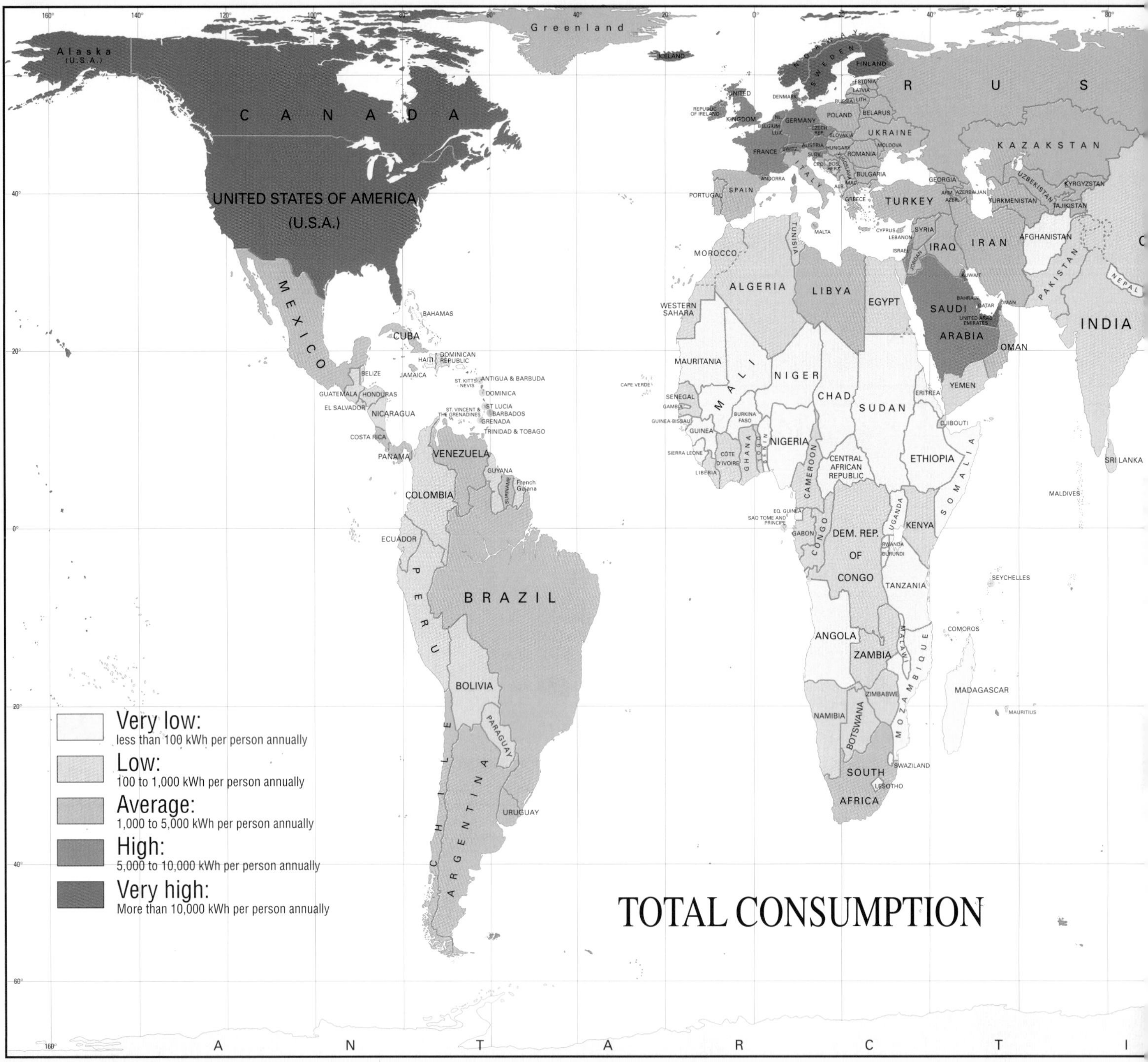

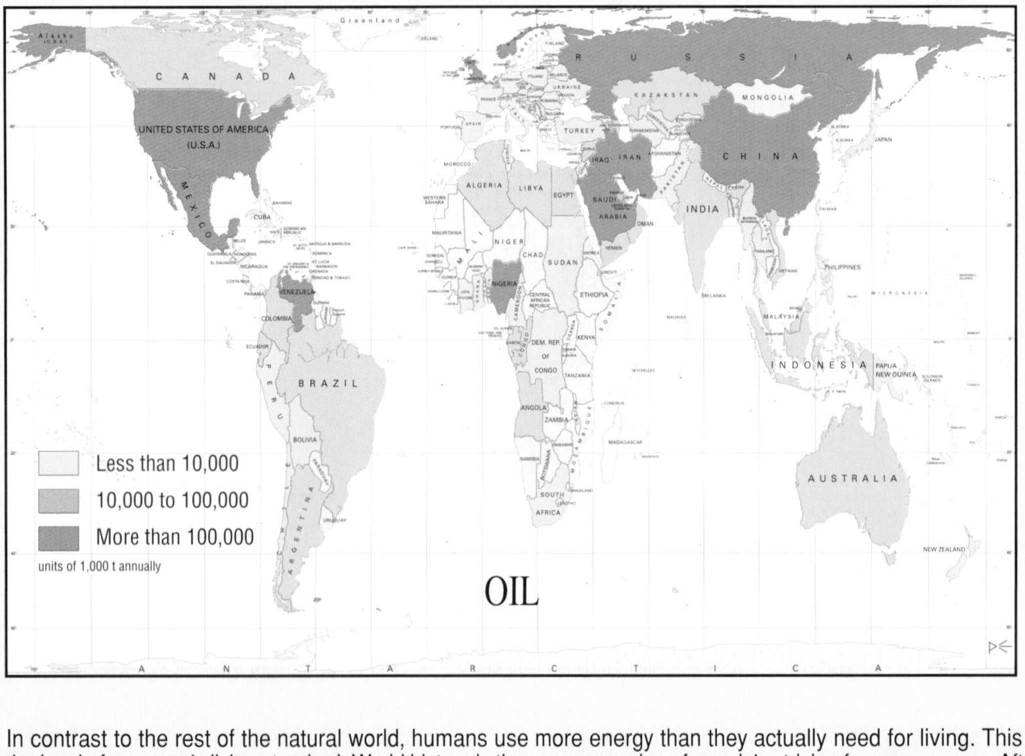

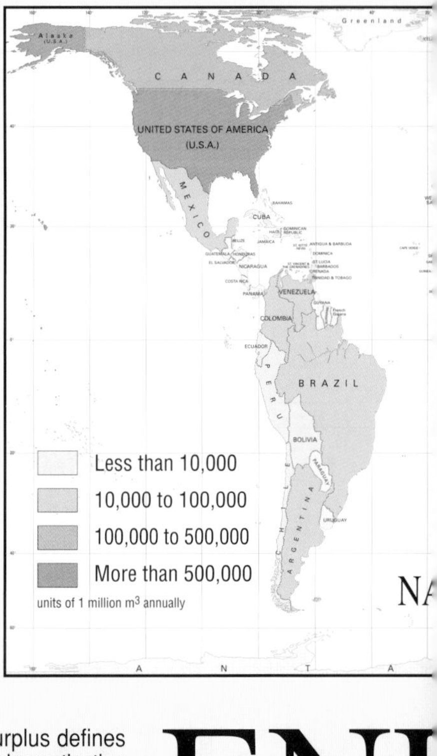

In contrast to the rest of the natural world, humans use more energy than they actually need for living. This surplus defines the level of a person's living standard. World history is thus an expression of people's striving for more energy. After domesticating animals men increased the energy available to them by using people (slaves, women, children, workers, employees). In our epoch humans can use the energy contained in matter to meet their needs without exploiting animals or people.

ENI

WATER POWER

Less than 10,000

10,000 to 100,000

More than 100,000

units of 1 million kWh annually

URANIUM

Less than 1,000

1,000 to 5,000

More than 5,000

units of t annually

COAL

Less than 10,000

10,000 to 100,000

100,000 to 500,000

More than 500,000

units of 1,000 t annually

AS

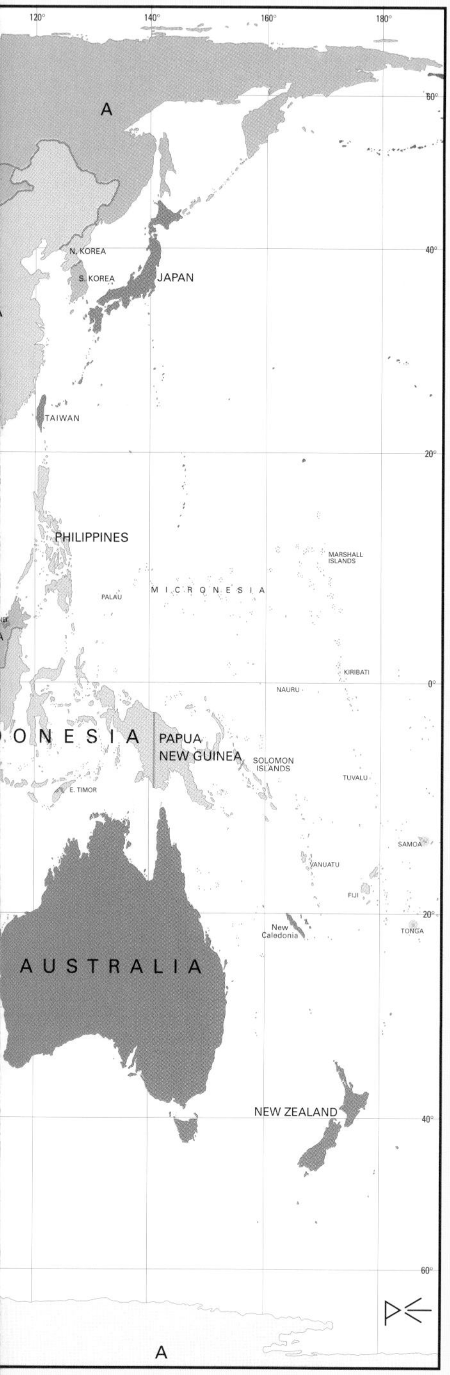

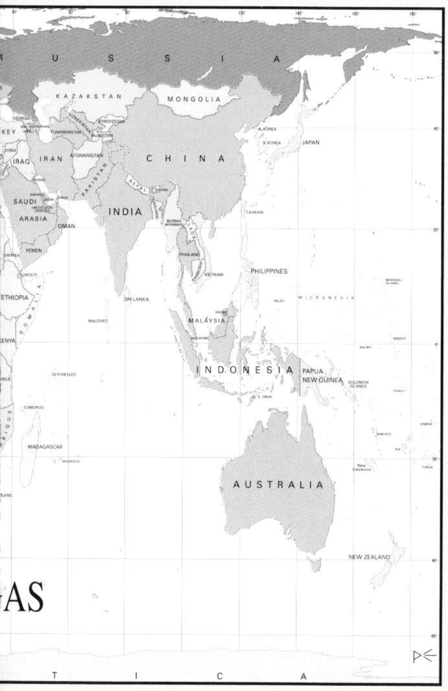

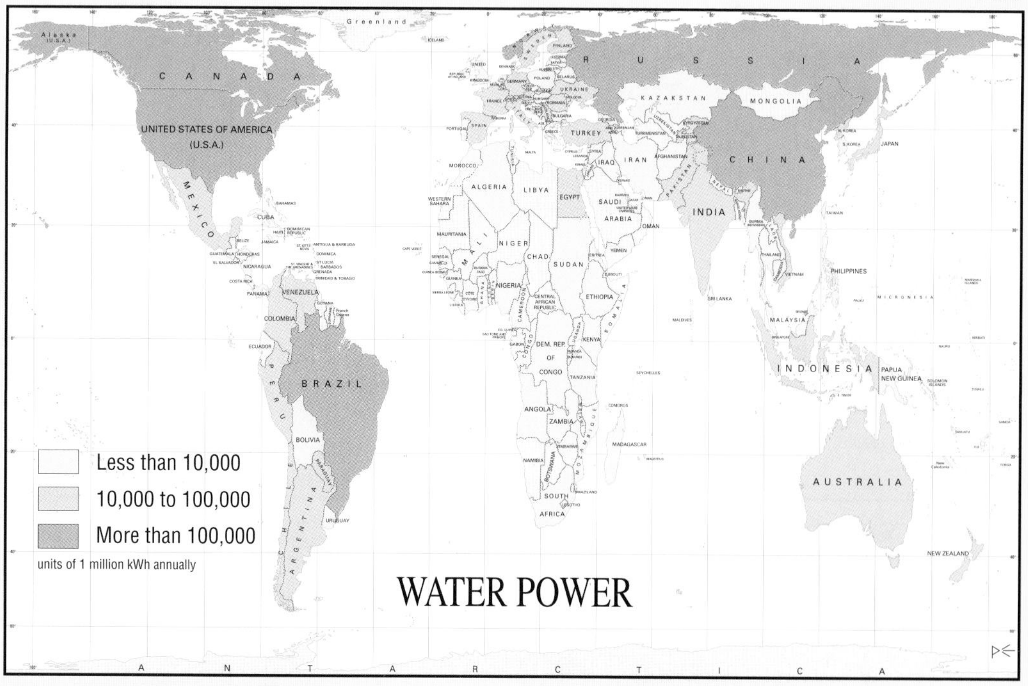

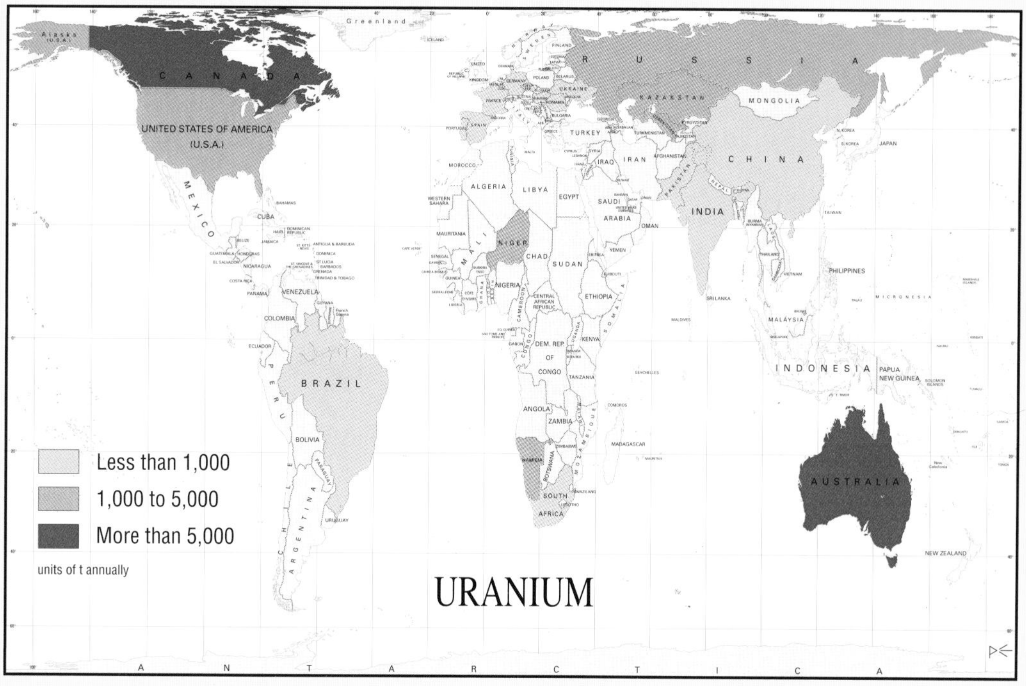

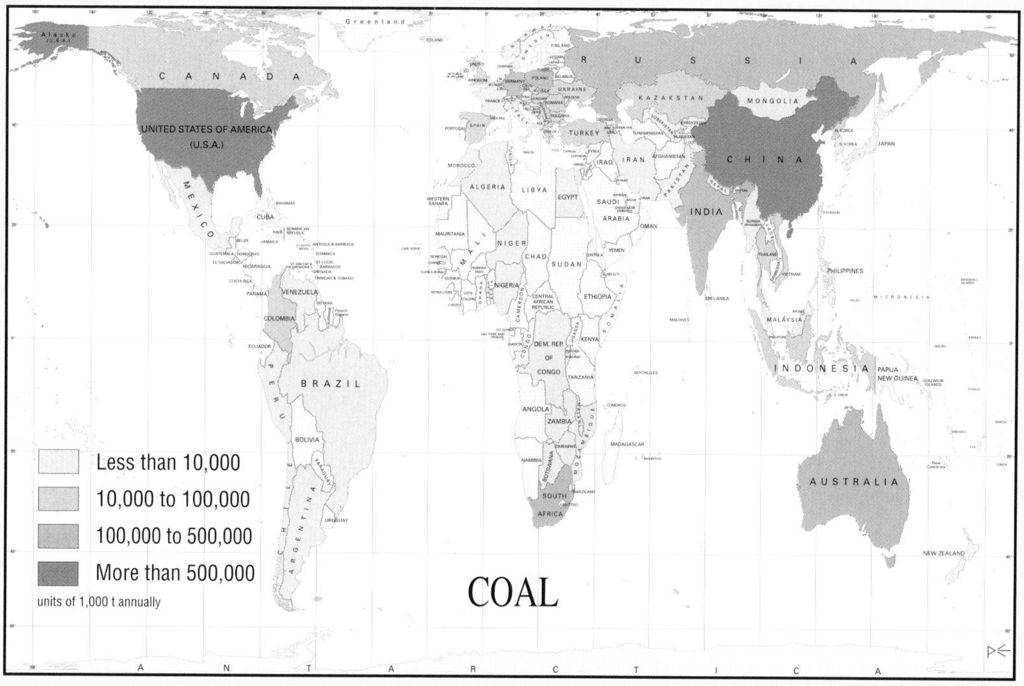

RGY

All our energy sources except water can be used only once. Water renews itself endlessly but covers only 3% of our needs; oil meets 43% of our energy needs, coal 32%, natural gas 18%, nuclear power 2%. Our increasing demand will exhaust natural energy reserves within a few decades, apart from hydro power, whose use could be increased six-fold. But in solar power we have inexhaustible reserves at our disposal. Eight minutes of sunshine could supply the entire energy needs of the world for one year.

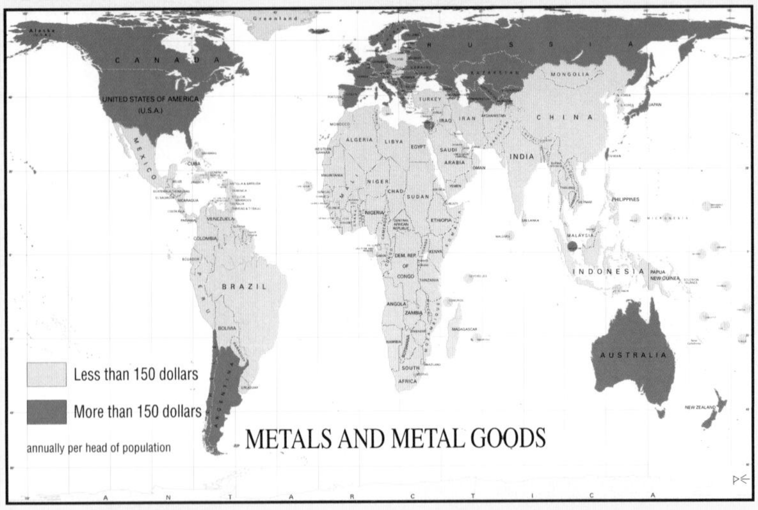

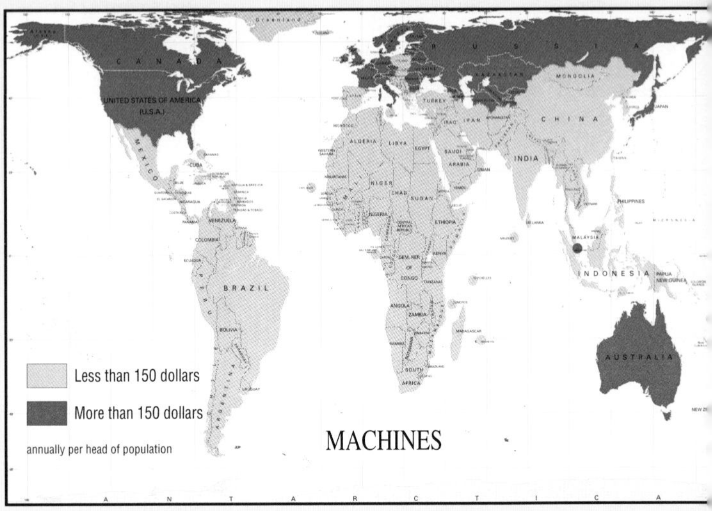

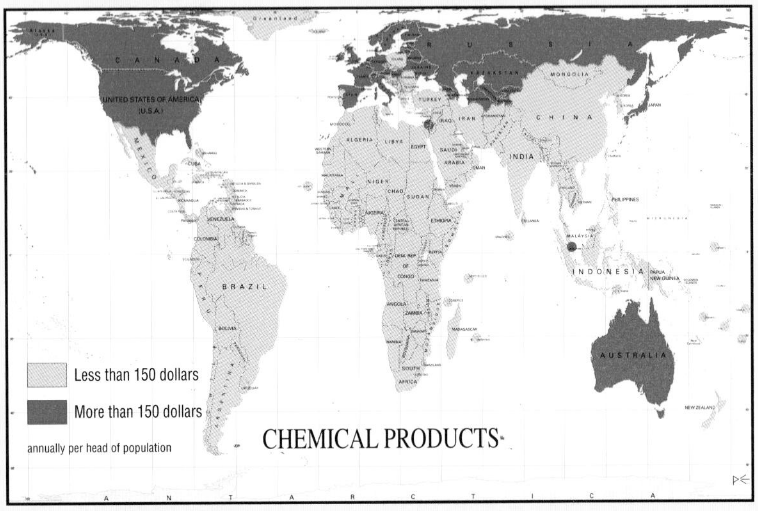

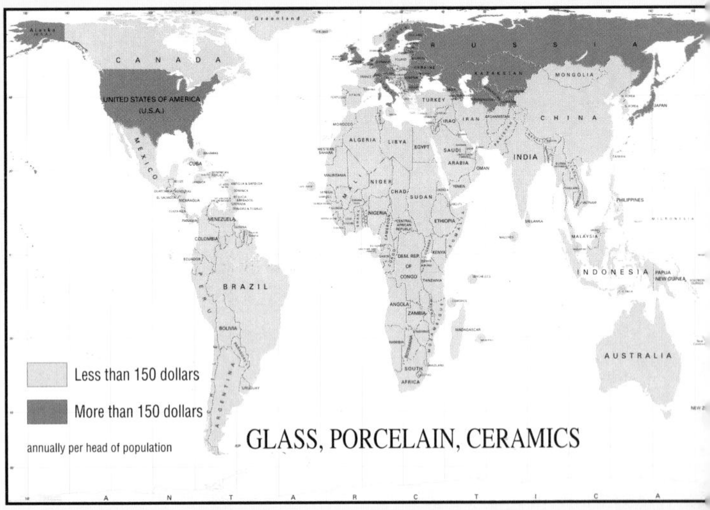

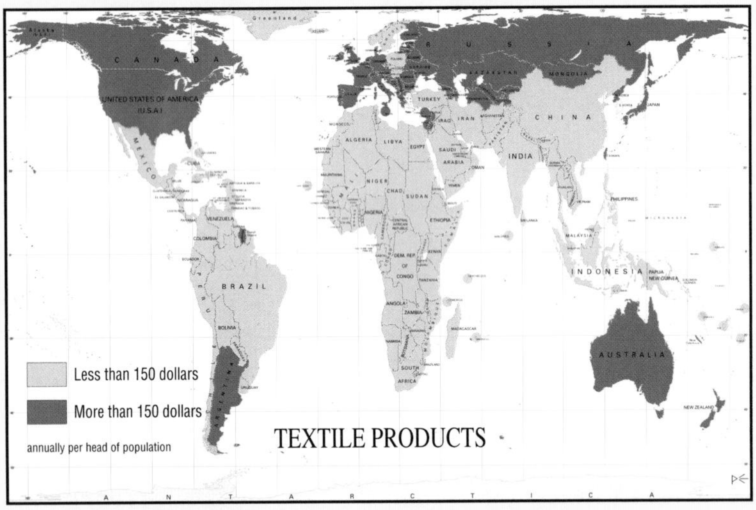

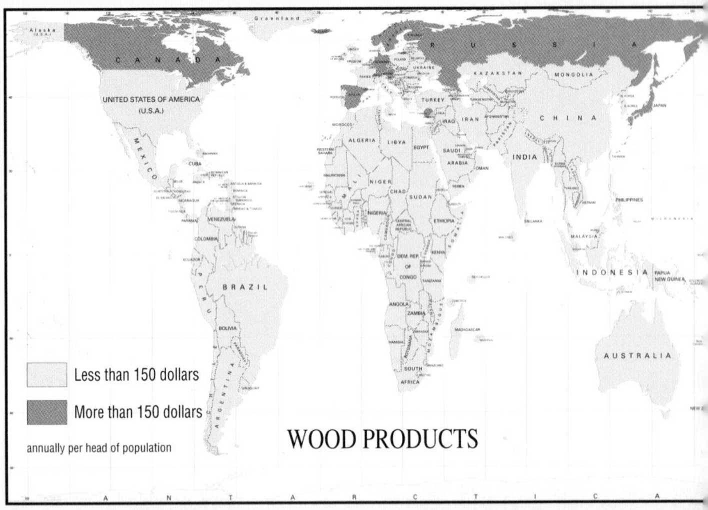

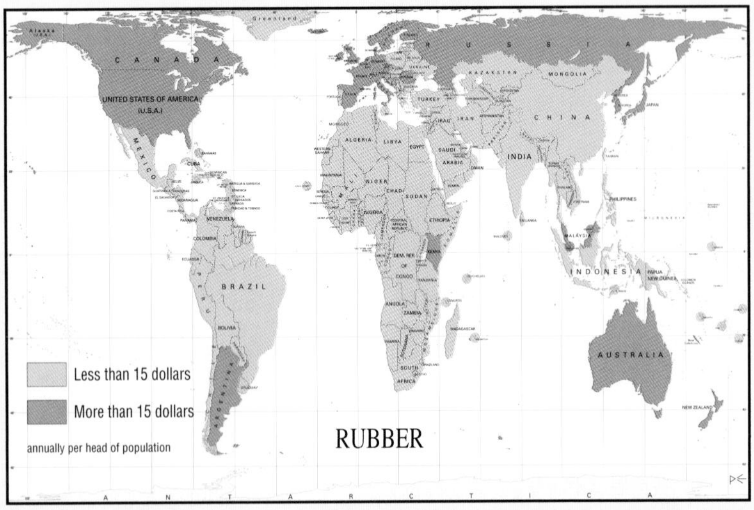

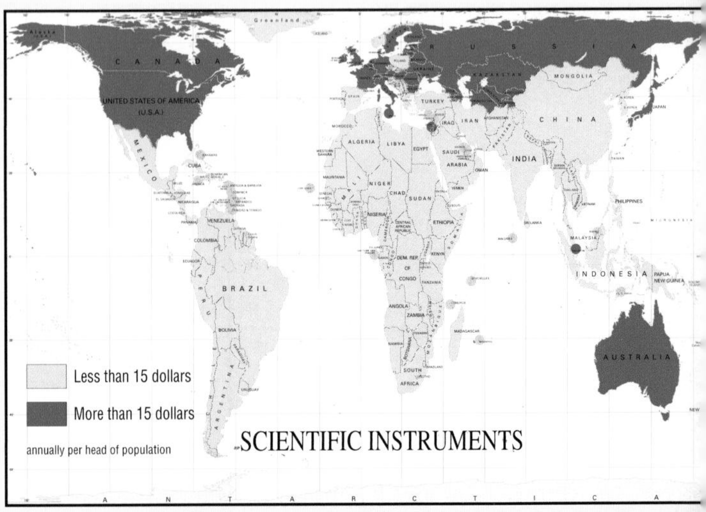

METALS AND METAL GOODS

Less than 150 dollars
More than 150 dollars
annually per head of population

MACHINES

Less than 150 dollars
More than 150 dollars
annually per head of population

CHEMICAL PRODUCTS

Less than 150 dollars
More than 150 dollars
annually per head of population

GLASS, PORCELAIN, CERAMICS

Less than 150 dollars
More than 150 dollars
annually per head of population

TEXTILE PRODUCTS

Less than 150 dollars
More than 150 dollars
annually per head of population

WOOD PRODUCTS

Less than 150 dollars
More than 150 dollars
annually per head of population

RUBBER

Less than 15 dollars
More than 15 dollars
annually per head of population

SCIENTIFIC INSTRUMENTS

Less than 15 dollars
More than 15 dollars
annually per head of population

If we define industry as covering all activities engaged in processing natural products, then we must include those manual crafts which all over the world continue to exist alongside industry in the strictest sense of the term and which to a great extent produce the same types of goods by means of machines. The branches of industry given in the maps on these two pages include those producing consumer goods or capital goods or undertaking the processing of raw materials.

INDUSTRIA

ELECTRICAL APPLIANCES

Less than 150 dollars
More than 150 dollars
ly per head of population

MEANS OF TRANSPORT

Less than 150 dollars
More than 150 dollars
annually per head of population

OIL AND COAL PRODUCTS

Less than 150 dollars
More than 150 dollars
y per head of population

PAPER, PAPER PRODUCTS

Less than 150 dollars
More than 150 dollars
annually per head of population

FOOD PRODUCTS

Less than 150 dollars
More than 150 dollars
per head of population

PLASTIC PRODUCTS

Less than 15 dollars
More than 15 dollars
annually per head of population

LEATHER AND FUR

Less than 1.5 dollars
More than 1.5 dollars
per head of population

SHOES

Less than 1.5 dollars
More than 1.5 dollars
annually per head of population

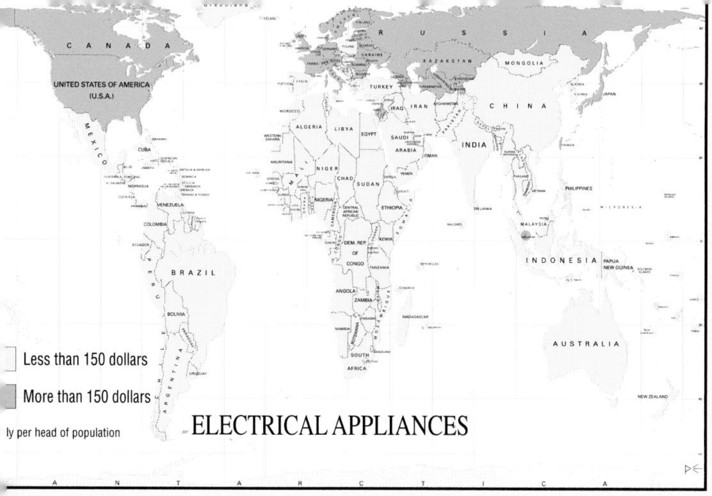

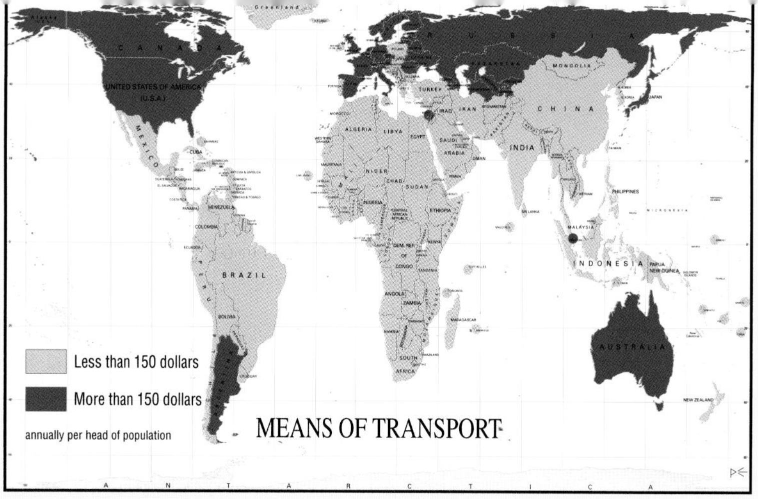

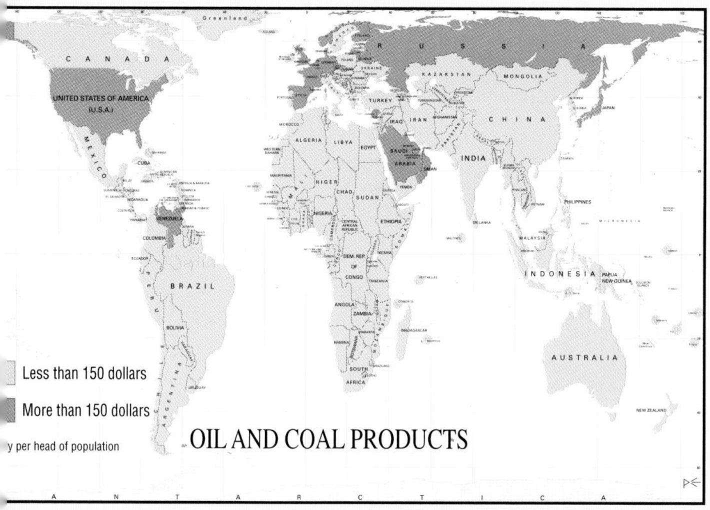

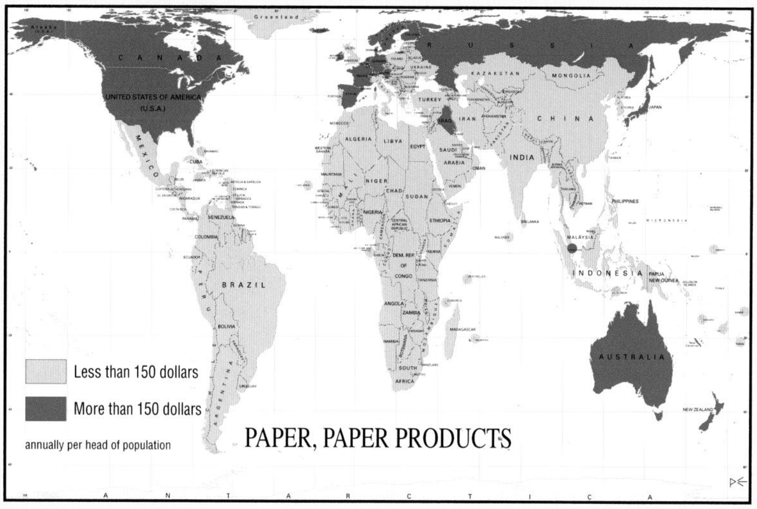

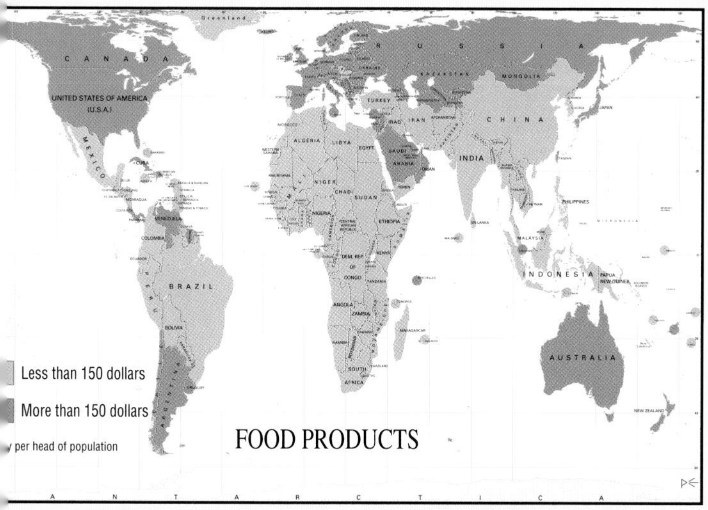

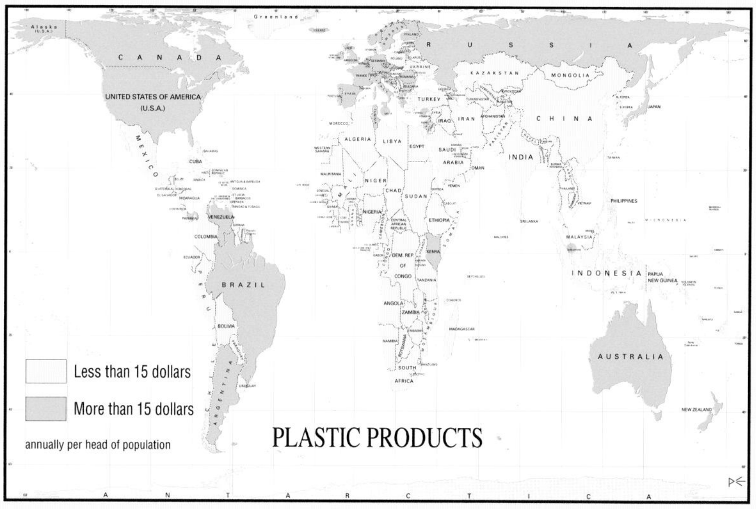

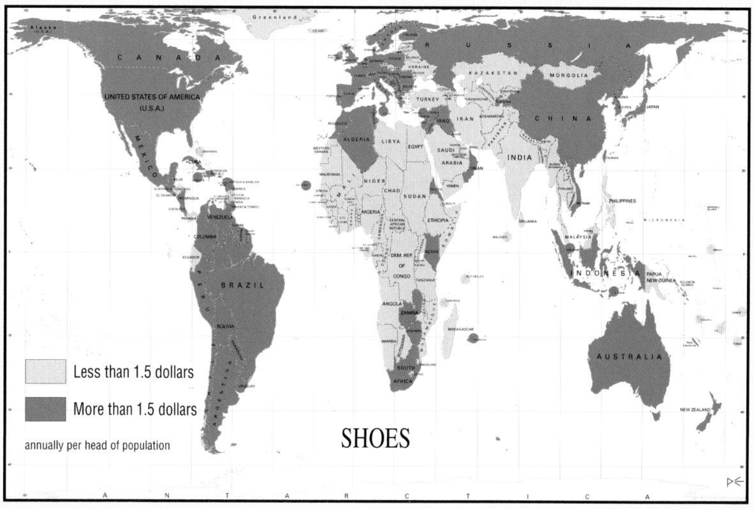

PRODUCTS

More than a dozen industrial countries have the highest output in nearly all areas of production. They achieve industrial production of $5,000 per head of the population. Fewer than half achieve more than $10,000, and only the Federal Republic of Germany achieves more than $14,000. Three-quarters of all countries in the world achieve less than $1,000 of industrial annual production per head, and nearly half of those less than $100.

Around 6,000 years ago the first cities appeared in Asia and Africa. About 3,000 years ago cities grew up in Europe. Initially they were only ruling foci that had to be supported by the surrounding rural populations, but they soon became centres of human culture. Arts, sciences and education all developed in cities. The new refined living conditions led to urban ways of life.

URBAN

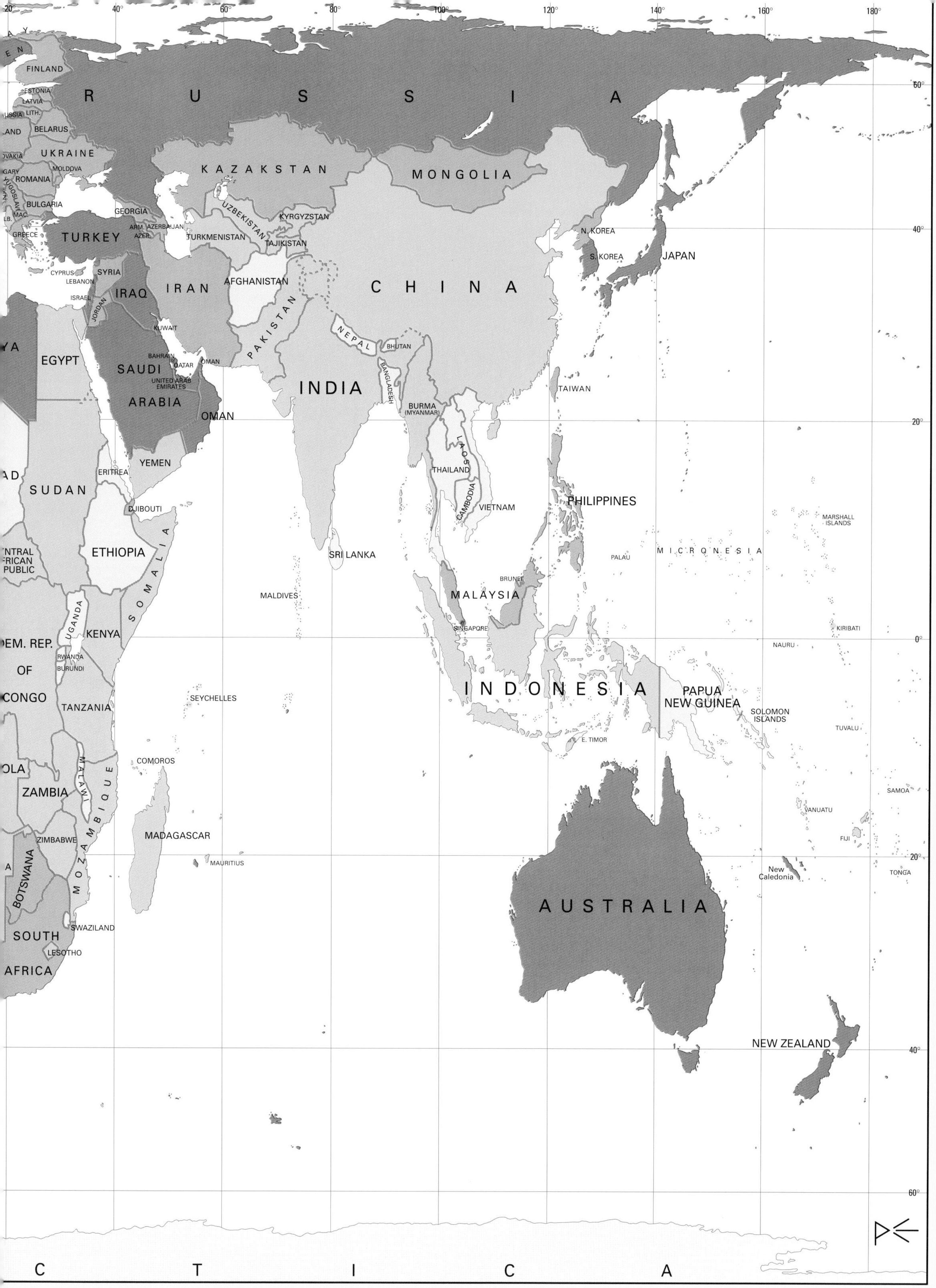

SATION

Over 100 years ago industry enabled cities to develop into centres of production. This led to a rapid increase in the number of their inhabitants. Nowadays more than three-quarters of the population of industrial countries live in cities (Britain 90%) but the same is also true of some developing countries (Venezuela 87%). In more than 50 countries of the world less than a quarter of the population lives in cities (Burundi 9%).

IMPORTS
NATURAL PRODUCTS

Less than 100 dollars
100 to 500 dollars
500 to 1,000 dollars
More than 1,000 dollars

annually per head of population

EXPORTS
NATURAL PRODUCTS

Less than 100 dollars
100 to 500 dollars
500 to 1,000 dollars
More than 1,000 dollars

annually per head of population

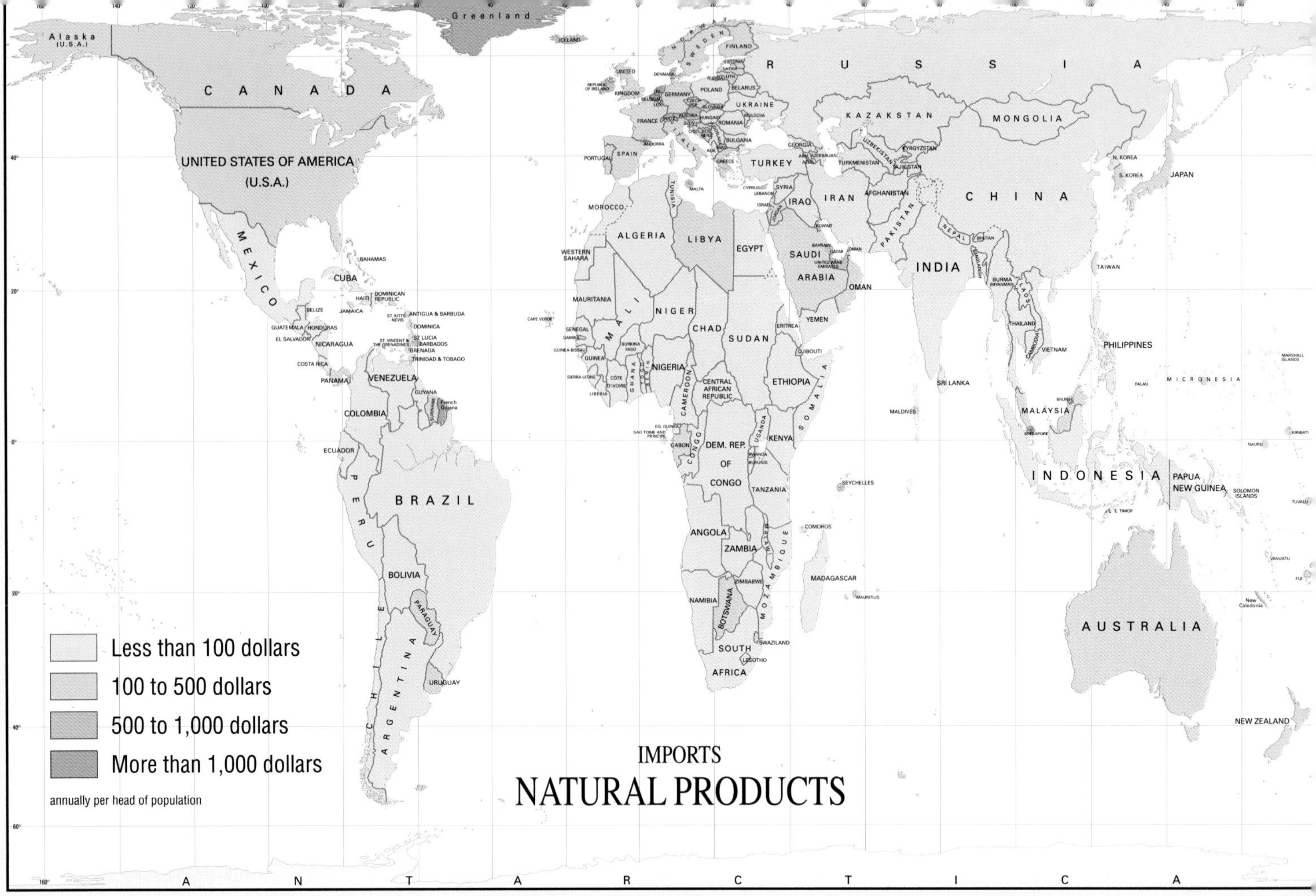

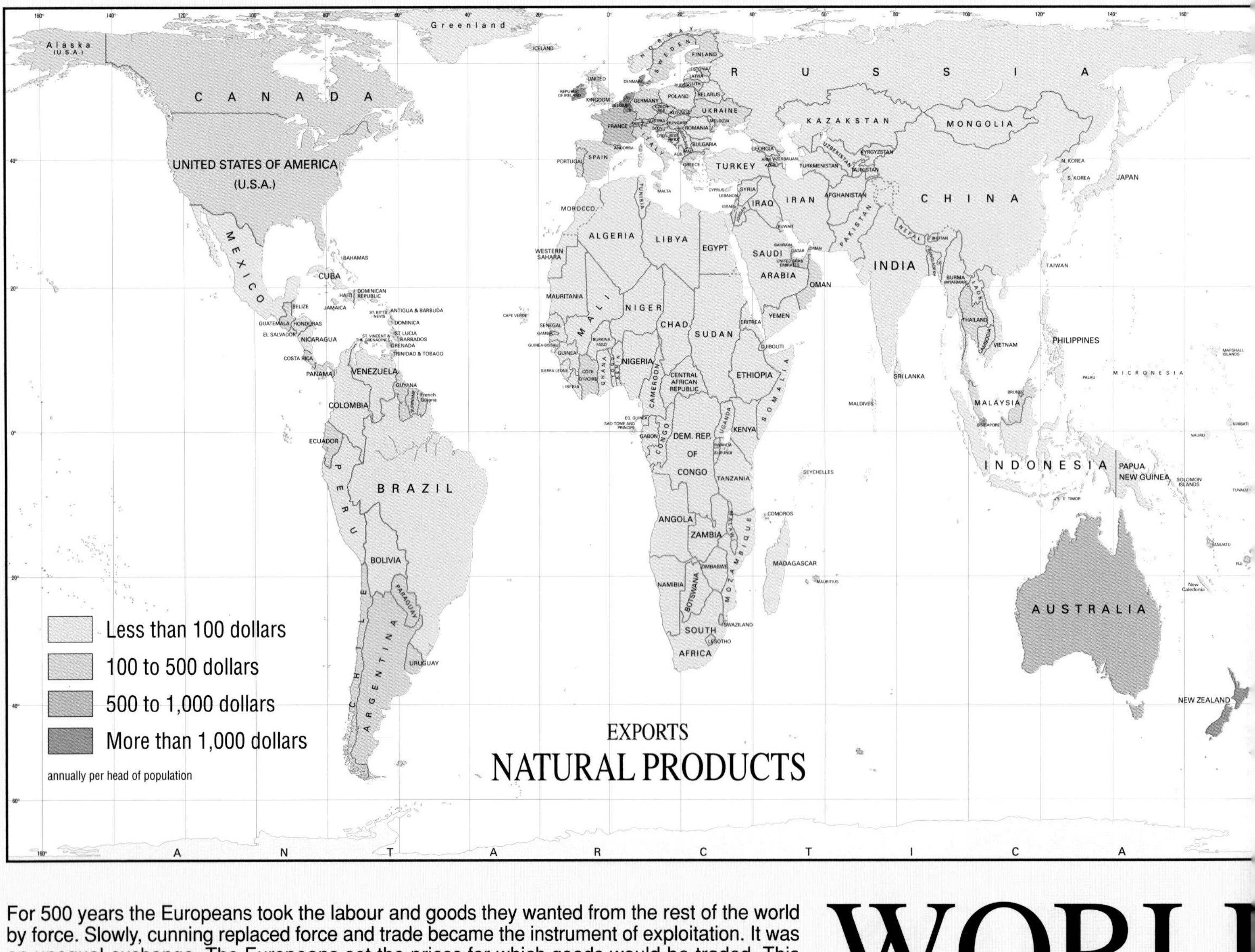

For 500 years the Europeans took the labour and goods they wanted from the rest of the world by force. Slowly, cunning replaced force and trade became the instrument of exploitation. It was an unequal exchange. The Europeans set the prices for which goods would be traded. This method of accumulating wealth was developed to such perfection that the Europeans could end their colonial domination in the second half of the twentieth century without losing its benefits.

WORLI

IMPORTS
INDUSTRIAL PRODUCTS

Less than 100 dollars
100 to 500 dollars
500 to 1,000 dollars
More than 1,000 dollars

annually per head of population

EXPORTS
INDUSTRIAL PRODUCTS

Less than 100 dollars
100 to 500 dollars
500 to 1,000 dollars
More than 1,000 dollars

annually per head of population

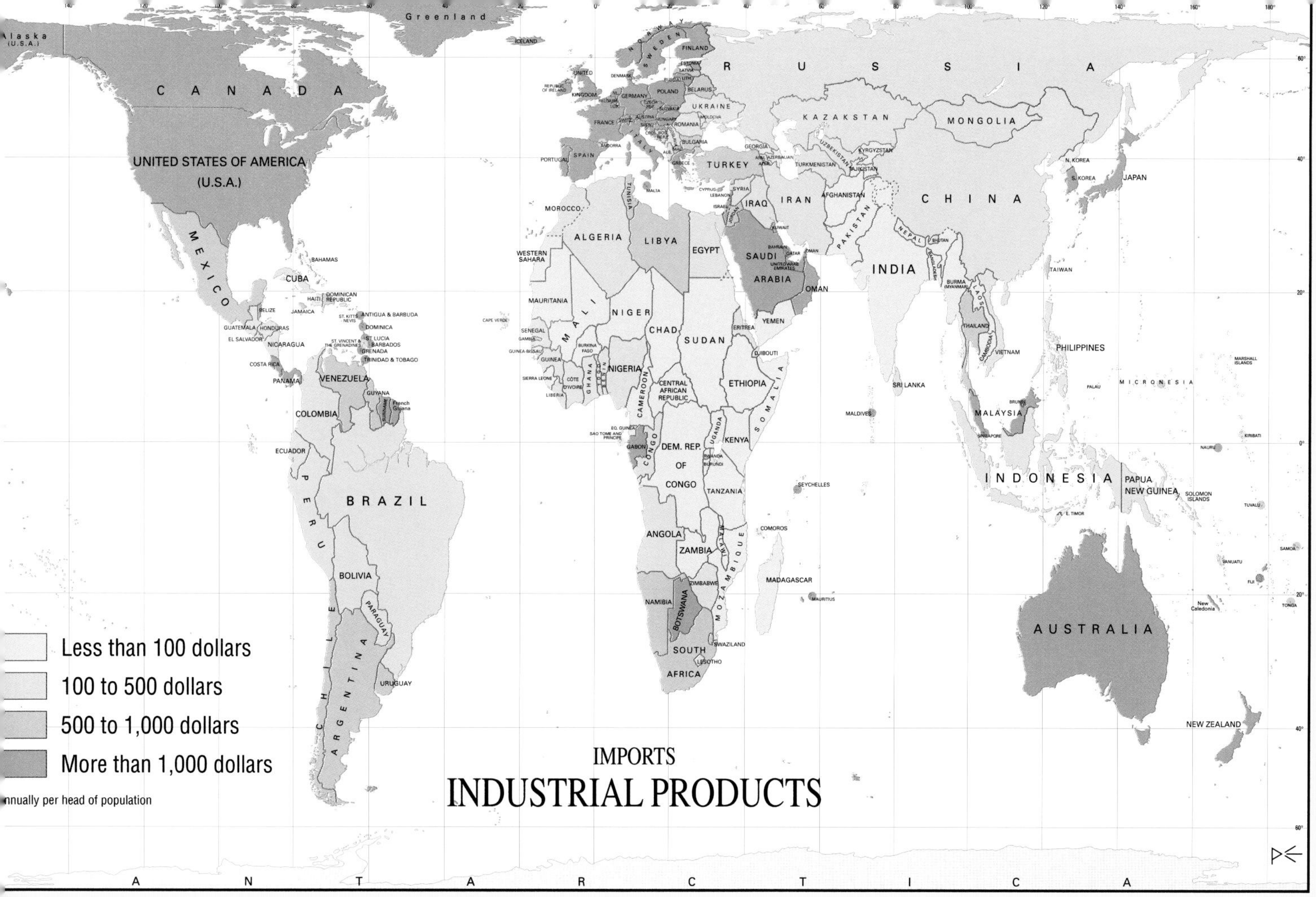

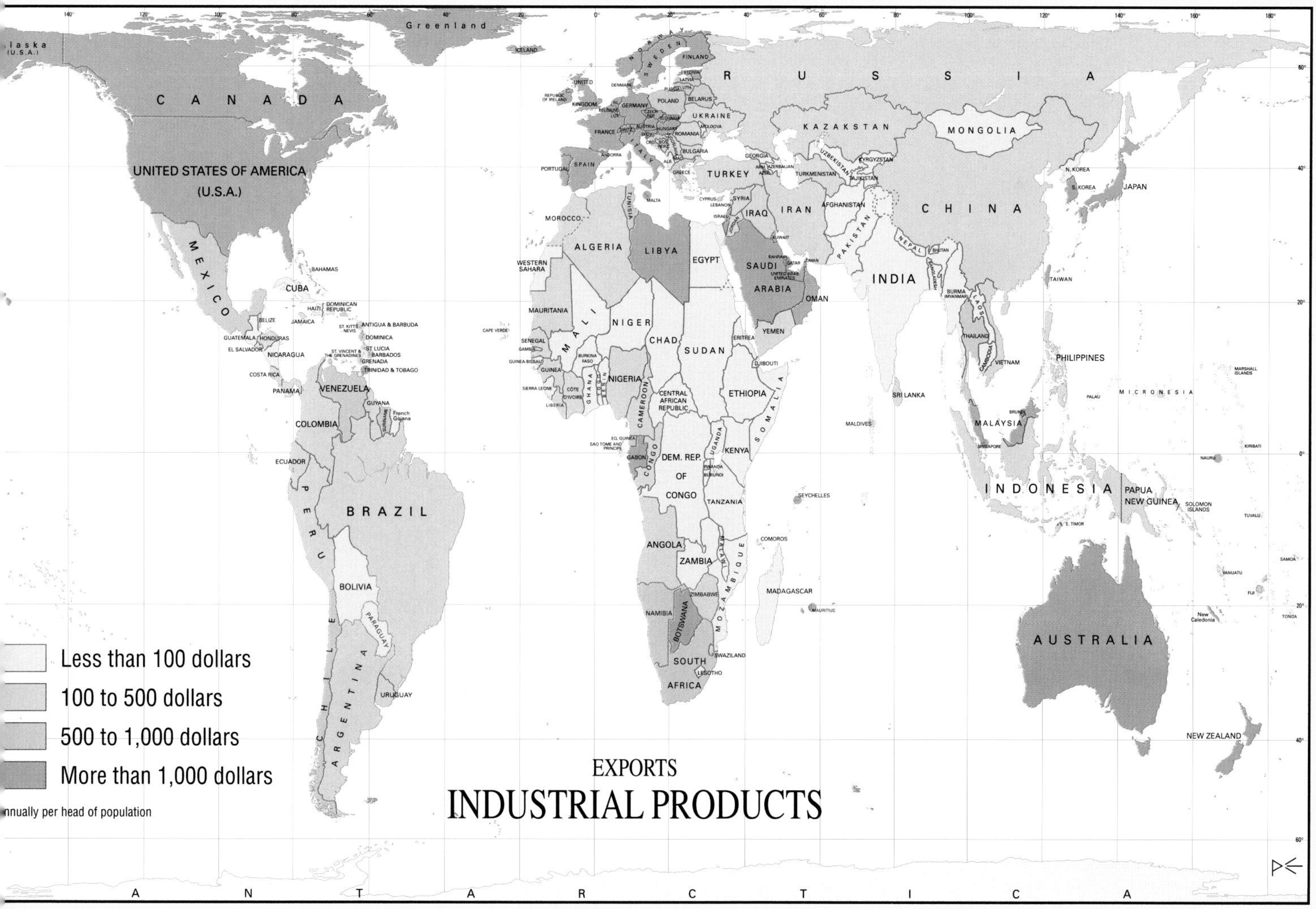

TRADE

Since the end of European colonial domination in the 1970s, prices for raw materials, which had already been far too low, fell by a third, whereas prices for industrial products increased fivefold. Within three decades this manipulation of world market prices caused the purchasing power of the developing countries to sink to an all-time low. Developing countries are to a large extent excluded from the world-wide exchange of goods because they have to hand over their products at a fraction of their real value.

Average income:

Less than 500 dollars
per person annually

500 to 1,000 dollars
per person annually

1,000 to 5,000 dollars
per person annually

5,000 to 10,000 dollars
per person annually

More than 10,000 dollars
per person annually

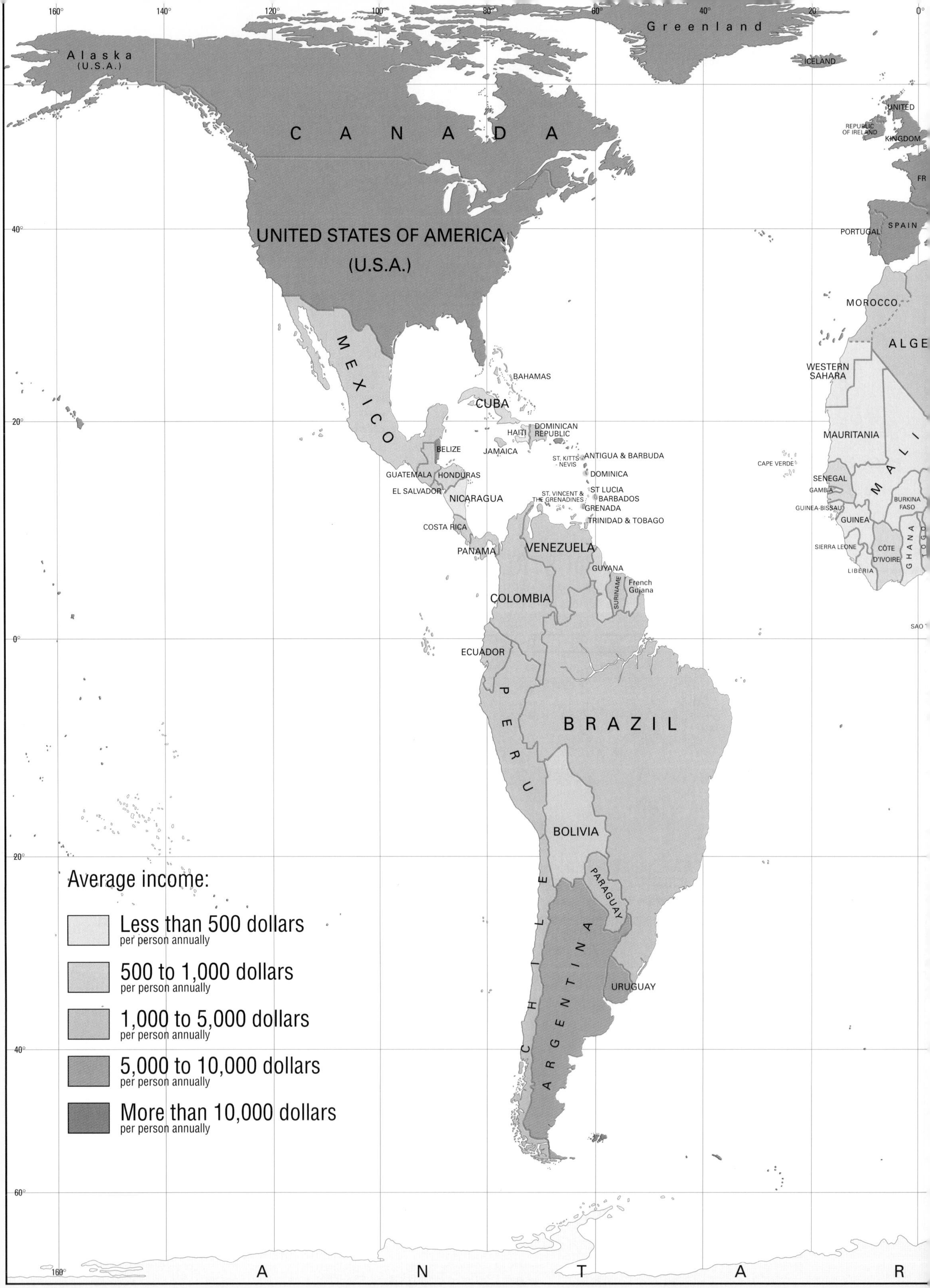

24% of the world's population consumes 83% of the world's income. That leaves just 17% of world income for the remaining 76%. Therefore each inhabitant of the rich countries has on average 16 times more of world income.

POOR NATION

RICH NATIONS

In the poorest countries the average income is $100-300 a year (Burundi $120, Ethiopia $100, Sierra Leone $130). In the richest nations the annual average income is more than one hundred times greater (Norway $33,000, Switzerland $38,000, Japan $32,000).

Annual economic growth
Less than 1%

Annual economic growth
1 to 2%

Annual economic growth
2 to 3%

Annual economic growth
3 to 4%

Annual economic growth
More than 4%

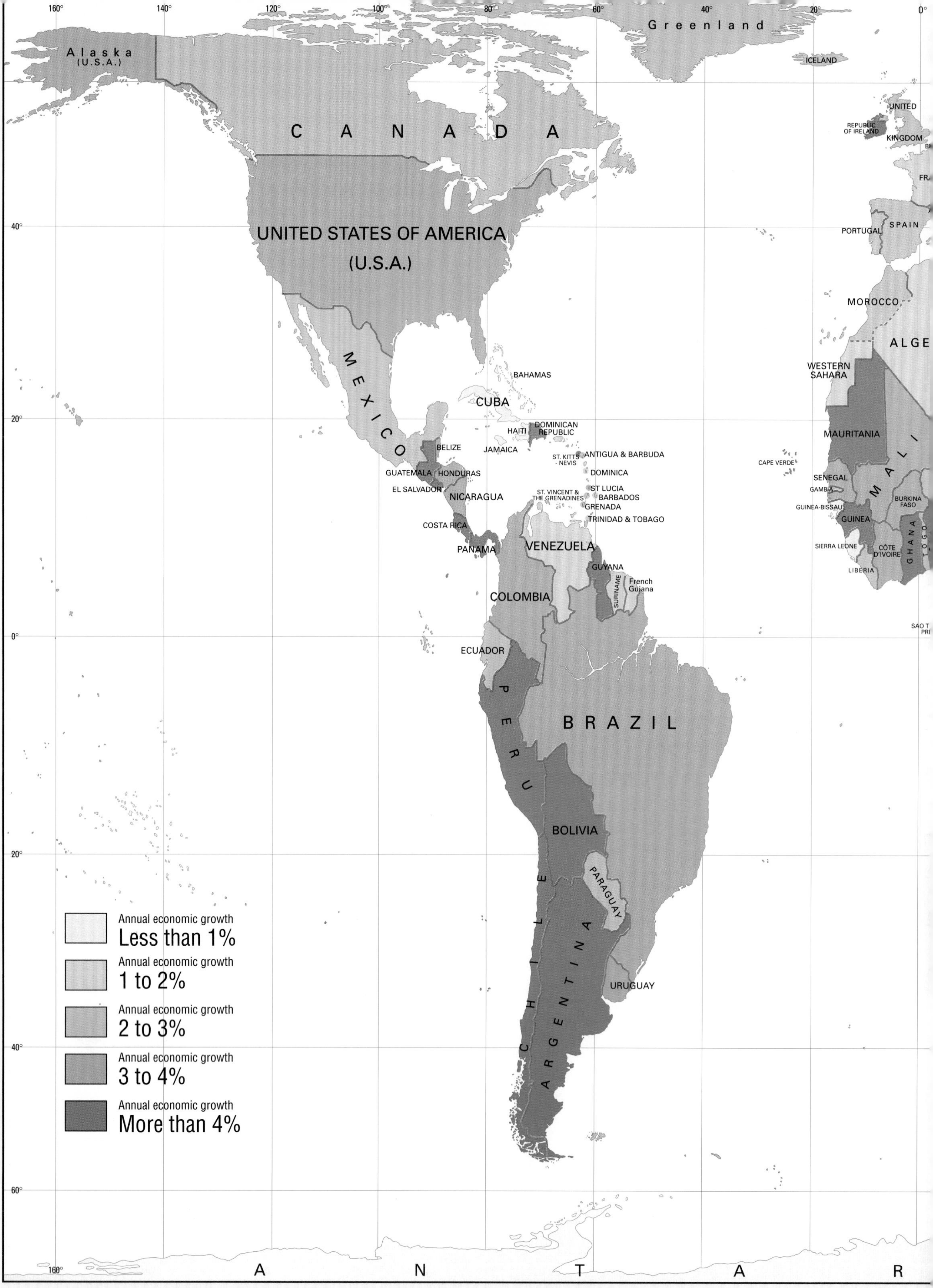

In the age of globalisation the economic growth of a country does not depend just on its own economic achievements. What is decisive today is the terms on which it exchanges its own products with the rest of the world. This relationship is defined by the rich industrial nations through world market prices.

ECONOMI

GROWTH

In the last ten years economic growth in Western countries has slowed: France 1.5%, Germany 1.7%, Britain 2.4%, Italy 1.2%, Switzerland 0.4%. Socialist countries have stabilised their economic growth: China 6.3%, Vietnam 8.4%, Laos 6.6%.

AGRICULTURE

Less than 10%
10 to 30%
30 to 50%
50 to 70%
More than 70%

of the workforce is employed in agriculture

T

Less than 2%
2 to 4%
4 to 6%
6 to 8%
More than 8%

of the workforce is employed in transport

MINING

Less than 1%
1 to 2%
2 to 3%
3 to 4%
More than 4%

of the workforce is employed in mining

Less than 3%
3 to 6%
6 to 9%
9 to 12%
More than 12%

of the workforce is employed in
building construction

ENERGY

Less than 0.5%
0.5 to 1%
1 to 1.5%
1.5 to 2%
More than 2%

of the workforce is employed in
energy production

SOCIA

Less than 10%
10 to 20%
20 to 30%
30 to 40%
More than 40%

of the workforce is employed in
social professions

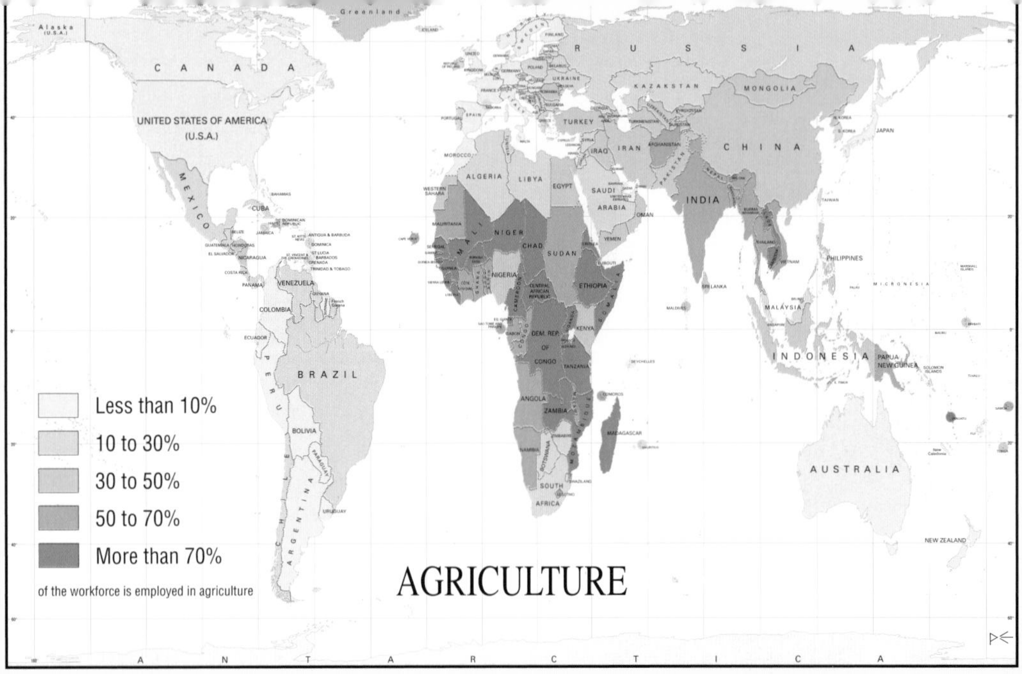

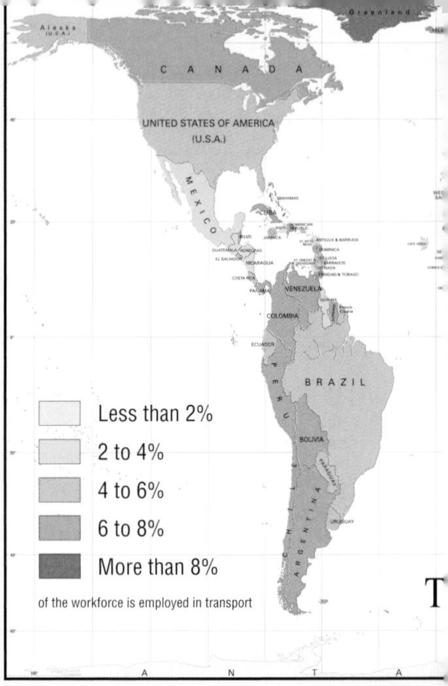

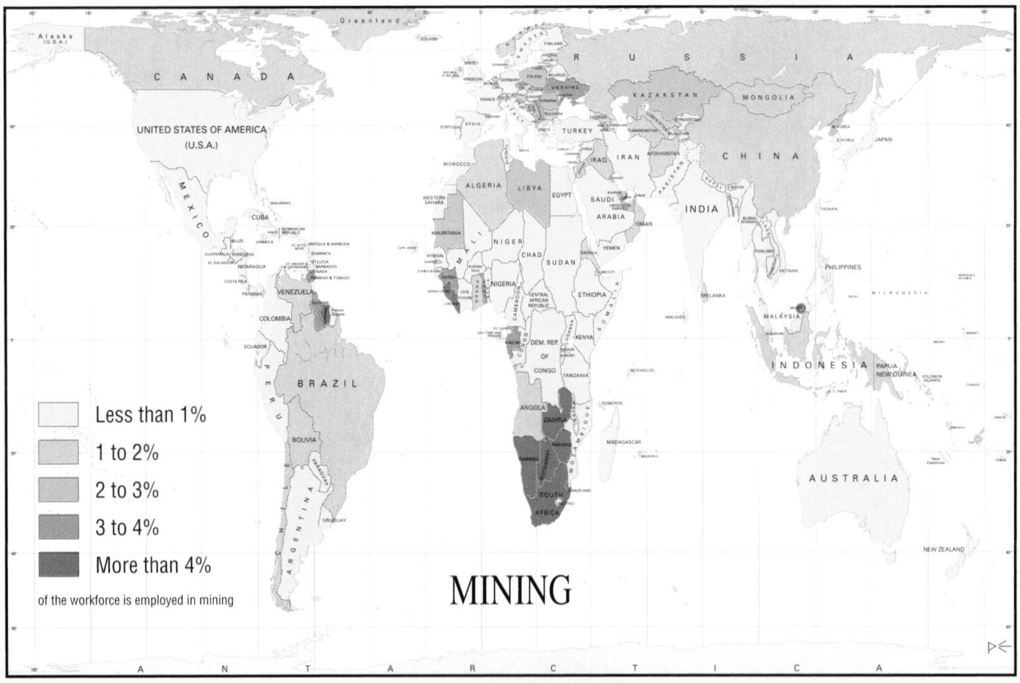

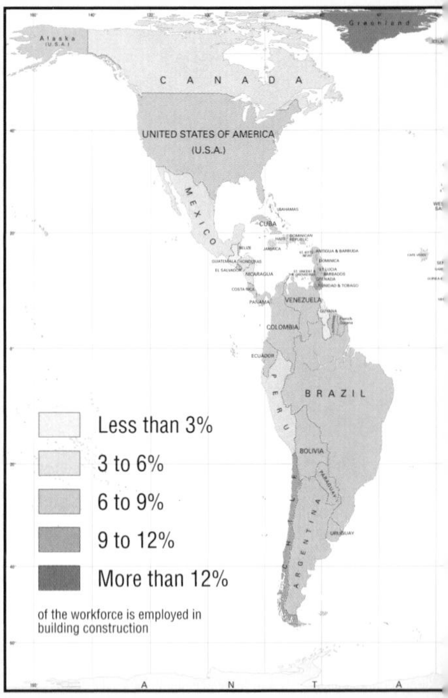

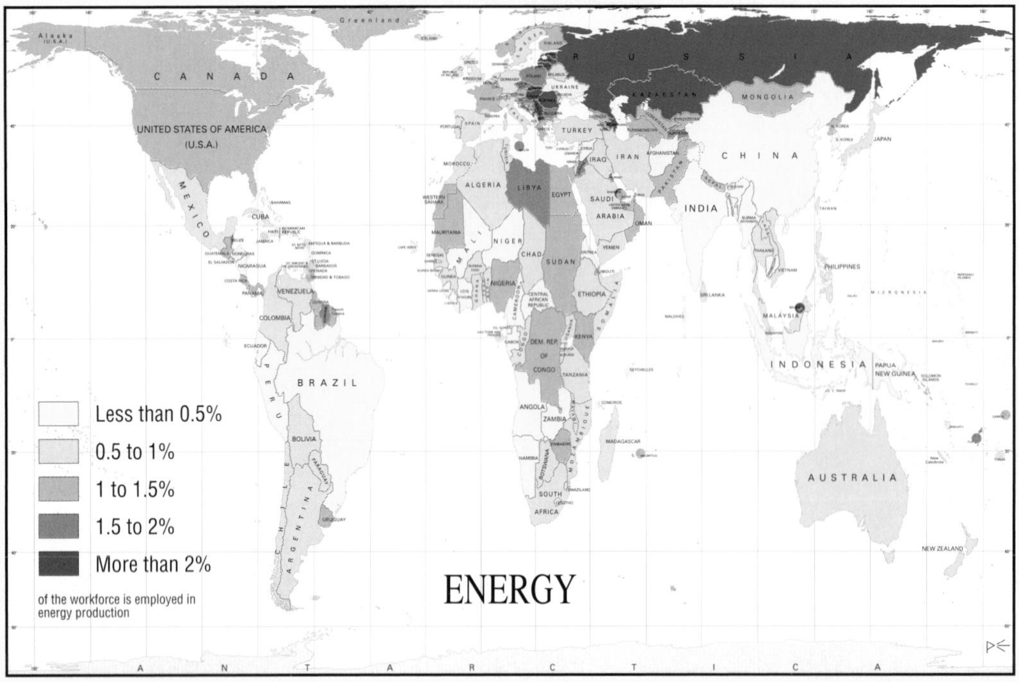

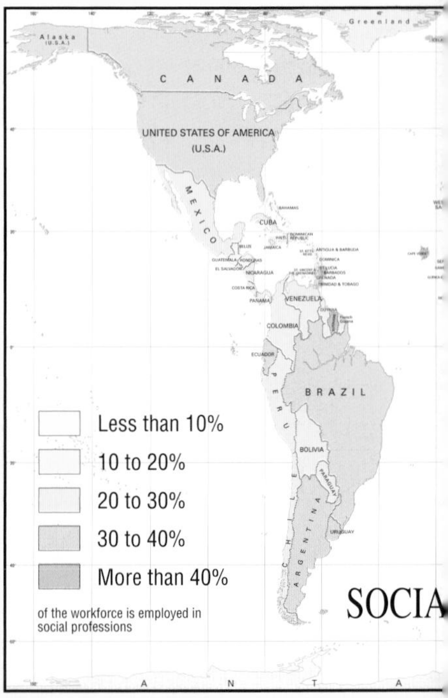

The distribution of employment among the various sectors of an economy
does not say anything about each sector's relative strength or productivity.
The US for example, where only 3% of its workers are in agriculture today,
is the greatest wheat supplier in the world, whereas Tanzania cannot even
feed its own population although 82% of its people work in agriculture.

EMPLOYMEN

Less than 5%
5 to 10%
10 to 15%
15 to 20%
20 to 25%
More than 25%
of the workforce is employed in industry

INDUSTRY

Less than 5%
5 to 10%
10 to 15%
15 to 20%
More than 20%
of the workforce is employed in trade

TRADE

Less than 1%
1 to 2%
2 to 4%
4 to 6%
6 to 8%
More than 8%
of the workforce is employed in banking

BANKING

T

SIONS

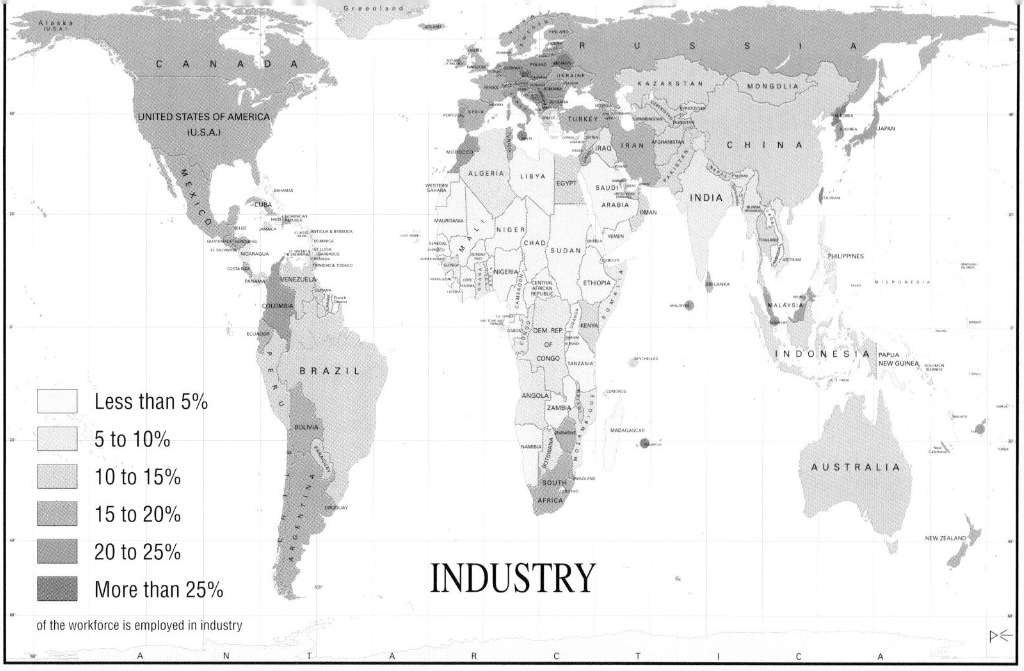

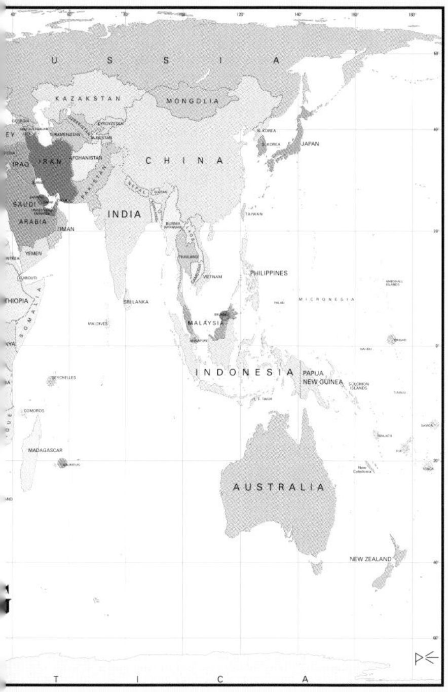

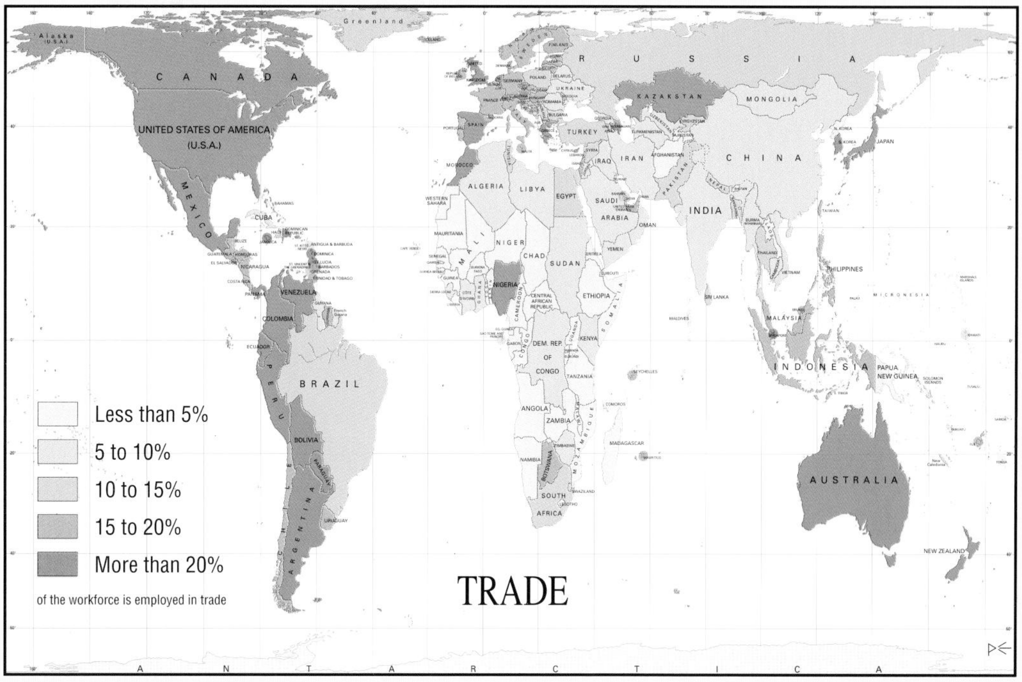

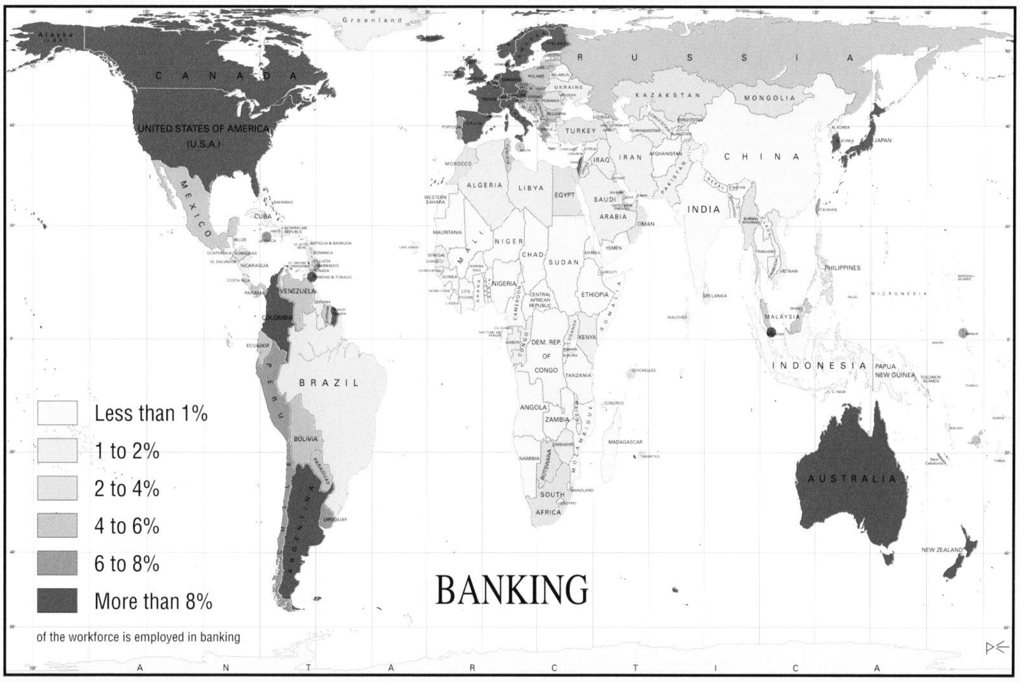

STRUCTURE

As a result of increasing automation in the industrial countries, in most cases fewer than a quarter of the workforce is now employed in industrial production, for example Germany and Italy. In such countries the emphasis of employment has shifted towards trade and services, (which has already overtaken industry in Canada and the US), and towards banking, which is increasingly shaping economies and states.

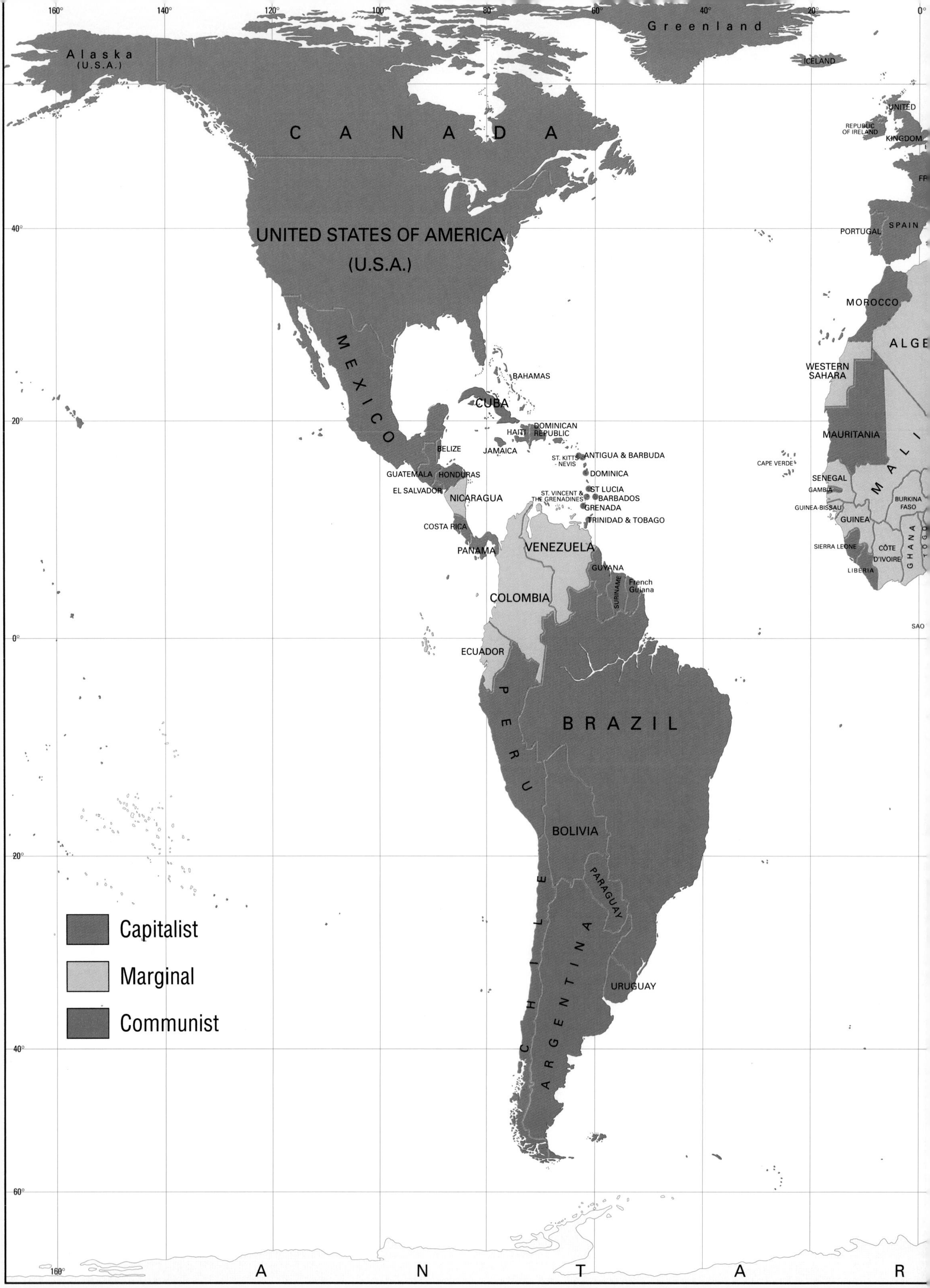

It is nearly a million years ago since the first people began to exchange products of equal value. With the beginning of farming and the domestication of animals about 10,000 years ago this economy of meeting immediate needs was slowly pushed aside by the market economy. Trade replaced barter, and striving for profit became the engine of economics. Rich and poor emerged, and with them domination and subservience, robbery and war.

ECONOM

R U S S I A

FINLAND
ESTONIA
LATVIA
SSIA LITH.
BELARUS
ND
UKRAINE
ARY
ROMANIA
MOLDOVA
BULGARIA
GREECE
TURKEY
GEORGIA
ARM. AZERBAIJAN
AZER.
CYPRUS
LEBANON
SYRIA
ISRAEL
JORDAN
IRAQ   IRAN
KUWAIT
EGYPT
BAHRAIN
SAUDI   QATAR   OMAN
UNITED ARAB
ARABIA   EMIRATES
OMAN
YEMEN
ERITREA
SUDAN
DJIBOUTI
ETHIOPIA

KAZAKSTAN

UZBEKISTAN
KYRGYZSTAN
TURKMENISTAN
TAJIKISTAN
AFGHANISTAN

PAKISTAN

MONGOLIA

CHINA

N. KOREA
S. KOREA
JAPAN

NEPAL
BHUTAN
BANGLADESH
INDIA
BURMA
(MYANMAR)
LAOS
THAILAND
CAMBODIA
VIETNAM

TAIWAN

PHILIPPINES

MARSHALL
ISLANDS

PALAU
M I C R O N E S I A

SRI LANKA

MALDIVES

BRUNEI
MALAYSIA
SINGAPORE

KIRIBATI

NAURU

NTRAL
RICAN
UBLIC
EM. REP.
OF
CONGO
UGANDA
KENYA
RWANDA
BURUNDI
TANZANIA
SOMALIA
SEYCHELLES

COMOROS

OLA
ZAMBIA
MALAWI
MOZAMBIQUE
ZIMBABWE
MADAGASCAR
MAURITIUS

BOTSWANA
SWAZILAND
SOUTH
LESOTHO
AFRICA

I N D O N E S I A
E. TIMOR
PAPUA
NEW GUINEA
SOLOMON
ISLANDS
TUVALU

SAMOA

VANUATU
FIJI

New
Caledonia
TONGA

A U S T R A L I A

NEW ZEALAND

50°
40°
20°
0°
20°
40°
60°

C   T   I   C   A

ORDER

The market economy reached its highest form in capitalism which has developed with the machine age over the past 250 years. With capitalism, the gulf between rich and poor grew immeasurably throughout the world. Over the past 100 years some countries have been trying, by abolishing private ownership of the means of production, to bring back the old economic system of meeting only real needs but at a higher level in the form of planned economies. Nearly a quarter of humankind, or 1.4 billion people, live in those socialist countries today.

Less than 1%
of the workforce is unemployed

1 to 5%
of the workforce is unemployed

5 to 10%
of the workforce is unemployed

10 to 20%
of the workforce is unemployed

More than 20%
of the workforce is unemployed

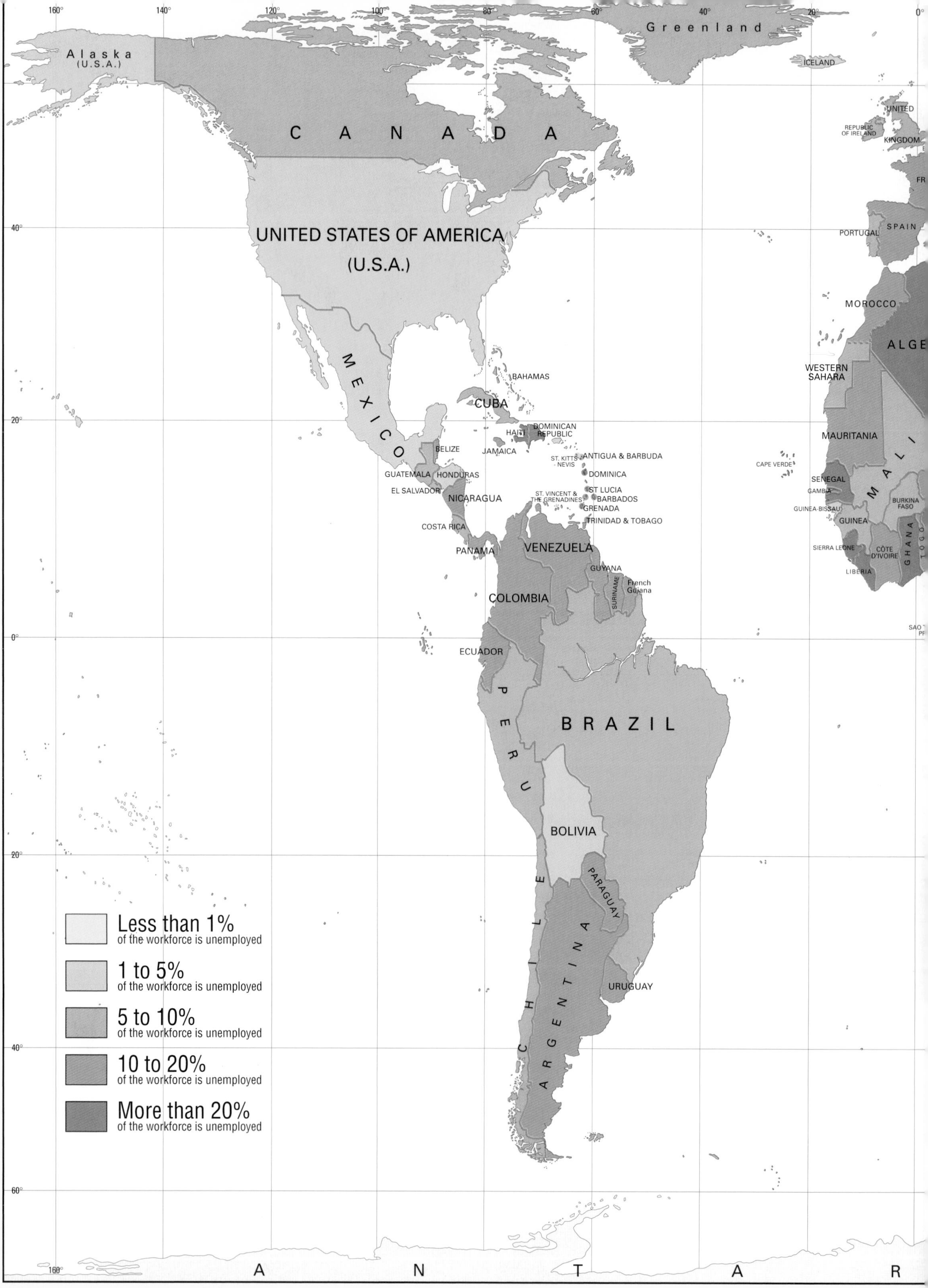

Work shapes the face of the earth and of man; it defines the way man lives, his language, behaviour and thinking; work brings about the progress of mankind and is the source of education, science and morals. To be excluded from work means the loss of personal fulfilment and exclusion from the community. A society which is unable to secure work for all its members on a lasting basis bears responsibility for hopelessness, self-neglect, flight from reality and criminality.

UNEMP

YMENT

According to official figures world-wide there are, today, about 150 million unemployed, of whom about 50m are in Western Europe. But in many countries only those entitled to unemployment benefit are counted so the real figure is higher. Unemployment was seen at the beginning of the 20th century as the worst form of economic crisis; today it is an integral part of the capitalist market economy. In socialist countries the right to work, which was in part established as a constitutional right, has been abandoned as a result of the partial restoration of the market economy.

Map labels

160°   140°   120°   100°   80°   60°   40°   20°   0°

Greenland

Alaska (U.S.A.)

ICELAND

UNITED KINGDOM

REPUBLIC OF IRELAND

FR.

C A N A D A

40°

UNITED STATES OF AMERICA

(U.S.A.)

PORTUGAL   SPAIN

MOROCCO

ALGE

WESTERN SAHARA

MEXICO

BAHAMAS

20°

CUBA

DOMINICAN REPUBLIC

HAITI

MAURITANIA

M A L I

BELIZE

JAMAICA

ANTIGUA & BARBUDA

ST. KITTS - NEVIS

CAPE VERDE

GUATEMALA   HONDURAS

DOMINICA

SENEGAL

BURKINA FASO

EL SALVADOR

ST LUCIA

GAMBIA

NICARAGUA

ST VINCENT & THE GRENADINES

BARBADOS

GUINEA-BISSAU

GRENADA

GUINEA

COSTA RICA

TRINIDAD & TOBAGO

SIERRA LEONE

CÔTE D'IVOIRE

GHANA

TOGO

0°

PANAMA

VENEZUELA

LIBERIA

GUYANA

SAO T

COLOMBIA

SURINAME

French Guiana

ECUADOR

P E R U

B R A Z I L

20°

BOLIVIA

PARAGUAY

C H I L E

A R G E N T I N A

URUGUAY

40°

60°

A N T A R

160°

Legend

Less than 5%
annual inflation

5 to 10%
annual inflation

10 to 25%
annual inflation

More than 25%
annual inflation

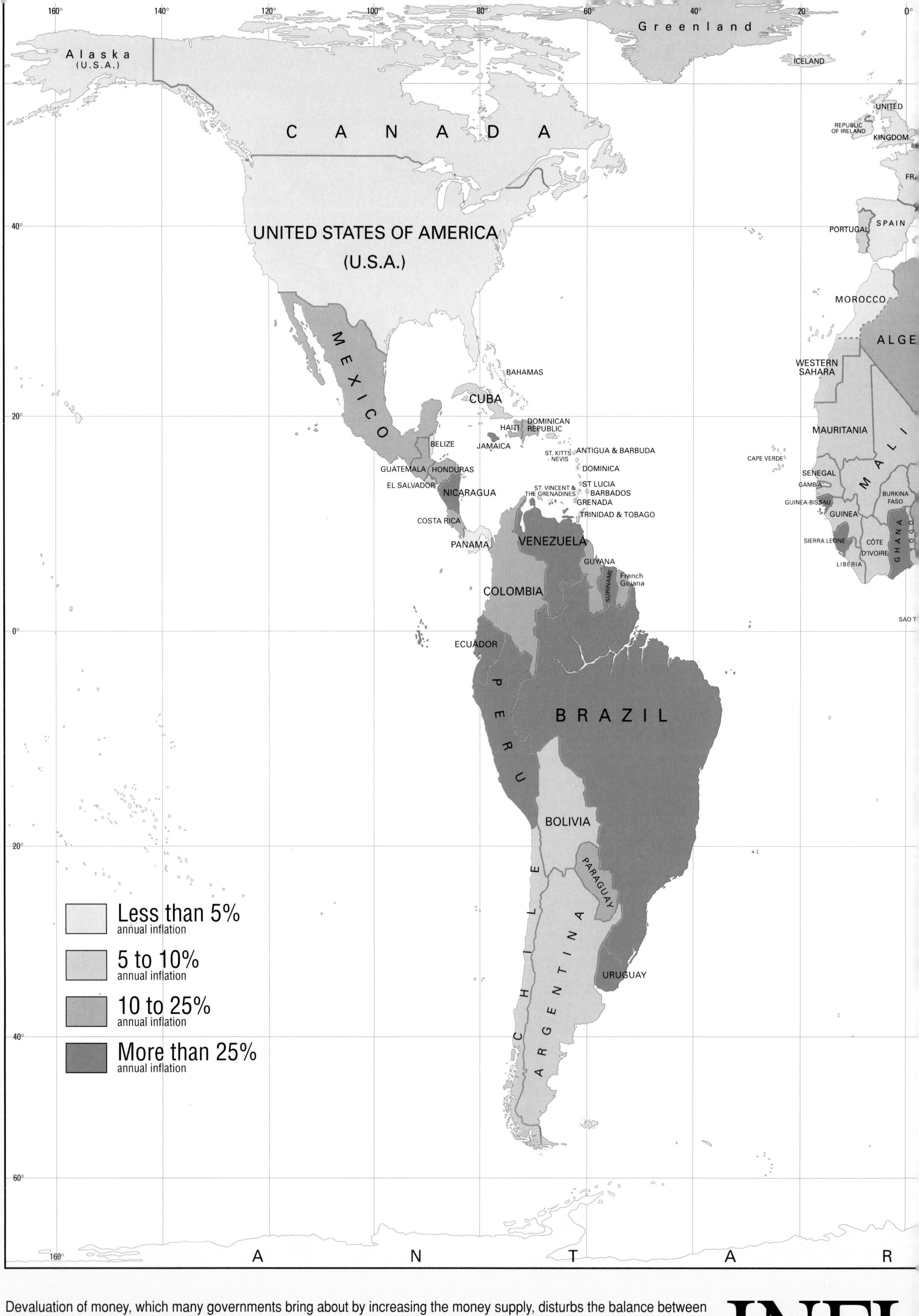

Devaluation of money, which many governments bring about by increasing the money supply, disturbs the balance between the supply of money and that of goods. It increases the prices of consumer goods without simultaneously increasing pay and is therefore at the expense of the waged and salary workers whose real income decreases. Those who profit are national governments, whose debts sink, and banks, who earn from the reduced value of their deposits, and the owners of capital assets which rise in value. If devaluation is not followed by increased production, inflation brings crises and unemployment.

INFL

FINLAND
ESTONIA
LATVIA
LITH.
BELARUS
UKRAINE
MOLDOVA
ROMANIA
BULGARIA
MAC.
GREECE
CYPRUS
LEBANON
ISRAEL
GEORGIA
ARM. AZERBAIJAN
AZER.
TURKMENISTAN

R U S S I A

KAZAKSTAN

MONGOLIA

N. KOREA
S. KOREA
JAPAN

UZBEKISTAN
KYRGYZSTAN
TAJIKISTAN

TURKEY
SYRIA
IRAQ
IRAN
AFGHANISTAN
PAKISTAN

C H I N A

JORDAN
KUWAIT
EGYPT
SAUDI
BAHRAIN
QATAR
UNITED ARAB
EMIRATES
OMAN
ARABIA

NEPAL
BHUTAN
BANGLADESH
I N D I A
BURMA
(MYANMAR)
LAOS
TAIWAN

OMAN
YEMEN
ERITREA
DJIBOUTI

THAILAND
CAMBODIA
VIETNAM
PHILIPPINES

SUDAN

MARSHALL
ISLANDS

SRI LANKA
MALDIVES
M I C R O N E S I A
PALAU

ETHIOPIA
SOMALIA

BRUNEI
KIRIBATI

NTRAL
RICAN
PUBLIC
UGANDA
KENYA
RWANDA
BURUNDI

MALAYSIA
SINGAPORE
NAURU

EM. REP.
OF
CONGO
TANZANIA
SEYCHELLES

I N D O N E S I A
PAPUA
NEW GUINEA
SOLOMON
ISLANDS
TUVALU

E. TIMOR

COMOROS

OLA
ZAMBIA
MALAWI
MOZAMBIQUE
MADAGASCAR
MAURITIUS

SAMOA
VANUATU
FIJI

ZIMBABWE

A U S T R A L I A

New
Caledonia
TONGA

BOTSWANA
SWAZILAND
SOUTH
LESOTHO
AFRICA

NEW ZEALAND

C T I C A

Paper money, which was introduced in Europe about 200 years ago to replace coins of precious metals, made possible the arbitrary increase of the money supply and hence inflation. For 150 years inflation remained the last resort to overcome breakdowns after wars and revolutions. But from the middle of the 20th century doses of inflation have been continually used by the rich industrial nations of the world as an instrument of monetary policy. Their inflation roughly keeps pace with rising incomes achieved by wage demands, whereas the inflation rate of developing countries adds to the poverty of their peoples (Zambia 63%, Somalia 75%, Sudan 74%, Brazil 350% a year.)

Less than 1 child
per thousand head of population

1 to 5 children
per thousand head of population

5 to 15 children
per thousand head of population

15 to 30 children
per thousand head of population

More than 30 children
per thousand head of population

under 15 years of age are in paid employment

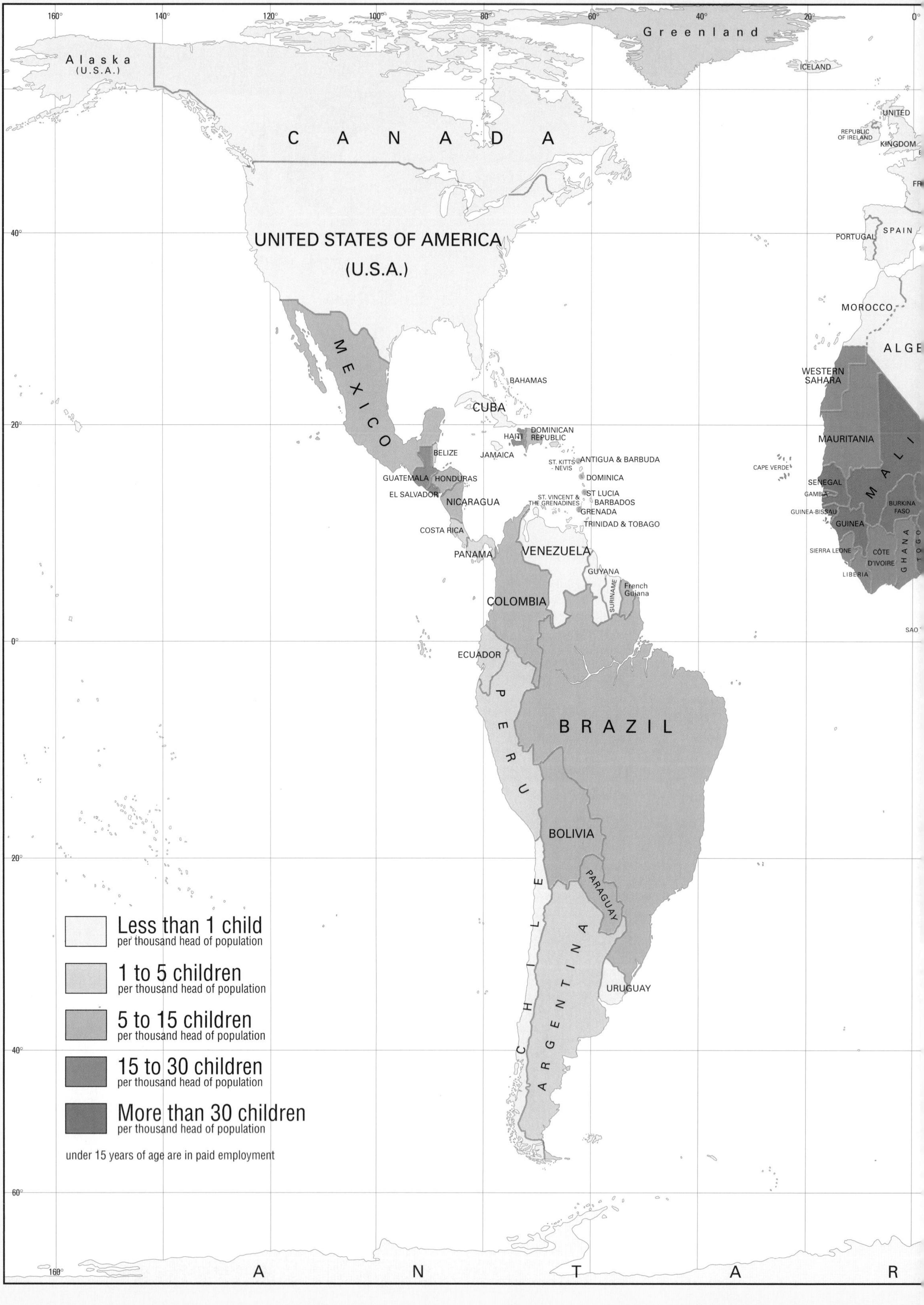

The use of children to help in the house and in the fields is as old as human culture. This help served a useful educational purpose when it did not overwork the children. During industrialisation child labour throughout Europe shifted from the parental house to workshops in which children were merely cheap labour. This paid child labour, the worst form of exploitation, was suffered only by children of the poorest people whose families were hungry and deprived. Today child labour is incompatible with regular attendance at school or learning a profession so it leads to lifelong social disadvantage.

ABOUR

As the most acute forms of exploitation shifted to the colonial areas so did most child labour. Political independence of colonies did not end exploitation because economic dependence continued. In the rich industrial countries, increasing condemnation of child labour led to a loss of educational opportunities at work but did not wholly eradicate child labour. Socialist countries are increasingly trying to bring work into education in polytechnic schools.

Approaching equality:
Total income of the richest 10% = total income of the poorest 20%

Moderate inequality:
Total income of the richest 10% = total income of the poorest 40%

Severe inequality:
Total income of the richest 10% = total income of the poorest 60%

Gross inequality:
Total income of the richest 10% = total income of the poorest 80%

(The percentage figures for the poorest refer to average values,
which can vary in the individual countries by up to 10%)

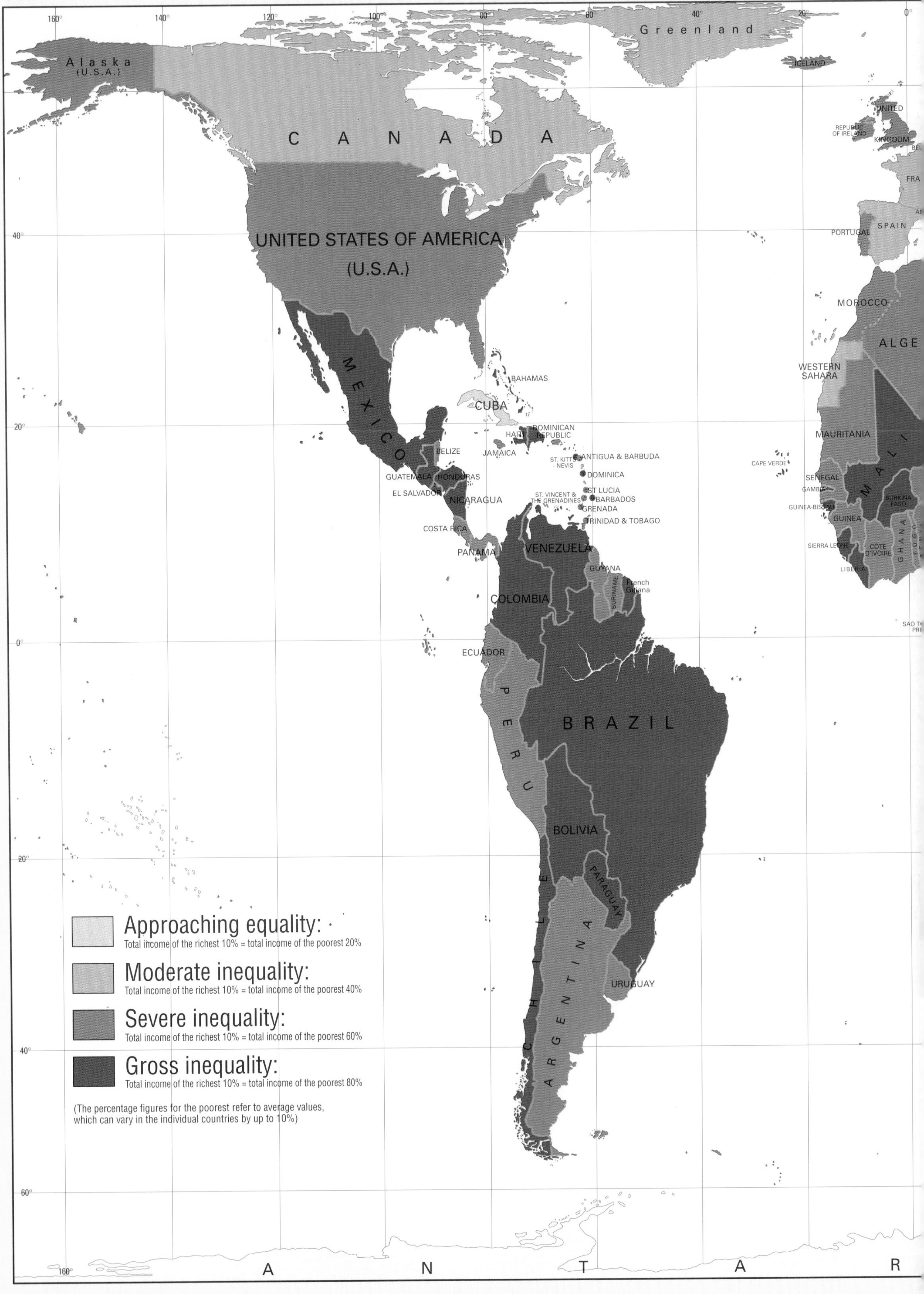

Increasing inequality which evolved with the beginnings of the market economy 6000 years ago has today reached a high point. Directors of big companies earn many millions yearly. Heads of big American concerns have annual salaries of $20-30m; thus in one minute they earn as much as the poorest people in the developing countries earn in their whole lives. The owners of big companies have annual incomes running into billions while every day world-wide more than 100,000 people starve to death.

INEQU

60°

AY
EN
FINLAND
ESTONIA
LATVIA
RUSSIA LITH.
LAND BELARUS
OVAKIA UKRAINE
NGARY MOLDOVA
ROMANIA
SLAVI MAC.
BULGARIA
GREECE
TURKEY
CYPRUS
LEBANON
ISRAEL
JORDAN
IRAQ
SYRIA
YA
EGYPT

R U S S I A

K A Z A K S T A N

MONGOLIA

GEORGIA
ARM. AZERBAIJAN
AZER.
TURKMENISTAN
UZBEKISTAN
KYRGYZSTAN
TAJIKISTAN
AFGHANISTAN

IRAN

40°

N. KOREA
S. KOREA
JAPAN

KUWAIT
BAHRAIN
QATAR OMAN
UNITED ARAB
EMIRATES
SAUDI
ARABIA
OMAN

P
A
K
I
S
T
A
N

N E P A L
BHUTAN

C H I N A

INDIA

BANGLADESH

20°

AD
SUDAN
ERITREA
YEMEN
DJIBOUTI
ENTRAL
RICAN
PUBLIC
ETHIOPIA
S
O
M
A
L
I
A

BURMA
(MYANMAR)
L
A
O
S
THAILAND
CAMBODIA
VIETNAM

TAIWAN

PHILIPPINES

MARSHALL
ISLANDS

SRI LANKA

MALDIVES

PALAU
M I C R O N E S I A

BRUNEI
MALAYSIA

KIRIBATI

SINGAPORE

NAURU

0°

EM. REP.
OF
CONGO
UGANDA
KENYA
RWANDA
BURUNDI
TANZANIA

SEYCHELLES

I N D O N E S I A

PAPUA
NEW GUINEA

SOLOMON
ISLANDS

TUVALU

E. TIMOR

COMOROS

OLA
ZAMBIA
M
A
L
A
W
I
M
O
Z
A
M
B
I
Q
U
E
ZIMBABWE
IA
BOTSWANA
SOUTH
SWAZILAND
AFRICA
LESOTHO

MADAGASCAR

MAURITIUS

VANUATU

SAMOA

FIJI

New
Caledonia

20°

TONGA

AUSTRALIA

NEW ZEALAND

40°

60°

C T I C A

ALITY

Income distribution in different countries does not depend on the size of average income. Inequality in poor developing countries is often greater than in the rich industrial nations. In South Africa the income of the richest mine owner is about $2 billion a year, three times as much as all five million inhabitants of Chad earn together in a year. The extreme inequality which comes from private ownership of the big companies has been overcome by a fifth of mankind in the socialist countries without, however, achieving real equality anywhere.

The most horrible form of exploitation of women, girls and children is prostitution. It developed with the emergence of the profit motive in market economies about 6,000 years ago. It was introduced by priests who made money from sacrificing young girls to the temple goddesses (Ishtar, Aphrodite, Venus). Prostitution was later adopted by city states (Athens and Corinth), then by slave dealers and finally by free entrepreneurs. The few people who still live in a state of pure nature do not know prostitution. The United Nations has declared prostitution a form of slavery and demanded its abolition.

PROST

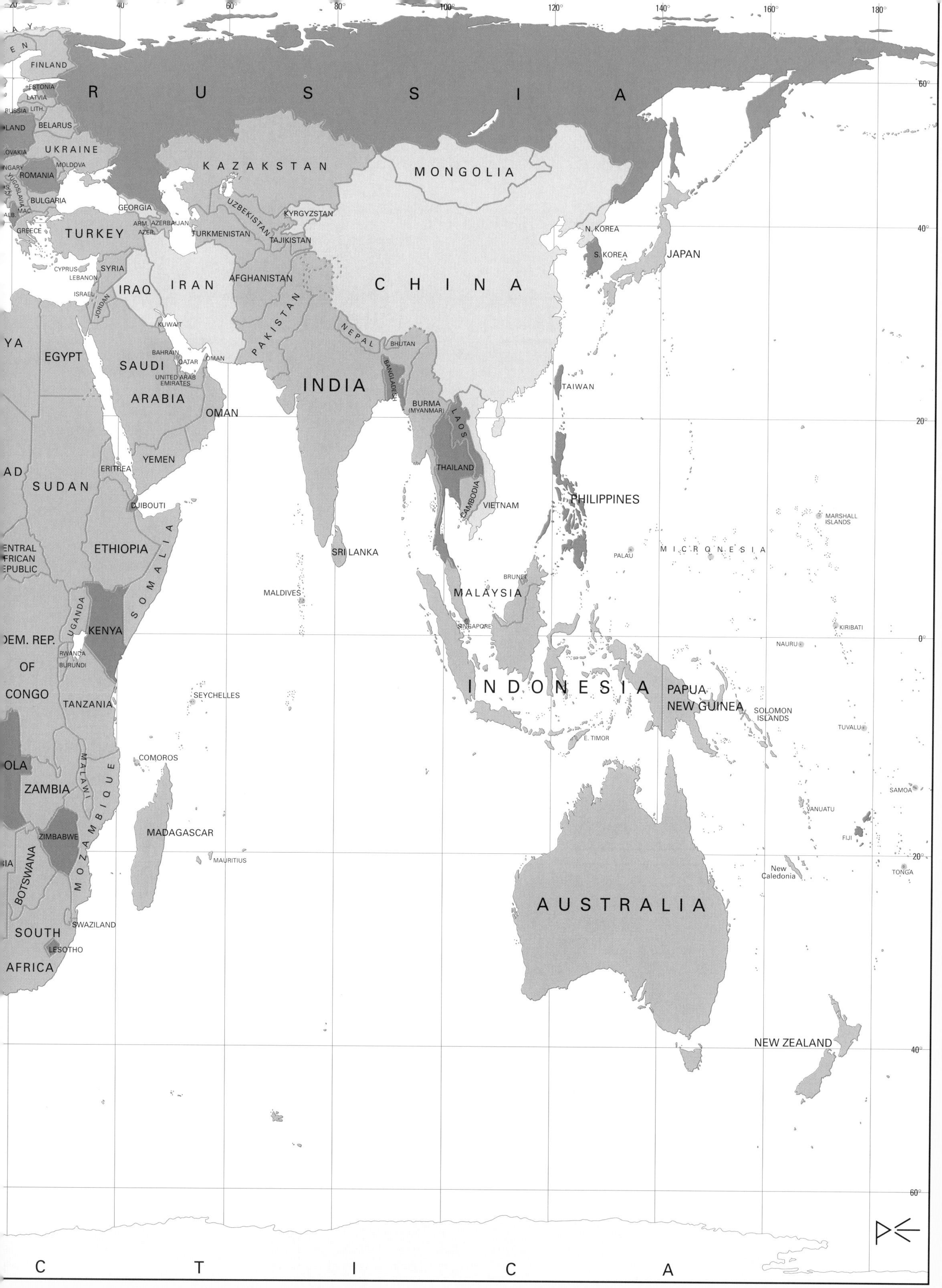

UTION

Because the worst exploitation is now in non-European countries the emphasis of prostitution has shifted there too. More and more men fly from Western Europe, Japan and North America to those countries in East Asia, Africa and Latin America in which bordello cities have developed (sex tourism). Apart from this more and more women, girls and children from Eastern Europe and the Third World are brought by organised trade to Western Europe, Japan and North America and are there forced into prostitution.

NUMBER OF CHILDREN

Each woman has an average of:

- Less than 2 children
- 2 to 3 children
- 3 to 4 children
- 4 to 5 children
- 5 to 6 children
- More than 6 children

HOUSEWORK

Each woman does on average:

- 60 to 70%
- 70 to 80%
- 80 to 90%
- More than 90%

of household work

PAID

- Less than 20%
- 20 to 30%
- 30 to 40%
- More than 40%

of the workforce are women

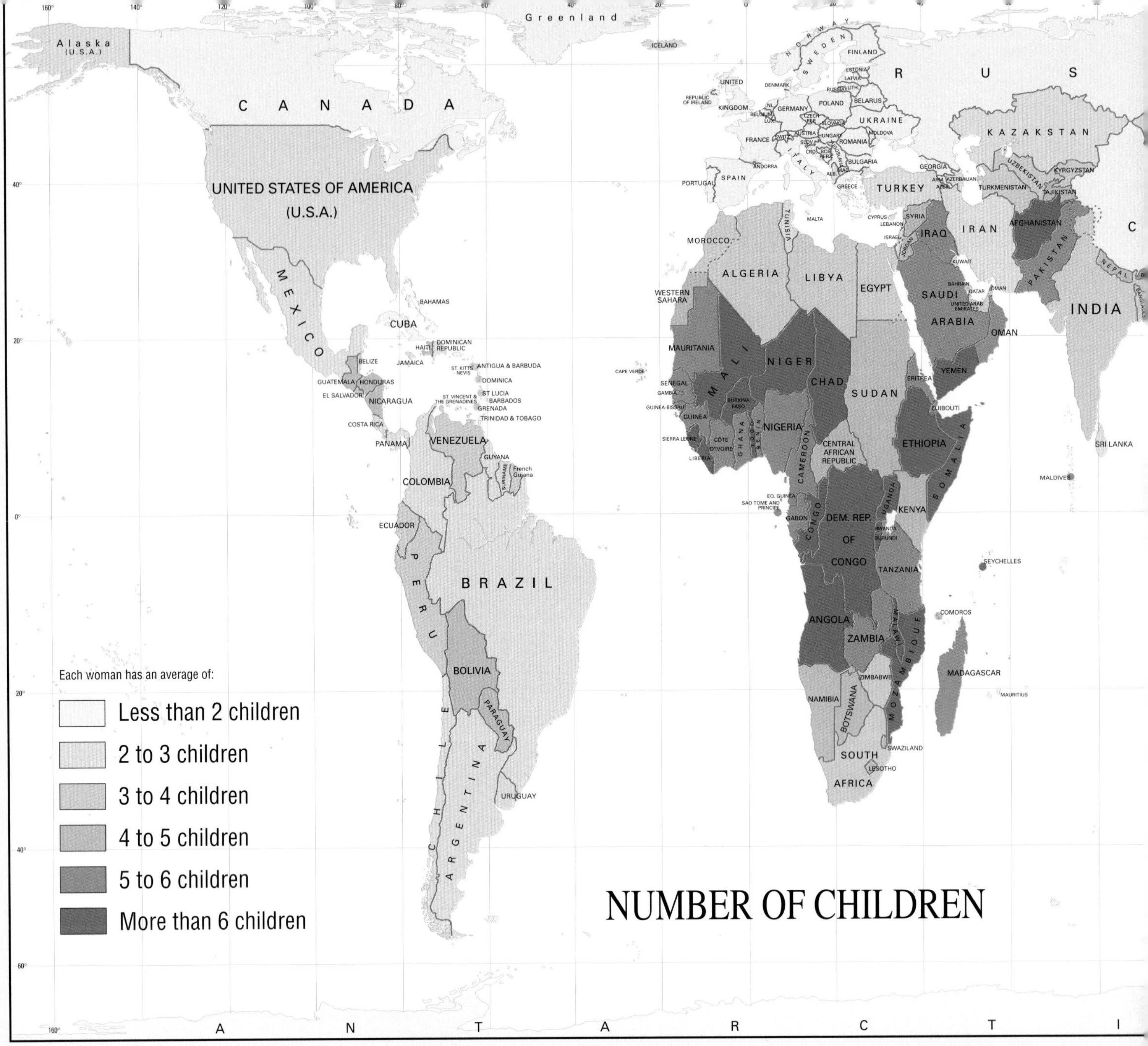

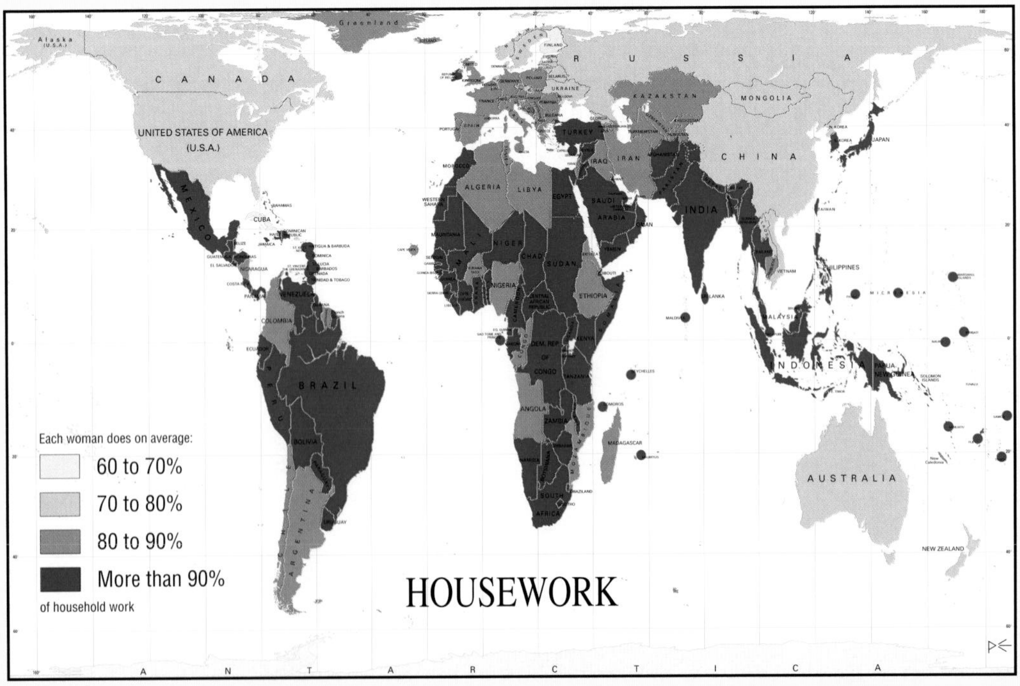

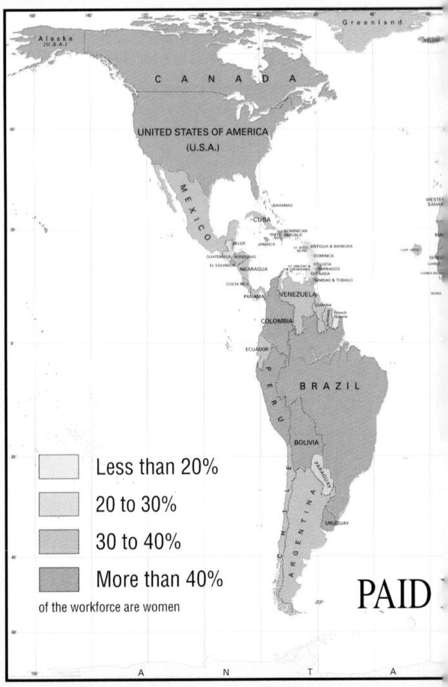

Half the world's people are women. They do two-thirds of the work, earn a tenth of the world's income and own a hundredth of the world's wealth. This statement by the United Nations in 1980 is still valid. The position of women in the rich industrial nations has somewhat improved in the meantime but not the position of four times as many women in the poor developing countries. Even in the socialist countries, equality of women is also not yet complete.

THE STATU

MONOGAMY/ POLYGAMY

Monogamy
legally prescribed

Polygamy
legally permitted

PARTICIPATION IN LEGISLATION

Less than 5%

5 to 10%

10 to 20%

20 to 30%

More than 30%

of Parliamentarians are women

HIGHER EDUCATION

Less than 20%

20 to 40%

40 to 60%

More than 60%

of enrolled students are women

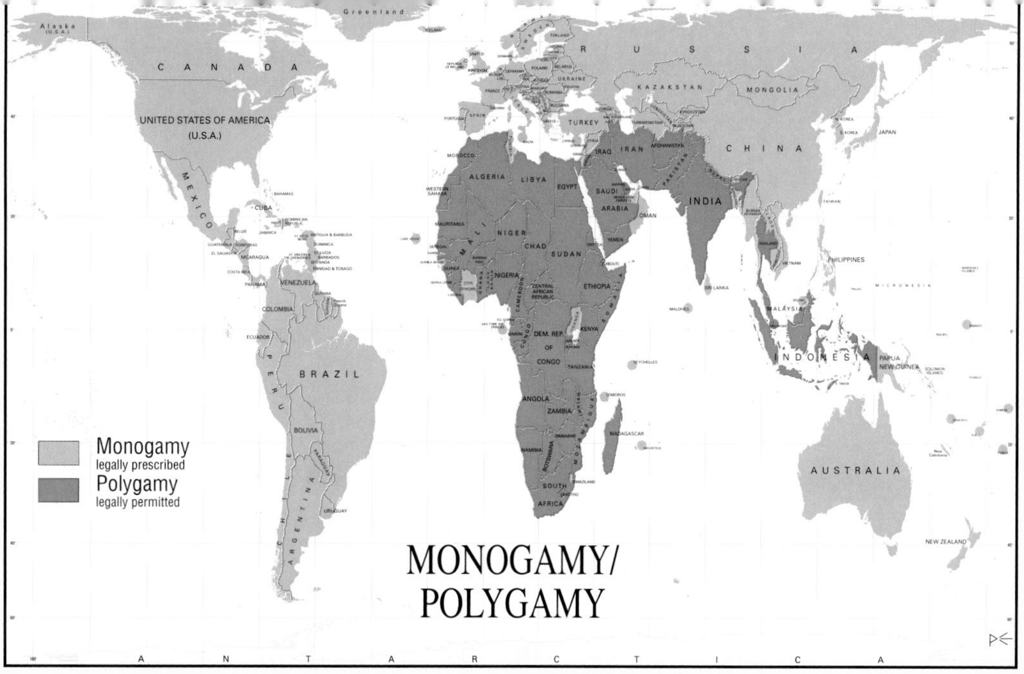

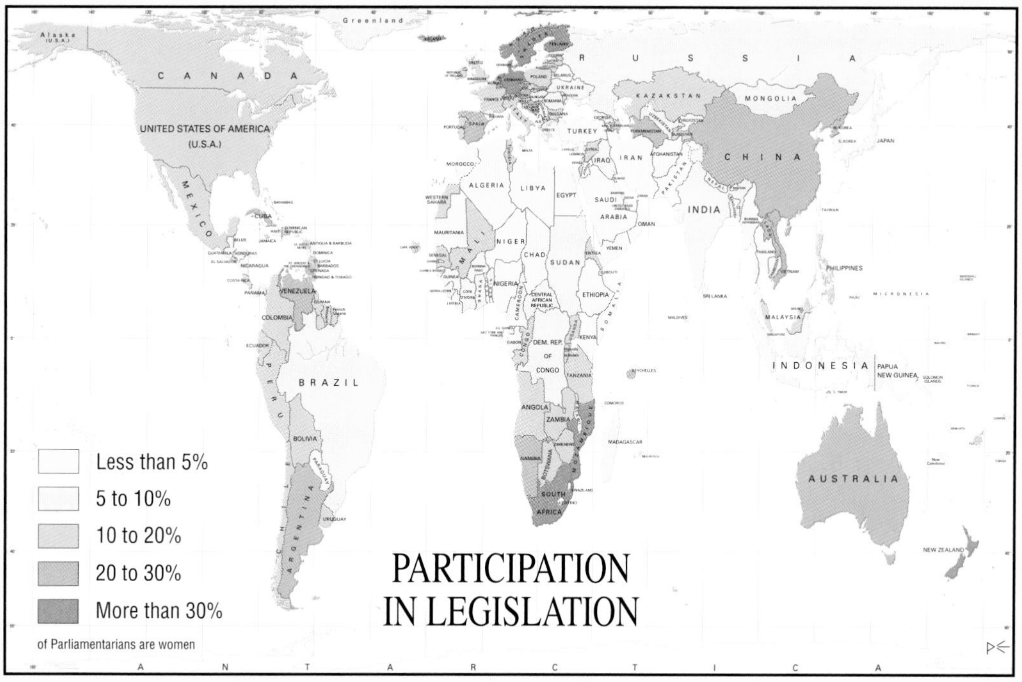

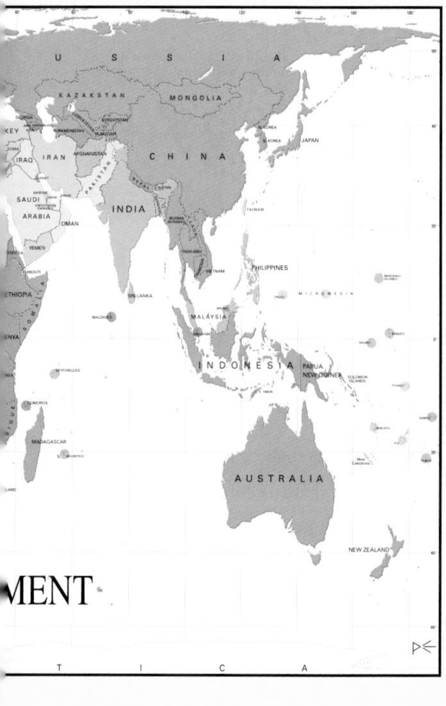

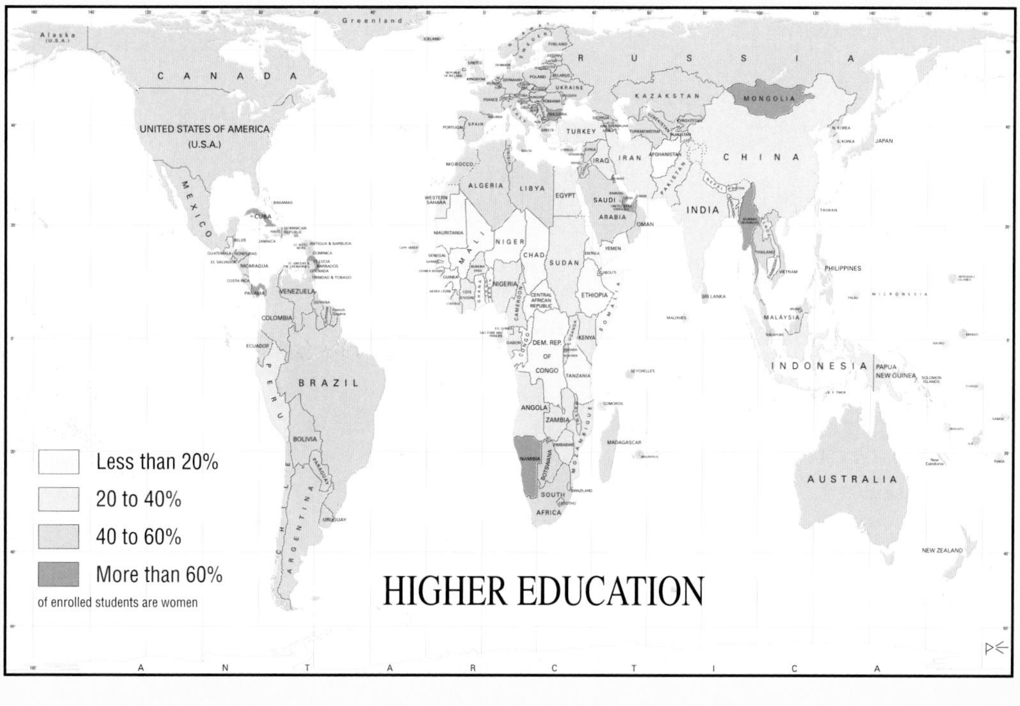

OF WOMEN

Besides bringing up children and doing the housework, more and more women are taking up employment. World-wide this threefold burden is the price of growing equality. Women seek paid employment in order to be liberated from the narrowness of domestic existence. Their hope that men will share domestic duties is only slowly being realised. And in only a few countries have women achieved full rights over their own bodies (the right to abortion) and equal participation in lawmaking.

ARMED FORCES

Less than 100,000
100,000 to 500,000
500,000 to 1 million
1 to 2.5 million
More than 2.5 million

TANKS

Less than 50
50 to 500
500 to 5,000
5,000 to 25,000
More than 25,000

NA

Less than 100
100 to 1,000
1,000 to 2,000
More than 2,000

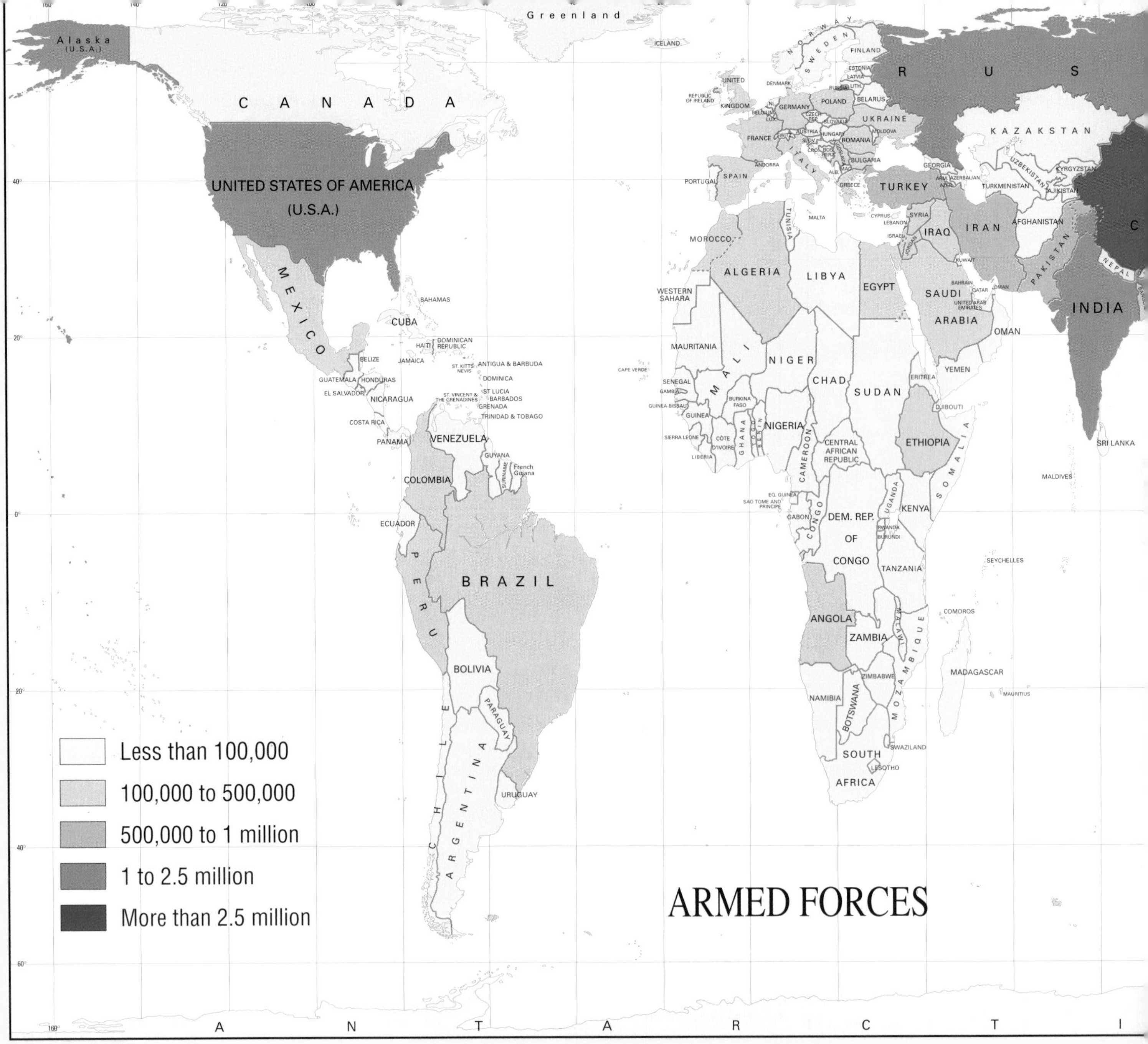

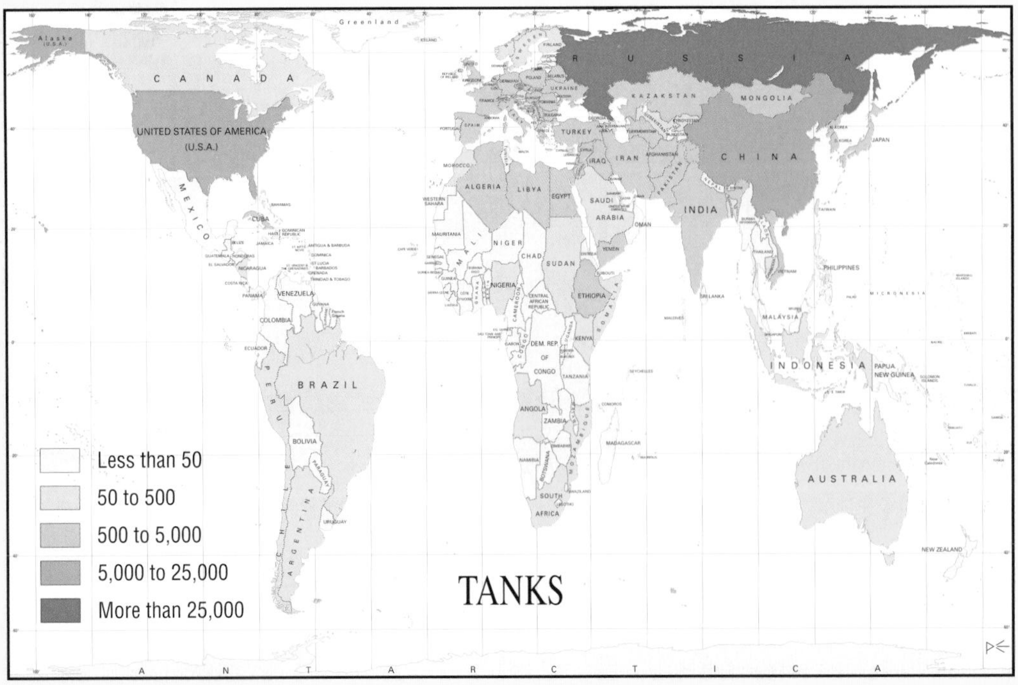

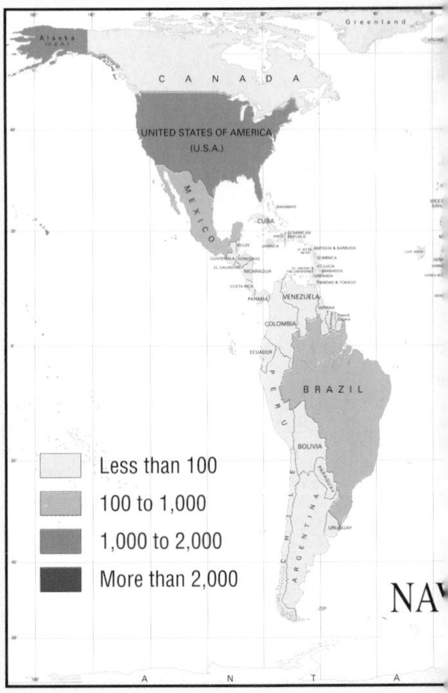

After the Second World War the Soviet Union deferred higher living standards to achieve military balance with the rich industrial nations so it could help the developing countries in their liberation struggles against their white colonial masters as well as giving military help to the spread of the socialist revolution.

RELATIVE MIL

FIGHTER PLANES

Less than 100
100 to 500
500 to 1,000
1,000 to 5,000
More than 5,000

NUCLEAR WEAPONS
(NUMBER OF ATOMIC WARHEADS)

Less than 100
100 to 1,000
More than 10,000

RESERVE FORCES
(AUXILIARIES OF ALL KINDS)

Less than 500,000
500,000 to 1 million
1 to 5 million
More than 5 million

ELS

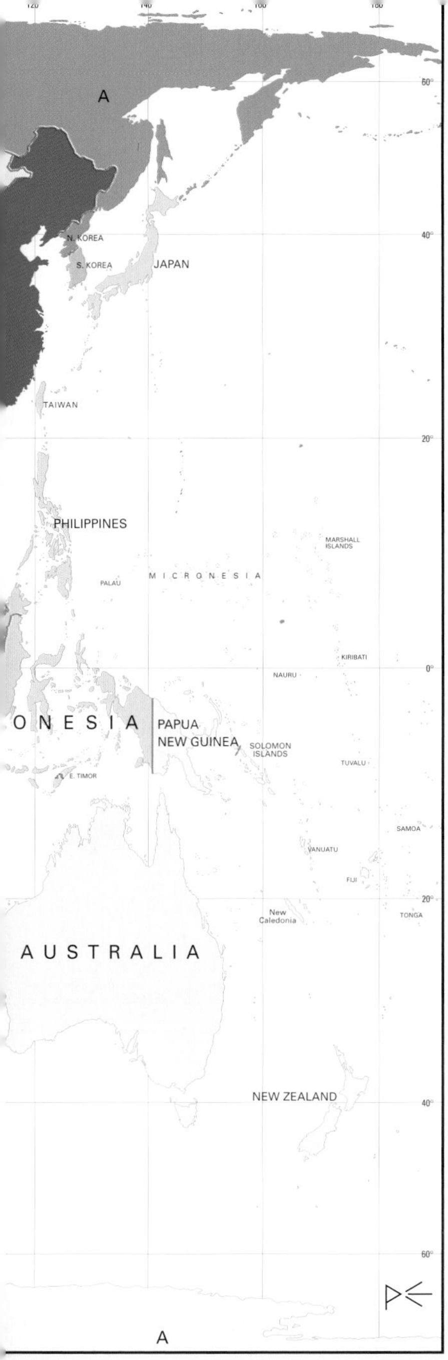

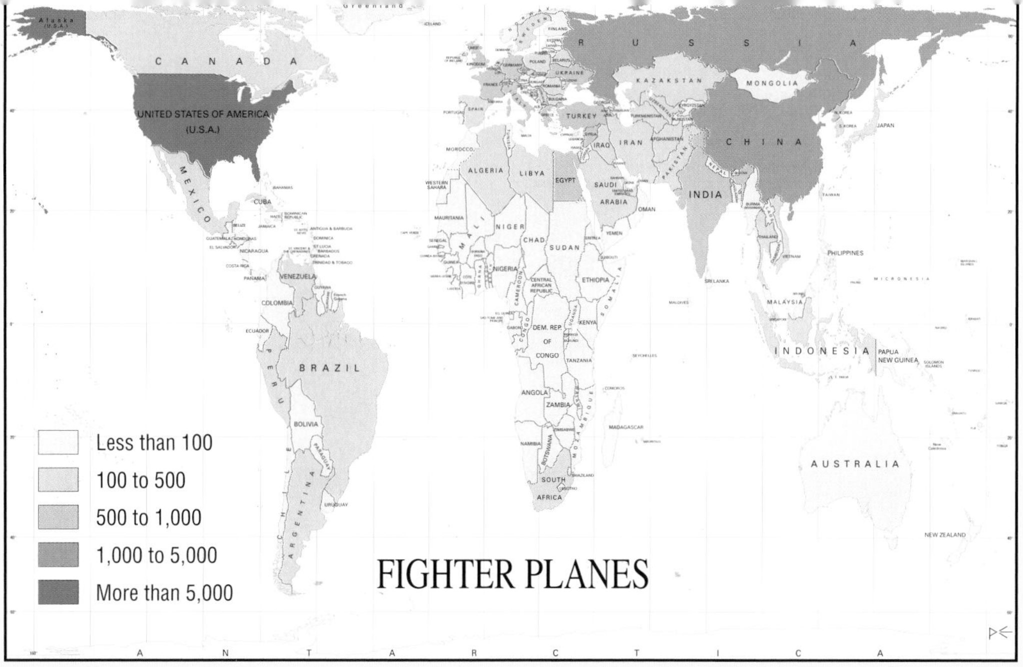

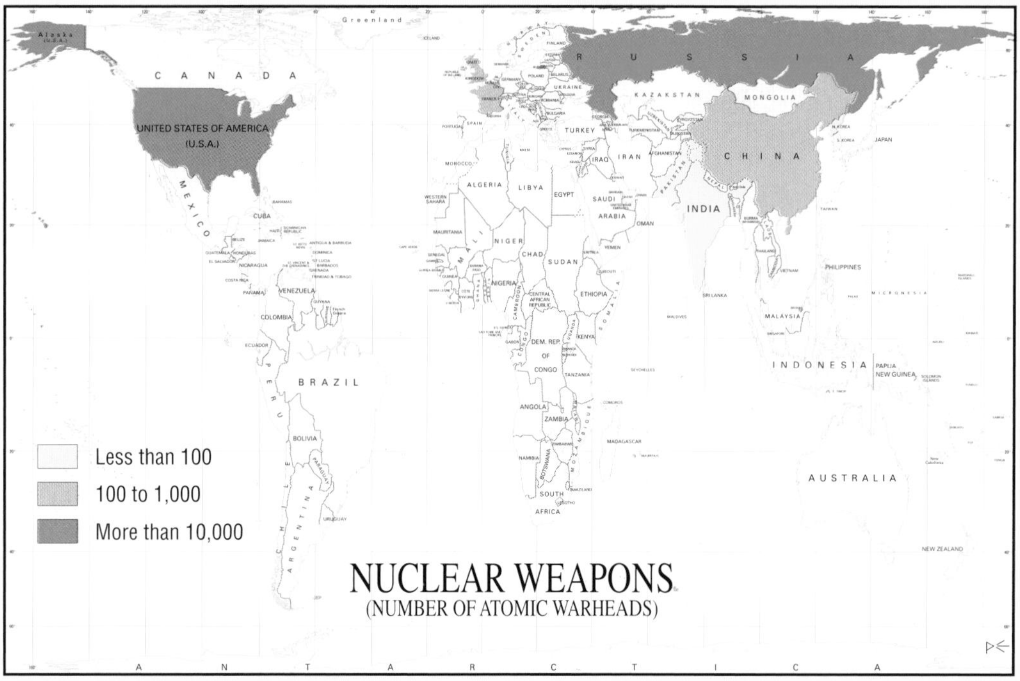

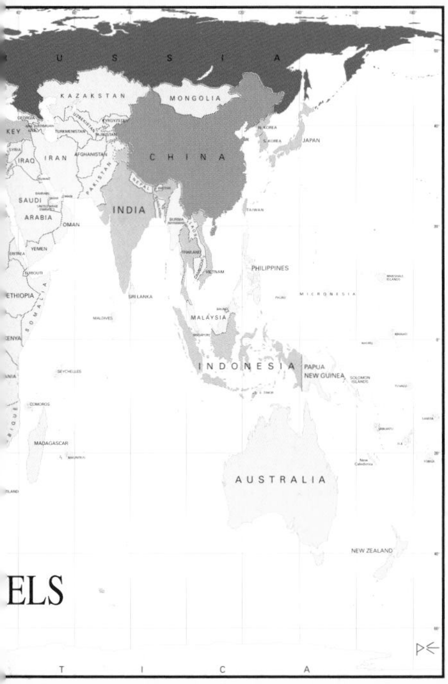

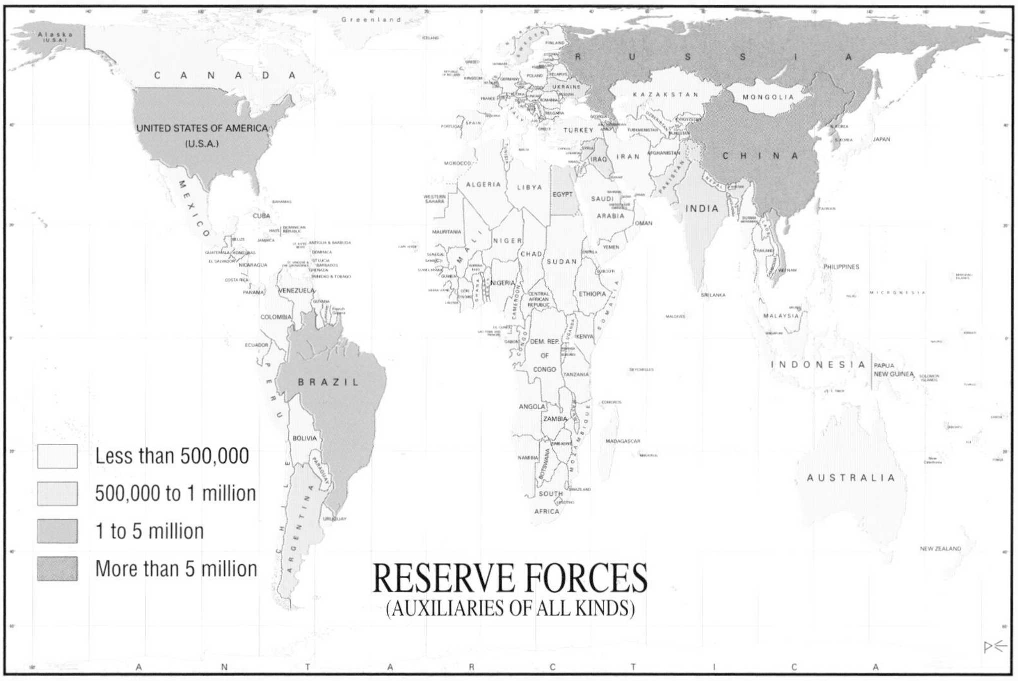

ARY STRENGTH

Since the disintegration of the Soviet Union the United States and
the rich industrial nations with just under 0.7 billion people confront
the socialist countries with 1.3 billion people and the developing
countries with 4 billion people. Thus the predominance of the rich
industrial nations rests on their technological/military superiority.

LAUNCHING SITES FOR SPACE FLIGHTS

X **First launching site**
Here space travel began on October 4 1957

X **Further launching sites**

Countries with manned spaceships

MANNED SPACE FLIGHTS

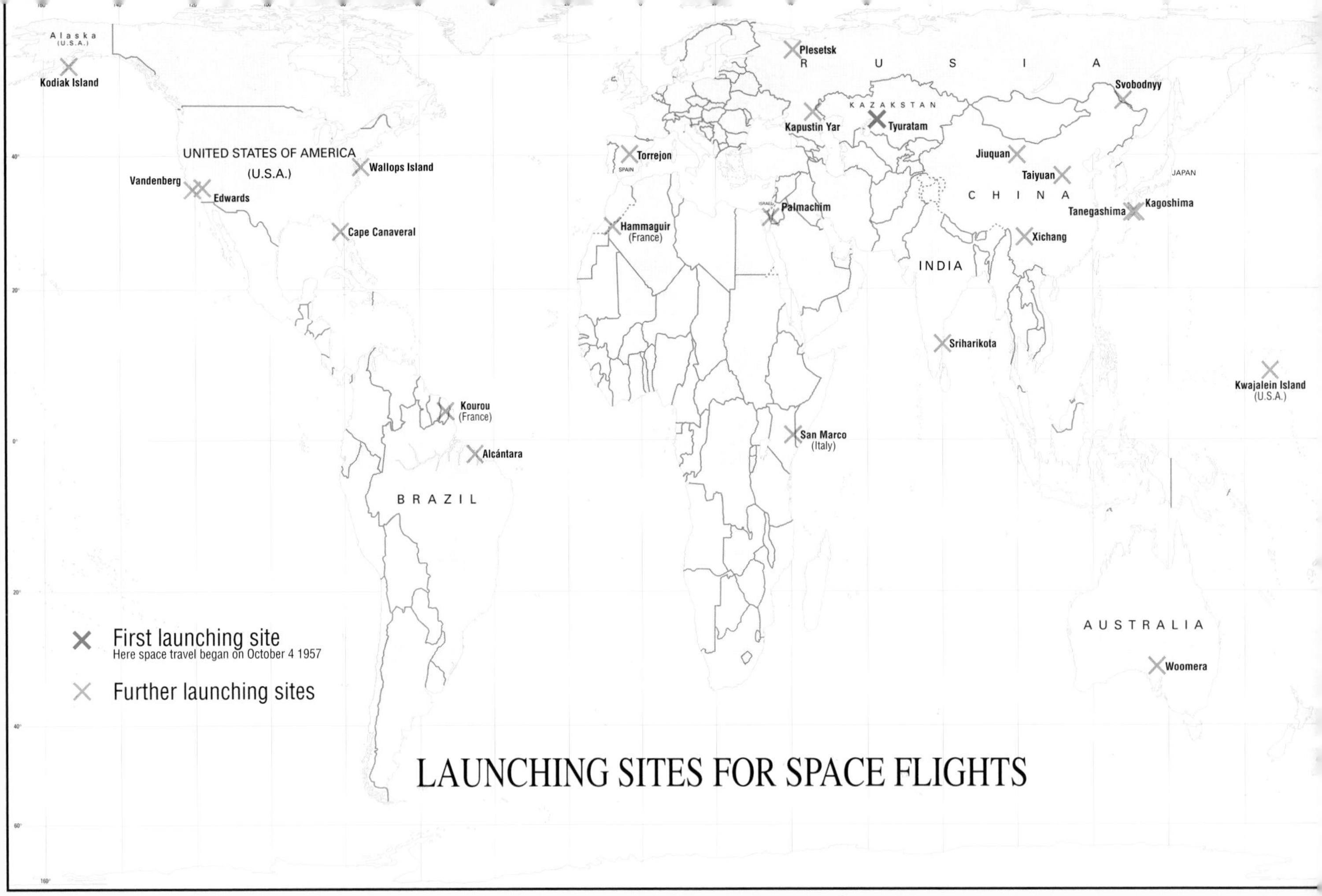

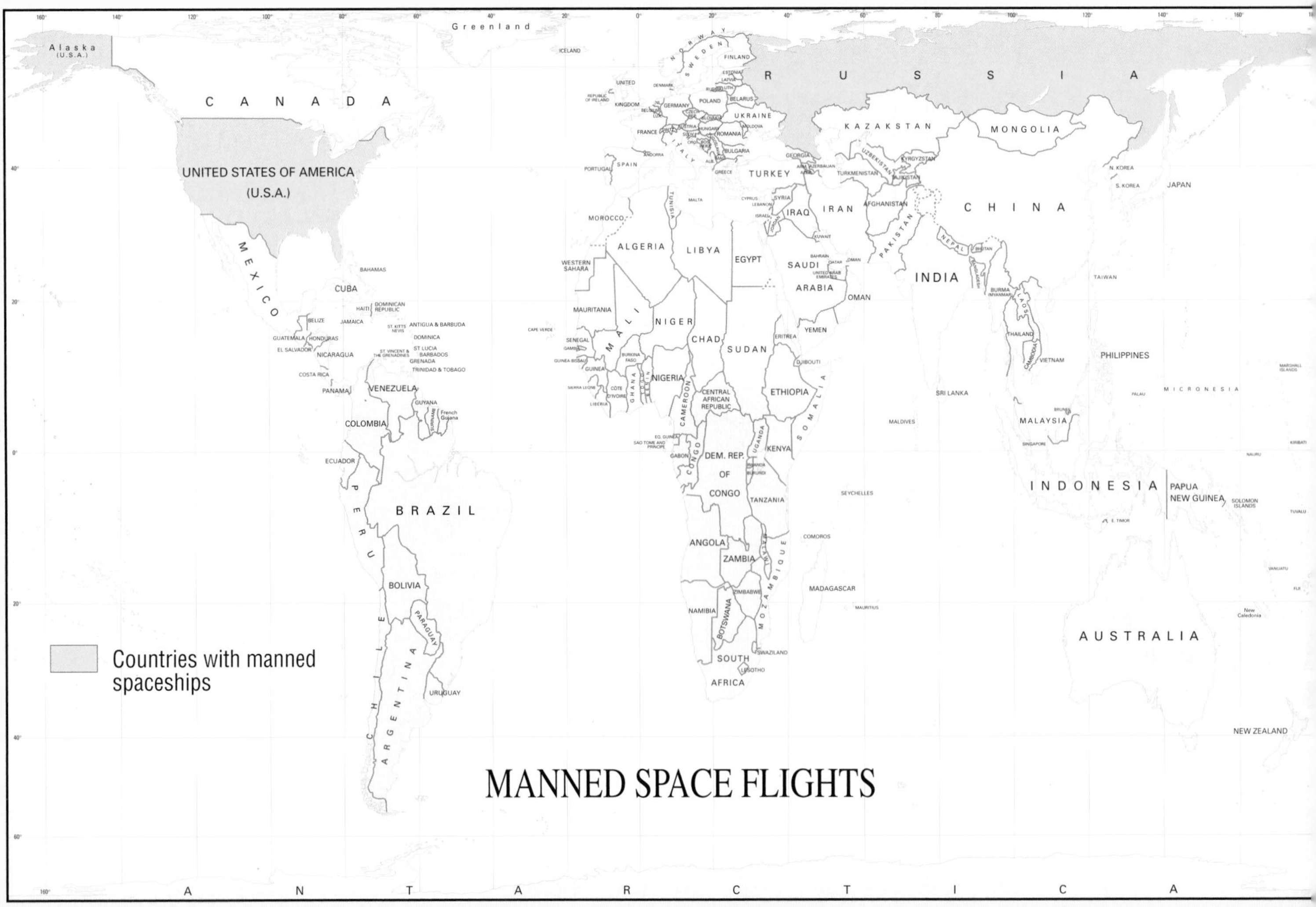

On 4 October 1957 the Soviet Union launched the first spacecraft (Sputnik). Four years later on 12 April 1961 the Russian, Yuri Gagarin, was the first person to fly into space. Thus began a new epoch in human history, opening unlimited new possibilities for mankind's urge to explore and act.

THE CONQU

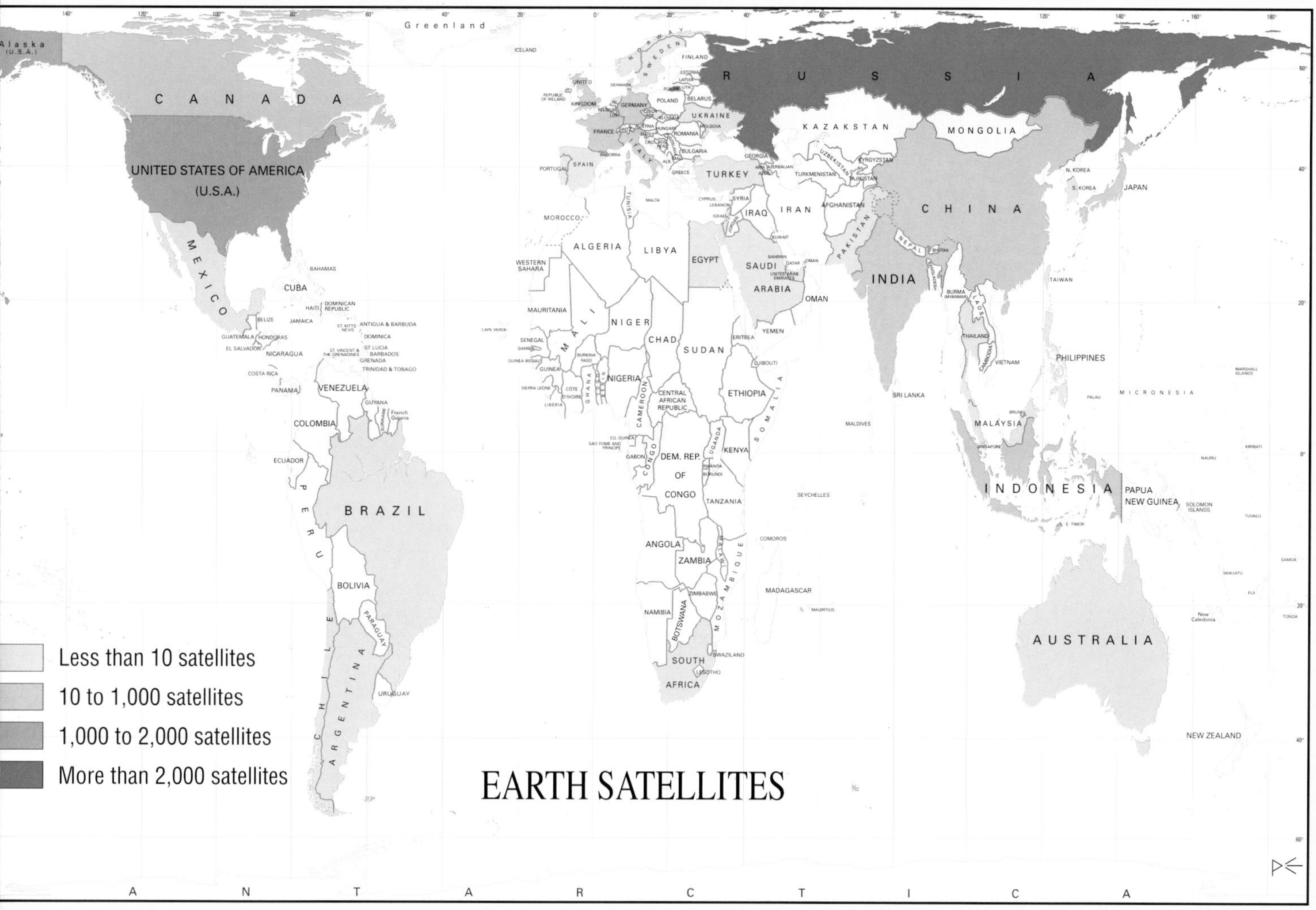

Earth Satellites

- Less than 10 satellites
- 10 to 1,000 satellites
- 1,000 to 2,000 satellites
- More than 2,000 satellites

EARTH SATELLITES

- Less than 50
- More than 50

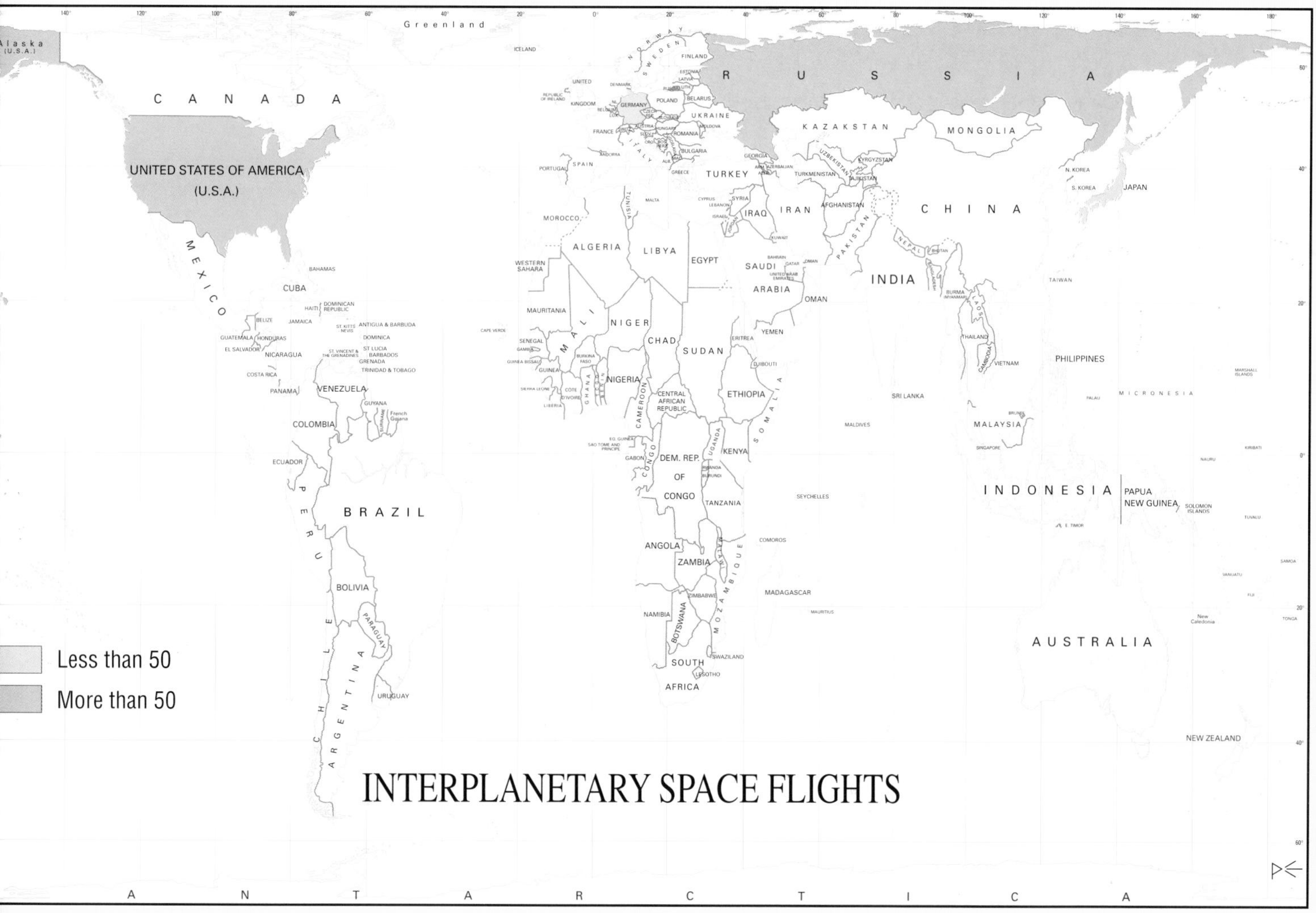

INTERPLANETARY SPACE FLIGHTS

ST OF SPACE

Since then hundreds of manned spacecraft and many thousands of probes and satellites have been sent into space from a good dozen launching sites. Men have landed on the moon and returned to earth (Armstrong and Aldrin). Pictures and data from Mars and other celestial bodies have been sent back to earth. Weather forecasting, navigation, telephone traffic, television and the internet have all been improved by satellites.

INDEX

Each name in the index is followed by a page number and a letter. On the page referred to, the letter can be found either at the top or at the bottom of the map frame. In the first case, the place is in the upper half of the map vertically below the letter; otherwise it is on the lower half of the map vertically above the letter. If a name extends over several letters, the given letter indicates its beginning.

Names such as countries or oceans which cover a large area on the map are listed with their page number only. However, if they extend over two pages, two page numbers are shown – the left-hand and right-hand page numbers being linked with a dash. Names of countries, oceans, rivers and mountains that extend over more than a double page are listed under each separate page. A dash between two nonconsecutive page numbers means that the place appears on all maps between and including those two pages.

The headwords are in alphabetical order. Names with prefixes like “Saint” or “Bad” can be looked up under the initial letter of the prefix. Place names appear on the maps in their widely-used Anglicised form, or in their local spelling or a standard transliteration of that local spelling. The index also includes local forms of names where the Anglicised form has been used on the map. In these cases the local name is followed by the Anglicised name in brackets. This indicates that the place name appears on the map, at the reference given, in the form shown in brackets, not in its local form.

Aachen **33** n
Aaro **25** v
Aargub **36** o
Aba (China) **62** h
Aba (Nigeria) **41** s
Aba (Dem. Rep. Congo) **42** w
Abadan **39** g
Abadeh **39** j
Abadla **36** k
Abaeté **29** g
Abaetetuba **26** l
Abag Qi **57** v
Abakan **56** i
Abakan (River) **56** h
Abakan Mountains **56** h
Abala **41** c
Abalessa **37** o
Aban **56** l
Abancay **24** z
Abarqu **39** k
Abay **55** j
Abay (River) **43** b
Abaya, Lake **43** e
Abbabis **48** h
Abbe, Lake **43** o
Abbeville **32** y
Abbotabad **60** m
Abbot Ice Shelf **80** m
Abd al Kuri **43** m
Abdulino **54** m
Abéché **42** c
Abengourou **40** x
Abeokuta **41** p
Aberdeen Lake **12** y
Aberdeen (South Africa) **49** n
Aberdeen (South Dakota) **15** h
Aberdeen (UK) **32** x
Aberdeen (Washington) **14** g
Aberfoyle **74** o
Aberystwyth **32** w
Abez' **50** l
Abha **39** p
Abidjan **40** x
Abilene **19** b
Abingdon Downs **73** l
Abitibi **16** i
Abitibi Lake **16** j
Abiyata, Lake **43** c
Abkit **53** k
Abminga **77** d
Abomey **41** o
Abong Mbang **41** w
Abou Deïa **42** b
Abqaiq **39** h
Abra Pampa **28** f
Abrolhos Archipelago dos **29** m
Abu al Abyad **39** x
Abu Dara, Ras **38** z
Abu Dhabi **39** x
Abu Habi **42** k
Abu Hadriyah **39** h
Abu Hamed **38** w
Abuja **41** f
Abu Kamal **39** b
Abu Madd, Ras **38** z
Abumonbazi **42** r
Abun **25** r
Abun (River) **25** q
Abune Yosef **43** c
Abu Shagara, Ras **38** z
Abu Simbel **38** v
Abu Tig **38** i
Abuye Meda **43** d
Abuyog **67** j
Abu Zabad **42** i
Acailandia **27** n
Acámbaro **19** n
Acampamento **26** i
Acampamento de Indios **25** w
Acaponeta **18** x
Acapulco **19** n
Acarai, Serra **25** l
Acaraú **27** f
Acarigua **23** d
Acatlán **19** p
Acayucan **19** r
Accra **40** z
Achacachi **25** p
Achénoumma **37** v
Achinsk **56** i
Achsu **54** w
Acklins **21** q
Acomayo **25** n
Aconcagua **28** p
Aconguija, Nev. de **28** s
Acre **25** p
Açu **27** u
Açu (River) **27** u
Acude Araras **27** s
Acude Orós **27** t
Ada **15** v
Adafer **36** s
Adak **10** v
Adale **43** v
Adam **60** o
Adam's Br. **64** u
Adamaoua, Highlands **41** u
Adan **66** c
Adana **35** z
Adanac **15** b
Adapazari **35** j
Adarama **38** x
Adare, Cape **86** s
Adavale **74** o
Ad Da'ain **42** g
Ad Darb **39** p
Ad Dawadimi **39** r
Ad Dibdibah **39** f
Addis Ababa **43** c
Addis Zemen **43** b
Ad Diwaniyah **39** e
Ad Dueim **42** k
Ad Duwaid **39** c
Adelaide **77** g
Adelaide Island **82** u
Adelaide Peninsula **12** m
Adelaide River **73** c
Adélieland **87** o
Aden **43** h
Aden, Gulf of **43** h
Aderbissinat **41** g
Adi Arkay **43** b
Adigrat **43** d
Adi Keyih **43** d
Adilabad **61** q
Adi Quala **43** c
Adirondack Mountains **16** z
Admiralty Inlet **13** d
Admiralty Islands **71** n
Ado **41** q
Adoni **64** f
Adour **34** f
Adrar **36** l
Adrar of the Iforas **36** z
Adré **42** d
Adriatic Sea **35** a
Adwa **43** c
Adycha **53** c
Adygalakh **53** f
Adzhima **59** b
Adzva **50** k
Aegean Sea **35** t
Affolé, Montagnes de l' **40** g
Afghanistan **55/60**
Afgoi **43** t
Afif **39** p
Afikpo **41** s
Aflou **34** t
Afmadu **43** s
Aftout **36** w
Afuá **26** l
Afyon **35** w
Agadem **41** j
Agadèz **37** r
Agadir **36** f
Agadyr' **55** k
Agailas **36** p
Agamor **41** a
Agan **51** q
Agapa **51** i
Agaro **43** a
Agartalā **61** z
Agassiz, Cape **82** w
Agassiz Ice Cap **13** h
Agata **51** j
Agboville **40** x
Agdam **54** v
Agdz **36** h
Agen **34** f
Agnew **76** g
Agnibilekrou **40** x
Agoare **41** c
Agra **61** c
Ağri **54** t
Agrigento **37** h
Agrínion **35** r
Agryz **54** m
Aguadas **22** z
Agua de Chale **18** e
Aguapei, Serra **25** w
Agua Prieta **18** i
Aguarico **22** y
Aguas Belas **27** u
Aguascalientes **18** z
Aguas Calientes, Sierra de **28** r
Aguaytía **24** x
Aguaytia (River) **24** x
Aguelock **36** z
Aguelt el Melah **36** s
Agueraktem **36** u
Aguilas **36** l
Agulhas **48** x
Agulhas, Cape **48** x
Aha, Mount **48** l
Ahaggar **37** p
Ahar **54** v
Ahmadi **39** g
Ahmadnagar **61** n
Ahmar Mountains **43** e
Ahmedabad **60** y
Ahnet **37** n
Ahome **18** h
Ahoskie **16** y
Ahuachapan **22** c
Ahwar **43** i
Ahwaz **39** g
Aibak **60** i
Aileron **73** r
Ailigandi **22** k
Aim **53** o
Aim (River) **53** n
Aimorés **29** k
Aïn Beïda **34** x
Ain Benimathar **36** k
Aïn ben Tili **36** s
Ain Oussera **34** u
Ain Sefra **34** s
Ain Sukhna **38** i
Aioun Abd el Malek **36** u
Aiquile **28** f
Aïr **37** r
Airo **25** h
Airy, Mount **16** w
Aitape **70** y
Aiwasedapur **51** r
Aix-en-Provence **34** j
Āizawl **62** o
Ajaccio **34** k
Ajaguz **56** c
Ajaguz (River) **56** b
Ajdabiyah **38** a
Ajmer **61** a
Ajni **55** u
Ajryk **55** m
Akabli **37** n
Akchar **36** o
Ak-Dovurak **56** i
Akelamo **69** m
Akespe **55** c
Aketi **42** r
Akhisar **35** v
Akhmîn **38** i
Akhtyrka **35** l
Akimiki Island **16** i
Akita **59** o
Akjoujt Faye **36** p
Akkabak **55** d
Akkani **10** k
Akkarga **55** d
Aklavik **11** k
Aknoul **34** q
Akobo **42** l
Akola **61** o
Akordat **43** b
Akoupé **40** x
Akpatok Island **13** x
Akqi **56** o
Akranes **32** b
Akreïjit **36** s
Akrerèb **41** g
Akritas, Cape **35** r
Aksakovo **54** m
Aksaray **35** y
Aksay **54** m
Akşehir **35** w
Aksu **55** j
Aksuat **55** f
Aksum **43** c
Aksumbe **55** u
Aktag **56** r
Aktau (Kazakstan) **54** y
Aktau (Kazakstan) **55** k
Aktaz **56** s
Aktogaj (Kyrgyzstan) **56** n
Aktogaj (Kazakstan) **56** c
Aktyubinsk **55** a
Akulivik **13** s
Akure **41** q
Akureyri **32** c
Akwanga **41** f
Alabama (River) **19** j
Alabama (State) **19** k
Al Abyar **35** r
Alachakh **53** p
Al Adam **35** s
Alagoinhas **27** u
Al Ain **39** y
Alajuela **22** g
Alakanuk **10** m
Alakol', Lake **56** d
Al Alamein **38** g
Al Amarah **39** g
Alamogordo **18** k
Alamos **18** i
Aland Islands **33** h
Alanya **35** x
Al Aqaylah **37** m
Al Artawiyah **39** e
Alaşehir **35** v
Alashan Desert **57** p
Al Ashkhirah **60** q
Alaska **11**
Alaska, Gulf of **11**
Alaska Peninsula **11** o
Alaska Range **11** e
Al Aswaa, Ras **39** n
Alat **55** r
Ala Tau **55** z
Alatyr **54** i
Alausí **22** x
Al Awaynat **37** t
Al Aziziyah (Iraq) **39** e
Al Aziziyah (Libya) **34** z
Albacete **34** r
Al Bad **38** k
al Baida **43** h
Al Balyana **38** i
Albanel Lake **17** a
Albania **35** d
Albany (Australia) **76** e
Albany (Georgia) **20** j
Albany (New York) **16** z
Albany (Oregon) **14** g
Albany (River) **16** h
Albany Downs **74** q
Al Bardi **35** t
Al Batinah **39** z
Al Bayda **35** r
Alberga **77** d
Alberta **14** l
Albert, Lake **42** w
Albert Lea **16** o
Albert Nile **42** x
Alberton **17** e
Al Bir **38** l
Ålborg **33** p
Albuquerque **15** p
Albury **78** o
Al Busaiyah **39** e
Alcantara **27** b
Alcova **15** p
Alcudia **34** u
Aldabra Island **47** d
Aldama **18** k
Aldan **52** x
Aldan (River) **53** a
Aldar **56** l
Aleg **40** d
Alej **56** d
Alejandro Sekirk **30** c
Alejsk **56** d
Aleksandrovskoye **51** q
Aleksandrovsko-Sakhalinskiy **53** r
Alekseyevka (Kazakstan) **55** j
Alekseyevka (Ukraine) **54** d
Alekseyevo **53** h
Além Paraiba **29** j
Alençon **34** f
Alenquer **26** h
Aleppo **54** q
Alert **91** g
Alert, Cape **89** t
Alerta **25** n
Alessandria **34** k
Ålesund **33** a
Aleutian Islands **10** u
Alevina, Cape **53** v
Alexander Archipelago **11** x
Alexander Bay **48** u
Alexander Island **82** w
Alexandra **79** r
Alexandra, Lake **77** t
Alexandra, Land **50** f
Alexandria (Australia) **73** s
Alexandria (Egypt) **38** g
Alexandria (Louisiana) **19** g
Alexandria (Minnesota) **15** j
Alexandria (Virginia) **16** y
Al Faiyûm **38** h
Al Farcia **36** f
Al Faw **39** g
al Fûla **42** i
Alga **55** a
Algarroho del Aguila **30** j
Algarve **34** n
Algatart **55** w
Al Gaydah **43** m
Algeciras **34** p
Alger (Algiers) **34** u
Algeria **34/36-37**
Al Ghaydah **39** w
Algiers **34** u
al Hadd, Ras **60** q
Al Hadithah (Iraq) **39** c
Al Hadithah (Saudi Arabia) **38** m
Al Hajar al Gharbi **39** z
Al Hajar ash Sharqi **60** p
Al Hammâm **38** h
Al Hanakiyah **39** o
Al Hasakah **54** r
Al Hazm **39** r
Al Hijaz **38** m
Al Hillah **39** s
Al Hoceima **34** q
Aliabad **39** l
Aliança **25** f
Ali-Bagata **53** a
Alicante **34** s
Alice Springs **73** r
Aligarh **61** c
Alijos, Rocas **18** d
Alindao **42** q
Alipxa **51** u
Ali-Sabieh **43** e
Al Isawiyah **38** m
Aliwal North **49** o
al Jabal al Akhdar **35** r
Al Jaghbub **38** d
Al Jalamid **39** b
Al Jawf (Libya) **38** p
Al Jawf (Saudi Arabia) **39** a
Al Jubayl **39** h
al Junayna **42** e
Aljustrel **36** g
Al Kamil **60** p
Al Karak **38** l
Al Khaburah **60** o
Al Khamasin **39** q
Al Khandaq **38** u
Al Khârga **38** u
Al Kharja Oasis **38** u
Al Khartum **42** k
Al Khaznah **39** y
Al Kut **39** f
al Kú, Wadi **42** g
Allahabad **61** r
Allakh-Yun' **53** c
Allegheny **16** w

Allegheny Mountains 16 w
Allende 19 a
Allentown 16 y
Alleppey 64 e
Alliance 15 r
Allier 34 h
Al Lith 39 n
Alma 17 a
Almaden 74 b
al Mado 43 j
al Mahdad 43 g
Al Maiyah 39 d
Al Majm'ah 39 e
Al Mansura 38 i
Al Marj 35 r
Almaty 55 z
Almaznyy 52 f
Almeirim 26 j
Al Mekhily 38 c
Almenara 29 k
Almería 34 r
Al'metyevsk 54 m
al Milk 38 u
Al Minyâ 38 h
Almirante 22 h
Almora 61 d
Al Mudauwara 38 l
Al Mughairah 38 m
Al Muglad 42 i
al Mukalla 43 k
al Mukha 43 f
Alor 69 w
Alor Setar 65 w
Alota 28 e
Alotau 74 f
al Ouaday 42 a
Alpena 16 h
Alpercatas, Serra das 27 p
Alpha 74 q
Alpine 18 l
Alps 34 j
Al Qahirah 38 i
Al Qaisumah 39 e
Al Qalibah 38 m
Al Qariyat 37 i
Al Qunfudhah 39 o
Al Qurain 39 q
Al Qurnah 39 f
Alroy Downs 73 t
Alta 33 i
Alta Gracia 28 t
Altah 56 h
Altai (Mountains) 56 e
Altaj 56 l
Altaj (High Altai) 56 y
Altamaha 20 l
Altamira (Brazil) 26 j
Altamira (Mexico) 20 t
Altamonte Springs 20 l
Altar Desert 18 f
Altares 18 m
Altat 51 w
Altay 56 h
Altejskij 56 f
Altiplano 28 d
Alto do Araguaia 29 a
Alto Hama 44 t
Alto Molócuè 49 k
Alton 16 q
Alton Downs 77 f
Altoona 16 x
Alto Paraiso de Goiás 29 f
Alto Parnaíba 27 n
Alto Purús 25 n
Altun Shan 56 u
Alturas 14 v
Altus 19 b
Alu 71 u
Al Udailiyah 39 t
al Udaiya 42 i
Al Ulaya 39 o
Al Uruq al Mutaridah 39 x
Alva 15 u
Alvarado 19 r
Alvares 25 e
Alvorada 26 y
Al Wafra 39 g
Al Wajh 38 l
Alwar 61 b
Alxa Zuoqi 57 q
Alyaskitovyy 53 d
Alygdzer 56 m
Amadeus, Lake 73 p
Amadjuak Lake 13 j
Amakinskiy 52 f
Amapá 26 k
Amara 43 b
Amarante 27 q
Amarillo 15 s
Amasin 36 p
Amata 77 a
Amatenango 19 t
Amazar 52 v
Amazon 25-26
Amazon (Solimões) 25 b
Ambala 61 b
Ambalavao 47 q
Ambam 41 v
Ambar 51 i
Ambarchik 10 a
Ambardakh 53 c
Ambato 22 z
Ambikapur 61 t
Ambilobe 47 e
Ambo 24 x
Ambohitralanana 47 g
Ambon 69 z
Ambositra 47 q
Ambovombe 47 q
Ambriz 44 e
Amchitka 10 u
Amderma 50 l
Amdo 61 l
Ameca 18 y
Americana 29 f
American Highlands 84 z
American Samoa 230 n
Amery Basin 85 p
Amery Ice Shelf 84 n
Ames 16 o
Amga 53 a
Amga (River) 53 a
Amguid 37 p
Amherst 17 f
Amiens 34 h
Amindivi Islands 64 b
Amistad Reservoir 19 a
Amizmiz 36 g
Amka 53 q
Amman 38 l
Ammassalik 90 y
Amo 52 b
Amol 54 y
Amolar 28 l
Amourj 40 h
Amoy 63 s
Ampanihy 47 o
Ampato 25 n
Amravati 61 p
Am Raya 41 m
Amritsar 61 a
Amsel 37 p
Amsterdam 33 n
Amsterdam Island 231 r
Amudarja 55 q
Amudat 42 z
Amund Ringnes Island 12 m
Amundsen Bay 84 m
Amundsen Gulf 12 d
Amundsen Scott 83 z
Amundsen Sea 81 n
Amur (River) 58 k
Amur (Sudan) 38 x
Amursk 58 m
Amysakh 52 h
Anabar 52 f
Anaco 23 h
Anaconda 14 m
Anadyr' 10 g
Anadyr, Gulf of 10 h
Anadyr Mountains 10 f
Anadyr' (River) 10 f
Anah 39 c
Anaheim 18 c
Anai 37 t
Anai Mudi 64 f
Anajás 26 l
Anaka 42 y
Anaktuvuk Pass 11 e
Anama 25 i
Anama, Lake 51 k
Anambas Islands 68 i
Anamur 35 x
Anamur, Cape 35 x
Ananjevo 55 z
Anantapur 64 f
Anantnag 61 a
Anápolis 29 e
Anar 39 l
Anarak 39 k
Anatolia 54 p
Añatuya 28 v
Anauá 26 d
Ancha 53 d
Anchorage 11 e
Ancohuma 25 p
Ancona 35 a
Ancud 30 g
Anda 58 f
Andahuaylas 24 z
Andalgalá 28 s
Åndalsnes 33 b
Andalusia 19 k
Andaman Sea 65 f
Andaman Islands 65 d
Andapa 47 f
Anderson (Canada) 89 b
Anderson (Indiana) 16 t
Anderson (South Carolina) 20 l
Andes 22-25/28/30
Andirlangar 56 r
Andižan 55 w
Andkhoy 55 s
Andoas 24 k
Andong 58 v
Andoom 73 j
Andorra 34 g
Andöya 33 f
Andradina 29 c
Andranovory 47 o
Andreanof Islands 10 v
Andreas, Cape 35 y
Andrées Land 91 r
Andreyevka 54 k
Andreyevskiy 52 t
Andriamena 47 q
Andros 35 t
Andros Island 21 n
Andulo 44 u
Andyngda 52 g
Anéfis 36 z
Aney 37 v
Angara 51 x
Angarsk 57 c
Angas Downs 73 q
Angel de la Guarda 18 f
Angeleri 42 w
Angeles 67 f
Angel Falls 23 v
Ångerman 33 g
Angers 34 f
Angkor 66 g
Anglesey 32 w
Ango 42 t
Angoche 46 l
Angola 44
Angostura Reservoir 19 t
Angoulême 34 g
Angra Dos Reis 29 i
Angren 55 v
Angu 42 s
Anguilla 21 y
Angurugu 73 f
Angwa 45 r
Anhua 63 a
Aniak 11 b
Anjouan 47 b
Anju 58 t
Anka 41 e
Ankacho 52 d
Ankang 62 m
Ankara 35 y
Ankazoabo 47 o
Ankazobe 47 q
Anking 63 e
Anlong 62 x
Annaba 34 x
An'Nahûd 42 i
Anna Plains 72 w
Annapolis 16 y
Annapurna 61 g
Ann Arbor 16 u
An Nashash 39 y
An Nasiriyah 39 e
Annecy 34 j
An Nimas 39 p
Anning 62 u
Annitowa 73 t
An Nukhaib 39 b
Anou Mellene 36 z
Ansab 39 d
Anschan 58 e
Anschluss 48 h
Anse d'Hainault 21 q
Anshun 62 x
Anson Bay 73 b
Ansongo 41 a
Antakya 35 z
Antalaha 47 f
Antalya 35 w
Antalya, Gulf of 38 h
Antananarivo 47 q
Antanimora 47 p
Antarctica 84
Antarctic Peninsula 82 u
Antelope Mine 49 d
Antequera 34 p
Anthonys Lagoon 73 s
Anti Atlas 36 g
Anticosti Island 17 f
Antigua and Barbuda 21 z
Antipayuta 51 d
Antipinskiy 52 m
Antipodes Islands 223 z
Antofagasta 28 b
Antofagasta de la Sierra 28 r
Antofalla 28 q
Antong (Dandong) 58 r
Antonovo 54 l
Antsalova 47 o
Antsirabe 47 q
Antsiranana 47 f
Antsohihy 47 d
An Tuc 66 k
Antuerpia 25 t
Antwerp 33 n
Antwerpen (Antwerp) 33 n
Anuradhapura 64 u
Anvers Island 82 s
Anxi 56 y
Anxious Bay 77 c
Anyang 63 d
Anzhero-Sudzhensk 56 f
Aomori 59 c
Aoraki (Mt. Cook) 79 r
Aosta 34 k
Aouderas 37 r
Aouk 42 c
Aoukr 40 g
Aoukarr 36 w
Aouker 36 s
Aoulef el Arab 36 m
Aozi 37 y
Apalachee Bay 20 j
Apan 19 p
Apaporis 25 a
Aparri 67 g
Apatou 26 i
Apatzingán 18 z
Apennines 34 m
Apere 25 r
Api 42 t
Api (River) 42 t
Apiacás, Serra dos 25 x
Apaiú, Serrado 23 v
Apizaco 19 p
Aplao 24 z
Apo 69 k
Apodi 27 u
Apoera 26 g
Apollo Bay 77 w
Apolo 25 p
Aporema 26 l
Apostle Islands 16 d
Apóstoles 28 z
Apoteri 23 y
Appalachian Mountains 16 v
Appleton 16 r
Apucarana 29 c
Apuka Chukotskaya 10 d
Apure 23 e
Apurimac 24 y
Aqaba 38 k
Aqaba, Gulf of 38 k
Aqcha 60 h
Aqqikkol, Hu 61 j
Aqua Clara 29 b
Aquidabán 28 m
Aquidauana 28 m
Aquidauana (River) 28 m
Araara 43 s
Arabelo 23 u
Arabian Desert 38 j
Arabian Gulf 39 i
Arabian Sea 60 s
Araca 25 g
Aracaju 27 u
Aracati 27 u
Araçatuba 29 d
Aracena 34 p
Aracui 29 j
Arad 35 e
Arafat 39 o
Arafura Sea 73 c
Aragarças 29 c
Araguacema 26 y
Araguaçu 26 y
Araguaia 26 z
Araguaína 26 z
Araguari 26 j
Arak 39 h
Arakan Mountains 62 o
Arak Bordj 37 n
Araks 54 v
Aral 56 q
Aral Sea 55
Aral'sk 55 d
Aralsor, Lake 54 j
Aramac 74 p
Aramberri 19 o
Aranos 48 k
Arapari 25 y
Arapey 28 y
Arapiraca 27 u
Ar'ar 39 b
Araracuara 24 m
Araranguá 29 r
Araraquara 29 f
Araras 26 v
Araras, Serra das 29 o
Ararat 77 v
Ararat, Mount 54 t
Arari 27 b
Ar Arish 38 j
Arauca 23 c
Arauca (River) 23 f
Aravalli Range 60 z
Araxá 29 f
Arba Minch 43 o
Arbil 39 d
Arcas 19 u
Archangel 50 q
Archei 38 o
Archer's Post 43 p
Arčman 55 n
Arco 14 z
Arcoverde 27 u
Arctic Bay 13 d
Arctic Circle 53 l
Arctic Ocean 10-11/32-33/89
Arctic Red River 11 m
Arctic Village 11 h
Arctowski 82 r
Ar Dăg 54 q
Ardahan 54 s
Ardakan 39 k
Arde 43 h
Ardebil 54 w
Ardencaple Fjord 91 t
Ardestan 39 j
Ar Dzargala 57 j
Arenas 19 u
Arendal 33 c
Arequipa 25 n
Arere 26 i
Areyonga 73 q
Arezzo 34 m
Arga 53 h
Argadargada 73 t
Arga Sala 52 d

Argentina 28-33
Argentino Lago 30 u
Arghandab 60 g
Argun 58 c
Argungu 41 d
Argun Youqi 58 c
Argun Zuoqi 58 d
Argut 56 g
Argyle, Lake 73 a
Århus 33 p
Ariamsvlei 48 x
Ariari 23 n
Arica (Bolivia) 28 c
Arica (Colombia) 25 a
Arica (Peru) 24 k
Arinos 29 g
Arinos (River) 25 x
Aripuan 25 w
Aripuan (River) 25 w
Ariquemes 25 t
Arizona 18 f
Arizpe 18 h
Arjeplog 33 g
Arjo 43 a
Arjona 22 m
Arka 53 r
Arkadelphia 19 f
Arkagala 53 g
Arkalyk 55 g
Arkansas 15 w
Arkansas City 15 v
Arkansas (River) 19 g
Arkansas (State) 19 f
Arkbajtal 55 x
Arkhangelsk (Archangel) 50 q
Arkhara 58 i
Arklow 32 v
Arkona, Cape 33 r
Arktichesgo Instituta 51 f
Arles 34 i
Arlington (Texas) 19 c
Arlington (Washington) 16 x
Arman 53 v
Armavir 54 s
Armenia 22 z
Armenia 54 u
Armidale 78 f
Armstrong (British Columbia) 14 i
Armstrong (Ontario) 16 e
Arnauti, Cape 35 x
Arnhem 33 n
Arnhem, Cape 73 g
Arnhem Land 73 d
Aroab 48 x
Arrah 61 u
Ar Ramadi 39 d
Ar Randa 39 p
Ar Rawda 43 i
Arrecifal 23 q
Arrecife 36 c
Arriaga 19 s
Ar Rifa 39 f
Arrilalah 73 y
Arrowsmith 79 s
Ar Rutbah 39 b
Ar Ruwais 39 i
Arsen'yev 58 k
Arsk 50 t
Arta 43 f
Artém 58 k
Artemovskiy 50 y
Artesia 18 l
Arthur 77 x
Arthurs Pass 79 t
Artigas 28 z
Artillery Lake 12 u
Art'omosk 56 k
Arturo Prat 82 s
Artyk (Russia) 53 f
Artyk (Turkmenistan) 55 o
Aru 42 w
Aru Islands 70 r
Arua 42 x
Aruaña 29 c
Aruba 23 c
Arum 25 h
Arun Qi 58 e
Arusha 45 i
Aruwimi 42 s
Arvaj Cheer 57 c
Arviat (Eskimo Point) 13 n
Ary 52 j
Arys' 55 u
Arys, Lake 55 g
Arzamas 54 g
Asab 48 v
Asadabad 60 k
Asahi-dake 59 d
Asahikawa 59 d
Asanib 48 j
Asansk 51 x
Asayta 43 e
Asbe Tafari 43 d
Ascensión Bay 20 v
Ascensión (Bolivia) 25 t
Ascensión (Mexico) 18 j
Ascensión Island 230 y
Ascoli 35 a
Asedjrad 37 n
Asela 43 d
Asha 55 a
Ashburton 79 t
Ashburton (River) 72 t
Ashburton Downs 72 s
Asheville 16 u
Ashgabat 55 o
Ashland (Montana) 15 c
Ashland (Wisconsin) 15 l
Ash Sha'am 39 l
Ash Sharmah 38 l
Ash Shihr 43 k
Ash Shubaiyai 39 d
Ash Shumlul 39 g
Ash Shwayrif 37 i
Ashtabula 16 v
Ashton 15 a
Asi 38 l
Asilah 34 p
Asimba 43 d
Asino 51 u
Asir 39 p
Askale 54 s
Asmara 43 c
Asosa 42 m
Aspiring 79 q
Assab 43 f
Assad Reservoir 39 a
Assale, Lake 43 d
As Salman 39 e
Assamakka 37 q
As Samawah 39 e
As Sawadah 39 r
As Sib 60 o
As Sidr 39 n
As Sila 39 v
Assiniboia 15 c
As Sua 39 p
As Sulaiyil 39 r
As Suq 39 p
As Suwaiq 60 o
Astakh 53 c
Astana 55 j
Astara 54 w
Astillero 25 o
Astoria 14 g
Astrakhan 54 i
Asuka 84 d
Asunción 28 y
Aswân 38 w
Asyût 38 h
Atacama Desert 28 p
Atakh-Yuryakh 52 i
Atakor 37 p
Atakpamé 41 n
Atalanka 57 b
Atalaya 24 y
Atambua 69 w
Atar 36 p
Atasu 55 i
Atbara 38 w
Atbara (River) 38 x
Atbasar 55 h
Atchison 15 w
Atebubu 40 z
Athabasca 14 m
Athabasca (River) 14 l
Athabasca, Lake 12 v
Athens (Georgia) 20 k
Athens (Greece) 35 t
Athens (Ohio) 16 v
Atherton 74 c
Athínai (Athens) 35 t
Athlone 32 u
Atholl, Cape 91 b
Ati 42 b
Atiak 42 x
Atico 24 y
Atikokan 16 c
Atikonak Lake 17 f
Atkarsk 54 h
Atka (USA) 10 w
Atka (Russia) 53 i
Atlanta 20 j
Atlantic City 16 z
Atlantic Ocean 230
Atlas Mountains 36/37
Atlasovo 53 y
Atlin, Lake 11 y
Atlixco 19 p
Atouat 66 j
Atoyac 19 o
Atrato 22 l
Attawapiskat 16 g
Attawapiskat Lake 16 e
Attikamagen Lake 17 d
At Timan 42 e
Attopeu 66 j
Attu 10 r
Atuel 30 k
Atyrau 54 l
Auckland 79 u
Auckland Island 231 x
Augathella 74 p
Augrabies Falls 48 x
Augsburg 34 l
Augusta (Georgia) 20 l
Augusta (Maine) 17 o
Augusta Victoria 28 d
Augustus 72 s
Augustus Downs 73 v
Augustus, Mount 72 t
Auld, Lake 72 x
Aurangabad 61 n
Aurillac 34 g
Aurora (Suriname) 26 h
Aurora (USA) 15 x
Aurukun 73 j
Aus 48 u
Aust. Capital Territory 78 d
Austin, Lake 76 e
Austin (Minnesota) 16 p
Austin (Nevada) 14 x
Austin (Texas) 19 d
Austral Downs 73 t
Australia 72-74/76-78
Austria 33-35
Autlán 18 y
Auxerre 34 h
aux Feuilles 13 v
Auzangate 25 n
Auzu 37 x
Avaré 29 e
Aveiro 34 a
Avenal 14 v
Avezzano 35 a
Avignon 34 i
Avila 34 c
Avispas 18 g
Avon 76 e
Avon Downs 73 t
Avon Park 20 l
Awaran 60 h
Awasa 43 p
Awash 43 d
Awash (River) 43 d
Awaso 40 y
Awat 56 p
Awaynat Wanin 37 h
Aweil 42 h
Awetu 43 r
Awjilah 38 b
Axel Heiberg Island 13 b
Ayacucho (Argentina) 31 c
Ayacucho (Peru) 24 y
Ayakkum Hu 56 u
Ayan 53 p
Ayan (Ilimpeya) 52 b
Ayan (Nepa) 52 o
Ayan (River) 51 k
Ayangba 41 s
Ayaviri 25 o
Ayaya 53 o
Aydabu 55 h
Aydin 35 v
Ayers Rock 73 p
Aykhal 52 e
Aylmer Lake 12 v
Ayoûn el Atroûs 40 g
Ayr (Australia) 74 q
Ayr (UK) 32 w
Ayshirak 55 i
Ayu Islands 70 c
Ayvalik 35 u
Azamgarh 61 s
Azángara 25 n
Azaouad 36 x
Azaouak 41 d
Azaouak (River) 37 o
Azaouak, Vallée de l' 41 c
Azefal 36 o
Azemmour 36 g
Azerbaijan 54 v
Azhbulat, Lake 55 m
Azna 39 h
Azogues 24 i
Azopol'ye 50 s
Azores 230 k
Azoum 42 d
Azov, Sea of 54 c
Azrou 36 i
Azuero Peninsula 22 i
Azúl 31 b
Azum 42 e
Azurduy 28 g
Az Zaydiyah 43 f
Az Zilfi 39 e
Az Zuqar 43 f

B

Baacagaan 57 n
Baalbek 38 l
Babaçulândia 26 z
Babahoyo 22 w
Bab al Mandab 43 f
Babanusa 42 i
Babar 70 o
Babati 45 i
Babel Thuap 70 f
Babile 43 f
Babo 70 r
Baboua 41 y
Babuyan Islands 67 l
Bababal 27 o
Bacajá 26 j
Bacan Islands 69 l
Bacău 35 h
Bachardok 55 p
Bachinivas 18 j
Bachu Liuchang 56 o
Back 12 m
Bac Ninh 62 x
Baco 67 g
Bacolod 67 i
Badain Jaran 57 o
Badajós 25 g
Badajós, Lago 25 g
Badajoz 34 o
Badgastein 35 a
Bad Hersfeld 33 p
Badillo 23 a
Badin 60 w
Badr Hunain 39 n
Badu 70 x
Badu (Island) 73 j
Baduen 43 w
Badulla 64 v
Baeza 22 y
Bafang 41 u
Bafang (River) 40 f
Bafatá 40 c
Baffin Bay 13 g
Baffin Island 13 g
Bafia 41 u
Bafoulabé 40 f
Bafoussam 41 u
Bafq 39 l
Baft 60 b
Bafwabalinga 42 u
Baga 41 j
Bagadzha 52 i
Bagamoyo 45 k
Bagan 62 e
Bagata 44 i
Bagazán 24 m
Bagdarin 52 s
Bagé 29 n
Baghdad 39 e
Baghin 60 a
Baghlan 60 j
Bago 67 h
Bagua 24 i
Baguinéda 40 i
Baguio 67 g
Bagzane 37 s
Bahamas 21 b
Bahariya, Oasis 38 g
Baharu 66 s
Bahawalpur 60 l
Baheh 39 e
Bahia Negra 28 k
Bahir Dar 43 b
Bahla 39 m
Bahrain 39 i
Bahrain, Gulf of 39 i
Bahr al Arab 42 g
Bahr al Ghazel 42 i
Bahr al Milh 39 d
Bahu Kalat 60 q
Baia Mare 35 f
Baio 26 l
Baïbokoum 41 y
Baicheng 58 e
Baidarata Bay 50 m
Baidoba 43 t
Baie Comeau 17 c
Baie-St.-Paul 17 a
Baihe 63 a
Bailundo 44 u
Baima 62 g
Baingoin 61 k
Baiquan 58 f
Baird Mountains 11 a
Bairin Youqi 57 y
Bairin Zouqi 57 x
Bairnsdale 78 p
Bais 67 h
Bait al Faqih 43 f
Baixingt 57 t
Baiyanghe 56 t
Baiyuda 38 v
Bajan 57 e
Bajan Baraat 57 d
Bajanchongor 57 a
Bajan-Dalaj 57 p
Bajanleg 57 n
Bajan-Öndör 56 z
Bajan Ovoo 57 h
Bajan-Uul 56 l
Bajan-Uul (Uldz Gol) 57 h
Bajeador, Cape 63 u
Bajo Caracoles 30 v
Bajram Ali 55 r
Bajsint 57 u
Bakchar 51 s
Baker (California) 14 x
Baker (Montana) 15 e
Baker (Oregon) 14 j
Baker, Lake 12 z
Baker Lake 12 z
Bakersfield 14 w
Bakhta 51 v
Bakhta (River) 51 w
Bakhtaran 39 f
Bakhynay 52 j
Bako 40 h
Bakrakondre 26 g
Baku 54 x
Balabac 67 q
Balabac Strait 67 q
Bala, Cerros de 25 p
Baladek 53 n
Balagannakh 53 c
Balagannakh 53 k
Balagannoye 53 u
Balagansk 57 c
Balaghat 61 r
Balaipungut 66 s

Balaka 46 i
Balakovo 54 j
Bala Murghab 60 f
Balancán 19 u
Balängir 61 t
Balashikha 54 d
Balashov 54 g
Balasore 61 v
Balaton, Lake 35 c
Balbi 71 u
Balboa 22 j
Bald Cape 76 e
Balearic Islands 34 t
Baley 57 j
Balgazya 56 l
Balgo 73 n
Bali 69 p
Bali Sea 69 q
Balikesir 35 v
Balikpapan 69 e
Balkans 35 g
Balkhab 60 i
Balkhash 55 l
Balkhash, Lake 55 k
Balladonia 76 j
Ballarat 77 w
Ballé 40 h
Ballenas Bay 18 f
Balleny Islands 86 w
Balombo 44 t
Balonne 78 d
Balotra 60 z
Balrampur 61 f
Balranald 77 j
Balsas (Brazil) 27 n
Balsas (Mexico) 19 n
Balsas (Peru) 24 i
Balta 25 n
Bălti 35 i
Baltic Sea 33 t
Baltîm 38 i
Baltimore 16 y
Baluchistan 60 e
Bam (Iran) 60 c
Bam (Russia) 52 w
Bama 41 k
Bamaga 73 k
Bamako 40 h
Bamba (Mali) 40 m
Bamba (Senegal) 40 e
Bambama 44 f
Bambamarca 24 i
Bambari 42 p
Bamberg 33 q
Bambesa 42 t
Bambesi 42 m
Bambili 42 t
Bamboi 40 m
Bamboo Creek 72 v
Bambui 29 g
Bambuyka 52 t
Bamenda 41 u
Bamian 60 i
Bamingui 42 b
Bampur 60 d
Bampur (River) 60 d
Bamyili 73 d
Banados del Atuel 30 k
Banados del Izozog 28 i
Banagi 45 h
Banalia 42 t
Banamba 40 i
Banana 74 s
Banas 61 o
Banas, Ras 38 y
Ban Ban 65 m
Banbar 62 c
Bancroft 16 k
Banda (India) 61 r
Banda (Demp. Rep. Congo) 44 j
Banda Aceh 65 s
Banda Sea 69 x
Bandama 40 w
Bandar Abbas 60 a
Bandar Anzeli 54 x
Bandar-e-Khomeini 39 h
Bandar-e-Lengeh 39 l
Bandar-e-Margam 39 j
Bandar-e-Rig 39 h
Bandarlampung (Telukbetung) 68 v
Bandar Seri Begawan 69 b
Bandar Sri Aman 68 m
Bandeirante 26 x
Bandera 28 v
Banderas Bay 18 x
Bandiagara 40 k
Bandirma 35 i
Bandundu 44 i
Bandung 68 x
Baneh 54 v
Banes 21 p
Banff 14 l
Banfora 40 k
Bangalore 64 f
Banganapalle 64 g
Bangassou 42 r
Bangeta 71 n
Banggai Islands 69 i
Banggi 67 q
Bangka 68 w
Bangkalan 69 n
Bangkok (Krung Thep) 66 e
Bangladesh 61
Bangor 17 c
Bangoran 42 c
Bangued 67 f
Bangui 42 n
Bangweulu, Lake 45 q
Bani 40 j
Bani Sar 39 p
Bania 41 y
Baniara 74 f
Banja Luka 35 b
Banjarmasin 69 o
Banjul 40 a
Banket 46 r
Banks Island (Canada) 12 d
Banks Islands (Micronesia) 75 e
Banks Peninsula 79 u
Banks Strait 78 p
Bankura 61 v
Ban Me Thout 66 k
Ban Na San 66 q
Bannu 60 k
Ban Pong 66 d
Ban Pu Kroy 66 j
Banswara 61 n
Ban Thateng 66 i
Banvalot 61 i
Banya Fort 43 n
Banyo 41 v
Banyuwangi 69 p
Banzare Coast 87 d
Banzart (Bizerte) 34 y
Baoji 62 l
Bao Loc 66 j
Baoshan 62 s
Baouna 40 l
Bap 60 m
Baqên 62 c
Ba'qubah 39 e
Bara (Nigeria) 41 h
Bara (Sudan) 42 j
Barabinsk 56 b
Baracoa 21 q
Baragoi 43 o
Barahona 21 s
Baralaba 74 r
Baram 69 b
Baran 61 o
Baranga 42 u
Baranoa 22 m
Baranof Island 11 x
Baranovichi 33 x
Barat Daya Islands 69 y
Barbacena 29 h
Barbados 23 k
Barbas, Cap 36 n
Barbuda 21 z
Barcaldine 74 p
Barcelona (Spain) 34 h
Barcelona (Venezuela) 23 g
Barcelos 23 u
Barcoo 74 o
Bardai 37 x
Barddhaman 61 v
Bardera 43 s
Bardeskan 60 b
Bareilly 61 d
Barentsburg 92 o
Barents Island 92 p
Barents Sea 50 d
Barga 61 e
Barguzin 52 q
Bari 35 c
Barinas 23 c
Baring, Cape 12 e
Baringo Lodge 43 n
Baripada 61 v
Bâris 38 u
Barisal 61 x
Barisan Mountains 68 s
Barito 69 c
Barka 38 z
Barkal 61 z
Barkam 62 i
Barkly East 49 p
Barkly Tableland 73 s
Barkly West 49 n
Barkol Hu 56 w
Barkol Kazak 56 w
Barlee, Lake 76 g
Barlow 11 j
Barmer 60 y
Barnaul 56 e
Barnes Ice Cap 13 i
Baro 41 e
Baroda (Vadodara) 60 z
Barquisimeto 23 c
Barra 27 p
Barraca da Boca 26 j
Barra de Navidad 18 x
Barra do Corda 27 o
Barra do So Manuel 25 k
Barranca 24 j
Barrancabermeja 23 a
Barrancas (Argentina) 30 j
Barrancas (Venezuela) 23 h
Barranquilla 22 m
Barre 17 n
Barreira do Campo 26 y
Barreiras 27 o
Barreiros 27 w
Barretos 29 e
Barrhead 14 l
Barrie 16 w
Barrier Range 77 h
Barrington Tops 78 f
Barrow 11 c
Barrow, Cape 11 c
Barrow Creek 73 r
Barrow Island 72 r
Barrow Strait 13 a
Barsa Kel'mes 55 c
Barsi 61 o
Barstow 14 x
Bartica 23 y
Bartle Frere 74 c
Bartlesville 15 v
Barumun 68 e
Baruun Turuun 56 k
Baruun-Urt 57 i
Barwani 61 n
Barysh 54 i
Basac 66 h
Basankusu 42 p
Bascuñan, Cabo 28 o
Bashi Channel 63 u
Basilan 67 t
Basilan (Island) 67 u
Bas-Kouilou 44 d
Basle (Basel) 34 k
Basoko 42 r
Basotho 49 b
Basra 39 g
Bassari 41 a
Bassas da India 46 y
Bassein 65 f
Basse Santa Su 40 d
Basseterre 21 y
Bassett 15 t
Bassikounou 40 i
Bassila 41 b
Bass Strait 77 x
Bastak 39 k
Bastia 34 k
Bata 41 u
Batagay 53 a
Batakan 69 o
Batama 42 u
Batamay 52 m
Batang 62 f
Batangafo 42 n
Batangas 67 g
Batan Islands 63 v
Batatais 29 f
Bataysk 54 e
Bat Cengel 57 b
Batchelor 73 b
Batha 42 b
Bathurst (Australia) 78 e
Bathurst (Canada) 17 e
Bathurst, Cape 12 a
Bathurst Inlet 12 i
Bathurst Island (Canada) 12 l
Bathurst Island (Australia) 73 b
Bati 43 d
Batista, Serra da 27 r
Batna 34 w
Batomga 53 p
Baton Rouge 20 e
Batouri 41 x
Batovi 29 b
Batsireet 57 g
Battambang 66 f
Batterbee Range 82 x
Batticaloa 64 w
Battle Creek 16 t
Battle Mountain 14 x
Batui 69 h
Batumi 54 s
Baturino 56 f
Baubau 69 v
Bauchi 41 h
Baunt 52 s
Baures 25 s
Baurú 29 d
Bavispe 18 i
Bawean 69 n
Bawîti 38 g
Bawku 40 m
Ba Xian 62 l
Baxoi 62 e
Bay Islands 20 v
Bayamo 21 o
Bayamón 21 v
Bayanga 41 z
Bayan Har Shan 62 f
Bayan Mod 57 p
Bayan Obo 57 s
Bayawan 67 h
Bay City 16 u
Bayir 38 l
Baykal, Lake 52 p
Baykalovo 51 n
Baykal'skiy Mountains 52 q
Baykal'skoye 52 q
Baykit 51 y
Baykonyr 55 g
Baymak 55 b
Bayneu 54 m
Bayombong 67 g
Bayonne 34 f
Bayóvar 24 g
Baytown 19 e
Baza 36 k
Bazaruto 46 v
Bazman 60 d
Beagle Bay 72 k
Beagle Gulf 73 b
Beardmore Glacier 86 c
Beardstown 16 q
Bear Island 92 p
Bearskin Lake 15 l
Beatrice 15 v
Beatty 14 x
Beaufort 69 d
Beaufort Sea 11/89
Beaufort West 48 z
Beaumont 19 e
Beaver (River, Canada) 15 b
Beaver (River, USA) 15 t
Beaver Creek 11 i
Beavermouth 14 j
Beawar 61 n
Béboura 41 z
Beckley 16 v
Bedajós 26 b
Bedajós, Lago 26 b
Bedele 43 a
Bedford 16 s
Bedopa 51 y
Bedourie 73 u
Beed 61 o
Beer Sheba 38 k
Beethoven Peninsula 82 x
Befale 42 p
Befandriana Av 47 e
Befori 42 r
Beger 56 z
Begichev 52 f
Behbahan 39 i
Behring Point 21 o
Behsud 60 i
Bei'an 58 g
Beihai (Pakhoi) 62 z
Beijing (Peking) 57 w
Beira 46 v
Beirut 38 k
Bei Shan 56 w
Beitbridge 49 e
Beitun 56 g
Bejaia 34 v
Beja (Portugal) 34 o
Beja (Tunisia) 34 x
Béka 41 w
Bekabad 55 v
Bekdas 54 y
Békéscsaba 35 d
Bela 60 v
Bel'agas 56 c
Belaja Šhola 56 d
Belarus 33 x
Bela Vista 49 t
Belaya Tserkov 33 z
Belcher Channel 13 a
Belcher Islands 13 s
Bélel 41 x
Belém 26 m
Belem de So Francisco 27 t
Belen (USA) 15 p
Belén (Argentina) 28 r
Belen'kaya 52 w
Beles 43 a
Belesc Cogani 43 r
Belet Huen 43 t
Beleutty 55 g
Belev 54 c
Beleya 43 a
Belfast 32 v
Belfield 15 e
Belgaum 64 d
Belgium 32-33/34
Belgorod 35 j
Belgrade 35 d
Beli 41 v
Belitung 68 y
Belize (City) 19 w
Belize (State) 19/20
Bel'kachi 53 n
Bel'kovskiy 53 b
Bell 49 p
Bellary 64 f
Bella Unión 28 y
Bella Vista (Argentina) 28 x
Bella Vista (Brazil) 28 m
Belle Isle, Strait of 17 j
Belleville 16 x
Bellingham 14 h
Bellingshausen 82 r
Bellingshausen Sea 80 l
Bello 22 m
Bell Peninsula 13 r
Bellyk 56 i
Belmopan 19 w
Belogorsk 58 h
Belo Horizonte 29 i
Beloit 16 r
Belo Monte 26 k
Belomorsk 50 n
Beloretsk 55 b
Belterra 26 h
Belyuen 73 b
Belyy Yar 51 t
Bembe 44 g
Bembéréké 41 c
Bemidji 15 j

Bena Dibele 44 l
Benadir 43 t
Bena-Tshadi 44 l
Bend 14 h
Benda Range 77 g
Bender Beila 43 l
Bendigo 77 x
Bene 46 g
Benevento 35 a
Bengal, Bay of 64 m
Bengamisa 42 t
Benghazi 35 q
Bengkolan Bay 66 x
Bengkulu 68 s
Benguela 44 r
Ben Guerdane 34 y
Benguerir 36 g
Beni 42 v
Beni Abbès 36 k
Beni Cunif 36 l
Beni Mazâr 38 h
Beni Mellal 36 i
Benin 41 b
Benin City 41 r
Beni (River) 25 q
Beni Saf 34 r
Beni Suef 38 i
Benito Juárez 31 b
Beni Walid 35 n
Benjamin Acéval 28 y
Benjamin Constant 25 b
Benmara 73 g
Bennetta 53 h
Benoni 49 q
Bentinck Island 73 i
Bentiu 42 j
Bentong 66 s
Benue 41 f
Beograd (Belgrade) 35 d
Berber 38 x
Berbera 43 h
Berberati 41 y
Berdale 43 w
Berdyansk 54 c
Berea 16 t
Bereda 43 l
Berekum 40 y
Berenice 38 x
Berens River 15 i
Berezniki 50 w
Berezovka 52 t
Berezovka (River) 53 k
Berezovo 50 z
Berezovo (Koryak Mountains) 10 e
Berezovskaya 52 u
Berga, Cape 51 m
Bergamo 34 l
Bergen 33 a
Berhala Strait 68 h
Berhampore 61 w
Berhampur 61 t
Beringovskiy 10 h
Bering Sea 10
Bering Strait 10 k
Berkakit 52 x
Berkner Island 83 s
Berlin (Germany) 33 r
Berlin (USA) 17 a
Bermejillo 18 l
Bermejo 28 g
Bermejo (River) 28 h
Bermejo (River) 28 r
Berne 34 j
Bernier Bay 13 b
Bernina 34 l
Bernstorff's Isfjörd 90 w
Beroubouay 41 c
Berrechio 36 h
Berriane 37 a
Bertes 53 f
Bertoua 41 w
Berwick upon Tweed 32 x
Besançon 34 j
Besar 69 q
Besham Qila 60 l
Besikama 69 x
Besima 60 h
Bessemer 20 h
Bestamak 56 b
Bestobe 55 k
Betafo 47 q
Bétaré-Oya 41 x
Betehor 43 c
Bethal 49 r
Bethanie 48 v
Bethany 15 w
Bethel 11 a
Bethlehem 49 p
Betioky 47 o
Betoota 77 h
Bet-Pak-Dala 55 i
Betpak-Dala Steppe 55 h
Betroka 47 p
Betsiboka 47 q
Bettiah 61 h
Betul 61 p
Betwa 61 q
Beverley Springs 72 l
Beyla 40 h
Beysehir, Lake 35 x
Bhadrachalam 64 i
Bhadrakh 61 v
Bhadra Reservoir 64 e
Bhadrathalam 61 r
Bhadravati 64 e
Bhagalpur 61 w
Bhaktapur 61 i
Bhamo 62 r
Bhandara 61 q
Bhanjanager 61 t
Bharatpur 61 b
Bharuch 60 z
Bhatinda 61 a
Bhavnagar 60 y
Bhawanipatna 61 s
Bheri 61 f
Bhilwara 61 n
Bhima 64 e
Bhojpur 61 i
Bhopal 61 p
Bhor 60 z
Bhubaneswar 61 u
Bhuj 60 x
Bhutan 61 k
Bia 62 v
Biak 70 t
Bialystok 33 v
Biankbuma 40 v
Biaza 51 r
Bickle Knob 16 w
Bida 41 e
Bidar 61 p
Bidokht 60 c
Bielsko-Biala 35 d
Bien Hoa 66 j
Bienville, Lake 17 a
Big Bell 76 e
Big Delta 11 g
Biggar 15 b
Big Island 90 e
Bignona 40 b
Big Sandy 15 a
Big Sioux 15 v
Big Spring 19 a
Big Trout Lake 16 d
Bihác 35 b
Bihar 61 u
Bija 56 g
Bijapur 64 e
Bijar 39 g
Bijiang 62 s
Bijie 62 k
Bijsk 56 f
Bikaner 60 m
Bikin 58 l
Bikin (River) 58 m
Bikoro 44 i
Bilaspur 61 s
Bilbao 34 d
Bilecik 35 w
Bili 42 t
Bili (River) 42 s
Bilir 53 q
Biliran 67 i
Billabalon 76 d
Billabong 77 y
Billiluna 73 n
Billings 15 b
Bilma 37 v
Bilma, Grand Erg de 37 v
Biloela 74 s
Biloku 23 x
Biloxi 20 g
Biltine 42 d
Bimbo 42 n
Binalbagan 67 h
Binatang 69 a
Bindura 49 f
Binga 46 p
Bing Bong 73 f
Binghampton 16 y
Bingöl 54 r
Binhai 63 g
Bintuhan 68 t
Bintulu 69 b
Binzert 37 f
Bio Bio 30 h
Bioko Island 41 t
Bir al Hasa 38 y
Birao 42 e
Biratnagar 61 j
Birdsville 77 g
Bir el Khzaim 36 t
Bir Enzarah 36 p
Bireuen 68 b
Bir Gandus 36 n
Birganj 61 h
Birikčul 56 i
Birilyussy 51 w
Birjand 60 d
Birmingham (UK) 32 x
Birmingham (USA) 19 j
Birnin Gwari 41 e
Bernin-Kebbi 41 d
Birobidzhan 58 k
Birou 40 f
Bir Oum Greine 36 r
Bir Shari 39 d
Biru 62 b
Bir Zar 34 y
Biscay, Bay of 34 d
Biscoe Island 82 t
Bishkek 55 x
Bishop 14 w
Biskra 34 w
Bismarck 15 g
Bismarck Archipelago 71 p
Bismarck Range 70 z
Bismarck Sea 71
Bison 15 f
Bissagos Islands 40 a
Bissau 40 b
Bitam 41 v
Bitkine 42 b
Bitola 35 e
Bitterfontein 48 w
Bitterroot Mountains 14 l
Biu 41 j
Biwa, Lake 58 z
Bjorne Peninsula 13 c
Bla 40 j
Blackall 74 p
Blackburn, Mount 11 h
Black Hills 15 r
Blackpool (UK) 32 w
Blackpool (USA) 14 i
Black Sea 35
Blackstone Camp 76 m
Black Volta 40 l
Blackwood 76 d
Blagoevgrad 35 f
Blagoveshchensk 58 h
Blagovščenka 56 c
Blair Athol 74 q
Blanca, Bahía 31 a
Blanca, Laguna 30 v
Blanche, Lake 72 x
Blanc, Mont 34 j
Blanco, R. 25 t
Blanding 15 o
Blanquilla 23 g
Blantyre 46 h
Blenheim 79 u
Blida 34 u
Blind River 16 h
Blitta 41 a
Bloemfontein 49 o
Bloemhof 49 o
Bloemhof Reservoir 49 o
Bloomington (Illinois) 16 r
Bloomington (Indiana) 16 s
Bluefield 16 v
Bluefields 22 g
Blue Mountains 14 k
Blue Nile 42 m
Bluenose Lake 12 e
Blue Ridge 16 u
Blue River 14 i
Bluff Knoll 76 f
Blumenau 29 r
Blumut 66 t
Blythe 18 e
Blytheville 16 q
Bo 40 e
Boac 67 g
Boa Esperanca Reservoir 27 o
Boa Esperança 29 g
Boa Fé 24 m
Boatasyn 53 s
Boa Vista 23 w
Bobo-Dioulasso 40 k
Bobruysk 33 y
Boca del Pao 23 g
Boca do Acará 25 g
Boca do Acre 25 q
Boca do Curequeté 25 r
Boca do Jari 26 j
Boca do Moaco 25 c
Boca do Mutúm 25 c
Boca Grande 23 j
Bocaranga 41 y
Boco Mavaca 23 t
Boconó 23 c
Bodala 42 q
Bodaybo 52 s
Bodēlē 42 a
Bodö 33 e
Boende 44 k
Boffa 40 c
Bogangolo 42 o
Boganida 51 l
Bogantungan 74 q
Bogda Feng 56 u
Bogdanovich 50 y
Bognes 33 f
Bogo 67 i
Bogor 68 w
Bogorodskoye 53 r
Bogotá 23 n
Bogotol 51 v
Bogra 61 x
Boguchany 51 y
Bogué 40 d
Bohemia Downs 72 z
Bohodou 40 g
Bohol 67 i
Boise 14 x
Boise City 15 s
Bojador 36 o
Bojador, Cap 36 o
Bojeador, Cape 67 f
Bojnurd 55 o
Boké 40 d
Boknfjörd 33 a
Boko 44 g
Bokol Mayo 43 r
Boktor 58 m
Bolaños 18 y
Bole (China) 56 q
Bole (Ghana) 40 l
Bolgatanga 40 m
Bolgrad 35 i
Bolia 44 i
Bolvar (Peru) 24 i
Bolivar (USA) 15 x
Bolivia 25/26/28
Bollon 74 q
Bolodzhak 53 n
Bologna 34 m
Bolognesi 24 y
Bolomba 42 o
Bolon 58 m
Bolonchén de Rejón 19 u
Bol'senarymskoje 56 f
Bolsevik 55 o
Bol'shaya Balakhnya 52 b
Bol'shaya Glushitsa 54 k
Bol'shaya Kheta 51 g
Bol'sherech'ye 51 q
Bol'shezemel'skaya Tundra 50 j
Bol'shiye Khatymy 52 x
Bol'shoy Lyakhovskiy 53 e
Bol'shoy Onguren 57 e
Bol'shoy Patom 52 t
Bol'shoy Shantar 95 j
Bol'shoy Yenisey 56 m
Bol'shoye Vlasévo 53 r
Bol'shoye Zimovye 53 g
Bolson de Mapimi 18 l
Bolu 35 k
Boluntay 62 b
Bolzano 34 l
Boma 44 e
Bomassa 41 z
Bombale 41 z
Bombay 60 z
Bomberai 70 r
Bömbögör 57 a
Bom Despacho 29 g
Bomi 62 d
Bomi Hills 40 s
Bomili 42 u
Bom Jardim 25 r
Bom Jesus da Lapa 27 q
Bom Jesus de Itabapoana 29 k
Bonaire 23 e
Bonaparte Archipelago 72 l
Bon, Cap 34 z
Bonda 44 e
Bondo 42 s
Bondoukou 40 k
Bone, Gulf of 69 t
Bonete 28 q
Bong 40 t
Bonga 43 n
Bongadanga 42 q
Bongor 41 l
Bongos, Massif des 42 d
Bonifacio 34 k
Bonifacio, Str. of 34 k
Bonin Islands 231 j
Bonito 28 m
Bonn 33 o
Bonner Ferry 14 k
Bonny 41 s
Böön Cagaan Nuur 57 n
Boonderoo 73 y
Boothby, Cape 85 a
Boothia, Gulf of 13 b
Boothia Peninsula 13 a
Booué 44 e
Booylgoo Springs 76 g
Boqueiro 27 p
Boquilla Reservoir 18 k
Bor 42 x
Bora 42 g
Borah Peak 14 m
Borås 33 e
Borazjah 39 i
Borba 25 j
Borborema, Planalto da 27 u
Bordeaux 34 e
Borden Island 12 g
Borden Peninsula 13 e
Bordj-Bou-Arreridj 34 v
Bordj Bourguiba 34 y
Bordj Flye Sainte Marie 36 k
Bordj Messouda 37 e
Bordj-Moktar 36 z
Bordj Omar Driss 37 e
Borisoglebsk 54 f
Borisov 33 y
Borja 24 j
Borkou 37 y
Borlänge 33 e
Borneo 69
Bornholm 33 s
Borodino 56 l
Borohoro Shan 56 p
Borolgustakh 52 i
Borovskoye 55 e
Borroloola 73 f
Borshchovochnyy Mountains 52 u
Boru 53 e
Borujerd 39 g
Bor-Yuryakh 52 h
Borzya 57 j

Bosaso 43 k
Bose 62 y
Bosing 63 f
Bosnia-Herzegovina 35 c
Bosobolo 42 p
Bosporus 35 i
Bossangoa 41 z
Bossembélé 41 z
Bosso 41 j
Bostan 56 r
Bosten Hu 56 t
Boston 17 o
Bothnia, Gulf of 33 h
Botoşani 35 h
Botswana 44/46/48-49
Bouaflé 40 w
Bou Akba 36 g
Bouaké 40 w
Bouanga 44 g
Bouar 41 y
Bou Arfa 36 k
Bouca 42 o
Boufarik 37 b
Bougainville, Cape 72 l
Bougainville (Island) 71 t
Bougouni 40 i
Bougtob 34 t
Bou Izakarene 36 e
Boukombé 41 b
Boulder 15 q
Boulder City 14 y
Boulia 73 v
Boulsa 40 m
Boumango 44 e
Boumba 41 x
Boûmdeid 40 e
Boundary Peak 14 w
Boundiali 40 i
Boundji 44 g
Boungo 42 q
Bountiful 14 z
Bounty Islands 79 y
Bourail 75 p
Bourem 40 m
Bouressa 37 n
Bourke 77 k
Bournemouth 32 x
Bou Saada 34 u
Bousso 41 m
Boutilimit 40 c
Bouvet Island 230 z
Bova Marina 37 j
Bowen 74 r
Bowling Green 16 s
Bowman 15 e
Bo Xian 63 d
Boxing 58 o
Boyabo 42 o
Boyarka 51 l
Boyoma Falls 42 t
Bozeman 15 a
Bozoum 41 y
Brac 35 b
Braco Menor do Araguaia 26 y
Bradenton 20 k
Braeburn 11 k
Braga 34 b
Bragança 27 a
Brahmaputra 61 y
Brainerd 15 j
Brak 37 i
Brali 55 f
Branco 25 h
Brandberg 48 g
Brandon (Canada) 15 g
Brandon (USA) 20 l
Brandvlei 48 y
Branson 15 x
Brasilandia 29 g
Brasileia 25 p
Brasilia 29 f
Brasilia Legal 26 g
Brasov 35 h
Brass 41 r
Bratislava 35 c
Bratsk 57 a
Bratskoye Reservoir 57 b
Brattleboro 17 n
Braunschweig (Brunswick) 33 p
Brava 43 t
Bravo del Norte 18 l
Bray 49 a
Brazil 23-29
Brazilian Plateau 29 h
Brazos 19 d
Brazzaville 44 f
Breadalbane 73 u
Breda 33 n
Bredy 55 c
Breeza Plains 74 b
Breidhi Fjord 32 a
Bremen 33 p
Bremerhaven 33 p
Bremerton 14 g
Brescia 34 l
Brest (France) 34 c
Brest (Belarus) 33 w
Bretaña 24 l
Breves 26 l
Brewarrina 78 c
Brewster, Cape 91 q
Brézina 34 t
Bria 42 q
Bridgeport 16 z
Bridgetown 23 k
Bridgewater 17 r
Brig 34 k
Brighton 32 y
Brikama 40 a
Brindisi 35 c
Brinkley 15 y
Brisbane 78 g
Bristol 32 x
Bristol Bay 11 o
Bristol Channel 32 w
British Columbia 11/14
Britstown 48 z
Brive 34 g
Brno 33 s
Broadus 15 d
Brockville 16 l
Brod 35 c
Brodeur Peninsula 13 c
Broken Hill 77 h
Brokopondo 26 h
Brookhaven 20 f
Brookings 15 i
Brooks 14 m
Brooks Range 11 c
Broome 72 w
Broome (Mount) 72 l
Broughton Island 13 l
Browning 14 m
Brownsville 19 d
Brownwood 19 c
Brumado 29 j
Brunei 69 c
Brunei Bay 69 o
Brunette Downs 73 s
Brunswick (Georgia) 20 m
Brunswick (Germany) 33 p
Brunswick (New Hampshire) 17 o
Brunswick Peninsula 30 u
Brunt Ice Shelf 83 g
Brussels 33 n
Bruxelles (Brussels) 33 n
Bruzual 23 d
Bryan 19 d
Bryanka 51 w
Bryansk 54 a
Bubiyan 39 g
Bubye 49 f
Buçaco 44 w
Bucaramanga 23 a
Buchanan 40 s
Buchanan, Lake 74 p
Buchan Gulf 13 h
Buchans 17 j
Buchara 55 r
Bucharest 35 h
Buckingham 16 l
Bucklin 15 t
Bucureşti (Bucharest) 35 h
Budapest 35 c
Budaun 61 d
Budd Coast 87 e
Budjala 42 p
Buea 41 t
Buena Esperanza 30 l
Buenaventura (Mexico) 18 j
Buenaventura (Colombia) 22 x
Buenos Aires (Argentina) 31 c
Buenos Aires (Colombia) 23 n
Buenos Aires, Lago 30 u
Buerát el Hsun 35 o
Buffalo (New York) 16 x
Buffalo (South Dakota) 15 e
Buffalo (Wyoming) 15 c
Buffalo Narrows 12 v
Bug 33 v
Bugarikta 51 v
Bugat 56 x
Bugorkan 52 c
Bugsuk 67 q
Bugul'ma 54 l
Bugun 55 d
Bugunda 52 s
Buguruslan 54 l
Bu Hasa 39 w
Bui 50 q
Buitepos 48 k
Bujant 56 m
Bujant-Ovoo 57 q
Bujba 56 k
Bujedžul' 56 j
Bujumbura 45 d
Bukačača 57 j
Bukavu 45 c
Bukittingti 68 e
Bukoba 45 f
Bula 70 p
Bulag Sum 57 w
Bulan 67 i
Bulanavo 54 m
Bulawayo 46 p
Buldana 61 n
Bulgan 57 p
Bulgan (High Altai) 56 w
Bulgan (Selenga) 57 b
Bulgar 57 i
Bulgaria 35
Bulguntay 56 t
Buller 78 o
Bulloo 77 j
Bulloo Downs (W.Australia) 72 v
Bulloo Downs (Queensland) 74 n
Bulo Burti 43 u
Bultfontein 49 o
Bulun 53 s
Bulun (River) 53 k
Bulungu 44 j
Bulukol 55 y
Bumba 42 q
Buna 43 q
Bunbury 76 d
Bundaberg 74 t
Bu Ndjem 37 j
Bungo Channel 58 x
Bunguran (Natuna) 66 x
Buni 41 i
Bunia 42 w
Bunkeya 45 o
Buntok 69 c
Buol 69 h
Bourkhaya Bay 52 m
Bourkhaya, Cape 53 a
Bur 52 p
Bur Acaba 43 s
Buraidah 39 d
Buramo 43 g
Buran 56 f
Burandzha 53 o
Burang 61 e
Bur Anod 43 i
Burao 43 h
Burdekin 74 p
Burden, Mount 12 p
Bure 43 b
Bureya 58 i
Bureya (River) 58 j
Burgakhchan 53 f
Burgas 35 i
Burgersdorp 49 o
Burgon 56 k
Burgos 34 d
Bürhanpur 61 o
Burias 67 h
Buri Ram 66 f
Burke Island 81 a
Burketown 73 v
Burkhala 53 h
Burkina Faso 40-41
Burlington (Colorado) 15 s
Burlington (Iowa) 15 y
Burlington (Vermont) 16 z
Burma 61/62/65/66
Burney 14 u
Burnie 77 x
Burni-Nkonni 41 d
Burns 14 w
Burns Junction 14 w
Burqin 56 g
Burra 77 g
Burro, Sierra 19 a
Burrundie 73 c
Bursa 35 j
Buru 69 y
Burundi 45 d
Burwash Landing 11 i
Burylbaytal 55 x
Busanga 44 l
Busanga (Congo River) 45 n
Bushehr 39 i
Bushenyi 42 w
Businga 42 p
Busira 44 j
Busselton 76 c
Busseri 42 u
Busu-Djanoa 42 q
Buta 42 s
Butembo 42 v
Butiá 29 p
Butte, Mount 14 m
Butterworth 66 r
Butuan 67 j
Butung 69 v
Buturlinovka 54 f
Butwal 61 g
Buwatah 39 n
Buyr-Nur 58 b
Buzuluk 54 l
Byam Martin Channel 89 p
Bychez 52 b
Bydgoszcz 33 t
Bylot Island 13 f
Byrd 81 g
Byro 76 d
Byrranga Mountains 51 k
Byssa 52 z
Bystryy 51 p
Bysyttakh 53 a
Bytantay 53 a
Byuchennyakh 53 f
Byyangnyr 53 g

C

Caala 44 t
Cáatingas 27 r
Caazapá 28 z
Caballococha 25 a
Cabanatuan 67 g
Cabezas 28 h
Cabimas 23 c
Cabinda 44 d
Cabonga Reservoir 16 l
Cabool 16 p
Caboolture 74 u
Cabo Pantoja 24 k
Cabora Bassa Reservoir 46 f
Caborca 18 f
Cabot Strait 17 h
Cabrobó 27 s
Caçador 29 p
Cáceres (Brazil) 25 x
Cáceres (Spain) 34 o
Cache Creek 14 h
Cachi 28 s
Cachi, Mount 28 s
Cachimbo 26 u
Cachimbo, Serra do 25 z
Cachingues 44 u
Cachoeira 27 s
Cachoeira do Arari 26 l
Cachoeira do Sul 29 o
Cachoeiro de Itapemirim 29 k
Cacolo 44 w
Caconda 44 t
Cacula 44 s
Cadan 56 j
Cadelga 77 h
Cadillac 16 t
Cadiz (Philippines) 67 i
Cádiz (Spain) 34 o
Cádiz, Gulf of 34 o
Čadobec 51 z
Caen 34 f
Caetité 27 q
Cafayate 28 s
Cagaan Bogd Uul 56 z
Cagaan Gol 56 h
Cagaan Nuur 56 h
Cagaan-Olom 56 l
Cagaan-Uul 56 m
Cagayan de Oro 67 w
Cagayan Sulu 67 r
Cágliari 34 y
Caguán 24 l
Caguas 21 w
Čagyl 55 n
Caia 46 v
Caiabis, Serra dos 25 y
Caiaponia 29 c
Caicara de Orinoco 23 f
Caicó 27 u
Caima 26 i
Caird Coast 83 f
Cairns 74 c
Cairo (Al Qahirah) (Egypt) 38 i
Cairo (Illinois) 16 r
Caiundo 44 u
Cajabamba 24 i
Cajamarca 24 i
Cajatamboo 24 w
Cajázeiras 27 t
Čajek 55 x
Cajueiro 26 v
Calabar 41 s
Calabozo 23 e
Calacoto 25 o
Calais 32 z
Calalaste, Cord. de 28 r
Calama (Brazil) 25 g
Calama (Peru) 28 d
Calamar (Colombia) 23 n
Calamar (Venezuela) 22 m
Calamian Group 67 f
Calanaque 25 f
Calang 65 s
Calapan 67 g
Calatayud 34 f
Calbayog 67 j
Calca 25 n
Calçoene 26 k
Calcutta 61 w
Caldera 28 o
Caldwell 14 x
Caledon 48 x
Caleta el Cobre 28 o
Caleta Olivia 30 x
Calexico 18 d
Calgary 14 l
Cali 22 y
Calicut 64 d
Calie Corar 43 t
Caliente 14 y
California 14 v
California, Gulf of 18 f
Calkini 20 s
Callao 24 w
Caloocan 67 g
Calpulalpan 19 p
Caltanissetta 35 n
Calulo 44 t
Calvert Hills 73 g
Calverton 17 n
Calvinia 48 x
Camabatela 44 g
Camaçari 27 t
Camacho 18 m
Camacupa 44 u
Camagüey 21 n
Camaná 24 z
Camaná (River) 24 z
Camaqu 29 p
Camaqu (River) 29 o

Camarones **30** y
Camaxilo **44** j
Camballin **72** y
Cambell River **14** f
Cambay, Gulf of (Gulf of Khambhat) **60** y
Cambodia **66**
Cambridge (Delaware) **16** y
Cambridge (Ohio) **16** v
Cambridge (UK) **32** y
Cambridge Bay **12** j
Camburinga **73** f
Camden **20** m
Cameroon **41**
Cameroon, Mount **41** t
Cametá **26** l
Camiguin **67** j
Camiri **28** h
Camisea **24** z
Camocim **27** e
Camooweal **73** u
Camopi **26** j
Campana **30** s
Campbell Island **231** y
Campbell, Mount **11** j
Campbelltown **17** d
Campeche **19** u
Campeche, Bay of **19** s
Campiègne **34** h
Campina Grande **27** v
Campinas **29** f
Campina Verde **29** e
Camp Alegre **26** x
Campobasso **35** a
Campo de Diauarum **26** w
Campo dos Parecis **25** w
Campo Grande **29** a
Campo Largo **29** q
Campo Major **27** q
Campo Mouro **29** b
Campos **29** k
Campos Belos **27** n
Campos (Region) **27** o
Campos Sales **27** s
Cam Ranh **66** k
Canada **11-17/88-90**
Cañada de Gómez **28** v
Canadian **15** t
Canadian (River) **15** r
Canairiktok **17** g
Canakkale **35** u
Canal do Norte (Brazil) **26** k
Canal do Sul **26** l
Canamaria **25** o
Cananea **18** h
Canary Islands **36** a
Canastra, Serra de **29** g
Canatlán **18** l
Canaveral, Cape **20** m
Canavierias **29** l
Canberra **78** d
Cancun **19** x
Candeias **27** t
Canelones **31** d
Cangchou **57** x
Cangkuang, Cape **68** v
Canguaretama **27** w
Canguçu **29** o
Caniapiscau **17** b
Caniapiscau Reservoir **17** b
Canicado **49** g
Canindé **27** t
Canindé (Juruá) **25** a
Canindé (River) **27** r
Canipole **18** g
Cannanore **64** d
Cannanore Islands **64** b
Canoas **29** q
Canobie **73** w
Canon City **15** q
Cantabrian Mountains **34** c
Cantaura **23** g
Canterbury Bight **79** t
Canterbury Plains **79** s
Can-Tho **66** i
Canto do Buriti **27** q
Canton (USA) **16** v
Canton (China) **63** p
Cantwell **11** f
Canudos **27** s
Canum **25** i
Canum (River) **25** j
Canyon **15** a
Canyushikino **54** k
Cao Bang **62** x
Caojian **62** s
Capanaparo **23** e
Capanema **27** a
Capo Bonito **29** f
Cap-de-la-Madeleine **17** a
Cap-Haïtien **21** r
Cape Coast **40** z
Cape Cora **20** l
Cape Cuvier **72** q
Cape Dorset **13** t
Cape Flattery **74** c
Cape Girardeau **16** q
Cape May **16** z
Cape Parry **12** c
Cape Town **48** w
Cape Verde **230** k
Cape York Peninsula **73** k
Capella **74** r
Capelongo **44** t
Capim **26** m
Capim Verde **29** a
Capivara, Serra de **29** g
Caponga **27** t
Caprivi Strip **44** x
Caquetá **25** a
Carabaya, Cord. de **25** n
Caracarai **23** v
Caracas **23** f
Caracol **27** p
Carajás **26** y
Carajás, Serra dos **26** x
Carandotta **73** u
Caráquez, Baia de **22** v
Caratianas **25** t
Caratinga **29** j
Carauari **25** d
Caravelas **29** l
Caravelí **24** y
Caraz **24** w
Carazinho **29** o
Carbó **18** g
Carcaraña **28** v
Carcar Mountains **43** j
Carcassonne **34** g
Carcross **11** k
Cardara **55** s
Cardarinskoje Reservoir **55** t
Cardenas **19** o
Cardiel, Lago **30** u
Cardiff **32** w
Cardona **31** d
Čardžou **55** r
Carey, Lake **76** i
Carhue **30** m
Cariamanga **24** h
Caribbean Sea **20-21**
Caribou **12** z
Caribou Mountains **12** s
Caripito **23** h
Carleton, Mount **17** d
Carlisle **32** w
Carlsbad **18** l
Carmacks **11** j
Carmelo **31** s
Carmem **25** z
Carmen **22** m
Carmen (Island) **18** h
Carmen Alto **28** d
Carmen de Patagones **30** m
Carmen, Sierra **18-19**
Carmila **74** r
Carnarvon (Australia) **72** q
Carnarvon (South Africa) **48** y
Carnarvon Range (Western Australia) **72** v
Carnarvon Range (Queensland) **74** r
Carnegie **76** i
Carnegie, Lake **76** h
Carney Island **81** p
Carnicobar **65** q
Carnot **41** y
Carolina (Brazil) **27** n
Carolina (Puerto Rico, USA) **21** w
Carolina (South Africa) **49** r
Caroline Islands **70** m
Caroni **23** u
Carora **23** c
Carpathians **35** f
Carpentaria, Gulf of **73** h
Carrington **15** g
Carrizal Bajo **28** o
Čarsk **56** c
Carson City **14** v
Cartagena (Spain) **34** s
Cartagena (Venezuela) **22** m
Cartago **22** y
Cartier Island **72** k
Cartwright **17** j
Caruarú **27** v
Carúpano **23** h
Čarysskoje **56** e
Casablanca **36** g
Casa Grande **18** f
Casamance **40** b
Casanare **23** o
Casa Nova **27** r
Casa Verde **29** b
Cascade **14** k
Cascade Range **14** u
Cascavel **29** n
Caserta **35** a
Casey **87** f
Casey Bay **84** l
Casigna **23** b
Casino **78** g
Casiquiare **23** s
Casma **24** v
Casper **15** p
Caspian Depression **54** j
Caspian Sea **54** x
Cassai **44** x
Cassamba **44** w
Cassiar **11** z
Cassilandia **29** c
Cassinga **44** t
Castanhal (Brazil) **26** m
Castanhal (Brazil) **26** p
Castelli **28** w
Castellón **34** s
Castilla **28** o
Castries **23** i
Castro (Brazil) **29** q
Castro (Chile) **30** g
Castrovirreyna **24** x
Cat **21** p
Catalo **29** f
Catamarca **28** s
Catandica **46** u
Catanduanes **67** j
Catania **35** o
Catanzaro **35** o
Cataract, 1st **38** w
Cataract, 2nd **38** u
Cataract, 3rd **38** u
Cataract, 4th **38** v
Cataract, 5th **38** x
Cataract, 6th **38** w
Catarman **67** j
Catatumbo **23** b
Catbalogan **67** j
Catende **27** v
Catengue **44** s
Catete **44** s
Catió **40** c
Catisimiña **23** u
Cat Lake **16** c
Catoche, Cape **20** v
Cato Island **74** w
Catriel **30** k
Catrimani **26** c
Catrimani (River) **26** b
Catskill Mountains **16** z
Catua **28** e
Catuane **49** t
Čatyrk'ol, Lake **55** x
Čatyrtăš **55** y
Cauca **22** m
Caucasia **22** m
Caucasus **54** t
Caungula **44** i
Caura **26** a
Cauvery **64** g
Cavally **40** u
Cavanayen **23** v
Caviana **26** l
Cavinas **25** q
Caxias **25** a
Caxias do Sul **29** q
Caxito **44** f
Cayambe **22** x
Cayenne **26** j
Cayman Brac **20** z
Cayman Islands **20** z
Cayos Miskitos **22** h
Cazombo **44** z
Ceará-Mirim **27** v
Cebu **67** i
Cebu (Island) **67** i
Cecerleg **57** a
Cedar City **14** z
Cedar Lake **15** g
Cedar Rapids **15** y
Cedros **18** d
Ceduna **77** c
Ceilândia **29** e
Čekisler **54** z
Cekunda **53** n
Celaya **19** n
Celébes (Sulawesi) **69** t
Celébes Sea **69** g
Celeken **54** z
Cel'us **56** g
Čemolgan **55** y
Cencher Mandal **57** f
Cenderawasih **70** q
Cenderawasih, Gulf of **70** s
Central African Republic **41-42**
Central Butte **15** c
Central City **16** s
Central Cordillera (Boliva) **28** f
Central Cordillera (Colombia) **22** z
Central Cordillera (Peru) **24** j
Centralia **14** g
Central Makran Range **60** g
Central Plateau **29** f
Central Siberian Uplands **52** b
Central Ural Mountains **50** x
Cephalonia **35** q
Ceram **69** z
Ceram Sea **69** z
Čeremchovo **57** b
Čerepovec **50** o
Ceres (Argentina) **28** v
Ceres (Brazil) **29** d
Čerkessk **54** s
Černogorsk **56** i
Cernysevsk **52** t
Cerritos **19** n
Cerro de Pasco **24** w
Cerro Pinacate **18** e
Cerros Colorados Reservoir **30** j
Cerro Sombrero **30** w
Cervantes Island **76** c
Česa Bay **50** f
Cesar **23** a
Česke Budějovice **35** a
Cess **40** t
Ceuta **34** p
Cevennes **34** i
Ceyhan **54** p
Chabahar **60** r
Chacabuco **31** b
Chachani **25** n
Chachapoyas **24** i
Chacharramendi **30** k
Chaco Austral **28** v
Chaco Boreal **28** j
Chaco Central **28** i
Chad **37/38/41/42**
Chad, Lake **41** k
Chadron **15** r
Chagai **60** h
Chagai Hills **60** g
Chagda **52** z
Chaghcharan **60** g
Chagos Archipelago **231** r
Chaibāsa **61** v
Chai Si **66** d
Chaim **52** q
Chaiten **30** h
Chaiyaphum **66** f
Chajari **28** y
Chakwal **60** m
Chala **24** y
Chalaxung **62** f
Chalbi Desert **43** o
Chalchaqui **28** w
Chalhuanca **24** z
Chalinze **45** k
Chalkidike **35** f
Chalkis **35** s
Challapata **28** f
Chalons-sur-Saône **34** i
Chama **45** s
Chamah **65** x
Chaman **60** i
Chamba (India) **61** b
Chamba (Tanzania) **45** w
Chambal **61** o
Chamberlain **15** t
Chamberlin, Mount **11** h
Chambeshi **45** r
Chamcha **52** f
Chamical **28** s
Chamo, Lake **43** o
Champaign **16** r
Champassak **66** i
Champlain, Lake **17** a
Champotón **20** s
Chañaral **28** o
Chan Bogd **57** r
Chancay **24** w
Chanch **57** a
Chanchiang **63** n
Chandigarh **61** c
Chandler **17** e
Chandpur **61** y
Chandrapur **61** q
Chang **66** f
Changada **51** m
Changara **46** u
Changchih **63** b
Changchow **63** r
Changchun **58** f
Changhua **63** t
Changji **56** t
Chang Jiang (Yangtze) **63** a
Changkiakow **57** w
Changma **56** z
Chang Mai **62** s
Changpai Shan **58** h
Changsha **63** c
Changshu **63** h
Changteh **63** b
Changwu **62** l
Chani **28** f
Channel Cape **76** f
Channel Islands (UK) **34** d
Channel Islands (USA) **18** b
Channel-Port-aux-Basques **17** i
Chantaburi **66** f
Chany, Lake **56** b
Chao'an **63** r
Chao Phraya **66** e
Chaoyang **63** r
Chapa **52** z
Chapada das Mangabeiras **27** n
Chapada Diamantina **27** r
Chapada do Araripe **27** s
Chapado dos Gauchos **29** c
Chapadinha **27** d
Chapais **16** m
Chapala, Lake **18** y
Chaparral **22** z
Chapayevo **54** k
Chapayevsk **54** k
Chapceranga **57** g
Chapeco **29** o
Chapleau **16** h
Chaplino **54** c
Chara **52** u
Chara (River) **52** u
Charaa **57** d
Charagua **28** h
Charaña **25** o
Charata **28** v
Charcas **19** n
Charcot Island **82** w

Chari 41 l
Charikar 60 j
Charleroi 33 n
Charleston (South Carolina) 20 m
Charleston (Virginia) 16 v
Charleville 74 p
Charlotte 20 m
Charlottesville 16 x
Charlottetown 17 f
Char Nuur 56 k
Charouïne 36 m
Charters Towers 74 p
Chartres 32 z
Char Us Nuur 56 j
Chasaat 57 b
Chascomús 31 c
Chasel'ka 51 r
Chasovnya-Vchurskaya 53 n
Chăsuri 54 t
Châteauroux 34 h
Chatgal 57 a
Chatrapur 61 q
Chatsworth (Australia) 73 v
Chatsworth (Zimbabwe) 49 e
Chattahoochee 20 j
Chattanooga 20 j
Chauk 62 p
Chaumont 33 n
Chau Phu 66 h
Chavantina 29 c
Chaves 26 l
Chavirga 57 j
Chaya 52 r
Chay-Povarnaya 53 d
Chebka du Mzab 34 u
Cheboksary 54 i
Chechaouen 34 q
Chech Erg 36 w
Cheduba 65 e
Cheepie 74 o
Cheetham, Cape 86 v
Cheffadene 37 t
Chegdomyn 58 k
Chegga 36 u
Chegutu 49 e
Cheju 58 t
Chekalio 54 c
Chekunda 58 k
Chekurovka 52 l
Chelago 43 q
Chelforó 30 k
Cheliff 34 t
Chelkar 55 c
Chellala 34 t
Chelyabinsk 55 d
Chembe 45 q
Chemdal'sk 52 o
Chemnitz 33 q
Chemult 14 u
Chenab 60 l
Chenachane 36 w
Chen Barag Qi 58 c
Chengchow 63 c
Chengdu (Chengtu) 62 j
Chengshan, Cape 58 r
Chengteh 57 x
Chengtu 62 j
Chennai (Madras) 64 h
Chenxi 63 a
Chen Xian 63 p
Chepes 28 r
Cherbourg 32 x
Cherchell 37 a
Cherdyn 50 w
Cherendey 52 u
Cherepanovo 56 e
Cherkashina 52 q
Cherkassy 35 k
Cherlak 55 l
Cherlen Gol 57 h
Chernaya 51 h
Chernaya (Pechora Sea) 50 j
Chernigov 33 v
Chernikovsk 55 a
Chernovtsy 35 g
Chernyshevskiy 52 e
Chernyy Mys 53 l
Chernyy-Yar 54 h
Cherpiya 51 n
Cherskiy 10 a
Cherskogo Mountains 53 d
Chertovo-Ulovo 53 p
Chesapeake Bay 16 y
Chester 15 a
Chesterfield Islands 74 y
Chesterfield Inlet 13 o
Chesterton Range 74 q
Chetumal 20 u
Chetwynd 12 p
Cheulik 53 c
Chevak 10 m
Chew Bahir, Lake 43 o
Cheyenne 15 r
Cheyenne (River) 15 r
Chhatarpur 61 q
Chhatrapur 61 u
Chhindwara 61 p
Chiai 63 u
Chiang Mai 66 d
Chianje 44 s
Chiapa de Corzo 19 t
Chiba 59 o
Chibagalakh 53 d
Chibagalakh (River) 53 d
Chibaranda 44 x
Chibembe 45 r
Chibia 44 s
Chibougamau 16 m
Chicago 16 s
Chicala 44 w
Chicama 24 i
Chicapa 44 k
Chichaoua 36 g
Chichas, Cordillera de 28 f
Chichón 19 t
Chickasha 15 u
Chiclayo 24 h
Chico (River) 30 w
Chico (USA) 14 u
Chicoutimi-Jonquiére 17 a
Chicualacuala 49 f
Chidley, Cape 13 y
Chiefland 20 k
Chiengi 45 d
Chifeng 57 x
Chifwefwe 45 q
Chignik 11 p
Chigorodó 22 m
Chigubo 49 h
Chigul'bach 53 p
Chihuahua 18 j
Chik Ballapur 64 f
Chikhacheva 53 g
Chikmagalur 64 d
Chikwa 46 g
Chilapa 19 o
Chilas 60 m
Childers 74 t
Chile 28/30
Chile Chico 30 u
Chilecito 28 r
Chililabombwe 46 c
Chillagoe 74 b
Chillán 30 h
Chilli 55 t
Chillicothe (Iowa) 15 x
Chillicothe (Ohio) 16 u
Chilliwack 14 h
Chiloe 30 f
Chilok 57 g
Chilok (River) 57 e
Chilonga 46 f
Chilpancingo 19 o
Chilumba 46 h
Chilung 63 v
Chilwa, Lake 45 v
Chimala 45 g
Chimanimani 49 g
Chimbay 55 p
Chimborazo 24 h
Chimbote 24 v
Chimoio 49 g
China (Mexico) 19 b
China (State) 52/55-58/61-63
Chinandega 22 e
Chincha Alta 24 w
Chincha Islands 24 w
Chincheros 24 y
Chinchilla 74 t
Chinchow 58 d
Chincolco 28 o
Chinde 49 j
Chindu 62 d
Chindwin 62 p
Chingola 46 c
Chinguetti 36 q
Chinju 58 u
Chinko 42 s
Chinle 15 o
Chinnamp 58 s
Chinsali 46 f
Chinsi 58 c
Chintalnar 61 r
Chíos 35 t
Chipata 46 f
Chipinge 49 g
Chiplun 60 z
Chippewa Falls 16 c
Chiquían 24 w
Chiquilá 19 x
Chiquita, Laguna 28 u
Chiredzi 49 f
Chirgis Nuur 56 j
Chirinda 51 m
Chiriqui, Gulf of 22 h
Chirripó 22 h
Chisasa 45 n
Chisasibi 16 j
Chisig-Ondŏr 57 b
Chisinău 35 i
Chiskovo 51 x
Chisoso 45 s
Chistoozernoye 55 l
Chistopol 54 k
Chita 57 h
Chitembo 44 u
Chitina 11 h
Chitradurga 64 f
Chitrāl 60 l
Chittagong 61 y
Chittoor 64 h
Chitunde 46 g
Chiume 44 x
Chiúta 46 g
Chivay 25 n
Chivhu 49 f
Chivilcoy 31 b
Chodzeili 55 p
Choele Choel 30 l
Choiseul 71 v
Choke Mountains 43 b
Chokudakh 53 h
Choma 46 p
Chon Buri 65 k
Ch'ŏngjin 58 i
Ch'ŏngju 58 u
Chongquing (Chungking) 62 l
Chŏnju 58 u
Chonos, Archipelago 30 s
Chorinsk 57 f
Chorog 55 w
Chorracho 27 t
Chorregon 74 n
Chōshi 59 p
Chos Malal 30 i
Choteau 14 m
Chotla, Cerro de 19 n
Chott Djerid 34 x
Chott ech Chergui 36 m
Chott Melrhir 34 w
Chotts ech Chergui 34 t
Choüm 36 q
Choushuidan 56 z
Chovd 57 o
Chovd Gold 56 i
Chövsgöl 57 s
Chövsgöl Nuur 57 a
Christchurch 79 t
Christensen Mountains 84 l
Christiana 49 o
Christian X Land 91 q
Christmas Creek 72 y
Christmas Island 68 u
Chubut 30 l
Chuchow 63 c
Chudinovo 55 e
Chudovo 33 m
Chugwater 15 q
Chuhoi 63 p
Chukchi Sea 10
Chukehagirskoye, Lake 53 p
Chuken 58 m
Chukochye 53 l
Chukot Peninsula 10 j
Chulucanas 24 h
Chulugli 52 t
Chuluman 25 q
Chulym 56 d
Chumakovo 56 d
Chumar 61 d
Chumbicha 28 s
Chumikan 53 o
Chum Phae 65 k
Chumphon 65 i
Chuna 51 y
Ch'unch'ŏn 58 u
Ch'ungju 58 u
Chungking 62 l
Chunguj Gol 56 k
Chunhuhub 20 t
Chunskiyo 57 a
Chunya 45 g
Chuquibamba 24 z
Chuquicamata 28 d
Chur 34 l
Churapcha 53 a
Churchill 13 n
Churchill, Cape 13 n
Churchill Lake 12 v
Churchill Peak 12 o
Churchill (River, Quebec) 17 f
Churchill (River, Saskatchewan) 12 w
Churu 61 a
Churunguara 23 c
Chushakyl' 55 b
Chushul 61 c
Chutag 57 b
Chuūronjang 58 i
Chu Xian 63 f
Chuxiong 62 x
Chuya 52 r
Chuya (River) 52 r
Chuyengo 52 b
Chyul'be 52 z
Cibitoke 45 d
Ciego de Avila 21 n
Ciénaga 23 a
Cienfuegos 20 z
Cilacap 68 y
Čilik 56 o
Cimarron 15 t
Čimkent 55 v
Cincinatti 16 t
Cintra, G. de 36 n
Cipó 27 t
Cirčik 55 u
Circle 11 h
Cirebon 68 y
Cisneros 22 m
Citlaltépetl 19 p
Citrusdal 48 x
Ciudad Acuña 19 a
Ciudad Altamirano 19 n
Ciudad Bolivar 23 h
Ciudad Camargo 18 l
Ciudad del Carmen 19 t
Cuidad Guayana 23 i
Cuidad Guzman 18 y
Ciudad Ixtepec 19 r
Ciudad Juárez 18 j
Ciudad Madero 19 p
Ciudad Mante 19 o
Ciudad Mier 19 b
Ciudad Obregón 18 h
Ciudad Ojeda 32 b
Ciudad Real 34 q
Ciudad Valles 19 o
Ciudad Victoria 19 p
Civitavecchia 34 m
Clanwilliam 48 x
Claraville 73 w
Clarence, Cape 13 b
Clarence Island 82 f
Clarión 18 r
Clarksburg 16 w
Clarksdale 20 f
Clarksville (Arkansas) 16 o
Clarksville (Kentucky) 16 s
Clavering Island 91 s
Clayton 15 r
Clear, Cape 32 t
Clearfield 16 x
Cleopatra Needle 67 e
Clermont 74 q
Clermont-Ferrand 34 h
Cleveland (North Carolina) 16 t
Cleveland (Ohio) 16 v
Clifton 78 f
Clifton Hills 77 g
Clingmans Dome 16 u
Clinton (Missouri) 15 x
Clinton (Oklahoma) 15 u
Clinton (South Carolina) 20 l
Clinton Colden Lake 12 v
Clinton Creek 11 i
Clipperton 230 e
Clocolan 49 p
Cloncurry 73 w
Cloquet 15 k
Clorinda 28 y
Cloud Peak 15 c
Clovis 18 m
Cluj Napoca 35 f
Clutha 79 r
Clyde 13 j
Coari 25 g
Coari (River) 25 f
Coast Range 14 t
Coast Mountains 14 g
Coats Island 13 r
Coats Land 83 g
Coatzacoalcos 20 q
Cobar 78 b
Cobija 25 p
Coca 22 y
Cocalzinho 27 b
Cochabamba 28 f
Cochin 64 e
Cochrane (Canada) 16 i
Cochrane (Chile) 30 t
Cockburn 77 h
Cockburn (Mount) 73 o
Coco 22 g
Cocobeach 41 t
Cocoparra Range 78 b
Cocos Islands 65 e
Cocula 18 y
Codajás 25 h
Cod, Cape 17 o
Codera, Cabo 23 f
Codó 27 p
Codrington 21 y
Čodro 56 h
Cody 15 b
Coen 73 k
Coeur d'Alene 14 k
Coffee Bay 49 f
Cogt-Ovoo 57 q
Coiba 22 i
Coihaique 30 u
Coimbatore 64 e
Coimbra 34 o
Coipasa, Lago de 28 e
Coixtlahuaca 19 q
Cojbalsan 57 i
Cojedes 23 e
Colatina 29 k
Colbeck, Cape 81 x
Cold Bay 11 n
Coles Bay 78 q
Colesberg 49 n
Colhué Huapi, Lago 30 w
Colima 18 y
Colima, Nevada de 18 y
Colinas 27 o
Collahuasi 28 d
College Park 20 j
Collie 76 d
Collier Bay 72 k
Collingwood 79 t
Collinsville 74 q
Colnett 18 d
Cologne 33 o
Colomb Bechar 36 k
Colombia 22-25
Colombo 64 u
Colón (Cuba) 20 z
Colón (Panama) 22 j

Colorado 15 q
Colorado (River, Texas) 19 d
Colorado (River, Arizona) 14 y
Colorado (River, Argentina) 30 m
Colorado Plateau 14 z
Colorado Springs 15 q
Colorados 28 q
Columbia (Missouri) 15 x
Columbia (South Carolina) 20 l
Columbia (Tennessee) 16 s
Columbia (River) 14 j
Columbia Plateau 14 w
Columbus (Georgia) 19 l
Columbus (Mississippi) 19 j
Columbus (Nebraska) 15 u
Columbus (Ohio) 16 u
Colville 11 e
Colville Lake 12 b
Comai 61 m
Comalcalco 20 q
Comarapa 28 g
Combarbala 28 o
Comilla 61 y
Comitán 19 t
Commandante Ferraz 82 r
Committee Bay 13 c
Communism, Mount 55 v
Como (China) 61 h
Como (Italy) 34 k
Comodoro Rivadavia 30 w
Comores Islands 47 a
Comorin, Cape 64 s
Comoros 47 b
Compiègne 32 z
Compostela 18 x
Cona 61 m
Conakry 40 d
Conceiço do Araguaia 26 y
Concepción (Argentina) 28 s
Concepción (Bolivia) 28 i
Concepción (Chile) 30 g
Concepción (Paraguay) 28 l
Concepción del Oro 19 a
Concepción del Uruguay 28 x
Concepción, Laguna 25 v
Conchi 28 d
Conchos 18 k
Concord 17 n
Concordia (Argentina) 28 x
Concórdia (Brazil) 25 e
Concordia (Peru) 24 k
Concordia (USA) 15 u
Conde 27 u
Condobolin 78 b
Congo 41-42/44
Congo, Democratic Republic of 42/44-45
Congo (River) 44-45
Conjuboy 73 z
Connecticut (River) 17 n
Connecticut (State) 17 n
Connemara 73 w
Conrad 14 m
Conselheiro Lafaiete 29 i
Constance, Lake 33 p
Constanţa 35 i
Constantine 34 w
Constitución 30 g
Consuelo Peak 74 q
Contact 14 y
Contamaná 24 l
Contas 27 r
Contendas do Sincorá 27 r
Contwoyto Lake 12 h
Conway 20 e
Coober Pedy 77 d
Cook 77 a
Cook, Mount 79 r
Cook Islands 230 o
Cook Strait 79 u
Cooktown 74 c
Coolah 78 e
Coolgardie 76 g
Cooma 78 q
Coonabarabran 78 d
Coonamble 78 c
Coonapoor 64 d
Coongoola 77 k
Cooper 77 h
Cooperation Sea 85 e
Coorabulka 73 v
Coorong, The 77 t
Coorow 76 d
Coos Bay 14 t
Cootamundra 78 d
Cooya Pooya 72 s
Copenhagen 33 p
Copiapo 28 p
Copiapo, Mount 28 p
Copiapo (River) 28 p
Copper Center 11 h
Copper Harbor 16 e
Coppermine 12 f
Copperton 48 z
Coqên 61 h
Coquimbo 28 o
Coracora 24 z
Coral Harbour 13 r
Coral Sea 74 f
Corcovado, Gulf of 30 g
Cordillera Central 67 g
Cordillo Downs 77 h
Córdoba (Argentina) 28 u
Córdoba (Mexico) 19 q
Córdoba (Spain) 36 j
Cordoba, Sierra de 28 t
Cordova 11 g
Corfield 73 x
Corfu 35 q
Corfu (Island) 35 q
Coricudgy 78 e
Corigliano 35 o
Corinda 73 h
Corinda (Lake Galilee) 73 y
Corinth 20 g
Corinth, Gulf of 35 s
Corinto 29 h
Coriolei 43 t
Cork 32 u
Corleone 37 i
Corner Brook 17 i
Corno, Monte 35 a
Cornwall 16 l
Cornwall Island 12 m
Cornwallis Island 12 m
Coro 23 d
Coroatá 27 p
Corocoro 25 p
Coroico 25 q
Coromandel Coast 64 h
Coronation Gulf 12 g
Coronation Island 82 f
Coronel Murta 29 j
Coronel Oviedo 28 z
Coronel Pringles 31 a
Coronel Suárez 31 a
Coropuna 24 z
Corowa 78 b
Corpus Christi 19 d
Corque 28 e
Corrente 27 o
Corrente (River) 27 p
Correntina 27 o
Corrientes 28 y
Corrientes, Cabo 22 x
Corrientes (River, Argentina) 28 x
Corrientes (River, Peru) 24 k
Corsica 34 k
Cortina 34 m
Corubal 40 c
Corum 54 o
Corumba 28 l
Corumbá (River) 29 e
Corunna 34 a
Cosalá 18 k
Coscomatepec 19 q
Cosenza 35 o
Cosmonaut Sea 84 j
Costa Blanca 34 s
Costa Brava 34 h
Costa del Sol 34 q
Costa Marques 25 s
Costa Rica 22 g
Cotabato 67 v
Cotagaita 28 f
Cotahuasi 24 z
Côte d'Ivoire 40
Cotonou 41 o
Cotopaxi 22 x
Cottbus 33 r
Cottonwood 14 z
Coulman Island 86 s
Coulomb Point 72 j
Council Bluffs 15 v
Courantyne 23 y
Coventry 32 x
Cowan, Lake 76 h
Cowargarzê 62 e
Cowarie 77 f
Cowell 77 e
Cowra 78 d
Cox's Bzr 61 y
Cozumel 20 v
Cradock 49 o
Craig 15 p
Craiova 35 f
Cranbrook 14 k
Crateús 27 s
Cravo Norté 23 p
Cree Lake 12 v
Creporizinho 25 l
Cres 35 a
Crescent City 14 t
Creston 15 w
Crestview 20 h
Creswell Downs 73 f
Crete (Island) 35 s
Crete, Sea of 35 t
Criciúma 29 r
Crimea 35 l
Cristalandia 26 y
Cristalina 29 f
Cristino Castro 27 p
Cristóbal Colón 23 a
Croker, Cape 73 d
Crooked Island 21 q
Crookston 15 i
Cross 41 s
Crowl 77 k
Crown Prince Christian Land 91 i
Crown Prince Olaf Coast 84 j
Crown Princess Martha Coast 83 h
Croatia 35 b
Croydon 73 w
Crozet Island 231 p
Cruz Alta 29 n
Cruz das Almas 27 s
Cruz del Eje 28 t
Cruzeiro do Oeste 29 b
Cruzeiro do Sul 24 m
Crystal River 20 k
Ču 55 x
Ču (River) 55 i
Cuamba 45 v
Cuando 44 y
Cuangar 44 w
Cuango 44 v
Cuanza 44 t
Cuatrociénegas 18 m
Cuauhtémoc 18 j
Cuba 20-21
Cubango 44 v
Cuchi 44 u
Cucuí 23 r
Cucúi 25 d
Cúcuta 23 a
Cuddalore 64 h
Cuddapah 64 g
Cue 76 e
Cuemba 44 v
Cuenca 24 h
Cuernavaca 19 o
Cuiabá 25 y
Cuiabá (River) 25 y
Cuito 44 w
Cuito Cuanavale 44 w
Cuiuni 25 f
Cuixi 63 e
Culbertson 15 d
Culiacán 18 j
Cullman 20 h
Culpeper 16 x
Culuene 26 w
Čuluut 57 a
Culver, Cape 76 j
Čulym 56 h
Cumaná 23 g
Cumberland 16 x
Cumberland, Lake 16 t
Cumberland Peninsula 13 k
Cumberland Plateau 16 t
Cumberland (River) 16 t
Cumberland Sound 13 k
Cunani 26 k
Cuñaré 23 n
Cundza 56 p
Cunene 48 g
Čunja 51 y
Cunnamulla 77 l
Cupica 22 l
Curaõao 23 d
Curacautin 30 h
Curacó 30 l
Curaray 24 j
Curbur 76 d
Curico 30 i
Curimatá 27 p
Curitiba 29 r
Curitibanos 29 q
Currais Novos 17 v
Currant 14 y
Currie 77 w
Curtin Springs 73 p
Curtis Island 79 m
Curua 26 u
Curua-Uná 26 i
Curupira, Serra 25 f
Curuzú Cuatiá 28 x
Curvelo 29 h
Cutral-Có 30 j
Cuttack 61 v
Cuvelai 44 u
Cuya 28 c
Cuyuni 23 j
Cuzco 25 n
Cyaring Hu 62 e
Cyclades 35 t
Cyprus 35/38
Cyrenaica 38 b
Czech Republic 33-35
Czestochowa 33 t

D

Da 62 w
Dabar Tichitt 36 s
Dabola 40 f
Dabou 40 x
Dabsan Hu 62 c
Dachechang 57 o
Dachstein 35 a
Dadanawa 23 x
Daet 67 h
Dagana 40 c
Dagandely 55 m
Dagupan 67 g
Dahab 38 k
Dahar Oualata 36 t
Daheba 62 f
Dahlak, Islands 43 d
Dahna 39 f
Dāhod 61 n
Dahongliutan 61 d
Dai Hai 57 u
Dailehk 61 f
Dainkog 62 e
Daintree 74 c
Dairen (Dalian) 58 q
Dairût 38 h
Dairy Creek 76 d
Dajarra 73 v
Dakar 40 a
Dakhla 36 n
Dakhla, Oasis 38 t
Dakshin Gangotri 84 b
Dal 33 f
Dala 44 x
Dalaba 40 e
Dalandzadgad 57 q
Dalandžargalan 57 s
Dalaoba 56 r
Da Lat 66 k
Dalbandin 60 g
Dalby 78 f
Dalgonally 73 w
Dalgoye 52 l
Dalhart 15 s
Dalhousie, Cape 11 m
Dalian 58 q
Dallas 19 d
Dal'nerechensk 58 l
Daloa 40 v
Dalou Shan 62 k
Dalrymple 74 r
Dal'stroy 53 c
Dalton 20 j
Dalton, Cape 91 q
Dalou 62 t
Daly 73 c
Daly River 73 b
Daly Waters 73 d
Damakar 41 j
Daman 60 z
Damanhûr 38 h
Damar 70 n
Damara 42 o
Damascus 38 l
Damaturu 41 i
Damavand 39 j
Damavand (Mount) 39 j
Damba 44 g
Dambulla 64 u
Dam Gamad 42 i
Damghan 54 z
Dammam 39 i
Damon 61 q
Dampier 72 s
Dampier Downs 72 w
Dampier Land 72 j
Dampier Strait 70 p
Dam Qu 62 b
Damxung 61 l
Dana 10 a
Danakil 43 e
Danané 40 u
Da Nang 66 k
Danba 62 h
Danbury 16 z
Dan, Cape 90 y
Dandelehura 61 d
Danells Fjord 90 t
Dang 56 y
Dangla 43 b
Dango 42 f
Daniel 15 n
Daniëlskuil 48 z
Dankhar 61 c
Dankowa, Pik 55 z
Danmark Fjord 91 i
Dannebrog Island 90 x
Dansville 16 x
Danube, Mouths of the 35 j
Danube 33 r
Danville (Illinois) 16 s
Danville (Virginia) 16 w
Danzig (Gdansk) 33 t
Danzig, Gulf of 33 t
Daora 36 d
Dao Timni 37 v
Dapango 41 a
Dapchi 41 i
Dapitan 67 v
Da Qaidam 56 y
Daqing 58 f
Daquan 56 y
Dar'a 38 l
Daran 39 h
Darasun 52 s
Daraut-Kurgan 55 w
Darband 60 d
Darbhanga 61 v
Darchan 57 d
Dar-el-Beida (Casablanca) 36 g
Dar-es-Salaam 45 k
Dargaville 79 h
Darién, Gulf of 22 l
Daringskiy 55 j
Darj 37 g
Darjeeling 61 j
Darlag 62 g
Darling 77 i
Darling Range 76 d
Darnah 35 s
Darnley, Cape 85 c
Dartmouth 17 f
Daru 70 y

Darvaza 55 o
Darvel Bay 67 r
Darwin 73 c
Darwin (Island) 22 n
Darwin River 73 b
Daryacheh-ye-Bakhtegan 39 l
Daryacheh-ye-Namak 39 i
Daryacheh-ye-Tashk 39 k
Darzin 60 c
Dashizhai 58 d
Dasht 55 n
Dasht (River) 60 r
Dasht-e-Kavir 39 k
Dasht-e-Lut 39 m
Dashuiqiao 62 f
Datong 57 v
Datu, Cape 68 l
Datuk Bay 68 m
Daugav'pils 33 x
Daulat Yar 60 h
Daule 22 w
Daund 61 n
Dauphin 15 g
Davangere 64 e
Davao 67 w
Davao Gulf 67 w
Davenport 16 q
Davenport Downs 73 v
Davenport Range 73 r
David 22 h
Davidson 15 d
Davidson Mount 73 p
Davies 76 m
Davis 85 q
Davis Sea 85 t
Davis Strait 13 m
Davlekanovo 54 m
Dawa 43 p
Dawson (Canada) 11 i
Dawson (USA) 19 m
Dawson Creek 12 q
Dawson Landing 12 t
Dawu 62 h
Daxian 62 l
Dayangshu 58 f
Dayong 63 a
Dayr az Zawr 39 a
Dayton 16 t
Daytona Beach 20 m
Dazhu 62 l
De Aar 49 n
Deacon, Cape 82 z
Deadhorse 11 f
Dead Sea 38 l
Deakin 76 m
Deán Funes 28 t
Dease Lake 11 z
Dease Strait 12 i
Death Valley 14 x
Debba 38 u
Debdou 36 k
Debin 53 i
Débo Lake 40 k
Deborah, Lake 76 f
Debre Birhan 43 d
Debrecen 33 u
Debre-Markos 43 b
Debre Tabor 43 c
Debre Zeit 43 c
Decatur (Alabama) 20 h
Decatur (Illinois) 16 r
Deccan 61 o
Dechang 62 i
Decorah 16 p
Dédougou 40 l
Dedza 46 h
Deep Well 73 r
Deer 15 a
Dêgê 62 f
Degeh Bur 43 g
Degtyarsk Sysert' 55 c
Dehak 60 d
Dehbid 39 k
Dehloran 39 g
Dehra Dun 61 c
Dehui 58 f
Deihuk 60 b
Dej 35 g
Dejen 43 c
De Juh 62 c
De Kalb 16 r
Dekar 48 l
De Kastruskoye 53 r
Dekemehare 43 c
Dekese 44 l
Dékoa 42 o
Delamere 73 c
Delano 14 w
Delareyville 49 n
Delaware 16 y
Delgado, Cape 45 y
Delger 56 m
Delgerdhaan 57 c
Delgo 38 u
Delhi 61 b
Delicias 18 l
Déline (Fort Franklin) 12 c
Delingha 56 z
Dell 14 m
Dellys 34 v
Deloge, Monts 16 k
Delphi 35 s
Del Rio 19 a
Delta 14 z
Delta Downs 73 j
Delta Junction 11 g
Demba 44 l
Dembia 42 s
Dembidolo 42 m
Deming 18 j
Demini 23 u
Demnate 36 h
Dempo 68 t
Demyanka 51 o
Dem'yanovka 55 f
Demyanskoye 51 n
Denau 55 t
Deneżkin Kamen 50 x
Dengkou 57 q
Dengqên 62 d
Denham 76 b
Deniliquin 77 x
Denison 15 w
Denizli 35 w
Denman Glacier 85 s
Denmark 33
Denmark Strait 32 a
Denpasar 69 p
D'Entrecasteaux Islands 71 r
D'Entrecastleaux, Cape 76 c
Denver 15 q
Deogarh 61 u
Depósito 23 w
Deputatskiy 53 d
Dêgên 62 f
Dera Bugti 60 k
Dera Ghazi Khan 60 k
Dera Ismail Khan 60 k
Derbent 54 w
Derby (Australia) 72 k
Derby (UK) 32 x
Dergachi 54 j
Derm 48 j
Dêrong 62 g
De Rose Hill 73 r
Derudeb 38 y
Derwent 77 y
Derzhavinsk 55 g
Desaquadero (River, Argentina) 28 r
Desaquadero (River, Bolivia) 28 d
Descalvados 25 x
Dese 43 c
Deseado 30 x
Desertas 36 a
Des Moines 16 o
Des Moines (River) 15 w
Desna 54 a
Desolación 30 t
Dessau 33 q
Desterrada Pérez 19 v
Dete 46 p
Detroit 16 u
Det Udom 66 h
Deva 35 f
Devils Lake 15 h
Devon Island 13 c
Devonport 77 x
Dez 39 h
Dezful 39 g
Dezhgan 39 l
Dhahran 39 h
Dhaka 61 y
Dhamar 34 g
Dhanbad 61 v
Dhandhuka 60 z
Dharmapuri 64 g
Dharmsala 61 b
Dharwar 64 d
Dhaulāgiri 61 g
Dhofar 39 x
Dhuburi 61 y
Dhule 61 n
Diaca 45 x
Dialafara 40 f
Dialakoto 40 d
Diamaa 34 w
Diamante 28 w
Diamante (River) 28 r
Diamantina 26 q
Diamantina (Minas Gerais) 29 i
Diamantina (River) 73 w
Diamantina Lakes 73 w
Diamantino 25 y
Diamou 40 e
Dian-Chi 62 v
Dianópolis 27 n
Diapaga 41 b
Dibba 60 n
Dibella 41 j
Dibrūgarh 62 c
Dickinson 15 e
Didesa 43 a
Didiéni 40 h
Didwana 61 a
Diego de Almargro 28 p
Diéma 40 g
Digne 34 j
Digos 67 w
Digul 70 w
Dijon 34 i
Dikhil 43 e
Dikimdya 52 w
Dikson 51 f
Dikwa 41 j
Dila 43 p
Dilaram 60 g
Dili 69 x
Di Linh 66 k
Dilling 42 j
Dillingham 11 p
Dillon 14 m
Dilolo 44 y
Dimas 18 w
Dimbelenge 44 m
Dimbokro 40 w
Dinagat 67 j
Dinajpur 61 w
Dinar 39 i
Dinaric Alps 35 b
Dinder 42 m
Dingbian 57 r
Dinggyê 61 j
Dinguiraye 40 f
Dingxi 62 j
Ding Xian 57 v
Dinsor 43 s
Diourbel 40 b
Dipolog 67 u
Dirâng 62 b
Dire Dawa 43 e
Dirkou 37 v
Dirranbandi 78 c
Disappointment, Lake 72 x
Discovery Bay 77 u
Discovery, Cape 91 g
Disko Bay 90 k
Diu 60 y
Divinópolis 29 h
Divisoes, Serra das 29 d
Divnoye 54 g
Divriği 54 q
Dixon Entrance 14 b
Diyala 39 e
Diyarbakir 54 r
Dja 41 x
Djado 37 u
Djado Plateau 37 u
Djamaa 37 c
Djanet 37 s
Djebel Amour 37 a
Djebel Bani 36 g
Djebel Serkout 37 q
Djebel Ouarkziz 36 f
Djebel Tahat Telertheba 37 q
Djelfa 34 u
Djenné 40 j
Djerba 37 g
Djermaya 41 l
Djibo 40 m
Djibouti (City) 43 f
Djibouti (State) 43 f
Djidjelli 37 c
Djolu 42 r
Djougou 41 b
Djúpivogur 32 f
Dmitrov 50 p
Dneprodzerzhinsk 35 l
Dnepropetrovsk 35 l
Dnieper 35 l
Dniester 35 g
Doab-i Mikhe Zarin 60 i
Doba 41 m
Dobryanka 50 w
Doce 29 j
Docker River 73 o
Doda Betta 64 f
Dodge City 15 t
Dodoma 45 h
Dogai Coring 61 j
Dogondoutchi 41 c
Do'gyaling 61 j
Doha 39 w
Doi Inthanon 62 s
Dois Irmos, Serra do 27 r
Dolak Island 70 u
Dolgany 51 j
Dolo 43 s
Dolomites 34 m
Dolon 56 b
Dolores 31 c
Dolphin and Union Strait 12 f
Domba 62 d
Dombarovskiy 55 c
Dombås 33 b
Dome Fuji 84 f
Domeyko 28 o
Dominica 23
Dominican Republic 21
Don 54 e
Donald 77 w
Dondo (Angola) 44 s
Dondo (Mozambique) 46 v
Dondo Bay 69 g
Dondra, Head 64 v
Donegal Bay 32 u
Donets 54 d
Donetsk 54 d
Dong 57 n
Dongbatu 56 y
Dongfang 62 z
Dongfanghong 58 k
Donggala 69 f
Dong Hoi 66 j
Dong Jian 63 q
Dongjingcheng 58 l
Dongkalang 69 g
Dongle 57 n
Dongliao 58 e
Donglük 56 u
Dongnan Quiling 63 o
Dongola 38 u
Dongou 42 n
Dongqiao 61 l
Dongsheng 57 t
Dong-Ujimqin Qi 57 x
Dongzhen 57 p
Donors Hill 73 v
Doomadgee 73 u
Dora Lake 72 w
Dorbod 58 f
Dordabis 48 j
Dordogne 34 g
Dori 40 m
Doro 40 m
Döröö Nuur 56 k
Dorowa 49 f
Dorrego 31 a
Dortmund 33 o
Doruma 42 u
Dos de Mayo 24 k
Doshi 60 j
Dosso 41 c
Dothan 19 l
Douala 41 u
Doualayel 41 w
Douaouir 36 x
Douentza 40 l
Douglas (UK) 32 w
Douglas (Arizona) 18 h
Douglas (Wyoming) 15 q
Douglas Range 82 w
Dourada, Serra 26 z
Dourados 29 a
Douro 34 b
Dove Bay 91 t
Dover 32 z
Dover, Strait of 34 g
Dover Foxcroft 17 b
Dovsk 33 z
Dowlatabad 60 b
Dracena 29 c
Drakensberg 49 q
Drake Passage 82 c
Drammen 33 c
Drava 35 c
Dreikikir 70 y
Dresden 33 r
Dresvyanka 50 j
Drosh 60 l
Drovyanaya 51 b
Dr. Pedro P. Pen 28 i
Drumheller 14 m
Drummondville 17 a
Druzhina 53 g
Dryden 15 k
Drygalski Island 85 t
Drysdale 72 m
Dschang 41 u
Dua 42 q
Duaringa 74 r
Duba 38 l
Dubai 39 y
Dubawnt Lake 12 x
Dubbo 78 d
Dublin (Ireland) 32 v
Dublin (USA) 20 k
Dubna 50 p
Dubois 14 m
Dubovskoye 54 g
Dubrovnik 35 c
Dubuque 16 q
Duchess 73 v
Duero 34 d
Dudinka 51 h
Dudypta 51 k
Duékoué 40 v
Duero 34 e
Dugiuma 43 s
Dukhan 39 v
Duki 53 o
Dukou 62 u
Dulan 62 e
Dulce 28 v
Dugla-Kyuyel' 52 r
Dulia 42 s
Duluth 15 k
Dumaguete 67 i
Dumai 68 f
Dumka 61 w
Dumont d'Urville Sea 87 o
Dumont d'Urville 87 o
Dumyat 35 x
Duna 35 c
Dunărea 35 g
Dunay 52 k
Dunbar 73 k
Dundalk 32 v
Dundas 91 b
Dundas Harbour 13 e
Dundas Peninsula 12 g
Dundee (South Africa) 49 r
Dundee (UK) 32 x
Dunedin 79 s
Dungas 41 g
Dungu 42 v
Dungun 66 t
Dungunab 38 y

Dunhua 58 h
Dunhuang 56 x
Dunkwa 40 z
Duqm 60 o
Durack Range 72 m
Durango (Mexico) 18 x
Durango (USA) 15 p
Duranzo 28 z
Durban 49 s
Durham 16 x
Duri 68 f
Durma 39 r
Durrës 35 d
Durrie 77 g
Dusak 55 p
Dusa Mareb 43 v
Dushan 62 y
Dushanbe 55 u
Düsseldorf 33 o
Dusti 55 u
Dutch Harbor 10 z
Dutlwe 49 a
Dvina 33/50
Dvina Bay 50 p
Dwangwa 45 t
Dwarka 60 w
Dwarsberg 49 c
Dyalinya 53 b
Dyer, Cape 13 m
Dyersburg 16 q
Dzachuj 56 y
Dzag 56 m
Džambul 55 v
Dzaoudzi 47 c
Dzavchan Gol 56 k
Dzereg 56 j
Dzerzhinsk 50 r
Dzerzhinsky 54 f
Dzhaksy 55 g
Dzhalinda 52 x
Dzhambul 55 e
Dzhamm 53 a
Dzhankoy 35 m
Dzhara 52 d
Dzhardzhan 52 k
Dzhelinde 52 f
Dzhelon 52 m
Dzhezkazgan 55 h
Dzhungdzhur Mountains 53 p
Dzhunkun 52 e
Dzhusaly 55 f
Džida 57 d
Džida (River) 57 d
Dzilam de Bravo 19 v
Dzioua 37 c
Džirgatal 55 v
Džizak 55 u
Dznankoy 54 b
Dznetygara 55 d

E

Eagle Plain 11 k
Eagle Summit 11 g
East Cape 79 x
East China Sea 63 k
Easter Group 76 b
Easter Island 230 r
Eastern Cordillera (Bolivia) 25 s
Eastern Cordillera (Colombia) 22-23
Eastern Cordillera (Peru) 24 k
Eastern Ghats 61 s
Eastern Sierra Madre 19 o
East Falkland 31 p
East London 49 q
Eastmain 16 k
Eastmere 74 p
East Millinocket 17 c
Easter Siberian Sea 53 i
East Timor 69 x
East Turkestan 56 o
Eau Claire 16 c
Eau Claire, Lac à l' 13 u
Eauripik Atoll 70 l
Ebe 52 j
Ebebiyin 41 u
Ebinur Hu 56 q
Ebola 42 q
Ebolowa 41 u
Ebro 34 f
Echo Bay (Port Radium) 12 e
Ecija 34 p
Eclipse Sound 88 y
Ecuador 22/24
Ed Damazin 42 m
Ede 41 q
Edéa 41 u
Eden 15 o
Edessa 35 e
Edge Island 92 p
Edinburgh 32 x
Edirne 35 h
Edith Ronne Ice Shelf 83 o
Edith Ronne Land 83 s
Edjeleh 37 f
Edmonton 14 m
Edmundston 17 c
Edsel Ford Range 81 u
Edson 14 k
Eduardo Castex 30 l
Edward, Lake 45 c
Edward River 73 j
Edwards Plateau 19 a
Edward VII Peninsula 81 x
Edzo 12 r
Efate 75 e
Effingham 16 r
Egadi 34 z
Egersund 33 a
Egijn Gol 57 b
Egmont 79 u
Eğridir, Lake 35 w
Egvekinot 10 h
Egypt 35/38
Eidfjord 33 b
Eight Degree Channel 64 o
Eighty Mile Beach 72 v
Eil 43 k
Eilerts-de-Haan-Gebergte 26 g
Einasleigh 73 y
Eindhoven 33 n
Eirunepé 25 b
Eje Volcanico 19 o
Ejido Insurgentes 18 f
Ejin Qi 57 n
Ejutla 19 q
Ekalaka 15 d
Ekibastuz 55 l
Ekimchan 53 n
Ekiti 41 q
Ekoli 44 m
Ekonda 52 b
El Arco 18 f
El Aaiún 36 d
El Aricha 36 k
Elat 38 k
Elato Atoll 71 a
Elaziğ 54 q
Elba 34 l
El Banco 23 a
El Barcat 37 t
El Baúl 23 e
El Bayadh 34 s
Elbe 33 q
Elbert, Mount 15 p
Elblag 33 u
El Bordo 22 y
Elbrus 54 s
El Bur 43 v
Elburz Mountains 54 x
El Cajon 18 c
El Calafate 30 u
El Callao 23 i
El Canton 23 c
El Carmen 25 t
El Carrizalillo 18 k
El Cerro 25 u
El Chilicote 18 l
El Chinero 18 e
El Dab 43 i
El Dere 34 v
El'dikan 53 b
El Djem 34 y
El Djouf 36 t
El Dorado (Arkansas) 19 g
Eldorado (Brazil) 29 a
Eldorado (Uruguay) 29 n
Eldorado (Canada) 12 c
El Dorado (Kansas) 15 v
El Dorado (Mexico) 18 w
El Dorado (Venezuela) 23 i
Eldoret 43 n
El Eglab 36 v
Elektrostal 54 d
Elemi Triangle 42 z
El Encanto 23 o
Elephant Island 82 e
Eleuthera 21 c
El Fasher 42 g
El Fuerte 18 i
El Fugha 37 k
El Gal 43 l
El Gezira 42 l
Elgin (UK) 32 k
Elgin (USA) 16 r
El Goléa 37 a
Elgon 42 z
El Hamurre 43 x
El Hank 36 t
El Hasheisa 42 m
Eliseu Martins 27 p
Elista 54 h
Elizabeth 16 z
Elizabeth City 16 y
Elizabeth Reef 78 k
Elizabethtown 16 t
El Jadida 36 f
El Jebelein 42 l
Elkedra 73 s
El Kere 43 s
El Khenachich 36 v
Elkins 16 w
Elko 14 x
Ellef Ringnes Island 12 k
Ellensburg 14 i
Ellesmere Island 91 f
Elliot (S. Africa) 49 q
Elliot Bay 77 x
Elliot, Mount (Queensland) 74 q
Elliott (Australia) 73 e
Elliott, Mount (W. Australia) 72 z
Ellisras 49 c
Ellsworth Land 81 b
Ellsworth Mountains 81 d
El Maia 36 x
El Maitén 30 i
El Mango 23 s
El Mansour 36 l
El Meghaier 37 c
Elmira 16 y
El Mreïti 36 t
El Obeid 42 j
El Oso 23 t
El Oued 34 w
El Paso 18 k
El Porvenir 18 k
El Real 22 k
El Salado 30 w
El Salto 18 x
El Salvador (State) 22
El Salvador (Chile) 28 p
El Sauz 18 k
Elsey 73 e
El Sherana 73 d
El Socorro 18 f
El Sombrero 23 e
El Sueco 18 k
Eltanin Bay 80 m
El Tigre 23 h
Elton 54 i
El Triunfo 18 u
El Tule 19 a
El Uach 43 r
Eluru 64 i
Elvira 24 m
El Wak 43 q
Ely 14 y
Emba 55 b
Emba (River) 55 a
Embarcación 28 g
Embu 43 o
Emden 33 o
Emerald 74 r
Emi Koussi 37 y
Emmen 33 n
Emmet 74 o
Emory Peak 18 m
Empalme 18 h
Emporia (Kansas) 15 v
Emporia (Virginia) 16 x
Empredrado 28 y
Emu 58 h
Emu (River) 77 v
Encarnación 28 z
Encounter Bay 77 s
Endako 14 f
Ende 69 u
Enderby Land 84 l
Endicott Mountains 11 d
Endybal 52 m
Eneabba 76 d
Engaño, Cape 67 h
Engel's 54 i
Engenheiro Dolabela 29 i
Engerdyakh 52 h
Enggano 68 s
England 32 x
English Channel 32 x
English River 16 d
Engoordina 77 d
Enid 15 u
Enkan 53 q
Enna 37 i
Ennadai Lake 12 x
Ennedi 38 p
Ennis 15 a
Enschede 33 o
Ensenada 18 c
Enshi 62 m
Entebbe 42 y
Enterprise 12 r
Entroncamento 27 n
Enugu 41 s
Envira 25 b
Envira (River) 25 n
Enyélé 42 n
Equatorial Guinea 41
Erba 38 y
Erdene 57 t
Erdene Büren 56 i
Erdene Cagaan 57 w
Erdenedalaj 57 p
Erdenet 57 c
Erdi 38 o
Erebus 86 r
Ereğlí 35 y
Ereğli (Black Sea) 35 j
Erenhot 57 u
Erexim 29 o
Erfoud 36 i
Erfurt 33 p
Ergedzhey 52 h
Erg el Ahmar 36 w
Erger Raoui 36 k
Erguig 42 a
Ergun 52 v
Ergun Yuoqi 52 v
Erie 16 w
Erie, Lake 16 v
Erigavo 43 j
Erimbet 55 r
Erimo 59 d
Eritrea 43 d
Erldunda 73 q
Ermelo 49 r
Er Mreyer 36 t
Ernabella 77 b
Ernakulam 64 e
Erode 64 f
Eromanga 73 x
Erozionnyy 53 h
Er Rahad 42 j
Errego 46 j
Erromango 75 s
Ershiyizhan 52 x
Ertai 56 u
Ertix He 56 f
Erzincan 54 r
Erzurum 54 s
Esbjerg 33 o
Escalante 15 n
Escanaba 16 f
Escondido 18 c
Escondido (River) 22 g
Escoumins 17 b
Escuinapa 18 x
Escuintla 22 c
Ese 42 u
Eséka 41 u
Eshowe 49 s
Esk 74 t
Eskimo Point 13 n
Eskişehir 35 w
Eslamada-e-Gharb 39 f
Esmeralda 73 x
Esmeraldas 22 w
Esmeraldas (River) 22 w
Espanola 16 i
Española 22 p
Esperance 76 h
Esperanza (Antarctica) 82 g
Esperanza (Argentina) 28 v
Esperanza (Argentina) 30 v
Esperanza (Mexico) 18 h
Esperanza (Peru) 25 n
Espinal 22 z
Espinnaco, Serra do 29 i
Espiritu Santo 75 d
Espiritu Santo Bay 20 u
Espiritu Santo (Island) 18 h
Espita 19 w
Espoo 33 j
Espungabera 49 g
Esquel 30 h
Esquina 28 x
Essaouira 36 f
Essen 33 o
Essendon, Mount 72 v
Essequibo 23 x
Esso 53 y
Estación Babicora 18 j
Estacion Trincheras 18 g
Estancia 27 u
Estcourt 49 r
Estelí 22 e
Estevan 15 e
Estherville 15 w
Estmain 16 l
Estonia 33 j
Etah 61 d
Etap Bajanmönch 57 t
Etawah 61 d
Ethiopia 42-43
Ethiopian Highlands 43 b
Etna 35 n
Etosha Pan 48 h
Etykan 53 g
Etzatlán 18 y
Eubboea 35 s
Eucla 76 m
Eucumbene, Lake 77 z
Eufaula 20 i
Eugene 14 g
Eulo 74 o
Euphrates 39 e
Eureka (California) 14 t
Eureka (Canada) 13 c
Eureka (Nevada) 14 x
Eureka (Utah) 14 z
Eurinilla 77 h
Europe Island 46 z
Evans Lake 16 j
Evans Strait 13 r
Evanston 15 n
Evansville 16 s
Everard, Lake 77 c
Everard Park 77 b
Everest 61 i
Everett 14 h
Everglades 20 m
Evinayong 41 u
Evje 33 b
Evora 34 o
Évreux 32 y
Ewirgol 56 t
Ewo 44 g
Exeter 32 w
Exeter Sound 13 m
Exmouth 72 q
Exmouth Gulf 72 r
Eyakit-Tërdë 52 f
Eyik 52 h
Eyre 76 k
Eyre, Lake 77 e
Eyre Peninsula 77 d

Ezequil Ramos Mexia
Reservoir 30 j
Ez Zemoul el Akbar 37 d

F

Fachi 37 t
Facundo 30 v
Fada 38 o
Fada-Ngourma 41 a
Faeroe Islands 32 i
Fafen 43 t
Faggo 41 h
Fagnano, Lago 30 w
Faguibine Lake 40 k
Faidzabad 55 v
Fairbanks 11 g
Fairmont (Minnesota) 15 w
Fairmont (W. Virginia) 16 w
Fairweather, Mount 11 x
Faisalabad 60 m
Faizabad 61 f
Fakfak 70 q
Falcon Reservoir 19 b
Falkland Islands/
Islas Malvinas 31 p
Fallon 14 w
Falster 33 q
Famagusta 35 y
Famatina, Sierra de 28 q
Fana 40 i
Fandriana 47 r
Fangshan 63 t
Fang Xian 63 a
Fangzheng 58 i
Fan si Pan 62 v
Faradje 42 w
Farafangana 47 r
Farafra 38 f
Farafra, Oasis 38 g
Farah 60 e
Farahrod 60 f
Farah Rud 60 f
Faranah 40 f
Farasen, Island 39 o
Faraulep Atoll 70 m
Farewell, Cape 90 t
Farewell Island 80 l
Fargo 15 i
Faribault 15 k
Faridpur 61 x
Farim 40 c
Farkovo 51 h
Farmington 15 o
Faro (Brazil) 26 g
Faro (Canada) 11 l
Faro (Portugal) 34 o
Farrukhabad 61 d
Farsi 60 f
Fartak, Ras 43 m
Fasa 39 k
Faskari 41 e
Fataki 42 x
Fatala 40 d
Fatehpur 61 r
Fátima 26 y
Fatsa 54 p
Fatunda 44 i
Fatzeh 54 b
Fauresmith 49 o
Fauro 71 u
Faxa Bay 32 a
Faya 37 z
Fayetteville (Arkansas) 15 w
Fayetteville (Carolina) 16 x
Fayetteville (Tennessee) 16 s
Fayu 71 d
Fazilka 60 m
Fdérik 36 q
Federated States of
Micronesia 71 c
Fedorovskiy 53 d
Fedulki 50 z
Feijó 25 o
Feira de Santana 27 s
Felipe Carrillo Puerto 20 u
Fengfeng 63 c
Fengje 62 m
Fengning 57 w
Fengqing 62 s
Feodosiya 54 p
Ferdows 60 b
Ferfer 43 u
Fergana 55 w
Fergus Falls 15 i
Fériana 34 x
Ferkéssédougou 40 k
Ferlo 40 c
Fernandina 22 o
Fernandina Beach 20 m
Fernando de Noronha 27 l
Fernandópolis 29 d
Ferrara 34 m
Ferreira Gomes 26 k
Ferreñafe 24 h
Fès 36 i
Feshi 44 i
Festus 16 q
Fethiye 35 w
Fetisovo 54 z
Fezzan 37 u
Fiambalá 28 r
Fianarantsoa 47 p
Fiche 43 c
Ficksburg 49 q
Figuig 36 l
Fiji 75 l
Fik 43 e
Filadelfia 28 k
Filchner Ice Shelf 83 t
Filingué 41 c
Filtu 43 r
Fimbul Ice Shelf 83 j
Finch Hatton 74 r
Findlay 16 u
Fingoè 45 r
Finike 35 w
Finisterre, Cape 34 a
Finke 77 d
Finke (River) 77 d
Finland 33
Finland, Gulf of 33 i
Firat 54 q
Firenze (Florence) 34 m
Firozpur 61 a
Firuzabad 39 j
Fish 48 x
Fisher Strait 13 q
Fishguard 32 w
Fiske, Cape 83 n
Fitzcarrald 24 z
Fitzroy (Queensland) 74 s
Fitzroy (Western Australia) 72 x
Fitzroy Crossing 72 z
Flagstaff 15 n
Flathead Lake 14 m
Flattery, Cape 14 f
Flensburg 33 p
Flinders 73 w
Flinders Bay 76 c
Flinders Island 78 q
Flinders Range 77 g
Flin Flon 15 f
Flint 16 u
Flint (River) 20 j
Floraville 73 v
Florence (Italy) 34 m
Florence (South Carolina) 20 m
Florence (Tennessee) 20 h
Florencia 22 z
Florentino Ameghino
Reservoir 30 y
Flores 20 s
Flores (Island) 72 j
Flores Sea 69 t
Floriano 27 p
Florianópolis 29 s
Florida (Uruguay) 31 d
Florida (USA) 20
Florida Bay 20 m
Florida, Straits of 20 m
Flower's Cove 17 j
Fly 70 x
Foggia 35 b
Foley 13 g
Fomich 52 c
Fond du Lac 16 r
Fonseca, Gulf of 22 d
Fontanillas 25 w
Fonte Boa 25 e
Fontur 32 e
Foochow 63 t
Forbes 78 c
Forécariah 40 d
Forel, Mt. 90 z
Formosa (Argentina) 28 x
Formosa (Brazil) 29 f
Formosa do Rio Preto 27 o
Formosa, Serra 25 z
Formoso 29 g
Forrest River 73 a
Forsayth 73 x
Forsyth 15 c
Fort Albany 16 i
Fortaleza (Bolivia) 25 q
Fortaleza (Brazil) 27 g
Fortaleza (Brazil) 25 s
Fort Beaufort 49 o
Fort Black 12 v
Fort Chipewyan 12 t
Fort Collins 15 q
Fort-de-France 23 i
Fort Dodge 15 w
Forte Carumbo 44 k
Fortescue 72 u
Forte Veneza 26 v
Fort-Foureau 41 k
Fort Frances 15 k
Fort Franklin 12 c
Fort Gardel 37 r
Fort Good Hope 12 a
Fort Hope 16 e
Fortin Garrapatal 28 i
Fortin General Diaz 28 j
Fortin Gral. Eugenio Garay 28 i
Fortin Hernandarias 28 i
Fortin Juan de Zalazar 28 k
Fortin Madrejón 28 k
Fortin Max Parades 28 k
Fortin Ravelo 28 j
Fort Lauderdale 20 m
Fort Laird 12 p
Fort Macleod 14 m
Fort McMurray 12 t
Fort McPherson 11 k
Fort Morgan 15 r
Fort Myers 20 l
Fort Nelson
(British Columbia) 12 p
Fort Nelson (Manitoba) 13 n
Fort Norman 12 o
Fort Peck Reservoir 15 d
Fort Pierce 20 m
Fort Portal 42 w
Fort Providence 12 r
Fort Qarain 38 d
Fort Resolution 12 t
For Rupert 16 k
Fort Sandeman 60 j
Fort Scott 15 w
Fort-Sevčenko 54 x
Fort Severn 13 p
Fort Simpson 12 p
Fort Smith (Canada) 12 u
Fort Smith (USA) 15 w
Fort St. John 12 q
Fort Stockton 18 m
Fort Walton Beach 20 i
Fort Wayne 16 t
Fort William 32 v
Fort Worth 19 c
Fort Yukon 11 g
Foshan 63 o
Fossil Bluff 82 x
Foumban 41 v
Foum El Aassane 36 g
Fourdou 40 d
Fouta Djalon 40 d
Foveaux Strait 79 q
Fowler's Bay 77 b
Foxe Basin 13 g
Foxe Channel 13 s
Foxe Peninsula 13 t
Fox Harbour 17 j
Fox Islands 10 z
Foz do Cunen 48 e
Foz do Iguaçú 29 n
Foz do Mamoriá 25 d
Foz do Pauini 25 d
Franca 29 f
France 32-33/34
Franceville 44 f
Francisco Beltro 29 o
Francistown 49 c
Frankfort 49 q
Frankfurt 33 r
Frankfurt (am Main) 33 p
Frankland 76 d
Frankland Range 78 o
Franklin Mountains 12 o
Franklin Strait 12 m
Franz Josef Land 50 h
Fraserburg 48 y
Fraserdale 16 i
Fraser (Newfoundland) 13 y
Fraser (River,
British Columbia) 14 h
Fraser Island 74 u
Fraser Range 76 i
Frazier Downs 72 w
Frederick 15 h
Frederick E. Hyde Fjord 91 j
Fredericksburg 16 x
Fredericton 17 d
Frederikshavn 33 c
Fredonia 16 w
Fredrikstad 33 d
Freeport 16 q
Freetown 40 d
Fregon 77 a
Freiburg 33 o
Fremantle 76 d
French Guiana 26 i
French Polynesia 230 p
Fresco 26 x
Fresnillo 18 z
Fresno 14 v
Frewena 73 r
Fria 40 d
Frias 28 s
Frio, Cabo (Brazil) 29 j
Frio, Cape (Namibia) 48 e
Frisian Islands 33 n
Frobisher Bay (Iqaluit) 13 w
Frobisher Lake 12 v
Frome, Lake 77 g
Frontera 19 t
Front Range 15 q
Frutal 29 e
Frylinckspan 48 z
Fuding 63 h
Fuerte 18 i
Fuerte Olimpo 28 k
Fuerteventura 36 c
Fujairah 39 y
Fujin 58 k
Fujiyama 59 n
Fuka 38 f
Fukui 58 z
Fukuoka 58 v
Fukushima 59 o
Fukuyama 58 x
Funchal 36 a
Fundy, Bay of 17 e
Fünen 33 p
Funhalouro 49 h
Funing 62 x
Funtua 41 f
Furmanovka 55 w
Furmanovo 54 k
Furnas Reservoir 29 g
Furneaux Group 78 p
Fury and Hecla Strait 13 e
Fushun 58 f
Fusin 58 d
Fu Xian 58 q
Fuyang 63 d
Fuyu 58 f
Fuyuan 58 l
Fuyun 56 h
Fuzhou (Foochow) 63 e

G

Ga 40 l
Gabela 44 t
Gabès 37 f
Gabès, Gulf of 34 y
Gabon 41/44
Gabon (River) 44 c
Gaborone 46 o
Gadag 64 e
Gadsden 19 l
Gaferut 71 a
Gafoua 41 k
Gafsa 37 e
Gagarin 54 b
Gagnoa 40 w
Gagnon 17 c
Gagyu Hu 63 g
Gainesville (Florida) 20 k
Gainesville (Georgia) 20 j
Gairdner, Lake 77 d
Gairo 45 i
Gai Xian 58 e
Gaktsynka 53 p
Gala 61 k
Galanino 51 x
Galapagos Islands 22 q
Galati 35 h
Galbraith 73 j
Galcaio 43 v
Galdhöpiggen 33 b
Galena 11 c
Galesburg 16 q
Galilee, Lake 73 z
Galimyy 53 k
Galiwinku 73 f
Galle 64 u
Gallegos 30 v
Gallinas, Cabo 23 b
Gällivare 33 h
Gallup 15 o
Galt 57 a
Galveston 19 e
Galway 32 u
Galway Downs 77 i
Gama 29 f
Gambaga 40 m
Gambela 42 m
Gambell 10 k
Gambia 40
Gambo 42 q
Gamboma 44 g
Gamboola 73 l
Gambos 44 s
Ganda 44 t
Gandadiwata 69 s
Gandajika 44 m
Gandak 61 g
Gander 17 k
Gandi 42 f
Gandia 34 s
Gandsya 54 v
Gandu 27 s
Gangan 30 j
Ganganagar 60 m
Gangapur 61 b
Gangaw 62 p
Gangca 57 n
Ganges 61 t
Ganges Delta 61 x
Ganhezi 56 u
Gan Jiang 63 d
Gannett Peak 15 o
Ganta 40 u
Gao 41 a
Gao'an 63 d
Gaotai 57 n
Gaoua 40 k
Gaoual 40 d
Garalo 40 i
Garanhuns 27 v
Garapu 26 w
Garba Tula 43 p
Garberville 14 t
Garda, Lake 34 m
Garden City 15 t
Gardez 60 j
Gardo 43 j
Garhchiroli 61 q
Garies 48 v
Garimpo Cumaru 26 x
Garissa 43 q
Garland 19 d
Garmabe 42 w
Garmenka 57 b
Garmsar 39 j

Garoe 43 j
Garonne 34 g
Garoua 41 j
Garoua Boulaï 41 x
Garry Lake 12 l
Garwa 61 t
Gary 16 s
Garyarsa 61 d
Gar Zangbo 61 e
Garzê 62 g
Garzón 22 z
Gascoyne 72 s
Gascoyne Junction 72 r
Gas Hu 56 v
Gashua 41 i
Gaspar Strait 68 w
Gaspé 17 e
Gastre 30 j
Gatton 74 t
Gauhati 61 z
Gavbandi 39 k
Gavio 27 s
Gävle 33 g
Gawan 59 b
Gawler 77 g
Gawler Ranges 77 d
Gaxun Nur 57 n
Gaya (India) 61 u
Gaya (Niger) 41 c
Gayndah 78 f
Gaza 38 k
Gaziantep 54 q
Gbadolite 42 p
Gbarnga 40 t
Gdansk 33 t
Gdynia 33 t
Gebe 67 z
Gedaref 43 a
Geelong 77 w
Geelvink Channel 76 c
Gê'gyai 61 e
Geidam 41 i
Geita 45 f
Gejiu (Kokiu) 62 v
Gela 35 n
Gelib 43 s
Gêlo 25 y
Gemena 42 p
Gemsa 38 j
Gemsbok 48 x
General Acha 30 l
General Alvear 30 k
General Belgrano 83 s
Beneral Belgrano Plateau 83 o
General Bernardo O'Higgins 82 s
General Carrera, Lago 30 t
General Conesa 30 l
General Güemes 28 t
General Juan Madariaga 31 d
General Pico 30 m
General Roca 30 k
General San Martin 82 v
General Santos 67 w
General Viamonte 31 a
General Villegas 30 m
Geneva 34 i
Geneva, Lake 34 j
Genève (Geneva) 34 i
Genoa 34 k
Genoa, Gulf of 34 k
Genova (Genoa) 34 k
Genovesa 22 p
Geographical Society Island 91 r
George 48 z
George IV Sound 82 z
George, Lake (USA) 20 l
George, Lake (Uganda) 45 d
George Land 50 h
Georgetown (Australia) 73 x
Georgetown (Cayman Islands, UK) 20 y
Georgetown (Gambia) 40 c
Georgetown (Guyana) 23 l
George Town (Pinang, Malaysia) 65 w
Georgetown (USA) 21 a
George V Land 86 y
Georgia 20 k
Georgia (State) 54 t
Georgian Bay 16 i
Georgia, Strait of 14 g
Georgiievka 56 d
Georgina 73 v
Georg von Neumayer 83 g
Gera 33 q
Geral de Goiás, Serra 29 f
Geral do Parana, Serra 29 f
Geraldton (Australia) 76 c
Geraldton (Canada) 16 f
Gerasmikova 51 p
Gerede 35 k
Gerlachovsky 35 d
Germania Land 91 t
Germany 33
Germiston 49 q
Gerona 34 h
Gêrzê 61 g
Gettysburg 15 g
Getz Ice Shelf 81 q
Geureudong 65 u
Gewane 43 d
Geyhan 35 z
Ghadames 37 f
Ghadir 43 g
Ghaem-Shahr 54 z
Ghaghara 61 t
Ghana 40-41
Ghandi Sagar Reservoir 61 n
Ghanzi 48 m
Ghardaia 34 u
Ghariyan 34 z
Ghat 37 s
Ghazaouet 36 k
Ghaziabad 61 c
Ghazipur 61 t
Ghazni 60 j
Ghelinsor 43 v
Ghent 34 h
Ghion 43 b
Ghorian 60 e
Ghubeish 42 h
Ghugri 61 v
Giahel 43 k
Giamama 43 s
Gibb River 72 m
Gibraltar 34 p
Gibraltar, Str. of 34 p
Gibson Desert 72 y
Gidgealpa 77 g
Gidgee 76 g
Gidole 43 o
Gifford 88 x
Gifu 58 z
Giganta, Siera de la 18 g
Gijón 34 c
Gila Desert 18 f
Gilbert River 74 a
Gilbués 27 o
Giles Meteorological Station 73 n
Gilf Kebir Plateau 38 r
Gilgil 43 n
Gilgit 61 a
Gillam 13 n
Gillette 15 d
Gimbi 43 a
Gingin 76 d
Gingoog 67 w
Giohar 43 u
Giresun 54 q
Giri 42 n
Girishk 60 g
Gironde 34 f
Gisborne 79 x
Gisenyi 45 d
Gitarama 45 d
Giza 38 h
Gizhduvan 55 r
Gizhiga 53 m
Gjoa Haven 12 m
Glace Bay 17 h
Gladmar 15 d
Gladstone 74 t
Glasgow (Kentucky) 16 t
Glasgow (Montana) 15 c
Glasgow (UK) 32 w
Glazov 50 v
Glenayle 76 h
Glendive 15 d
Glenelg 77 u
Glen Falls 16 z
Glengyle 77 g
Glen Helen 73 q
Glen Innes 78 f
Glenmorgan 78 d
Glennallen 11 g
Glenns Ferry 14 y
Glenormiston 73 u
Glenroy 72 m
Glenwood Springs 15 p
Globe 18 h
Glubinnoye 58 l
Goa 64 d
Goageb 48 v
Goalpara 61 y
Goba 43 q
Gobabis 48 k
Gobernador Gregores 30 v
Gobi 56-57
Gochas 48 j
Godavari 64 i
Gode 43 s
Goderich 16 v
Godhavn 90 k
Godhra 60 z
Godinlave 43 v
Gods Lake 15 j
Godthåb (Nuuk) 90 u
Goiána 27 w
Goianésia 29 e
Goiânia 29 d
Goiás 29 d
Goiatuba 29 d
Gokwe 46 q
Gol (Norway) 33 b
Gol (Russia) 52 t
Golan Heights 38 l
Gol'chikha 51 g
Gold Coast (Australia) 78 g
Gold Coast (Ghana) 40 z
Golden 14 k
Goldfield 14 x
Goldsboro 16 x
Goldworthy 72 u
Golmud 62 c
Golyshmanovo 55 g
Goma 45 c
Gombari 42 w
Gombe 41 i
Gomel 33 y
Gomera 36 a
Gómez Palacio 18 l
Gonaïves 21 r
Gonam 52 z
Gonam (River) 52 z
Gonbad-e-Kavus 54 z
Gonder 43 b
Gongbo'gyamda 62 b
Gonggar 61 l
Gonghe 62 g
Gongola 41 h
Gongpoquan 56 z
Gongshan 62 f
Gongxi 63 e
Gonzales 19 d
Good Hope, Cape of 48 w
Gooding 14 y
Goodnews Bay 11 n
Goondiwindl 78 e
Gooty 64 f
Gorakhpur 61 f
Gordon 77 x
Gordon Downs 73 n
Gore (Chad) 41 m
Gore (Ethiopia) 43 a
Gore (New Zealand) 79 r
Goreis 48 h
Gorel'de 55 q
Gorelova 53 m
Gorgan 54 z
Gorgona 22 x
Gorgora 43 b
Gor'kiy (Nizhiy Novgorod) 50 r
Gorlovka 54 d
Gornak 56 d
Gorno-Chuyskiy 52 r
Gornyy 58 m
Gornyy Kazymsk 51 a
Goroka 70 z
Gorongosa 46 u
Gorontalo 69 i
Gorotiré 26 x
Gorshechnoye 54 d
Gorzow-Wikp 33 s
Gosford 78 f
Göteborg 33 d
Gotland 33 g
Göttingen 33 p
Goudoumaria 41 i
Gouin Reservoir 16 m
Goukou 58 d
Goulburn 78 e
Goulmina 36 i
Goumeré 40 x
Goundam 40 k
Goura 41 g
Gourara 36 m
Gouré 41 h
Gouro 37 z
Gov'Chonin 56 w
Governador Valadares 29 j
Govorovo 52 l
Goya 28 x
Goyder's Lagoon 77 g
Goyoum 41 x
Goz Beïda 42 d
Gozo 35 n
Graaff-Reinet 49 n
Grabo 40 v
Gracias á Dios, Cape 22 h
Gradaús, Serra 26 x
Grafton (Australia) 78 g
Grafton (USA) 15 h
Graham Bell Island 50 m
Graham Island 13 b
Graham Land 82 u
Grahamstown 49 o
Grain Coast 40 t
Grajaú 27 n
Grajaú (River) 27 o
Granada (Nicaragua) 22 f
Granada (Spain) 34 q
Gran Canaria 36 b
Gran Chaco 28 h
Grand Bahama Island 21 a
Grand Bank 17 j
Grand-Bassam 40 x
Grand Caicos 21 s
Grand Canal 57 w
Grand Canyon 14 z
Grand Cayman 20 z
Grand Centre 15 a
Grande (Brazil) 29 h
Grande (Nicaragua) 22 g
Grande (Venezuela) 23 i
Grande, Bahia 30 w
Grande Cache 14 j
Grande Comore 47 b
Grande de Gurapa 26 k
Grande de Santiago, Rio 18 y
Grande Prairie 14 j
Grand Erg de Bilma 37 u
Grande, Rio (River, Bolivia) 28 g
Grande, Rio (River, Campos, Brazil) 27 p
Grande, Rio (River, Brazil) 29 h
Grande, Rio (River, USA) 19 b
Grand Forks 15 i
Grand Island 15 u
Grand Junction 15 o
Grand-Lahou 40 w
Grand Marais 16 d
Grand-Mére 17 a
Grand Pantanal 28 m
Grand Rapids (Minnesota) 15 k
Grand Rapids (Michigan) 16 t
Grand Santi 26 i
Grangeville 14 k
Granite Downs 77 c
Granite Peak (Australia) 76 h
Granite Peak (USA) 15 a
Gran Laguna Salada 30 x
Gran Sabana 23 v
Grant Island 81 r
Grants 15 p
Grants Pass 14 t
Granville 32 x
Gravatá 27 v
Gray, Cape 87 o
Grayling 16 g
Graz 35 b
Great Abaco Island 21 b
Great Anyuy 10 a
Great Australian Bight 76 k
Great Bahama Bank 21 n
Great Barrier Reef 74 b
Great Barrier Island 79 i
Great Basin 14 x
Great Bear Lake 12 d
Great Bitter Lake 38 j
Great Britain and Northern Ireland 32
Great Dividing Range 78
Great Eastern Erg 34 w
Great Exuma Island 21 p
Great Falls 15 a
Great Fish 49 o
Great Inagua Island 21 q
Great Karasberg 48 w
Great Karoo 48 z
Great Khingan Mountains 58 d
Great Plain 63 c
Great Salt Lake 14 z
Great Sandy Desert 72 x
Great Slave Lake 12 t
Great Smoky Mountains 16 u
Great Tiraz 48 u
Great Victoria Desert 76 l
Great Wall 57 u
Great Western Erg 36/37
Great Whale River 16 l
Greater Antilles 20/21
Greece 35
Greeley 15 q
Greely Fjord 91 e
Green Bay 16 e
Green Head 76 c
Greenland 90-91
Greenland Sea 91 w
Greenough 76 d
Green River 15 n
Green River (River) 15 o
Greensboro 16 w
Greensburg 16 w
Greenvale 74 o
Greenville (Alabama) 20 i
Greenville (Liberia) 40 t
Greenville (Mississippi) 20 f
Greenville (North Carolina) 16 x
Greenville (South Carolina) 20 k
Gregory Downs 73 u
Gregory, Lake 72 z
Gregory Range 74 n
Greifswald 33 r
Grenada 23 j
Grenoble 34 j
Grey Bull 15 b
Greymouth 79 s
Grey Range 77 i
Greytown 49 s
Gribingui 42 b
Griekwastad 48 z
Griffith 77 k
Grinell Peninsula 13 a
Grise Fjord 13 e
Groblersbrug 46 p
Groblersdal 46 q
Groblershoop 48 y
Grodno 33 w
Grong 33 d
Groningen (Netherlands) 33 n
Groningen (Suriname) 26 g
Groot 49 n
Groote Eylandt 73 g
Grootfontein 48 j
Groot Winterhoek 48 x
Grosseto 34 m
Gross Glockner 34 m
Groznyi 54 u
Grudziadz 33 t
Grünau 48 w
Grungedal 33 b
Gryazi 54 e
Guaçu 29 a
Guadalajara (Mexico) 18 z
Guadalajara (Spain) 34 e
Guadalcanal 71 x

Guadalquivir 34 p
Guadalupe 18 z
Guadalupe (Island) 18 c
Guadalupe Peak 18 l
Guadalupe Victoria 18 y
Guadalupe-y-Calvo 18 j
Guadeloupe 21
Guadiana 34 o
Guadix 36 k
Guafo, Gulf of 30 f
Guaicurus 28 l
Guainia 23 q
Guaira 29 n
Guajará Mirim 25 r
Guajira Peninsula 23 b
Gualeguay 28 x
Gualeguay (River) 28 x
Gualeguaychu 28 x
Guallatiri 28 c
Guam 231 j
Guamini 31 a
Guanahacabibes Peninsula 20 w
Guanaja 20 v
Guanajuato 19 n
Guanambi 29 i
Guanare 23 d
Guandacol 28 q
Guangnan 62 x
Guangyuan 62 k
Guangzhou (Canton) 63 p
Guanipa 23 h
Guantiánamo 21 p
Guan Xian 62 i
Guapi 22 x
Guaporé 25 s
Guaqui 25 o
Guarabira 27 v
Guarai 26 z
Guarapuava 29 p
Guarantinguetá 29 g
Guarda 34 b
Guardafui, Cape 43 l
Guàrico 23 e
Guarulhos 29 f
Guasave 18 i
Guásimas 18 h
Guatemala 19/22
Guatemala (City) 22 c
Guaviare 23 q
Guayabero 23 n
Guayaquil 24 g
Guayaquil, Gulf of 24 g
Guaymas 18 g
Guazapares 18 j
Guba 43 a
Gubakha 50 w
Gudur 64 h
Gudvangen 33 a
Guéckedou 40 g
Guedi 42 b
Guelb er Richat 36 r
Guélengdeng 41 l
Guelma 37 d
Guelta Zemmur 36 q
Guémar 37 d
Güera 36 n
Guerara 34 v
Guercif 36 j
Guernsey 34 e
Guga 53 p
Gugu 43 d
Guguang 69 d
Guia 36 b
Guiana Highlands 23 s
Guidjiba 41 k
Guiglo 40 u
Guijá 46 t
Guimaras 67 h
Guinan 62 g
Guinea 40
Guinea Bissau 40
Guinea, Gulf of 41 p
Güines 20 y
Guir 36 k
Güiria 23 i
Guiyang (Kweiyang) 62 x
Gujarkhan 60 m
Gujranwala 60 m
Gujrat 60 m
Gulbarga 61 p
Gul'ča 55 x
Gulf of Mexico 20
Gulfport 20 g
Gulian 52 v
Gulistan 55 u
Gulkana 11 h
Gulu 42 x
Gulya 52 v
Gumare 48 l
Gumbiro 45 v
Gumti 61 s
Gümüşhane 54 q
Guna 61 p
Guna (Mount) 43 c
Gungu 44 j
Gunnbjrn Fjeld 91 n
Gunnedah 78 e
Gunpowder 73 v
Gunter 61 r
Guntur 64 h
Guoju 63 i
Gurdaspur 61 a
Gurgei 42 f
Gurguéia 27 p
Gurha 60 y
Guri, Lago de 23 i
Guro 46 u
Gurskoye 59 a
Gurué 46 j
Gurun 54 q
Gurupi 26 y
Gurupi (River) 27 a
Gurupizinho 26 m
Guru Sikhar 60 z
Gurvan Ozagal 57 i
Gusau 41 e
Gushan 58 r
Gusinoozersk 57 e
Gutara 56 m
Guthrie 15 u
Guyana 23/25/26
Guyang 57 t
Guymon 15 s
Guyuan 62 k
Gvardeyets 53 g
Gwa 62 p
Gwai 49 c
Gwai River 49 c
Gwalior 61 p
Gwanda 49 d
Gweru 49 e
Gwydir 78 d
Gyaring Co 61 j
Gyda 51 e
Gydan Bay 51 d
Gydan Peninsula 51 d
Gyirong 61 h
Gyldenlves Fjord 90 w
Gympie 78 g
Gynym 52 z
Györ 35 c

H

Haarlem 48 z
Haast 79 q
Haast Bluff 73 p
Hab 60 v
Habaswein 43 q
Hab Chauki 60 v
Habshan 39 x
Hachioji 59 n
Ha Coi 62 y
Hadarba, Ras 38 z
Haddad 42 c
Hadejia 41 h
Hadejia (River) 41 g
Hadera 38 k
Hadilik 56 s
Hadley Bay 12 i
Hadramaut 43 j
Haeju 58 s
Haena 18 p
Hafun, Ras 43 l
Hagadera 43 q
Hagere Hiywot 43 c
Hagerstown 16 x
Ha Giang 62 x
Hague, The 33 n
Hagunia 36 d
Haifa 38 k
Haikow 63 n
Ha'il 39 b
Hailar 58 c
Hailar (River) 58 b
Hainan 63 n
Hainan Strait 63 n
Haines 11 x
Haines Junction 11 k
Haiphong 62 y
Haiti 21
Haiya 38 y
Haiyan 62 h
Hajiabad 39 l
Hajjah 43 f
Hakkâri 54 t
Hakodate 59 c
Halaban 39 q
Halaib 38 z
Halawa 18 r
Halcon 67 g
Hale 76 e
Hal Flood Range 81 t
Halifax 17 s
Halil Rud 60 b
Hall Beach 13 e
Halle 33 q
Hallett 86 s
Halley Bay 83 f
Hall Island 50 j
Hall Islands 71 e
Hall Land 91 f
Hall Peninsula 13 x
Halls Creek 73 n
Halmahera 69 m
Halmstad 33 r
Ham 41 l
Hama 38 m
Hamada du Guir 36 j
Hamada du Tinrhert 37 d
Hamada el Haricha 36 w
Hamada el Homra 37 g
Hamada of Dra 36 h
Hamadan 39 h
Hamada Safia 36 v
Hamadat Tingharat 37 g
Hamamatsu 59 n
Hamar 33 d
Hamarro Hadad 43 f
Hambantota 64 v
Hamburg 33 p
Hämeenlinna 33 i
Hamelin Pool 76 c
Hamersley Range 72 s
Hamhung 58 u
Hami 56 x
Hamilton (Alaska) 11 a
Hamilton (Australia) 77 v
Hamilton (Canada) 16 w
Hamilton (Idaho) 14 l
Hamilton (New Zealand) 79 v
Hamilton Downs 73 q
Hamilton Inlet 17 i
Hammami 36 t
Hammam Lif 37 g
Hammerfest 33 j
Hammond 20 f
Hamoud 40 e
Hampton (Oregon) 14 v
Hampton (Virginia) 16 y
Hampton Tableland 76 l
Hamrat al Shaikh 42 h
Hamun-e Jaz Murian 60 c
Hancheng 63 a
Handeni 45 j
Handgai 57 l
Hangayn Mountains 57 a
Hangchow 63 h
Hanggin Houqi 57 q
Hangzhou (Hangchow) 63 h
Hankö 33 i
Hann 72 l
Hanna 14 m
Hannah Bay 16 j
Hannibal 16 p
Hannover 33 p
Hanoi 62 x
Hanover (Hannover) 33 p
Hanover (Island) 30 s
Hanover (South Africa) 49 n
Hanover (USA) 17 n
Han Shui 63 b
Hantan 57 v
Hanzhong 62 k
Haouach 38 n
Happy Valley-Goose Bay 17 g
Hapur 61 c
Harad 39 u
Harare 46 s
Haraza 42 j
Haraze Mangueigne 42 c
Harbin 58 g
Harda 61 p
Hardangerfjörd 33 a
Hardec Králove 33 s
Hardin 15 c
Harding 49 r
Hardy 16 p
Harer 43 e
Hargeisa 43 g
Hargele 43 s
Har Hu 56 z
Hari 68 h
Hari Rud 60 f
Harlingen 19 c
Harlowtown 15 a
Harper 40 u
Harper Island 13 y
Harqin 58 c
Harricana 16 k
Harrington Harbour 17 h
Harrisburg 16 y
Harrismith 49 q
Hartford 17 n
Harts Range 73 s
Harudj el Asued 37 l
Hasa 39 h
Hasalbag 56 n
Hassan 64 e
Hassel Sound 12 l
Hassi bel Guebbour 37 d
Hassi Inifel 37 b
Hassi Maroket 38 a
Hassi Messaoud 34 w
Hassi Touareg 37 c
Hastings (New Zealand) 79 w
Hastings (USA) 15 u
Hatches Creek 73 s
Ha Tinh 62 x
Hat Lek 66 g
Hatteras, Cape 16 y
Hattiesburg 20 f
Hat Yai 66 q
Hauberg 83 o
Haugesund 33 a
Hauraki Gulf 79 v
Haute Kotto 42 r
Hauts Plateaux 36 m
Havana 20 x
Haverhill 17 o
Havre 15 a
Havre-St-Pierre 17 f
Hawaii 18 r
Hawaiian Islands 18 o
Hawera 79 u
Hawi 18 r
Hawke Bay 79 w
Hawr al Hammar 39 f
Hawthorne 14 w
Hay 77 j
Hay River 12 s
Hay River (River) 12 r
Hayes 13 a
Hayes Halv 91 c
Haynan 43 j
Hays (USA) 15 t
Hays (Yemen) 43 f
Hazard 16 u
Hazaribagh 61 u
Hazelton 14 e
Head of Bight 77 a
Healesville 78 o
Heard Island 231 r
Hearst 16 h
Hearst Island 82 x
Hebel 74 q
Heber City 15 n
Hebrides 32 h
Hecate Strait 14 c
Hechi 62 y
Hefei 63 f
Hefeng 63 a
Heihe 58 g
Heilbron 62 p
Helena, Mount 14 m
Helen Reef 70 d
Heligoland Bight 33 o
Hell-Ville 47 e
Helmand 60 f
Helmeringhausen 48 v
Helsingborg 33 r
Helsingfors (Helsinki) 33 j
Helsingör 33 q
Helsinki 33 j
Helwân 38 i
Henbury 73 q
Hendersonville 16 u
Hendijan 39 h
Hendrik Verwoerd Reservoir 49 o
Hengchun 63 u
Hengduan Shan 62 e
Hengyang 63 b
Henrietta Maria, Cape 16 i
Henryetta 15 v
Henry Kater Peninsula 13 j
Henties Bay 48 g
Henzada 65 f
Heppner 14 i
Herat 60 f
Herbert Vale 73 u
Heredia 22 g
Hereford 15 s
Hermosillo 18 g
Herrick 78 p
Herschel 11 j
Hervey Bay 74 u
Hexigten Qi 57 x
Heze 63 d
Hibbing 15 k
Hibbs, Point 77 x
Hickory 16 v
Hidalgo del Parral 18 k
Hidden Valley 73 d
High Altai 56 v
High Atlas 36 h
High Knob 16 u
Highlands (Scotland) 32 w
High Level 12 s
High Prairie 12 r
High River 14 l
Hiiumaa 33 i
Hilla 39 e
Hillsboro 16 u
Hilo 18 s
Hima' 16 r
Himalaya 61
Himatnagar 60 z
Himeji 58 y
Himeville 49 r
Hindmarsh, Lake 77 u
Hindu Kush 60 j
Hinlopen Strait 92 o
Hirafok 37 q
Hirakud Reservoir 61 t
Hiroshima 58 x
Hisar 61 a
Hoa Binh 62 x
Hoare Bay 13 l
Hobart (Tasmania) 77 y
Hobart (USA) 15 u
Hobbs 18 m
Hochfeld 48 j
Hochwan 62 k
Ho Chi Minh (Saigon) 66 j
Hodal 61 b
Hodda 43 k
Hoddur 43 s
Hodeida 43 f
Hoeryōng 58 i
Hohoi 63 c
Hoh Xil Shan 61 l
Hoima 42 x
Hoit Taria 56 y
Hokang 58 i
Hokitika 79 s
Hokkaidō 59 d
Hola 43 q

Holbrook 15 n
Hold with Hope Peninsula 91 s
Holguín 21 p
Hollick Kenyon Plateau 81 d
Holman Island 12 e
Holstebro 33 o
Holt Sum 57 x
Holy Cross 11 b
Holyhead 32 w
Hombori 40 l
Home Bay 13 k
Homodji 41 k
Homs 38 m
Honda 22 z
Honda Bay 67 e
Hondo 20 t
Hondo Reservoir 28 t
Hondo (River) 19 w
Honduras 19-20/22
Honduras, Gulf of 20 v
Hönefoss 33 c
Hong Ha 62 w
Hong Kong 63 q
Hongliuyuan 56 y
Hongyuan 62 i
Hongze 63 g
Honiara 71 x
Honolulu 18 p
Honshú 59 n
Hood Cape 76 g
Hooker, Cape 86 t
Hooker Creek 73 p
Hooker Island 50 i
Hooper Bay 10 m
Hopa 54 s
Hope 14 h
Hopedale 17 h
Hopes Advance, Cape 13 w
Hopetown 49 n
Hopin 62 q
Hopkins, Lake 73 n
Hormuz, Strait of 39 m
Horn, Cape (Chile) 30 x
Horn, Cape (Iceland) 32 b
Horn, Cape (Norway) 91 p
Hornavan 33 g
Horqin Youyi Qianqi 58 d
Horqin Zuoyi Zhongqi 58 e
Horsham 77 v
Hoseinabad 39 l
Hoshab 60 t
Hoshangabad 61 p
Hoshiarpur 61 b
Hospet 64 e
Hossororo 23 k
Hoste 30 w
Hotan 56 p
Hotan (River) 56 p
Hotazel 48 z
Hot Springs 15 r
Hottah Lake 12 e
Houailu 75 p
Houck 15 o
Houghton 16 e
Houma (China) 63 a
Houma (USA) 19 h
Houndé 40 l
Houston 19 d
Houtman Abrolhos 76 b
Houxia 56 t
Howar 38 q
Howe, Cape 78 r
Howship 73 d
Howship (Mount) 73 d
Hoyo 42 w
Hradec Králové 35 b
Hsinchu 63 u
Hsuchang 63 c
Huachinango 20 n
Huacho 24 v
Huacrachuco 24 w
Huadian 58 g
Huahaizi 56 x
Hau Hin 65 j
Huai 63 d
Huai'an 57 v
Huaibei 63 e
Huaiji 63 o
Huainan (Hwainan) 63 e
Huairen 57 u
Huaiyin 63 g
Huajuapan de León 19 p
Hualien 63 v
Huallaga 24 k
Huamanrazo 24 y
Huancabamba 24 h
Huancané 25 o
Huancapi 24 y
Huancavelica 24 x
Huancayo 24 y
Huanchaca, Serra de 25 v
Huang 63 a
Huangchuan 63 d
Huan Jiang 62 l
Huanren 58 f
Huanta 24 y
Huánuco 24 x
Huapanapan 19 p
Huaping 62 u
Huara 28 c
Huaral 24 w
Huaraz 24 v
Huarmey 24 v
Huascaran 24 w
Huasco 28 o
Huasco (River) 28 p
Huashixia 62 f
Huatabampo 18 h
Huauchinango 19 p
Hudiksvall 33 g
Hudson 16 z
Hudson, Cape 86 y
Hudson Bay 13 q
Hudson Bay (Saskatchewan) 15 f
Hudson Land 91 s
Hudson Strait 13 v
Hue 66 j
Huehuetenango 19 u
Huelva 34 o
Huesca 34 f
Huéscar 36 j
Hufuf 39 u
Hughenden 73 y
Hughes 11 d
Hugli 61 w
Huhehot 57 u
Hŭichŏn 58 t
Huila, Nev. de 22 y
Huili 62 u
Huinan 58 f
Huinca Renancó 30 m
Huixtla 19 t
Huize 62 v
Huizhou 63 q
Hulaifah 39 a
Hulin 58 k
Hull 16 l
Hulls Cove 17 p
Huluun Nuur 57 j
Huma 58 g
Humahuaca 28 f
Humaitá 26 o
Humansdorp 49 n
Humboldt 14 w
Humera 43 b
Hume Reservoir 78 c
Humphreys Peak 15 n
Hun 37 j
Húna Bay 32 b
Hunchun 58 i
Hungary 33/35
Hungchui 62 y
Hungtze, Lake 63 f
Hunter Island 77 w
Huntington 16 u
Hunt, Mount 12 n
Huntsville (Canada) 16 j
Huntsville (Texas) 19 e
Huntsville (Tennessee) 19 k
Hunyani 46 e
Huolongmen 58 g
Huo Xian 63 b
Hurghada 38 k
Huron 15 h
Huron, Lake 16 h
Hutanopan 68 d
Hutchinson 15 u
Huth 43 g
Huxley, Mount 72 z
Huyani 49 e
Hval Sound 91 c
Hvar 35 b
Hwainan 63 e
Hwang (Huang He) 63 f
Hwange 46 o
Hwangju 58 t
Hwangshih 63 d
Hyderabad (India) 61 q
Hyderabad (Pakistan) 60 w
Hyesanjin 58 h
Hyndman Peak 14 y

I

Iaco 25 p
Iaşi 35 h
Iba 67 f
Ibadan 41 q
Ibagué 22 z
Ibarra 24 i
Ibb 43 g
Ibba 42 v
Ibembo 42 s
Iberia 25 o
Ibi 41 h
Ibiapaba, Serra da 27 r
Ibicui 28 z
Ibitunane 27 q
Ibiza 34 t
Ibologero 45 g
Ibotirama 27 q
Ibra 42 f
Ibri 39 z
Ica 24 x
Içá 25 b
Ica (River) 24 x
Içana 25 d
Iceland 32
Içel (Mersin) 35 y
Icha 53 x
Ichang 63 a
Ichera 52 q
Ichilo 25 s
Ichinskaya Sopka 53 y
Ich'on 58 t
Icó 27 t
Icy, Cape 11 a
Idaho 14 k
Idaho Falls 14 z
Idaye 41 i
'Idd al Ghanam 42 e
Ideles 37 p
Iderijn Gol 57 a
Idfu 38 w
Idhan Awbari 37 g
Idhan Murzuq 37 u
Idi 65 u
Idiofa 44 j
Idlib 38 l
Idri 37 i
Idutywa 49 q
Idyum 52 z
Idžim 56 j
Ifakara 45 i
Ifalik Atoll 70 l
Ife 41 q
Iférouane 37 r
Iffley 73 w
Igaluit 90 f
Iganga 42 y
Igarka 51 h
Igbetti 41 c
Ighil 36 h
Igli 36 k
Igluligaarjuk (Chesterfield Inlet) 13 o
Igombe 45 f
Igra 50 v
Iguaçú 29 o
Iguala 19 o
Iguatu 27 s
Iguidi Erg 36 i
Iharaña 47 f
Ihosy 47 p
Ija 57 a
Ijebu Ode 41 q
Ika 52 p
Ikanbujmal 56 u
Ikela 42 r
Ikelenge 44 z
Ikerasassuaq 90 t
Ikerre 41 q
Ikom 41 t
Il'a 57 h
Ilagan 67 h
Ilam 39 f
Ilan 63 v
Ilaro 41 p
Ilbenge 52 k
Ilebo 44 k
Ie de France 91 u
Ilek 54 l
Ilesha 41 g
Ilha do Bananal 26 y
Ilhéus 29 l
Ili 56 p
Iliamna Lake 11 q
Iligan 67 v
Ilimniir 53 i
Ilimpeya 52 b
Ilimsk 57 c
Ilir 57 a
Ilirney 10 c
Illampu 28 d
Illapel 28 o
Illéla 41 d
Illela 41 d
Illimani 25 q
Illinois 16 q
Illizi 37 r
Illmani 28 e
Ilmer, Lake 33 m
Ilo 25 n
Iloilo 67 h
Ilorin 41 d
Il'pyrskiy 10 a
Imataca, Serrania de 23 i
Imatra 33 l
Imbros 35 t
im Chapyeva 53 i
im Gastello 53 g
Imi 43 s
Imilili 36 o
Imperatriz 27 n
Imperia 34 k
Imperial 15 s
Impfondo 42 n
Imphäl 62 p
In Abalene 37 n
In Afeleh 37 s
In Alay 36 x
Inambari 25 o
In Amenas 37 e
In Amguel 37 p
Iñapari 25 o
Inari, Lake 33 k
In Azaoua 37 r
In Azaraf 37 n
Inca de Oro 28 p
Ince, Cape 35 m
Inch'ŏn 58 t
Independence 15 w
Independence Fjord 91 i
Inderborskiy 54 k
India 60-61/64
Indiana (Australia) 73 s
Indiana (USA) 16 s
Indianapolis 16 s
Indian Head 15 e
Indian Ocean 231-231
Indiara 29 d
Indigirka 53 g
Indonesia 68-70
Indore 61 n
Indragiri 68 g
Indravati 61 r
Indus 60
Indus Delta 60 v
In Ebeggi 37 q
In Ekker 37 p
Inezgane 36 f
Infiernillo Reservoir 18 z
Inga 44 f
Ingende 44 j
Ingeniero Guillermo Nueva Juárez 28 i
Ingeniero Jacobacci 30 j
Ingham 74 c
Ingili 53 o
Inglefield Land 91 d
Inglewood 78 e
Ingoda 52 t
Ingolf Fjord 91 j
Ingraj Bazar 61 w
Ingrid Christensen Coast 85 n
In Guezzam 37 p
Inhambane 46 v
Inhaminga 46 v
Inhassoro 46 v
Ining 56 q
Inirida 23 q
Inja 56 g
Injaptuk 57 f
Injune 74 r
Inkerman 73 j
Inkisi-Kisantu 44 g
Inland Sea 58 x
Inn 33 q
Innamincka 77 h
Inner Mongolia 57
Innisfail 74 c
Innsbruck 34 m
Inongo 44 i
Inoni 44 g
In Salah 37 a
Inscription, Cape 76 a
Insein 65 g
Inta 50 k
In Talak 41 c
Intelewa 26 h
International Dateline 86 q
International Falls 15 k
Inthanon 66 c
Inukjuak 13 t
Inuvik 11 k
Invercargill 79 q
Inverell 78 e
Inverness 32 j
Inverway 73 b
Investigator Strait 77 r
Investigator Group 77 c
Inya 53 s
Inya (River) 53 s
Inyanga 46 t
Inza 54 h
Iolotan 55 r
Iona 48 f
Ionian Sea 35 p
Iowa 16 o
Iowa City 16 p
Ipameri 29 f
Ipatinga 29 j
Ipiales 24 j
Ipiau 29 l
Ipin 62 j
Ipixuna 25 g
Ipoh 66 r
Iporanga 29 r
Ipswich (Australia) 74 u
Ipswich (UK) 32 z
Ipu 27 r
Iqaluit (Frobisher Bay) 13 w
Iqe 56 x
Iquique 28 c
Iquitos 24 m
Iracema 25 u
Irai 29 o
Iráklion 35 t
Iramaia 27 r
Iran 39/54-55/60
Iranshahr 60 e
Irapuato 19 n
Iraq 39/54
Irbid 38 l
Irebu 44 h
Irece 27 r
Ireland 32
Irgiz 55 d
Irharharene 37 d
Irigui 40 j
Iringa 45 h
Iriomote 63 w
Iriri 26 v
Irish Sea 32 w
Irkestam 55 x
Irkutsk 52 o
Irondro 47 q
Iron Knob 77 e

Iron Mountain 16 e
Iron Range 73 l
Ironwood 16 d
Irrawaddy 62-65
Irrawaddy, Mouths of the 65 f
Irta 50 t
Irtysh 51 n
Irving 19 d
Iryupinsk 54 f
Isabal, Lago de 20 s
Isabela 22 o
Isabella 22 g
Isabella, Cordillera 22 f
Isačenko 51 h
Isa Fjord 92 o
Isafjördur 32 a
Isalo Mountains 47 p
Isangi 42 s
Isangila Falls 44 f
Isayevskiy 51 l
Isbil 43 g
Iseyin 41 c
Isfahan 39 j
Ishasha River 45 d
Isherton 23 x
Ishim 51 n
Ishim (River) 51 o
Ishinomaki 59 p
Isil'kul 55 j
Isinga 57 g
Isiolo 43 o
Isiro 42 v
Isisford 73 y
Iskenderun 35 z
Iskine 54 l
Islamabad 60 m
Island Falls 12 x
Island Lagoon 77 e
Island Lake 51 j
Islands, Bay of 79 h
Islay 32 v
Ismâilîya 38 j
Isna 38 v
Isoka 45 s
Israel 35/38
Israelite Bay 76 j
Issyk-Kul 55 y
Issyk-Kul, Lake 56 n
Istanbul 35 i
Istlán 18 y
Itabaiana 27 u
Itaberaba 27 r
Itaboca 26 o
Itabuna 29 l
Itacaiúnas 26 y
Itacajá 27 n
Itacoatiara 25 j
Itaituba 25 l
Itajai 29 r
Italy 34-35
Itamaraju 29 l
Itamataré 27 a
Itanagar 62 b
Itaobim 29 j
Itapetinga 29 k
Itapetininga 29 e
Itapeva 29 e
Itapicuru 27 t
Itapicuru (Serra das Alpercatas) 27 p
Itapicuru Mirim 27 c
Itapicuru, Serra do 27 o
Itapipoca 27 f
Itaporanga 27 t
Ithaca 16 y
Itigi 45 g
Itinga 26 z
Itiquira 25 y
Itonamas 25 s
Ittoqqortoormiit 91 r
Itui 25 a
Ituiutaba 29 d
Itumbiara 29 d
Itungi 45 t
Ituri 42 t
Iturup 59 g
Ituxi 25 r
Iuaretê 25 b
Iultin 10 h
Ivaipor 29 p
Ivalo 33 k
Ivangrad 35 d
Ivanhoe 78 a
Ivano Frankovsk 35 g
Ivanovo 50 q
Ivdel' 50 y
Ivinhema 29 b
Ivittuut 90 t
Ivohibe 47 q
Ivory Coast 40 v
Ivujivik 13 t
Iwaki 59 p
Iwo 41 p
Ixiamas 25 p
Ixopo 49 r
Ixtlán 18 y
Izadkhast 49 j
Izamal 19 v
Izhevsk 50 v
Izhma 50 v
Izimbiri 42 r
Izki 60 p
Izmir 35 u
Izmit 35 j
Izúcar de Matamoros 19 p
Izvestkovyy 58 j
Izyum 54 c

J

Jabal adh Dhanna 39 w
Jabal al Qamar 39 w
Jabal al Qara 39 x
Jabal at Tinef 39 a
Jabal Nuqay 37 y
Jabalpur 61 q
Jabal Tuwaya 39 s
Jablanica 35 c
Jaboato 27 w
Jabung, Cape 68 i
Jaburu 25 f
Jaca 34 f
Jaçara 29 c
Jacaré 27 r
Jacareacanga 25 k
Jacaretinga 25 v
Jaciara 25 z
Jaciparaná 25 s
Jackson (Alabama) 19 j
Jackson (Michigan) 16 t
Jackson (Mississippi) 19 i
Jackson (Tennessee) 16 r
Jackson (Wyoming) 15 n
Jackson Island 50 j
Jacksonville (Florida) 20 m
Jacksonville (Illinois) 16 q
Jacksonville (North Carolina) 21 a
Jacmel 21 r
Jacobabad 60 i
Jacobina 27 r
Jacona 18 z
Jacques Cartier, Mount 17 d
Jacui 29 o
Jacundá 26 y
Jacundá (River) 26 l
Jadu 34 z
Jaen 24 h
Jaén 34 q
Jafene 36 u
Jaffa (Yafo) 38 k
Jaffna 64 h
Jafura 39 v
Jagdalpur 61 s
Jaggang 61 d
Jaghbub, Oasis 38 d
Jaghin 60 b
Jagtial 61 q
Jaguaro 29 o
Jaguaribe 27 t
Jagüe 28 q
Jahra 39 g
Jahrom 39 k
Jaicós 27 r
Jailolo 69 l
Jaipur 61 b
Jaisalmer 60 k
Jakarta 68 w
Jakes Corner 11 l
Jakobstad (Pietarsaari) 33 i
Jalaid Qi 58 e
Jalalabad 60 k
Jalapa 19 q
Jalaula 39 e
Jalda 54 o
Jalgaon 61 n
Jalingo 41 i
Jalna 61 o
Jalpaiguri 61 k
Jalu 38 b
Jalu Oasis 38 b
Jamaica 21
Jamalpur 61 y
Jamanxim 25 l
Jamari 25 t
Jamarovka 57 g
Jambi 68 h
Jambogan 67 q
James (River, S.Dakota) 15 h
James (River, Virginia) 16 x
James Bay 16 k
James Bay (Bay) 16 i
Jameson Land 91 q
James Ross Island 82 t
Jamestown (North Dakota) 15 h
Jamestown (Pennsylvania) 16 w
Jammu 61 a
Jammu and Kashmir 61 a
Jamnagar 60 x
Jamshedpur 61 u
Jamuna 61 x
Jamysevo 56 b
Janaúba 29 i
Janaucú 26 l
Jane Peak 79 q
Janesville 16 r
Jangijul' 55 u
Jánina 35 q
Janjira 60 z
Jan Mayen 32 h
Janos 18 j
Januária 29 h
Janzur 37 h
Japan 58-59
Japan, Sea of 58 y
Japurá 25 c
Jaramillo 30 x
Jardim 28 m
Jari 26 j
Jarma 37 u
Jaroslavl 50 p
Jartai 57 q
Jarú 25 t
Jarud Qi 58 d
Jaruu 56 m
Jashpurnagar 61 t
Jask 60 o
Jason Pensinsula 82 u
Jasper (Canada) 14 j
Jasper (Indiana) 16 s
Jasper (Texas) 19 f
Jatai 29 c
Jati 60 w
Jatobá 26 w
Jatobal 26 y
Jatuarana 25 i
Jaú 25 g
Jauaperi 26 c
Jauja 24 x
Jaumave 19 o
Jauperi 25 h
Java 68 x
Java Sea 69 z
Jawand 60 g
Jawhar 60 z
Jaya (Mount) 70 t
Jayapura 70 w
Jaypur 61 s
Jebba 14 d
Jebel Ali 39 y
Jebel Igdet 36 g
Jebel Marra 42 f
Jeberos 24 j
Jebri 60 h
Jeddah 39 n
Jefferson City 16 p
Jeffreys Bay 49 n
Jekabpils 33 w
Jeleninskij 52 s
Jember 69 o
Jenda 45 t
Jens Munk Island 13 f
Jequié 27 s
Jequitinhonha 29 k
Jerbent 55 p
Jeremoabo 27 t
Jerez 18 z
Jerez de la Frontera 34 p
Jerramungup 76 p
Jersey 32 x
Jerusalem 35 y
Jessore 61 x
Jesup 20 l
Jesús Carranza 20 p
Jevlach 54 v
Jhang-Maghiana 60 l
Jhansi 61 q
Jialing Jiang 62 k
Ji'an 63 p
Jianchuan 62 t
Jiangcheng 62 u
Jiangjumiao 56 u
Jiangjuntai 56 z
Jiangmen (Kongmoon) 63 o
Jiangquanzi 56 z
Jianping 57 y
Jianshui 62 v
Jianyang 62 j
Jiaohe 58 h
Jiao Xian 58 p
Jiaozuo 63 c
Jiayin 58 i
Jiayuguan 56 z
Jibóia 25 b
Jieyang 63 q
Jigzhi 62 h
Jihlava 33 s
Jijiga 43 f
Jili Hu 56 g
Jilin (Kirin) 58 g
Jima 43 b
Jiménez 19 p
Jiménez (Mexican Plateau) 18 l
Jinan (Tsinan) 63 e
Jinchang 57 o
Jinchuan 62 h
Jingdong 62 u
Jinghong 62 t
Jingning 62 k
Jing Xian 62 z
Jingyu 58 g
Jingyuan 62 j
Jinhe (Borohoro Shan) 56 r
Jinhe 58 d
Jining 63 e
Jinja 42 z
Jinka 43 n
Jinping 62 v
Jinsha 62 k
Jinsha Jiang 62 t
Jiparaná 25 u
Jipijapa 24 g
Jirin Gol 57 x
Jishou 62 m
Jiuding Shan 62 j
Jiuquan 56 z
Jiwani 60 r
Jizan 43 f
Joaçaba 29 p
Joo Monlevade 29 i
Joo Pessoa 27 w
Joaquín V. González 28 u
Jodhpur 60 z
Joensuu 33 l
Jofane 49 h
Johannesburg 49 p
John Day 14 j
John Day (River) 14 i
Johnsons Crossing 11 l
Johnston, Lakes 76 g
Johnstown 16 w
Johor 68 h
Johor Baharu 68 h
Joinville 29 r
Joinville Island 82 g
Jojoca 26 v
Jojutla 19 o
Joliet 16 r
Jolo 67 t
Jolo Group 67 t
Jomda 62 e
Jonesboro 16 q
Jones Sound 13 d
Jönköping 33 e
Joplin 15 w
Jordan (USA) 15 c
Jordan (State) 38
Jorhāt 62 p
Jorullo 19 n
Jos 41 g
José Bonifácio 25 v
José de San Martin 30 v
Joseph Bonaparte Gulf 73 a
Joseph, Lake 17 e
José Rodrigues 26 x
Jryupinsk 54 f
Juan Aldama 18 z
Juan de Fuca, Strait 14 g
Juan de Nova (Island) 47 a
Juan Fernández Islands 30 c
Juanjuí 24 j
Juan Sola 28 h
Juarez, Sierra de 18 d
Juàzeiro 27 s
Juàzeiro do Norte 27 s
Juazohn 40 u
Juba 42 x
Jubany 82 s
Juba (River) 43 s
Jubbah 39 b
Júcar 34 s
Juchatengo 19 q
Juchipila 18 z
Juchitán 20 p
Juiz de Fora 29 i
Juli 25 o
Juliaca 25 o
Julia Creek 73 w
Julian 62 j
Juliana Top 23 y
Jullundur 61 a
Junagadh 60 x
Junan 63 g
Junction City 15 v
Jundah 77 i
Jundiai 29 g
Juneau 11 y
Junee 78 c
Junggar Pendi 56 t
Junín 31 a
Junin de los Andes 30 h
Juntuliang 57 s
Jura 34 j
Juruá 25 d
Juruena 25 w
Juruena (River) 25 w
Justo Daract 28 s
Jutaí 25 c
Juatí (River) 25 c
Juticalpa 22 e
Jutland 33 p
Juyom 39 k
Jwaneng 49 a
Jyväskylä 33 k

K

K2 55 z
Kaabong 42 z
Kabaena 69 u
Kabakly 55 q
Kabala 40 f
Kabale 45 d
Kabalebo Reservoir 23 z
Kabalo 45 b
Kabanjahe 68 c
Kabba 41 r
Kabinda 45 a
Kabo 42 a
Kabompo 44 z
Kabompo (River) 44 z
Kabondo Dianda 45 n
Kabongo 45 a
Kaboudia, Cape 34 z
Kabul 60 j
Kabul (River) 60 l
Kabului 18 r

Kabunga 45 c
Kabwe 45 p
Kabyrga 55 e
Kachalola 45 r
Kachikattsy 52 m
Kachiry 56 a
K'achta 57 e
Kadali 52 s
Kadan 65 h
Kadina 77 f
Kadiri 64 g
Kadnoye 54 d
Kadoma 49 e
Kadugli 42 j
Kaduna 41 f
Kaduna (River) 41 e
Kadzherom 50 w
Kadzhi 51 s
Kaédi 40 d
Kaesōng 58 t
Kafanchan 41 f
Kafue 46 d
Kafue, Lake 49 c
Kaga 55 b
Kaga Bandoro 42 o
Kagan 55 s
Kagizman 54 t
Kagora 41 g
Kagoschima 58 v
Kahal Tabelbala 36 k
Kahama 45 f
Kahan 60 j
Kahemba 44 j
Kahnuj 60 b
Kahoolawe 18 q
Kahului 18 r
Kaiama 41 d
Kaidu 56 s
Kaifeng 63 d
Kai Islands 70 q
Kaikoura 79 u
Kaili 62 y
Kailua 18 r
Kailu He 58 d
Kaimana 70 r
Kainji Reservoir 41 d
Kairouan 34 y
Kaiser Franz Josephs Fjord 91 r
Kaitaia 79 g
Kaiyuan 58 f
Kaiyuan 62 v
Kajaani 33 k
Kajabbi 73 v
Kajiado 45 i
Kajnar 56 a
Kajo-Kaji 42 x
Kajrakkumskoje Reservoir 55 v
Kaka 43 c
Kakamas 48 y
Kakamega 42 z
Kakenge 44 l
Kakhovskoye Reservoir 54 c
Kakinada 64 j
Kaktovik 11 h
Kakuma 42 z
Kalaallit Nunaat (Greenland) 90-91
Kalabagh 60 l
Kalachinsk 55 l
Kalach-na-Donu 54 g
Kalahari 48 m
Kalakan 52 u
Kalamai 35 r
Kalamare 49 b
Kalamazoo 16 t
Kalamba 42 o
Kalandula 44 u
Kalao 69 u
Kalaqi 58 d
Kalar 52 u
Kalasin 66 g
Kalat 60 i
Kalbarri 76 b
Kalekol 43 n
Kalemie 45 d
Kalemyo 62 p
Kalevala 33 m
Kalgoorlie 76 g
Kalima 45 b
Kalimantan 69
Kaliningrad 33 u
Kalininsk 54 g
Kaliro 42 y
Kalispell 14 l
Kalisz 33 t
Kalkfeld 48 h
Kalkfontein 48 l
Kalkrand 48 i
Kalli 76 e
Kalmar 33 s
Kalni 61 y
Kaloko 45 a
Kalole 45 c
Kalomo 45 n
Kalpa 61 c
Kaltag 11 b
Kaluga 54 c
Kalumburu 72 m
Kalyazin 50 p
Kama 50 v
Kamanga 52 n
Kamanjab 48 g
Kamba 41 c
Kambia 40 e
Kambove 45 n
Kamchatka 10/53
Kamchatsk 10 n
Kamen 51 k
Kamenets-Podol'skiy 33 x
Kamenka 54 g
Kamenka (Angara) 51 x
Kamenka (Don) 54 e
Kamen-na-Obi 56 c
Kamensk 57 e
Kamensk-Shakhinskiy 54 e
Kamensk-Ural'skiy 50 y
Kamet 61 d
Kamiji 44 m
Kamileroi 73 v
Kamina 45 a
Kamkaly 55 v
Kamloops 14 i
Kamo 51 y
Kamoa Mts. 23/26
Kampala 42 x
Kampar 66 r
Kampar (River) 66 s
Kampene 45 b
Kamskoje Reservoir 50 v
Kamuli 42 y
Kamyshin 54 h
Kan 56 k
Kanaaupscow 16 l
Kanab 14 z
Kananda 52 b
Kananga 44 l
Kanash 54 i
Kanawolo 40 j
Kanazawa 58 z
Kanbe 66 a
Kanbetlet 62 p
Kanchanaburi 65 i
Kanchipuram 64 h
Kanchow 63 p
Kand 60 i
Kandahar 60 h
Kandalaksa 50 a
Kandalaksa Gulf 50 a
Kandangan 69 p
Kandi 41 c
Kandrian 71 p
Kandy 64 v
Kandychan 53 v
Kane 16 x
Kánea 35 t
Kane Basin 91 e
Kanem 41 l
Kaneohe 18 q
Kang 48 m
Kangalassay 52 m
Kangan (Australia) 72 u
Kangan (Iran) 39 j
Kangaroo Island 77 r
Kangavar 39 f
Kangchenjunga 61 j
Kangding 62 h
Kangean 69 p
Kangerlussuaq 91 n
Kangiqsualujjuaq 13 x
Kangiqsujuaq 13 v
Kangmar 61 k
Kangmar (Zhari Namco) 61 h
Kangnūng 58 v
Kangro 61 h
Kangto 62 b
Kangxiwar 61 d
Kani 40 i
Kaniama 44 m
Kanin Nos, Cape 50 d
Kanin Peninsula 50 e
Kankakee 16 r
Kankan 40 g
Kanker 61 s
Kankossa 40 f
Kankroli 60 z
Kannapolis 16 w
Kannauj 61 e
Kano 41 g
Kanona 45 r
Kanpur 61 d
Kansas 15 u
Kansas City 16 o
Kansk 56 l
Kantchari 41 a
Kantemirovka 54 e
Kanuku Mts. 23/26
Kanye 49 a
Kanyu 49 a
Kaohsiung 63 t
Kaolack 40 b
Kaoma 45 n
Kaoyui Lake 58 o
Kapalala 45 q
Kapanga 44 m
Kapatu 46 e
Kapčagaj 55 y
Kapchagayskoye Reservoir 56 o
Kapedo 43 n
Kapia 44 j
Kapingamarangi Atoll 71 g
Kapiri Mposhi 46 d
Kapka 42 d
Kapoeta 42 z
Kapona 45 d
Kapsabet 43 n
Kapsan 58 h
Kapuas 69 a
Kapuskasing 16 h
Kapustin-Yar 54 i
Karaaul 56 b
Kara-Balta 55 x
Karabas 55 m
Kara-Bogaz-Gol 54 z
Karabük 35 k
Karabutak 55 c
Karachi 60 v
Kara Dag 54 q
Karaganda 55 k
Karagayly 55 l
Karaginskiy Island 10 o
Karaj 39 i
Karakax 61 c
Karakoram Range 61 a
Karakore 43 d
Karakul, Lake 55 x
Kara Kum 55 o
Karakumskiy Canal 55 r
Karalon 52 t
Karalundi 76 f
Karaman 35 y
Karamay 56 r
Karamea Bight 79 s
Karamysheva 51 z
Karana 39 v
Karanambo 23 x
Karand 39 e
Karang 40 b
Karaozek 55 o
Karasaj 55 z
Karasay 56 r
Karasayo 61 g
Karasburg 48 w
Kara Sea 50 l
Karashoky 55 l
Karasino 51 h
Karasuk 56 b
Karatal 56 n
Kara Tau 55 v
Karaton 54 m
Karaul 51 g
Karaulkeldy 55 a
Karayulgun 56 p
Karazhingil 55 j
Karbala 39 d
Karbi 65 v
Karchev 54 b
Karet 36 s
Kargasok 51 s
Kargil 61 b
Kargo 51 l
Kargopol 50 p
Kari 41 h
Kariba 46 q
Kariba Reservoir 46 q
Karima 38 v
Karimata 68 l
Karimata Strait 68 k
Karīmganj 61 z
Karimnagar 61 q
Karisimbi 45 d
Karkheh 39 f
Karkinitskiy Bay 35 k
Karla-Aleksandra 50 k
Karlik Shan 56 x
Karlovac 35 b
Karlsbad 33 r
Karlskrona 33 s
Karlsruhe 33 p
Karlstad 33 d
Karma 42 c
Karmé 41 l
Karnak 38 j
Karnal 61 b
Karnali 61 f
Karnaprayag 61 d
Karoi 49 e
Karonga 46 h
Karora 38 z
Karoy 55 l
Kárpathos 35 u
Karrats Fjord 90 m
Karridale 76 c
Kars 54 t
Karshi 54 y
Karsi 55 t
Karskiye Vorota, Proliv 50 j
Kartaly 55 d
Karumba 73 i
Karun 39 h
Karunjie 72 m
Karwar 64 c
Karymskoje 57 i
Kasai 44 j
Kasaji 44 z
Kasala 43 a
Kasama 45 r
Kasambule 45 b
Kasanga 45 e
Kasar, Ras 39 n
Kasba Lake 12 x
Kasembe 45 p
Kasempa 45 n
Kasenga 45 p
Kasese 42 w
Kashan 39 j
Kashgar 55 y
Kashgert 50 z
Kashing 63 h
Kashiwazaki 59 n
Kashkanteniz 55 j
Kashmar 60 c
Kashmir 61 a
Kasindi 45 d
Kaskalen 55 y
Kasli 55 c
Kasongo 45 b
Kasongo-Lunda 44 h
Kass 42 f
Kassel 33 p
Kasserine 34 y
Kastamonu 35 l
Kasulu 45 e
Kasungu 45 t
Kasur 61 a
Kata 52 n
Kataba 49 a
Katamobagu 67 w
Katanda 44 m
Katanning 76 e
Katchall 65 r
Katesh 45 h
Katete 45 s
Katgi 61 r
Katherina 38 j
Katherine 73 c
Kathiawar 60 x
Kathmandu 61 h
Kati 40 h
Katima Mulilo 49 a
Katiola 40 j
Katompi 45 a
Katoomba 78 d
Katowice 33 t
Katsina 41 f
Kattakurgan 55 s
Kattegat 33 q
Katun' 56 f
Katyl'ga 51 q
Kauai 18 p
Kaula 18 o
Kaunas 33 v
Kaura Namoda 41 f
Kavalerovo 58 l
Kavali 64 h
Kaval'kan 53 p
Kaválla 35 f
Kavendou 40 e
Kavieng 71 r
Kavkaz 54 p
Kavumu 42 v
Kaw 26 j
Kawambwa 45 q
Kawasaki 59 n
Kawatop 26 h
Kawio 69 k
Kawio Islands 67 w
Kawlin 62 q
Kaya 40 m
Kayan 69 d
Kayanza 45 d
Kaycee 15 p
Kayes 40 e
Kayonza 45 e
Kaysatskoye 54 i
Kayseri 35 z
Kayunga 42 y
Kazabegi 54 u
Kazach 54 u
Kazachinskoye 57 f
Kazach'ye 53 c
Kazakdarya 55 p
Kazakstan 55 e
Kazak Uplands 55 k
Kazalinsk 55 d
Kazan' 54 j
Kazandžik 55 n
Kazerun 39 j
Kazhim 50 u
Kazumba 44 l
Kazungula 49 a
Kazym 51 o
Kazymskaya 51 n
Kazyr 56 k
Kearney 15 t
Keban Lake 54 q
Kebili 37 f
Kebkabiya 42 f
Kebnekaise 33 g
Kebri Dehar 43 t
Kediri 69 n
Kédougou 40 e
Kedrovyy 51 n
Kedva 50 v
Keele Peak 11 m
Keeroongooloo 77 i
Keetmanshoop 48 w
Keflavík 32 a
Kegen 56 p
Keibeb 48 j
Keimoes 48 y
Kéita ou Doka 42 b
Kekuk 53 y
Kel' 52 k
Kelafo 43 t
Kelang 68 f
Kelantan 66 s
Kelem 43 n
Kélibia 34 z

Kéllé 44 g
Kellerberrin 76 e
Kellog 51 u
Kelo 41 l
Kelowna 14 i
Keluang 68 h
Kembolcha 43 d
Kemerovo 56 f
Kemi 33 j
Kemi (River) 33 k
Kemijärvi 33 k
Kemkara 53 q
Kemmerer 15 n
Kemp Land 85 a
Kempsey 78 g
Ken 61 r
Kenadsa 36 j
Kenai 11 e
Kenai Peninsula 11 e
Kenamuke Swamp 42 z
Kencha 53 q
Kendari 69 v
Kendégué 42 b
Kenema 40 s
Kenge 44 h
Kenhardt 48 y
Kenitra 36 h
Kenmare 15 f
Kenmaur 49 d
Kennedy 62 p
Kenner 19 h
Kennya 53 c
Keno Hill 11 k
Kenora 15 j
Kenosha 16 r
Kentau 55 u
Kent Group 78 p
Kenton 16 u
Kentucky 16 s
Kenya 43/45
Kenya (Mount) 43 o
Kenzou 41 x
Keokuk 16 p
Kerch' 54 c
Kerekyano 52 k
Kerema 71 n
Keren 43 b
Kerguelen 231 r
Kericho 43 n
Keirči 55 s
Kerinci 68 f
Keriske 53 a
Keriya 61 f
Kerkenna Islands 34 z
Kerma 38 u
Kermadec Islands 79 l
Kerman 60 b
Kérouané 40 h
Kerrville 19 b
Kerzaz 36 l
Kesagami Lake 16 j
Kesen 59 p
Keshvar 39 g
Ket 51 s
Keta, Lake 51 i
Ketapang 68 l
Ketchikan 11 y
Key Afer 43 n
Keyano 17 a
Keyi 56 q
Key Largo 20 m
Key West 20 y
Kez 50 v
Khabalakh 52 r
Khabarovsk 58 m
Khabary 56 b
Khairpur 60 j
Khakhar 53 o
Khakhea 48 m
Khalesavoy 51 r
Khal'mer-Yu 50 m
Khamasin 39 r
Khambhat 60 y
Khamis Mushait 39 q
Kham-Keut 66 h
Khammam 64 h
Khampa 52 j
Khamra 52 s
Khandwa 61 o
Khandyga 53 b
Khangokurt 50 z
Khanh Hung 66 i
Khani 52 v
Khanka, Lake 58 k
Khantau 55 x
Khantayka 51 h
Khantayskoye, Lake 51 i
Khantayskoye Reservoir 51 h
Khanty-Mansiysk 51 n
Khanyangda 53 r
Khara-Aldan 53 a
Kharabalio 54 i
Kharagpur 61 v
Kharalakh 52 k
Kharan 60 h
Khara-Tala 53 j
Khara-Tas 53 b
Khargon 61 o
Kharkov 54 c
Kharstan 53 d
Khartoum 42 k
Khartoum North 42 l
Khasalakh 52 k
Khash 60 e
Khashm al Girba 43 a
Khash Rud 60 f
Khastakh 53 e
Khatanga 52 a
Khatanga (River) 52 a
Khatyngnakh 53 n
Khatyngnakh (Chereskogo Mountains) 53 g
Khatyrka 10 f
Khay 39 o
Khayber 39 a
Khemarat 66 h
Khemis Miliana 34 t
Khemisset 36 h
Khenchela 34 w
Kherson 35 k
Kheta 51 m
Kheta (River) 51 m
Khiaw 65 k
Khmel'nitskiy 35 h
Khobolchan 53 d
Khochot 52 j
Khokiley 51 f
Kholmsk 59 c
Khomokashevo 52 p
Khomotovka 54 b
Khoms 35 n
Khong 66 i
Khongo 53 i
Khongsey 53 i
Khon Kaen 65 l
Khonu 53 f
Khoppuruo 52 v
Khor (Iran) 39 l
Khor (Russia) 58 l
Khordogoy 52 g
Khorgo 52 f
Khorixas 48 g
Khormuj 39 i
Khoronkhu 52 m
Khoronnokh 52 j
Khorramabad 39 g
Khorramshahr 39 g
Khouribga 36 h
Khoy 54 u
Khroma 53 f
Khrom-Tau 55 b
Khuff 39 q
Khujand 55 u
Khulais 39 n
Khulm 60 i
Khulna 61 x
Khurais 39 t
Khurasan 55 o
Khurd 60 h
Khusf 60 c
Khuzdar 60 i
Khuzdzhakh 53 f
Khyber Pass 60 l
Kiambi 45 c
Kiamusze 58 j
Kibangou 44 e
Kiberg, Cape 33 m
Kibiti 45 k
Kibombo 45 a
Kibondo 45 e
Kibre Mengist 43 q
Kibuye 45 d
Kichi Kichi 37 x
Kidal 37 n
Kidira 40 e
Kiel 33 p
Kiel Bay 33 p
Kielce 33 u
Kieta 71 u
Kiev 35 j
Kiev Reservoir 33 y
Kiewietskuil 48 z
Kiffa 40 e
Kigali 45 d
Kigilyakh 53 d
Kigisa 13 k
Kigoma 45 d
Kiik 55 j
Kiikkaškan 55 m
Kii Strait 58 y
Kijabe 43 n
Kikagati 45 e
Kikao 49 a
Kikiakki 51 s
Kikki 60 s
Kikondja 45 a
Kikori 70 z
Kikwit 44 i
Kilembe 44 k
Kilibo 41 o
Kilifi 45 l
Kilimanjaro 45 j
Kilindoni 45 k
Kilkoris 42 z
Killarney 32 u
Killeen 19 c
Kil'mez 50 u
Kilosa 45 i
Kimball, Mount 11 h
Kimberley 49 n
Kimberley Downs 72 l
Kimberley Plateau 72 m
Kimchaek 58 i
Kimpese 44 f
Kimvula 44 g
Kinabulu 67 p
Kindersley 15 b
Kindia 40 d
Kindu 45 a
Kineshma 54 f
Kinesma 50 r
Kingaroy 74 t
King Christian IX Land 90 z
King Christian X Land 91 r
King City 14 u
King Frederick VI Coast 90 v
King Frederick VIII Land 90 n
King George Island 82 e
King Island 77 w
King Leopold and Queen Astrid Coast 85 r
King Leopold Range 72 l
Kingman 14 z
Kingombe 45 b
Kingoonya 77 d
King Oscars Fjord 91 r
King Peninsula 81 a
Kingri 60 k
King Salmon 11 p
King Sound 72 k
Kingsport 16 u
Kingston (Canada) 16 y
Kingston (Jamaica) 21 o
Kingston (USA) 16 z
Kingston upon Hull 32 y
Kingstown 23 j
Kingsville 19 c
Kingtehchen 63 f
King Wilhelm II Land 85 s
King William Island 12 m
King Williams Town 49 p
Kinhwa 63 g
Kinkala 44 g
Kinoosao 12 x
Kinshasa 44 g
Kintampo 40 m
Kintus 51 o
Kinyeti 42 y
Kipaka 45 b
Kipembawe 45 g
Kipushi 45 o
Kirakira 75 a
Kirbey 52 b
Kirbey (Arga-Sala) 52 d
Kirenga 52 q
Kirensk 52 q
Kirgiz Steppe 55 a
Kiri 44 j
Kiribati 231 l
Kirikkale 35 y
Kirim 42 i
Kirin 58 g
Kirinyaga (Kenya) 43 o
Kirit 43 h
Kiritimati 230 b
Kiriwina or Trobriand Island 71 r
Kiriyestyakh 52 l
Kirkenes 33 l
Kirkland Lake 16 j
Kirkpatrick, Mt. 86 c
Kirksville 15 x
Kirkuk 39 e
Kirkwood 49 o
Kirov 50 t
Kirovakan 54 u
Kirovograd 35 k
Kirovsk 50 a
Kirovskiy 58 l
Kirrikkale 54 o
Kirs 50 u
Kirsanov 54 g
Kirthar Range 60 i
Kiruna 33 h
Kirundu 45 a
Kisangani 42 s
Kisarawe 45 k
Kiseleva 53 h
Kisel'ovsk 56 g
Kishtwar 61 a
Kisi 58 j
Kisigu 45 g
Kisii 45 h
Kisima 43 o
Kisimaio 43 s
Kiska 10 t
Kislovodsk 54 s
Kissidougou 40 g
Kisumu 45 g
Kita 40 g
Kita-Kjūshū 58 v
Kitale 43 n
Kitami 59 d
Kit Carson 15 r
Kitchener-Waterloo 16 w
Kitgum 42 y
Kithira 38 c
Kitimat 14 d
Kitui 45 j
Kitunda 45 f
Kitutu 45 c
Kitwe 45 p
Kiukiang 63 e
Kivitoo 13 l
Kivu, Lake 45 c
Kizema 50 r
Kizilirmak 35 l
Kiziltepe 54 r
Kiz'lar 54 v
Kizyl-Arvat 55 n
Kizyl Jilga 61 d
Klabat 67 w
Klaeng 65 k
Klagenfurt 35 a
Klamath Falls 14 u
Klar 33 e
Klerksdorp 49 e
Kliapeda 33 u
Klin 57 k
Klin (Moscow) 50 o
Klintsy 54 a
Knob, Cape 76 f
Knox Coast 87 f
Knoxville (Iowa) 15 x
Knoxville (Tennessee) 16 u
Knud Rasmussens Land 91 d
Knysna 48 z
Kobbo 43 d
Kobdo 56 i
Kobe 58 y
København (Copenhagen) 33 q
Kobenni 40 g
Koblenz 33 o
Kobuk 11 c
Kobya 52 l
Kočečum 51 m
Koch Bihr 60 k
Kochechum 52 b
Kochi 58 y
Kochikha 51 k
Kochubey 54 v
Kodarma 61 v
Kodiak 11 r
Kodiak (Island) 11 r
Koës 48 x
Koforidua 40 z
Kogon 40 c
Koh-e-Baba 60 i
Kohīma 52 o
Koidern 11 j
Koidu 40 f
Kokand 55 v
Kokaral 55 c
Kokchetav 55 i
Kokiu 62 v
Kok-Jangak 55 x
Kokkola 33 i
Kokoma 16 s
Kokonau 70 t
Kokpekty 56 d
Koksoak 13 w
Kokstad 49 r
Kokuora 53 f
Kokwo 43 n
Kola 50 c
Kolaka 69 u
Kolar 64 g
Kolari 33 j
Kolarovgrad 35 h
Kolbio 43 r
Kolda 40 c
Kolding 33 p
Kole 42 t
Kolesovo 53 i
Kogujev 50 g
Kolhapur 64 c
Kolik'yegan 51 q
Kolin 33 s
Kolkata (Calcutta) 61 w
Kolmya 53 j
Köln (Cologne) 33 o
Kolokani 40 h
Kolomna 54 e
Kolomyya 35 g
Kolono 69 u
Kolpashevo 51 t
Kolpino 33 m
Koltovkinda 52 u
Kolva 50 w
Kolva (Bol'shezemel'skaya Tundra) 50 j
Kolwezi 46 b
Kolyma 53 j
Kolmyskiy Mountains 53 j
Kolymskiy Plain 53 j
Komadugu 41 j
Komanda 42 w
Komandor Islands 10 p
Komatipoort 49 g
Komelek 53 a
Komoé 40 x
Kom Ombo 38 w
Komotini 35 g
Kompong Cham 66 i
Kompong Chhnang 66 h
Kompong Som 66 g
Komsberg 48 y
Komsomolets 55 e
Komsomolets (Island) 51 k
Komsomol'sk 51 u
Komsomol'skaya 85 n
Komsomol'skiy 50 z
Komsomol'sk-na-Amure 53 p
Konda 51 n
Kondakovo 53 i
Kondoa Irangi 45 i
Kondon 58 m
Kong 40 k
Kongbo 42 q
Kongmoon 63 o

Kongor 48 m
Kongor 42 x
Kongsvinger 33 d
Kongwa 45 i
Koniakari 40 f
Konkouré 40 d
Konongo 40 z
Konosa 50 p
Konotop 54 a
Konqi 56 t
Konso 43 o
Kontagora 41 e
Kontum 66 j
Konya 35 y
Konzaboy 53 l
Kopet Dag 55 o
Kopiago 70 y
Korča 35 e
Korčula 35 b
Korda 51 y
Kordofan 42 j
Korea, North 58
Korea, South **58/63**
Korea Bay 58 r
Korea Strait 58 v
Korennoye 52 c
Koreyver 50 k
Korf 10 b
Korhogo 40 j
Kor-i-Hisar 60 h
Korinth 35 s
Kōriyama 59 o
Korkodon 53 j
Korkodon (River) 53 k
Korla 56 s
Korliki 51 s
Koro 40 i
Korobovskiy 55 l
Korogwe 45 j
Koronadal 67 w
Koror 70 f
Koro Sea 75 m
Korosten 35 i
Koro Toro 42 b
Korsakov 59 d
Korti 38 v
Korti Linchang 56 g
Koryaken Mountains 10 d
Kos-Agač 56 h
Kosciuszko, Mount 77 z
Kosha 38 u
Košice 35 d
Kosrae 71 m
Kossou Reservoir 40 v
Kosti 42 l
Kostino 51 u
Kostroma 50 q
Kosyu 50 x
Kószalin 33 s
Kota 61 o
Kota Baharu 66 s
Kotabaru 69 q
Kotabumi 68 u
Kota-i Ashro 60 j
Kota Kinabalu 69 c
Kotamobagu 69 j
Kotel'nich 50 t
Kotel'nikovo 54 g
Kotel'nyy 53 b
Kotel'nyy (Island) 53 d
Kotido 42 z
Kotikova 58 l
Kotka 52 k
Kotlas 50 s
Koto 59 b
Kotri 60 v
Kotto 42 q
Kotturu 64 e
Kotui 51 l
Kotuykan 52 b
Kotzebue 11 a
Kotzebue Sound 10 m
Kouango 42 p
Koudougou 40 l
Kougouleu 41 u
Kouilou 44 d
Koukdjuak 13 i
Koulamoutou 44 d
Koulikoro 40 i
Koulou 41 c
Koumpentoum 40 c
Koumra 41 m
Kounala 40 j
Koundara 40 d
Koundougou 40 k
Kourou 26 j
Kouroussa 40 g
Koutouba 40 k
Kouyou 44 g
Kova 51 z
Kovel' 33 w
Kovrizhka 10 a
Kovroy 54 f
Kowares 48 g
Kowloon 63 q
Koxlax 56 p
Koyma Reservoir 64 c
Koyuk 11 a
Kozan 35 z
Kozáni 35 r
Kozhevnikovo 52 e
Kpalimé 41 n
Kpandu 41 n
Kpessi 41 a
Kra, Isthmus of 66 d
Krakatau 68 v
Krakow 33 t
Kramatorsk 54 c
Kramfors 33 f
Krasino 50 i
Krasnaya Yaranga 10 j
Krasnoarmeyesk 55 i
Krasnoarmeyskiy 10 e
Krasnobrodskij 56 g
Krasnodar 54 r
Krasnojarsk 56 j
Krasnokamsk 50 v
Krasnosel'kup 51 s
Krasnoslobodsk 54 h
Krasnotur'insk 50 x
Krasnoufimsk 50 w
Krasnousol'skiy 55 a
Krasnoyarskiy 55 b
Krasnoyarskoye Reservoir 56 i
Krasnyye-Baki 50 s
Krasnyy-Yar 54 i
Kratie 66 i
Kreb en Naga 36 u
Kremenchug 35 l
Kremenchugskoye Reservoir 35 l
Kresty 51 i
Krichev 33 z
Krishna 64 g
Krishnagiri 64 f
Kristianstad 33 r
Kristiansund 33 b
Krivoy Rog 35 k
Krk 35 a
Kronok 53 z
Kronprins Frederiks Bjaerge 90 z
Kroonstad 49 p
Kropotkin 54 f
Kropotkin (Patomskoye Plateau) 52 t
Krotovka 54 l
Kruglikovo 58 m
Kruis, Cape 48 f
Krung Thep (Bangkok) 66 e
Ksabi 36 l
Ksabi Talsinnt 36 j
Ksar el Boukhari 37 a
Ksar el Kebir 34 o
Ksar es Souk 36 j
Ksar Torchane 36 q
Kuala Belait 69 b
Kuala Kubu Baharu 68 f
Kuala Lipis 66 s
Kuala Lumpur 66 r
Kuala Terengganu 66 t
Kuancheng 57 y
Kuandang 69 i
Kuandian 58 f
Kuango 44 h
Kuantan 66 t
Kuba 54 w
Kuban' 54 d
Kubor 70 z
Kuching 68 m
Kudu-Kyuyel' 52 v
Kudymkar 50 v
Kufrah Oasis 38 p
Kugluktuk (Coppermine) 12 f
Kugulta 54 g
Kuhak 60 f
Kuh Lab, Ras 60 q
Kuito 44 u
Kukan 58 k
Kul 39 l
Kul'ab 55 u
Kulagino 54 k
Kulai 68 h
Kulakshi 55 a
Kulaly 54 x
Kulanoy 55 b
Kular 53 a
Kule 48 k
Kulgera 77 b
Kulinda 52 o
Kul'sary 54 m
Kultay 54 y
Kulu 61 c
Kulunda 56 b
Kulundinskaya Steppe 56 b
Kulundinskoje, Lake 56 b
Kulynigol 51 s
Kuma 54 t
Kumari 54 t
Kumamoto 58 w
Kumanovo 35 e
Kumarina 76 f
Kumasi 40 z
Kumertau 55 a
Kumkuduk 56 w
Kunar 60 l
Kunašir 59 f
Kuná-Urgenč 55 o
Kunduz 60 j
Kungrad 55 o
Kungu 42 o
Kungur 50 w
Kungur (Mount) 55 y
Kunlun Shan 61 h
Kunming 62 v
Kunsan 58 t
Kuntuk 53 t
Kununurra 73 a
Kuogastakh 53 a
Kuopio 33 k
Kuoyka 52 i
Kupang 69 v
Kupino 56 b
Kuqa 56 q
Kura 54 t
Kuragino 56 j
Kuraj 56 g
Kurčum 56 e
Kŭrdžali 35 g
Kureyka 51 j
Kureyskaya 52 r
Kurgal'dzhino 55 i
Kurgan 55 f
Kurgan-T'ube 55 u
Kuria Muria Islands 60 n
Kuri Bay 72 i
Kuril Islands 59 g
Kurleja 57 l
Kurmuk 42 m
Kurnool 64 f
Kursk 54 c
Kurtalan 54 s
Kurtamysh 55 e
Kuruman 48 z
Kurundi 73 s
Kurunegala 64 u
Kurun Uryak 53 o
Kur'ya 50 w
Kusagan-Olokh 53 a
Kushiro 59 e
Kushmurun 55 f
Kuska 60 e
Kuskokwim 11 b
Kuskokwim Mountains 11 c
Kustanay 55 e
Kut 66 f
Kutacane 68 d
Kütahya 35 v
Kutaisi 54 t
Kutch, Gulf of 60 w
Kutch, Rann of 60 x
Kutno 33 t
Kutu 44 i
Kuujjuaq 13 w
Kuujjuarapik 16 k
Kuusamo 33 i
Kuwait 39 g
Kuwait (State) 39
Kuybyschevskoye Reservoir 54 j
Kuyygan 55 x
Kuzmov'ka 51 w
Kuznetsk 54 i
Kvigtind 33 e
Kwale 45 k
Kwanga 45 a
Kwangju 58 t
Kwango 44 h
Kweilin 63 n
Kweiyang 62 x
Kwe Kwe 46 r
Kwethluk 11 a
Kwigillingok 11 a
Kwiha 43 d
Kwikila 74 d
Kwilu 44 i
Kwoko 70 q
Kyaikto 65 h
Kyaka 45 e
Kyanjojo 42 x
Kyaukme 62 r
Kyaukpyu 62 o
Kyauktaw 62 o
Kycham-Kyuyel' 53 g
Kyrgyzstan 55 x
Kynuna 73 x
Kyoga, Lake 42 y
Kyōto 58 z
Kyrbana 53 j
Kyren 57 b
Kyrgyday 52 j
Kyrta 50 w
Kystatyam 52 j
Kysyl-Suluo 53 c
Kysyl-Yllyk 52 f
Kytyl-Zhura 52 k
Kyuekh-Bulung 52 f
Kyushe 55 n
Kyūshū 58 w
Kyusyur 52 l
Kyyiv (Kiev) 33 z
Kyyjärvi 33 j
Kyzyk 54 y
Kyzyl 56 k
Kyzyl-Chaja 56 h
Kyzyl-Chem 56 l
Kyzyl-Dzhar 55 i
Kyzyl Kum 55 r
Kyzyl-Orda 55 s
Kyzyluy 55 f
Kzyltu 55 j

L

La Almarcha 34 r
La Asunción 23 h
La Banda 28 t
La Barca 18 z
Labaz, Lake 51 l
Labé 40 e
Labe (Elbe) 33 r
Laboulaye 30 m
Labrador 17 e
Labrador City 17 c
Labrador Sea 13 z
Lábrea 25 e
Labuha 67 y
Labuk Bay 67 q
Labytnangi 50 m
La Calera 28 o
La Campana 18 m
La Carbonera 19 c
La Carlota 28 u
La Ceiba 19 x
Lacepede Bay 77 t
Lachlan 78 a
La Chorrera 24 m
Lac la Martre 12 r
La Concepción 23 b
Laconia 17 n
La Crosse 16 q
Ladoga, Lake 33 m
Lady Frere 49 p
Lady Grey 49 p
Ladysmith (South Africa) 49 r
Ladysmith (USA) 16 d
Lae 71 o
Laem Ngop 66 g
La Escalera 23 w
La Esmeralda 23 t
La Esperanza 25 u
Lafayette (Indiana) 16 s
Lafayette (Lousiana) 19 g
Lafia 41 g
Laghouat 34 u
Lagos (Nigeria) 41 p
Lagos (Portugal) 36 g
La Grande 14 j
La Grande Rivière 16 m
Lagrange 72 w
Laguna de Bay 67 g
Lagunas 28 c
Lagunillas 28 g
Lahad Datu 69 e
Lahat 68 u
Lahej 43 g
La Higuera 28 o
Lahore 61 a
Lahti 33 j
Lai 41 m
Laibin 62 z
Lai Chau 62 v
Laichou Bay 58 p
Laingsburg 48 y
Laisamis 43 p
Laiyang 58 q
Laiyuan 57 v
Lajeado 29 o
Lajes 29 q
Lajes (Cáatingas) 27 v
Lajinha 25 k
La Julia 30 v
La Junta 15 r
La Junta 18 j
Lake Charles 19 g
Lake City (Florida) 20 l
Lake City (South Carolina) 20 m
Lake Harbour 13 w
Lake Havasu CIty 18 e
Lake Jackson 19 d
Lakeland 20 l
Lake Nash 73 u
Lake Ozark 15 x
Lake Providence 20 e
Lake River 16 h
Lake Seul 15 k
Lakeview 14 v
Lakhpat 60 w
Lakki 60 l
Lakota 40 w
Lakselv 33 j
Lakshadweep 64 b
Lalara 44 d
Laleh Zar 60 b
Lalin 58 g
Lalitpur 61 p
Lalyo 42 x
Lama-Kara 41 a
La Mancha 18 m
Lama, Lake 51 i
Lamar 15 s
La Martre, Lake 12 r
Lambaréné 44 c
Lambasa 75 m
Lambayeque 24 g
Lambert Glacier 84 y
Lambert Land 91 i
La Merced 24 x
Lamia 35 s
La Misión 18 c
Lamon Bay 67 h
La Montaña **24/25**
Lamotrek Atoll 71 a
Lampalla 24 y
Lampang 66 d
Lampedusa 34 z
Lanai 18 q
Lanbi 65 h
Lancang 62 t

Lancang Jiang 62 t
Lancaster 14 w
Lancaster (California) 18 c
Lancaster (Pennsylvania) 16 y
Lancaster Sound 13 d
Lanchow 62 j
Lândana 44 d
Landeck 34 l
Lander 15 o
Landes 34 f
Landless Corner 45 p
Land's End 32 v
La'nga Co 61 e
Langano, Lake 43 c
Langdon 15 h
Langhko 62 r
Langkawi 66 q
Langöyo 33 e
Langsa 66 p
Lang Son 62 x
La Noria 25 v
Lansing 16 t
Lanus 31 c
Lanxi 58 g
Lanzarote 36 c
Lanzhou (Lanchow) 62 j
Laoag 67 f
Laoang 67 j
La Oroya 24 x
Laos 62/65-66
La Palma 22 k
La Paragua 23 h
La Parilla 18 y
La Paz (Argentina) 28 r
La Paz (Bolivia) 25 p
La Paz (Honduras) 22 d
La Paz (Mexico) 18 u
La Paz (Paraná, Argentina) 28 x
La Paz Bay 18 h
La Pedrera 25 b
La Pérouse Strait 59 c
La Piedad 18 z
La Plata 31 c
Lappeenranta 33 k
Lappland 33 j
Laptev Sea 52 h
Laptev Strait 53 e
La Puntilla 24 g
La Quiaca 28 f
Lar 39 k
Larache 36 h
La Radisson 16 k
Laramie 15 q
Laranjal 25 k
Larba 52 w
Laredo 19 b
Largo 20 k
La Rioja 28 r
Lárisa 35 s
Larkana 60 i
Larnaca 35 y
La Rochelle 34 e
La-Roche-sur-Yon 34 e
La Romana 21 u
La Ronge, Lake 15 d
La Rons'yer 50 l
Laropi 42 x
Larrimah 73 e
Larsen Ice Shelf 82 v
Larvik 33 c
Lar'yak 51 s
Las Anod 43 i
Las Bocas 18 h
Las Cruces (Mexico) 18 u
Las Cruces (USA) 18 j
Las Davé 43 j
Las Entimias 18 m
La Serena 28 o
Las Flores 31 b
Las Heras 30 w
Lashio 62 r
Lashkargah 60 g
Lasho Joāyin 60 e
Las Koreh 43 j
Las Lajas 30 i
Las Lajitas 28 t
Las Lomas 24 h
Las Lomitas 28 w
Las Palmas 36 b
La Spezia 34 l
Las Piedras 25 n
Las Plumas 30 x
Lastoursville 41 w
Las Trincheras 23 g
Las Vegas (Arizona) 14 y
Las Vegas (New Mexico) 15 q
Latacunga 24 h
Latady Island 82 x
Latady Range 82 z
La Tagua 24 k
Latakia 35 z
Latina 34 m
La Tuque 17 a
Latur 61 o
Latvia 33 w
Launceston 77 y
La Unión 24 w
Laura 73 l
La Urbana 23 f
Laurel 19 i
Laurie Island 82 g
Lausanne 34 j
Laut 69 q
Lavapié, Punta 30 g
La Vega 21 s
La Venturosa 23 q
La Vibora 18 m
La Victoria 23 f
Lavumisa 49 s
Lawa 62 r
Lawdar 43 h
Lawn Hill 73 u
Lawra 40 l
Lawrenceburg 16 s
Lawton 19 c
Layla 39 s
Lazarev Sea 83 j
Learmonth 72 q
Leavenworth 15 w
Lebanon (State) 38
Lebanon (USA) 16 p
Lebap 55 q
Lebú 30 g
Lecce 35 c
Leduc 14 m
Leeds 32 x
Leesburg 20 l
Leeton 78 b
Leeuwarden 33 n
Leeward Islands 21 x
Legazpi 67 i
Leghorn (Livorno) 34 l
Legnica 33 s
Leh 61 c
Le Havre 34 f
Leiah 60 k
Leicester 32 y
Leigh Creek 77 f
Leipzig 33 q
Leiria 34 n
Leiyang 63 o
Le Kef 34 x
Lekki 41 p
Le Mans 34 g
Lema Shilindi 43 s
Lemmon 15 f
Lemsid 36 p
Lena 52 l
Leng Hu 56 w
Lenina 55 w
Leningradskaya 86 w
Leninsk 55 e
Len'ki 56 c
Lensk 52 s
Léo 40 l
Leoben 35 b
Leonardville 48 j
León (Mexico) 19 n
León (Nicaragua) 22 e
León (Spain) 34 c
Leonora 76 h
Lepsy 56 b
Le Puy 34 h
Lerdo 18 l
Lerida 73 y
Lérida (Colombia) 25 b
Lérida (Spain) 34 g
Lerwick 32 k
Lesbos 35 t
Les Cayes 21 q
Leschenault, Cape 76 c
Leskovac 35 e
Lesnaya 53 z
Lesosibirsk 51 w
Lesotho 49 p
Lesozavodsk 58 l
Lesser Antilles 23 e
Lesser Slave Lake 12 s
Lesser Sunda Islands 69 r
Lesser Zab 39 d
Leszno 33 s
Lethbridge 14 m
Lethem 23 x
Leticia 25 b
Leti Islands 69 z
Letlhakane 49 b
Letlhakeng 49 a
Letsok-Aw 66 c
Leuser 65 u
Levelland 18 m
Levêque, Cape 72 j
Levkas 35 q
Lewis 32 i
Lewis Hill 17 i
Lewiston (Idaho) 14 k
Lewiston (Maine) 17 o
Lewiston (Montana) 15 b
Lexington 16 t
Lexington Park 16 y
Leyte 67 j
Lhari 62 b
Lhasa 61 l
Lhazê 61 j
Lhazhong 61 i
Lhokseumawe 65 u
Lhoksukon 65 u
Lhorong 62 d
Lhozhag 61 l
Lhünzë 62 b
Liadong Wan 57 z
Liangcheng 63 g
Liangpran 69 c
Lianjiang 63 n
Lian Xian 63 o
Lianyuan 63 b
Liao 58 e
Liaodun 56 w
Liaotong Bay 58 d
Liaoyang 58 e
Liaoyuan 58 f
Liard 12 o
Libby 14 k
Libenge 42 o
Liberal 15 t
Liberdade 25 e
Liberia (State) 40
Liberia (Costa Rica) 22 f
Libertador General San Martin 28 g
Liboi 43 q
Libreville 41 t
Libya 37/38
Libyan Desert 38 d
Libyan Plateau 38 e
Licancabur 28 e
Licata 37 i
Lichinga 46 i
Lichtenburg 46 o
Lichuan 62 m
Lida 33 w
Lidköping 33 e
Liebig, Mount 73 p
Liechtenstein 34
Liège 34 i
Lienyunkang 63 g
Liepāja 33 u
Ligurian Sea 34 k
Lihue 18 p
Lijiang 62 g
Likasi 45 o
Likati 42 r
Likoto 45 a
Likouala 41 x
Likouala-aux-Herbes 41 z
Lille 32 z
Lillehammer 33 d
Lilongwe 45 t
Lima (Paraguay) 28 m
Lima (Peru) 24 w
Lima (USA) 16 t
Limassol 35 y
Limay 30 j
Limbe (Cameroon) 41 t
Limbe (Malawi) 46 i
Limerick 32 u
Lime Village 11 d
Limmen Bight 73 f
Limnos 35 t
Limoeiro 27 v
Limoges 34 g
Limon 15 r
Limón 22 h
Limpopo 49 g
Linah 39 d
Linares 19 b
Lincang 62 t
Lincoln (Argentina) 31 a
Lincoln (USA) 15 v
Lincoln Sea 91 h
Linda Downs 73 u
Linde 52 k
Linden 23 y
Lindi 45 x
Lindi (River) 42 t
Lindo 28 l
Line Islands 230 a
Linganamakki Reservoir 64 d
Lingayen 67 f
Lingayen Gulf 67 f
Lingbao 63 a
Lingga Islands 68 i
Lingomo 42 q
Lingshan 62 z
Lingsugur 64 f
Linguère 40 c
Linhai 58 f
Linhares 29 l
Linhe 57 r
Linkiang 58 g
Linköping 33 f
Linkou 58 i
Linosa 34 z
Linqing 63 d
Lins 29 d
Linsia 62 i
Lintao 62 i
Linton 15 g
Linxi 57 x
Linz 35 a
Linze 57 n
Lion, Gulf of 34 i
Liouesso 41 y
Lipa 67 g
Lipari Islands 35 n
Lipetsk 54 e
Lipez, Cord. de 28 e
Lira 42 y
Lisala 42 p
Lisboa (Lisbon) 34 n
Lisbon 34 n
Lisburne, Cape 10 m
Lishui 63 g
Lismore 78 g
Listowel Downs 77 k
Listv'anka 57 c
Litang 62 z
Litang 62 g
Litchfield 16 q
Lithgow 78 e
Lithuania 33 v
Litke 53 q
Litke (Novaya Zemlya) 50 j
Litovko 58 m
Little Andaman 65 d
Little Anyuy 10 a
Little Cayman 20 z
Little Current 16 i
Little Diomede 10 l
Little Falls 15 j
Little Karoo 48 y
Little Khinggan Mountains 58 h
Little Rock 15 x
Little Salmon 11 l
Little Scarcies 40 e
Little Swartberge 48 y
Litunde 45 v
Liuba 62 l
Liuchou 62 z
Liuhe 58 g
Liupo 45 y
Liushuquan 56 w
Live Oak 20 k
Liverpool 32 w
Liverpool Land 91 r
Livingston 15 a
Livingstone 46 o
Livingstone Mountains 45 u
Livingstonia 46 h
Livingston Island 82 s
Livny 54 d
Livorno 34 l
Liwa Oasis 39 x
Li Xian 63 a
Li Yuba 42 u
Lizarda 27 n
Ljamin 51 o
Ljubljana 35 a
Ljungan 33 f
Ljusnan 33 f
Llanos 23 b
Llanos de Chiquitos 28 i
Llanos de los Caballos Mestenos 18 l
Llanos de Mojos 25 s
Llanquihue, Lago 30 g
Llata 24 w
Llera 19 o
Lloydminster 15 a
Llullaillaco 28 q
Loa 28 c
Lobatse 46 o
Lobaye 42 n
Loberia 31 b
Lobito 44 r
Lobos 31 b
Lobos, Cape 18 f
Lobos Island 24 g
Lobva 50 x
Lockhart River 73 l
Loddon 77 w
Lodja 44 m
Lodwar 43 n
Łódź 33 t
Loeriesfontein 48 x
Loffa 40 s
Lofoten Islands 33 d
Log 54 g
Logan 15 n
Logan, Mount 11 i
Logone 41 l
Logroño 34 e
Loikaw 65 h
Loi-lem 62 r
Loire 34 f
Loiyangalani 43 o
Loja 24 h
Lokandu 45 a
Lokichar 43 n
Lokichokio 42 z
Lokitaung 43 n
Lokoja 41 r
Lokomo 41 x
Lokori 43 n
Lokshak 52 z
Lolland 33 q
Lolworth 74 p
Lomami 45 a
Loma Mts 40 f
Lombarda, Serra 26 j
Lombardina 72 j
Lombok 69 q
Lomé 41 o
Lomela 44 m
Lomela (River) 44 k
Lomza 33 u
Londonderry 32 v
Londonderry, Cape 72 m
London (Canada) 16 v
London (UK) 32 y
Londrina 29 d
Longa 44 w
Long Beach 18 b
Longchuan 63 q
Longhua 57 x
Long Island (Bahamas) 21 p
Long Island (USA) 17 n
Longjiang 58 e
Longlac 16 f
Long Range 17 i

Longreach 73 y
Long Strait 10 g
Longview (Texas) 19 e
Longview (Washington) 14 g
Longxi 62 j
Long Xuyen 66 h
Longyan 63 r
Longyearbyen 92 o
Longzhen 58 g
Lonkin 62 q
Lönsdal 33 e
Lontra 26 x
Lookout Mountain 17 f
Loongana 76 l
Lop Buri 65 j
Lopcha 52 w
Lopez 67 h
Lop Nur 56 v
Lopori 42 q
Loptyuga 50 t
Lora 60 h
Loralai 60 j
Lorca 34 r
Lord Howe Island 78 k
Lordsburg 18 i
Lorenço 26 j
Loreto (Bolivia) 25 s
Loreto (Mexico) 18 g
Lorica 22 m
Lorient 34 d
Loruk 45 i
Lorukumu 43 n
Los Alamos 15 p
Los Angeles (Chile) 30 h
Los Angeles (Mexico) 18 f
Los Angeles (USA) 18 f
Losap Atoll 71 f
Los Blancos 28 i
Los Burros 18 g
Los Menucos 30 j
Los Mochis 18 i
Los Vientos 28 p
Lot 34 g
Lotta 33 l
Louangphrabang 62 v
Loubomo 44 e
Louchuan 62 b
Louga 40 b
Lougheed Island 12 j
Louisiade Archipelago 74 g
Louisiana 20 d
Louis Trichardt 49 e
Louisville 16 t
Louis XIV, Point 16 j
Lovat 33 m
Lovelock 14 w
Løvenørn, Kap 90 x
Lowa 45 b
Lower California 18 f
Lower Egypt 38 h
Lower Hutt 79 v
Lower Red Lake 15 j
Loxton 48 z
Loyalty Islands 75 r
Loyang 63 b
Loyoro 42 z
Luachimo 44 k
Lua Dekere 42 p
Luambo 45 o
Luan 57 w
Luanda 44 e
Luang 66 q
Luang Prabang 65 l
Luang, Thale 66 r
Luangua 45 r
Luangwa 45 s
Luanhaizi 62 b
Luanshya 45 p
Luapula 45 p
Luau 44 y
Luba 41 t
Lubang 67 f
Lubango 44 s
Lubao 45 a
Lubbock 19 a
Lübeck 33 p
Lübeck Bay 33 p
Lubefu 44 m
Lubero 45 c
Lubilanji 44 m
Lublin 33 v
Lubny 35 l
Lubuklinggau 68 t
Lubuksikaping 68 e
Lubumbashi 45 p
Lubungu 45 n
Lubutu 45 b
Lucala 44 t
Lucapa 44 k
Lucas 25 z
Lucena (Philippines) 67 g
Lucena (Spain) 36 j
Lucerne 34 k
Luchegorsk 58 l
Luchou 62 k
Lüchun 62 v
Lucira 44 r
Luckhoff 49 n
Lucknow 61 e
Lucusse 44 x
Lucy Creek 73 t
Lüda (Dalian) 58 q
Luddington 16 s
Lüderitz 48 t
Ludhiana 61 b
Ludlow 18 d
Luebo 44 k
Luena (Angola) 44 w
Luena (River) 44 y
Luena (Zaïre) 45 n
Luengué 44 x
Lüeyang 62 k
Lufeng 63 q
Lufkin 19 e
Luga 33 l
Lugansk 54 e
Lugenda 45 v
Lugh Ganana 43 s
Lugovatka 51 u
Lugovoi 55 w
Lugu 61 g
Luhombero 45 w
Luiana 44 y
Luidzhi 50 i
Luiza 44 l
Luján 31 b
Lujlang 63 e
Lukacheck 53 n
Lukenie 44 k
Lukolela 44 i
Lukuga 45 b
Lukula 44 e
Lukulu 44 z
Lukumburu 45 u
Lukunskiy 52 b
Lule 33 h
Luleá 33 i
Luleburgaz 35 i
Lulong 57 y
Lulonga 42 o
Lulonga (River) 42 o
Lumbala 44 y
Lumbala N'Guimbo 44 x
Lumberton 21 a
Lumbo 45 y
Lumding 62 o
Lumi 70 x
Lumsden 79 q
Lumu 69 f
Lün 57 d
Lundazi 45 s
Lunga 45 o
Lunggar 61 g
Lungue-Bungu 44 y
Luni 60 y
Luobei 58 j
Luobuzhuang 56 t
Luocuan 62 m
Luoding 63 n
Luoguhe 57 m
Luohe 63 c
Luoshan 63 c
Luozi 44 f
Lupar 68 m
Luputa 44 m
Luqu 62 h
Luremo 44 i
Lúrio 45 w
Lusaka 46 c
Lusambo 44 m
Lushoto 45 k
Lusk 15 q
Lutembo 44 x
Luton 32 y
Lutselk'e (Snowdrift) 12 u
Lutsk 35 g
Lützow Holm Bight 84 h
Luvua 45 b
Luvuei 44 x
Luwingu 45 r
Luxembourg (City) 33 n
Luxembourg (State) 33-34
Luxi 62 s
Luxor 38 j
Luzi 44 x
Luzon 67 f
Luzon Strait 63 u
L'viv 35 g
L'vovka 51 q
Lycksele 33 g
Lydenburg 49 e
Lynchburg 16 w
Lyndhurst 74 o
Lyndon 72 r
Lynn Lake 12 x
Lynwood 74 n
Lyon (Lyons) 34 i
Lyon Inlet 13 e
Lyons (France) 34 i
Lyons (River) 72 r
Lyubinskiy 55 j

M

Ma'an 38 l
Maas (Netherlands) 33 n
Maas (Somalia) 43 v
Maasin 67 j
Maatsuyker Island 77 x
Maba 42 d
Mabote 49 h
Mabrouk 36 y
Macaé 29 j
McAlester 15 v
McAllen 19 c
MacAlpine Lake 12 k
McArthur 73 f
Macane 49 g
Macao 63 p
Macapá 26 k
Macas 24 i
Macau 27 u
Macauley Island 79 m
McClintock 13 n
McClintock Channel 12 k
McClintock Island 50 j
McClure Strait 12 d
McComb 20 f
McCook 15 t
McDermitt 14 w
Macdonald, Lake 73 n
Macdonell Ranges 73 q
Macedonia (F. Y. R.) 35 e
Maceió 27 v
Macenta 40 g
McGrath 11 d
Mach 60 i
Machachi 24 h
Machačkala 54 w
Machaila 49 g
Machakos 45 j
Machala 24 g
Macharetí 28 h
Machettie, Lake 73 v
Macheng 63 d
Machilipatnam 64 i
Machiques 23 b
Machuan 61 g
Macia 49 g
Macina 40 j
Mack 15 o
Mackay 74 r
Mackay, Lake 73 o
Mackenzie 12 p
Mackenzie (River) 11-12
Mackenzie Bay 11 j
Mackenzie King Island 12 g
Mackenzie Mountains 12 o
Mackinaw City 16 g
McKinlay 73 w
McKinley, Mount 11 e
Maclear 49 q
McLennan 12 s
McLeod Lake 14 g
McLeod, Lake 72 q
Macmillan 11 l
McMurdo 86 r
Macomia 45 y
Mâcon 34 i
Macon (Georgia) 20 k
Macon (Missouri) 16 p
Macquarie 78 d
Macquarie Harbour 77 w
Macquarie Island 231 x
MacRobertson Land 85 b
Macuarichic 18 j
Macuje 24 m
Macusani 28 c
Macuspana 19 t
Madagascar 47
Mada'in Salih 38 m
Madama 37 u
Madang 71 n
Madaoua 41 e
Madeira (Island) 36 a
Madeira (River) 25 j
Madenijet 56 b
Madera 18 j
Madidi 25 p
Madikeri 64 e
Madimba 44 g
Madingou 44 f
Madison 16 r
Madiun 69 n
Mado Gashi 43 q
Madoi 62 f
Madrakah 39 o
Madrakah, Ras 60 p
Madras (India) 64 h
Madras (USA) 14 h
Madre de Dios 25 q
Madre, Laguna 19 d
Madre, Sierra 67 g
Madre del Sur, Sierra 19 p
Madre Occidental, Sierra 18 k
Madre Oriental, Sierra 19 o
Madrid 34 d
Madula 42 t
Madura 69 o
Madura Strait 69 o
Madurai 64 f
Madziwadzido 49 d
Maebashi 59 o
Mae Sot 66 d
Maevatanana 47 q
Mafeteng 49 p
Mafia Island 45 l
Mafra 29 q
Mafraq 38 l
Magadan 53 v
Magadi 45 i
Magdagachi 52 y
Magdalen Islands 17 g
Magdalena (Argentina) 31 c
Magdalena (Bolivia) 25 s
Magdalena (Island) 30 t
Magdalena (Mexico) 18 h
Magdalena (River) 22 z
Magdalena (USA) 18 j
Magdeburg 33 q
Magelang 68 z
Magellan Straits 30 v
Maggieville 73 j
Maghama 40 e
Magnetic North Pole 89 r
Magnitogorsk 55 c
Magrur 42 g
Maguarinho, Cabo 26 m
Magude 49 g
Magwe 62 q
Mahabad 54 v
Mahabo 47 p
Mahaddei Uen 43 u
Mahagi 42 x
Mahajan 60 m
Mahajanga 47 d
Mahakam 69 d
Mahalapye 49 c
Mahalevona 47 f
Mahallat 39 h
Mahânadi 61 s
Mahanoro 47 r
Maha Sarakham 65 l
Mahavavy 47 p
Mahbubnagar 64 f
Mahd adh Dhahab 39 o
Mahdia 37 g
Mahenge 45 i
Mahesana 60 y
Maicao 23 b
Maiduguri 41 k
Maigudo 43 o
Maihar 61 r
Maiko 42 t
Maimana 60 h
Maimeča 51 m
Main 34 l
Mai-Ndombe, Lake 44 i
Maine 17 b
Mainé-Soroa 41 i
Mainling 62 b
Mainoru 73 e
Maiodao Islands 57 z
Maiquetía 23 e
Mait 43 i
Maitencillo 28 o
Maitri 83 m
Maizhokunggar 61 m
Majene 69 s
Maji 43 n
Makjadikgadi Pans 46 n
Makalu 61 i
Makambako 45 h
Makanza 42 o
Makarikha 50 j
Makarov 59 d
Makarova 51 g
Makassar Strait 69 e
Makat 54 m
Makaw 62 r
Makeni 40 e
Makeyevka 54 d
Makgadikgadi Pans 49 b
Makinsk 55 i
Makkovik 17 h
Makokou 41 w
Makongolosi 45 g
Makopong 48 m
Makoua 44 g
Makrah 43 l
Makri 61 s
Maksimicha 57 f
Maksimovka 59 a
Makteir 36 r
Maku 54 u
Makurdi 41 t
Makushino 55 g
Makuyuni 45 i
Mâl 40 d
Mal. Lyakhovskiy 53 e
Malabar Coast 64 d
Malabo 41 t
Malacca 68 f
Malacca, Strait of 68 d
Malad City 14 z
Málaga (Colombia) 23 b
Málaga (Spain) 34 q
Malagarasi 45 e
Malaita 71 y
Malakal 42 k
Malang 69 n
Malanga 45 v
Malange 44 u
Mälar, Lake 33 f
Malargue 30 i
Malaripó 26 h
Malaspina 30 x
Malatya 54 q
Malawi 45-46/49
Malawi, Lake 46 i
Malaya (Malaysia) 66 s
Malaya (Russia) 53 i
Malaya Baranikha 10 b
Malayan Peninsula 66 r
Malayan Sea 67 o
Malaybalay Bislig 67 w
Malayer 39 h
Malaysia 65-69
Malčin 56 j

Maldives 64
Maldonado 31 e
Male 64 p
Maléa, Cape 35 s
Malegaon 61 n
Malekula 75 d
M. Alémán Reservoir 19 q
Malemba Nkulu 45 b
Malème-Hodar 40 c
Malhada 29 i
Malheur Lake 14 w
Mali 36-37/40-41
Malik 69 i
Malindi 45 l
Malka 53 x
Malkachan 53 x
Mallapunyah 73 f
Mallorca 34 u
Malmesbury 48 w
Malmö 33 r
Malmyzh 50 u
Maloca 26 h
Maloca Velha 26 h
Malonga 44 z
Målöy 33 a
Malozemelskaja Tundra 50 h
Malpelo 22 v
Malta (State) 35/37
Malta (USA) 15 b
Maltahöhe 48 i
Maluwe 40 l
Malykay 52 g
Malyutka 52 z
Malyy Lyakhovskiy 53 e
Mama 52 s
Mama (Cherskogo Mountains) 53 f
Mamadysh 54 k
Mamanguape 27 w
Mamantel 19 u
Mamazair 55 x
Mambasa 42 v
Mamberamo 70 v
Mamfe 41 t
Mamoré 25 r
Mamoriá 25 d
Mamou 40 e
Mampikony 47 e
Mampong 40 z
Man 40 u
Man, Isle of 32 w
Mana (French Guiana) 26 i
Mana (Hawaiian Islands) 18 o
Mana (River) 56 j
Mana Elena 28 c
Manacapuru 25 h
Manado 69 j
Managua 22 f
Managua, Lake 22 e
Manakara 47 q
Manama 39 i
Manambolo 47 o
Manamo 23 i
Mananara 47 f
Mananara (River) 47 q
Mananjary 47 r
Manankoro 40 i
Manar 43 g
Manas 56 t
Manas Hu 56 s
Manaus 25 j
Manchan 56 i
Manchester (UK) 32 x
Manchester (USA) 17 n
Manchouli 57 j
Manchuria 58 f
Máncora 24 g
Mand 39 j
Mandabe 47 p
Mandach 57 r
Mandal 57 e
Mandal (Hangayn Mountains) 57 a
Mandala 70 w
Mandalay 62 q
Mandalgov' 57 r
Mandal-Ovoo 57 p
Mandasor 61 n
Mandaue 67 i
Mandera 43 r
Mandimba 46 i
Mandla 61 r
Mandoto 47 p
Mandritsara 47 e
Mandurah 76 d
Mandvi 60 w
Mandya 64 e
Mangalmé 42 e
Mangalore 64 d
Manglares, Cabo 24 h
Mangnai 56 w
Mangochi 46 i
Mangoky 47 o
Mangole 69 k
Mangueni Plateau 37 u
Mangui 52 w
Manhattan 15 v
Manhuaçu 29 j
Mani 40 t
Maniamba 46 i
Manicoré 25 i
Manicouagan 17 c
Manicouagan Reservoir 17 c
Maniitsoq 90 v
Manila 67 f
Manila Bay 67 f
Manily 10 b
Maningrida 73 e
Manipa, Strait of 69 y
Manisa 35 v
Manitoba 15 g
Manitoba, Lake 15 h
Manitoulin Island 16 i
Manitouwadge 16 g
Manitowoc 16 s
Maniwaki 16 l
Manizales 22 z
Manjacaze 49 h
Manjimup 76 d
Manjra 61 p
Manjuri 25 e
Man Kabat 62 e
Mankato 15 j
Manlaj 57 r
Manley Hot Springs 11 f
Mannar 64 u
Mannar, Gulf of 64 t
Mannheim 33 p
Manning 12 r
Manoa 25 r
Manokwari 70 r
Manombo 47 n
Manonga 45 g
Manono 45 b
Mano River 40 s
Manpojin 58 g
Mansa 45 q
Mansel Island 13 e
Mansfield (Ohio) 16 u
Mansfield (Pennsylvania) 16 y
Mansi 62 q
Manso 29 b
Mansôa 40 b
Manta 24 g
Mantalingajan 67 r
Mantaro 24 x
Mantecal 23 d
Mantena 29 k
Mantiqueira, Serra da 29 h
Manú 25 n
Manuel 19 p
Manuel Urbano 25 o
Manuelzinho 25 m
Manyami 45 k
Manyapa 69 d
Manych Gudilo Lake 54 g
Manyoni 45 g
Manyuan 57 o
Manzanillo 21 o
Manzini 49 s
Manzurka 57 d
Mao (Chad) 41 l
Mao (Dominican Republic) 21 s
Maoke (Mountains) 70 t
Mapaga 69 f
Mapai 49 g
Mapam Yumco 61 f
Mapati 44 f
Mapia Islands 70 f
Mapinhane 49 i
Maple Creek 15 a
Mappi 70 v
Mapuera 25 k
Maputo 49 t
Maqên 62 g
Maqên Gangri 62 f
Maquela do Zombo 44 g
Maquinchao 30 j
Mar, Serra do 29 r
Mara 45 g
Mara 25 e
Marabá 26 y
Maracá 26 l
Maracaçumé 27 b
Maracaibo 23 b
Maracaibo, Lake 23 b
Maracaju 29 a
Maracaju, Serra de 29 a
Maracay 23 e
Maradah 37 l
Maradi 41 f
Maragheh 54 v
Marajó 26 l
Marajó Bay 26 m
Maralal 43 n
Marambio 82 t
Marand 54 v
Maranguape 27 t
Maranoa 78 c
Marañón 24 k
Marape 25 y
Maraş 54 p
Marathon 16 f
Maravatio 19 o
Maraveh-Tappeh 55 n
Marawah 39 w
Marawi 67 v
Marble Bar 72 u
Marcelino 25 d
Marchena 36 i
Marchena (Island) 22 p
Marcy, Mount 16 z
Mardan 60 m
Mar del Plata 31 c
Mareeba 74 b
Margai Caka 61 i
Margaret River 72 z
Margarita 23 g
Margaritovo 58 m
Margherita Peak 42 w
Margilan 55 w
Marhoum 34 s
Maria Cleofas 18 x
Maria Madre 18 w
Marea Magdalena 18 w
Mariana Islands, Northern 231 j
Marianna 20 j
Maribor 35 a
Maridi 42 w
Maridi (River) 42 w
Marie Byrd Land 81 d
Marihamn 33 h
Mariental 48 j
Marietta (Georgia) 20 j
Marietta (Ohio) 16 v
Mariinsk 56 g
Mariinskoye 53 q
Marilia 29 d
Marinduque 67 g
Marinette 16 f
Maringa (Dem. Rep. Congo) 42 q
Maringá (Brazil) 29 b
Marioka 59 p
Marion 16 v
Marion Downs 73 v
Maripa 23 g
Mariscal Estigarribia 28 j
Maritime Alps 34 j
Mariupol 54 d
Markakol', Lake 56 f
Markam 62 f
Markapur 64 g
Marken 49 d
Markha 52 g
Markit 56 o
Markoka 52 f
Markovo 10 d
Marlborough (Australia) 74 s
Marlborough (Guyana) 23 k
Marmara, Sea of 35 i
Marmarica 35 s
Marneuli 54 u
Maro 42 b
Maroantsetra 47 e
Maroochydore 74 u
Maroua 41 k
Marovoay 47 c
Marowijne 26 h
Marqua 73 t
Marquesas Islands 230 p
Marquette 16 f
Marrakech 36 g
Marree 77 f
Marresale 51 a
Marrupa 45 w
Marsa Alam 38 x
Marsabit 43 p
Marsala 34 z
Marsa Matruh 35 u
Marseilles 34 i
Marsella 24 k
Marshall (Arkansas) 15 x
Marshall (Minnesota) 15 i
Marshall (Missouri) 15 x
Marshall (Texas) 20 c
Marshall Islands 231 l
Marshal'skiy 53 d
Marshfield 16 d
Martaban, Gulf of 65 g
Martinez 31 b
Martinez de la Torre 19 q
Martinique 23 j
Martinique Passage 23 i
Martinsville 16 w
Martuk 55 a
Marungu Mountains 45 d
Mary 55 q
Maryborough (Queensland) 74 u
Maryborough (Victoria) 77 v
Marydale 48 y
Maryevka 54 j
Mar'yevka 55 h
Mary Kathleen 73 v
Maryland 16 y
Maryvale 73 y
Masai Steppe 45 i
Masaka 42 x
Masalembo 69 p
Masamba 69 t
Masan 58 u
Masasi 45 x
Masawa 43 d
Masbate 67 i
Masbate (Island) 67 i
Mascara 36 m
Maseru 49 p
Mashhad 55 p
Masia-Mbio 44 h
Masi-Manimba 44 i
Masindi 42 x
Masinloc 67 f
Masirah 60 p
Masisea 24 y
Masisi 45 c
Masjed-e-Soleiman 39 h
Maskana 38 m
Mason City 15 x
Massachusetts 17 n
Massaguet 41 l
Massakori 41 l
Massangena 49 g
Massangulo 45 u
Massenya 41 l
Massif Central 34 h
Massinga 49 i
Massingir 49 g
Mastabah 39 n
Mastakh 52 j
Masteksay 54 k
Masterton 79 v
Mastuj 60 m
Masturah 39 n
Masuda 58 w
Masuguru 45 x
Masvingo 49 f
Matadi 44 f
Matagalpa 22 f
Matagami 16 k
Mataj 56 o
Matam 40 d
Matamoros 19 d
Matamoros (Mexican Plateau) 18 m
Matane 17 d
Matankari 41 c
Matanzas 20 y
Matapan, Cape 35 r
Mataram 72 f
Mataranka 73 d
Mategua 25 t
Matehuala 19 n
Mateur 37 f
Mathura 61 b
Matías Romero 20 p
Mato Grosso 25 w
Mato Grosso Plateau 26/29
Mato, Sierra de 23 t
Matruh 38 f
Matsue 58 x
Matsumoto 59 n
Matsusaka 58 z
Matsuyama 58 x
Matucana 24 w
Matun 60 k
Matundu 42 s
Maturín 23 h
Maturuca 23 w
Matyl'ka 51 t
Mau, Cape 66 u
Maúa 45 w
Maués 25 k
Maués (River) 25 k
Maui 18 r
Maule 30 h
Maulvī Bazār 61 y
Maumere 69 v
Maun 48 m
Mauna Kea 18 r
Mauna Loa 18 r
Maunaloa 18 q
Maurice, Lake 77 a
Mauritania 36/40
Mauritius 47 y
Mavinga 44 x
Mawson 85 b
Maxcanú 19 u
Maxwelton 73 x
May, Cape 16 z
Maya 68 l
Maya (River) 53 n
Maya (River) 53 p
Mayaguana Island 21 r
Mayagüez 21 v
Mayamba 44 h
Mayamey 55 n
Maychew 43 d
Mayer 18 g
Maykain 55 l
Maykop 54 r
Maymakan 53 o
Maynopil'gyn 10 g
Mayo 11 k
Mayo (River) 24 j
Mayoko 44 e
Mayon 67 i
Mayor-Krest 53 f
Mayotte 47 c
May Pen 21 n
Maysville 16 u
Mayumba 44 c
Mayupa 23 v
Mayuram 64 h
Mayya 52 m
Mazabuka 49 c
Mazalet 41 g
Mazán 24 m
Mazanillo 18 y
Mazar 56 n
Mazar-i Sharif 60 i
Mazaruni 23 w
Mazatenango 22 a
Mazatlán 18 w
Mazo Cruz 25 o
Mazunga 49 e
Mazunzut 62 e
Mbabane 49 s
Mbaïki 42 n
Mbaké 40 c

Mbala 46 f
Mbale 42 z
Mbalmayo 41 v
Mbandaka 44 i
M'Banza-Congo 44 g
Mbanza-Ngungu 44 g
Mbarara 42 x
Mbari 42 r
Mbé 41 k
Mbesuma 45 s
Mbeya 45 f
Mbini 41 t
Mbini (River) 41 u
Mbomou 42 s
Mbour 40 a
Mbout 40 e
Mbrés 42 p
Mbuji Mayi 44 m
Mbulu 45 h
Mbuyuni 45 i
Mcherrah 36 i
Mchinji 46 g
Mdrak 66 k
Mead Lake 14 y
Meadow Lake 15 b
Meadville 16 w
Mearim 27 n
Mecejana 27 g
Mecca 39 n
Méchéria 34 s
Medan 68 d
Medea 37 a
Medellín 22 z
Médenine 34 y
Mederdra 40 c
Medford 14 t
Medi 42 x
Medicine Hat 15 a
Medina 39 n
Mediterranean Sea 34-35
Medje 42 u
Mednogorsk 55 a
Mednyy, Cape 51 j
Medvežjegors 50 o
Meekatharra 72 u
Meerut 61 c
Mega 43 p
Megalo 43 r
Meghna 61 y
Meharry, Mount 72 u
Mehdia 36 h
Mehran 39 f
Mehriz 39 k
Meiganga 41 x
Meighen Island 12 l
Meigu 62 i
Meiktla 62 q
Meishan 62 i
Mei Xian 63 r
Mejicana 28 q
Mejillones 28 b
Mékambo 41 w
Mekele 43 c
Meknès 36 i
Mekong 66 g
Mekong Delta 66 i
Mekongga 69 u
Melambes 35 t
Melanesia 74 i
Melbourne (Australia) 77 x
Melbourne (USA) 20 m
Meletsk 51 v
Melfi 42 a
Melfort 15 d
Melilla 34 r
Melitopol 35 m
Melo 29 n
Melville 15 e
Melville Bay 91 b
Melville Island (Canada) 12 g
Melville Island (Australia) 73 c
Melville Lake 17 h
Melville Land 91 i
Melville Peninsula 13 d
Memmingen 33 p
Memphis (Egypt) 38 h
Memphis (USA) 16 q
Ménaka 41 b
Menawashei 42 g
Mendebo Mountains 43 q
Menderes 35 v
Mendi (Ethiopia) 42 m
Mendi (Papua New Guinea) 70 y
Mendocino, Cape 14 s
Mendoza 28 q
Mengoub 36 k
Menkere 52 j
Menominee 16 f
Menongue 44 v
Menorca 34 v
Menyapa 67 p
Menyuan 62 h
Menza 57 f
Menzies 76 g
Meoqui 18 k
Meraia 36 u
Merak 68 w
Merauke 70 w
Merca 43 t
Merced 14 v
Mercedario 28 p
Mercedes (Argentina) 30 l
Mercedes (Buenos Aires, Argentina) 31 b
Mercedes (Corrientes, Argentina) 28 y
Mercedes (Uruguay) 31 c
Mergenevo 54 l
Mergol 56 x
Mergui 65 i
Mergui Archipelago 65 h
Mérida (Mexico) 19 v
Mérida (Spain) 34 p
Mérida (Venezuela) 23 b
Mérida, Cordillera de 23 b
Meridian 20 g
Merir 70 d
Meriruma 26 h
Merowe 38 v
Merrill 16 d
Mersa Metruh 38 f
Mersa Teklay 39 n
Mersín 35 y
Mértola 36 g
Mertz Glacire 87 n
Meru 45 j
Meru (Mount) 45 i
Mesa 18 g
Mesa del Nayar 18 y
Mesa de Yambi 25 a
Meseta del Cerro Jáua 23 t
Meseta de Somuncurá 30 k
Mesfinto 43 b
Messaad 34 u
Messalo 46 j
Messina (Italy) 35 n
Messina (Zimbabwe) 49 e
Messoyakha 51 e
Meta 23 r
Meta Incognita Peninsula 13 w
Metán 28 t
Metema 43 a
Metlaoui 37 e
Metlili Chaamba 34 u
Metoro 45 y
Metsiamonong 49 a
Metu 43 a
Metz 33 n
Meulaboh 65 t
Mexiana 26 l
Mexicali 18 d
Mexican Plateau 18-19
Mexican Water 15 o
Mexico 18-19/20
Mexico City 19 o
Meymeh 39 i
Mezcalapa 20 q
Meždurečensk 56 g
Mezen' 50 e
Mezen' Gulf 50 e
Mezen' (River) 50 t
Mezquital 18 y
M'guiden 37 a
Mhangura 49 e
M. Hidalgo Reservoir 18 i
Mhow 61 n
Miahuatlán 19 q
Miami (Florida) 20 m
Miami (Oklahoma) 15 w
Mianeh 54 w
Miang 65 j
Mianwali 60 l
Mianyang 62 j
Mianyang 63 c
Miaodao Qundao 58 q
Miarinarivo 47 r
Michigan 16 t
Michigan, Lake 16 s
Michurinsk 54 f
Micronesia 71 a
Midar 36 j
Middelburg 49 n
Middelburg 49 r
Middle Andaman 65 e
Middle Atlas 36 i
Middleboro 15 j
Middlesbrough 32 y
Middleton (Australia) 73 w
Middleton (Canada) 17 e
Middleton Reef 78 k
Midelt 36 i
Midi 39 p
Midland (Canada) 16 w
Midland (Michigan) 16 u
Midland (Texas) 18 m
Midway Island 223 m
Mieso 43 d
Miguel Auza 18 l
Mikhaylova 54 i
Mikhaylova (Taimyr Peninsula) 51 g
Mikhaylovka 54 g
Mikumi 45 j
Mikun 50 t
Milan 34 k
Milang 62 u
Milano (Milan) 34 k
Mildura 77 i
Mile 62 v
Miles 78 e
Miles City 15 d
Milestone 15 d
Mileura 76 e
Milford 14 z
Milford Sound 79 p
Milgun 76 f
Milingimbi 73 e
Milk 15 b
Mil'kovo 53 y
Milk River 14 m
Mille, Lake 15 k
Millerovo 54 e
Millicent 77 u
Millstream 72 t
Millungera 73 x
Milne Land 91 p
Milos 35 t
Milparinka 77 i
Milwaukee 16 r
Mimongo 44 d
Mina 56 k
Minab 39 m
Minas 31 e
Mina Saud 39 g
Minas Gerais 29 h
Minatitlán 19 s
Minch 32 i
Mindanao 67 x
Minden 19 f
Mindoro 67 f
Mindoro Strait 67 f
Mineiros 29 b
Minfeng 56 q
Minga 45 p
Mingecaurskoje Reservoir 54 v
Mingenew 76 d
Mingoyo 45 x
Mingshui 56 y
Minhe 62 i
Minicoy 64 p
Min Jiang 63 r
Min Jiang (Wuyi Shan) 62 i
Minle 57 n
Minna 41 f
Minneapolis-St. Paul 16 b
Minnedosa 15 g
Minnesota (State) 15 j
Minnesota (River) 15-16
Minnie Creek 72 s
Miño 34 a
Minot 15 f
Minqing 63 s
Minsk 33 x
Minto Atoll 71 h
Minto Inlet 12 e
Minto, Lake 13 u
Minusinsk 56 j
Min Xian 62 j
Minya Konka 62 h
Min'yar 55 b
Mirabad 60 e
Miracema do Norte 26 z
Miraflores 24 m
Miramar 31 c
Miran 56 u
Miranda 28 m
Miranda Downs 73 k
Mirbat 39 y
Mirbat, Ras 39 y
Miri 69 b
Miriam Vale 74 t
Mirim, Lagoa 29 o
Mirjaveh 60 e
Mirny 85 s
Mirnyy 52 f
Mirpur Khas 60 w
Kirsale 43 w
Mirzapur 61 t
Miscou, Point 17 e
Misgar 61 a
Misheguk Mountain 11 a
Misión San Fernando 18 e
Miskolc 35 d
Misool 70 o
Missinaibi 16 h
Mississippi (State) 20 f
Mississippi (River) 16 q
Mississippi Delta 20 g
Missoula 14 l
Missour 36 j
Missouri (River) 15 w
Missouri (State) 15 x
Mistassini 17 a
Mistassini, Lake 16 m
Misurata 35 o
Mitatib 43 a
Mitchell (Australia) 78 c
Mitchell (USA) 15 u
Mitchell (River) 73-77
Mitchell River 73 j
Mitla 19 q
Mito 59 o
Mitrovica 35 d
Mitú 25 b
Mitumbar Mountains 45 b
Mitwaba 45 b
Mitzic 41 v
Miyako 63 x
Miyazaki 58 w
Miyun 57 x
Mizan Teferi 43 n
Mizda 34 z
Mjösa, Lake 33 c
Mkomazi 45 j
Mkumbura 46 f
Mkuze 49 t
Mmabatho 49 n
Moab 15 o
Moa (Island) 73 k
Moa (River) 40 s
Moanda 44 e
Mobe 45 d
Mobaye 42 p
Mobayi-Mbongo 42 q
Mobeka 42 o
Mobile 20 h
Mobridge 15 g
Mocajuba 26 m
Moçambique 45 y
Mocimboa da Praia 45 y
Mocoa 24 j
Moctezuma 18 h
Moctezuma (River) 19 o
Mocuba 45 v
Modena 34 l
Modesto 14 u
Modjamboli 42 q
Moe 77 x
Moengo 26 h
Moenkopi 15 n
Mogadishu 43 u
Mogdy 58 l
Mogilev 33 z
Mogilev Podol'skiy 35 i
Mogoča 52 u
Mogochin 51 s
Mogojto 52 r
Mogok 62 r
Mohammadia 34 s
Moheli 47 a
Mohoro 45 k
Moincêr 61 e
Mointy 55 k
Mo-i-Rana 33 e
Mojave 14 w
Mojo 28 f
Mojones 28 r
Moju 26 m
Mokambo 45 p
Mokil Atoll 71 l
Mokolo 41 k
Mokowe 45 l
Mokp'o 58 t
Molde 33 b
Moldova 35 i
Molepolole 49 b
Molgary 56 b
Moline 16 q
Mollendo 24 z
Molócuè 46 k
Molodetschno 33 x
Molodezhnaya 84 l
Molodo 52 j
Molokai 18 q
Molopo 49 n
Moloundou 41 y
Moluccas 69 l
Molucca Sea 69 k
Moma 46 y
Mombasa 45 k
Momboyo 44 j
Mompós 23 a
Monaco 34 k
Monapo 46 l
Mona-Quimbundo 44 x
Mončegorsk 50 a
Mönch Chajrchan 56 j
Monclova 19 a
Moncton 17 e
Mondo 41 l
Mondy 57 a
Monga 42 r
Mongalla 42 y
Monghyr 61 v
Möng Küng 62 r
Mongo 42 b
Mongola 42 p
Mongolia, 56-57
Mongolo 52 d
Möng Ton 62 s
Mongu 44 y
Monguno 41 j
Möng Yai 62 r
Monkira 77 h
Monkoto 44 k
Mono 71 u
Mon'obut 52 z
Monroe 19 g
Monrovia 40 s
Montalvo 24 j
Montana 15 a
Mont aux Sources 49 q
Monte Alegre 26 i
Monte Alto 29 e
Monte Dourado 26 j
Montego Bay 21 n
Montemorelos 19 b
Montepuez 45 x
Monte Quemado 28 u
Monterey 14 u
Montería 22 l
Montero 25 t
Monteros 28 s
Monterrey 19 b
Montes Claros 29 i
Montevideo (Uruguay) 31 d
Montevideo (USA) 15 i
Montgomery 20 i
Monticello 15 o

Mont-Joli....17 c
Mont Laurier....16 m
Montmagny....17 b
Monto....74 s
Montpelier....15 n
Montpellier....34 h
Montréal....16 m
Montrose....15 o
Monts des Ouled Nail....37 b
Montserrat....21 y
Montsinery....26 j
Monywa....62 p
Moomou....42 s
Moonie....78 e
Moora....76 d
Moore, Lake....76 e
Moorhead....15 i
Moose Jaw....15 d
Moose Lake....15 g
Moosonee....16 i
Mopeia....46 v
Mopti....40 k
Moquegua....25 n
Moradabad....61 d
Morafenobe....47 p
Moran....15 n
Morava (River, Slovakia)..35 b
Morava (River, Yugoslavia)35 e
Moray Firth....32 j
Mordaga....57 l
Morden....15 h
Mordovo....54 f
Moree....78 e
Morehead....16 u
Morehead City....21 b
Morelia....19 n
Morella....74 o
Morelos....19 s
Moreton Island....78 g
Morgan....77 g
Morichal....23 p
Morin Dawa....58 f
Morley River....11 m
Mornington....73 h
Mornington (Island)....73 h
Moro....60 j
Morobe....71 o
Morocco....36
Morogoro....45 j
Moro Gulf....67 u
Morokovo....10 e
Morokweng....49 n
Moroleón....19 n
Morombe....47 n
Morón....21 n
Mörön....57 a
Morona....24 j
Morondava....47 o
Morondo....40 i
Moroni....47 a
Moron Us He....61 m
Morotai....69 m
Moroto....42 z
Morozovsk....54 g
Morrinhos....29 d
Morris....16 r
Morro Grande....26 h
Morshansk....54 f
Morteros....28 v
Mortes....26 x
Mortlock Islands....71 g
Morven....74 q
Morvi....60 y
Moryakovskiy Zaton....51 s
Moscow (Russia)....54 c
Moscow (USA)....14 k
Mosegda....52 u
Moses Lake....14 i
Mosetse....49 b
Moshi....45 j
Mösjöen....33 d
Moskva (Moscow)....54 c
Mosomane....49 b
Mosquitos Coast....22 g
Mosquitos, Gulf of....22 i
Mossaka....44 h
Mosselbaai....48 z
Mossendjo....44 e
Mossman....74 b
Mossoró....27 u
Mostaganem....34 s
Mosting, Cape....90 w
Mosul....54 t
Mota....43 b
Motagua....22 c
Motihari....61 h
Motorchuna....52 i
Motril....36 j
Motul....20 t
Motykleyka....53 u
Moudjéria....40 e
Mouila....44 d
Moul....41 j
Mould Bay....12 e
Moulins....34 h
Moulmein....65 h
Moulouya....36 j
Moundou....41 l
Mount Coolon....74 q
Mount Dalrymple....74 r
Mount Darwin....49 f
Mount Douglas....74 q
Mount Dutton....77 d
Mount Elliot....74 q
Mount Fletcher....49 q
Mount Florence....72 t
Mount Frere....49 r
Mount Gambier....77 u
Mount Hagen....70 z
Mount House....72 m
Mount Isa....73 v
Mount Magnet....76 f
Mount Minnie....72 s
Mount Morgan....74 s
Mount Seabrook....76 e
Mount Sturgeon....74 n
Mount Surprise....74 b
Mount Vernon (Australia)..72 t
Mount Vernon (Illinois)....16 r
Mount Vernon (Washington)....14 h
Mount Wedge....73 q
Mountain Village....11 a
Moura....25 h
Mourdi Depression....38 o
Moussoro....41 m
Moutong....69 h
Moutouroua....41 k
Moven....77 l
Mowming....63 y
Moxico....44 x
Moyale....43 p
Moyeni....49 q
Moyero....52 b
Moyobamba....24 j
Moyu....61 d
Mozambique....45-46/49
Mozambique Channel....46 z
Mozhaysk....54 c
Mozyr....33 y
Mpaathutlwa Pan....48 l
M'Pala....44 f
Mpanda....45 e
Mpata....44 j
Mpessoba....40 i
Mpika....45 s
Mporokoso....45 r
Mpulungu....46 e
Mpwapwa....45 i
Msaken....37 g
Msata....45 j
Mtito Andei....45 j
Mtubatuba....49 t
Mtwara....45 y
Muanda....44 d
Muang Chiang Rai....65 i
Muang Khoa....62 u
Muar....68 g
Muarabadak....69 e
Muarabungo....68 g
Mubarek....55 s
Mubende....42 x
Mubi....41 j
Mucajá....25 k
Muchinga Mountains....45 r
Muconda....44 x
Mucubela....46 x
Mucuim....25 f
Mucuri....29 k
Mucusso....48 l
Muddy Gap....15 p
Mudgee....78 e
Mudginbarry....73 d
Mueda....45 x
Muerto Meer....20 p
Mufulira....45 p
Muğla....35 v
Mugrab....55 r
Muhairiqah....39 r
Muhammad Qol....38 z
Muhammad, Ras....38 k
Mühling Hoffman Mountains....83 j
Muinak....55 p
Muji....56 o
Mukachevo....33 v
Mukana....45 o
Mukden (Shenyang)....58 c
Mukuku....45 q
Mukumbura....49 f
Mulanje....46 i
Mulata....26 i
Mulga Park....77 a
Mulgrave....17 g
Mulhouse....34 j
Muligort....50 z
Muling....58 j
Mull....32 v
Mullaittivu....64 v
Mullewa....76 d
Mulongo....45 b
Multan....60 l
Mulu....67 o
Mulundo....44 t
Mulym'ya....50 z
Mumbai (Bombay)....60 z
Mumbué....44 v
Mumbwa....45 o
Mumra....54 j
Muna (Island)....69 v
Muna (River)....52 h
München (Munich)....34 l
Muncie....16 t
Mundo Novo....27 s
Mundri....42 x
Mundubbera....74 s
Mundybas....56 g
Mungindi....78 d
Munich....34 l
Münster....33 o
Muntok....68 i
Munugudzhak....53 l
Mununga....45 q
Muonio....33 j
Muqdisho (Mogadishu)....43 u
Muraé....29 j
Murallón....30 t
Murashi....50 t
Murat Nehri....54 r
Muratus Mountains....69 p
Murchison....76 d
Murchisson....41 g
Murcia....34 r
Murdochville....17 e
Mures....35 e
Murfreesboro....16 s
Murgab (River, Afghanistan)....60 h
Murgab (River, Tajikistan).55 w
Murgenella....73 d
Murgon....74 t
Murgoo....76 d
Muriege....44 x
Murillo Atoll....71 f
Murmansk....50 a
Murom....54 f
Muroran....59 c
Murray....77 g
Murray Bridge....77 g
Murray Lake....70 x
Murrumbidgee....77 j
Murukta....52 a
Mururoa....230 p
Murwillumbah....78 g
Murzuq....37 v
Musa Ali....43 f
Musala....35 f
Musandam, Ras....60 n
Muscat....60 p
Musgrave Ranges....77 a
Muskegon....16 s
Muskogee....15 w
Muslimbagh....60 j
Musmar....38 y
Musoma....45 g
Mussende....44 u
Mussera....44 f
Mustahil....43 t
Mustang....61 g
Musters, Lago....30 w
Muswellbrook....78 f
Mût....38 t
Mutankiang....58 h
Mutare....49 g
Mutoko....49 g
Mutomo....45 k
Mutoray....51 z
Muttaburra....74 o
Mutuali....45 w
Muxima....44 s
Muzaffarabad....60 m
Muzaffarnagar....61 c
Muzaffarpur....61 u
Muztag....61 j
Muztag (Yurungkax He)....61 e
Muz Tau....56 f
Mvolo....42 w
Mvomero....45 j
Mvurwi....46 s
Mwanza....45 f
Mwatate....45 k
Mweka....44 k
Mwene Ditu....44 m
Mwenezi....49 e
Mwenga....45 c
Mweru, Lake....45 c
Mwingi....45 j
Mwinilunga....44 z
Myajlar....60 x
Myakit....53 i
Myanaung....66 a
Myanmar (Burma)..62/65/66
Myingyan....62 q
Myitkyina....62 r
Mymensingh....61 x
Mynaral....55 x
Mynbulak....55 q
Myroodah....72 x
Myrtle Beach....21 a
Mys....53 m
Mysore....64 f
Mys Shmidta....10 h
Mys Zelaniya....51 a
My Tho....66 i
Mytisci....54 d
Myylybulak....55 l
Mzimba....45 t
Mzuzu....45 t

N

Naalehu....18 r
Naba....62 q
Nababeep....48 v
Nabberu, Lake....76 g
Naberezhnyje Celny....54 l
Nabk....38 l
Nabk Abu Qasr....39 a
Nabukjuak....13 g
Nacala....45 y
Nacaome....22 e
Nacaroa....45 y
Nachičevan....54 u
Nachingwea....45 w
Nachodka....58 k
Nacogdoches....19 e
Nadiad....60 z
Nador....36 j
Nadym....51 p
Nafud....39 h
Naga....67 i
Nagano....59 n
Nagarjuna Reservoir....64 g
Nagasaki....58 v
Nagaur....60 m
Nagercoil....64 s
Nagornyy....52 x
Nagoya....58 z
Nagpur....61 p
Nagqu....61 l
Nagykanizsa....35 c
Naha....63 z
Nahanni Butte....12 p
Nahuel Huapi, Lago....30 h
Naiband....60 b
Naij Tal....62 c
Naiman Qi....58 d
Nain (Canada)....13 z
Nain (Iran)....39 k
Nairobi....45 j
Naivasha....45 i
Najaf....39 d
Najafabad....39 i
Najd....39 c
Najin....58 j
Najran....39 q
Nakamura....58 x
Nakasongola....42 x
Nakfa....38 z
Nakhl....38 k
Nakhodka....51 e
Nakhon Pathom....65 j
Nakhon Ratchasima....65 k
Nakhon Sawan....65 j
Nakhon Si Thammarat....65 w
Nakina....16 f
Naknek....11 p
Nakonde....45 s
Nakuru....45 i
Nal'čik....54 t
Nalgonda....61 q
Nalut....34 z
Nalychevo....53 y
Nama....28 d
Namaacha....49 t
Namacurra....46 w
Namakzar-e Shadad....60 c
Namanga....45 i
Namangan....55 v
Namanyere....45 e
Namapa....46 l
Nambour....78 g
Nambuangongo....44 f
Nam Can....66 u
Nam Co....61 k
Namco....61 l
Nam Dinh....62 x
Nametil....46 l
Namialo....45 x
Namib....48 g
Namibe....48 e
Namibia....44/48
Namies....48 x
Namjagbarwa Feng....62 c
Nam Kaub....48 k
Namlea....69 y
Namoi....78 d
Namolok....71 f
Namonuito Atoll....71 c
Nampala....40 j
Nampula....46 k
Namutoni....44 u
Namwala....45 n
Nan....65 j
Nanaimo....14 g
Nanbu....62 k
Nancha....58 i
Nanchang....63 e
Nanchung....62 k
Nancy....34 i
Nanda Devi....61 d
Nanded....61 p
Nandi....75 k
Nanfeng....63 e
Nanga Eboko....41 w
Nanga Parbat....61 a
Nanga Pinoh....69 a
Nanga Sokan....68 m
Nangdoi....62 h
Nangomba....45 w
Nangqên....62 e
Nangsin Sum....57 r
Nangtud....67 h
Nangurukuru....45 k
Nang Xian....62 b
Nan Hulsan Hu....62 d
Nanjing (Nanking)....63 g
Nanking....63 g
Nanning....62 z

Nanortilak 90 s
Nanpang Jiang 62 w
Nanping 63 s
Nansen Land 91 i
Nansen Sound 89 s
Nanshan Islands 67 a
Nansio 45 g
Nantes 34 f
Nantulo 45 x
Nantung 63 h
Nanuque 29 k
Nanxiong 63 p
Nanyang 63 b
Nanyuki 43 o
Nanzhang 63 a
Nanzhao 63 b
Nao, Cabo de la 34 s
Napalkovo 51 c
Nape 62 w
Napier 79 w
Naples (Florida) 20 l
Naples (Italy) 35 a
Napo 24 k
Napoleon 16 t
Napoli (Naples) 35 a
Nara 40 i
Naracoorte 77 u
Narasun 57 h
Narat 56 r
Narathiwat 65 x
Narbonne 34 h
Nares Strait 91 d
Naribis 48 h
Narijnteel 57 n
Narmada 60 z
Narodnaja 50 k
Narodnaya 50 x
Narok 45 h
Narrabri 78 e
Narrandera 78 b
Narrogin 76 e
Narromine 78 c
Narsarsuaq 90 t
Narsimhapur 61 q
Narsinghgarh 61 p
Narubis 48 w
Narva 33 k
Narvik 33 f
Nar'yan Mar 50 i
Naryn 56 m
Naryn (Naryn Taragay) 55 y
Narynkol 56 p
Naryn Taragay 56 n
Nashville 16 s
Näsi, Lake 33 j
Nasik 60 z
Nasir 42 l
Naskaupi 17 g
Nassau 21 b
Nasser, Lake 38 v
Nata 49 b
Natal 27 w
Natanz 39 i
Natashquan 17 g
Natashquan (River) 17 g
Natchitoches 20 d
Nathan River 73 f
Natitingou 41 b
Natividade 26 z
Natron, Lake 45 i
Natuna 66 x
Natuna Islands 66 x
Naulila 44 t
Nauru 231 y
Naurzum 55 f
Nauta 24 l
Nauzad 60 g
Navadwip 61 w
Navarin, Cape 10 h
Navio, Serra do 26 j
Navirai 29 a
Navlya 54 b
Navoi 55 s
Navojoa 18 h
Navolato 18 i
Navrongo 40 m
Navsari 60 z
Náxos 35 t
Nayakhan 53 l
Naykhin 58 m
Nazaré 27 t
Nazarovka 54 f
Nazarovo 56 i
Nazas 18 l
Nazca 24 y
Nazimovo 51 w
Nazina 51 r
Nazret 43 d
Nazwa 60 o
Nazym 51 n
Nazyyayevsk 55 i
Nchelenge 45 q
N'Dalatando 44 t
Ndareda 45 h
Ndélé 42 c
Ndendé 44 d
N'Djamena 41 l
Ndji 42 e
Ndjolé (Cameroon) 41 v
Ndjolé (Gabon) 41 v
Ndola 46 d
Neagh, Lough 32 v
Neale, Lake 73 o
Near Islands 10 r
Nebit-Dag 54 z
Nebo 74 r
Nebraska 15 s
Nebraska City 15 v
Nechako Reservoir 14 e
Nechi 22 m
Necochea 31 c
Necoclí 22 l
Nêdong 61 m
Neds Creek 76 f
Neepawa 15 g
Neftekamsk 54 m
Negage 44 g
Negele 43 q
Negoiu 35 g
Negola 44 t
Negotka 51 s
Negro Reservoir 28 z
Negro (River, Argentina) 30 m
Negro (River, Brazil) 25 e
Negro (River, Uruguay) 29 n
Negros 67 h
Nehbandan 60 d
Nehe 58 f
Nehri 54 s
Neijiang (Neikiang) 62 k
Neiriz 39 k
Neishabur 55 o
Neiva 22 z
Nekempt 43 b
Neleger 52 m
Nel'gese 53 b
Nelidovo 50 n
Nel'kan 53 p
Nellore 64 h
Nelson (Canada) 14 k
Nelson (New Zealand) 79 t
Nelson (River) 13 n
Nelson Forks 12 p
Nelson Strait 30 s
Nelspruit 49 s
Néma 40 i
Nembudziya 46 r
Nemen 33 v
Nemuro 59 e
Nemuy 53 p
Nenana 11 f
Nenjiang 58 f
Nen Jiang (River) 58 f
Neosho 15 w
Nepa 52 q
Nepal 61
Nepalganj 61 f
Nepa (River) 52 p
Nephi 14 z
Nepoko 42 v
Nera 53 f
Nerčа 52 t
Nerchinskiy Zavod 52 u
Nerpich'ye, Lake 53 m
Nerrima 72 x
Neryungri 52 w
Ness, Loch 32 j
Neter 53 r
Netherlands 33
Netherlands Antilles 21 x/23 e
Netta 37 e
Nettilling Lake 13 j
Neubrandenburg 33 r
Neuquén 30 k
Neuquén (River) 30 i
Neuruppin 33 r
Neuva Alejandría 24 l
Nevada (Missouri) 15 w
Nevada (State) 14 w
Nevada, Mount 28 q
Nevada, Sierra 36 k
Nevado, Sierra del 30 j
Nevanka 56 m
Nevel' 33 y
New 23 y
Newala 45 x
New Amsterdam 23 y
Newark (New York) 16 z
Newark (Ohio) 16 u
New Bedford 17 o
New Bern 16 y
New Braunfels 19 c
New Britain 71 q
New Brunswick 17 d
Newburgh 16 z
New Caledonia 75 o
Newcastle (Australia) 78 f
Newcastle (Canada) 17 d
Newcastle (South Africa) 49 r
Newcastle (USA) 15 q
Newcastle upon Tyne 32 x
Newcastle Waters 73 d
New Crown 77 d
New Delhi 61 b
Newfoundland 17 g
New Georgia 71 w
New Georgia Islands 71 v
New Glasgow 17 f
New Guinea 70
New Hampshire 17 n
New Haven 17 n
New Hebrides 75 f
New Iberia 19 g
New Ireland 71 s
New Jersey 16 z
New Kandla 60 x
New Liskeard 16 j
Newman 72 v
Newman, Mount 72 u
New Meadows 14 k
New Mexico 15 p
New Norfolk 77 y
New Orleans 20 f
New Plymouth 79 u
Newport (Arkansas) 16 p
Newport (Tennessee) 16 u
Newport News 16 y
New Providence Island 21 o
New Richmond 17 d
New Siberian Islands 53 d
New South Wales 78 c
Newton 15 x
New Ulm 15 j
New York (City) 16 z
New York (State) 16 y
New Zealand 79
Neyto, Lake 51 a
Nezhin 33 z
Ngabang 68 m
Ngamring 61 i
Ngangala 42 y
Ngangla Ringco 61 g
Ngaoundéré 41 x
Ngatik Atoll 71 j
Ngauruhoe 79 v
Ngidinga 44 g
N'Giva 48 h
Ngo 44 g
Ngoring 62 e
Ngoura 41 m
Ngouri 41 l
Ngourti 41 j
Ngudu 45 g
Nguigmi 41 j
Ngukurr 73 f
Ngulu Atoll 70 h
Nguru 41 h
Nhamunda 25 k
Nha Trang 66 l
Nhill 77 u
Nhulunbuy 73 g
Niafounké 40 k
Niagara Falls 16 w
Niak 61 h
Niamey 41 b
Niangara 42 u
Nia Nia 42 u
Nias 68 c
Nicaragua 22
Nicaragua, Lake 22 f
Nice 34 j
Nichatka, Lake 52 u
Nicholls Town 21 a
Nicholson 73 n
Nička 55 r
Nicobar 65 q
Nicobar, Great 65 r
Nicobar, Little 65 r
Nicosia 35 y
Nicoya, Gulf of 22 g
Nicoya Peninsula 22 f
Nidym 51 z
Niefang 41 u
Niemba 45 c
Niénokoué 40 v
Nieuw Nickerie 23 z
Nieuwoudtville 48 x
Niğde 35 z
Niger 37/41
Niger (River) 41 e
Nigeria 41
Nihau 18 o
Niigata 59 o
Nikolayev 35 k
Nikolayevsk 54 h
Nikolayevsk-na-Amure 53 r
Nikol'sk 50 s
Nikol'skiy 55 g
Nikopol 35 l
Nikshahr 60 q
Nilang 61 d
Nile 38 u
Nile Delta 35 w
Nilka 56 q
Niman 53 n
Nîmes 34 h
Nimule 42 y
Ninbing 73 a
Nindigully 74 r
Nine Degree Channel 64 p
Ninety Mile Beach (Australia) 77 z
Ninety Mile Beach (New Zealand) 79 g
Ning'an 58 i
Ningde 63 t
Ningdu 63 q
Ningjin Shan 62 d
Ningming 62 y
Ningpo 63 h
Ningshan 62 m
Ningyuan 63 o
Ninnis Glacier 86 z
Niobrara 15 s
Nioki 44 h
Niokolo Koba 40 d
Nioro du Sahel 40 g
Nipigon 16 e
Nipigon Lake 16 d
Niquero 21 n
Nis 35 e
Nishinoyima 58 y
Nitchequon 17 b
Niterói 29 i
Niubiziliang 56 v
Nizamabad 64 f
Nizhinevartovsk 51 q
Nizhneangarsk 57 f
Nizhneimbatskoye 51 v
Nizhniy Novgorod 50 r
Nizhniy Tagil 50 x
Nizhniy Yenangsk 50 s
Niznaya Tunguska 52 a
Nižneudinsk 56 m
Niž Taimyra 51 m
Njombe 45 u
Nkambe 41 u
Nkawkaw 40 z
Nkayi 49 d
Nkhata Bay 45 u
Nkhotakota 45 t
Nkolabona 41 v
Nkongsamba 41 u
Noatak 11 a
Noatak River 11 a
Nochixtlán 20 o
Nockatunga 77 i
Nogales 18 h
Noginsk 54 d
Noginskiy 51 v
Nohar 61 a
Nok Kundi 60 f
Kokou 41 l
Nola 41 y
Nolinsk 50 u
Nom 56 x
Nome 10 m
Nomgon 57 q
Nomhon 62 e
Nonacho Lake 12 v
Nonburg 50 h
Nong Khai 65 l
Noonamah 73 c
Noorvik 11 b
Noranda 16 j
Nordenshel'da Arch. 51 k
Nordostrundingen 91 k
Nordvik 52 e
Nordvik, Cape 52 f
Norfolk (Nebraska) 15 u
Norfolk (Virginia) 16 y
Norfolk Island 79 d
Noril'sk 51 h
Normanby (Island) 74 g
Normanton 73 j
Norman Wells 12 b
Norovtin 57 h
Norrköping 33 f
Norrtälje 33 g
Norseman 76 h
Norte, Cabo 26 l
Norte, Puntá 30 m
Norte, Puntá (Samboronbón Bay) 31 d
Norte, Serra do 25 w
Northam 76 e
Northampton 76 c
North Andaman 65 e
North Anyuskiy Mountains 10 b
North Battleford 15 b
North Bay 16 j
North Baykal Plateau 52 r
North, Cape (Canada) 17 h
North Cape (New Zealand) 79 g
North Cape (Norway) 33 k
North Caribou Lake 16 c
North Carolina 16 v
North Channel (UK) 32 v
North Dakota 15 f
North Dvina 50 r
North East Land 92 c
Northern Ireland 32 v
Northern Mariana Islands 231 j
Northern Sporades 35 t
Northern Territory 73 q
Northern Ural Mountains 50 x
Northern Uvaly 50 s
North Fork 14 x
North Horr 43 o
North Island 79 u
North Lincoln Land 13 f
North Natuna 68 k
North Pagai 68 r
North Platte 15 t
North Pole 92 a
North Saskatchewan 15 a
North Sea 32 z
North Sosva 50 y
Northumberland Strait 17 f
Northway Junction 11 h
North West Cape 72 q
North-West River 17 g
Northwest Territories 11-12
Norton 15 t
Norton Sound 11 a
Norvegia, Cape 83 g
Norway 33
Norway House 15 h
Norwegian Bay 13 b
Norwegian Sea 33

Norwich 32 z
Noshul' 50 t
Nosratabad 60 c
Nossob 48 y
Nosy-Bé 47 e
Nosy Boraha 47 s
Noto 37 j
Nôtre Dame Bay 17 k
Nottingham 32 y
Nottingham Island 13 s
Nouâdhibou 36 n
Nouâdhibou, Cape 36 n
Nouakchott 36 n
Nouamrhar 36 o
Nouméa 75 q
Nouna 40 k
Nova Alvorada 29 a
Novabad 55 v
Nova Crixas 29 d
Nova Gaia 44 u
Nova Goleg 46 u
Nova Olinda do Norte 25 j
Novara 34 k
Nova Russas 27 r
Nova Scotia 17 f
Novay 51 m
Novaya Kakhova 54 b
Novaya Kakhovka 35 l
Novaya Sibir' 53 h
Novaya Zemlya 50 j
Novgorod 33 l
Novillo Reservoir 18 h
Novisad 35 d
Novo Aripuan 25 i
Novocherkassk 54 e
Novodolinka 55 k
Novo Friburgo 29 j
Novograd Volynskiy 33 x
Novo Hamburgo 29 q
Novoilinovka 59 a
Novoishimskiy 55 h
Novokiyevskiy Uval 58 i
Novokuzneck 56 g
Novolazarevskaya 83 m
Novomoskovsk (Russia) 54 e
Novomoskovsk (Ukraine) 54 c
Novorossiyka 52 z
Novorossiysk 54 q
Novoryonye 52 b
Novoshakhtinsk 54 e
Novosibirsk 56 e
Novo Uzensk 54 j
Novo-Vyatsk 50 u
Novoyerundinskiy 51 x
Novyy 52 c
Novyy (Vilyuy) 52 f
Novyy Port 51 b
Nowgong 62 o
Nowra 78 e
Noyabr'sk 51 q
Nsah 44 g
Nsanje 46 v
Ntadembele 44 h
Ntam 41 w
Ntoroko 42 w
Nuanetsi 49 g
Nuatja 41 n
Nuba Mountains 42 j
Nubian Desert 38 x
Nueltin Lake 12 y
Nueva Rosita 19 a
Nueve de Julio 31 a
Nuevitas 21 o
Nuevo 20 r
Nuevo Casas Grandes 18 j
Nuevo Gulf 30 m
Nuevo Laredo 19 a
Nu Jiang 62 e
Nukiki 71 w
Nullagine 72 v
Nullarbor 77 a
Nullarbor Plain 76 l
Numan 41 i
Numkaub 48 k
Numto 51 p
Nunap Isua
(Cape Farewell) 90 t
Nunatak 13 k
Nunavut 12-13
Nungnain Sun 57 y
Nungo 45 w
Nunivak 10 m
Nunligran 10 j
Nuoro 34 k
Nura 55 i
Nurabad 39 i
Nuremberg 34 m
Nuri 18 i
Nürnberg (Nuremberg) 34 m
Nur Turu 56 w
Nuru 55 k
Nusaybin 54 s
Nushki 60 h
Nutak 13 z
Nutwood Downs 73 e
Nuuk 90 u
Nuussuaq Halv 90 l
Nuweiba 38 k
Nuyts Archipelago 77 c
Nuyts, Cape 76 d
Nyahururu 43 o
Nyainqentangla Shan 62 c
Nyainrong 61 m
Nyakanazi 45 e
Nyaksimvol 50 y
Nyala 42 f
Nyalam 61 i
Nyamapanda 49 g
Nyamboyoto 51 e
Nyanga 49 g
Nyanyadzi 49 f
Nyasa, Lake
(Lake Malawi) 45 u
Nyazepetrovsk 55 b
Nyda 51 c
Nyeboe Land 91 g
Nyêmo 61 l
Nyima 61 j
Nyimba 45 r
Nyingchi 62 c
Nyíregyháza 35 e
Nyiri Desert 45 j
Nyiru 43 n
Nylstroom 49 d
Nyngan 78 c
Nyong 41 u
Nysh 53 r
Nyunzu 45 c
Nyurba 52 h
Nyurchan 53 v
Nyuya 52 t
Nyuya (River) 52 r
Nyvrovo 53 r
Nzega 45 f
Nzérékoré 40 u
N'Zeto 44 e

O

Oahe, Lake 15 g
Oahu 18 p
Oajazeiras 27 t
Oakes 15 h
Oakland 14 u
Oaklands 78 o
Oakley 15 t
Oak Ridge 16 t
Oala Panja 55 w
Oamaru 79 s
Oates Land 86 w
Oatlands 77 y
Oaxaca 20 o
Ob' (River) 56 e
Ob', Gulf of 51 c
Obbia 43 w
Oberá 29 n
Obi 69 l
Obidos 25 m
Obihiro 59 d
Oblukovino 53 x
Obninsk 54 c
Obo 42 u
Obo Liang 56 w
Obombo 48 g
Oboyan' 54 c
Obrique 36 i
Obsči Syrt 54 l
Obuasi 40 z
Ocala 20 l
Ocaña 23 a
Ocean Falls 14 d
Oceanside 18 c
Ocha 53 r
Ocoña 24 z
Ocoña (River) 24 z
Ocotlán 18 z
Oda (Ghana) 40 z
Oda (Mountain) 38 y
Odemira 36 f
Odense 33 p
Oder 33 r
Odessa (USA) 18 m
Odessa (Ukraine) 35 k
Odienné 40 i
Odintsovo 54 c
Oeiras 27 q
Oenpelli 73 d
Ofira 38 k
Ogaden 43 t
Ogbomosho 41 c
Ogden 14 z
Ogeechee 20 l
Ogilvie Mountains 11 i
Ogoamas 69 g
Ogoja 41 t
Ogoki 16 f
Ogooué 44 c
Ogoron 52 z
Ogun 41 p
Ogurčinskij 54 y
Ohanet 37 e
O' Higgins, Lago 30 t
Ohio (State) 16 u
Ohio (River) 16 u
Ohrid Lake 35 d
Oiapoque 26 k
Ōita 58 w
Ojgun Nuur 56 l
Ojinaga 18 l
Ojo Caliente 18 z
Ojo de Liebre, Lac 18 e
Ojos del Salado 28 q
Oka 54 f
Oka (Vostochny
Mountains 57 a
Okahandja 48 i
Okakarara 48 j
Okara 60 m
Okaukuejo 48 h
Okavango 48 m
Okavango Delta 48 m
Okayama 58 x
Okeechobee, Lake 20 l
Okene 41 r
Okha 53 s
Okhotsk 53 s
Okhotsk, Sea of 59 g
Okhotskiy-Perevoz 53 b
Oki 58 x
Okinawa 63 z
Oklahoma 15 t
Oklahoma City 15 u
Okondja 44 e
Okoyo 44 g
Oktyabr'isk 51 y
Oktyabrskiy 52 z
Oktyabr'skiy 54 m
Oktyabr'skiy (Kamchatka) 53 x
Oktyabr'skoy Revolutsii 51 k
Öland 33 s
Olavarría 31 a
Olbia 34 l
Old Crow 11 j
Oldéani 45 h
Olds 14 l
Olean 16 x
Olekma 52 v
Olekminsk 52 v
Olenëk 52 e
Olenëk (River) 52 g
Olëng-Sala 52 h
Oleni 51 d
Ölgij 56 j
Olinda 27 w
Oliva 28 u
Oliva, Cord. de 28 p
Olivares 28 p
Oliveira 29 h
Ollague 28 d
Ollita, Cord. de 28 p
Olmos 24 h
Oloitokitok 45 i
Ol'okama 52 v
Olomouc 33 s
Olongapo 67 f
Olov'annaja 57 i
Oloyskiy Mountains 10 a
Olsztyr 33 u
Olympia 14 g
Olympus 35 y
Olyutorskiy 10 d
Olyutorskiy, Cape 10 q
Ōma 59 c
Omaha 15 v
Omak 14 i
Oman 39/60
Oman, Gulf of 60 p
Omaruru 48 h
Omboué 44 b
Ombu 61 i
Omchali 54 z
Omdurman 42 k
Omeo 78 p
Omnya 53 n
Omo 43 n
Omolon 53 l
Omoloy 53 a
Omsk 55 k
Omsukchan 53 k
Onangué, Lake 41 u
Oncócua 48 f
Ondangwa 48 h
Ondo 41 q
Öndör 57 j
Öndör Chaan 57 g
Ondor Sum 57 u
Onega 50 p
Onega Bay 50 o
Onega, Lake 50 o
Onega (River) 50 p
Onegva Yar 51 q
O'Neill 15 u
Onekotan 59 k
Ongjin 58 s
Ongniud Qi 57 x
Ongole 64 h
Onitsha 41 s
Onkuchakh 52 f
Onon Gol 57 g
Onseepkans 48 w
Onslow 72 r
Ontario 14 k
Ontario (Province) 16 c
Ontario, Lake 16 x
Oobagooma 72 k
Oodnadatta 77 d
Ooldea 77 b
Oologah Lake 15 w
Ooratippra 73 t
Ootacamund 64 e
Opal 55 y
Opala 42 s
Opelika 20 i
Ophir 68 e
Opienge 42 u
Opochka 33 y
Opornyy 54 m
Oporto 34 a
Oppdal 33 c
Opuwa 48 f
Oradea 35 e
Orai 61 q
Oran (Algeria) 34 s
Orange 78 d
Orange (River) 48 y
Orange, Cabo 26 k
Orangegebirgte 26 h
Orbost 78 q
Orcadas 82 g
Orchontuul 57 d
Ord (Mount) 72 l
Ord (River) 73 a
Ord River 73 a
Ordos 57 s
Ordynskoye 56 d
Örebro 33 e
Orechovo-Zujevo 54 e
Oregon 14 h
Orel 54 c
Orel', Lake 53 q
Orellana 24 i
Orellana (Ucayali) 24 k
Orenburg 54 m
Orense 34 a
Orgejev 35 i
Orgon Tal 57 u
Orillia 16 j
Orinoco 23 h
Orinoco Delta 23 i
Oristano 34 x
Orìximiná 25 m
Orizaba 19 q
Orkney Islands 32 k
Orlando 20 m
Orléans 32 z
Orleans, Isle d' 17 b
Orlik 57 a
Orlinga 57 d
Ormara 60 t
Ormoc 67 j
Ornsköldsvik 33 g
Orocué 23 o
Orog Nuur 57 n
Orög Nuur 56 i
Oroluk Atoll 71 i
Oron (Russia) 57 h
Oron (Russia) 52 t
Oronoque 23 y
Oroqen Zizhiqi 58 e
Oroquieta 67 v
Orotukan 53 i
Oroumieh 54 u
Orovada 14 w
Oroville (California) 14 u
Oroville (Washington) 14 i
Oroyek 53 j
Orsha 33 y
Orsk 55 b
Orto-Ayan 52 m
Orto-Kyuyel' 52 m
Ortonville 15 i
Orupembe 48 f
Oruro 28 e
Os 55 w
Ōsaka 58 z
Oscrovnoy 94 i
Oshakati 48 h
Oshawa 16 w
Oshkosh 16 r
Oshmarino 51 f
Oshogbo 41 d
Oshtoran 39 h
Oshwe 44 j
Osijek 35 c
Osinovo 51 v
Oskaloosa 15 x
Oskara, Cape 51 l
Oslo 33 d
Oslofjord 33 c
Osnabrück 33 o
Osóriô 29 q
Osorno 30 g
Ossa 77 x
Ossora 10 o
Ostashkov 50 n
Ostend 32 z
Östersund 33 e
Ostrava 35 c
Ostrov 33 l
Ostrovnoy 10 b
Ōsumi Channel 58 v
Osvaldo Cruz 29 d
Otaru 59 b
Otavalo 24 i
Otavi 48 i
O.T.Downs 73 e
Otish Mountains 17 b
Otjiwarongo 48 h
Otog Qi 57 r
Ot-Siyen 52 i
Ottawa (Canada) 16 m
Ottawa (USA) 15 w
Ottawa (River) 16 k
Ottawa Islands 13 s
Ottuk 55 y
Ottumwa 15 x
Oturkpo 41 t
Otuzco 24 i
Otway, Cape 77 v

Ouadane 36 r
Ouadda 42 e
Ouagadougou 40 m
Ouagat 42 d
Ouahigouya 40 l
Ouahila 36 i
Ouake 42 p
Oualata 36 u
Oualidia 36 f
Ouallam 41 b
Ouandago 42 o
Ouandja 42 d
Ouangolodougou 40 i
Ouaqui 26 i
Ouara 42 s
Ouarane 36 s
Ouargla 34 v
Oubangui 42 p
Oudeïka 36 y
Oudtshoorn 48 y
Oued Zem 36 h
Ouémé 41 b
Ouerrha 36 j
Ouesso 41 y
Ouezzane 36 i
Ouham 42 a
Ouidah 41 o
Oujda 34 r
Oujeft 36 q
Ouled Djellal 34 v
Oulou 42 d
Oulu 33 j
Oulu, Lake 33 k
Oum 36 g
Oum Hadjer 42 b
Ounianga Kebir 38 n
Ouricuri 27 s
Ourinhos 29 d
Ourique 36 g
Outat-el-Hadj 36 j
Outjo 48 h
Ouyen 77 v
Ouyu Bezze Denga 41 j
Ovalle 28 o
Ovamboland 48 i
Oviedo 34 c
Ovoot 56 k
Ovoot Chural 57 o
Övre Årdal 33 b
Owando 44 h
Owensboro 16 s
Owen Sound 16 i
Owen Stanley Range 71 o
Owo 41 r
Owyhee 14 x
Oxapampa 24 x
Oxford 32 x
Oyapock 26 j
Oyem 41 v
Oyero Arys 55 g
Oymyakon 53 e
Oyo 41 p
Oysurdakh 53 j
Oyun-Kyuyel' 53 c
Oyun-Yurege 53 a
Ožalilabad 54 w
Ozamiz 67 v
Ozark Plateau 15 x
Ozhogina (River) 53 x
Ozhogino, Lake 53 g
Ozhogino 53 h

P

Paamiut 90 t
Pabna 61 x
Pacáas Novos, Serra dos 25 s
Pacajá 26 k
Pacaraima, Serra 23 v
Pacasmayo 24 h
Pacaya 24 k
Pachino 37 j
Pachitea 24 y
Pachuca 19 o
Pacific Ocean 230-231
Pacoval 26 i
Padang 68 e
Padangpanjang 68 f
Padangsidempuan 68 d
Padauiri 25 f
Padre Bernardo 29 e
Padre Paraiso 29 k
Padua 34 m
Paducah 16 r
Padunskoje, More 33 m
Paektu-san 58 h
Pafuri 49 f
Pag 35 a
Paga-Conta 26 u
Pagadian 67 u
Pagalu 41 r
Page 15 n
Pahokee 20 m
Päijänne, Lake 33 j
Paita 24 g
Pajule 42 y
Pakanbaru 68 g
Pakaraima Mountains 26
Pakhoi 62 z
Pakistan 60
Pakkoku 62 p
Pak Sane 66 g
Pakse 66 i
Pala 41 k
Palana 53 z
Palangkaraya 69 b
Palanpur 60 z
Palapye 49 c
Palata 20 l
Palatka 53 v
Palau 70 e
Palawan 67 d
Paleleh 69 h
Palembang 68 u
Palenque 20 r
Palermo (Colombia) 24 m
Palermo (Italy) 35 n
Palghat 64 f
Palgrave 72 s
Palgrave, Mount 72 s
Pali 60 z
Palk Strait 64 h
Palliser, Cape 79 v
Palma 34 u
Palmares 27 w
Palma Soriano 21 p
Palmeirais 27 p
Palmeira los Indlos 27 v
Palmeiras 27 n
Palmer (Alaska) 11 f
Palmer (Graham Land) 82 t
Palmer Land 82 x
Palmerston North 79 v
Palmira 22 y
Palm Springs 18 d
Palmyra 38 m
Palmyra Island 230 a
Palmyras Point 61 w
Paloich 42 l
Palomani 25 p
Palopo 69 t
Palo Santo 28 x
Palpa 24 x
Palparara 73 w
Palu 69 g
Pamangkat 68 k
Pambarra 49 h
Pamir 55 x
Pamlico Sound 16 y
Pampa de las Salinas 28 r
Pampa de los Guanacos 28 v
Pampas 24 y
Pampas (River) 24 y
Pamplona (Colombia) 23 b
Pamplona (Spain) 34 f
Pamyat 56 j
Pamzal 61 c
Panaji 64 c
Panamá (City) 22 j
Panama 22
Panamá Canal 21 j
Panamá, Gulf of 22 j
Panay 67 g
Panda 49 h
Pandamatenga 49 a
Pandharpur 61 n
Pandie Pandie 77 g
Panevėžhys 33 w
Panfilov 56 o
Pangi 45 b
Pangin 62 c
Pangi Range 61 a
Pangkalanbrandan 68 d
Pangkalanbuun 69 n
Pangkal Kalong 66 s
Pangkalpinang 68 j
Pangnirtung 13 l
Pangody 51 c
Pangong Tso 61 d
Panipat 61 b
Panjgur 60 g
Pankshin 41 h
Panna 61 r
Pannawonica 72 s
Panovo 51 o
Panova (Angara) 51 z
Pantelleria 34 z
Panter Downs 72 l
Pánuco 19 p
Pan Xian 62 w
Panyabungan 68 e
Paoting 57 v
Paotow 57 t
Papai 23 z
Papantla 19 q
Paphos 35 x
Paposo 28 o
Papua, Gulf of 70 z
Papua New Guinea 70-71/73/74
Pará 26 m
Parabel 51 r
Paraburdoo 72 t
Paracatu 29 f
Paracatu (River) 29 g
Paracel Islands 66 m
Paragominas 27 a
Paraguá (Brazil) 25 u
Paragua (Venezuela) 23 u
Paraguacu 27 s
Paraguai 25 x
Paraguaná Peninsula 23 d
Paraguari 28 z
Paraguay 28-29
Paraiba 27 v
Paraiba do Sul 29 j
Paraïso 29 b
Paraíso do Norte de Goiás 26 y
Parakou 41 c
Paramaribo 26 h
Paramirim 27 q
Paramušir 59 l
Paraná (Argentina) 28 w
Paraná (Brazil) 26 z
Paraná (River, Argentina) 28-29
Paraná (River, Brazil) 26
Paranaguá 29 s
Paranaiba 29 d
Paranam 26 h
Paranapanema 29 c
Paranapiacaba, Serra 29 r
Paranavai 29 c
Paraparaumu 79 u
Parapeti 28 i
Paratunka 53 y
Parbhani 61 o
Parbig 51 s
Parding 61 j
Pardo 29 b
Pardo (Brazilian Plateau) 29 l
Parepare 69 s
Parecis, Serra dos 25 u
Pariaguán 23 g
Paria, Gulf of 23 i
Parima, Serra 23 u
Pariñas, Cabo 24 f
Parintins 25 l
Paris (France) 34 h
Paris (USA) 19 e
Parkano 33 i
Parker Range 76 f
Parkersburg 16 v
Parkes 78 c
Parma 34 l
Parnaíba 27 e
Parnaíba (River) 27 d
Parnamirim 27 s
Parnu 33 j
Paromay 53 s
Paroo 77 k
Parras 18 m
Parry Islands 12 h
Parry Sound 16 j
Parsons 16 n
Partida, Roca 18 s
Paru 26 i
Paru de Oeste 25 l
Parvatipuram 61 t
Paryang 61 g
Parys 49 p
Pasadena 19 e
Pasangkayu 69 f
Pascagoula 20 g
Pasig 67 g
Pasni 60 t
Paso de los Indios 30 w
Paso de los Toros 28 z
Paso Limay 30 i
Paso Real 20 p
Passau 35 a
Passmore 77 g
Passo Fundo 29 o
Passos 29 g
Pastakh 53 i
Pastaza 24 j
Pasto 24 j
Pastos Bons 27 p
Patagonia 30 u
Patandar 60 g
Paterson 16 z
Pathankot 61 a
Patia 24 i
Patiala 61 b
Patience 26 i
Pativilca 24 v
Patkai Mountains 62 p
Patna 61 u
Patnos 54 t
Pato Branco 29 o
Patom 52 u
Patomskoye Plateau 52 s
Patos 27 u
Patos de Minas 29 f
Patos, Lagoa dos 29 p
Patquía 28 r
Pátrai (Patras) 35 r
Patras 35 r
Patrasuy 50 x
Patrocinio 29 f
Patta Island 43 r
Pattani 68 f
Pattullo, Mount 11 z
Patuca 22 g
Patzcuaro 19 n
Pau 34 f
Pau de Ferros 27 u
Pauini 25 c
Paulatuk 12 c
Paulistana 27 r
Paulo Alfonso 27 t
Pauri 61 d
Pausa 27 p
Pavlodar 55 m
Pavlogard 54 c
Pavlovsk 54 e
Pavlovsk 56 d
Pavon 23 o
Paxson 11 g
Payakumbuh 68 f
Pay-Khoy 50 l
Paynes Find 76 e
Paysandú 28 y
Payturma 51 k
Pay-yer 50 m
Peace River 12 s
Peace (River) 12 t
Peak Charles 76 g
Peak Downs 74 r
Peak Hill 76 f
Pearl City 18 p
Pearsall 19 b
Pearson Island 77 c
Peary Channel 89 r
Peary Land 91 i
Pebane 46 x
Pebas 25 a
Pečenga 33 m
Pechora 50 w
Pechora (River) 50 w
Pechora Sea 50 i
Pecked 77 m
Pecos 18 m
Pecos (River) 18 m
Pecs 35 c
Pedasi 22 j
Pedirka 77 d
Pedra Azul 29 k
Pedreiras 27 o
Pedro Alfonso 26 z
Pedro Gomes 25 z
Pedro Luro 30 m
Peel Bay 76 c
Peel Sound 12 m
Peg Ariak 70 r
Pegu 65 g
Pehuajó 31 a
Peipus, Lake (Lake Chud) 33 l
Peixe 26 z
Pekalongan 68 z
Peking 57 w
Pelagie Islands 34 z
Peleng 69 i
Peljesac 35 c
Pelly 11 l
Pelly Bay 13 b
Pelly (Bay) 13 b
Pelly Crossing 11 j
Pelotas 29 p
Pelsart Group 76 b
Pelvoux 34 j
Pematangsiantar 66 q
Pemba 45 y
Pemba Island 45 l
Pembroke 16 k
Penas Gulf 30 s
Pendembu 40 f
Pendleton 14 j
Penedo 27 v
Pene-Tungu 42 t
Penganga 61 p
Penge 45 a
Penglai 58 q
Pengpu 63 e
Penitente, Serra do 27 n
Penki 58 e
Penner 64 h
Pennsylvania 16 w
Penny Ice Cap 13 k
Penong 77 c
Penonomé 22 i
Pensacola 20 h
Pensacola Mountains 83 u
Penticton 14 i
Pentland 74 p
Pentland Firth 32 i
Penukonda 64 f
Penza 54 h
Penzance 34 c
Penzhino 10 c
Penzhinskaya, Gulf of 10 a
Penzhinskiy Mountains 10 b
Peoria 16 q
Perabumulih 68 v
Perak 66 r
Perambalur 64 g
Percival Lakes 72 y
Pereira 22 z
Pereshchepino 35 m
Pérez 20 t
Pergamino 31 a
Péribonca 17 a
Pericos 18 j
Perija, Sierra de 23 b
Periquitos 29 q
Perito Moreno 30 v
Perlas Archipelago 22 j
Perm' 50 w
Perote 19 p
Perpignan 34 h
Perry 20 k
Perry Island 12 k
Perryton 15 t
Perryville 16 q
Persepolis 39 j
Perseverancia 25 t
Perth (Australia) 76 d
Perth (Canada) 16 l
Perth (UK) 32 w
Peru 24-25
Perugia 34 m

Pervomaysk 33 z
Pervoural'sk 50 x
Pesagi 68 u
Pescara 35 a
Peschanyy, Cape 92 j
Peshawar 60 l
Peski 55 g
Pesqueira 27 v
Petaling Jaya 68 f
Petatlán 19 n
Petauke 45 r
Peterborough (Australia) 77 g
Peterborough (Canada) 16 x
Peter Island 80 j
Petermann Range 76 m
Peter Pond Lake 12 u
Petersburg 16 x
Peters Mine 23 x
Petitsikapau Lake 17 d
Peto 19 v
Petoskey 16 g
Petra 38 k
Petrel 82 g
Petrolina 27 r
Petropavlovka 52 y
Petropavlovsk 55 i
Petropavlovsk-Kamchatskiy 53 y
Petrópolis 29 i
Petrovka 55 h
Petrovsk-Zabajkal'skij 57 f
Petrozavodsk 50 n
Petukhovo 55 g
Petushkova 10 e
Peureulak 65 u
Pevek 10 d
Phalaborwa 49 f
Phalsund 60 y
Phangan 65 j
Phatthalung 68 e
Phayao 65 j
Phenix City 20 i
Phetchabun 65 k
Phetchaburi 65 i
Phiafay 66 i
Philadelphia 16 z
Philippines 67
Philippine Sea 231 i
Philipsburg 21 y
Phitsanulok 65 j
Phnom Penh 66 h
Phoenix 18 g
Phoenix Island 231 z
Phongsali 62 u
Phrae 65 j
Phu Chong 66 i
Phuket 65 u
Phulabāni 61 t
Phu Quoc 66 g
Piacenza 34 l
Pianguan 57 t
Piauí 27 q
Piauí, Serra de 27 q
Pibor Post 42 z
Pico da Neblina 25 e
Pico de Aneto 34 g
Picos 27 r
Pico Truncado 30 w
Picton 79 u
Pic Toussidé 37 w
Picuún Leufú 30 i
Pidi 45 a
Pidurutalagala 64 v
Piedrabuena 30 w
Piedras Negras 19 a
Pielis, Lake 33 l
Pierce 14 k
Pierre 15 g
Pietarsaari (Jakobstad) 33 i
Pietermaritzburg 49 s
Pietersburg 49 d
Piet Retief 49 r
Pietrosu 35 g
Pigu 40 m
Pigüe 31 a
Pijijiapan 19 t
Pik-Aborigen 53 i
Pikelot 71 b
Pikes Peak 15 q
Pikeville 16 u
Pik Grandioznyi 56 l
Pikhtovka 56 d
Pikounda 41 y
Pik Pobedy 56 p
Pilo Arcada 27 q
Pilar 28 y
Pilaya 28 g
Pilcomayo 28 g
Pilibhit 61 d
Pilsen (Plzen) 35 a
Pim 51 o
Pimenta Bueno 26 q
Pimenteiras 25 v
Pinacate Desert 18 c
Pinang (Indonesia) 68 l
Pinang (George Town, Malaysia) 65 w
Pinang (Island) 65 w
Pinar del Río 20 w
Pinawa 15 i
Pindobal 26 m
Pindus 35 r
Pine Bluff 19 g
Pine City 15 k
Pine Creek 73 c
Pinega 50 r
Pinega (River) 50 r
Pine Island Bay 81 b
Pingelap Atoll 71 l
Pingguo 62 y
Pingle 63 n
Pingliang 62 l
Pingnan 63 n
Pingsiang 63 c
Pingtingshan 63 b
Pingtung 63 u
Pingxiang 62 x
Pinheiro 27 b
Pini 65 v
Pinnaroo 77 u
Pinos 19 n
Pinos, Isla de 20 y
Pinotepa Nacional 19 p
Pinsk 33 w
Pinta 22 p
Pintados 28 c
Pinto 28 u
Pioner 51 j
Pionerskaya 85 r
Pionerskiy 50 y
Piorini 25 f
Piorini, Lago 25 g
Piotrków 33 u
Pipangikum Lake 15 k
Pipmuacan Reservoir 17 b
Piquiri 29 o
Piracuruca 27 d
Piraeus 35 s
Pirajiba 27 p
Piraju 29 e
Pirané 28 x
Piranhas 25 g
Pirapetinga 25 g
Pirapora 29 h
Pires do Rio 29 e
Piripiri 27 q
Piritu 23 g
Pirot 35 f
Pisa 34 l
Pisagua 28 c
Pisco 24 x
Pishin 60 r
Pissis 28 q
Pita 40 e
Pitcairn Island 230 q
Pite 33 h
Piteşti 35 g
Pithara 76 e
Pittsburgh 16 w
Pittsfield 16 z
Piura 24 g
Piura (River) 24 g
Pixa 61 d
Pizhma 50 s
Pjasina 51 i
Pjasina, Lake 51 h
Pjatigorsk 54 t
P.K.le Roux Reservoir 49 n
Placa 29 b
Placetas 21 n
Plainview 19 a
Plamennyy 10 f
Plara-Açu 26 v
Plast 55 d
Platbakkies 48 w
Plate, River 31 d
Plato 22 m
Platte 15 u
Plauen 34 m
Plavsk 54 c
Playa Azul 18 z
Plaza Huincul 30 j
Pleiku 66 j
Plenty, Bay of 79 w
Plétipi, Lake 17 b
Pleven 35 g
Plibo 40 u
Ploieşti 35 h
Plovdiv 35 g
Plumtree 49 c
Plymouth 32 w
Plymouth (Island) 21 z
Plzen 35 a
Po 40 m
Po (River) 34 m
Pocatello 14 z
Poconé 25 y
Pocos de Caldas 29 g
Podgorica 35 c
Podkamennaya Tunguska 51 w
Podkamennaya Tunguska (River) 51 x
Podolsk 54 d
Podporoze 50 o
Podukkottai 64 g
Podutesnaya 10 p
Pofadder 48 x
Pogo 40 j
Po Hai 57 y
Poinsett, Cape 87 g
Pointe-à-Pitre 21 z
Pointe-Noire 44 d
Point Hope 10 m
Poitiers 34 g
Pokacheva 51 p
Pokaran 60 l
Pokhara 61 g
Poko 42 u
Pokrovka 56 a
Pokrovsk 52 l
Pokrovsk (Vostochny Mountains) 56 m
Poland 33
Poli 41 j
Poligus 51 x
Polillo Islands 67 h
Politovo 50 t
Polkan 51 w
Pol'kyko 51 m
Polotsk 33 y
Polovinka 53 n
Polovinka (Patomskoye Plateau) 52 t
Polson 14 l
Poltava 35 m
Polui 51 a
Polunochnoye 50 y
Polur 64 h
Pol'yanovo 50 z
Pomeranian Bay 33 r
Pomona 48 u
Pon 33 h
Ponape 71 h
Ponca City 15 v
Ponce 21 v
Pondicherry 64 h
Pond Inlet 13 g
Pongo 42 u
Pongola 49 s
Ponta Branca 29 b
Ponta da Pedra 25 x
Ponta Grossa 29 q
Ponta Pora 28 m
Pontdrif 49 d
Ponterrada 34 b
Pontianak 68 l
Pontine Mountains 54 o
Ponton 76 i
Poopó, Lake 28 e
Popayán 22 y
Popigay 52 d
Popigay (River) 52 e
Poplar Bluff 16 q
Popocatépetl 19 o
Popokabaka 44 h
Popomanaseu 71 y
Popondetta 71 p
Porangatu 26 y
Porbandar 60 w
Porcupine 11 i
Porog 50 w
Poronaysk 59 d
Porpoise Bay 87 q
Portachuelo 25 s
Portadown 32 v
Portage 16 q
Portage la Prairie 15 h
Port Albert 78 p
Portales 18 l
Port Alfred 49 p
Port Alsworth 11 d
Port Angeles 14 g
Port Arthur 78 p
Port Augusta 77 f
Port-au-Prince 21 r
Port-Bergé-Vaovao 47 d
Port Burwell 13 x
Port-Cartier 17 d
Port Charlotte 20 k
Port Davey 77 x
Port-de-Paix 21 q
Port Edward 49 r
Portel 26 k
Port Elgin 16 v
Port Elizabeth 49 o
Port-Gentil 41 t
Port Harcourt 41 r
Port Hardy 14 e
Port Hedland 72 t
Portimo 36 f
Port Keats 73 b
Portland (Australia) 77 u
Portland (Maine, USA) 17 o
Portland (Oregon, USA) 14 g
Port Lincoln 77 d
Port Louis 47 x
Port Macquarie 78 g
Port Menier 17 e
Port Moresby 71 n
Port Nolloth 48 v
Porto (Oporto) 34 a
Pôrto Alegre 29 p
Pôrto Alegre (Purus) 25 q
Pôrto Alegre (Serra do Roncador) 26 x
Pôrto Alegre (Xingu) 26 w
Porto Alexandre (Tômbua) 48 d
Porto Amboim 44 r
Pôrto Artur 26 u
Pôrto Atlántico 25 y
Pôrto de Moz 26 j
Pôrto do Cajueiro 25 z
Pôrto dos Gauchos 25 x
Pôrto dos Meinacos 26 w
Pôrto Esperança 28 l
Pôrto Esperidio 25 w
Pôrto Franco 27 n
Port of Spain 23 i
Pôrto Grande 26 k
Pôrto Jofre 25 y
Pôrto Murtinho 28 k
Pôrto Naçional 26 z
Porto Novo 41 o
Pôrto Poet 26 i
Pôrto Santana 26 k
Pôrto So José 29 b
Porto Seguro 29 l
Pôrto Velho 25 s
Portoviejo 24 g
Port Philip Bay 77 x
Port Pirie 77 f
Port Radium 12 e
Port Safaga 38 k
Port Said 35 x
Port Shepstone 49 s
Portsmouth (New Hampshire) 17 o
Portsmouth (Ohio) 16 u
Portsmouth (Virginia) 16 y
Port St. Johns 49 r
Port Sudan 38 z
Portugal 34
Porva 54 m
Porvenir (Bolivia) 25 p
Porvenir (Chile) 30 v
Posadas 28 z
Poso 69 g
Pospelicha 56 c
Posse 29 g
Postavy 33 x
Postmasburg 48 z
Posto Alto Manissaua 26 u
Posto Cocraimore 26 w
Posto Curuá 25 m
Potapovo 51 h
Potchefstroom 49 p
Poteau 20 c
Potenza 35 b
Potgietersrus 49 e
Poti (Brazil) 27 q
Poti (Georgia) 54 s
Potiskum 41 h
Potosí 28 f
Potrero del Llano 20 n
Potsdam 33 q
Pottuvil 64 w
Pouso Alegre 29 g
Povungnituk 13 t
Powder 15 d
Powell Basin 82 g
Powell, Lake 15 n
Powell River 14 f
Poyang, Lake 63 e
Poza Rica 19 q
Poznan 33 t
Pozo Colorado Monte 28 k
Pozo del Tigre 28 w
Prachin Buri 65 k
Prachuap Khiri Khan 65 j
Prague 35 a
Praha (Prague) 35 a
Prainha 26 i
Prainha Nova 25 i
Pratt 15 u
Precordillera 28 q
Predivinsk 51 x
Preparis 65 e
Prescott 18 f
Presidencia de la Plaza 28 w
Presidencia Roque Sâenz Peña 28 w
Presidente Dutra 27 o
Presidente Hermes 25 u
Presidente Prudente 29 c
Presnogor'kovka 55 g
Presnovka 55 g
Prešov 35 e
Prespa Lake 35 e
Presque Isle 17 c
Prestea 40 y
Prêto do Igapó-Acu 25 i
Pretoria 49 p
Priargunsk 57 k
Pribilof Islands 10 y
Price 15 n
Prieska 48 z
Priluki 35 k
Primavera 82 s
Primorsk 54 h
Primorsko-Akhtarsk 54 d
Prince Albert 15 d
Prince Albert Peninsula 12 f
Prince Albert Road 48 y
Prince Albert Sound 12 f
Prince Albert, Cape 12 b
Prince Charles Island 13 g
Prince Charles Mountains 84 m
Prince Edward Island (Canada) 17 f
Prince Edward Island (S. Africa) 231 o
Prince George 14 g
Prince Gustav Adolf Sea 12 i
Prince Harald Coast 84 g
Prince Karls Forland 91 z
Prince of Wales Strait 12 e
Prince of Wales Island (Canada) 12 l
Prince of Wales Island (USA) 11 y

Prince of Wales Island (Australia) 73 j
Prince Patrick Island 12 d
Prince Regent Inlet 13 b
Prince Rupert 14 c
Princess Astrid Coast 83 l
Princess Charlotte Bay 73 l
Princess Elizabeth Land 85 q
Princess Ragnhild Land 84 c
Princess Ragnhild Coast 84 d
Princeton 16 r
Principe 41 s
Prinzapolca 22 h
Pripet 33 y
Pripet marshes 33 x
Pristina 35 d
Prizren 35 e
Probolinggo 69 o
Prochladnyl 54 t
Prof. van Bloomenstein Lake 26 h
Progreso 20 s
Prokopjevsk 56 f
Prome 65 f
Propriá 27 u
Proserpine 74 r
Providence 17 o
Providencia 25 n
Providencia (Island) 22 i
Provideniya 10 k
Provo 15 n
Prudhoe Bay 11 f
Prudhoe Land 91 c
Prut 35 h
Przemyśl 33 v
Przeval'sk 55 z
Pskov 33 l
Pskov, Lake 33 l
Pucallpa 24 y
Pucheng 63 f
Pudukkottai 64 g
Puebla 19 p
Pueblo 15 q
Puelches 30 l
Pu'er 62 t
Puerto Acosta 28 d
Puerto Aisén 30 t
Puerto Alegre 25 u
Puerto Angel 19 q
Puerto Armuelles 22 h
Puerto Asis 24 k
Puerto Ayacucho 23 r
Puerto Barrios 19 v
Puerto Berrio 23 a
Puerto Boyaca 23 n
Puerto Cabello 23 e
Puerto Cabezas 22 h
Puerto Carreño 23 r
Puerto Cisnes 30 t
Puerto Cortés (Honduras) 19 w
Puerto Cortés (Costa Rica) 22 g
Puerto Cumarebo 23 d
Puerto del Rosario 36 c
Puerto Deseado 30 y
Puerto Escondido 19 p
Puerto Heath 25 p
Puerto Huitoto 24 l
Puerto Inca 24 y
Puerto Juárez 19 x
Puerto La Cruz 23 f
Puerto Leguizamo 24 l
Puerto Lempira 22 g
Puerto Limón 23 n
Puertollano 34 q
Puerto Lobos 30 l
Puerto Lopez 23 o
Puerto Madryn 30 l
Puerto Maldonado 25 o
Puerto Marquez 25 r
Puerto Miraña 25 a
Puerto Montt 30 g
Puerto Morelos 19 x
Puerto Natales 30 t
Puerto Nuevo 23 q
Puerto Pardo 24 k
Puerto Peñasco 18 e
Puerto Piñasco 28 l
Puerto Plata 21 t
Puerto Portillo 24 z
Puerto Presidente Stroessner 29 n
Puerto Princesa 67 e
Puerto Rico (Bolivia) 25 q
Puerto Rico (Peru) 24 y
Puerto Rico (USA) 21 v
Puerto San Augustín 25 a
Puerto San Julián 30 w
Puerto Sastre 28 k
Puerto Suárez 28 l
Puerto Vallarta 18 y
Puerto Villamil 22 o
Puerto Villarroel 25 s
Puesta Varadero 24 z
Pugal 60 m
Pujehun 40 r
Pukaki, Lake 79 s
Pukch'ong 58 h
Pula 35 a
Pular 28 d
Pullman 14 k
Pulo Anna 70 d
Pulog 67 g
Pulu 61 e
Pumasillo 24 z
Puná 24 h
Pune 60 z
Punia 42 u
Puno 25 o
Punta Aguja 24 f
Punta Alta 31 a
Punta Arenas 30 u
Punta Chirambirá 22 x
Punta Delgada (Chile) 30 w
Punta Delgada (Argentina) 30 m
Punta Galera 22 v
Punta Manzanillo 22 k
Punta Norte 30 m
Punta Prieta 18 e
Puntarenas 22 f
Punto Fijo 23 c
Puquio 24 y
Pur 52 j
Pur (Siben'an Uvaly) 51 e
Pura 51 h
Puri 61 v
Puricama 23 u
Purnia 61 v
Purros 48 f
Pursat 66 g
Purtuniq 13 u
Puruliya 61 v
Purus 25 h
Purwokerto 68 y
Pusan 58 v
Pushchino 53 y
Pushkino 54 i
Pusur 61 x
Putao 62 e
Putian 63 s
Putorana Mountains 51 j
Putrajaya 68 f
Putre 28 c
Puttalam 64 u
Putumayo 24 l
Puzla 50 v
Pweto 45 c
Pyaozero, Lake 33 m
Pyapon 65 g
Pyasina Bay 51 f
Pyatigory 50 v
Pyinmana 62 q
Pymta 53 x
Pyŏngyang 58 s
Pyramid Lake 14 v
Pyramids 38 h
Pyrenees 34 f
Pyrgos 35 r
Pyu 62 r

Q

Qaanaaq (Thule) 91 c
Qaen 60 c
Qagan 57 k
Qagan Nur 57 v
Qagcaka 61 f
Qahan Qulut 57 k
Qaisar 60 g
Qala Panja 60 l
Qal'at Bishah 39 p
Qalat-i Chilzai 60 h
Qamar, Bay 39 w
Qamdo 62 e
Qaminis 35 q
Qânâq (Thule) 91 c
Qapqal 56 p
Qaqortoq 90 t
Qara 38 e
Qarah Tarai 60 h
Qareh Su 39 h
Qarhan 56 y
Qarqan 56 t
Qarqi 56 s
Qaryat al 'Ulya 39 f
Qasr 38 g
Qatar 39 v
Qatrun 37 v
Qattara Depression 38 f
Qazvin 54 x
Qen 57 n
Qena 38 j
Qeqertarsuaq (Godhavn) 90 k
Qeqertarsuaq (Island) 90 l
Qeshm 60 a
Qeshm (Island) 60 a
Qeys 39 k
Qian Gorlos 58 f
Qianjiang 62 m
Qianning 62 g
Qiansuo 62 t
Qianwei 62 j
Qian Xian 62 l
Qianyang 63 a
Qiaowan 56 z
Qiemo 56 s
Qijiang 62 k
Qijiaojing 56 w
Qila Ladgasht 60 f
Qila Saifullah 60 j
Qilian Shan 56 y
Qing'an 58 h
Qingchuan 62 j
Qingdao (Tsingtao) 58 p
Qinghai Hu 57 n
Qingyang 62 l
Qingyuan 58 f
Qing Zang Gaoyuan 62 a
Qinhuangdao 57 y
Qinling Shan 62 l
Qinzhou 62 z
Qionglai 62 i
Qiqian 52 v
Qiqihar (Tsitsihar) 58 f
Qiquanhu 56 u
Qira 61 e
Qitai 56 u
Qitaihe 58 j
Qi Xian 63 c
Qlom 53 a
Qma 61 g
Qojur 54 w
Qom 39 i
Qomsheh 39 i
Qotbabad 60 a
Quala-I Nau 60 f
Quanzhou 63 n
Quarai 28 z
Quchan 55 o
Queanbeyan 78 d
Québec 17 a
Quebec (Province) 13 u
Queen Astrid and King Leopold Coast 85 r
Queen Charlotte Strait 14 e
Queen Charlotte Islands 14 b
Queen Elizabeth Islands 12 d
Queen Louise Land 91 s
Queen Mary Land 85 s
Queen Maud Gulf 12 k
Queen Maud Land 84 c
Queen Maud Range 81 k
Queensland 74 r
Queenstown (Australia) 77 x
Queenstown (New Zealand) 79 r
Queenstown (South Africa) 49 p
Queimada 26 k
Queimadas 27 s
Quélésseboougou 40 i
Quelimane 46 w
Quelpart Island (Cheju) 58 t
Querétaro 19 o
Querrha 34 p
Quesnel 14 h
Quetta 60 i
Quezaltenango 22 b
Quezon 67 g
Quibala 44 t
Quibaxe 44 g
Quibdo 22 y
Quilán, Cabo 30 f
Quillabamba 24 z
Quillacollo 28 f
Quillagua 28 c
Quilon 64 r
Quilpie 77 j
Quimbele 44 h
Quince Mil 25 n
Quincy 16 p
Quines 28 s
Quinghai Hu 62 g
Quinhon 66 l
Quiñones 18 t
Quirinópolis 29 d
Quissico 49 i
Quitapa 44 v
Quiteve 44 t
Quitexe 44 g
Quito 24 h
Quixadá 27 s
Qujing 62 w
Qumar Heyan 62 b
Qumarlêb 62 d
Qunaitra 38 l
Qungtag 61 j
Quorn 77 f
Quraiyat 60 p
Qus 38 j
Qusair 38 k
Quseima 38 k
Quynh Luu 62 x
Quzhou 63 g

R

Raahe 33 j
Raas Caseyr (Cape Guardafui) 43 l
Raba 72 h
Rabableh 43 j
Rabak 42 l
Rabang 61 e
Rabat 36 h
Rabaul 71 r
Rabbit Lake 12 x
Rabyanah 38 o
Race, Cape 17 l
Rach Gia 66 h
Racine 16 r
Radhanpur 60 x
Radom 33 u
Rae 12 s
Rae Isthmus 13 c
Rae Lakes 12 r
Raeside, Lake 76 h
Rafaela 28 v
Rafaii 42 r
Rafha 39 d
Rafsanjan 39 l
Raga 42 g
Ragusa 35 n
Raha 69 v
Rahad 43 a
Rahad al Berdi 42 f
Rahimyar-Khan 60 l
Raichur 64 f
Rainier, Mount 14 h
Rainy Lake 15 k
Raipur 61 s
Raisut 39 x
Rajada 27 s
Rajahmundry 64 i
Rajang 69 a
Rajanpur 60 k
Rajasthan Canal 60 m
Rajgarh 61 o
Rajkot 60 x
Raj Nandgaon 61 r
Rakaposhi 61 a
Raka Zangbo 61 i
Raleigh 16 x
Rama 22 g
Ramah 13 y
Ramanathapuram 64 t
Ramdurg 64 d
Rameswaram 64 u
Ramhormoz 39 h
Ramlat al Wahiba 60 p
Ramlat Rabyana 37 x
Ramlu 43 e
Ramos 26 i
Rampur 61 d
Rampur (Rann of Kutch) 60 w
Rampura 61 n
Ramree 65 e
Ramsar 54 x
Ramshir 39 h
Ramu 43 r
Ramu (River) 70 z
Rancagua 30 i
Ranchi 61 u
Ranco, Lago de 30 h
Randa 43 f
Randers 33 p
Randolph 15 v
Rangoon 65 g
Rangpur 61 x
Raniganj 61 w
Rankin Inlet 13 n
Ranong 65 i
Rantauprapat 68 e
Rantekombola 69 s
Rantoul 16 r
Rao Go 66 h
Rapak 69 e
Rapel 30 h
Rapid City 15 e
Rapti 61 g
Rapulo 25 r
Raqqah 39 a
Ras al Khaimah 39 l
Ras-al-Ma 36 l
Ras Dashén 43 c
Ras Ghârib 38 j
Ras Halileh 39 i
Rasht 54 x
Ras Koh 60 h
Raskoh 60 g
Ras Nuh 60 s
Rason, Lake 76 j
Rassokha 53 h
Ras Tannurah 39 i
Ratangarh 61 a
Rat Islands 10 t
Ratlam 61 n
Ratnagiri 64 c
Raton 15 q
Ratta 51 t
Ratz, Mount 11 y
Raub 65 x
Raub Kuala Kubu 66 s
Rauch 31 b
Ravansar 39 e
Ravenna 34 m
Ravensthorpe 76 g
Ravor 60 b
Rawalpindi 60 m
Rawlinna 76 k
Rawlins 15 p
Rawson 30 l
Raya 69 a
Raychikhinsk 58 h
Rayones 19 a
Rayong 65 k
Razan 39 h
Razdolnoye 53 i
Razmak 60 k
Reading (USA) 16 y
Reading (UK) 32 x
Read Island 12 g
Reboly 33 m
Rebricha 56 d
Recherche Archipelago 76 i
Recife 27 w
Reconquista 28 w
Recovery Glacier 83 v

Recreio 25 w
Recreo 28 s
Red Bluff 14 u
Red Deer 14 m
Redding 14 u
Redenço 26 y
Redeyef 37 d
Red Lake 15 k
Red Pass 14 j
Red River (Canada) 15 i
Red River (USA) 20 d
Red Sea 38 y
Red Wing 15 k
Regensburg 34 m
Reggane 36 y
Reggio 35 o
Regina 15 d
Régina 26 j
Registan 60 g
Registro 29 s
Rehoboth 48 i
Reims 34 i
Reindeer Lake 12 x
Reitz 49 q
Reivilo 49 n
Reliance 12 v
Relizane 34 t
Remada 34 y
Remanso 27 q
Remarkable, Mount 73 a
Remeshk 60 c
Renascença 25 d
Rengat 68 g
Renk 42 l
Renland 91 q
Renmark 77 h
Rennell Island 74 m
Renner Springs 73 r
Rennes 34 e
Rennick Glacier 86 u
Reno 14 v
Repetek 55 r
Republican 15 u
Repulse Bay 13 c
Requena 24 l
Resistencia 28 x
Resolute 12 m
Resolution Island 13 y
Retkucha 10 d
Retreat 77 j
Réunion 47 w
Revelstoke 14 j
Revilla Gigedo Islands 18 t
Rewa 61 r
Rewari 61 b
Rey 22 k
Reyes 25 q
Reykjanes 32 a
Reykjavik 32 b
Reynosa 19 b
Rhallamane 36 s
Rhine 34 k
Rhinelander 16 e
Rhode Island 17 o
Rhodes 35 v
Rhodes (Island) 35 v
Rhodope 35 g
Rhône 34 i
Riau Islands 68 h
Ribas do Rio Pardo 29 a
Ribat 60 e
Ribauè 46 k
Ribeiro Preto 29 f
Riberalta 25 r
Riboiro Gonçalves 27 o
Rice Lake 15 l
Rich 36 j
Richards Bay 49 t
Richardson 11 g
Richfield 14 z
Richland 14 i
Richmond (Australia) 74 n
Richmond (Indiana) 16 t
Richmond (Virginia) 16 x
Richmond Range 79 t
Richwood 16 v
Riddle 14 x
Ridgecrest 14 w
Rif 36 i
Rifle 15 p
Rift Valley 42/45
Riga (Latvia) 33 w
Riga (Russia) 52 p
Riga, Gulf of 33 i
Riggins 14 k
Rigolet 17 i
Rig-Rig 41 k
Rihand Reservoir 61 s
Riiser Larsen Peninsula 84 h
Riiser Larsen Sea 84 d
Riiser Larsen Ice Shelf 83 g
Rijeka 35 a
Rime 42 b
Rimini 34 m
Rimouski 17 c
Rinčin Lchumbe 57 a
Ringwood 73 s
Riobamba 24 h
Rio Branco 25 p
Rio Claro 29 f
Río Colorado 30 m
Rio Cuarto 30 m
Rio de Janeiro 29 i
Rio de Oro 36 n
Río Gallegos 30 w
Rio Grande (Argentina) 30 x
Rio Grande (Brazil) 29 p
Rio Grande (Mexico) 18 z
Riohacha 23 a
Rioja 24 j
Rio Largo 27 v
Río Mayo 30 v
Rio Mulatos 28 e
Riosucio 22 l
Río Tercero 28 t
Río Turbio 30 u
Río Verde (Mexico) 19 n
Rio Verde (Brazil) 29 c
Rio Verde de Mato Grosso 29 a
Riposto 37 j
Rissani 36 i
Rito 44 w
Ritscher Highland 83 i
Rivadavia 30 m
Rivas 22 f
Rivera 28 z
River Falls 15 k
Riversleigh 73 u
Riverton (Canada) 15 i
Riverton (USA) 15 o
Rivière du Loup 17 b
Rivungo 44 y
Riwoqê 62 d
Riyadh 39 s
Riyan 43 k
Rjazan 54 e
Roanoke 16 w
Roanoke (River) 16 y
Roanoke Rapids 16 x
Roatán 20 v
Robe 77 h
Roberval 17 a
Robinhood 73 y
Robinson, Cape 82 v
Robinson Crusoe 30 d
Robinson River (Papua New Guinea) 74 e
Robinson River (Australia) 73 g
Roboré 28 k
Robson, Mount 14 j
Roçadas 44 s
Roca, General 30 k
Rocas, Atol das 27 w
Rocha 31 e
Rochelle 16 r
Rochester (Maine) 17 o
Rochester (Minnesota) 16 p
Rochester (New York) 16 x
Rockefeller Plateau 81 g
Rockford 16 r
Rockhampton 74 t
Rock Hill 20 l
Rockingham 20 m
Rock Springs 15 o
Rockstone 23 x
Rockwood 16 t
Rocky Harbour 17 i
Rocky Mount 16 x
Rocky Mountains 12/14
Rocky Mountain House 14 g
Roda Velha 27 o
Rodeo 18 l
Rodina 51 x
Rodino 56 c
Rodrigues 24 m
Roebuck Plains 72 x
Roes Welcome Sound 13 p
Rogachevka 54 e
Rogaguado, Lago 25 r
Rogagua, Lago 25 r
Rogers, Mount 16 v
Rohtak 61 b
Roi Et 66 g
Rokel 40 e
Rolla 16 p
Rolleston 74 q
Roma 74 r
Roma (Rome) 34 m
Romaine 17 f
Romania 33/35
Romano, Cape 20 l
Romanova 57 b
Romanovka 57 h
Rome 34 m
Rommani 36 h
Roncador, Serra do 26 w
Ronda (Pakistan) 61 a
Ronda (Spain) 36 i
Rondônia 25 u
Rondonópolis 29 a
Rong'an 62 z
Rongjiang 62 z
Ronne Entrance 82 y
Roodepoort 49 p
Roosevelt Island 81 z
Roper 73 f
Roper Bar 73 e
Roques, Islas los 23 f
Roraima 26 d
Roraima, Mount 23 w
Rosa, Monte 34 k
Rosário 27 c
Rosario 28 f
Rosario (Paraná) 28 w
Rosario de Arriba 18 d
Rosario de la Frontera 28 t
Rosário do Sul 29 n
Rosario Oeste 25 y
Rosarito 18 c
Rosarito (Sabastían Vizcaino Bay) 18 e
Rosa Zárate 24 h
Roscrea 32 u
Roseau (Dominica) 23 j
Roseburg 14 t
Roseires, Lake 42 m
Rose River 73 f
Rosetown 15 b
Rosetta 38 h
Rosiori 35 g
Roslavl 54 a
Ross Barrier 86 o
Ross Ice Shelf 81 l
Ross Island 86 r
Rosso 40 b
Ross River 11 m
Ross Sea 81 v
Rossville 73 m
Rostock 33 q
Rostov 54 e
Roswell 18 l
Rothera 82 v
Roti 69 v
Rotorua 79 w
Rotterdam 33 n
Rouen 34 g
Round 78 f
Roundup 15 b
Rourkela 61 v
Rovno 35 h
Rovnoye 54 i
Rowley 90 k
Rowley Island 13 g
Roxas 67 h
Rosborough Downs 73 u
Roydale Isle 16 e
Rtishchevo 54 h
Ruacana 48 g
Ruahine Range 79 v
Ruapehu 79 v
Rubačje 56 n
Rub'al Khali 39 t
Rubcovsk 56 d
Ruby 11 d
Rudbar 60 f
Rudnaya Pristan 58 m
Rudnya 54 g
Rudolf 50 k
Rufiji 45 j
Rufino 31 a
Rufunsa 46 e
Rugby 15 g
Rügen 33 r
Ruhengeri 45 d
Rui Barbosa 27 r
Ruijin 63 r
Ruki 44 i
Rukwa, Lake 45 f
Rumbek 42 w
Rum Cay 21 q
Rumford 17 b
Rumphi 45 t
Rundu 48 k
Rungu 42 v
Rungwa 45 g
Rungwa (River) 45 f
Rungwe 45 t
Ruoqiang 56 u
Rupat 68 f
Rupert 16 l
Rupisi 49 f
Rupununi 26 e
Rurópolis 26 u
Rusape 46 t
Ruse 35 h
Russas 27 t
Russell Range 76 i
Russia 10/33/50-59
Russkaya 81 s
Russkaya (River) 51 f
Russkaya Gavan 50 l
Russkiy 51 l
Rustavi 54 u
Rustenburg 49 p
Ruteng 69 t
Rutenga 46 s
Rutland 17 n
Rutshuru 42 v
Ruvuma 46 j
Ruzayevka 55 g
Rwanda 42/45
Rybinsk 50 p
Rybinsker Reservoir 50 p
Rycroft 12 r
Ryūkyu Islands 63 x
Rzeszów 35 e
Ržev 54 b

S

Saadatabad 39 k
Saarbrücken 34 j
Saaremaa 33 h
Sab'Abar 38 m
Sabah 69 d
Sabana de Cardona 23 s
Sabaya 28 d
Sabha 37 i
Sabie 49 e
Sabinas 19 a
Sabinas Hidalgo 19 a
Sabkhat Matti 39 w
Sable, Cape (Canada) 17 r
Sable, Cape (USA) 20 l
Sabrina Coast 87 e
Sabun 51 s
Sabyndy 55 i
Sabzevar 55 n
Sabzevaran 60 c
Šachrisabz 55 t
Sachs Harbour 12 c
Saco Uen 43 s
Sacramento 14 u
Sacramento (River) 14 u
Sacramento, C. del 31 c
Sa'dah 43 g
Sado 59 n
Safaniyah 39 g
Safar 60 g
Safford 18 h
Safi 36 f
Saga (China) 61 h
Saga (USSR) 55 e
Šagan 56 b
Sagar 61 q
Sagastyr 52 l
Sagastyr 52 l
Saginaw 16 u
Sagiz 54 m
Šagonar 56 k
Sagres 36 f
Sagua la Grande 20 z
Sagyr 52 a
Sahara 36/37
Saharan Atlas 36/37
Saharanpur 61 c
Sahel 40 i
Sahil al Jazir 60 o
Sahiwal 60 m
Sahuaripa 18 i
Sahuayo 18 z
Sai Buri 65 x
Saigon (Ho Chi Minh) 66 j
Saihan Toroi 57 n
Saikhoa Ght 62 d
Saimaa, Lake 33 k
Ste-Agathe-des-Monts 16 m
St. Alban's 17 j
Sto. André 29 g
Ste-Anne-des-Monts 17 d
St. Anthony 17 k
St.-Augustin 17 i
St.-Augustin (River) 17 i
St. Augustine 20 m
St. Brieuc 34 d
St. Catharines 16 w
St. Christopher and Nevis 21 x
St. Cloud 15 j
St. Croix 21 w
Saint-Denis 47 w
St. Eleanors 17 f
St. Elias Mountains 11 j
St. Étienne 34 h
Ste-Foy 17 a
St. George (Australia) 74 q
St. George (USA) 14 z
Saint George's 23 i
St.-Georges (Canada) 17 b
St. Georges (French Guiana) 26 j
St. George's Channel 32 v
St. Helena 230 z
St.-Hyacinthe 17 a
St. Jean, Lac 17 a
St.-Jérôme 16 m
Saint John 17 d
St. John's (Antigua and Barbuda) 21 z
St. John's (Canada) 17 l
St. Joseph 15 w
St. Joseph, Lake 15 l
St. Kitts/Nevis 21 x
St. Laurent 26 i
St. Lawrence 74 r
St. Lawrence, Gulf of 17 g
Saint Lawrence Island 10 l
St. Lawrence (River) 17 c
St. Louis (Senegal) 40 b
St. Louis (USA) 16 q
Saint Lucia 23 j
St. Lucia, Lake 49 t
St. Lucia Passage 23 j
St. Malo, Gulf of 32 x
St.-Marc 21 r
Ste.-Marguerite 17 d
Sta. Maria de Nieva 24 i
St. Martin 21 y
St. Marys 78 q
Saint Matthew 10 k
St. Matthew's 66 c
St. Nazaire 34 d
St. Paul (Liberia) 40 t
St. Paul (River) 17 i
St. Paul Island 231 r
St. Paul-Minneapolis 16 b
St. Petersburg (Russia) 33 l
St. Petersburg (USA) 20 k
St. Pierre and Miquelon 17 j
St. Quentin 34 h

St. Roch Basin 12 m
St.-Siméon 17 b
St. Stephen 17 c
St. Thomas 16 v
Saint Vincent and Grenadines 23 j
St. Vincent, Cape 34 n
St. Vincent Gulf 77 f
St. Vincent Passage 23 j
Saintes 34 f
Sajak 56 b
Sajama 25 p
Sajanogorsk 56 j
Sajnsand 57 s
Sak 48 y
Saka 43 q
Sakai 58 z
Sakakah 39 b
Sakakawea Reservoir 15 f
Sakami 16 m
Sakata 59 o
Sakhalin 53/59
Sakhandzha 52 l
Sakhon Nakhon 66 h
Sakir 60 i
Salaberry-De-Valleyfield 16 m
Salada Laguna 18 d
Saladillo 31 a
Salado 30 k
Salado (Bahia Samboronbón) 31 c
Salado (Chaco Austral) 28 u
Salaga 40 m
Salajar 69 t
Salal 42 a
Salalah 39 x
Salamanca (Chile) 28 o
Salamanca (Mexico) 19 n
Salamanca (Spain) 34 c
Salamat 42 b
Salar de Antofalle 28 q
Salar de Arizaro 28 r
Salar de Atacama 28 d
Salar de Pipanaco 28 s
Salar de Pocitos 28 r
Salar de Uyuni 28 d
Salar Punta Negra 28 p
Saldanha 48 v
Sale 77 y
Salé 36 h
Salekard 50 m
Salem (India) 64 f
Salem (USA) 14 g
Salerno 35 a
Salgueiro 27 t
Sali 36 z
Salima 45 u
Salina (Kansas) 15 u
Salina (Utah) 14 z
Salina Cruz 20 p
Salinas (Brazil) 25 w
Salinas (Ecuador) 24 g
Salinas (Mexico) 19 n
Salinas (USA) 14 u
Salinas Grande 28 t
Salinas Grandes 28 f
Salinópolis 27 a
Salisbury 16 z
Salisbury Island (Canada) 13 t
Salisbury Island (Russia) 50 i
Saljany 54 w
Salluit 13 u
Sallûm 35 t
Sal'um 50 k
Salmon 14 l
Salmon (River) 14 l
Salmon River Mountains 14 l
Salsacate 28 s
Sal'sk 54 f
Salta 28 t
Saltillo 19 a
Salt Lake City 14 z
Salt Lakes 76 g
Salto 28 y
Salton Sea 18 d
Salvador 27 t
Salvatierra 19 n
Salwa 39 v
Salween 65 h
Salzburg 35 a
Samagaltaj 56 l
Samar 67 j
Samara 54 k
Samarga 59 a
Samarinda 69 d
Samarkand 55 t
Samatiguila 40 i
Samaumá 25 j
Samba 45 a
Samba (Maringa) 44 l
Samba Caju 44 g
Sambalpur 61 u
Sambas 68 l
Sambava 47 f
Sambhar 61 a
Samborombón Bay 31 d
Same 45 j
Samfya 45 q
Samirah 39 c
Samoa 231 z
Sámos 35 u
Sampit 69 o
Samrong 66 g
Samsang 61 g
Samsun 35 m
Samui 65 j
San'a 43 g
San 40 j
Sanae 83 i
Sanaga 41 v
San Agustín de Valle Fértil 28 r
Sanandaj 39 f
San Andrés 22 i
San Andrés Tuxtla 19 r
San Angelo 19 b
San Antonio (Chile) 30 h
San Antonio (USA) 19 c
San Antonio de los Cobres 28 r
San Antonio Oeste 30 l
Sanaw 39 v
San Benedicto 18 u
San Bernardino 18 c
San Bernardo 30 i
San Blas 18 i
San Blas, Cape 20 i
San Borja 25 q
San Buenaventura 19 a
San Carlos (Colombia) 23 r
San Carlos (Luxon, Philippines) 67 f
San Carlos (Mexico) 18 g
San Carlos (Negros, Philippines) 67 i
San Carlos (Nicaragua) 22 g
San Carlos de Bolivar 31 a
San Carlos de Bariloche 30 i
San Carlos del Zulia 23 b
Sanch 57 b
Sanchakou 56 o
San Clemente 18 b
San Cristobal 75 a
San Cristóbal (Argentina) 28 v
San Cristóbal (Columbia) 24 m
San Cristóbal (Ecuador) 22 q
San Cristóbal (Venezuela) 23 b
San Cristóbal las Casas 19 t
Sancti Spiritus 21 n
Sandakan 69 e
Sanderson 18 m
Sandia 25 o
San Diego 18 c
San Diego, Cabo 30 y
Sandoa 44 y
Sandoway 62 p
Sandpoint 14 k
Sandstone 76 f
Sandusky 16 u
Sandy Bay 76 i
Sandy Cape 77 w
Sandy Lake 15 k
San Estanislao 28 z
San Felipe (Chile) 28 o
San Felipe (Lower California, Mexico) 18 e
San Felipe (Mexico) 19 n
San Felipe (Venezuela) 23 d
San Fernando (Chile) 30 i
San Fernando (Philippines) 67 g
San Fernando (Venezuela) 23 j
San Fernando de Atabapo 23 r
San Fernando de Apure 23 e
San Francisco (Argentina) 28 u
San Francisco (USA) 14 t
San Francisco de Macoris 21 t
San Francisco de Rincón 18 z
San Francisco del Oro 18 k
San Gabriel 22 y
Sangan 60 g
Sangareddi 61 p
Sange 45 c
Sanggau 68 m
Sangha 41 z
Sanghar 60 w
Sangihe 69 k
Sangihe Islands 69 k
Sangijn Dalaj Nuur 56 m
Sangli 61 n
Sangmelima 41 w
Sangre de Cristo Range 15 q
Sangruma 62 f
Sangyyakhtakh 52 x
San Guillermo 18 k
San Ignacio (Apere, Bolivia) 25 r
San Ignacio (Argentina) 28 y
San Ignacio (Bolivia) 25 v
San Ignacio (Peru) 24 i
San Ignacio, Laguna 18 f
San Ildefonso Peninsula 67 h
San Javier 25 u
San Joaquin 25 s
San Jorge 22 m
San Jorge, Gulf of 30 x
San Jose (USA) 14 u
San José (Mexico) 18 h
San José (Costa Rica) 22 g
San Jose (Philippines) 67 g
San José (Venezuela) 23 r
San José de Amacuro 23 j
San Jose de Buenavista 67 g
San José de Chiquitos 25 v
San José de Jáchal 28 q
San José del Guaviare 23 o
San Jose de Mayo 31 d
San José de Ocune 23 p
San Juan (Argentina) 28 q
San Juán (Chile) 24 x
San Juan (Dominican Republic) 21 s
San Juan (Puerto Rico) 21 w
San Juan (Venezuela) 23 s
San Juan (River, Columbia) 22 y
San Juan (River, USA) 15 n
San Juan (River, Argentina) 28 r
San Juan (River, Costa Rica) 22 g
San Juan Bautista 28 z
San Juan del Norte 22 g
San Juan de los Lagos 18 z
San Juan do los Morros 23 e
San Juan Mountains 15 p
San Juanico 18 f
San Julián 30 w
San Justo 28 w
Sankuru 44 m
San Lázaro, Cape 18 f
San Lorenzo (Ecuador) 24 h
San Lorenzo (USA) 18 j
San Lorenzo (Mount) 30 u
San Lucas 18 u
San Lucas, Cape 18 u
San Luis 28 s
San Luis de la Paz 19 o
San Luis de Tapajós 25 l
San Luis, Lago de 25 s
San Luis Obispo 14 v
San Luis Potosi 19 n
San Luis-Rio Colorado 18 e
San Malo, Golfe de 34 e
San Marcos 19 o
San Marino 34 m
San Martin (Argentina) 28 q
San Martin (Bolivia) 25 t
San Martín de los Andes 30 i
San Martin (River) 25/28
San Matías 25 w
San Matias Gulf 30 m
Sanmenhsia 63 a
San Miguel (Bolivia) 25 t
San Miguel (El Salvador) 22 d
San Miguel del Monte 31 c
San Miguel de Tucumán 28 t
Sanming 63 s
San Nicolas (Argentina) 31 a
San Nicolas (USA) 18 a
Sanniquellie 40 u
Sanouyah 40 f
San Pablo (Bolivia) 28 e
San Pablo (River, Bolivia) 25 u
San Pablo (Philippines) 67 g
San Pédro 40 v
San Pedro (Argentina) 28 t
San Pedro (Paraguay) 28 y
San Pedro (Paraná, Argentina) 28 w
San Pedro de Atacama 28 d
San Pedro de las Colonias 18 m
San Pedro de Lloc 24 h
San Pedro Sula 19 w
San Rafael (Argentina) 30 j
San Rafael (Venezuela) 23 b
San Ramón de la Nueva Orán 28 g
San Salvador 22 d
San Salvador (Island, Bahamas) 21 q
San Salvador (Island, Ecuador) 22 p
San Salvador de Jujuy 28 s
Sansanné-Mango 41 a
San Sebastián 34 e
Santa 24 v
Santa Ana (Beni, Bolivia) 28 e
Santa Ana (Bolivia) 25 r
Santa Ana (Serra de Santiago, Bolivia) 28 k
Santa Ana (El Salvador) 22 c
Santa Ana (Mexico) 18 h
Santa Ana (USA) 18 c
Santa Barbara (Mexico) 18 k
Santa Barbara (USA) 14 v
Santa Barbara (Venezuela) 23 s
Santa Catalina (Chile) 28 p
Santa Catalina (Island, USA) 18 c
Santa Catalina (Island, Mexico) 18 h
Santa Clara (Colombia) 25 b
Santa Clara (Cuba) 20 z
Santa Clotilde 24 l
Santa Corazón 25 w
Santa Cruz (Bolivia) 28 h
Santa Cruz (Brazil) 24 m
Santa Cruz (Chile) 28 o
Santa Cruz (Peru) 24 h
Santa Cruz (Spain) 36 b
Santa Cruz (USA) 14 u
Santa Cruz (Island, California) 18 a
Santa Cruz (Island, Eduador) 22 p
Santa Cruz (River, Argentina) 30 v
Santa Cruz Island 75 d
Santa Elena, Cabo 22 f
Santa Elena de Uairen 23 v
Santa Fé (Argentina) 28 w
Santa Fe (USA) 15 q
Santa Filomena 27 o
Santa Helena 25 l
Santai 62 k
Santa Inés (Brazil) 27 b
Santa Inés (Chile) 30 t
Santa Isabel (Argentina) 30 k
Santa Isabél (Brazil) 25 v
Santa Isabel (Ecuador) 24 h
Santa Isabel (Peru) 24 l
Santa Isabel (Solomon Islands) 71 x
Santa Lucia 24 m
Santa Maria (Amazon, Brazil) 25 j
Santa Maria (Argentina) 28 r
Santa Maria (Brazil) 29 o
Santa Maria (Ecuador) 22 o
Santa Maria (Mexico) 18 k
Santa Maria (Peru) 24 l
Santa Maria (Venezuela) 23 e
Santa Maria da Vitória 27 p
Santa Maria di Leuca, Capo 35 p
Santa Marta 23 a
Santana 27 p
Santana do Araguaia 26 x
Santana do Ipanema 27 u
Santana do Livramento 29 n
Santander (Colombia) 22 y
Santander (Spain) 34 d
Santanghu 56 x
Santarém (Brazil) 25 m
Santarém (Portugal) 34 o
Santa Rosa (Argentina) 30 l
Santa Rosa (Brazil) 25 n
Santa Rosa (California) 14 t
Santa Rosa (Colombia) 23 p
Santa Rosa (Honduras) 22 d
Santa Rosa (New Mexico) 15 q
Santa Rosa (Island) 18 a
Santa Rosa del Conlara 28 s
Santa Rosalia 18 g
Santa Teresa 73 r
Santa Teresinha 26 x
Santiago (Argentina) 29 n
Santiago (Chile) 28 o
Santiago (Dominican Republic) 21 t
Santiago (Panama) 22 l
Santiago (River) (Mexico) 18 y
Santiago (River) (Peru) 24 i
Santiago de Chuco 24 v
Santiago de Compostela 34 b
Santiago de Cuba 21 p
Santiago del Estero 28 t
Santiago Ixcuintla 18 x
Santiago Papasquiaro 18 k
Santiago, Serra de 28 k
San Tiburcio 19 n
Santo Amaro 27 t
Santo Angelo 29 n
Santo Antônio 25 t
Santo Antônio (Negro) 25 i
Santo Antônio de Içá 25 d
Santo Antônio de Jesus 27 s
Santo Corazón 28 k
Santo Domingo 21 t
Santos 29 g
Santos Dumont 25 c
Santo Tomás 24 z
Santo Tomé 28 z
San Valentin 30 t
San Vincente 18 c
San Vicente de Cañete 24 w
San Yanaro 23 q
Sanyati 45 q
Sanyuan 62 m
Sanza Pombo 44 h
São Borja 28 z
São Carlos 29 e
São Félix 26 z
São Félix (Illha do Bananal) 26 x
São Félix do Xingu 26 x
São Francisco (Island) 29 s
São Francisco (River) 29 i
São Francisco, Serra 27 r
São Gabriel 29 n
Sao Hill 45 h
São Joo de Araguaia 26 z
São Joo do Piauí 27 q
São José 29 r
São José (Negro) 25 d
São José do Anauá 25 h
São José do Egito 27 u
São José do Rio Preto 29 d
São José do Ribamar 27 c
São José dos Campos 29 g
São José do Xingu 26 w
Saolat 69 m
São Lorenço 25 z
São Luis 27 b
São Luis de Montes Belos 29 c
São Marcos Bay 27 c
São Mateus 29 l
São Miguel de Gyamá 27 a
São Miguel do Araguaia 26 x

São Miguel dos Campos 27 v
São Paulo 29 g
São Paulo de Olivença 25 c
São Pedro do Piauí 27 q
São Raimundo das Mangabeiras 27 n
São Raimundo Nonato 27 q
São Romo 29 g
São Roque, Cabo 27 w
Sâo Sebastiâo 26 v
São Sebastio (São Paulo) 29 h
São Tomé 41 s
São Tomé (Island) 41 r
São Tomé and Principe 41/44
Sapele 41 r
Saposoa 24 j
Sapporo 59 c
Sapri 35 o
Sapt Kosi 61 i
Saqqez 54 v
Saquenay 17 b
Sarajevo 35 c
Sarakhs 55 q
Saraktash 55 a
Saran 55 j
Sarangani Islands 67 w
Sarangarh 61 s
Saranpaul 50 y
Saransk 54 h
Sarapul 54 m
Sarapulskoye 58 l
Sarar 39 g
Sarasota 20 k
Saratov 54 i
Saravan 60 e
Sarawak 69 b
Saraya 40 e
Saraysu 55 g
Sarbaz 60 e
Sarbisheh 60 d
Sarbulak 56 h
Sardinia 34 l
Sarek 33 g
Sarempaka 69 d
Sargasso Sea 21 d
Sargento Lores 24 i
Sargodha 60 l
Sarh 42 b
Sari Bulak 56 n
Sari-i Pul 60 h
Sarikei 68 m
Sarina 74 r
Sarkand 56 p
Šarlauk 55 n
Sarmi 70 v
Sarmiento 30 w
Sarmiento Peninsula 30 w
Särna 33 e
Sarnia 16 v
Sarolangun 68 t
Sarychik 54 l
Saryg-Sop 56 l
Sarykamysskoje, Lake 55 n
Saryozek 55 z
Sásabe 18 g
Sasaram 61 t
Sasebo 58 v
Saser 61 c
Saskatchewan (Province) 12/15
Saskatchewan (River) 15 e
Saskatoon 15 c
Saskylakh 52 f
Sassandra 40 w
Sassandra (River) 40 v
Sassari 34 k
Sasykkol', Lake 56 c
Satadougou 40 f
Satara (India) 64 d
Satara (South Africa) 49 f
Satawal 71 b
Satawan Atoll 71 g
Satipo 24 y
Šatlyk 55 o
Sātpura Range 61 n
Satu Mare 33 v
Satun 65 w
Saucillo 18 l
Saudi Arabia 38-39
Saul 26 i
Sault Ste. Marie 16 g
Sauqira, Bay 39 z
Sauré 25 k
Saurimo 44 x
Sava 35 c
Savalou 41 o
Savannah Downs 73 x
Savannah (Georgia) 20 m
Savannah (Tennessee) 20 g
Savannakhet 66 h
Savanur 64 d
Savate 44 u
Saveh 39 h
Savé (Benin) 41 o
Save (Mozambique) 49 h
Sawla 40 l
Sawu 69 u
Sawu Sea 69 u
Say 41 b
Sayaboury 62 u
Sayan Mountains 56 i
Saydy 53 b
Sayhut 43 l
Sayram Hu 56 q
Sayula 18 y
Sayun 43 k
Say-Utes 54 z
Sayylyk 53 b
Sbaa 36 m
Scarborough 23 j
Ščerbakty 56 b
Schefferville 17 c
Schenectady 16 z
Schizuoka 59 n
Schmidta 51 i
Schreiber 16 f
Schuangliao 58 e
Schwabenland 83 k
Schwangyashan 58 j
Schweizer-Reneke 49 o
Schwerin 33 q
Sciacca 34 z
Scoresby Land 91 q
Scoresby Sound 91 q
Scorpion Bay 76 m
Scotia Sea 82 d
Scotland 32 w
Scott Base 86 r
Scottsbluff 15 r
Scranton 16 y
Sea of Crete 38 e
Seabra 27 q
Searchlight 14 y
Seattle 14 h
Sebastian Vizcaino Bay 18 e
Sebuku Bay 69 e
Sedalia 16 o
Sedan 34 i
Seddon, Kap 91 b
Sededema 53 i
Sedova 50 i
Sefid 54 x
Sefrou 36 i
Segamat 65 y
Segera 45 k
Ségou 40 j
Segovia 34 d
Seguedine 37 v
Séguéla 40 i
Segura 34 r
Sehwan 60 i
Seine 34 g
Seke Banza 44 f
Sekoma 49 a
Sekondi-Takoradi 40 z
Selaru 70 p
Selatan, Cape 69 p
Selby 15 g
Selebi-Phikwe 49 d
Selenga 57 e
Selety-Tengiz Lake 55 j
Sélibabi 40 e
Šelichov 57 c
Selma 20 h
Semarang 68 z
Sembé 41 x
Semeru 69 n
Semipalatinsk 56 c
Seman 39 k
Semnu 37 j
Semonaicha 56 d
Sem-Tripa 26 v
Sena 45 u
Senador Pompeu 27 s
Sena Madureira 25 o
Senanga 44 z
Sencha 52 l
Sendai 59 p
Seneca, Lake 16 x
Senegal 40
Senegal (River) 40 c
Senekal 49 p
Seney 16 f
Senhor do Bonfim 27 s
Senja 33 f
Senjavin Group 71 k
Sennar 42 m
Senneterre 16 k
Seoni 61 q
Seoul 58 u
Sepik 70 y
Sepone 66 i
Sepopa 48 l
Sept-les 17 d
Serebr'ansk 56 d
Sere Kunda 40 a
Seremban 68 f
Serengeti 45 h
Serenje 45 q
Sergach 54 h
Sergino 50 z
Sergiyev Posad 50 p
Sermata 70 o
Serowe 49 b
Serpent's Mouth 23 i
Serpuchovo 54 d
Sérrai 35 f
Serra Acarai 25 l
Serra Aguapei 25 w
Serra Curupira 25 f
Serra da Batista 27 r
Serra da Canastra 29 g
Serra da Capivara 29 g
Serra da Ibiapaba 27 r
Serra da Mantiqueira 29 h
Serra das Alpercatas 27 p
Serra das Araras 29 o
Serra das Divisoes 29 c
Serra da Tabatinga 27 p
Serra de Huanchaca 25 v
Serra de Maracaju 29 a
Serra de Pianí 27 q
Serra de Santiago 28 k
Serra do Apiaú 23 v
Serra do Cachimbo 25 z
Serra do Dois Irmos 27 r
Serra do Espinnaco 29 i
Serra do Itapicuru 27 o
Serra do Mar 29 r
Serra do Navio 26 j
Serra do Norte 25 w
Serra do Penitente 27 n
Serra do Roncador 26 w
Serra dos Apiacás 25 x
Serra dos Caiabis 25 y
Serra dos Carajás 26 x
Serra dos Pacáas Novos 25 s
Serra dos Parecis 25 u
Serra do Tiracambu 27 a
Serra do Tombador 25 x
Serra Dourada 26 z
Serra do Urucui 27 o
Serra do Valentim 27 p
Serra Formosa 25 z
Serra Geral de Goiás 27 n
Serra Geral do Parana 29 f
Serra Gradaús 26 x
Serra Lombarda 26 j
Serra Pacaraima 23 u
Serra Paranapiacaba 29 r
Serra Parima 23 u
Serra So Francisco 27 r
Serra Talhada 27 t
Serra Tapirapecó 23 t
Serra Tumucumaque 26 i
Serrania de Imataca 23 i
Serrinha 27 t
Sêrtar 62 g
Serule 49 c
Sêrxu 62 e
Sesayap 69 d
Sese Islands 42 y
Sesheke 44 z
Sesriem 48 h
Sessa 44 x
Sete Lagoas 29 i
Setif 34 v
Settat 36 h
Setúbal 34 n
Seul, Lac 16 c
Sevan, Lake 54 u
Sevastopol 35 k
Severn 16 e
Severnaja 51 i
Severnaya Zemlya 51 j
Severnoye 54 l
Severodvinsk 50 q
Severomuysk 52 u
Sevi 56 k
Sevilla 34 p
Seville (Sevilla) 34 p
Sewa 40 f
Seward 11 f
Seward Peninsula 10 m
Seychelles 231 p
Seym 54 b
Seymchan 53 j
Seymour 77 x
Sfax 34 y
Shache 55 z
Shackleton Ice Shelf 85 t
Shackleton Range 83 u
Shadrinsk 55 e
Shahdol 61 r
Shahgarh 60 k
Shahjahanpur 61 e
Shahjui 60 i
Shahr-e-Kord 39 i
Shajapur 61 o
Shakamku 48 k
Shakawe 48 l
Shakhty (Russia) 54 e
Shakhty (Kazakstan) 55 b
Shala, Lake 43 b
Shaliangzi 56 x
Shamattawa 13 o
Shamrock 15 t
Shandan 57 o
Shangdu 57 v
Shanghai 63 i
Shangjao 63 f
Shangkiu 63 d
Shangnan 63 a
Shangshui 63 d
Shang Xian 62 m
Shangyi 57 v
Shangzhi 58 h
Shannon (Island) 91 t
Shannon (River) 32 u
Shanshan 56 v
Shantar 53 p
Shantung 58 p
Shaohing 63 h
Shaokwan 63 p
Shaowu 63 f
Shaoyang 63 b
Shaqra 39 r
Sharbithat 39 y
Sharbithat, Ras 60 o
Sharjah 39 y
Shark Bay 76 b
Sharlyk 54 m
Sharqat 39 d
Shashe 46 q
Shashemene 43 p
Shashi 49 d
Shasi 63 b
Shasta, Mount 14 u
Shatsk 54 f
Shaunavon 15 b
Shawinigan 17 a
Shawnee 15 v
Shay Gap 72 v
Shazaoyuan 56 x
Shcherbakovo 53 m
Shchuch'ye 51 a
Sheberghan 60 h
Sheboygan 16 r
Sheffield 32 x
Shelayevo 56 m
Shelburne 17 r
Shelby 14 m
Shelekhova, Gulf of 53 x
Shenandoah 16 n
Shenber 55 f
Shendi 38 w
Shenmu 57 t
Sheno 43 d
Shepparton 77 x
Sherbro Island 40 q
Sherbrooke 17 a
Sherda 37 x
Sheridan 15 c
Sherman 19 d
Sherman Basin 12 m
Sherman Island 80 m
Shestakova 53 g
Shetland Islands 32 k
Shetpe 54 y
Shevli 53 n
Sheya 52 h
Shibeli 43 e
Shibing 62 l
Shiguaigou 57 t
Shihezi 56 s
Shihkiachwang 57 u
Shihtsuishan 57 q
Shikar Pur 60 i
Shikoku 58 x
Shilabo 43 t
Shiliguri 61 k
Shilkan 53 t
Shillong 62 n
Shimanovsk 52 y
Shimonoseki 58 v
Shinas 39 z
Shindand 60 e
Shingwedzi 49 f
Shintuya 25 n
Shinyanga 45 g
Shiping 62 u
Shiquanhe 61 d
Shir 39 k
Shirane-san 59 n
Shiraz 39 j
Shisanzhan 58 g
Shishinda 43 n
Shishmaref 10 l
Shivera 51 w
Shivpuri 61 o
Shiyan 63 a
Shkodër 35 d
Shokal'skogo Str. 51 m
Sholapur 61 o
Shomvukva 50 u
Shorobe 49 a
Shoshong 46 o
Shostka 54 a
Showak 43 a
Show Low 18 h
Shreveport 19 f
Shuangcheng 58 g
Shuangjiang 62 s
Shuangliao 58 e
Shubra al Kheima 38 h
Shuga 55 l
Shuga (Gulf of Ob') 51 b
Shule 56 x
Shumikha 55 e
Shumougou 57 l
Shunte 63 p
Shuo Xian 57 t
Shurgaz 60 d
Shush 39 g
Shwangliao 58 e
Shwebo 62 q
Shyok 61 c
Si 63 o
Siakwan 62 t
Sialkot 61 a
Sian 62 m
Siangfan 63 b
Siangtan 63 b
Siargao 67 k
Siauliai 33 v
Šibenik 35 b
Siberia 51 o
Siberian Uvaly 51 w
Siberut 68 e
Sibi 60 j
Sibirjakov 51 e

Sibiti 44 e
Sibiu 35 g
Sibolga 68 d
Sibu 69 a
Sibut 42 o
Sibuyan 67 h
Sicasica 28 e
Sichuan Pendi 62 j
Sicilian Channel 34 z
Sicily 35 n
Sicuani 25 n
Sidatun 58 l
Sīdi Barrâni 38 e
Sidi-bel-Abbes 34 s
Sidi Bennour 36 g
Sidi Ifni 36 e
Sidi Kacem 36 i
Sidley, Mount 81 f
Sidney (Montana) 15 e
Sidney (Nebraska) 15 r
Sidorovoko 51 f
Siedlce 33 v
Siegen-Kyugel 52 m
Siena 34 l
Sierra Blanca Peak 18 k
Sierra Burro 19 a
Sierra Carmen 18/19
Sierra Colorada 30 j
Sierra de Aguas Calientes 28 r
Sierra de Cordoba 28 t
Sierra de Famatina 28 q
Sierra de Juarez 18 d
Sierra de la Giganta 18 g
Sierra del Nevado 30 j
Sierra de Mato 23 t
Sierra de Perija 23 b
Sierra de Velasco 28 r
Sierra Leone 40
Sierra Madre 67 g
Sierra Morena 34 p
Sierra Nevada (Spain) 34 q
Sierra Nevada (USA) 14 v
Sierra Vista 18 h
Sigil 65 t
Signy 82 g
Siguiri 40 g
Sihabuhabu 65 v
Sihochac 19 u
Sikar 61 a
Sikasso 40 i
Sikhote-Alin 58 m
Sikonge 45 g
Siktyakh 52 k
Silao 19 n
Silay 67 h
Silchar 62 o
Silet 37 o
Silifke 35 y
Siligir 52 f
Siling Co 61 k
Siljan, Lake 33 e
Šilka 57 j
Silkwood 73 m
Sillanjnuay 28 d
Silver City 18 i
Simao 62 t
Simcoe, Lake 16 j
Simenga 52 d
Simeulue 68 b
Simferopol' 54 o
Simikot 61 f
Simla 61 c
Simpson Desert 73 t
Simpson Peninsula 13 b
Simušir 59 i
Sinadogo 43 u
Sinai Peninsula 38 j
Sinawan 37 g
Sincelejo 22 m
Sinclair Mills 14 h
Sind 61 p
Sindi 42 f
Šinedžinst 57 n
Sines 34 n
Sinewit 71 r
Singa 42 m
Singapore 66 t
Singatoka 75 k
Sing Buri 65 j
Singida 45 h
Singkawang 68 l
Singkep 68 i
Singkilbaru 66 p
Singtai 63 c
Sining 57 o
Sinjai 69 t
Sinjar 54 s
Sinkat 38 y
Sinn 58 m
Sinnamary 26 j
Sinop 35 m
Sintang 68 m
Sinú 22 m
Sinugif 43 j
Sinŭiju 58 s
Sinyaya 52 k
Sinyuga 52 s
Sioux City 15 v
Sioux Falls 15 v
Sioux Lookout 16 c
Siple (Mountain) 81 b
Siple (Research Sta.) 81 q
Siple Island 81 q
Sipora 68 e
Siquijor 67 i
Sira 56 i
Siracha 65 j
Siracusa (Syracuse) 35 o
Siraj 60 b
Sir Edward Pellew Group 73 g
Siret 35 h
Sirha 61 i
Sir James McBrien, Mount 12 o
Sirjan 60 a
Sir Joseph Banks Group 77 e
Sirohi 60 z
Sironcha 64 h
Sirpur 64 g
Sirsa 61 a
Sirte 35 o
Sirte Desert 37 k
Sirte, Gulf of 35/38
Sirwa 43 h
Si Sa Ket 66 g
Sishen 48 z
Sisimiut 90 i
Sisophon 66 g
Sisseton 15 i
Sitapur 61 e
Sitka 11 x
Sittang 65 g
Sittwe 62 o
Siuri 61 w
Sivas 54 p
Siverek 54 r
Sivuch 53 v
Siwa 38 e
Siwa, Oasis 38 e
Sixtymile 11 i
Siziman 59 b
Skagen, Cape 33 c
Skagerrak 33 b
Skagway 11 x
Skardu 61 a
Skeena 14 d
Skellefte 33 g
Skellefteå 33 h
Skibotn 33 h
Skikda 34 w
Sklad 52 j
Skoer Fjord 91 u
Skopin 54 e
Skopje 35 e
Skovorodino 52 x
Skukuza 49 f
Skye 32 v
Slamet 68 y
Slana 11 h
Slave Coast 41 o
Slave Lake 14 l
Slave River 12 u
Slessor Glacier 83 u
Slidell 19 i
Sligo 32 u
Slippers Bay 48 w
Sliven 35 h
Slonim 33 w
Slovakia 35 c
Slovenia 35 a
Sl'ud'anka 52 n
Słupsk 33 s
Slutsk 33 x
Smallwood Reservoir 17 f
Smara 36 r
Smederevo 35 e
Smidovich 50 j
Smith 14 l
Smith Bay 13 g
Smithfield 49 o
Smith's Falls 16 l
Smithton 77 w
Smolensk 33 z
Smyley Island 82 z
Snag 11 i
Snake 14 j
Snake River (USA) 15 a
Snare River 12 s
Snares Islands 79 p
Snowdrift 12 u
Snowy 78 q
Snowy Mountains 78 q
Soai Dao 65 k
Sobat 42 k
Sobradinho Reservoir 27 r
Sobral 27 f
Soči 54 r
Socompa 28 q
Socorro (Colombia) 23 n
Socorro (USA) 18 j
Socorro (Island) 18 u
Socotra 231 c
Soda Springs 15 n
Söderhamn 33 g
Södertälje 33 f
Sodiri 42 j
Sodo 43 o
Sofala Bay 46 v
Sofia 35 f
Sofiya (Sofia) 35 f
Sofiysk 53 o
Sofiysk (Amur) 59 b
Sogamoso 23 o
Sogeri 71 o
Sognefjörd 33 a
Sogo Nur 57 o
Sohâg 38 i
Sohar 39 z
Soje 49 b
Šokalsky 51 c
Sokcho 58 v
Sokodé 41 a
Sokolo 40 i
Sokoto 41 d
Sokoto (River) 41 c
Sokyrbulak 55 b
Soledade 25 b
Solikamsk 50 w
Sol Iletsk 54 m
Solimões 23 s
Solodniki 54 h
Solok 68 f
Sololo 43 p
Solomon Islands 71/74
Solomon Sea 74 k
Solor Islands 69 v
Solovjevsk 57 i
Solwezi 45 n
Somalia 43
Somerset 16 t
Somerset East 49 n
Somerset Island 13 a
Son 61 t
Sonaly 55 i
Søndrestrømfjord 90 w
Søndre Strømfjord (Fjord) 90 w
Songea 45 u
Songkhla 65 w
Songo 45 s
Sonhat 61 s
Sonoyta 18 f
Sonsonate 22 c
Sonsorol 70 d
Sopo 42 g
Sorabai 60 k
Sordongnokh (Russia) 53 f
Sordongnokh (Russia) 53 p
Soria 34 e
Sorocaba 29 f
Sorochinsk 54 m
Sorol Atoll 70 j
Sorong 70 p
Soroti 42 y
Söröya 33 i
Sorsk 56 i
Sorsogon 67 i
Sortavala 33 m
Sosna 52 b
Sosnovka 57 f
Sos'va 50 y
Sosyko 54 e
Souanké 41 x
Soubré 40 v
Souk-Ahras 34 w
Sŏul (Seoul) 58 u
Sounda 44 e
Souré 26 m
Sousse 34 y
South Africa 46/48-49
Southampton Island 13 q
Southampton (UK) 34 f
Southampton (USA) 17 n
South Andaman 65 e
South Anyuskiy Mountains 10 b
South Australia 77 b
South Bend 16 s
South Bug 35 k
South Carolina 20 m
South China Sea 66-67
South Dakota 15 g
South East Cape 77 y
Southend 12 w
Southend-on-Sea 32 y
Southern Alps 79 r
Southern Cross 76 f
Southern Indian Lake 12 z
Southern Ocean 87 t
Southern Sierra Madre 19 p
Southern Sporades 35 u
South Georgia Islands 31 y
South Horr 43 o
South Island 79 r
South Magnetic Pole 87 q
South Natuna Islands 68 l
South Orkney Islands 82 g
South Pagai 68 r
South Platte 15 s
South Pole 81 m
South Saskatchewan 15 a
South Scotia Ridge 82 f
South Shetland Islands 82 r
Southwest Cape 79 p
Sovetsk 33 v
Sovetskaya 84 w
Sovetskiy 50 z
Soyapa 18 i
Soyo 44 e
Spaatz Island 82 z
Spain 34/36
Spanish Town 21 o
Spartanburg 20 l
Spassk Dal'niy 58 k
Spearfish 15 e
Spence Bay 13 a
Spencer 15 w
Spencer, Cape 77 r
Spencer Gulf 77 e
Spitsbergen 92 p
Split 35 b
Spokane 14 j
Spratly Islands 66 z
Springbok 48 w
Springdale 17 j
Springfield (Colorado) 15 s
Springfield (Illinois) 16 q
Springfield (Massachusetts) 17 n
Springfield (Missouri) 15 x
Springfield (Ohio) 16 u
Springs 46 q
Springsure 74 r
Spruce Knov 16 w
Squaw Habor 11 n
Sredinnyy Mountains 53 y
Srednekolymsk 53 j
Sredniy 53 w
Sredniy Kalar 52 t
Sretensk 57 k
Srikakulam 64 k
Sri Lanka 64
Sri Mohangarh 60 k
Srinagar 61 a
Stafonovo 50 f
Stakhanov 54 d
Stampriet 48 j
Standerton 49 r
Stanford 15 a
Stanley (Falkland Is.) 31 p
Stanley (N. Dakota) 15 f
Stannakh-Khocho 52 i
Stanovoy Mountains 52 y
Stanthorpe 78 f
Staraja Russa 33 m
Stara Zagora 35 h
Star.Dom 53 d
Stargard 33 s
Staritsa 51 s
Staritsa (Moscow) 50 n
Star. Kayakhnyy 52 b
Star. Kheydzhan 53 s
Staryy Nadym 51 p
Staryy Oskol 54 d
Staten Island 30 z
Statesboro 20 l
Stavanger 33 a
Stavropol' 54 t
Stavropolka 55 f
Steamboat 12 p
Steamboat Springs 15 p
Steelpoort 49 e
Steenkool 70 q
Steenstrup Glacier 91 b
Stefansson Island 12 j
Steinhausen 48 i
Steinkier 33 d
Steinkopf 48 w
Stephenville 17 h
Stepnyak 55 i
Sterling 15 r
Sterlitamak 55 a
Stettin (Szczecin) 33 r
Stevens Point 16 d
Stewart (British Colombia) 11 z
Stewart (Yukon Territory) 11 i
Stewart Crossing 11 k
Stewart Island 79 p
Stewart, Mount 74 p
Stewart (River) 11 k
Steynsburg 49 o
Steytlerville 49 n
Stikine 11 z
Stilbaai 48 y
Stirling 32 w
Stockholm 33 g
Stockton 14 u
Stoke-on-Trent 32 w
Stolbovoy 50 i
Stolbovoy (Island) 53 c
Stonehenge 77 i
Stony Rapids 12 v
Stony River 11 c
Store Koldewey 91 u
Storkerson Peninsula 12 i
Storm Bay 77 z
Storm Lake 16 n
Stors, Lake 33 e
Storuman 33 f
Strahan 77 x
Stralsund 33 q
Strand 48 w
Strasbourg 34 j
Strathleven 73 k
Strathmay 73 k
Streaky Bay 77 c
Strelka 53 i
Strelka (Yenisey) 51 w
Strelka-čunja 52 a
Strezhevoy 51 q
Strickland 70 x
Strömsund 33 f
Stryy 35 f
Stung Treng 66 i
Sturge Island 86 v
Sturgeon Bay 16 f
Sturgeon Falls 16 j
Sturt Creek 73 n
Sturt Desert 77 h
Stutterheim 49 p
Stuttgart 34 l

Styr 33 w
Suakin 38 z
Suanhwa 57 w
Suata 23 g
Subotica 35 d
Suceava 35 h
Süchbaatar 57 d
Suchow (Xuzhou) 63 f
Suchow (Suzhou) 63 h
Suchumi 54 r
Suckling, Mount 74 e
Sucre 28 f
Sucuaro 23 q
Sucunduri 25 j
Sucuriu 29 b
Sucurundi 25 j
Sudan 38/42-43
Sudbury 16 i
Sudd 42 j
Suddie 23 k
Sudety 35
Sudocje, Lake 55 o
Sudr 38 j
Sue 42 u
Suez 38 j
Suez Canal 38 j
Suez, Gulf of 38 j
Sugdža 57 e
Suglan 53 a
Sugoy 53 k
Sugun 55 y
Suhai Hu 56 x
Suhait 57 q
Suhsien 63 e
Suide 57 t
Suifenhe 58 j
Suihua 58 g
Suileng 58 g
Suining 62 k
Sui Zian 63 c
Suj 57 r
Sukabumi 68 w
Sukhana 52 h
Sukhinichi 54 b
Sukhona 50 r
Sukkur 60 j
Suknah 37 j
Sulaiman 60 k
Sulaimaniyah (Iraq) 39 e
Sulaimaniyah (Saudi Arabia) 39 t
Sulaiman Range 60 k
Sula Islands 69 k
Sulan Cheer 57 s
Sulawesi (Celébes) 69 t
Suleya 55 b
Suli Hu 56 x
Sullana 24 g
Sullivan 16 p
Sulphur Springs 19 e
Sultan 60 f
Sultanpur 61 s
Sulu Archipelago 67 s
Sulu Sea 67 s
Sulzberger Ice Shelf 81 v
Sum 56 l
Sumaih 42 i
Sumail 60 o
Sumarokovo 51 v
Sumatra 68 f
Sumba 69 s
Sumbawa 69 r
Sumbawa Besar 69 r
Sumbawanga 45 f
Sumbe 44 s
Sümber 57 e
Sumbu 45 e
Sumgait 54 x
Sumprabum 62 r
Sumy 35 l
Sunan 57 n
Suncho Corral 28 u
Sundance 15 d
Sundargarh 61 t
Sunda Strait 68 v
Sunderland 32 y
Sundsvall 33 g
Sungaigerung 68 v
Sungai Ko-lok 65 x
Sungaipenuh 68 f
Sungai Petani 66 q
Sungai Siput Utara 65 x
Sungari 58 i
Sun Kosi 61 i
Suntar 52 g
Sunwu 58 g
Sunyani 40 y
Suolama 52 e
Suon-Tit 52 x
Suordakh 53 c
Superior 15 k
Superior, Lake 15 m
Suphan Buri 66 d
Sur (Oman) 60 q
Sur (Lebanon) 60 q
Surab 60 h
Surabaya 69 o
Surakarta 68 z
Surat (Australia) 74 r
Surat (India) 60 z
Suratgarh 60 m
Surat Thani 65 w
Surgat 51 p
Surigao 67 j
Surin 65 m
Suriname 23/26
Susanville 14 v
Šusenskoje 56 j
Susquehanna 16 y
Sutam 52 y
Sutherland 48 x
Sutlej 60 m
Suttor 74 p
Sutun'ya 52 m
Suva 75 l
Suvorka 57 c
Suwałki 33 v
Suwar 39 b
Suyevatpaul 50 y
Suzun 56 d
Svalbard 92 o
Svartenhuk 90 m
Svartisen 33 e
Sveg 33 e
Svendborg 33 q
Sverdlovsk (Yekaterinburg) 50 y
Sverdrup Channel 89 r
Sverdrup Islands 12 k
Svetlaya 59 a
Svetlovodnaya 58 m
Svetozarevo 35 e
Svobodny 58 h
Swakopmund 48 g
Swan 76 d
Swan Hill 77 v
Swan Island 19 z
Swan River 15 f
Swansea (Australia) 77 z
Swansea (UK) 32 w
Swat 60 m
Swatow 63 r
Swaziland 46/49
Sweden 33
Sweeney Range 83 n
Sweetwater 19 a
Sweetwater (River) 15 o
Swellendam 48 y
Swift Current 15 b
Switzerland 33/34
Syagannakh 53 f
Sydney (Australia) 78 f
Sydney (Canada) 17 h
Sydney Ice Cap 13 d
Syktyvkar 50 t
Sylhet 61 y
Sym 51 u
Sym (River) 51 v
Symya 50 m
Syowa 84 i
Syracuse (USA) 16 y
Syracuse (Sicily) 35 o
Syrdarja (River) 55 s
Syria 38-39/54
Syrian Desert 38 m
Syzran 54 j
Szczecin 33 r
Szczecinek 33 s
Szeged 35 d
Szeping 58 f

T

Tabah 39 c
Tabajara 25 u
Tabarka 34 x
Tabas 39 m
Tabatinga, Serra da 27 p
Tabelbala 36 j
Tablas 67 h
Table Island 13 a
Tableland 72 m
Tabletop 72 x
Tabor 53 i
Tabora 45 f
Tabou 40 v
Tabriz 54 v
Tabuk 38 l
Tacámbaro 19 n
Tachakou 56 r
Tacheng 56 e
Tacloban 67 j
Tacna 25 n
Tacoma 14 h
Tacora 25 o
Tacuarembó 28 z
Tacutu 23 w
Tademait, Hama da 36 m
Tadjourah 43 f
Tadmur 38 m
Taegu 58 v
Taejon 58 u
Tafassâsset, Ténéré du 37 s
Taftan 60 e
Taganrog 54 d
Tagant 36 r
Tagap Ga 62 d
Tagbilaran 67 i
Taghit 36 k
Tagounite 36 h
Taguatinga 27 n
Tagum 67 x
T'agun 56 f
Tagus 34 o
Tahifet 37 q
Tahiti 230 o
Tahlequah 16 n
Tahoua 41 e
Tahrud 60 c
Tai 40 v
Tai'an 63 e
Taibus Qi 57 w
Taichow 58 p
Taichung 63 t
Ta'if 39 o
Taigu 57 u
Tailai 58 e
Tai, Lake 63 g
Taima 38 m
Taimba 51 y
Taimura 51 z
Taimyr 51 l
Taimyr, Lake 51 m
Taimyr Peninsula 51 i
Tainan 63 u
Taiobeiras 29 j
Taipei 63 v
Taiping 65 w
Taitao Peninsula 30 s
Taiwan 63
Taiwan Strait 63 t
Taiyuan 57 u
Ta'izz 43 g
Tajarhi 37 v
Tajikistan 55 v
Tajito 18 g
Tajo 34 q
Tajsara, Cord. de 28 g
Tajura 37 i
Tak 65 i
Takamatsu 58 y
Takatshwaane 48 m
Ta-Kaw 62 s
Takestan 39 h
Takhta Bazar 55 r
Takijuak Lake 12 g
Takla Makan Desert 56 r
Takpa Shiri 62 b
Takua Pa 65 u
Takum 41 u
Talak 37 p
Talandzha 58 j
Talara 24 g
Talata Mafara 41 e
Talaud Islands 69 l
Talavera de la Reina 34 p
Talawana 72 v
Talbot 76 k
Talca 30 h
Talcahuano 30 g
Talcher 61 u
Taldy-Kurgan 56 n
Talhada, Serra 27 t
Taliabu 69 j
Taliqan 60 k
Talitsa 50 z
Talkeetna 11 f
Tall'Afar 39 c
Tallahassee 20 j
Tall Kalakh 38 l
Tal'menka 56 e
Talodi 42 j
Talon 53 u
Taloyoak (Spence Bay) 13 a
Taloye 52 y
Taltal 28 o
Taluma 52 w
Talwood 78 e
Tamala 76 c
Tamale 40 m
Tamanrasset 37 p
Tamassoumit 36 p
Tamazula 18 z
Tamazunchale 19 p
Tambacounda 40 d
Tambara 49 h
Tambelan Islands 68 j
Tambey 51 b
Tambo (Australia) 74 b
Tambo (Peru) 24 y
Tambo (Peru) 25 n
Tambor 48 f
Tambov 54 f
Tambura 42 u
Tamč 56 k
Tamchaket 36 r
Tamentit 36 l
Tamiahua Lagune 19 q
Tamitatoala 26 v
Tampa 20 k
Tampere 33 j
Tampico 19 p
Tamsagbulag 57 k
Tamshiyaco 24 m
Tamu 62 p
Tamworth 78 e
Tanabe 58 z
Tanacross 11 h
Tanahbala 68 d
Tanahjampea 69 u
Tanahmerah 70 v
Tana (Kenya) 43 q
Tana (Norway) 33 l
Tana (River, Norway) 33 k
Tana, Lake 43 b
Tanama 51 e
Tanami Desert 73 p
Tanana 11 e
Tanbar 77 h
Tanchoj 57 d
Tandil 31 b
Tanega 58 w
Tanezrouft 36 y
Tanezrouft-n-Ahenet 36/37
Tanga (Tanzania) 45 k
Tanga (Russia) 57 g
Tanganyika, Lake 45 d
Tanggula Shan 61 k
Tanghe 63 c
Tangier 34 p
Tangorin 74 o
Tangra Yumco 61 i
Tangshan 57 y
Tangub 67 u
Tanguiéta 41 b
Tanimbar Islands 70 o
Tanjung 69 c
Tanjungbalai 65 w
Tanjungkarang 68 v
Tanjungpandan 68 x
Tanjungpura 65 v
Tanjungredeb 69 e
Tannu Mountains 56 j
Tano 40 y
Tanot 60 k
Tanout 41 g
Tanque El Revés 18 m
Tanta 38 h
Tantan 36 e
Tanzania 42/45/46
Tao'an 58 d
Taolañaro 47 q
Taoudenit 36 w
Taourirt 36 k
Taouz 36 j
Taoyüan 63 u
Tapachula 19 t
Tapajós 25 l
Tapaktuan 65 t
Tapanahoni 26 h
Tapauá 25 f
Tapauá (River) 25 e
Tapeta 40 t
Tapirapecó, Serra 23 t
Tapirapua 25 x
Tapis 68 g
Tapsui 50 y
Tapti 60 z
Tapurucuara 25 f
Taquaras 25 s
Taquari 28 m
Tara 55 k
Tara (River) 55 m
Tarabuco 28 g
Taracuá 25 c
Taragay 55 y
Tarakan 69 e
Taran 51 c
Taranto 35 c
Taranto, Gulf of 35 p
Tarapoto 24 j
Taraq 39 x
Tararua Range 79 v
Tarat 37 s
Tarata 25 o
Tarauacá 25 n
Tarauacá (River) 25 a
Tarbagatay Mountains 56 d
Tarbaj 43 q
Tarbes 34 f
Tarcoola 77 c
Taree 78 g
Tareya 51 j
Tarfaya 36 d
Tarhuna 35 n
Tarialan 57 b
Tariat 57 d
Tariat (Hangayn Mountains) 57 a
Tarif 39 x
Tarija 28 g
Tarim 56 q
Tarim (River) 56 r
Tarim Basin 56 q
Tarim Liuchang 56 t
Tarime 45 g
Tarim Kot 60 h
Tarka La 61 k
Tarkwa 40 z
Tarlac 67 f
Tarnak 60 i
Taroom 74 r
Taroudannt 36 g
Tarragona 34 g
Tarso Ahon 37 y
Tartagal 28 h
Tartary, Gulf of 59 b
Tartu 33 k
Tartus 35 z
Tarutung 68 d
Tasauz 55 p
Tashigang 61 l
Tachkent 55 v
Tasik Malaya 68 x
Task 41 h
Taskesken 56 c
Tas-Kumsa 53 a
Tas-Kumyr 55 w
Tasman Bay 79 t
Tasmania 77 w
Tasman Sea 78 v

Tassili-n-Ajjer 37 r
Tassili Oua-n-Hoggar 37 p
Tasso Fragoso 27 o
Tastagol 56 g
Tas-Tumus 52 m
Tastyp 56 h
Tas-Yuryakh 52 f
Tata 36 g
Tatarsk 55 l
Tataurovo 57 e
Tathlina Lake 12 r
Tathlith 39 q
Tatty 55 x
Tatung 57 o
Tatvan 54 s
Tauá 27 s
Taubaté 29 g
Taumarunui 79 v
Taumaturgo 24 z
Taunggyi 62 r
Taupo 79 w
Taupo, Lake 79 w
Tauranga 79 w
Taurus 35 x
Tavda 50 z
Tavda (River) 50 z
Tavira 36 g
Tavoy 65 h
Tavua 75 l
Tawau 69 e
Tawitawi 67 s
Tawitawi Group 67 s
Taxco 19 o
Tayabamba 24 w
Tayebad 60 d
Taygonos, Cape 53 z
Taymylyr 52 j
Tayshet 56 m
Taz 51 f
Taz (River) 51 f
Taz Bay 51 d
Taza 36 j
Tazenakht 36 h
Tazirbu 38 a
Tazovskiy 51 e
Tazzarine 36 i
Tbilisi 54 u
Tchibanga 44 c
Tchien 40 u
Tchin-Tabaradene 41 e
Tcholliré 41 k
Te Anau 79 p
Te Araroa 79 x
Tea Tree 73 r
Tebessa 34 x
Tebicuary 28 y
Teboursouk 34 y
Techiman 40 z
Tecka 30 i
Tecomán 18 y
Tecpan 19 n
Tecuala 18 x
Tedžen 55 p
Teelin 56 m
Tefé 25 f
Tefé (River) 25 e
Tegal 68 y
Tegguidda-n-Tessoum 41 e
Tegina 41 e
Tegucigalpa 22 e
Teguldet 51 v
Tegyulte-Terde 52 z
Tehchow 57 w
Tehran 39 j
Tehuacan 19 q
Tehuantepec 19 r
Tehuantepec, Gulf of 19 r
Tehuantepec, Isthmus of 19 s
Teide, Pico de 36 a
Tekax 19 v
Tekes 56 q
Tekes (River) 56 q
Tekeze 43 c
Tekiliktag 61 e
Tekirdağ 35 h
Teku 69 i
Tela 19 w
Tel-Aviv-Yaffa 38 k
Tele 42 s
Teleckoje, Lake 56 g
Telefomin 70 x
Telegraph Creek 11 y
Telemaco Borba 29 q
Telemba 57 h
Telémélé 40 e
Teles Pires 25 x
Tell Atlas 34 t
Teller 10 m
Telmen Nuur 56 l
Telsen 30 k
Telukbetung
(Bandarlampung) 68 v
Tema 41 n
Temacine 37 d
Tembenchi 51 y
Tembenchi (River) 51 k
Tembo 41 v
Temir 55 b
Temirtau 55 j
Témiscaming 16 j
Temnikov 54 g
Temosachic 18 j
Temple 19 d
Temuco 30 g
Tena 24 j
Tenacatita 18 x
Tenali 64 i
Tenalr 53 h
Tenasserim (River) 65 i
Tenasserim Coast 65 h
Tendaho 43 d
Ten Degree Channel 65 d
Tendelti 42 k
Tendrara 36 k
Ténéré 37 s
Ténéré, Erg du 37 t
Tenerife 36 a
Tenerife (Island) 36 b
Ténès 34 t
Tenchong 62 s
Tengiz, Lake 55 h
Tenkasi 64 s
Tenke 52 g
Tenkeli 53 e
Tenkodogo 40 m
Tennant Creek 73 r
Tennessee (State) 16 r
Tennessee (River) 16 r
Tenosique 19 t
Tensift 36 f
Tenterfield 78 f
Teófilo Otoni 29 j
Tepatitlán 18 z
Tepeji 19 o
Tepi 42 z
Tepic 18 x
Téra 41 a
Terbu 37 w
Terek 54 u
Terensay 55 c
Teresina 27 q
Terezinha 26 j
Termes de Rio Hondo 28 t
Termez 55 t
Termination Island 76 h
Terminos, Laguna de 19 u
Termit, Massif de 41 i
Termit N. 41 h
Ternate 69 l
Terney 58 m
Terni 34 m
Ternopol' 35 g
Terrace 14 d
Terrace Bay 48 f
Terra Firma 48 z
Terra Preta 25 j
Terra Haute 16 s
Terror 86 r
Teruel 34 f
Terutao 66 q
Tesig 57 c
Teslin 11 l
Tessalit 36 z
Tessaoua 41 f
Tete 46 g
Tété 42 d
Tetere 52 o
Tetuan 34 p
Tetyushi 54 j
Teuco 28 w
Teulada, Cape 34 x
Tevriz 51 o
Têwo 62 i
Texarkana 19 e
Texas 19 a
Texas City 19 e
Texcoco 19 p
Teya 51 w
Tezejet 55 p
Tezew 33 t
Teziutlán 19 p
Tezpur 62 n
Thabazimbi 49 c
Thailand 62/65/66
Thailand, Gulf of 66 e
Thakhek 66 h
Thallon 78 d
Thamarit 39 x
Thames 32 x
Thamud 39 u
Thane 60 z
Thanh Hoa 62 x
Thanjavur 64 h
Thap Put 65 u
Tharad 60 y
Thar Desert 60 k
Thargomindah 77 j
Tharthar, Lake 39 c
Thasos 35 g
Thaton 65 h
Thatta 60 v
Thayetmyo 65 f
Thebes 38 i
Theda 72 m
The Dalles 14 h
Thedford 15 t
Thelon 12 w
Theodore 74 s
Theodore Roosevelt 26 q
The Pas 15 f
Thermai, Gulf of 35 s
The Sound 33 q
Thessalonika 35 f
Thessaloniki
(Thessalonika) 35 f
Thief River Falls 15 i
Thiès 40 b
Thika 45 j
Thimphu 61 k
Thingangyun 65 g
Thionville 34 i
Thiruvananthapuram
(Trivandrum) 64 r
Thistle I. 77 e
Thlewiaza 12 z
Thollon 77 m
Thomasville 20 j
Thompson 12 y
Thompson Falls 14 l
Thomson 74 n
Thon Buri 65 j
Thorntonia 73 v
Three Hummock Island 77 x
Three Kings Island 79 g
Three Rivers (Australia) 76 f
Three Rivers (USA) 19 c
Thule 91 c
Thunder Bay 16 e
Thurso 32 k
Thurston Island 80 m
Thylungra 77 j
Tiancang 57 n
Tiancheng 57 n
Tianguá 27 e
Tianjin (Tientsin) 57 x
Tianjun 56 z
Tianlin 62 x
Tiaret 36 m
Tibati 41 v
Tibé 40 h
Tibesti 37 y
Tibet 61 g
Tiburon 18 f
Tichitt 36 s
Tichla 36 o
Tichvin 50 n
Ticul 19 v
Tidikelt 37 n
Tidjikja 36 q
Tidra 36 n
Tielongtan 61 d
Tien Shan 56
Tienshui 62 k
Tientsin 57 x
Tierra Blanca 19 q
Tierra Colorada 19 o
Tierra del Fuego 30 w
Tiete 29 d
Tieyon 77 c
Tifariti 36 r
Tifton 20 k
Tigieglo 43 t
Tigil' 53 y
Tigre (Peru) 24 k
Tigre (Venezuela) 23 h
Tigris 39 d
Tiguentourine 37 e
Tijuana 18 c
Tikhoretsk 54 e
Tikrit 39 d
Tiksi 52 m
Tilamuta 69 i
Tilemsés 41 d
Tilemsi 36 z
Tillabéri 41 b
Tillamook 14 g
Tillia 41 d
Tilrhemt 34 u
Timané 28 k
Timan Ridge 50 h
Timaru 79 s
Timbaúba 27 v
Timbedgha 40 g
Timber Creek 73 b
Timbouctou (Timbuktu) 40 l
Timbuktu 40 l
Timeiaouine 37 n
Timétrine 36 y
Timia 37 r
Timimoun 36 m
Timiris, Cap 36 n
Timişoara 35 e
Timmins 16 i
Timón 27 q
Timor 69 x
Timor Sea 69 x
Timpton 52 y
Timsah 37 w
Tindouf 36 g
Tiné 42 e
Tinerhir 36 i
Tinfouchy 36 i
Tingo María 24 x
Tingri 61 i
Tinogasta 28 r
Tinos 35 t
Tinrhert Hamada 37 e
Tinsukiā 62 d
Tintina 28 u
Tinyay 53 a
Tin Zaouatene 37 o
Tioman 68 h
Tipperary 73 c
Tiracambu, Serra do 27 a
Tirana 35 d
Tiranë (Tirana) 35 d
Tiraspol 35 j
Tirekh 52 m
Tirekhtyakh 53 c
Tirgelir 53 e
Tirgu Mureş 35 g
Tirich Mir 60 l
Tiroungoulou 42 e
Tiruchchirappalli 64 f
Tirunelveli 64 t
Tiruntán 24 l
Tirupati 64 h
Tisdale 15 e
Tisisat Falls 43 b
Tisza 35 d
Tit 37 p
Titaf 36 m
Tit-Ary 52 l
Titicaca, Lake 25 o
Titule 42 t
Titusville 20 m
Tizimïn 19 w
Tizi Ouzou 34 v
Tiznit 36 f
Tlacotalpan 19 r
Tlalamabele 49 b
Tlaltenango 18 z
Tlapacoyan 19 q
Tlaxiaco 19 p
Tlemcen 34 s
Tlisen 37 l
Tmed Bu Haschlscha 37 y
Toamasina 47 r
Toba & Kakar Ranges 60 j
Tobago 23 j
Toba, Lake 68 d
Tobelo 67 y
Tobermorey 73 t
Tobermorey (Australia) 73 x
Tobermorey (Canada) 16 i
Tobi 70 c
Tobo 70 o
Tobol' 55 e
Tobol' (River) 55 d
Tobol'sk 51 n
Tobruk 38 e
Tocache Nuevo 24 w
Tocantínia 26 z
Tocantinópolis 26 z
Tocantins 26 z
Tocopilla 28 c
Tocorpuri 28 e
Tocuyo 23 d
Todertang 43 n
Todos Santos (Bolivia) 25 r
Todos Santos (Mexico) 18 u
Toéssé 40 m
Togiak 11 n
Togliatti 54 k
Togo 41
Togtoh 57 t
Togyz 55 d
Tok 11 h
Tokar 38 z
Tokko 52 u
Tokko (River) 52 v
Tokoroa 79 v
Toktogul 55 x
Toktogul Reservoir 55 w
Tokuma 53 a
Tokushima 58 y
Tōkyō 59 o
Tolbo Nuur 56 i
Toledo (Brazil) 29 o
Toledo (Philippines) 67 i
Toledo (Spain) 34 q
Toledo (USA) 16 u
Toledo Bend Reservoir 20 d
Tolga 37 c
Toli 56 r
Toliara 47 n
Tolka 51 s
Tolka (River) 51 r
Tolo, Gulf of 69 h
Tolon 52 r
Tolstoy, Cape 53 x
Toluca 19 o
Tolybay 55 d
Tom' 56 g
Tomah 16 q
Tomar 55 l
Tomatlán 18 y
Tombador, Serra do 25 x
Tombigbee 20 h
Tombôco 44 f
Tômbua
(Porto Alexandre) 48 e
Tomé-Açu 26 m
Tomi 42 o
Tomini, Gulf of 69 g
Tommot 52 y
Tomo 23 q
Tompo 53 b
Tom Price 72 t
Tom Price, Mount 72 t
Tomra 61 i
Tomsk 51 t
Tomtor 53 a
Tomtor (Cherskogo
Mountains) 53 e
Tonalá 19 s
Tonatins 23 r
Tondano 67 w
Tonga 42 k
Tonga (State) 231 z

Tongguzbasti 56 q
Tonghae 58 v
Tonghai 62 u
Tongian Islands 67 u
Tongjiang 58 k
Tongliao 58 e
Tongren 62 h
Tongren (Wu Jiang) 62 m
Tongsa Dzong 61 l
Tongshan 63 d
Tongtian 62 e
Tongtianheyan 62 b
Tongulakh 52 j
Tongxin 57 q
Tongyu 58 e
Tongzi 62 l
Toni 42 v
Tonk 61 o
Tonking 62 w
Tonking, Gulf of 62 y
Tonkling 63 f
Tonle Sap 65 m
Tonnel'nyy 57 h
Tonopah 14 x
Tonsina 11 g
Tontantins 25 c
Tonzang 62 p
Toolebuc 73 v
Toompine 77 j
Toora-Chem 56 l
Toowoomba 78 f
Topeka 15 v
Topia 18 k
Topko 53 p
Top Springs 73 c
Torbat-e-Heidariye 60 d
Torbat-e-Jam 60 d
Torbert, Mount 11 d
Torgo 52 u
Torim 18 h
Torino (Turin) 34 k
Torit 42 y
Torne 33 i
Torngat Mountains 13 y
Tornio 33 i
Toro 28 p
Torodi 41 b
Toro Doum 41 m
Toro, Lago del 30 t
Toronto 16 w
Tororo 42 z
Torrabai 48 f
Torrens Creek 74 o
Torrens, Lake 77 e
Torreón 18 l
Torres Strait 73 k
Tortkuduk 55 k
Tortolas 28 p
Tortosa 34 g
Tortuga 23 f
Torud 39 l
Torun 33 t
Torzhok 50 n
Toson Cengal 56 m
Tostado 28 v
Toteng 48 m
Totma 50 q
Totness 23 z
Totora 28 f
Tottori 58 y
Touba 40 i
Toubkal 36 g
Touboro 41 k
Touggourt 34 w
Tougué 40 e
Toukoto 40 g
Toulépleu 40 u
Toulon 34 j
Toulouse 34 g
Toungoo 62 r
Tours 34 g
Toussoro 42 e
Touws River 48 x
Townsend 15 a
Townsville 74 q
Toxkan 56 o
Toyama 58 z
Toyon-Tirekh 52 m
Tozeur 34 x
Trabzon 54 r
Trail 14 j
Traill Island 91 r
Trang 65 v
Transantarctic Mountains 83 v
Trans Canada Highway 16 c
Transhimalaya 61 g
Trapani 34 z
Traralgon 77 y
Trarza 40 c
Travers 79 t
Treinta-y-Tres 31 f
Trelew 30 l
Trenque Lauquen 31 a
Trenton 16 z
Tres Arroyos 31 b
Três Bocas 25 a
Tres Coraçoes 29 h
Tres Isletas 28 w
Tres Lagos 30 u
Tres Marias 29 g
Tres Marias Islands 18 w
Tres Marias Reservoir 29 g
Tres Puntas, Cabo 30 y
Tres Rios 29 i
Triangulos 19 t
Trichur 64 e
Trier 34 j
Trieste 35 a
Tríkala 35 r
Trincomalee 64 v
Trinidad and Tobago 23 j
Trinidad (Bolivia) 25 s
Trinidad (Colombia) 23 o
Trinidad (Cuba) 20 z
Trinidad (USA) 15 q
Trinity Peninsula 82 t
Tripolis (Greece) 35 s
Tripoli (Lebanon) 38 l
Tripoli (Libya) 37 i
Tripolitania 37 h
Tristan da Canha 222 y
Trivandrum 64 r
Trobriand or Kiriwina Island 71 r
Trofimovsk 52 l
Troickoje 56 f
Trois Rivières 17 a
Troitsk 55 d
Troitsko-Pechorsk 50 w
Troitskoye 55 a
Trombetas 25 l
Trompsburg 49 n
Tromsö 33 g
Trondheim 33 c
Trondheimsfjord 33 c
Trosh 50 j
Troy 35 u
Troyekurovo 54 e
Troyes 34 i
Troynoy 51 f
Trujillo (Honduras) 20 v
Trujillo (Peru) 24 u
Trujillo (Spain) 34 p
Truk Islands 71 e
Truro 17 f
Tsaidam Basin 56 w
Tsaochuang 63 f
Tsaratanana Mountains 47 e
Tsau 48 m
Tsavo 45 j
Tsavo National Park 45 k
Tschita 52 r
Tsentral'nyy 56 g
Tsévié 41 n
Tshabong 48 z
Tshane 48 l
Tshele 44 e
Tshikapa 44 k
Tshimbalanga 44 z
Tshofa 45 a
Tsholotsho 49 c
Tshuapa 44 l
Tsihombe 47 p
Tsimafana 47 o
Tsimlyanskoye Reservoir 54 g
Tsinan 63 e
Tsingtao 57 z
Tsining 57 u
Tsinling Shan 56 z
Tsiribihina 47 p
Tsiroanomandidy 47 p
Tsitsihar 58 f
Tsoe 49 a
Tsugaru Channel 59 b
Tsumeb 48 j
Tsumkwe 48 k
Tsunyi 62 l
Tsuruga 58 z
Tsushima 58 v
Tswiza 49 f
Tuamotu Archipelago 230 p
Tuan Giao 62 v
Tuangku 65 u
Tuapse 54 r
Tuareg 40 m
Tubaro 29 r
Tubuai Islands 230 o
Tubutama 18 g
Tuckanarra 76 f
Tucson 18 g
Tucumá 26 x
Tucumcari 15 r
Tucupita 23 i
Tucuruí 26 l
Tuekta 56 f
Tueré 26 k
Tugela 49 r
Tugolukovo 54 f
Tuguegarao 67 g
Tugur 53 p
Tugur (River) 53 o
Tukalan 52 a
Tukangbesi Islands 69 v
Tuktoyaktuk 11 l
Tula (Mexico) 19 o
Tula (Russia) 54 d
Tula Mountains 84 m
Tulancingo 19 p
Tulcán 24 i
Tulcea 35 i
Tuli 49 d
Tuli (River) 49 d
Tulia 15 s
Tulihe 57 m
Tulit'a (Fort Norman) 12 b
Tully 74 c
Tulsa 15 v
Tulua 22 y
Tulum 19 w
Tulun 57 a
Tumaco 24 h
Tumanskiy 10 g
Tumany 53 k
Tumat 53 d
Tumatumari 23 x
Tumba, Lake 44 i
Tumbangsamba 69 b
Tumbes 24 g
Tumen 58 i
Tumkur 64 f
Tumu (Ghana) 40 l
Tumu (Libya) 37 v
Tumucumaque, Serra 26 i
Tunduma 45 t
Tunduru 45 v
Tungabhadra Reservoir 64 e
Tungabhadra (River) 64 f
Tungaru 42 k
Tungchuan 62 m
Tungchwan 62 v
Tunghwa 58 f
Tungtin, Lake 63 b
Tungus-Khaya 52 k
Tunguskoye Mountains 51 w
Tuni 61 s
Tunis 34 y
Tunis, Gulf of 34 y
Tunisia 34/37
Tunja 23 n
Tunor 52 c
Tunuyán 28 q
Tunuyán (River) 28 r
Tunxi 63 f
Tuolba 52 w
Tuostakh 53 c
Tuostakh (River) 53 c
Tupanacca 25 h
Tupelo 19 i
Tupik 52 v
Tupinambarama, Ilha 25 k
Tupiza 28 f
Tupper 12 q
Tupungato 30 i
Tuquan 58 d
Túquerres 24 i
Turabah 39 o
Tura (China) 56 s
Tura (India) 61 y
Tura (Russia) 51 z
Tura (River) 50 y
Turaif 39 a
Turbah 43 g
Turbat 60 s
Turee Creek 72 u
Turgattal 55 e
Turgay 55 e
Turgayskaya Valley 55 e
Turgen 56 i
Türgen (High Altai) 56 x
Turhal 35 m
Turiaçu 27 b
Turin 34 k
Turinsk 50 z
Turkana, Lake 43 n
Turkannakh 52 j
Turkestan 55 u
Turkey 35/54
Turkey Creek 73 a
Turkmenbashi 54 z
Turkmenistan 55 o
Turks and Caicos Islands 21 s
Turku 33 h
Turneffe Islands 19 w
Túrnovo 35 h
Turnu-Severin 35 f
Turočak 56 g
Turpan 56 u
Turrialba 22 h
Turtkul' 55 q
Turkhan 51 h
Turukhansk 51 h
Turum 42 k
Tuscaloosa 20 h
Tuticorin 64 t
Tutóia 27 d
Tutonchany 51 x
Tutonchany (River) 51 j
Tuul Gol 57 d
Tuvalu 231 y
Tüvsinsiree 57 g
Tuxpan 18 x
Tuxpan (Bay of Campeche) 19 q
Tuxtepec 20 o
Tuxtla Gutiérrez 19 s
Tuyen Quang 62 x
Tuyun 62 y
Tuz, Lake 35 y
Tuz Khurmatu 39 e
Tuzla 35 d
Tvayan 53 x
Tver 50 o
Twee Rivier 48 k
Twee Rivieren 48 y
Twilight Cove 76 k
Twin Falls (Canada) 17 e
Twin Falls (USA) 14 y
Twin Rocks 76 h
Twizel 79 s
Tyler 19 e
Tym 51 s
Tymovskoye 59 d
Tynda 52 w
Tynset 33 d
Tyre (Sour) 38 k
Tyrma 58 k
Tyrrhenian Sea 34 z
Tyry 53 c
Tyubelyakh 53 e
Tyugene 52 l
Tyugyuren 53 e
Tyukalinsk 55 j
Tyukyan 52 h
Tyumen 50 z
Tyung 52 h
Tyungulyu 52 m
Tzaneen 49 e
Tzekung 62 j
Tzepo 57 x

U

Uainambi 25 b
Uanle Uen 43 u
Uaroo 72 r
Uatum 25 j
Uaupés 25 d
Uaupés (River) 25 c
Ubari 37 u
Ube 58 w
Ubeda 34 q
Uberaba 29 e
Uberaba, Lagoa 28 l
Uberlandia 29 e
Ubon Ratchathani 66 h
Ubundu 45 a
Ucayali 24 l
Uch 60 l
Uchami 51 y
Uchami (River) 51 x
Uchiura Bay 59 c
Uchkuduk 55 r
Uchur 53 n
Uda 53 n
Uda (Vostochny Mountains) 56 m
Uda (Yablon Mountains) 57 g
Udachnyy 52 e
Udaipur 60 z
Udanna 53 f
Uddevaua 33 d
Udd, Lake 33 f
Udine 34 m
Udokan 52 u
Udon Thani 65 l
Udskoye 53 n
Uebonti 69 h
Uele (Russia) 52 g
Uele (Dem. Rep. Congo) 42 r
Uelen 10 l
Uel'kal 10 h
Uengan, Cape 50 m
Ufa 55 a
Ufa (River) 55 a
Ugagli 52 y
Ugalla 45 e
Uganda 42/45
Ugashik 11 o
Ughelli 41 r
Ugoyan 52 x
Ugulan 53 x
Ugun 52 z
Uige 44 g
Uil 54 m
Uil (River) 55 a
Uinta Mountains 15 n
Uis Mine 48 g
Uitenhage 49 n
Ujjain 61 o
Ujung Pandang 69 s
Ukerewe, Islands 45 f
Ukhta 50 v
Ukiah 14 t
Ukraine 35 j
Ukta 53 g
Ukukit 52 g
Ukwi 48 l
Ulaan Uul 56 m
Ulaanbaatar (Ulan Bator) 57 e
Ulaga 53 a
Ulakhan Botuobuya 52 e
Ulan 56 z
Ulan Bator 57 e
Ulan-Khol 54 v
Ulansuhai Nur 57 s
Ulan-Ude 57 e
Uldz Gol 57 i
Ulety 57 h
Ulgij 56 h
Ulgumdzha 52 h
Ulgumun 52 g
Uliastaj 56 m
Ulindi 45 c
Ul'kan 57 e

Ul'kenkaroy, Lake 55 j
Ullawarra 72 r
Ulovo 53 j
Ulsan 58 v
Ulua 22 d
Ulukuut 53 o
Ulundi 49 s
Ulungur 56 h
Ulungur Hu 56 g
Uluru (Ayers Rock) 77 a
Ulu Tau 55 g
Ul'ya 53 r
Ul'yanovsk 54 i
Ul'yanovskoye 55 k
Umala 25 p
Uman' 35 j
Umbakumba 73 g
Ume 33 g
Umeå 33 h
Umm as Samim 39 y
Umm as Sawin 60 n
Umm el Abid 37 j
Umm Inderaba 42 j
Umm Keddada 42 h
Umm Luj 38 z
Umm Mirdi 38 w
Umm Qasr 39 g
Umm Ruwaba 42 k
Umm Saggat 42 e
Umm Sa'id 39 w
Umm Saiyala 42 k
Umnak 10 y
Umtata 49 q
Umzinto 49 s
Unaí 29 f
Unaizah 39 d
Unalakleet 11 b
Unalaska 10 y
Unare 23 g
Uncia 28 f
Ungava Bay 13 x
Ungava Peninsula 13 u
Unio 27 q
Unio da Vitória 29 q
Unio dos Palmares 27 v
Unimak 10 z
Unimak Pass 10 z
Unini 23 v
Unión 30 l
United Arab Emirates 39
United States of America 11/14-20
United States Range 91 g
Unža 50 r
Uoyan 57 n
Upata 23 i
Upemba, Lake 45 b
Upernavik 90 m
Upington 48 y
Upper Egypt 38 v
Upper Red Lake 15 j
Uppsala 33 f
Uqlat al Suqur 39 b
Urad Qianqi 57 s
Ura J'ube 55 u
Urak 53 r
Ural 54 l
Ural'sk 54 k
Urals, South 55 b
Urandangi 73 u
Uranium City 12 u
Uraricoera 23 w
Uraricoera (River) 23 v
Urbano Santos 27 c
Urcos 25 n
Urdakh 53 h
Urdžar 56 d
Uren 50 s
Urengoy 51 e
Urfa 54 r
Urga 55 o
Urgal 58 k
Urgenč 55 p
Urho 56 f
Uriariti 25 x
Uritskiy 55 f
Uritskoye 52 w
Urluk 57 e
Urmia, Lake 54 u
Urru Co 61 j
Uruaçu 29 e
Uruapan 18 z
Urubamba 24 z
Urubamba (River) 24 z
Urucará 25 k
Urucu 25 f
Uruçui 27 p
Uruçui, Serra do 27 o
Uruguaiana 28 z
Uruguay 28-29/31
Uruguay (River) 28 x
Urumchi 56 t
Urup 59 h
Urusha 52 w
Uruzgan 60 i
Uryung-Khaya 52 f
Usa 50 j
Usakos 48 h
Usal'gin 53 p
Us'-Bel'dir 56 m
Useless Loop 72 p
Ushiarah 39 f
Ushakova 51 e
Ushuaia 30 w
Ushumun 52 y
Usino 71 n
Üsküdar 35 j
Usman 52 x
Usolje Sibirskoje 57 b
Uspenskiy 55 k
Ussuri 58 l
Ussuriysk 58 k
Ust'-Avam 51 j
Ust'-Belaya 10 f
Ust'-Belogolovoye 53 x
Ust'-Charky 53 c
Ust'-Chayka 52 p
Ust'-Džilinda 57 h
Ust'-Ilimpeya 52 b
Ust'-Kada 57 b
Ust'-Kamengorsk 56 e
Ust'Kamo 51 y
Ust'-Kara 50 m
Ust'-Karenga 52 t
Ust'-Karsk 57 k
Ust'-Kata 55 b
Ust'Kolik'yegan 51 q
Ust'Kulom 50 u
Ust'-Kureyka 51 h
Ust'-Kut 52 o
Ust'-Kuyga 53 b
Ust'Ilimsk 52 n
Ust'-Maya 53 n
Ust'-Mil 53 n
Ust'-Muya 52 t
Ust'-Nera 53 e
Ust'Niman 53 n
Ust'Nyukzha 52 v
Ustobe 56 n
Ust-Olenëk 52 h
Ust'Omchug 53 h
Ust'-Ordynskij 52 o
Ust'Ozernoye 51 u
Ust'-Ozilinda 52 s
Ust'Pit 51 w
Ust'-Port 51 g
Ust'-Sopochnoye 53 w
Ust'-Sugoy 53 j
Ust'-Tigil' 53 y
Ust'-Timpton 52 y
Ust'Tsil'ma 50 u
Ust'Tym 51 s
Ust'Tyrma 58 j
Ust'-Un'ya 52 z
Ust-Urt Plateau 54 z
Ust'-Uyskoye 55 e
Ustya 50 r
Usu 56 r
Usumacinta 19 u
Utah 14 z
Utah Lake 15 n
Utica 16 z
Utila 20 v
Utkholok 53 x
Utopia 73 s
Utrecht (Netherlands) 33 n
Utrecht (South Africa) 49 r
Utsunomiya 59 o
Utta 54 i
Utubulak 56 g
Uummannaq 90 m
Uvalde 19 b
Uvinza 45 e
Uvs Nuur 56 j
Uweinat 38 r
Uyandi 53 d
Uyandina 53 e
Uyar 56 k
Uyëdey 53 c
Uyole 45 g
Uyuk 55 v
Uyuni 28 e
Uzbekistan 55 r
Užgorod 35 f
Uzhur 56 h
Užice 35 d
Uzynkair 55 q

V

Vaal 49 q
Vaal Reservoir 49 p
Vaalwater 49 c
Vaasa 33 i
Vác 35 d
Vacaria 29 q
Vach 51 r
Vachs 55 u
Vadodara 60 z
Vaduz 34 k
Vaga 50 r
Vaigač 50 k
Valcheta 30 l
Valdés Peninsula 30 m
Valdez 11 g
Valdivia 30 g
Val-d'Or 16 k
Valdosta 20 k
Vale de Sonho 29 b
Valenç 27 t
Valença do Piauí 27 q
Valence 34 i
Valencia (Spain) 34 s
Valencia (Venezuela) 23 e
Valenciennes 34 h
Valentim, Serra do 27 p
Valentine 15 t
Valera 23 c
Valga 33 k
Valki 35 m
Valladolid (Mexico) 19 w
Valladolid (Spain) 34 d
Valle de la Pascua 23 f
Valle de Santiago 19 n
Valledupar 23 a
Valle Grande 25 s
Vallejo 14 u
Vallenar 28 o
Valletta 35 n
Valley City 15 h
Valleyview 14 k
Valparaíso 28 o
Valsad 60 z
Vals, Cape 70 u
Valuyki 54 d
Vanado Tuerto 28 v
Vanavara 52 n
Van Buren 17 d
Vancouver 14 g
Vancouver Island 14 e
Vandalia 16 r
Van Diemen, Cape 73 b
Van Diemen Gulf 73 c
Vänern, Lake 33 e
Vangaindrano 47 r
Van Gölu 54 t
Vangou 58 l
Vangunu 71 w
Vang Vieng 62 v
Van Horn 18 l
Vanimo 70 x
Van, Lake 54 t
Van Rees Mountains 70 u
Vanrhynsdorp 48 x
Vanrook 73 k
Vansittart Island 13 e
Vantaa 33 j
Vanua Levu 75 m
Vnuatu 75 d
Van Wyksvlei 48 y
Vanzevat 50 z
Vanzhil'kynak 51 s
Varanasi 61 s
Varaždin 35 b
Vargas Guerra 24 j
Varillas 28 c
Varna (Russia) 55 d
Varna (Bulgaria) 35 i
Várzea Grande 25 y
Vasa Barris 27 t
Vasjugan 51 r
Västerås 33 f
Västervik 33 f
Vasyuganye 51 p
Vatican City 34 m
Vatnajökull 32 d
Vättern, Lake 33 e
Vatyna 10 e
Vaughn 15 q
Vaughn (Montana) 15 a
Vaughn (New Mexico) 18 l
Vaupés 25 a
Växjö 33 s
Vayalpad 64 g
Vayvida 51 x
Vegreville 14 m
Vel 50 q
Velasco, Sierra de 28 r
Veles 35 e
Velhas 29 h
Velichayevskoye 54 u
Velikaya 10 f
Velikaya Kema 58 m
Velikije Luki 33 z
Velikiy Ustyug 50 s
Velikovisochnoye 50 i
Vella Lavella 71 u
Vellore 64 g
Velmo 1-oye 51 w
Velsk 50 r
Venada 49 e
Venado Tuerto 31 a
Vendenga 50 t
Venezia (Venice) 34 m
Venezuela 23/26
Venezuela, Gulf of 23 c
Veniaminof, Mount 11 p
Venice 34 m
Venice, Gulf of 34 m
Ventuari 23 s
Ventura 14 w
Vera 28 w
Veracruz 19 q
Vera, Laguna 28 y
Veraval 60 x
Verde, Cape 40 a
Verde Grande 29 i
Verde (River) (Brazil) 29 b
Verde (River) (Mexico) 19 o
Verde (River) (Paraguay) 28 j
Verdigris 15 w
Vereeniging 46 q
Vergemont 73 x
Verissimo-Sarmento 44 k
Verkhneimbatskoye 51 v
Verkhneural'sk 55 c
Verkhnevilyuysk 52 i
Verkhniy Tura 50 x
Verkhnyaya Amga 52 y
Verkhnyaya Taimyra 51 l
Verkhnyaya Toyma 50 s
Verkhoyansk 53 a
Verkhoyanskiy Mountains 52 k
Vermelha, Lagoa 29 p
Vermont 17 n
Vernadsky 82 t
Vernal 15 o
Verona 34 l
Versino-Darasunskij 57 j
Veshenskaya 54 f
Vest Fjord 33 e
Véstia 29 c
Veszprém 35 c
Vetekhtina 52 u
Vetluga 50 s
Vetluzhskiy 50 s
Vetrenyy 53 h
Vey Vozh 50 v
Vezdekhodnaya 52 d
Viacha 25 p
Vicenza 34 m
Vichada 23 q
Vichadero 29 n
Vicksburg 19 h
Victor Harbor 77 s
Victoria (Argentina) 28 w
Victoria (Brazil) 26 j
Victoria (British Columbia) 14 g
Victoria (Chile) 30 h
Victoria (Hong Kong) 63 q
Victoria (Texas) 19 c
Victoria de las Tunas 21 o
Victoria Falls 49 b
Victoria Island 12 h
Victoria, Lake 45 f
Victoria Land 86 t
Victoria (Mount, Burma) 62 o
Victoria, Mount (Fiji) 75 l
Victoria (Mount, Papua New Guinea) 71 o
Victoria Range 76 c
Victoria River Downs 73 b
Victoria (River) 73 b
Victoria (State) 77 w
Victoria Strait 12 l
Victoria West 48 z
Victorica 30 l
Victorino 23 r
Vicuña Mackenna 30 m
Vidim 57 c
Vidin 35 f
Viedma 30 m
Viedma, Lago 30 u
Vienna 35 b
Vien Pou Kha 62 u
Vientiane 62 v
Vietnam 62/66
Vigan 67 f
Vigia 26 m
Vigo 34 a
Vijayawada 64 i
Vikna 33 c
Vila 75 e
Vila Bittencourt 25 b
Vila de Sena 46 u
Vila Velha 29 k
Vila Velha (Serra Lombarda) 26 k
Vilhena 25 v
Viliga-Kushka 53 l
Viljujskoje Reservoir 52 e
Vilkitskogo 92 k
Vilkicky 51 d
Villa Ahumada 18 k
Villa Angela 28 v
Villa Bella 25 r
Villa Delores 28 s
Villaguay 28 x
Villa Guillermina 28 w
Villa Hayes 28 y
Villahermosa 19 t
Villa Iris 30 m
Villa Maria 28 u
Villa Media Agua 28 q
Villa Montes 28 h
Villa Ocampo 18 k
Villa Ojo de Aqua 28 u
Villarrica 30 h
Villa San Martín 28 t
Villa Unión (Argentina) 28 q
Villa Unión (Mexico) 18 x
Villavicencio 23 n
Villazón 28 f
Vilnius 33 w
Vilyuy 52 j
Vilyuy Mountains 52 d
Vilyuysk 52 j
Vindhya Range 61 n
Vineland 16 z
Vinh 62 x
Vinita 16 n
Vinnitsa 35 i
Vinson Massif 81 d
Vioolsdrif 48 v
Virac 67 i
Virawah 60 x

Virden 15 f
Virginia (Minnesota) 15 k
Virginia (State) 16 x
Virginia Range 76 i
Virgin Islands 21 x
Virú 24 x
Virundunagar 64 g
Visalia 14 v
Visby 33 g
Vischarv 55 w
Viscount Melville Sound 12 g
Viseu 27 a
Vishakhapatnam 61 t
Vista Alegre 25 c
Vistula 35 e
Vitebsk 33 z
Viterbo 34 m
Vitichi 28 f
Viti Levu 75 k
Vitim 52 r
Vitim (River) 52 s
Vitim Plateau 52 s
Vitimskiy 52 s
Vitoria 34 d
Vitória 29 k
Vitória da Conquista 29 j
Vivi 51 y
Vivi (River) 51 k
Vivi, Lake 51 k
Vize 51 d
Vizeaino Desert 18 e
Vizianagaram 61 t
Vizinga 50 t
Vladikavkaz 54 u
Vladimir 54 f
Vladivostok 58 k
Vlorë 35 d
Vltava 35 a
Vohidiala 47 r
Volcán Tres Virgenes 18 f
Volga 54 h
Volga Heights 54 h
Volgograd 54 h
Volksrust 49 r
Volochanka 51 j
Volochsk 53 m
Volodarskoye 55 h
Vologda 50 q
Volokolamsk 50 o
Volokon 52 o
Volonga 50 g
Vólos 35 s
Vol'sk 54 i
Volta Lake 41 n
Volta Redonda 29 i
Vorkuta 50 l
Vorob'yeva 52 n
Voronezh 54 e
Vorontsovka 52 s
Vorozheyka 56 h
Vosburg 48 z
Vostochny Mountains 56 l
Vostok I 85 o
Votkinsk 50 v
Vovodo 42 s
Voyeykov Ice Shelf 87 e
Voyvozh 50 w
Vozrozhdeniya 55 p
Vraca 35 f
Vrendenburg 48 w
Vrsac 35 e
Vryburg 49 n
Vryheid 49 s
Vung Tau 66 j
Vyaz'ma 54 b
Vyborg 33 l
Vyčegda 50 v
Vydrino 56 m
Vym' 50 u
Vyngapur 51 q
Vysni Volocek 50 o
Vyzakova 54 i

W

Wa 40 l
Wabag 70 z
Wabash 16 s
Wabowden 15 h
Wabush 17 d
Waco 19 d
Waco-Kungo 44 t
Wad 60 i
Wad Banda 42 i
Waddan 37 k
Waddington, Mount 14 f
Wadi ad Dawasir 39 q
Wadi al Akhdar 38 m
Wadi al Arish 38 j
Wadi al Batin 39 f
Wadi al Ghadaf 39 c
Wadi al Hamd 38 m
Wadi al Hamim 38 c
Wadi al Hayl 39 a
Wadi al Jarin 39 p
Wadi al Jawf 39 r
Wadi al Jiz 39 v
Wadi Allaqi 38 w
Wadi Araba 38 k
Wadi Ar'ar 39 b
Wadi ar Rimah 39 d
Wadi as Sirhan 38 m
Wadi Aswad 39 z
Wadi ath Thartar 39 c
Wadi bin Khawtar 39 x
Wadi Bishah 39 p
Wadi Gabgaba 38 w
Wadi Garara 38 w
Wadi Hadain 38 x
Wadi Halfa 38 v
Wadi Hawran 39 b
Wadi Ibib 38 y
Wadi Masilah 39 u
Wadi Oitbit 39 y
Wadi Oko 38 y
Wadi Qena 38 j
Wadi Seidna 38 v
Wadi Shihan 39 w
Wadi Tathlith 39 q
Wadi Tibal 39 b
Wad Medani 42 m
Wager Bay 13 b
Wagga Wagga 77 y
Wagin 76 e
Wagon Mound 15 q
Wagontire 14 v
Waigeo 70 c
Waikabubak 69 s
Waikato 79 v
Wailuku 18 q
Waingapu 69 t
Wainwright (Canada) 15 a
Wainwright (USA) 11 b
Waipahu 18 p
Waipara 79 t
Wairoa 79 x
Waitaki 79 s
Wajir 43 q
Waka 42 p
Wakatipu, Lake 79 q
Wakayama 58 z
Wake Island 231 l
Wakkanai 59 c
Walagan 52 x
Wałbrzych 35 b
Walcott 14 e
Waldburg Range 76 e
Walden 15 p
Wales (UK) 32 w
Wales (USA) 10 m
Wales Island 13 c
Walewale 40 m
Walgett 78 c
Walgreen Coast 81 c
Walikale 45 c
Walinga 71 o
Wallabi Group 76 b
Wallace 14 k
Wallal Downs 72 v
Walleroo 77 f
Walla Walla 14 j
Walsenburg 15 q
Walsh 74 b
Walterboro 20 m
Walvis Bay 48 g
Wamba (Nigeria) 41 g
Wamba (River) 44 i
Wamba (Dem. Rep. Congo) 42 v
Wamena 70 v
Wanaaring 78 a
Wandels Sea 91 j
Wandingzhen 62 s
Wandoan 78 e
Wanganui 79 u
Wanganui (River) 79 v
Wangaratta 78 o
Wangmo 62 x
Wangqing 58 i
Wang Saphung 65 k
Wanhsien 62 l
Wanning 63 n
Wannoo 76 c
Wanyuan 62 l
Warangal 64 h
Waratah Bay 77 x
Warburton 72 z
Warburton (River) 77 f
Warburton Lake 12 t
Warder 43 u
Wardha 61 q
Warin Chamrap 66 h
Warmbad 46 q
Warner Robins 20 k
Waroona 76 d
Warrabri 73 r
Warrawagine 72 v
Warrego 74 p
Warrenton 49 n
Warri 41 r
Warrnambool 77 v
Warsaw 33 u
Warta 33 t
Warwick 74 t
Warzawa (Warsaw) 33 u
Washington DC 16 y
Washington (State) 14 h
Washington, Cape 86 s
Washington Court House 16 u
Washington Land 91 f
Washington, Mount 17 o
Washita 15 v
Watampone 69 t
Waterbury 17 n
Waterford 32 y
Waterloo 16 p
Waterton 16 y
Watertown 15 i
Waterval Boven 49 r
Waterville 17 b
Watsa 42 v
Watsi 44 k
Watsi Kengo 44 k
Watson Lake 12 n
Wau 42 h
Wauchope 73 r
Wau el Kebir 37 x
Wau en Namus 37 y
Wausau (Massachusetts) 17 n
Wausau (Wisconsin) 16 d
Wave Hill 73 c
Wawa (Canada) 16 g
Wawa (Nigeria) 41 c
Waxxari 56 t
Waycross 20 k
Webster City 15 x
Weda 69 m
Weda Bay 69 m
Weda, Tulek 69 m
Weddell Sea 82 y
Wei 62 k
Weichang 57 x
Weifang 58 o
Weimar 33 q
Weinan 62 m
Weining 62 j
Weipa 73 k
Weiser 14 k
Weisse 51 b
Weiya 56 x
Welbourn Hill 77 c
Weldiya 43 d
Welkite 43 c
Welkom 49 o
Wellesley Islands 73 i
Wellington (Australia) 78 d
Wellington (Chile) 30 s
Wellington (New Zealand) 79 v
Wellington (South Africa) 48 x
Wells 14 y
Wema 44 l
Wenatchee 14 i
Wenchhow 63 h
Wendo 43 p
Wendover 14 y
Wenlock 74 a
Wenquan 56 q
Wenquan (Tanggula Shan) 61 m
Wenshan 62 w
Wentworth 77 i
Wepener 49 p
Wernecke Mountains 11 k
Weser 33 p
Wessel Islands 73 g
West Bank 38 l
West Cape 79 p
West Cape Howe 76 r
Western Australia 76 f
Western Cordillera 24-25/28
Western Cordillera (Colombia) 22 y
Western Ghats 60/64
Western Sahara 36
Western Sierra Madre 18 k
West Falkland 31 o
West Fayu 71 a
West Frankfort 16 r
Westgate 77 l
West Group 76 h
Westhope 15 f
West Ice Shelf 85 r
Westlock 14 m
Westmar 74 s
West Memphis 16 q
Westmoreland 73 h
West Palm Beach 20 m
West Papua 70 u
Westport (Ireland) 32 t
Westport (New Zealand) 79 s
West Siberian Sea 51 g
West Virginia 16 v
West Wyalong 78 b
Wetar 69 x
Wetaskiwin 14 m
Wewak 70 z
Wexford 32 v
Weyburn 15 e
Whakatane 79 w
Whale Cove 13 n
Whangarei 79 h
Wheeler Peak (Nevada) 14 y
Wheeler Peak (New Mexico) 15 q
Wheeling 16 w
Whidby Point 77 d
Whim Creek 72 t
White 15 y
White Cliffs 77 i
Whitecourt 14 k
Whitefish Lake 12 v
Whitehorse 11 l
White Island 92 d
White, Lake 73 o
White Nile 38/42
White River (Canada) 16 g
White River (USA) 15 t
White Sea 50 b
White Volta 40 m
Whitewood 73 y
Whitney, Mount 14 w
Whittle, Cape 17 h
Wholdaia Lake 12 w
Whyalla 77 e
Wichita 15 v
Wichita Falls 19 b
Wien (Vienna) 35 b
Wiesbaden 34 j
Wight, Isle of 32 y
Wilcannia 77 i
Wilczek Island 50 l
Wilhelmshaven 33 o
Wilkes Land 87 a
Wilkins Sound 82 w
Wilemstad 23 d
Willeroo 73 c
Williamsburg 16 y
Williams Lake 14 h
Williamson 16 v
Williamsport 16 x
Willis Islands 74 f
Williston (S.Africa) 48 y
Williston (USA) 15 e
Williston Lake 12 p
Willmar 15 j
Willow 11 f
Willowmore 48 z
Willowra 73 q
Wills, Lake 73 n
Wilmington (Carolina) 21 a
Wilmington (Delaware) 16 y
Wilpena 77 g
Wilson Bluff 76 m
Wilson's Promontory 77 y
Wiluna 76 g
Winburg 49 p
Windau 33 h
Windhoek 48 i
Windorah 77 i
Windsor (Canada) 17 j
Windsor (USA) 16 u
Winisk 16 g
Winisk (River) 16 f
Winisk Lake 16 f
Winnemucca 14 w
Winning 72 r
Winnipeg 15 i
Winnipeg, Lake 15 h
Winnipeg (River) 15 j
Winnipeg Beach 15 i
Winnipegosis 15 g
Winnipegosis, Lake 15 g
Winona (Mississippi) 19 i
Winona (Wisconsin) 16 p
Winslow 15 n
Winston Salem 16 w
Winter Garden 20 l
Winterhoek, Groot 48 x
Winton 73 x
Wisconsin 16 q
Wiseman 11 f
Wismar 33 q
Witbank 49 r
Witherspoon, Mount 11 g
Witpütz 48 v
Witrivier 49 f
Witsand 48 x
Wittenberge 33 q
Wittenoom 72 u
Witvlei 48 j
Włocławek 33 t
Woleai Atoll 70 l
Wolf 22 o
Wolf Creek 14 m
Wolf Point 15 d
Wollaston Foreland 91 t
Wollaston Lake 12 w
Wollaston Peninsula 12 f
Wollogorang 73 h
Wollongong 78 f
Wolmaransstad 49 o
Wonarah 73 t
Wondoola 73 w
Wonganoo 76 h
Wōnju 58 u
Wōnsan 58 u
Wonthaggi 77 x
Woodgreen 73 r
Woodlark 71 r
Woods, Lake of the 15 k
Woodstock 17 d
Woodward 15 t
Woomera 77 e
Worcester (South Africa) 48 x
Worcester (USA) 17 n
Worland 15 o
Worthington 15 v
Wotu 69 u
Wowan 74 s
Wrangel Island 10 h
Wrangell 11 y
Wrangell Mountains 11 h

Wrath, Cape 32 j
Wright Peak 80 m
Wrigley 12 p
Wrocław 33 t
Wuchow 63 o
Wuda 57 q
Wudao 57 z
Wudil 41 g
Wudinna 77 d
Wudu 62 j
Wuhan 63 d
Wuhsi 63 h
Wuhu 63 f
Wüjang 61 e
Wu Jiang 62 l
Wukari 41 u
Wular, Lake 61 a
Wuliang Shan 62 t
Wunnummin Lake 16 e
Wuqi 57 r
Würzburg 34 k
Wutunghliao 62 i
Wuwe 62 i
Wuwei 57 p
Wuyiling 58 i
Wuying 58 i
Wuyi Shan 63 r
Wuyo 41 i
Wuyuan 57 s
Wuzhong 57 r
Wyandra 77 k
Wyloo 72 s
Wyndham 73 a
Wynyard 15 d
Wyoming 15 o
Wytheville 16 v

X

Xainza 61 k
Xai-Xai 49 h
Xamavera 48 k
Xambioá 26 z
Xam Nua 62 w
X-Muteba 44 v
Xapuri 25 p
Xar Burd 57 p
Xar Hudak 57 v
Xar Moron 57 z
Xar Moron (Inner Mongolia) 57 t
Xhumo 49 a
Xi 58 c
Xiachengzi 58 i
Xiamen (Amoy) 63 s
Xiangcheng 62 g
Xiang Jiang 63 o
Xiangquan 61 e
Xiangride 62 e
Xi'an (Sian) 62 m
Xianyang 62 l
Xiao'ergou 58 e
Xide 62 i
Xieng Khouang 62 v
Xifeng 62 l
Xi Jiang (Si) 63 o
Xikou 57 m
Xilin Hot 57 w
Xilin Qagan Obo 57 u
Ximiao 57 n
Xin'anjiang 63 g
Xin Barag Youqi 57 k
Xin Barag Zouqi 57 l
Xincai 63 c
Xinge 44 w
Xingsagoinba 62 g
Xingu 26 v
Xingu (River) 26 w
Xinguara 26 y
Xingxingxia 56 y
Xingyi 62 w
Xingzi 63 d
Xinhe 56 q
Xinhuang 62 m
Xinkai 58 d
Xinmin 58 e
Xin Xian 57 u
Xinyang 63 c
Xinyu 63 d
Xinyuan 56 q
Xique-Xique 27 q
Xitieshan 56 y
Xi Ujimqin Qi 57 x
Xiushui 63 d
Xixabangma Feng 61 i
Xixiang 62 l
Xorkol 56 v
Xuancheng 63 g
Xuanwei 62 w
Xueweng 63 u
Xungba 61 f
Xunke 58 h
Xuwen 63 n
Xuyong 62 k

Y

Ya'an 62 i
Yabassi 41 u
Yabelo 43 o
Yablonovy Mountains 57 g
Yabrai Yanchang 57 p
Yacimiento 30 u
Yacuiba 28 h
Yada 51 b
Yadrin 54 h
Yafo 38 k
Yagra 61 f
Yahuma 42 r
Yakeshi 57 l
Yakima 14 i
Yako 40 l
Yakoma 42 r
Yakovlevka 51 g
Yakrik 56 q
Yaku 58 w
Yakutat 11 w
Yakutsk 52 m
Yala (Ghana) 40 m
Yala (Thailand) 65 x
Yalata 77 b
Yali 44 k
Yalifafu 44 l
Yalinga 42 r
Yallalong 76 d
Yalleroi 74 p
Yalong Jiang 62 h
Yalu 58 f
Yalutorovsk 50 z
Yama 53 w
Yamagata 59 o
Yamaguchi 58 w
Yamal Peninsula 51 a
Yambio 42 v
Yamburg 51 d
Yambuya 42 s
Yamma Yamma, Lake 77 h
Yamussoukro 40 w
Yamsk 53 w
Yamuna 61 r
Yamzho Yumco 61 l
Yana 53 b
Yan'an 57 s
Yanbu al Bahr 38 z
Yanchang 63 a
Yandja 44 h
Yandun 56 x
Yangambi 42 s
Yangarey 50 l
Yangbajain 61 k
Yangchow 63 f
Yangchuan 57 v
Yangd Sum 57 w
Yangjiang 63 o
Yangoda 51 h
Yangon (Rangoon) 65 g
Yangtze 63 a
Yanhuqu 61 f
Yankton 15 u
Yanov Stan 51 g
Yanqi Huizu Zizhixian 56 t
Yanrey 72 r
Yanshan 57 x
Yantai 63 h
Yany-Kurgan 55 t
Yanzhou 63 e
Yaoundé 41 v
Yapen 70 t
Yapeyú 28 z
Yap Islands 70 h
Yaptiksale 51 b
Yaqui 18 h
Yaraka 77 j
Yaransk 50 t
Yaransu 54 j
Yarda 37 z
Yarkant 56 o
Yarkino 51 y
Yarlung Zangbo Jiang 61 k
Yarmouth 17 q
Yarongo 51 a
Yarraloola 72 s
Yarraman 78 f
Yarrie 72 v
Yarroto, Lake 51 b
Yartsevo 51 v
Yarumal 22 m
Yashikera 41 c
Yashkino 53 o
Yashkul' 54 h
Yasin 55 x
Yasnaya Polyana 58 m
Yasothon 66 h
Yata (Bolivia) 25 r
Yata (Central African. Rep.) 42 e
Yathkyed Lake 12 y
Yatolema 42 s
Yatsushiro 58 w
Yauri 25 n
Yauyos 24 w
Yavari 24 m
Yavatmal 61 p
Yaxian 62 z
Yazd 39 k
Yazdan 60 d
Ye 65 h
Yebbi Bou 37 y
Yecheng 55 z
Yécora 18 i
Yeggueba 37 v
Yei 42 w
Yekana 42 r
Yekaterinburg 50 y
Yelets 54 d
Yeletskiy 50 m
Yelizavety, Cape 53 r
Yelkhovka 54 k
Yellowknife 12 t
Yellow River (Huang He) 63 f
Yellow Sea 58 r
Yellowstone 15 c
Yelma 76 h
Yeloguy 51 u
Yeloguy (River) 51 t
Yelvertoft 73 u
Yelwa 41 d
Yemen 39/43
Yenakiyevo 54 d
Yendi 41 a
Yengisar 56 r
Yengisu 56 t
Yenisey 51 u
Yenisey Bay 51 f
Yenisey Mountains 51 w
Yeniseysk 51 w
Yenki 58 i
Yenyuka 52 w
Yeo, Lake 76 j
Yepachic 18 i
Yepoko 51 d
Yeppoon 74 t
Yerbogachen 52 c
Yerema 52 q
Yerevan 54 t
Yermak 55 l
Yermaki 57 f
Yermakovo 51 p
Yermakovo (Yenisey) 51 g
Yermentau 55 k
Yermo 18 l
Yeropol 10 c
Yerupaja 24 w
Yesil' 55 f
Yessey 52 a
Yet 43 s
Yet-Kyuyel' 52 i
Yetti 36 t
Yeva-Liv 50 m
Yeyka 52 c
Yeysk 54 d
Yguazú 29 n
Ygyatta 52 g
Yi'an 58 f
Yichun 58 i
Yidin 62 g
Yidu 63 a
Yimuhe 57 l
Yinchuan 57 q
Yingde 63 o
Yingkow 57 z
Yipinglang 62 u
Yirrkala 73 g
Yirshi 57 l
Yishan 62 y
Yiwu 56 x
Yi Xian 57 z
Yiyang 63 b
Ylas-Yuryakh 52 c
Ynykchanskiy 53 q
Yogyakarta 68 z
Yokadouma 41 x
Yoko 41 w
Yokohama 59 o
Yokosuka 59 o
Yola 41 j
Yolin Mod 58 d
Yolombo 44 m
Yondeng 57 p
Yong'an 63 s
Yongchuang 62 k
Yongden 62 i
Yongding 57 w
Yongren 62 u
Yopal 23 o
Yopurga 55 z
York 32 y
York, Cape (Australia) 73 k
York, Cape (Greenland) 91 b
York Factory 13 o
Yorke Peninsula 77 f
Yorkton 15 f
Yoshkar Ola 54 j
Yōsu 58 u
Youngstown 16 v
Youshashan 56 v
Youyang 62 m
Yozgat 35 z
Ypé Jhú 28 m
Yreka 14 u
Ystad 33 r
Ytyk-Kyuyel' 53 a
Yuan Jiang 63 a
Yuanjiang 62 u
Yuanlin 57 m
Yuanshanzi 57 n
Yuba City 14 u
Yubi, Cap 36 c
Yucatán Peninsula 20 t
Yucatán, Straits of 20 v
Yuci 63 b
Yudoma 53 q
Yudoma-Krestovskaya 53 q
Yuendumu 73 q
Yueyang 63 c
Yugorenok 53 p
Yugoslavia 35
Yugo-Tala 53 i
Yu Jiang 62 y
Yukhta 57 e
Yukon 11 b
Yukon Territory 11 j
Yukta 52 c
Yule 72 t
Yuli 56 t
Yulin 63 n
Yulin (Great Wall) 57 s
Yulongxue Shan 62 g
Yuma 18 e
Yun 63 e
Yunhe 63 g
Yunmeng 63 c
Yurga 51 t
Yuribey 51 d
Yurimaguas 24 j
Yurungkax 61 e
Yushu 62 d
Yushu (Manchuria) 58 g
Yuti 28 i
Yutian 61 e
Yutze 57 u
Yu Xian 57 v
Yuzhno-Sakhalinsk 59 d

Z

Zabad 43 f
Zabol 60 e
Zabré 40 m
Zacatecas 18 z
Zacatecoluca 22 c
Zacualtipan 19 p
Zadar 35 b
Zadoi 62 d
Zagazig 38 i
Zaghouan 34 y
Zagora 36 i
Zagreb 35 b
Zagros Mountains 39 i
Zahedan 60 d
Zahksykan 55 h
Zahlé 38 l
Zahran 39 q
Zajsan 56 e
Zajsan, Lake 56 e
Zakamensk 57 c
Zakopane 35 d
Zakouma 42 b
Zalanga 41 h
Zalantun 58 e
Zalari 57 b
Zalim 39 p
Zalingei 42 f
Zambeke 42 t
Zambezi 44 y
Zambia 44-45/46/49
Zamboanga 67 u
Zamko 41 h
Zamora (Ecuador) 24 h
Zamora (Mexico) 18 z
Zamora (Spain) 34 c
Zamość 33 v
Zamzor 56 m
Zanda 61 d
Zangguy 56 o
Zangla 61 b
Zanjan 54 w
Zanjón 28 q
Zante 35 q
Zanzibar 45 k
Zanzibar Island 45 k
Zapala 30 i
Zaporozh'ye 35 m
Za Qu 62 d
Zarafshan 55 s
Zaragoza 22 m
Zarand 39 m
Zarand (Tehran) 39 i
Zaranj 60 e
Zárate 31 b
Zaraza 23 g
Zard 39 h
Zarghunshar 60 j
Zargun 60 i
Zaria 41 f
Zaris 48 h
Žarma 56 c
Zarqa 38 l
Žursuat 56 c
Zarumilla 24 g
Zarzis 34 z
Zaskar 61 c
Zastron 49 p
Zatish'ye 53 l
Zavitinsk 58 i
Zawa 56 o
Zayü 62 e
Zealand 33 q
Zebak 55 v
Zedness 36 r
Zeerust 49 b
Zêkog 62 h
Zelenga 54 j
Zella 37 l
Zel'onoje Ozero 52 u
Zémio 42 s

Zemmour ....36 r
Zenica ....35 c
Zeya ....52 y
Zeya (River) ....52 z
Zeydan ....39 i
Zeyski ....52 z
Zhagaly ....54 k
Zhag'yab ....62 e
Zhaltyr ....55 i
Zhamshi ....55 l
Zhanay ....55 q
Zhangjiaquan ....56 x
Zhangpu ....63 r
Zhaosu ....56 p
Zhaotong ....62 j
Zhaoyuan ....58 f
Zhari Namco ....61 i
Zharkamys ....55 a
Zhaxi Co ....61 h
Zhecheng ....63 d
Zhelezinka ....55 l
Zheleznodorozhnyy ....50 u
Zhenghe ....63 g
Zhenghuang Qi ....57 v
Zhenglan Qi ....57 w
Zhengzhou (Chengchow) ....63 c
Zhenning ....62 x
Zhenping ....63 a
Zhenyuan ....62 u
Zhidoi ....62 d
Zhigansk ....52 j
Zhirkova ....53 k
Zhitomir ....35 i
Zhizdra ....54 b
Zholymbet ....55 j
Zhongba ....61 g
Zhongdian ....62 g
Zhongshan ....85 p
Zhongwei ....57 p
Zhongye Islands ....67 b
Zhoushan Islands ....63 i
Zhoushan Qundao ....58 r
Zhungqu ....62 j
Zhupanovskiy ....53 y
Zichang ....62 m
Žigalovo ....57 c
Zigazê ....61 j
Zighan ....38 o
Ziguinchor ....40 b
Zihuatenejo ....19 n
Zilinan ....35 c
Zima ....57 b
Zimbabwe ....49 s
Zimbabwe (State) ...45/46/49
Zinapécuaro ....19 n
Zinder ....41 g
Zinga ....42 n
Zintan ....37 h
Žioj ....54 x
Zipaquirá ....23 n
Zirō ....62 c
Zitácuaro ....19 n
Ziway, Lake ....43 c
Ziya ....57 w
Zlatoust ....55 c
Zliten ....37 j
Zmiyevka ....54 c
Znamenka ....35 k
Znojmo ....33 s
Zogang ....62 e
Zoigê ....62 i
Zolotoy ....53 c
Zomba ....45 u
Zongo ....42 o
Zoo Baba ....37 v
Zorritos ....24 g
Zorzor ....40 t
Zouar ....37 x
Zouerate ....36 q
Zq'gya-Zangbo ....61 l
Zrenjanin ....35 d
Zubova-Polyana ....54 g
Zug ....36 p
Zugspitze ....34 m
Zumbo ....45 r
Zürich ....34 k
Zuru ....41 e
Zuwarah ....34 z
Zuwaylah ....37 w
Zvishavane ....49 e
Zvolen ....35 c
Zyryanka ....53 i
Zyryanka (Yenisey Bay) ...51 f